In two minds

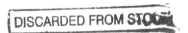

In two minds:
Dual processes and beyond

Edited by

Jonathan St. B. T. Evans
Centre for Thinking and Language
School of Psychology
University of Plymouth
Plymouth, UK
and

Keith Frankish
Department of Philosophy
The Open University
Walton Hall
Milton Keynes, UK

OXFORD
UNIVERSITY PRESS

OXFORD
UNIVERSITY PRESS

Great Clarendon Street, Oxford OX2 6DP

Oxford University Press is a department of the University of Oxford.
It furthers the University's objective of excellence in research, scholarship,
and education by publishing worldwide in

Oxford New York

Auckland Cape Town Dar es Salaam Hong Kong Karachi
Kuala Lumpur Madrid Melbourne Mexico City Nairobi
New Delhi Shanghai Taipei Toronto

With offices in

Argentina Austria Brazil Chile Czech Republic France Greece
Guatemala Hungary Italy Japan Poland Portugal Singapore
South Korea Switzerland Thailand Turkey Ukraine Vietnam

Oxford is a registered trade mark of Oxford University Press
in the UK and in certain other countries

Published in the United States
by Oxford University Press Inc., New York

A catalogue record for this title is available from the British Library

Data available

Library of Congress Cataloging in Publication Data

In two minds : dual processes and beyond / edited by Jonathan St. B.T.
Evans and Keith Frankish.
   p. cm.
 Includes bibliographical references.
 ISBN 978-0-19-923016-7
1. Thought and thinking. 2. Cognition. 3. Dual-brain psychology.
I. Evans, Jonathan St. B. T., 1948- II. Frankish, Keith.
BF441.I5 2009
153.4'2—dc22

2008043743

Typeset by Cepha Imaging Private Ltd., Bangalore, India
Printed by
the MPG Books Group in the UK

ISBN 978-0-19-923016-7

10 9 8 7 6 5 4 3 2 1

05447477

Preface

This volume presents a collection of essays on the increasingly popular topic of dual-process theory, or what we may more grandly term, the 'two minds' hypothesis. Dual-process theories hold that human thought processes are subserved by two distinct mechanisms, one fast, automatic, and nonconscious, the other slow, controlled, and conscious, which operate largely independently and compete for behavioral control. In their boldest form, they claim that humans have, in effect, two separate minds.

We feel that work in this area is reaching a pivotal stage. Dual-process theories are currently attracting a lot of attention, and researchers in many fields are beginning to explore their implications. Yet there is still relatively poor communication between dual-process theorists themselves, and the substantial bodies of work on dual processes in cognitive psychology and social psychology remain largely insulated from each other. Moreover, some of the leading proponents of dual-process theory are currently reassessing their views and recognizing that their theories require revision and complication. Given this, we feel there is a need for a volume that brings together leading researchers on dual processes, in order to summarize the state of the art, highlight key issues, present different perspectives, explore implications, and provide a stimulus to further work. This book seeks to meet this need. It is no mere survey volume but includes much new thinking about the human mind both by contemporary philosophers interested in broad theoretical questions about mental architecture and by psychologists specializing in traditionally distinct (and often isolated) fields of what is now a very large area of empirical study. We hope the volume will advance dual-process theorizing, promote interdisciplinary communication, and encourage further applications of dual-process approaches.

We open the volume with an historical perspective on dual-process theory (Chapter 1). As we show, philosophers and other academics have proposed versions of the two minds hypothesis over many centuries. The idea that there are fast, automatic, and unconscious thought processes that combine and compete with those that are slow, deliberative, and conscious, has been proposed many times by many authors, often in ignorance of each other's writings. Even in the modern, post-war history of this topic, dual-processing accounts developed more or less independently in several distinct fields of psychology, including learning, reasoning, and social cognition. Only recently have philosophers and psychologists started to connect up this large and diverse set of studies and to explore its implications for the nature of the human mind as a whole. The idea that these two forms of processing reflect two distinct systems, known as System 1 (fast, intuitive) and System 2 (slow, conscious) has attracted particular interest and is the focus for discussion in many of the current chapters.

The bulk of the book is organized into three broad categories. In Part 1, *Foundations*, the authors address fundamental questions about the architecture of the human mind, and about the proper formulation and interpretation of dual-process theories. How exactly should claims about dual systems be understood? What is the relation between the two systems? How could the mind be structured so that separate and competing processing systems can generate behaviour which nonetheless seems coherent and in line with the goals of the individual? We present here the latest thinking of two psychologists (Evans, Stanovich) and three philosophers (Frankish, Samuels, Carruthers) on these important questions. Both Evans and Stanovich argue that the dual-system theory they helped to develop is currently oversimplified, and they set about decomposing System 1 and System 2 (respectively) into distinct parts, while also each presenting an integrated theory of the mind as a whole. Frankish re-examines dual-system theory in the light of the philosophical distinction between the personal and subpersonal levels, arguing that System 2 reasoning is best thought of as a personal-level activity, in contrast to subpersonal System 1 processes. Samuels aims to clarify some current confusions in thinking about two systems, distinguishing *type* and *token* versions of dual-process theory and defending the former against the latter. Carruthers considers how dual-process theory may be reconciled with a massively modular theory of the mind, and proposes that System 2 is partly realized in cycles of System 1 activity, involving the mental rehearsal of action schemata.

In Part 2, *Perspectives*, contributors add further thoughts about cognitive architecture while discussing the dual-process theory from more specific perspectives, including evolutionary psychology, metacognition, social psychology, and learning theory. Adopting an evolutionary and massively modularist framework, Mercier and Sperber argue for a distinction between two kinds of inferences—intuitive and reflective—and explore its implications for dual-process theory. Thompson develops a new perspective on human reasoning by examining the role played by metacognition, or self-knowledge, in the determination of the mode of processing that people adopt. Smith and Collins provide a review of dual-process theories in social psychology and consider how these various theories can be reconciled with each other and with the dual-process accounts favored by cognitive psychologists. Buchtel and Norenzayan review a substantial body of work on differences in thinking styles across cultures and the implications this work has for dual-processing accounts of the mind. Sun, Lane, and Mathews focus on dual-process accounts of learning and develop a theoretical and computational account of the architecture involved.

In Part 3, *Applications*, the contributors explore the implications of dual-process theory for a number of fields of study (and vice versa). Klaczynski covers the very important developmental perspective. If the mind has a two-system architecture, then what does this imply for the development of cognitive abilities in children, and to what extent does research on children's thinking support this distinction? Lieberman writes from the perspective of the rapidly expanding field of study that is social neuroscience, addressing the fundamentally important question of what it is that we can do with slow, reflective thinking that we cannot do by use of fast, automatic processes. Dual-process theory raises some important questions about human rationality, which are the focus of C. Saunders and Over's contribution. The authors consider the various types of mental conflict that are possible within a mind structured along dual-process lines, and argue that it is neither possible nor desirable to eliminate them all. In the final chapter, L. Saunders explores an application of dual-process theory in moral philosophy, showing how a two-systems approach can help to solve an important problem posed by the existence of recalcitrant moral intuitions.

This book is loosely based on an international conference entitled 'In two minds: Dual-process theories of reasoning and rationality', organized by K.F. and J.E., together with Carolyn Price of the Open University, and held in Cambridge in the summer of 2006. The event was organized under the auspices of the Open University and was funded jointly by grants from the Mind Association, the Economic and Social Research Council of the UK, and the Open University. It was the first major conference specifically on dual-process theory and included contributions from leading researchers from several different disciplines.

Many (but not all) of the speakers have contributed chapters to the current volume, and most (but not all) of the contributors to this book spoke at the meeting. We would therefore like to take this opportunity to thank the speakers and poster presenters, and their co-authors, who made stimulating contributions at this meeting, but are not among the contributors to the current volume. These were (in alphabetical order): Linden Ball, Philip Barnard, Jean-Francois Bonnefon, Sacha Bourgeois-Gironde, Matthew Carmody, Nick Chater, Laurence Claes, Zoltan Dienes, Michael Eid, Shira Elqayam, Aidan Feeney, Vinod Goel, Pierre-Stanislas Grialou, Constantinos Hadjichristidis, Saïd Jmel, Uri Leron, Jon May, Fiona Montijn-Dorgelo, Agnes Moors, Mike Oaksford, Magda Osman, Valerie Reyna, Robin Scaife, Steven Sloman, Keith Stenning, John van den Bercken, Stéphane Vautier, Christopher Viger, and Cilia Witteman. We would also like to thank Veli Mitova and Asbjørn Steglich-Petersen, who helped with the running of the conference, and Danielle Bertrand, who provided secretarial support.

Both editors benefited from significant periods of funded research leave during the preparation of this work. Jonathan Evans would like to acknowledge the extended research fellowship awarded to him by the ESRC (RES 000–27–0184), as well as stimulating discussions on dual-process theory with several colleagues not contributing to current volume, including Simon Handley, Steven Sloman, Tim Wilson, and Shira Elqayam. Keith Frankish gratefully acknowledges a research leave award made to him by the UK's Arts and Humanities Research Council, and thanks his colleagues at the Open University for their support during his work on this project, mentioning in particular Alex Barber, Tim Chappell, Derek Matravers, and Carolyn Price. He is also deeply indebted to Maria Kasmirli for her patience, support, and excellent advice.

Jonathan St. B. T. Evans
University of Plymouth

Keith Frankish
The Open University

May 2008

Contents

Part 3 **Applications**

List of contributors

Emma E. Buchtel
Department of Psychology,
University of British Columbia,
Vancouver, BC, Canada.

Peter Carruthers
Department of Philosophy,
University of Maryland,
Skinner Building, MD, USA.

Elizabeth C. Collins
Department of Psychological and Brain
Sciences,
Indiana University,
Bloomington, IN, USA.

Jonathan St. B. T. Evans
Centre for Thinking and Language,
School of Psychology,
University of Plymouth,
Plymouth, UK.

Keith Frankish
Department of Philosophy,
The Open University,
Walton Hall,
Milton Keynes, UK.

Paul A. Klaczynski
School of Psychological Sciences,
McKee Hall,
University of Northern Colorado,
Greeley, CO, USA.

Sean M. Lane
Department of Psychology,
Louisiana State University,
Baton Rouge, LA, USA.

Matthew D. Lieberman
Department of Psychology,
University of California,
Los Angeles, CA, USA.

Robert C. Mathews
Department of Psychology,
Louisiana State University,
Baton Rouge, LA, USA.

Hugo Mercier
Institut Jean Nicod,
EHESS-ENS-CNRS,
Paris, France.

Ara Norenzayan
Department of Psychology,
University of British Columbia,
Vancouver, BC, Canada.

David E. Over
Department of Psychology,
Durham University,
Science Laboratories,
Durham, UK.

Richard Samuels
Department of Philosophy,
The Ohio State University,
Columbus, OH, USA.

Clare Saunders
Subject Centre for Philosophical and
Religious Studies,
University of Leeds,
Leeds, UK.

Leland F. Saunders
Department of Philosophy,
University of Maryland,
Skinner Building, MD, USA.

Eliot R. Smith
Department of Psychological and Brain
Sciences,
Indiana University,
Bloomington, IN, USA.

Dan Sperber
Institut Jean Nicod,
EHESS-ENS-CNRS,
Paris, France.

Keith E. Stanovich
Department of Human Development
and Applied Psychology,
University of Toronto,
Toronto, ON, Canada.

Ron Sun
Cognitive Science Department,
Rensselaer Polytechnic Institute,
Troy, NY, USA.

Valerie A. Thompson
Department of Psychology,
University of Saskatchewan,
Saskatoon, SK, Canada.

Chapter 1

The duality of mind: An historical perspective

Keith Frankish and Jonathan St. B. T. Evans

In recent years an exciting body of work has emerged from various quarters devoted to exploring the idea that there is a fundamental duality in the human mind. Since the 1970s *dual-process* theories have been developed by researchers on various aspects of human psychology, including deductive reasoning, decision making, and social judgment. These theories come in different forms, but all agree in positing two distinct processing mechanisms for a given task, which employ different procedures and may yield different, and sometimes conflicting, results. Typically, one of the processes is characterized as fast, effortless, automatic, nonconscious, inflexible, heavily contextualized, and undemanding of working memory, and the other as slow, effortful, controlled, conscious, flexible, decontextualized, and demanding of working memory. Dual-process theories of learning and memory have also been developed, typically positing a nonconscious *implicit* system, which is slow learning but fast access, and a conscious *explicit* one, which is fast learning but slow access.

More recently, some theorists have sought to unify these localized dual-process theories into ambitious theories of mental architecture, according to which humans have, in effect, two minds. Such theories claim that human central cognition is composed of two multi-purpose reasoning systems, usually called *System 1* and *System 2*, the operations of the former having fast-process characteristics (fast, effortless, automatic, nonconscious, etc.), and those of the latter slow-process ones (slow, effortful, controlled, conscious, etc.) (e.g. Evans and Over 1996; Sloman 1996; Stanovich 1999, 2004). It is often claimed that System 2 is unique to humans, and that it is the source of our capacity for decontextualized abstract thinking, in accordance with logical norms. These all-encompassing theories are sometimes referred to as *dual-system* theories, in contrast to more localized *dual-process* ones, but 'dual-process theory' is also used as an umbrella term for both, and for convenience we shall often adopt this usage.

In the form just outlined, dual-process theories are the product of the last thirty years or so, but it would be a mistake to think that hypotheses about mental division are unique to contemporary psychology. In fact, modern dual-process theories can be seen simply as the latest and most sophisticated development of ideas that have been around for centuries. In this chapter we shall survey this history of thinking about mental duality, looking at precursors and related theories in philosophy and psychology, and giving a detailed account of the origins of modern dual-process and dual-system theories themselves. We shall not aim to identify patterns of influence, except for some fairly modest ones in recent work. In many cases, the ideas discussed appear to have been developed quite independently, and in any case claims of influence are hard to establish—sometimes even for the theorists involved (see Evans 2004). Rather, we shall aim to show how theories of mental duality have emerged independently in different contexts. It strikes us as greatly significant that dual-process ideas have been continually discovered and rediscovered by many authors throughout the history of philosophy and psychology. We suspect this reflects on the nature of the object of study that all these authors have in common: the human mind.

The chapter is organized by themes rather than strict chronology. The first section looks at theories of mental division from Plato to Freud, focusing in particular on claims in the philosophical literature. The second section surveys relevant work in experimental psychology from the nineteenth through to the mid-twentieth century. The third section charts the history of modern dual-process theories in specific fields, and section four describes the subsequent development of dual-system approaches. The fifth section considers the contribution of contemporary philosophy, where several researchers have developed dual-process theories of their own, and the final section offers some speculations about the future development of dual-process ideas.

Division in the mind: Plato to Freud

The idea that the mind is partitioned is an ancient one. Perhaps the most famous account before Freud's is Plato's, who claimed that the soul is divided into three parts: *reason*, *spirit*, and *appetite*, understood as mini-agents, each with its own goals and reasoning powers (Plato 1993, pp.144–52, pp.354–61; for discussion see Annas 1981, ch.5). Reason seeks truth and pursues what is best for the person as a whole; spirit loves honour and winning; and appetite judges by appearances and seeks superficially gratifying things. Harmony within the soul comes when reason controls the other two parts, training spirit to serve its goals and regulating appetite in line with its judgements of what is genuinely desirable. This is fanciful psychology, of course, and heavily influenced by Plato's political theory (the three elements in the soul correspond to the three classes in his conception of the ideal society), but there are nonetheless some analogies with dual-process approaches. Like dual-process theory, Plato's account is designed to explain psychological conflict—to show how we can harbor conflicting attitudes towards the same object. And Plato's conception of reason is similar to some modern conceptions of System 2, being that of an analytic system, which seeks the good of the individual as a whole, and is able to override more superficial judgments and desires originating in the other parts of the mind.

Anticipations of dual-process theory can also be found in philosophical debates about animal mentality. Many philosophers have held that humans exhibit a qualitatively different kind of mentality from other animals. Indeed, some have denied that animals have minds at all, at least in the sense of a capacity for rational thought. Aristotle, Aquinas, and Descartes all took this view. Such views partially anticipate those of many dual-process theorists, who see System 2 as uniquely human and as conferring reasoning capacities different in kind from those of animals. Descartes's views on this topic are particularly interesting. Descartes famously denied that animals have minds, which he equated with incorporeal souls. Language use, he argued, is the only sure sign of thought, and animal behavior can be mechanistically explained without reference to genuinely mental processes. Yet Descartes did not ignore the complexity of animal psychology (as we would call it). He held that animals have perceptions, memories, appetites, and passions, albeit of a nonconscious kind, which are complex physiological states and which guide action mechanically, without the involvement of a soul (Descartes 1664/1985, p.108). Moreover, he held that much *human* behavior is the product of similar mechanical processes, including such everyday activities as walking and singing, when they take place without the mind attending to them (Descartes 1642/1984, p.161; Cottingham 1992). Though Descartes may not have thought of it as such, this is a rudimentary dual-process view.

Other writers have argued for the uniqueness of human reasoning without denying that animals can think. Leibniz maintained that animal behavior is guided solely by inductive reasoning, as is the larger portion of our own (he says 'three-fourths'; 1714/1989, p.208). However, he held that humans also have a capacity for 'true reasoning'—that is, *a priori* reasoning based on necessary truths, such as those of logic and mathematics. This capacity, he held, derives from our possession of reflective consciousness, which enables us to form metaphysical concepts, such as those of substance, cause, and effect (Leibniz 1702/1989, pp.188–91, 1714/1989, pp.208–9). Locke, too, held that there is a 'perfect distinction' between human and animal reasoning powers. Animals can think about particular things, as presented to their senses, but they lack the power of *abstraction*. That is, they cannot form general ideas of features common to many instances—the idea of whiteness, for example, as opposed to ideas of particular white things. This is evident, Locke argues, from the fact that animals lack language, and with it, signs for general ideas (Locke 1706/1961, Vol. 1, pp.126–7). Other writers have argued for the uniqueness of human mentality on the grounds that thought (at least of the distinctively human kind) constitutively involves language—that we can, in some sense, 'think in' language. This view was proposed by both Herder and Hamman in the late eighteenth century (see Cloeren 1988), and, as we shall see later, it is advocated by several contemporary philosophers of mind. Again, all of these accounts contain the seeds of a dual-process approach, and they partially anticipate modern theorists who characterize System 1 reasoning as associative, context-bound, and non-linguistic, and System 2 reasoning as rule-based, abstract, and language-involving.

We turn now to the theme of unconscious mentality, where the clearest anticipations of dual-process theory can be found. It is sometimes assumed that the concept of the unconscious originated with Freud, but this in fact is far from the case. It is true that many philosophers resisted the idea of unconscious mentality, following Descartes in identifying mind with consciousness. But there is, nonetheless, a long history of theorizing about the unconscious, though in many cases no distinction is made between mental states that are not present to consciousness and ones that are not available to it—*preconscious* versus *unconscious*, in Freud's terms (for surveys, see Ellenberger 1970; Reeves 1965; Whyte 1978). References to unconscious memories and perceptions crop up in various ancient and early modern philosophers; examples can be found in, among others, Plato, Plotinus, Augustine, Aquinas, Pascal, Spinoza, and Leibniz. Leibniz, in particular, made important observations about unconscious perception and memory. He distinguished between bare *perception* and conscious *appreciation*, and held that we continually experience a multitude of unattended *petites perceptions*, which are below the threshold of consciousness but which collectively shape our conscious experience (Leibniz 1714/1989, p.208, 1765/1996, pp.53–5). He also noted that we often retain information which we cannot consciously recall but which nonetheless influences our thoughts and behavior (Leibniz 1765/1996, pp.106–7).

With the rise of German idealism and Romantic aesthetics in the late eighteenth and early nineteenth centuries, claims about the unconscious became common. There are frequent references to unconscious mental states in Herder, Schelling, Hegel, and Schopenhauer, among others, as well as in creative writers such as Goethe, Richter, and Wordsworth. These writers' conceptions of the unconscious had strong metaphysical and mystical overtones. The German idealists thought of the unconscious as part of the underlying structure of reality, rather than as a postulate of empirical psychology (Gardner 1999, 2003), and the Romantic writers saw it as a source of inspiration and creative energy. Nonetheless, some interesting psychological observations can be found in their work.

Schopenhauer's writings are particularly relevant from our perspective. Schopenhauer held that there is a blind 'will to life' at work throughout nature, which shapes our conscious intellects to its own ends, in line with powerful primitive impulses, especially sexual ones. (In a striking metaphor, he likens the relationship between the will and the intellect to that of a strong blind man carrying a sighted lame man on his shoulders; Schopenhauer 1819/1966, Vol. 2, p.209.) Anticipating (and probably influencing) Freud, Schopenhauer claimed that the will represses ideas it finds painful and promotes ones it finds comforting. Moreover, like many modern dual-process theorists, he stressed the limitations of our self-knowledge and the relative impotence of the conscious intellect. He held that we possess unconscious desires, emotions, and resolutions—sometimes shameful ones—which we discover only indirectly, through observing our reactions. And he suggested that we are often ignorant of the true motives for our actions and that our conscious resolutions require backing from unconscious processes if they are to be effective (ibid. Vol 2; pp.209–11).

Philosophers continued to develop broadly metaphysical theories of the unconscious throughout the nineteenth century (Gardner 2003). Eduard von Hartmann's widely read 1868 book *Philosophy of the unconscious* synthesized Hegel and Schopenhauer, and Nietzsche and Bergson each produced influential accounts of their own. This work is, however, of marginal interest from our perspective, though it offered ammunition for philosophers and psychologists working to combat Cartesian conceptions of the mind and provided the intellectual context for the work we discuss next.

We turn now to another strand of thinking about the unconscious. Several nineteenth-century philosophers and physicians developed a view of the unconscious as a set of automatic processing systems for everyday tasks—a view which directly prefigures the modern conception of the cognitive, or 'adaptive', unconscious invoked in contemporary dual-process theories. Again there is a rich history here, and we can mention only a few milestones.

A largely forgotten pioneer in this area is the French philosopher known as Maine de Biran, who wrote on the influence of habit on thinking (Maine de Biran 1803/1929;

for discussion see Schacter and Tulving 1994). Maine de Biran noted that habitual actions could become so ingrained as to be completely automatic and unconscious, and he drew a distinction between habit-based memory systems and conscious memory, positing two systems for habitual responses: *mechanical memory* and *sensitive memory*—the former for motor skills, the latter for affective responses. Conscious memory was assigned to a third system, *representative memory*. In making such distinctions, based on function and content, Maine de Bain anticipated modern distinctions between implicit and explicit memory systems.

Another important development was the gradual recognition of the existence of unconscious mental *processes* underlying conscious thought and action—a view now commonplace, but radical in the nineteenth century. Helmholtz was one of the first to posit unconscious inferences, in his work on perception (Helmholtz 1867/1962; Hatfield 2002). The case for the existence and importance of unconscious processes was also made by a group of British philosophers and physicians, notably Thomas Laycock, William Hamilton, and William Carpenter, whom Timothy Wilson has dubbed the parents of the modern theory of the adaptive unconscious (Wilson 2002, p.10). Laycock developed the doctrine of the *cerebral reflex*—the view that many higher brain functions are effected by sophisticated but unconscious reflex processes, similar in kind to the more primitive ones in the brain stem and spinal cord. Laycock suggested that instinctive and emotional responses could be explained in this way, as could some aspects of intelligence (Laycock 1845, 1860). Hamilton vigorously attacked his Cartesian contemporaries and defended a doctrine he called *mental latency*—the view that the mind contains far more 'mental furniture' than consciousness reveals—pointing to evidence for unconscious processing in perception, the association of ideas, and the performance of habitual and skilled actions (Hamilton 1860, Vol. 1, pp.235–52). As Hamilton put it, 'the sphere of our conscious modifications is only a small circle in the center of a far wider sphere of action and passion of which we are only conscious through its effects' (ibid. p.242). Carpenter gathered evidence for what he called 'unconscious cerebration' (he regarded the term 'unconscious reasoning' as contradictory). He cited cases where people recall knowledge they do not know they possess (as in the phenomenon of 'automatic writing'), and highlighted the role of unconscious processes in generating insights, modifying emotions, and supporting unacknowledged prejudices (Carpenter 1874, pp.515–43).

William James's views deserve mention here, too. James is often thought of as having opposed the positing of unconscious mental states, and as thereby exerting a retrograde influence on psychology (Baars 1986, pp.34–9).There is material to support this view (James 1890, Vol. 1, pp.162–76), but it can be argued that James's target was a metaphysically-laden conception of the unconscious (Weinberger 2000), and James talks freely about states and processes at the margins of consciousness, if not completely outside it (see in particular his 1902 book on religious experience). Moreover, James himself contributed to the development of the modern conception of the cognitive unconscious with his account of *habit* (James 1890, Vol. 1, ch.4). He describes how sequences of actions can become automatized through repetition, thus freeing up conscious attention for other tasks. James cites everyday routines such as dressing and opening cupboards: 'Our lower centres know the order of these movements', he writes, 'and show their knowledge by their 'surprise' if the objects are altered so as to oblige the movement to be made in a different way. But our higher thought-centers know hardly anything about the matter' (ibid. p.115). James notes that we can access this knowledge only indirectly, by performing or mentally rehearsing the actions in question. This account harmonizes well with the views of modern dual-process theorists, who treat habit formation as involving a transfer of control from the conscious volitional system to the unconscious automatic one (e.g. Stanovich, this volume).

We turn now to a further tradition of theorizing about the unconscious, which came to overshadow the one just discussed—some would say with detrimental consequences. This is the appeal to the unconscious in psychiatry, which established itself as a discipline during this period. Nineteenth-century scientists made extensive studies of mental disorder, especially what was called *hysteria*—a catch-all term for anxiety disorders, psychosomatic illnesses, and dissociative conditions such as amnesia and multiple personality disorder. These conditions were often seen as manifestations of unconscious states, and in the later decades of the century several theorists developed sophisticated *dynamic* accounts of mental disorder in terms of unconscious motivations. The pre-eminent name here is of course that of Sigmund Freud, who drew on clinical work by Pierre Janet and Josef Breuer, among others, and on the philosophy of Schopenhauer and Nietzsche. Freud developed a precise, detailed, and far-reaching theory of what he called the 'dynamic unconscious', which was designed to explain not only hysteria and other psychopathologies but also many aspects of normal development and behavior. This work had a huge impact on early and mid-twentieth-century psychiatric theory and practice, as well as on the popular imagination, but in recent decades it has attracted severe criticism, and today many regard it as wholly discredited (e.g. Grünbaum 1984; Macmillan 1997). (Many contemporary cognitive scientists prefer to speak of 'nonconscious' processes rather than 'unconscious' ones, precisely in order to distance themselves from Freud.) This is not the place to enter into debates about the value of Freud's work and legacy, however, and we shall confine ourselves to noting how Freud's conception of the unconscious differed from that in play in modern dual-process theories. Freud's views are complex and changed considerably over the years, so we shall paint with a very broad brush.

Freud can certainly be described as a dual-process theorist. He held that the human mind is composed of two systems, a conscious one and an unconscious one, commonly labeled *Ucs* and *Cs*, respectively. (He also posited a third, *preconscious* system, *Pcs*, which for many purposes can be regarded as a part of *Cs*.) He held that these systems operated in different modes ('primary process' and 'secondary process'), the former associative, the latter logical. He also held that the contents of the unconscious system were inaccessible to the conscious one, and that the unconscious system was a source of motivation and mental conflict. So far, modern dual-process theorists can agree. However, there are huge differences between Freud's *Ucs* and System 1, as standardly conceived. We shall mention three.

First, *Ucs* consists largely of repressed impulses (or, in Freud's earlier work, memories) that have been prevented from becoming conscious because of their traumatic nature. (Freud thought that material naturally progressed from *Ucs* to *Cs* if not repressed.) By contrast, the notion of repression has no role in modern dual-process theory.

System 1 is assumed to have its own propriety knowledge base and goal structure, formed by routine belief-forming and desire-forming mechanisms, in response to perceptual information, bodily needs, and so on. And although some of its goals are genetically determined ones, which may conflict with those of System 2, these are not thought of as having been repressed. Second, *Ucs* is not a reasoning system; it does not represent negation, probability, time, or external reality, and seeks only to maximize pleasure and minimize pain, in accordance with the 'pleasure principle' (Freud 1915/2005, pp.69–70). System 1, on the other hand, is a set of inferential mechanisms for the control of various aspects of everyday behavior, and has a rich representational structure. Third, the influence of *Ucs* is indirect and often harmful. It has no direct access to motor control (ibid. p.70) and can influence conscious thought and action only indirectly, through its 'derivatives'—dreams, neurotic symptoms, and activities that symbolically represent the fulfilment of repressed impulses (ibid. pp.73–4). System 1, by contrast, has a far more direct and beneficial role. Some theorists hold that it can control action directly, bypassing System 2 altogether, others that it generates default responses, which are then vetted by System 2. Either way, its outputs are direct outcomes of its goals, rather than the indirect, symbol-laden influences characteristic of *Ucs*.

In his later writing Freud proposed a tripartite division of the human mind into *id*, *ego*, and *superego*, which cut across the earlier distinction between *Ucs* and *Cs* (Freud 1927). The id is a primitive pleasure-seeking system, the superego a moral system embodying social norms, and the ego the rational self, which deals with the external world and tries to reconcile the competing demands of the other two systems. Again, there are superficial similarities with a dual-process approach. System 1, like the id, harbors primitive, genetically programmed goals, whereas System 2, like the ego, pursues the goals of the individual as a whole. But there are also huge differences. For example, System 1, unlike the id, is capable of representing and engaging with external reality, and the functions of the superego are not unique to either System 1 or System 2. (It is plausible to think that social norms can be internalized by both; see Saunders, this volume.) In the end, whatever their value as therapeutic tools, Freud's taxonomies have little more relevance to contemporary dual-process theories than does Plato's tripartite division of the soul.

Experimental psychology: The first 100 years (or so)

In the first section, we sketched the history of thinking about dual processes through ancient philosophy down to the writings of Sigmund Freud. This work was conceptual or theoretical in nature and mostly based on informal observations of human behavior and/or personal introspection by the authors. A very different kind of influence emerged with the discipline of experimental psychology. In order to appreciate this, we need to turn the clock back a little from the end of the first section to the mid nineteenth century, when researchers began to conduct systematic psychological experiments, mostly in German universities. Such early psychological research was, in fact, based primarily on the study of *conscious* mental processes, and the use of introspective reporting was common. Of particular importance were the psychophysical schools of Gustav Fechner and Wilhelm Wundt. Psychophysics is essentially the study of the relationship between the properties of physical stimuli and the perceptual experiences that they give rise to. It remains an active field to the current day, and many of the methods established in this early period are still in use.

Despite the long history of writing about unconscious processes, described in the previous section, early evidence of unconscious processing in psychological experiments generated considerable controversy in the fledgling discipline of psychology (for reviews, see Humphrey 1951; Mandler and Mandler 1964). The problems began with the studies of the Wurzburgh school, around the turn of the nineteenth and twentieth centuries, with their new methodology. These researchers asked people to perform simple cognitive tasks, such as word association, and then to give an introspective report immediately afterwards on what was going on in their minds. The researchers expected, in accordance with a long tradition of associationist philosophy, to find mediating images linking stimulus and response. For example, if the experimenter said 'egg' and the participant 'bacon', it was expected that they would then report an image of a breakfast table with a plate of bacon and eggs on it. Sometimes this is what happened, but participants also reported on many occasions that no conscious experience intervened between stimulus and response, or else that they had an experience of an indescribable nature—the so-called 'imageless thoughts'. Wundt objected to the retrospective nature of the reporting, foreshadowing the famous critique of introspective reporting in modern psychology by Nisbett and Wilson (1977). Other psychological greats of the time, including Titchener, objected to the very idea that such things as imageless thoughts could exist—foreshadowing modern debates about the nature of mental imagery.

Outside of German psychology, the great British Victorian scientist, Sir Francis Galton, independently concluded that most brain work was automatic and unconscious. He used word association tests (which he invented) to explore unconscious associative processes, analyzing the ideas generated for their rate, character, age, tendency to recurrence, and so on. He conducted these introspective experiments on himself and (remarkably) noticed how little of the brain's mental work was reflected in the contents of consciousness. The experiments, Galton concluded, revealed 'the multifariousness of the work done by the mind in a state of half-unconsciousness' and indicated the existence of 'still deeper strata of mental operations, sunk wholly below the level of consciousness' (1879b, p.162). He went on to stress the extent and importance of unconscious mental operations, and suggested that consciousness was little more than a 'helpless spectator' of the bulk of automatic brain work—a claim which prefigures the views of some contemporary theorists (1879a, p.433). (In a poetical metaphor, Galton likened unconscious mental operations to waves traveling by night over an expanse of ocean, with consciousness being the line of breakers on the shore.)

The real hammer blow for introspective psychology, however, came from the foundation of the school of behaviorism by J. B. Watson in the early twentieth century, following publication of his famous paper, 'Psychology as the behaviourist views it' (1913). This began what some observers see as a 'long dark age' in psychology that lasted some 50 years or more, until the cognitive revolution eventually swept it away. Even when the second author (J. E.) was studying psychology in the 1960s, the behaviorist B. F. Skinner was easily the most famous psychologist in the world, and his writings were still taken very seriously by many readers. Watson built on Pavlov's work on classical conditioning to construct a stimulus-response psychology that was stripped bare of mentalistic thinking. In philosophical terms, Watson was an extreme empiricist (as opposed to nativist), a firm believer in the *tabula rasa* or blank slate theory of the mind, so strongly advocated by the British empiricist philosophers, such as Locke. Thus Watson believed that, with the right conditioning, anyone could be made to be any kind of person. However, behaviorism had many ramifications beyond empiricism. It banished not only introspectionism but any form of mentalism—that is, the description of internal mental processes that mediate behavior—as 'unscientific', on the grounds that science must be confined to what can be objectively observed. It also set a fashion of studying psychology through animal experimentation, with endless studies of rats and pigeons being conducted throughout this period, with the apparent objective of understanding the fundamental principles of learning in humans. With hindsight, we can see this as an extreme example of a System 1 research program, in which habit learning was the only show in town.

Although behaviorism was the dominant school of psychology in the first half of the twentieth century, there were other schools of a much more cognitive nature, such as Piaget's emerging theory of cognitive development. An important influence was Gestalt psychology, which flourished in Germany in the interwar period. The German word 'Gestalt' means form or shape, and the movement was based on a holistic approach to perception and cognition, founded on the principle that the whole was greater than the sum of the parts. Originally applied to perception, Gestalt theorists also turned their attention to the study of thinking and problem solving. They challenged behaviorism by studying 'insight' problems—those that are solved by a sudden, discontinuous process of thought—which defy explanation in terms of gradual habit learning. There are dual-process ideas to be found in the Gestalt work on problem solving. For example, they contrasted 'blind' with 'productive' thinking, the former based on habit learning so beloved of behaviorists. Wertheimer (1945/1961) caricatured the then current fashion in Germany for teaching children mathematics by drill and rote learning, showing how it could lead to silly mistakes when the problem was slightly unfamiliar in form. Gestalt psychologists showed how people could acquire unhelpful 'sets' in problem solving through habit learning, or fail to solve problems due to 'functional fixedness' (Duncker 1945; Luchins 1942) in which they would not think of using an object for an unfamiliar purpose. The approach was highly evaluative, with habitual thinking, of the type promoted by behaviorism, being regarded as 'bad', while productive, insightful thinking was 'good'. However, we can see here an anticipation of contemporary applications of dual-process theory, in which System 2 thinking is seen as necessary to intervene upon default, habitual System 1 thinking, in order for people to solve problems of an abstract or novel nature (Stanovich 1999). Gestalt psychology also provides the earliest reference in experimental psychology to the idea that thinking can be influenced by hints that are not consciously noticed (Maier 1931).

Before concluding this review of pre-modern psychological thinking, we should mention some work on the relationship between language and thought. Contemporary authors have strongly associated the possession of the uniquely human faculty of language with System 2 thinking (Evans and Over 1996), with the idea that such thought is realized through 'inner speech' being particularly emphasized by some contemporary philosophers, as discussed later in the fifth section. The contemporary study of executive working memory, which we see as a System 2 research program, is one in which inner speech is also thought to play a major role (Baddeley 2007). In fact, this idea was well developed in writings of the Russian psychologist Lev Vygotsky (1934/1962) in the 1930s. Piaget (1926) had observed that young children exhibit 'egocentric speech' in which they appear to give themselves instructions while playing. Piaget believed that infants are essentially autistic and take some years to learn to become social beings and to decenter their thinking. Correspondingly, he observed that egocentric speech was dominant in preschool children but decreased rapidly from about the age of 7 or 8 years. Vygotsky, however, reinterpreted Piaget's work assisted by findings of his own studies. For example, he showed that when children were frustrated and faced with difficult problems to solve, the proportion of egocentric speech increased markedly. Vygotsky (1934/1962, p.18) viewed egocentric speech not as disappearing, as Piaget suggested, but as being internalized, commenting that 'the inner speech of the adult represents his "thinking for himself"' rather than social adaptation: i.e. it has the same function that egocentric speech has in the child', adding that 'when egocentric speech disappears from view it does not simply atrophy but "goes underground", i.e. turns into inner speech'. (See fifth section for contemporary applications of this idea.)

Inner speech is also what gave behaviorists such as Watson, and later Skinner, a way out when forced to confront the issue of apparently conscious thinking. To Watson, for example, thought was simply subvocalization, which together with vocalization was merely a system of motor habits. However, language was to be the final battleground for behaviorism. When Skinner published his account of language in terms of operant conditioning, in the book *Verbal behavior* (Skinner 1957), it was hailed as a masterpiece. Triumph turned to disaster, however, when a young linguist called Noam Chomsky wrote one of the most devastating and influential book reviews in the history of academia (Chomsky 1959). Chomsky's critique went much deeper than the particulars of the book, exposing the fundamental weaknesses and limitations of the behaviorist approach. This was one of several key publications around this time that laid the foundation for the cognitive revolution to follow.

The modern history of dual-process theories

The modern history of dual-process theories, so far as we are concerned, concerns those that developed after the start of the cognitive revolution in psychology, which occurred during the 1960s and 1970s. We shall discuss here the origin of contemporary dual-process theories, in the narrower sense, in the order in which they roughly developed, in the fields of learning, reasoning, social cognition, and decision making. The further development of dual-system theories is covered in the fourth section.

It would be easy in an historical review such as this to create the impression that things developed in an orderly fashion, with each set of authors reading the previous and related work before engaging in their own research. In the case of dual-process theories, this would be particularly fictitious; most of these modern developments were little influenced either by the history outlined in earlier sections, or by earlier and parallel developments in the other fields of psychology. For example, the origin of modern dual-process theories is sometimes cited as stemming from the distinction between controlled and automatic processes in attention made by Schneider and Shiffrin (1977; also, Shiffrin and Schneider 1977). It is true that this work provided a major stimulus for the development of dual-processing accounts in social cognition from the 1980s onwards, but it actually played no part at all in the development of dual-process accounts of learning and reasoning which predated this publication. Reber's theory developed from his program of experimental study of implicit learning, which began in the 1960s (see Reber 1993 for a review). Reber's work in turn played no part in the early development of the dual-process theory of reasoning which started with collaboration between Peter Wason and Jonathan Evans in the mid-1970s. Reber's work only came to influence the account of Evans and Over (1996) some twenty years later (see Evans 2004). In the study of social cognition, where dual-process theories have formed the dominant paradigm for the past 20 years and more, the great majority of publications show no awareness at all of either the learning or the reasoning tradition.

This disconnectedness of the various fields is a reflection of modern psychology. There is now so much research conducted and reported in various fields that authors struggle to keep up with the literature in their own traditions and favored paradigms. For example, few cognitive psychologists take the time to read social psychology and vice versa. This state of affairs permits parallel discovery of phenomena and theoretical ideas, and this is precisely what seems to have happened in the case of dual-process theories in cognitive and social psychology. There are many striking similarities in the theories developed in these different traditions, as well as some important differences of emphasis (Evans 2008).

We shall start by reviewing the origins of various modern theories that distinguish between what we shall call type 1 processes (fast, automatic, unconscious) and type 2 processes (slow, conscious, controlled). Later we shall discuss the development of dual-*system* theories, which attempt to integrate work from different traditions and make stronger assumptions about the cognitive architecture of the human mind, leading to the popular terms 'System 1' and 'System 2'. Because it is the oldest work in the modern history, we start with Arthur Reber's studies of implicit learning.

By the mid 1960s the cognitive revolution was well underway in psychology, with the field of *cognitive psychology* recognizing its own identity with the publication of Neisser's (1967) book of that name. One of the most curious aspects of the revolution was its effect on the study of learning and memory. For the preceding 50 years of the behaviorist age, learning had been the dominant paradigm. The processes studied were slow and incremental, as in the many studies of classical and operant conditioning in animals, and in attempts to produce comparable paradigms in humans that required associative learning. With the cognitive revolution, however, researchers apparently stopped studying learning and started studying memory! Instead of studying gradual acquisition processes, researchers effectively studied one-trial learning. Methods such as free recall (which has older origins) became popular. In this paradigm, participants are read a list of words just once, and then try to recall them in any order. This was one of the methods that quickly led cognitive psychologists in this period to distinguish between short-term and long-term memory systems (Atkinson and Shiffrin 1968).

As one who studied psychology in the 1960s, the second author (J. E.) recalls being puzzled by this development at the time. How could learning and memory be different things? With hindsight, we can see that what actually happened was that researchers mostly shifted from studying implicit to explicit forms of memory. We now know that there are multiple memory systems in the brain, some of which are implicit and others explicit, a fact established beyond doubt by numerous neuropsychological studies (Eichenbaum and Cohen 2001). There is an explicit learning system located in the hippocampus and quite separate implicit learning systems residing in regions of the brain associated with motor skills and emotional processing. These can be dissociated from each other by specific kinds of brain damage: for example, patients with hippocampal damage, known as amnesics, suffer impairment of explicit learning and memory, while retaining the ability to learn new skills and habits.

Starting his work well in advance of the neuropsychological studies, Reber is notable as one who continued to study human learning, while adapting to the cognitive revolution that was occurring around him. He was one of the first psychologists to coin the term 'cognitive unconscious' to refer to the idea that many cognitive processes occur outside of consciousness. In the 1960s Reber devised new paradigms for the study of implicit learning, defined as the 'acquisition of knowledge that takes place largely independently of conscious attempts to learn and largely in the absence of explicit knowledge about what was acquired' (Reber 1993, p.5). One of the most famous of these is the artificial grammar learning (AGL) paradigm. Participants are presented with letter strings to memorize, which, unknown to them, have been generated according to rules embedded in a finite state grammar. Such grammars allow one to move through them using various branches and loops, with each move generating a letter. In this way, a large number of different grammatical strings can be generated.

In a second stage of the method, participants are told that the strings were rule-governed and then asked to classify new sets of strings as being 'grammatical' or 'ungrammatical'. As has been shown many times, participants are able to do this at levels well above chance, but without the ability to describe what rules they are using. Interestingly, this applies also when the AGL paradigm is administered to amnesic patients who have lost the ability to form new explicit memories (Knowlton et al. 1992). Such patients can learn to classify new strings, despite the fact that they have no recall of the training experience. In spite of findings like this, Reber's claim that participants extract rule information without explicit effort or awareness remains somewhat controversial. Critics have doubted whether implicit learning is wholly unconscious (Shanks and St John 1994) or whether rules are really being abstracted (Redington and Chater 2002). From the viewpoint of dual-process theory, however, the critical issue is whether the study of implicit learning implicates a distinct system of learning and knowledge from that involved in explicit memory tasks. The neuropsychological evidence appears to us to be conclusive on this point, strongly supported by evolutionary arguments for multiple memory systems (Carruthers 2006; Sherry and Schacter 1987). We should note also that evidence of implicit rule learning has been demonstrated in a range of experimental paradigms other than AGL and by a number of different laboratories (for reviews, see Berry and Dienes 1993; Reber 1993; Sun 2001).

Reber did more than provide evidence for distinct implicit and explicit learning processes: he also developed a dual-system theory of learning that has had a considerable influence on the generic dual-system theory of thinking, and we discuss his ideas below. Another major influence on dual-system theory was the development of dual-process accounts of deductive reasoning, an enterprise in which J. E. was involved from the start (for a detailed history, see Evans 2004). There are actually two distinct origins of this theory, both in the 1970s, but not connected up until some years later. The first was the observation of a dissociation between behavior and introspective reports, similar to that so famously discussed by Nisbett and Wilson (1977). Wason and Evans (1975) investigated some apparently discrepant findings on the Wason selection task. One the one hand, it seemed that participants were choosing cards according to a primitive 'matching bias' (Evans and Lynch 1973), which determines attention to items specifically mentioned in a conditional statement. On the other hand, participants were prone to give rational-sounding explanations of their choices, in terms of the instruction to choose cards that verified or falsified the conditional statement (Goodwin and Wason 1972). Wason and Evans concluded that matching bias was an unconscious determinant of responding, and that introspective reports were mere *post hoc* rationalizations (see Lucas and Ball 2005 for a recent replication of key findings). They also were the first to use the terms 'type 1' and 'type 2' processing to refer to the unconscious and conscious processes respectively. If there was an historic influence on this, it was that of Freud, for Peter Wason was a barely in-the-closet Freudian.

The main stimulus for dual-process theories of reasoning, however, was the observation of the fact that logical processes seemed to compete with non-logical biases in determining behavior on various deductive reasoning tasks (Evans 1977). What became the paradigm case of this was the apparent conflict between logic and belief bias in content-rich versions of syllogistic reasoning tasks, first documented by Evans, Barston, and Pollard (1983; see Evans, this volume). Subsequent research using a variety of methods has suggested that belief bias reflects a type 1 process, whereas successful logical reasoning on this task requires type 2 processing. Work of this kind led to the development of the heuristic-analytic theory of reasoning (Evans 1989, 2006) and later to the dual-system theory discussed below. None of this early work was influenced by dual-process accounts of learning, memory, and social cognition; rather, it was driven by an attempt to understand the experimental findings.

Next in the story, chronologically speaking, comes the development of dual-process theories of social cognition (see Smith and Collins, this volume, for a detailed review). Apart from some historic influence of Freud (Epstein 1994), however, the origin of dual-process theories in social psychology seems to come from two main sources. First, analogous to (but in ignorance of) the work of Wason and Evans, social psychologists needed to explain the dissociation between explicitly stated attitudes and actual social behavior that was firmly established in experimental research conducted in the 1960s and 1970s. As Smith and Collins (this volume) document, the earliest models, developed in the 1980s, were designed to deal with persuasion and attitude change.

One major tradition of work has focused on lack of self-insight in social behavior and the tendency for people to confabulate accounts of unconsciously caused behavior (Wilson 2002). A number of the (numerous) dual-processing accounts of social cognition that have been developed since have been strongly influenced by developments in mainstream cognitive psychology that paradoxically had little or no influence on the development of dual-process theories of reasoning. One was the distinction between automatic and controlled processing, already mentioned, which has been developed into a highly influential theory of automaticity in social judgment by John Bargh (see Bargh 2006).

Work on automaticity includes studies which show that stereotypes are powerful implicit knowledge structures that influence social behavior in spite of explicit attitudes that are egalitarian. The main methodology for such studies has been that of *priming*, borrowed from the study of implicit memory (Kihlstrom et al. 2007; Schacter 1987) in cognitive psychology. Unconscious knowledge structures, such as implicit stereotypes and attitudes, can be primed by using apparently unrelated prior tasks that include content that activates the relevant knowledge. This then affects performance on the main task of social judgment or perception that follows. Another method favored by social psychologists is the correlation of social judgments with measures of individual differences in thinking style, such as Need for Cognition (Cacioppo and Petty 1982) or the Rational-Experiential Inventory (Epstein et al. 1996). However, it is debatable whether differences in thinking style are related to dual-process theories founded in distinct cognitive systems (see Evans, this volume; Buchtel and Norenzayan, this volume).

The dual-process approach to decision making has been popularized recently by Kahneman and Frederick (2002) drawing upon generic dual-system theory, discussed below. However, the distinction between intuitive and reflective decision making has been around for a long time. In fact, it is implicit in some of Tversky and Kahneman's earlier writing about the heuristics and biases research program. For example, Kahneman and Tversky (1982), who distinguished errors of application from errors of understanding, discussed both intuition and rule-based reasoning: 'It has been demonstrated that many adults do not have generally valid intuitions corresponding to the law of large numbers ... But it is simply not the case that every problem to which these rules are relevant will be answered incorrectly or that the rules cannot appear compelling in particular contexts' (p.449). They did not quite join up the dots at this stage by specifying (as Kahneman and Frederick now have done) that type 1 heuristics compete with type 2 rule-based reasoning in determining responding on such tasks.

Research on judgment and decision making is not necessarily cognitively oriented, with much research focused on the adequacy of normative or other descriptive models to account for behavior. However, sundry examples of dual-process thinking are to be found in these literatures, of which we shall briefly mention a few. In the tradition of work called social judgment theory (Doherty 1996), which dates from the ecological psychology of Brunswick, there is an account called *cognitive continuum theory* (Hammond 1996), which posits a distinction between intuitive and analytic thinking. However, as the name suggests, this is seen as a continuum rather than reflecting discrete cognitive systems. Fuzzy-trace theory (Reyna 2004) posits a distinction between verbatim and gist memory, which are argued to underlie reflective and intuitive decision making, respectively. Reyna is one of an increasing number of authors to emphasize the idea that intuitive decision making can be highly effective and often superior to that based on reflection (Dijksterhuis et al. 2006; Gigerenzer 2007; Gladwell 2005; Myers 2002). Most of these also point out that intuition can be unreliable and lead to cognitive biases as well.

The development of dual-system theory

As already observed, dual-process theories distinguish fast, automatic (type 1) processes from slow, deliberative (type 2) processes. Dual-*system* theories attribute the origin of these processes to two distinct cognitive systems. (For a further distinction between type 1 and 2 systems, see Samuels, this volume.) As a result, such theories tend also to attribute long lists of additional features to distinguish the two forms of processing (see Table 1.1). The terms 'System 1' and 'System 2' were coined by Stanovich (1999), but the dual-system theory was devised by a combination of authors, and has much earlier origins. Reber (see 1993, ch. 3) argued for the 'primacy of the implicit', proposing that consciousness was a late arrival in evolutionary terms, preceded by unconscious perceptual and cognitive functions by a considerable margin. He suggested that consciousness provided a unique executive function in human beings but that this had led to an illusory belief in consciousness as the primary cognitive system. In other words, unconscious cognition is the default and dominant system, while conscious cognition is a uniquely human and recently acquired plug-in that does a great deal less than we generally assume.

Table 1.1 Features attributed by various theorists to the two systems of cognition

System 1	System 2
Evolutionarily old	Evolutionarily recent
Unconscious, preconscious	Conscious
Shared with animals	Uniquely (distinctively) human
Implicit knowledge	Explicit knowledge
Automatic	Controlled
Fast	Slow
Parallel	Sequential
High capacity	Low capacity
Intuitive	Reflective
Contextualized	Abstract
Pragmatic	Logical
Associative	Rule-based
Independent of general intelligence	Linked to general intelligence

Reber (1993) went on to make a number of claims about the nature of implicit learning and implicit systems that helped to build the feature list of the generic dual-system theory shown in Table 1.1. We have already seen that his theory included age of evolution, implicit and explicit knowledge, and the idea that implicit but not explicit cognition is shared with other animals. In addition he also argued that implicit function had low variability across individuals and was independent of general intelligence. He seems to have been the first author to have developed these ideas, which are now incorporated in the generic dual-system theory. However, mention should also be made of Epstein, whose cognitive-experiential self-theory evolved from publications in the early 1970s.

In a landmark development, Epstein (1994) proposed an integration of Freudian and cognitive ideas about the unconscious. Among contemporary dual-process theorists he is unusual, if not unique, in crediting the Freudian dual-process distinction between primary and secondary process thinking, and also in firmly attaching emotional processing to what has now become known as System 1. In this paper, Epstein also reviewed various cognitive research (although not that in the psychology of reasoning) and concluded (p.714) that 'There is widespread agreement among the various theories on the existence of a conscious, deliberative, analytical system that could reasonably be labeled a rational system'. This he contrasted with an experiential system that was 'not limited to nonverbal processing of information, as emotion-arousing verbal stimuli also evoke experiential processing'. As with Reber, the evolutionary argument for two systems of cognition is also to be found in this paper. Epstein asserts (p.714) that 'Higher order organisms evolved in a manner that replaced instinct with a cognitive system that ... could direct behavior on the basis of learning from past experience. This system operates in a very different manner from a system developed much later that solves problems by use of symbols and logical inference.'

Evans and Over (1996) developed their dual-system account of reasoning and judgment primarily under the influence of the early dual-process theories of Evans, but with a substantial input from Reber's ideas and other writing in the field of implicit learning (Berry and Dienes 1993). They were not, however, aware of Epstein's work at that time, nor of the many developments of dual-process theories in the field of social cognition. The initial focus of their 1996 book was on the idea of two kinds of rationality. Initially, Evans and Over argued that instrumental rationality (achieving one's goals) need not involve normative rationality, in the sense of *explicitly* following rules prescribed by a normative system such as logic or probability theory. They argued that participants in reasoning experiments are often described as irrational because they fail to comply with instructions and violate norms. A good example is the influence of belief bias in reasoning described earlier. Because the instructions require people to assume the truth of the premises and draw logically necessary conclusions, any influence of belief is deemed to be erroneous (normatively irrational). However, as Evans and Over (1996) argued, it is (instrumentally) rational in everyday life to reason from *all relevant belief*. Thus they suggested that it is adaptive for our reasoning to be automatically contextualized with prior knowledge.

Evans and Over (1996) developed the notion of implicit and explicit cognitive systems, drawing upon the evolutionary ideas of Reber. Like Epstein, they emphasized the experiential nature of the implicit system, which they proposed to be based mostly on personal learning. In discussing the explicit system, they focused on how slow, limited in capacity, and high effort it is by comparison with the implicit system and hence raised the question of what functional advantage it could provide. They commented (p.154) that 'The advantage of the dual-process system is that conscious reflective thought provides the flexibility and foresight that the tacit system cannot, by its very nature, deliver. Most of the time our decision making is automatic and habitual, but it does not have to be that way … consciousness gives us the possibility to deal with novelty and anticipate the future.' The most distinctive aspect of Evans and Over's contribution, perhaps, is their emphasis on the idea of *hypothetical thinking*, which requires imagination of possibilities and mental simulations and the ability to decouple suppositions from actual beliefs. This kind of thinking they argued to be distinctively human and to require the recently evolved, second cognitive system.

Evans and Over (1996) acknowledged a parallel but highly relevant development in the shape of Sloman's (1996) proposal of two systems of reasoning, described as associative and rule-based respectively. Sloman's paper proved highly influential and helped to popularize the dual-process approach. It also helped inspire an integrative account of dual-process theories of social cognition under the same labels (Smith and DeCoster 2000; Smith and Collins, this volume). Sloman's scope was intentionally more limited than most of the dual-system accounts we have described, however, in that he restricted his account to reasoning and judgment and refrained from broader evolutionary arguments. However, he proposed a very clearly parallel architecture (see Evans, this volume) for the two systems and made a number of specific proposals about how two forms of reasoning could occur.

The final major contribution to the dual-system account of reasoning was that of Keith Stanovich (1999; 2004; this volume), who coined the terms 'System 1' and 'System 2'. Along with his collaborator Rich West, Stanovich ran a series of major studies of individual differences in reasoning and decision making. In interpreting their findings, he drew upon the dual-process theory of Evans and Over, but added back in the element of Reber's account which they had overlooked. This is the idea that System 2, but not System 1, is linked to individual differences in general intelligence. A good example of Stanovich and West's approach is the work reported in their (1998), which involved administering both abstract and deontic versions of the Wason selection task to large numbers of students. The abstract version is known to be very difficult, but the deontic version (which uses realistic contents) is much easier. Stanovich and West showed that the minority who can solve the abstract problem are of unusually high general intelligence (estimated from SAT scores), but that IQ confers little advantage in solving the deontic versions, where people can draw upon experiential learning and background knowledge. They thus inferred that abstract reasoning draws heavily upon System 2. In a large number of studies reviewed by Stanovich (1999) it was shown that students with high SAT scores generally perform much better on a range of reasoning and judgment tasks as assessed by standard normative systems.

In addition to developing the individual differences approach to dual-process research, Stanovich (1999, 2004; Stanovich and West 2003) has also contributed significantly to the debate concerning rationality and evolution. In doing so, he takes strong issue with the arguments of evolutionary psychologists such as Cosmides and Tooby (e.g. 1992). His essential argument is that evolution will not necessarily confer adaptive advantages in a modern technological society because the modern environment differs so radically from that in which we evolved. Thus System 1 procedures often result in cognitive biases when we try to engage in abstract and decontextualized forms of reasoning. Thus Stanovich does not support what he calls the Panglossian position of assuming that people are invariably rational. On the contrary, he suggests that much educational effort must be devoted to developing System 2 thinking skills. He also suggests that, uniquely among animals, we have a cognitive system (2) on a 'long leash' from the genes, which allows us to rebel and pursue our goals as individuals, and not necessarily those programmed by evolution.

The contribution of contemporary philosophy

We turn now to work by contemporary philosophers, some of whom have also developed dual-process theories of the mind—showing again how such views have been rediscovered in different traditions. A central concern in this area is with the analysis of everyday commonsense, or 'folk', psychology. It is important to stress that by 'folk psychology', philosophers do *not* mean the explicit beliefs that laypeople happen to have about the mind—'folksy psychology' as one philosopher dubs it (Botterill 1996). Rather, they mean the basic concepts and principles by which we explain and predict each other's actions—in particular, the concepts of *belief* and *desire* and the principles that guide our application of them. Many philosophers argue that folk psychology in this sense constitutes a theory of the internal structure and functioning of the mind, which is tacitly known by almost all adult humans (e.g. Botterill 1996; Botterill and Carruthers 1999; Churchland 1981). This theory is sometimes likened to the tacitly known generative grammar that, according to Chomskyan linguists, guides our language use. (Folksy psychology, by contrast, corresponds to people's explicit beliefs about grammar, of the kind once taught in schools.) This view, known as the 'theory-theory', is controversial, however, and other philosophers take a different view of the status of folk psychology. Some argue that it is more craft than science—a heuristic device, which involves no assumptions about the structure of the mind (e.g. Dennett 1987, 1991c). Others argue that our skill at everyday psychological prediction derives from an ability to run mental *simulations* of each other, rather than from a knowledge of theoretical principles (e.g. Goldman 1989; Gordon 1986; Heal 1986).

The debate about folk psychology focuses in particular on the analysis of the concepts of belief and desire. A key issue is whether in attributing beliefs and desires to people we implicitly commit ourselves to claims about the internal structure of their minds. Views on the matter can be characterized as deflationary or inflationary (the terms are ours). On deflationary views the criteria for possession of beliefs and desires are mostly or wholly behavioral. The extreme deflationary position is analytic or 'logical' behaviorism, according to which attributions of mental states are simply attributions of complex behavioral dispositions or patterns (e.g. Ryle 1949). This view was influential in the first half of the twentieth century, and versions of it still have powerful advocates, most notably Daniel Dennett (e.g. Dennett 1987, 1991b). On inflationary views, by contrast, there are strict internal criteria for the possession of mental states, instead of, or in addition to, the external ones. The most popular view of this kind—functionalism—treats beliefs and desires as discrete representational states, defined by the role they play in mediating between stimuli and overt action (e.g. Fodor 1987; Lewis 1972). In one form or another, functionalism has been the dominant position in philosophy of mind from the 1960s onwards.

Philosophers of mind have also taken a strong interest in scientific models of the mind and in the question of their compatibility with folk psychology. On deflationary readings, folk-psychological descriptions involve few or no assumptions about internal structure and are compatible with a wide range of scientific models of the mind. On inflationary readings, by contrast, folk psychology does make such assumptions and is incompatible with some models. For example, some inflationary views assume that beliefs and desires are internal representational states, which are functionally discrete and can be selectively activated. Such a view is compatible with many computationalist models, but appears incompatible with some connectionist ones, which (arguably) do not support discrete representations of this kind. Some writers argue that if such connectionist models should prove correct, then folk psychology will be refuted and the concepts of belief and desire will have to be eliminated from serious discourse about the mind (e.g. Ramsey et al. 1990). Others prefer to adopt a more deflationary view, on which the potential for conflict between science and folk psychology is reduced (e.g. Clark 1993; Horgan and Graham 1990).

For the most part, these debates have proceeded within a unitary framework; it assumed that there is just one basic type of belief and desire, and one kind of mental processing. However, some writers have argued that there are important distinctions to be drawn among everyday mental concepts, which point to the existence of different types of belief, or belief-like state, associated with different reasoning systems. (The focus is typically on belief, though it is usually implied that a similar distinction can be made for desire.) We shall briefly review some suggestions along these lines.

Norman Malcolm distinguishes *thinking* and *having thoughts* (Malcolm 1973). To say that someone has the thought that p, Malcolm notes, is to say that they have formulated that proposition, or that it has occurred to them, or crossed their mind. To say that someone thinks that p, by contrast, does not imply any of these things. Seeing a dog barking up a tree, we might say 'He thinks the cat went up that tree', without implying that the creature had formulated or thought of the proposition *The cat went up that tree*. Malcolm focuses on conceptual issues and does not offer a substantive account of either of these psychological phenomena, though he argues that the ability to have thoughts is dependent on the possession of language. He concludes that there is no single paradigm or prototype of thinking, and suggests that it was by rashly taking *having thoughts* as the paradigm that Descartes was led to deny that animals can think.

Daniel Dennett draws a related distinction between *belief* and *opinion* (Dennett 1978, ch.16, 1991c). Belief in Dennett's sense is a basic mental state, common to humans, animals, and even mechanical systems, and the criteria for its possession are entirely behavioral. Opinions, on the other hand, are more sophisticated, 'linguistically infected' states, which are possessed only by humans. To have an opinion is to be committed to the truth of a sentence in a language one understands (to have 'bet' on its truth), often as result of consciously *making up* or *changing* one's mind. Dennett suggests that the psychology of belief and opinion is very different, and that a mental architecture that will support non-linguistic animal-type beliefs may be quite inadequate to support opinions. Confusion between the two states, Dennett claims, lies at the root of many philosophical misconceptions about belief, and lends spurious plausibility to inflationary views of belief (1991c).

Another duality can be found in the work of Jonathan Cohen, who makes a distinction between *belief* and *acceptance* (Cohen 1992). Belief in Cohen's sense is a disposition, though not a disposition to action; to believe something is to be disposed to *feel it true*. Acceptance, on the other hand, is a mental action or pattern of action; to accept something is to have a policy of taking it as a premise in conscious, rule-based reasoning. Belief is passive, graded, non-linguistic, and exhibited by animals as well as humans, whereas acceptance is active, binary, linguistically formulated, and not exhibited by animals. Cohen argues that this distinction is implicit in everyday thinking about the mind and that it is crucial to the explanation of many familiar psychological phenomena. This duality of mental states implies a duality of mental processes, and Cohen notes that it corresponds well with the division between connectionist and computational models in psychology. Belief, he argues, being parallel, graded, and not rule-governed, can be modeled by connectionist networks, whereas acceptance, which is sequential, ungraded, and rule-governed, is better modeled by digital computer programs (Cohen 1992, pp.56–8).

Frankish (2004) argues that the folk-psychological term 'belief' is used to refer to two different types of state: one nonconscious, implicit, passive, graded, and non-linguistic, the other conscious, explicit, active, binary, and language-involving. This hypothesis, he argues, explains various tensions in folk psychology and can reconcile the competing intuitions that support deflationary and inflationary positions. A deflationary perspective is appropriate for talk about nonconscious beliefs, which guide spontaneous, unreflective behavior. We attribute such beliefs freely to a wide range of creatures without assuming that they are discretely represented, and we cite them in explanation of actions without implying that they were individually activated. However, a more inflationary, functionalist, perspective is required for conscious beliefs, which can be individually called to mind, and whose activation may cause radical deviations from our normal patterns of behavior. Building on Cohen's account of acceptance, Frankish develops a model of conscious beliefs as premising policies, which are actively adopted and executed in response to beliefs and desires of the nonconscious type. This model of conscious belief, he argues, is functionalist in spirit but also compatible with a wide range of views about the internal structure of the cognitive system. To highlight the dependency relation between the two types of belief, Frankish dubs the nonconscious type *basic belief* and the conscious one *superbelief*.

There is a common theme to these distinctions: there is one type of belief that is implicit, non-linguistic, and common to humans and animals, and another (thought, opinion, acceptance, superbelief) that is explicit, conscious, language-involving, and uniquely human. And there are suggestions that each type is associated with a different kind of processing—parallel and connectionist in the first case, serial and rule-governed in the second. There is a clear, though not perfect, correspondence here with dual-process theories in psychology—the implicit form of belief corresponding to System 1 and the explicit form to System 2. (Of course, if implicit beliefs are behavioral dispositions, then they cannot be thought of as *inputs* to System 1 reasoning, but they can be regarded as manifestations of System 1 activity.) We think this correspondence offers further support for a dual-process model. Folk psychology, we suggest, is tracking, albeit obscurely, the same fundamental duality that scientific psychology has identified. Of course, this is not the only possible explanation of the correspondence. It could be that the dual-process perspective implicit in folk psychology has influenced explicit theorizing about the mind by philosophers and psychologists—resulting in the pattern of rediscovery we have highlighted in this chapter. We cannot conclusively rule out this hypothesis, but it seems to us a much less plausible one, given the diverse theoretical concerns of the writers discussed and the variety of methodological approaches they have employed.

The work discussed above was driven primarily by concerns with the analysis and evaluation of everyday psychological discourse, but contemporary philosophers have also contributed more directly to the development of dual-process theories by engaging in empirically based theorizing about mental architecture. In particular, many philosophers have been attracted to the idea that possession of language makes possible a new type of reasoning, different in character from the non-linguistic sort. This view is often coupled with the idea that the language-based reasoning system is a soft-wired one—a 'virtual machine' as Dennett puts it—which emerges from the interaction of pre-existing components. We shall briefly review some of this work, which can be seen as complementing the folk-psychologically-based dualities discussed above.

We begin with Dennett's account of the conscious mind (1991a). The biological brain, Dennett claims, is a collection of specialized hardwired subsystems, operating in parallel and competing for control of action. The conscious mind, on the other hand, is a virtual machine, which we create for ourselves by engaging in various learned behaviors—principally habits of private speech, either overt or silent. Dennett claims that such speech serves as a form of self-stimulation, and he suggests that it performs important executive functions, focusing the resources of different neural subsystems and promoting sustained and coherent patterns of behavior. There are echoes here of Skinner's account of thinking as automatically reinforcing verbal behavior, mentioned earlier. By engaging in private speech, Dennett argues, we effectively reprogram our biological brains, causing their parallel machinery to mimic the behavior of a serial computer. Dennett dubs this softwired system the *Joycean machine*—alluding to James Joyce's depictions of the stream of consciousness.

A somewhat similar view is proposed by Paul Smolensky—a cognitive scientist whose work has been much discussed by philosophers. Smolensky (1988) argues that a connectionist system could simulate the behavior of a rule-governed serial processor by encoding natural language sentences expressing production rules (rules of the form 'If condition A obtains then do action B'). When the condition of an encoded production rule holds, Smolensky argues, associative processes would trigger the activity pattern encoding the linguistic representation of the entire rule, and the representation of the action part of the rule would then tend to trigger the action itself, thus constraining the system to obey the rule. The effect would be to create a virtual rule-based serial processor—a 'Conscious Rule Interpreter'—implemented by parallel associative processes. (Smolensky suggests that the activities involved would be conscious in virtue of the fact that they would involve stable large-scale activity patterns.)

Frankish also characterizes the conscious mind as a language-dependent virtual machine (2004, this volume). Conscious reasoning, he argues, is an intentional activity, which involves producing and manipulating sentences of inner speech and other forms of mental imagery, in order to execute various problem-solving strategies. These actions, Frankish claims, are motivated and supported by nonconscious metacognitive attitudes (desires to solve problems, beliefs about the strategies that may work, and so on), and they influence action in virtue of a nonconscious desire to act on the results of one's conscious reasoning. The result is a two-level picture in which the conscious mind is a virtual structure—Frankish calls it the *supermind*—which is implemented in metacognitive processes at the nonconscious level.

Finally, another variant of the 'virtual system' approach is found in Carruthers's work (2002, 2006, this volume). Carruthers advocates a massively modular view of the mind, according to which central cognition is composed of numerous semi-independent domain-specific subsystems. A major challenge for such a view is to explain the existence of flexible, domain-general thinking, of the distinctively human kind. In response, Carruthers argues that such thinking is performed by a virtual system, which is the product of our capacity for the mental rehearsal of action schemata—in particular, ones for the production of utterances. In the case of utterances, Carruthers argues, such rehearsal generates auditory feedback (inner speech) that is processed by the speech comprehension subsystem and tends to produce effects at the modular level appropriate to the thoughts the utterances express. Since utterances may combine outputs from different modules, this implements a form of domain-general thinking, and cycles of mental rehearsal create a flexible domain-general reasoning system, using only the basic resources of a modular mind equipped with a language faculty.

The virtual-system approach proposed by these writers can be seen as a form of dual-process theory, which treats the second system as emergent from the first, rather than distinct from it. As the writers stress, this approach has particular attractions from an evolutionary perspective, showing how a radically new form of cognitive activity could develop without massive changes to neural hardware. From the viewpoint of cognitive and neural architecture, however, such virtual dual-process theories clearly differ significantly from those that describe System 2 as instantiated in mechanisms distinct from those of System 1. This is a debate which may ultimately be settled by work mapping type 1 and 2 processes onto underlying neural systems (see Lieberman, this volume, for examples of such research). If type 2 processing is an emergent property of type 1 systems, then we should not expect a switch to wholly distinct neural areas when this kind of thinking is activated. The issue is not a simple one, however, since virtual-system theorists need not claim that *all* type 1 systems are involved in supporting type 2 reasoning, and they typically allow that some other systems are involved as well, notably language and motor control (for some empirical predictions of one version of virtual-system theory, see Carruthers, this volume).

Future directions

How will dual-process theory develop? We can see three main trends in current research, which we expect to continue and flourish. The first involves reflection on the foundations of dual-process theory itself. We are confident that some form of two-systems theory will survive, but we also expect to see important modifications and qualifications to it. Many dual-process theorists are currently rethinking their views and recognizing that the original framework needs to be substantially revised. There are two aspects to this. One involves backing off from definitions of the two systems in terms of the processing styles involved—heuristic and associative on the one hand, analytic and role-governed on the other (see the chapters in this volume by Buchtel and Norenzayan, Evans, Frankish, and Stanovich). Theorists are increasingly recognizing the diversity of the processes in both systems, and seeking to redraw the distinction between the two systems in other terms, distinguishing System 2 by its association with working memory (Evans, this volume), high-level control (Stanovich, this volume), or personal control (Frankish, this volume). The second aspect involves the recognition of the range of processes involved in supporting System 2 reasoning. In recent work, for example, Evans posits *type 3* processes, which are involved in triggering System 2 activity and mediating between the two systems (Evans, this volume). In short, it is likely that future two-*systems* theories will need to posit multiple kinds of cognitive *processing*.

The second trend is one of increasing integration between dual-process theorists in different fields. In the past, work on dual processes in social psychology and cognitive psychology proceeded largely in parallel, with little communication between researchers. This is changing now (see Smith and Collins, this volume; Klaczynski, this volume), and we believe there is scope for significant experimental collaboration and theoretical integration in the future. We also feel that it is important to integrate dual-process theories of reasoning more closely with theories of perception, emotion, memory, and motor control, in order to develop overarching conceptions of mental architecture. An example is the application of the notion of 'metacognition', primarily developed in the study of memory, to dual-process accounts of reasoning and judgment (see Thompson, this volume). A narrow focus is necessary in experimental work, but it is important to keep pulling back to consider the wider theoretical picture, as some philosophers of psychology have urged. Peter Carruthers's 2006 book on the architecture of the mind, mentioned in the previous section, provides a good example of the kind of integrative theorizing we favor.

The third trend involves the application of dual-process theory, both within and beyond the academic world. Contemporary academic developments include computational modeling of dual-system architectures (see Sun et al., this volume) and the search for evidence of dual processes and systems through the methods of neuropsychology and neuroscience (see Goel 2005, 2007; Lieberman, this volume). Authors with a strong evolutionary orientation are now trying to reconcile dual-process theory with a massively modular view of the human mind (see Mercier and Sperber, this volume; Carruthers, this volume). The theory is influencing the approach of moral philosophers, too (see L. Saunders, this volume), and impacting strongly on the debate about human rationality (see Evans and Over 1996; Stanovich 1999; C. Saunders and Over, this volume).

The idea that we have 'two minds', only one of which corresponds to personal, volitional cognition, also has wide implications beyond cognitive science. The fact that much of our thought and behavior is controlled by automatic, subpersonal, and inaccessible cognitive processes challenges our most fundamental and cherished notions about personal and legal responsibility. This has major ramifications for social sciences such as economics, sociology, and social policy. As implied by some contemporary researchers (e.g. Stanovich, this volume; Klaczynski, this volume) dual-process theory also has enormous implications for educational theory and practice. As the theory becomes better understood and more widely disseminated, its implications for many aspects of society and academia will need to be thoroughly explored. In terms of its wider significance, the story of dual-process theorizing is just beginning.

Acknowledgments

The authors would like to thank Shira Elqayam for her detailed and thoughtful comments on an earlier draft of this chapter. They also thank Alex Barber, Stuart Brown, Tim Chappell, John Cottingham, and Carolyn Price for helpful discussions of philosophical precursors of dual-process theory. Keith Frankish's work on this chapter was supported by a research leave award from the Arts and Humanities Research Council, and Jonathan Evans's by a personal research fellowship from the Economic and Social Research Council (RES–000–27–0184).

References

Annas, J. (1981) *An introduction to Plato's republic.* Oxford University Press, Oxford.

Atkinson, R.C. and Shiffrin, R.M. (1968) Human memory: A proposed system and its control processes. In K.W. Spence (ed.) *The psychology of learning and motivation: Advances in research and theory,* 89–195. Academic Press, New York.

Baars, B.J. (1986) *The cognitive revolution in psychology.* Guilford Press, New York.

Baddeley, A. (2007) *Working memory, thought and action.* Oxford University Press, Oxford.

Bargh, J.A. (ed.) (2006) *Social psychology and the unconscious.* Psychology Press, New York.

Berry, D.C. and Dienes, Z. (1993) *Implicit learning.* Erlbaum, Hove.

Botterill, G. (1996) Folk psychology and theoretical status. In P. Carruthers and P.K. Smith (eds) *Theories of theories of mind,* 105–18. Cambridge University Press, Cambridge.

Botterill, G. and Carruthers, P. (1999) *The philosophy of psychology.* Cambridge University Press, Cambridge.

Cacioppo, J.T. and Petty, R.E. (1982) The need for cognition. *Journal of Personality and Social Psychology,* 42, 116–31.

Carpenter, W.B. (1874) *Principles of mental physiology with their applications to the training and discipline of the mind and the study of its morbid conditions.* Henry S. King & Co., London.

Carruthers, P. (2002) The cognitive functions of language. *Behavioral and Brain Sciences,* 25, 657–719.

Carruthers, P. (2006) *The architecture of the mind*. Oxford University Press, Oxford.

Chomsky, N. (1959) A review of B.F. Skinner's *Verbal Behavior*. *Language*, **35**, 25–58.

Churchland, P.M. (1981) Eliminative materialism and the propositional attitudes. *Journal of Philosophy*, **78**, 67–90.

Clark, A. (1993) *Associative engines: Connectionism, concepts and representational change*. MIT Press, Cambridge, MA.

Cloeren, H.J. (1988) *Language and thought: German approaches to analytic philosophy in the 18th and 19th centuries*. De Gruyter, Berlin.

Cohen, L.J. (1992) *An essay on belief and acceptance*. Oxford University Press, Oxford.

Cosmides, L. and Tooby, J. (1992) Cognitive adaptations for social exchange. In J.H. Barkow, L. Cosmides, and J. Tooby (eds) *The adapted mind: Evolutionary psychology and the generation of culture*, 163–228. Oxford University Press, New York.

Cottingham, J. (1992) Cartesian dualism: Theology, metaphysics, and science. In J. Cottingham (ed.) *The Cambridge companion to Descartes*, 236–57. Cambridge University Press, Cambridge.

Dennett, D.C. (1978) *Brainstorms: Philosophical essays on mind and psychology*. MIT Press, Cambridge, MA.

Dennett, D.C. (1987) *The intentional stance*. MIT Press, Cambridge, MA.

Dennett, D.C. (1991a) *Consciousness explained*. Little Brown and Co., Boston, MA.

Dennett, D.C. (1991b) Real patterns. *Journal of Philosophy*, **88**, 27–51.

Dennett, D.C. (1991c) Two contrasts: Folk craft versus folk science and belief versus opinion. In J. Greenwood (ed.) *The future of folk psychology: Intentionality and cognitive science*, 135–48. Cambridge University Press, Cambridge.

Descartes, R. (1642/1984) Objections and replies. In R. Descartes, *The philosophical writings of Descartes: Volume 2* (J. Cottingham, R. Stoothoff, and D. Murdoch, trans.), 63–383. Cambridge University Press, Cambridge.

Descartes, R. (1664/1985) Treatise on man. In R. Descartes, *The philosophical writings of Descartes: Volume 1* (J. Cottingham, R. Stoothoff, and D. Murdoch, trans.), 99–108. Cambridge University Press, Cambridge.

Dijksterhuis, A., Bos, M.W., Nordgren, L.F., and von Baaren, R.B. (2006) On making the right choice: The deliberation-without-attention effect. *Science*, **311**, 1005–7.

Doherty, M.E. (ed.) (1996) *Social judgement theory* (*Thinking and Reasoning* special issue, vol. 2, nos 2/3). Psychology Press, Hove.

Duncker, K. (1945) On problem solving. *Psychological Monographs*, **58** (whole number 270).

Eichenbaum, N.J. and Cohen, N.J. (2001) *From conditioning to conscious reflection: Memory systems of the brain*. Oxford University Press, New York.

Ellenberger, H.F. (1970) *The discovery of the unconscious: The history and evolution of dynamic psychiatry*. Basic Books, New York.

Epstein, S. (1994) Integration of the cognitive and psychodynamic unconscious. *American Psychologist*, **49**, 709–24.

Epstein, S., Pacini, R., Denes-Raj, V., and Heier, H. (1996) Individual differences in intuitive-experiential and analytic-rational thinking styles. *Journal of Personality and Social Psychology*, **71**, 390–405.

Evans, J.St.B.T. (1977) Toward a statistical theory of reasoning. *Quarterly Journal of Experimental Psychology*, **29**, 297–306.

Evans, J.St.B.T. (1989) *Bias in human reasoning: Causes and consequences*. Erlbaum, Brighton.

Evans, J.St.B.T. (2004) History of the dual-process theory of reasoning. In K.I. Manktelow and M.C. Chung (eds) *Psychology of reasoning: Theoretical and historical perspectives*, 241–66. Psychology Press, Hove.

Evans, J.St.B.T. (2006) The heuristic-analytic theory of reasoning: Extension and evaluation. *Psychonomic Bulletin and Review*, **13**, 378–95.

Evans, J.St.B.T. (2008) Dual-processing accounts of reasoning, judgment and social cognition. *Annual Review of Psychology*, **59**, 255–78.

Evans, J.St.B.T. and Lynch, J.S. (1973) Matching bias in the selection task. *British Journal of Psychology*, **64**, 391–7.

Evans, J.St.B.T. and Over, D.E. (1996) *Rationality and reasoning*. Psychology Press, Hove.

Evans, J.St.B.T., Barston, J.L., and Pollard, P. (1983) On the conflict between logic and belief in syllogistic reasoning. *Memory & Cognition*, **11**, 295–306.

Fodor, J.A. (1987) *Psychosemantics: The problem of meaning in the philosophy of mind*. MIT Press, Cambridge, MA.

Frankish, K. (2004) *Mind and supermind*. Cambridge University Press, Cambridge.

Freud, S. (1915/2005) *The unconscious*. (G. Frankland, trans.) Penguin, London.

Freud, S. (1927) *The ego and the id*. (J. Riviere, trans.) Hogarth Press, London.

Galton, F. (1879a) Psychometric facts. *The Nineteenth Century*, **5**, 425–33.

Galton, F. (1879b) Psychometric experiments. *Brain*, **2**, 149–62.

Gardner, S. (1999) Schopenhauer, will, and the unconscious. In C. Janaway (ed.) *The Cambridge companion to Schopenhauer*, 375–421. Cambridge University Press, Cambridge.

Gardner, S. (2003) The unconscious mind. In T. Baldwin (ed.) *The Cambridge history of philosophy, 1870–1945*, 107–15. Cambridge University Press, Cambridge.

Gigerenzer, G. (2007) *Gut feelings*. Penguin, London.

Gladwell, M. (2005) *Blink*. Penguin, London.

Goel, V. (2005) Cognitive neuroscience of deductive reasoning. In K. Holyoak and R.G. Morrison (eds) *The Cambridge handbook of thinking and reasoning*, 475–92. Cambridge University Press, Cambridge.

Goel, V. (2007) Anatomy of deductive reasoning. *Trends in Cognitive Sciences*, **11**, 435–41.

Goldman, A. (1989) Interpretation psychologized. *Mind and Language*, **4**, 161–85.

Goodwin, R.Q. and Wason, P.C. (1972) Degrees of insight. *British Journal of Psychology*, **63**, 205–12.

Gordon, R.M. (1986) Folk psychology as simulation. *Mind and Language*, **1**, 158–71.

Grünbaum, A. (1984) *The foundations of psychoanalysis: A philosophical critique*. University of California Press, Berkeley, CA.

Hamilton, W. (1860) *Lectures on metaphysics and logic*, 2 vols. Gould and Lincoln, Boston, MA.

Hammond, K.R. (1996) *Human judgment and social policy*. Oxford University Press, New York.

Hartmann, E. von (1868/1931) *Philosophy of the unconscious: Speculative results according to the inductive method of physical science* (W.C. Coupland, trans.). Kegan Paul, London.

Hatfield, G. (2002) Perception as unconscious inference. In D. Heyer and R. Mausfeld (eds) *Perception and the physical world: Psychological and philosophical issues in perception*, 115–43. John Wiley & Sons, Ltd., New York.

Heal, J. (1986) Replication and functionalism. In J. Butterfield (ed.) *Language, Mind, and Logic*, 135–50. Cambridge University Press, Cambridge.

Helmholtz, H. von (1867/1962) *Helmholtz's treatise on physiological optics*. (J.P.C. Southall trans. 3rd ed.) Dover Publications, New York.

Horgan, T. and Graham, G. (1990) In defense of southern fudamentalism. *Philosophical Studies*, **62**, 107–34.

Humphrey, C. (1951) *Thinking: An introduction to its experimental psychology*. Methuen, London.

James, W. (1890) *The principles of psychology*. Henry Holt and Co., New York.

James, W. (1902) *The varieties of religious experience: A study in human nature*. Longmans, Green and Co., New York.

Kahneman, D. and Frederick, S. (2002) Representativeness revisited: Attribute substitution in intuitive judgement. In T. Gilovich, D. Griffin, and D. Kahneman (eds) *Heuristics and biases: The psychology of intuitive judgment*, 49–81. Cambridge University Press, Cambridge.

Kahneman, D. and Tversky, A. (1982) On the study of statistical intuitions. *Cognition*, **11**, 123–41.

Kihlstrom, J.F., Dorfman, J., and Park, L. (2007) Implicit and explicit learning and memory. In M. Velmans and S. Schneider (eds). *The Blackwell companion to consciousness*, 525–39. Blackwell, Oxford.

Knowlton, B.J., Ramus, S., and Squire, L.R. (1992) Intact artificial grammar learning in amnesia. *Psychological Science*, **3**, 172–9.

Laycock, T. (1845) On the reflex function of the brain. *British and Foreign Medical Journal*, **19**, 298–311.

Laycock, T. (1860) *Mind and brain, or, The correlations of consciousness and organisation*. Sutherland and Knox, Edinburgh.

Leibniz, G.W. (1702/1989) Letter to Queen Sophie Charlotte of Prussia, on what is independent of sense and matter. In G.W. Leibniz, *Philosophical essays* (R. Ariew and D. Garber, trans.), 186–92. Hackett, Indianapolis.

Leibniz, G.W. (1714/1989) Principles of nature and grace, based on reason. In G.W. Leibniz, *Philosophical essays* (R. Ariew and D. Garber, trans.), 206–13. Hackett, Indianapolis.

Leibniz, G.W. (1765/1996) *New essays concerning human understanding*. (P. Remnant and J.F. Bennett, trans.) Cambridge University Press, Cambridge.

Lewis, D. (1972) Psychophysical and theoretical identifications. *Australasian Journal of Philosophy*, **50**, 249–58.

Locke, J. (1706/1961) *An essay concerning human understanding,* 5th ed. J.W. Youlton (ed.)) Dent, London.

Lucas, E.J. and Ball, L.J. (2005) Think-aloud protocols and the selection task: Evidence for relevance effects and rationalisation processes. *Thinking and Reasoning*, **11**, 35–66.

Luchins, A.S. (1942) Mechanisation in problem solving. *Psychological Monographs*, **54** (whole number 248).

Macmillan, M. (1997) *Freud evaluated: The completed arc*. MIT Press, Cambridge, MA.

Maier, N.R.F. (1931) Reasoning in humans II. The solution of a problem and its appearance in consciousness. *Journal of Comparative Psychology*, **12**, 181–94.

Maine de Biran, F.P.G. (1803/1929) *The influence of habit on the faculty of thinking*. (M.D. Boehm, trans.) Baillière & Co., London.

Malcolm, N. (1973) Thoughtless brutes. *Proceedings and Addresses of the American Philosophical Association*, 1972–73, **46**, 5–20.

Mandler, J.M. and Mandler, G. (1964) *Thinking: From association to gestalt*. Wiley, New York.

Myers, D.G. (2002) *Intuition: Its powers and perils*. Yale University Press, New Haven, CT.

Neisser, U. (1967) *Cognitive psychology*. Appleton, New York.

Nisbett, R.E. and Wilson, T.D. (1977) Telling more than we can know: Verbal reports on mental processes. *Psychological Review*, **84**, 231–95.

Piaget, J. (1926) *The language and thought of the child*. Routledge, London.

Plato (1993) *Republic* (R. Waterfield, trans.) Oxford University Press, Oxford.

Ramsey, W., Stich, S.P., and Garon, J. (1990) Connectionism, eliminativism and the future of folk psychology. In J.E. Tomberlin (ed.) *Philosophical perspectives, 4: Action theory and philosophy of mind*, 499–533. Ridgeview Publishing Company, Atascadero, CA.

Reber, A.S. (1993) *Implicit learning and tacit knowledge*. Oxford University Press, Oxford.

Redington, M. and Chater, N. (2002) Knowledge representation and transfer in artificial grammar learning. In R.M. French and A. Cleeremans (eds) *Implicit learning and tacit knowledge*, 121–50. Psychology Press, Hove.

Reeves, J.W. (1965) *Thinking about thinking: Studies in the background of some psychological approaches*. Secker & Warburg, London.

Reyna, V.F. (2004) How people make decisions that involve risk: A dual-processes approach. *Current Directions in Psychological Science*, **13**, 60–6.

Ryle, G. (1949) *The concept of mind*. Hutchinson, London.

Schacter, D.L. (1987) Implicit memory: History and current status. *Journal of Experimental Psychology-Learning Memory and Cognition*, **13**, 501–18.

Schacter, D.L. and Tulving, E. (1994) What are the memory systems of 1994? In D.L. Schacter and E. Tulving (eds) *Memory systems 1994*, 1–38. MIT Press, Cambridge, MA.

Schneider, W. and Shiffrin, R.M. (1977) Controlled and automatic human information processing I: Detection, search and attention. *Psychological Review*, **84**, 1–66.

Schopenhauer, A. (1819/1966) *The world as will and representation*, 2 vols (E.F. Payne, trans.). Dover Publications, New York.

Shanks, D.R. and St John, M.F. (1994) Characteristics of dissociable human learning systems. *Behavioral and Brain Sciences*, **17**, 367–447.

Sherry, D.F. and Schacter, D.L. (1987) The evolution of multiple memory systems. *Psychological Review*, **94**, 439–54.

Shiffrin, R.M. and Schneider, W. (1977) Controlled and automatic human information processing II: Perceptual learning, automatic attending and a general theory. *Psychological Review*, **84**, 127–89.

Skinner, B.F. (1957) *Verbal behavior*. Prentice-Hall, Englewood Cliffs, NJ.

Sloman, S.A. (1996) The empirical case for two systems of reasoning. *Psychological Bulletin*, **119**, 3–22.

Smith, E.R. and DeCoster, J. (2000) Dual-process models in social and cognitive psychology: Conceptual integration and links to underlying memory systems. *Personality and Social Psychology Review*, **4**, 108–31.

Smolensky, P. (1988) On the proper treatment of connectionism. *Behavioral and Brain Sciences*, **11**, 1–23.

Stanovich, K.E. (1999) *Who is rational? Studies of individual differences in reasoning*. Lawrence Elrbaum Associates, Mahwah, NJ.

Stanovich, K.E. (2004) *The robot's rebellion: Finding meaning the age of Darwin*. Chicago University Press, Chicago, IL.

Stanovich, K.E. and West, R.F. (1998) Cognitive ability and variation in selection task performance. *Thinking and Reasoning*, **4**, 193–230.

Stanovich, K.E. and West, R.F. (2003) Evolutionary versus instrumental goals: How evolutionary psychology misconceives human rationality. In D.E. Over (ed.) *Evolution and the psychology of thinking*, 171–230. Psychology Press, Hove.

Sun, R. (2001) *Duality of mind: A bottom-up approach towards cognition*. Lawrence Erlbaum Associates, Hillsdale, NJ.

Vygotsky, L. (1934/1962) *Thought and language*. MIT Press, Harvard.

Wason, P.C. and Evans, J.St.B.T. (1975) Dual-processes in reasoning? *Cognition*, **3**, 141–54.

Watson, J.B. (1913) Psychology as the behaviorist views it. *Psychological Review*, 20, 158–77.

Weinberger, J. (2000) William James and the unconscious: Redressing a century-old misunderstanding. *Psychological Science*, **11**, 439–45.

Wertheimer, M. (1945/1961) *Productive thinking*. Tavistock, London.

Whyte, L.L. (1978) *The unconscious before Freud*. St Martin's Press, New York.

Wilson, T.D. (2002) *Strangers to ourselves: Discovering the adaptive unconscious*. Belknap Press, Cambridge, MA.

Part 1

Foundations

Chapter 2

How many dual-process theories do we need? One, two, or many?

Jonathan St. B. T. Evans

Dual-process theories of cognition are to be found everywhere in psychology although the literatures concerned may contain little or no cross referencing to each other. These theories come under many labels, but at least superficially all seem to be making a similar distinction (see Evans 2008; and Frankish and Evans, this volume). One question addressed in this chapter is that of whether we need to have this great multiplicity of theories, or whether there is one grand unifying dual-process theory that can incorporate them all. The literature already contains dual-system theories which purport to integrate many if not all accounts in this way (see Evans 2003; Stanovich, this volume; Evans and Over 1996; Smith and DeCoster 2000; Stanovich 1999) and one objective is here is to assess the adequacy of such accounts. However, I shall argue that such theories fall into two distinct groups from the viewpoint of the cognitive architecture they imply. There is also a third notion (cognitive styles) which can all too readily be confused with such two-process accounts.

In previous reviews of this topic (e.g. Evans 2003), I have followed the fashion started by Stanovich (1999) for referring to System 1 and System 2 processes. I shall not do so in this chapter, except when referring specifically to dual-system theories. Instead I will talk of *type* 1 and 2 processes, a terminology first used over 30 years ago in the literature on reasoning (Wason and Evans 1975). Although, it is common to refer to type 1 processes as unconscious or preconscious and type 2 processes as conscious, this also begs some important questions. A minimal definition of the difference is the following:

- ◆ Type 1 processes: fast, automatic, high processing capacity, low effort.
- ◆ Type 2 processes: slow, controlled, limited capacity, high effort.

These definitions apply to all dual-process theories of higher cognition, including those in the fields of reasoning, decision making, and social cognition (Evans 2008). However, few theorists confine themselves to these properties. The most common additions imply some kind of basis for the type 1 and 2 distinction in cognitive architecture (see below). These include the ideas that (a) that type 2 processes are intrinsically sequential whereas type 1 processes can be massively parallel and (b) that type 2, but not type 1 processes are related to individual differences in cognitive capacity. By cognitive capacity, theorists mean either general intelligence or working memory capacity which are in any case very highly correlated measures (Colom et al. 2004).

Table 2.1 Some properties typically associated with dual-system theories of cognition

System 1	System 2
Evolutionarily old	Evolutionarily recent
Shared with animals	Distinctively human
Unconscious, preconscious	Conscious
Controlled, volitional	Automatic
Fast, parallel	Slow, sequential
Associated with language	Independent of language
Associative	Rule-based
Belief-based, pragmatic reasoning	Abstract, logical reasoning
Implicit knowledge	Explicit knowledge
Independent of cognitive capacity	Dependent on cognitive capacity
Personal	Subpersonal

Finally, dual-*system* theories, as currently conceived, hold that there are two distinct systems: Systems 1 and 2, which are responsible for type 1 and type 2 processing respectively. In such theories, these systems may be distinguished by other character-istics such as consciousness, access to linguistic representations, age of evolution, neurological location, and specificity to human beings (Epstein and Pacini 1999; Evans and Over 1996; Evans, Over, and Handley 2003; Reber 1993; Stanovich 1999; Stanovich 2004). For a list of typical System 1 and 2 attributes see Table 2.1.

On cognitive architecture: Systems, processes, modes, and minds

Cognitive architecture is concerned with identifying various components of the mind and their connection with one another. The term 'system' is somewhat vague because systems can be defined at many levels. For example, when Sloman (1996) talks of two systems of reasoning, or Reber (1993) of two systems of learning, they would seem to be referring to quite limited components of the human mind. The term 'system' as used by these authors nevertheless implies an architectural basis for these dual-process theories. That is, the two processes result from the operation of distinct cogni-tive components. However, the dual-system theories that were developed in an attempt to integrate much wider sets of phenomena (Evans and Over 1996; Stanovich 1999, 2004), now known popularly as Systems 1 and 2, are specified at a much higher level of generality, seeming to take in between them almost the whole human mind, or at least its higher aspects. In this view, System 1 is an old form of cognition, which evolved early and is shared with animals and includes both implicit learning and modular cognition. In contrast, System 2 is recent, uniquely human, related to working memory, general intelligence, and so on.

There are a number of reasons, which will become clear, why it may be a good idea to get away from the Systems 1 and 2 terminology. It would be more useful to describe this grand unifying form of dual-process theory as the 'two minds hypothesis' (Evans 2003; Stanovich 2004). Here I define 'mind' as a high-level cognitive system capable of representing the external world and acting upon it in order to serve the goals of the organism. The two minds hypothesis is that the human brain contains not one but two parallel systems for doing this. Animals, according to this view, have but one system corresponding to the 'old mind' in human beings. Humans have a second 'new' mind, which coexists in uneasy coalition with the first, sometimes coming into direct conflict with it. This is a strong, even startling hypothesis, which makes it very interesting (if probably wrong!).

As applied to date, the two minds hypothesis would seem to provide the architectural foundation for type 1 and 2 processing and hence potentially allow all dual-process theories to be reduced to one. Actually, I shall argue later that this is a mistake and that two minds do not have to equal only one kind of dual-process theory. However, this chapter is concerned only with dual-process theories that have some kind of foundation in cognitive architecture. That is, theories that imply the operation of some distinct cognitive systems at whatever level of definition. These may be contrasted with theories that merely propose two *modes* of processing, or two kinds of *cognitive style*. Such theories may well concern only the manner in which a single cognitive system is employed.

There are, in fact, dual-process distinctions to be found in the literature that are really about processing styles, and not about architecture at all. For example, the distinction between holistic and analytic thinking styles that differentiates Eastern and Western cultures (Nisbett et al. 2001) should not be confused with dual-process theories of cognition, in the sense that the term is used here (but see Buctel and Norenzayan, this volume). Such styles are malleable—they depend upon personality and education and can change when a person moves into another environment or culture. Dual-process accounts also cannot be architectural, if they posit a *continuum* between one form of thinking and another as in Hammond's (1996) cognitive continuum theory of judgment and decision making. Those authors who have argued that dual-process theories of reasoning should posit such a continuum (Newstead 2000; Osman 2004; Stevenson 1997) are hence implicitly rejecting the architectural foundation of such theories.

Stanovich (1999) is admirably clear about the distinction between dual-process theories and cognitive styles. He primarily uses the distinction between processes whose effectiveness do and do not correlate with individual differences in general intelligence to define processing that is type 2 rather than type 1. Having taken into account the correlation with general intelligence, he then analyses *residual variance*, which he shows to be related to dispositional factors inherent in different cognitive styles. Stanovich (this volume) has recently elaborated these two separate sources of individual differences into his definition of the *algorithmic* and *reflective* minds, which he explicitly sees as a partition of System 2 or what I am calling the new mind. I will not follow him down this path, however, as this distinction does not capture my definition of a mind as a system which has the self-contained ability to represent and act upon the world. I rather see his distinction as being between two properties of the same mind: its capacity and capability on the one hand, and the strategic use to which it is put, on the other.

Other dual-process theorists, by contrast, appear to confuse the distinction between dual processes and thinking styles. This is particularly true of the cognitive-experiential self-theory of Epstein (1994; Epstein and Pacini 1999). On the one hand, Epstein proposes a distinction between 'experiential' and 'rational' *systems* which share many of the familiar System 1 and 2 features. Thus we are told that the experiential system has 'a very long evolutionary history and is the same system through which nonhuman, higher-order animals adapt to their environments ...' (Epstein and Pacini 1999, p.463). It operates in manner which is automatic, effortless, and preconscious, contrasting with the rational system which is conscious, effortful, slow, conscious, analytical etc. This is an almost perfect match to the features of the generic dual-system theory of reasoning (Evans 2003) which was developed independently and published in a parallel literature. On the other hand, Epstein and colleagues talk about rational and experiential processing as styles of thinking that people can be persuaded to adopt in psychological experiments and which can be measured as stable personality characteristics using the rational-experiential inventory, or REI, a psychometric tool developed by Epstein. The use of such a scale also requires, of course, a continuum of measurement between experiential and rational. I fail to understand how systems and styles can be combined in the one theory in this way.

Another dual-process account that seems not to be founded on a clear distinction in cognitive architecture is the heuristic-systematic theory of Shelly Chaiken, which has been popular for many years in the social cognition literature (Chaiken 1980; Chen and Chaiken 1999). The distinction between a quick and dirty heuristic form of processing, and a slow and careful systematic form could, *but need not*, reflect an architectural distinction. It is clear that this kind of distinction is architectural in what I call *default-interventionist* dual-processing theories (Evans 2007b), discussed later. However, it is also possible that type 2 thinking can be applied in either a quick and careless or slow and careful manner in which case we are talking about thinking styles. While dual-process theorists have tended to emphasize the ability to follow normative rules in System 2 in earlier publications (Evans and Over 1996; Stanovich 1999), they are increasingly pointing to the poor thinking and cognitive biases that can also arise from this system (Evans 2007a; Stanovich, this volume).

To add to the problems, the term 'heuristic' is deeply ambiguous. While 'heuristic processing' has been used by me and other dual-process theorists to refer to the type 1—fast, automatic, preconscious—processes, the word 'heuristic' can also refer to a rule which is consciously learnt and applied (see Frankish 2004, p.102 for a similar distinction). In my recent book on research strategy, for example (Evans 2005), I list a number of research design heuristics that can be explicitly adopted to simplify the process of choosing an appropriate experimental design. Now, Chaiken and colleagues refer to heuristic and systematic processing modes that are low and high in effort respectively, but this criterion is ambiguous for reasons given above. They also talk about heuristics as knowledge structures that have to be retrieved from memory and applied, presumably by some conscious, analytic thought process. This is not at all what is meant by heuristic processing in the heuristic-analytic theory, discussed below. In a dual-process theory such as Sloman's (1996) that distinguishes between associative and rule-based processes, it seems that Chaiken's heuristics (as well as her systematic processes) would have be regarded as rule-based. While some reviewers give a two-system interpretation to the Chaiken model (see Smith and DeCoster 2000; Smith and Collins, this volume) others have seen the theory as more to do with cognitive styles (Strack and Deutsch 2004).

Dual-system theory and working memory

Dual-system theorists have tended to equate System 1 with implicit (unconscious, preconscious) processes and System 2 with explicit (conscious) processes. Frankish (2004; this volume) has also linked the distinction with that between a personal (mostly conscious) level of belief and reasoning (System 2) and a subpersonal level (System 1) which functions largely through automatic and unconscious processes. System 2 thinking is characterized as slow, sequential and correlated with cognitive capacity measures, which sounds like the stream of consciousness—or the flow of information through working memory—and this in turn leads us to think of System 2 as conscious. Some authors specifically frame their dual-process accounts in terms of conscious and nonconscious processing (e.g. Wilson 2002) and others rely heavily on the implicit/explicit distinction (e.g. Evans and Over 1996; Reber 1993).

Access to working memory seems a safer basis for defining the distinction between type 1 and 2 processing than does consciousness. While the notion of conscious thinking seems to involve particularly the contents of *verbal* working memory, the notion of conscious experience seems much broader and more slippery. The capacity of visual consciousness, for example, does not seem to be sharply limited given the richness and complexity of visual percepts. Nor would we be very safe to argue that animals lack conscious perceptual experiences, such as pain, that are similar to our own. We are, after all, closely biologically linked and the behavioral and physiological indicators of such states are essentially the same. But working memory does nothing on its own. It requires, at the very least, *content*. And this content is supplied by a whole host of *implicit* cognitive systems. For example, the contents of our consciousness include visual and other perceptual representations of the world, extracted meanings of linguistic discourse, episodic memories, and retrieved beliefs of relevance to the current context, and so on. So if there is a new mind, distinct from the old, it does not operate entirely or even mostly by type 2 processes. On the contrary, it functions mostly by type 1 processes.

Dual-process theorists broadly recognize that what has been called System 1 is really a multiplicity of systems that takes in a wide variety of implicit or type 1 processing (Evans 2008; Stanovich 2004; Wilson 2002). System 2 seems like a better case for a treatment as a single system, as it requires use of a singular working memory system. However, it would be a mistake surely to equate System 2 with working memory, as that would imply a single system able to do all the many cognitive tasks that are correlated with working memory capacity (Barrett et al. 2004). Do we really want to say that working memory is *a* system that does reading, reasoning, planning, explicit learning, etc.? A different approach is suggested by Samuels (this volume) who argues that we should think in terms of type 1 and type 2 systems that are distinguished by the list of type 1 and 2 attributes.

We can take the Samuels approach one step further by a definition of a type 2 system as one that requires access to a single central working memory system *among other resources*. What those other resources are depends on which type 2 system we are talking about. A type 2 system for deductive reasoning, for example, would require input from systems for attention, language processing, memory retrieval, and so on. A type 2 system for reading might require some common components and some different. The only common feature of a type 2 system is that (unlike type 1 systems) it requires access to working memory. However, this requirement has profound implications. There is only one working memory system to be had and it is slow and capacity limited. Consequently, only one type 2 system can effectively be active at a given time and all type 2 systems will be slow and correlated, in their effectiveness, with individual differences in cognitive capacity. And in so far as the fleeting contents of working memory are conscious, *something* about the working of a type 2 system will become conscious.

Note that this definition of type 1 and 2 systems does not map comfortably on to the definition of type 1 and 2 processes. The reason is that only processes accessing working memory have the type 2 characteristics. The other components of a type 2 system, for example those that rapidly supply relevant knowledge from memory operate through *type 1* processes. So if System 1 is a collection of (relevant) type 1 systems, as current theorists are suggesting, where does that leave System 2? Not, I suggest, as a single system (equal to working memory or the conscious mind or the personal level) but really as a relevant *category* of type 2 systems that carry out reasoning and decision making. Thus the 'System 2' that does decontextualized reasoning for Stanovich (1999) is not necessarily the same 'System 2' that does decision making for Kahneman and Frederick (2002). There may not be any stable versions of System 2 at all—just as set of interacting units (including working memory) that get activated to deal with a particular task. In favor of this rather anarchic view of System 2 is the evidence of neural imaging studies of reasoning tasks (Goel 2007). These studies indicate activation of multiple brain areas, with no clear-cut correspondence from one study to the next. It appears that there is no neural centre for reasoning. From this perspective we might argue that we do in fact need *many* dual-process theories, as each theory contrasts the relevant type 1 and 2 systems for the task and domain in question.

If it makes no sense to talk of two systems, can we still have a two minds hypothesis? Yes, I believe we can. There could be a mind which operates largely through type 1 systems and draws on forms of knowledge that are inherently implicit—for example, those encapsulated in modular systems or acquired associative or procedural knowledge stored as weightings in neural networks. There could be another mind which operates primarily through type 2 systems, drawing heavily on the use of explicit and personal knowledge and making use of central working memory. But on what basis should we deem these to be two minds? One basis, drawn from dual-system theory, would be the idea that Mind 1 is evolutionarily old and shared with other animals and that Mind 2 is recently evolved and distinctively human. We turn to this idea next.

Old mind/new mind?

The argument that 'System 2' is *uniquely* human is hard to maintain even if we restrict its definition to processing that involves executive working memory and 'controlled attention' (Barrett et al. 2004). There is a strong argument for a distinction between stimulus-controlled and higher-order controlled behavior in higher animals that is related to the System 1 and 2 distinction (Toates 2004, 2006). Dual-system theorists would hence be safer to assert that System 2 is uniquely *developed* in humans. I find this claim more attractive than the 'uniquely human' hypothesis. It means that we do not have to tell an improbably unique evolutionary story for humans: we can suggest instead that relatively small cognitive facility in animals became magnified greatly in humans. No odder, say, than a giraffe's neck or an elephant's trunk. It is only species-arrogance that leads us to believe that our overdeveloped forebrains are a mark of superiority. They could yet prove to be one of nature's great blunders, if they lead to destruction of the planet through nuclear warfare or catastrophic pollution of the atmosphere.

Of course, human beings are unique among animals in the kinds of cognitive acts that they can perform. No other species has developed mathematics and science, studied their own history as well as the cosmos in which they are placed, composed and performed complex music, built space ships or transmitted pictures and sounds at large distances. Although cultural transmission of knowledge does occur on a limited scale in intelligent species such as apes and whales, its use is dwarfed by our own. This seems quite compellingly to suggest that if we do not have a unique form of cognition, then we at least have some system which is much more greatly developed. As I have observed elsewhere (Evans 2007a; Evans and Over 1996), we have the capability for hypothetical thinking—mental simulation of possibilities—and a higher form of rationality that results from this. Like other animals, we can respond with what worked in the past, either for our evolving ancestors or in our personal experience of the world. Unlike other animals, however, we can base our decisions on simulation and imagination of their consequences.

But where do our unique abilities come from and are they located in System 2 as currently defined? An important issue here is that of cognitive modules. Fodor (1983) famously argued for a cognitive architecture comprised of 'input modules', such as vision and language, that are domain-specific and central cognitive system that is general purpose—a form of dual-process theory. He defined modules in a very specific way that included many criteria such as encapsulated and impenetrable information processes, innateness, neurological specificity, specific patterns of development and malfunction, and so on. Later authors tried to argue on evolutionary grounds for *massive* modularity, such that the mind is composed mostly or entirely of modular cognitive systems that are innate, domain-specific, and encapsulated and unlike Fodor's modules, capable of controlling higher order reasoning and decision making without need for a central and domain-general system (Tooby and Cosmides 1992). This idea was very controversial and unsurprisingly was attacked by dual-process theorists (e.g. Over 2003; Stanovich and West 2003) and by Fodor himself (Fodor 2001). However, there has been a progressive weakening of the criteria for modularity in the recent literature which makes a massively modular architecture easier to defend (Barrett and Kurzban 2006; Carruthers 2006; Samuels 2000; Sperber 2000). Nor need this approach be incompatible with dual-system theory. For example, Carruthers (2006) argues that System 2 and working memory exist but function as *virtual* systems that emerge from the interaction of a number of modular cognitive systems.

I agree with Carruthers (2006) that cognitive modules should be permitted to interact with one another. For example, if modules are to be domain-specific we would need to regard language as separate from the systems responsible for storing and retrieving knowledge about the world. However, language comprehension is well known to be a pragmatic process that goes well beyond syntax and semantics (see Sperber and Wilson 1995). To understand what someone says you must draw on your shared knowledge of the world, not just your knowledge of language. Hence, linguistic and pragmatic modules must be able to interact with each other in some rapid dialectical process for language comprehension to be possible.

In this sense of modularity, plausible candidates for modular cognition include vision and other perceptual systems, language, theory of mind and several forms of memory (episodic, semantic, procedural). Now here is the problem. Dual-system theorists have generally written as though modules belong to System 1 (Evans and Over 1996; Stanovich 2004) due to their type 1 manner of functioning (rapid, unconscious, automatic), but this now seems problematic to me. Language appears to be modular in the strong sense but (a) is uniquely human and (b) is an essential prerequisite for type 2 processing, facilitating higher order and explicit representations of knowledge. A similar problem applies to social intelligence or theory of mind. While there is evidence of a rudimentary theory of mind in chimpanzees (Mithen 1996), humans have highly developed abilities for metarepresentation both within and without the social domain (Cosmides and Tooby 2000; Sperber 2000). Yet it is obvious that a lot of our type 2 processing is concerned with reasoning or conversing (i.e. gossiping) about the social world, and theorizing about the mental states and motivations of the people who occupy it.

The fact that the human mind has distinct components that evolved at different times is not sufficient in itself to support the two minds hypothesis. However, the distinction between type 1 and 2 systems is helpful in this regard. If we think of the new mind as operating via type 2 *systems* (rather than processes) then it is evident that such systems require many inputs for processing through working memory, which can themselves be modular in origin. Perhaps a new mind did evolve in humans, the key platform for which was the evolution of modules, especially language, which could support abstract and metarepresentational thought. The evolution of executive working memory to exploit this—and which gives the new mind its type 2 characteristics—was possible only because of these modular developments.

Accounting for biases and conflict

The main reason that dual-process theories have been developed in the psychology of reasoning and decision making has been to account for cognitive biases and their apparent conflict with logical reasoning or normative, rule-based judgment and decision making. In fact, dual-process theorists in reasoning and decision making have until recently tended to associate System 1 with belief-based reasoning and cognitive biases and System 2 with abstract, rule-based reasoning and normatively correct responding (Evans 1989; Evans and Over 1996; Kahneman and Frederick 2002; Klaczynski and Cottrell 2004; Sloman 1996; Stanovich 1999; Stanovich 2004). However, there are considerable dangers in this if a one to one relationship is assumed. This leads to a fallacy in which the normative correctness of responding is taken as diagnostic of the nature of the underlying process. In fact, type 1 processing can lead to normatively correct answers and type 2 processing to errors (see Evans 2007a for extensive discussion of cognitive biases caused by type 2 processing, and Stanovich, this volume, for discussion of shallow, error-prone type 2 thinking). There is also nothing in the working memory based definition of type 2 thinking given in this chapter which implies that such processes are necessarily abstract and decontextualized, let alone normatively correct. In fact, recent dual-process accounts of reasoning have attributed belief-based reasoning to both systems (Evans et al. 1999; Verschueren et al. 2005; Weidenfeld et al. 2005).

The traditional allocation of belief biases to System 1 has also been questioned by Vinod Goel who has conducted a number of neural-imaging studies of reasoning (Goel 2005; Goel and Dolan 2003). Belief bias is almost the paradigm case for dual-process theories of reasoning (Evans 2003; Stanovich 1999). The general method involves giving people syllogisms—logical arguments with two premises and a putative conclusion—and asking them whether the conclusion necessarily follows from the premises. Some arguments are valid and some invalid. Some conclusions of are believable and some unbelievable, but this is irrelevant to the logical task set. People accept more valid than invalid conclusions, but they also accept more believable than unbelievable conclusions—the belief bias effect. Logic and belief appear to compete for control of people's responding on a within-person basis as originally demonstrated by Evans et al. (1983; for a recent extensive study of the effect, see Klauer et al. 2000).

Of particular interest are belief-logic conflict problems where conclusions are valid but unbelievable, or believable but invalid. The ability to resolve such conflict in favor of logic seems to require working memory and slow, type 2 processing. For example, this ability declines in old age (Gilinsky and Judd 1994), under requirement of give a very fast decision (Evans and Curtis-Holmes 2005) and under concurrent working memory load (De Neys 2006). Also consistent with dual-process theory, Goel and Dolan (2003) found that successful reasoning with belief-logic conflict problems activates an area of the pre-frontal cortex associated with inhibition and executive control. So far, so good for System 2. However, they also found that when belief bias dominates, another area of the pre-frontal cortex associated with semantic memory is activated. That is, belief bias originates within in the new brain, not the old.

On reflection, this should not be at all surprising. How can you have belief bias without a modern human belief system? However, it does indicate an oversimplification in the dual-system theories of Evans and Over (1996) and Stanovich (1999). Belief bias does appear to reflect a type1 processes—fast and preconscious—but it is not part of the old mind. So something is wrong. Either System 1 is not entirely old, or System 2 is not entirely comprised of type 2 processes. While there is a case to be made for a form of the two minds hypothesis, not all dual-process theories concern this distinction, and some deal entirely with issues within the new mind. Before I get to this, I need to say something about modularity and the multiplicity of forms of type 1 processing in the brain.

A duality of dual-process theories

To summarize progress to date, there is no problem in defining a distinction between type 1 and 2 processes where the latter require use of controlled attention or executive working memory. Type 1 processes, which can manage without this special resource, are hence fast, automatic, parallel, low effort and independent of individual differences in working memory capacity. There are, however, great difficulties in assuming that there is a System 1 comprised of type 1 processing and a System 2 comprised of type 2 processing. If System 2 requires working memory then as a *system*, it must also include many other resources, such as explicit knowledge and belief systems together with powerful, type 1 processes, for identifying and retrieving data that is relevant in the current context, not to speak of the role of attention, language, and perception in supplying content for type 2 processing. Many of these essential support systems for working memory also seem to have a modular nature, so how can modules be described as lying in System 1?

A way to get out of this mire may be to introduce some new terminology. Let us distinguish between two kinds of what I have been calling type 1 processes. *Autonomous* processes are those that can control behavior directly without need for any kind of controlled attention. I am avoiding the common term 'automatic' because that has been applied also to the other kind of type 1 processing. For want of a better term, *preattentive* processes are those that supply content into working memory. These correspond to what some authors (e.g. Velmans 2000) call preconscious processes. 'Preattentive' is accurate, because it refers to processes that precede and provide content for focal attention, defined as the contents of working memory. I hesitate to use the term because it has traditionally been associated only with perceptual processing whereas it applies here to also to processes which access and retrieve memories and beliefs. However, it is better than *preconscious*, as I am also trying to avoid the use of consciousness as a defining property of type 2 processing!

In place of type 2 processes, we can talk of *analytic* processes are those which manipulate explicit representations through working memory and exert conscious, volitional control on behavior. We can combine these together in a simple diagram which constitutes a first attempt at visualizing the implied architecture of the human mind (see Figure 2.1).

Basic though Figure 2.1 is, it serves some useful purposes. For example, we can see that a dual-system approach or a parallel form of dual-process theory might be one that contrasts autonomous and analytic control of behavior. Sequential forms of dual-process theory, by contrast, concern the biasing of analytic processing by preattentive cues that shape its contents and locus of attention. In a recent paper (Evans 2007b), I discussed the problem of conflict resolution when type 1 and type 2 processes favor different decisions. I actually showed that three architecturally distinct descriptions of this were possible, but I will focus on the two most plausible here.

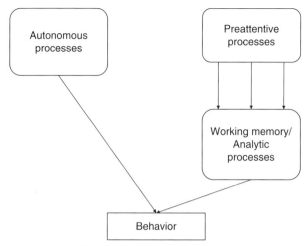

Fig. 2.1 A simple representation of the difference between autonomous and preattentive type 1 processes.

These, I called *parallel-competitive* and *default-interventionist*. In the former, two parallel processes propose their own judgments or decisions which may or may not conflict. In this approach, one or the other kind of process ultimately takes control of the behavior. In the default-interventionist approach, a fast type 1 process provides default intuitions which are always subject to at least minimal scrutiny by type 2 processes which may approve them or intervene with effortful analytic reasoning. Because one theory has a parallel and the other a sequential structure, inspection of Figure 2.1 suggests that the former may concern autonomous and the latter preattentive forms of processing. However, we need to examine the actual proposals in more detail.

Parallel form dual-process theories

Dual-process theories which propose a parallel processing architecture all seem to include the idea that there are two kinds of knowledge, implicit and explicit. This idea is intrinsic to dual-process theories of learning (e.g. that of Reber 1993) but also to theories of reasoning and social cognition that contrast associative with rule-based processing (Sloman 1996; Smith and DeCoster 2000). The very term 'associative' suggests implicit forms of learning in the 'old mind' and its description by Sloman as a system that 'encodes and processes statistical regularities of its environment, frequencies and correlations amongst various features of the world' (Sloman 2002, p.381) suggests a form of cognitive processing that could well be shared with other animals. In contrast, the description of rules as abstract, propositional entities seems to put them in domain of explicit human knowledge. Moreover, Sloman clearly describes the two kinds of processes as being parallel competitors for the control of behavior:

> Both systems seem to try, at least most of the time to generate a response. The rule based system can suppress the response of the associative system in the sense that it can overrule it.

> However, the associative system always has its opinion heard and, because of its speed and efficiency, often precedes and neutralizes the rule-based response. (Sloman 2002, p.391)

Although Sloman does not invoke some of the wider features of dual-system theories, he does make the following claim: 'When a response is produced by the associative system, we are conscious only of the results of the computation, not the process. In contrast, we are aware of both the result and the process in rule-based computation.' (Sloman 2002, p.83). Awareness of process might be taken to indicate that the process passes through working memory in line with my earlier definition of type 2 processes. Does 'awareness of result', however, not sound more like the outcome of a preattentive or preconscious process rather than an autonomous one? This is not really the case, since by the current definition, preattentive processes are those which deliver content to working memory before a decision is made. In contrast, the outcome of an autonomous process provides a direct behavioral propensity. However, Sloman is right in saying that such propensities may register consciously as an intuition that we are about to behave in a given way. Such intuitions may also be accompanied by metacognitive feelings of confidence or rightness (see Thompson, this volume).

This is what Sloman has in mind with his criterion S when he talks of people believing in two contradictory responses simultaneously and experiencing a conflict between them. It is true that we sometimes become aware of dual-process conflict, as when a man who wishes to visit his sick mother is unable to cope with his flying phobia, or when a compulsive gambler cannot overcome her habit by rational reasoning about chance and probability. In general, however, I think that Criterion S is too strong for many applications of parallel-form dual-process theories. For example, there is much evidence of automatic and nonconscious processing in social cognition (Bargh 2006; Forgas et al. 2003; Wilson 2002) where people do not generally seem to be aware of conflict. If people respond according to an implicit attitude or implicit stereotype, they must generally lack awareness that these behaviors are in conflict with their explicit attitudes and beliefs in order to maintain their core beliefs about themselves. Instead they may rationalize or confabulate reasons for actions that are unconsciously caused and there is much evidence for this in the social psychological literature (Wilson 2002). Introspective reports in reasoning research may also appear to be rationalizations of choices which lack awareness of the true causes (Wason and Evans 1975).

Another parallel form of dual-process theory is that of Smith and DeCoster (2000; see also Smith and Collins, this volume). These authors are highly explicit about both the parallel nature of the processing and its foundation in two forms of knowledge. They start by arguing for two kinds of memory, a slow-process which is implicit and associative and a fast-process that is mediated by the hippocampus. This is the distinction between associative and implicit learning on the one hand and explicit learning and the formation of episodic memories on the other. (Note that slow acquisition equals fast application and vice versa.) They then say that these two kinds of memory lead to two kinds of processing that are associative and rule-based respectively, pointing out that 'rules' are defined here to be explicit or propositional in format. Further, the theory is explicitly parallel: 'We assume that the two processing modes generally operate simultaneously rather than as alternatives in sequence' (p.112). Smith and

DeCoster apply their distinction to phenomena in social psychology, such as implicit and explicit stereotypes, and also attempt to reconcile this scheme with a number of dual-process theories of social cognition.

To take one more example, Lieberman (2003; this volume) proposes a distinction between reflexive (System 1) and reflective (System 2) cognition, with corresponding neurological systems called X and C (as in refleXive and refleCtive). It is notable that the X system includes the basal ganglia (linked to explicit learning) and the C system the temporal lobe incorporating the hippocampus which is linked to explicit learning. The theory is parallel in that either system may take control of behavior and activation of one system may inhibit the other. On this basis, we could explain why people may learn complex tasks less well when they make explicit effort (Reber 1993) or make better judgments when they are not trying to engage in explicit reasoning (Reyna 2004). It seems that the C system is activated (by the anterior cingulate cortex) when the X system is failing to cope (e.g. automated driving in hazardous conditions) and hence needs to inhibit the X system in order to take control. If the X system does something better (learning complex rules) then instructional sets which activate the C system can have a deleterious effect on performance.

Sequential form dual-process theories

In sequential dual-process theories, authors assume that a fast automatic (therefore type 1) process precedes and shapes subsequent conscious and effortful (type 2) reasoning. If we need theories like this as well as the parallel-form, then they must be describing a different kind of type 1 process: preattentive rather than autonomous (see Figure 2.1). The heuristic-analytic theory is of this type and has survived many years since its original publication (Evans 1984). Heuristic processes are specifically described as preattentive and their purpose is to provide content for further processing by analytic processes and not to control behavior directly. Mostly, heuristic processes are described as attentional, linguistic and pragmatic processes that contribute to explicit knowledge representations in working memory.

Heuristic or preattentive processes are distinct from autonomous ones that recruit implicit knowledge of an associative nature. In their pragmatic aspect, they rather concern the *implicit* processing of *explicit* knowledge. These (clearly type 1) processes solve the 'frame problem' by rapidly and effortlessly contextualizing our thought, retrieving stored memories and beliefs that are relevant to the current context. These powerful preattentive pragmatic processes can, however, be the cause of cognitive biases as an earlier work (Evans 1989) explained in detail. If preattentive processing fails to encode logically relevant information, or encodes irrelevant information then subsequent analytic processing may cause biased responding. In the recent revision of the heuristic-analytic theory (Evans 2006b, 2007a) this idea is retained, but a major source of bias in analytic processing is also identified (not relevant for our present purposes). The dual-process account of Stanovich (1999) appears to have a similar structure, as he puts great emphasis on the biasing effects of contextualization and the need for people to inhibit belief based reasoning and to *decontextualize* in order to think abstractly and rationally. Decontextualization is a concept that presupposes contextualization and hence a sequential form of theory.

A problem for sequential dual-process theories is the existence and resolution of conflict that appears to be prompted by two different processes. However, I recently (Evans 2006b) dealt with this issue by suggesting that heuristic processes provide default mental models for analytic processing. Where such processing is shallow and careless a default response prompted by such models is enacted which is effectively a heuristic response. However, depending upon motivation, cognitive ability, instructional set, time available and so on, there may be an intervention by analytic processing which leads to revision and replacement of such default models and more effortful reasoning. One form of such revision could be what Stanovich (1999) calls decontextualization—stripping out concrete content with its associated beliefs to reveal the underlying logical structure.

The dual-process theory of judgment and decision-making put forward by Kahneman and Frederick (2002, 2005) has been having considerable impact. Although they use the terms System 1 and 2, their statements seem to imply a sequential architecture, not unlike that of the heuristic-analytic theory. That is, they suggest that analytic (System 2) processes are always involved, even if their role is shallow and minimal. They state (p.51), 'In the particular dual-process model we assume, System 1 quickly proposes intuitive answers to judgment problems as they arise, and System 2 monitors the quality of these proposals, which it may endorse, correct or override'. In common with me and Stanovich, then, they assume that analytic processes may optionally intervene to apply high effort reasoning, or may simply approve default intuitive responses cued by heuristic processes. That is why I call this class of theories 'default-interventionist'.

One reason to argue that hypothetical thinking tasks will necessarily involve analytic thinking is that they require interpretation of experimental instructions. If there is an innate frequency processing model (Cosmides and Tooby 1996) it surely would not manifest itself on quantitative word problems of the kind that its proponents have investigated. Such a device would be designed for encoding regularities in the environment, not reading and reasoning about contingency tables. Along with others (Evans et al. 2000; Girotto and Gonzalez 2001; Sloman et al. 2003) we have shown that frequency formats facilitate statistical reasoning instead by prompting the formation of explicit mental models that encode set relationships. With this representation, analytic processes easily find the solution. Another example is the 'recognition heuristic' (Goldstein and Gigerenzer 2002). Foreigners may be able better to judge the size of German cities than natives, by using a simply heuristic based on the familiarity of the city name. Should we regard this as an autonomous process in direct control of the behavior? No, because people will only use the heuristic where it provides a sensible basis for judgment. If they recognize the name because they know the city, and know that it is in fact small, they will not judge it to be large (Oppenheimer 2003). Thus the decision to use the feeling of familiarity as a basis of answering the question given is an analytic process.

The hybrid model and 'type 3' processing

Leaving aside for the moment the question of whether we need two systems (or two minds) it seems we do in fact need both kinds of dual-process theories. The type 1 and type 2 distinction is too simple and fails to recognize the multiple kinds of type 1 (fast, implicit, low effort) processes that operate in the human mind. In fact, type 2 processing seems to refer only to the kind that uses working memory. The evidence strongly supports two forms of knowledge, but it seems evident that the autonomous processes that control behavior via implicit knowledge and habitual learning are distinct from the preattentive processes that retrieve and apply explicit knowledge in the contextualization of type 2 thinking. Thus parallel dual-process theories concern two systems that provide alternative routes to behavioral control, while sequential theories concern the interactions between working memory and its many support systems.

The failure to recognize this distinction previously has resulted, however, in a confusing and complicated literature on dual-processing. We may need both kinds of theory, but this does not mean that all the authors are correct in all the claims they make. In particular, parallel dual-process theorists like Sloman (1996) have offered explanations of some phenomena, such as the Wason selection task or the Linda problem, that sequential theorists like me have explained in terms of the heuristic-analytic theory (Evans 2007a). If the distinction between autonomous and preattentive processes is as clear as I am suggesting, then we cannot both be right! It may seem, however, that what we need is a hybrid model that will combine elements of both types of theory within a single cognitive architecture.

Before describing the hybrid model, I need to say a little more about the problem of conflict resolution and control (see also Evans 2007b). In my first attempt to model dual-processes in reasoning, some 30 years ago, I discovered that I needed not two but *three* parameters to do the job (see also Evans 1977; Klauer et al. 2007; Krauth 1982). The first parameter (h) provides the probability of responding given that a heuristic (type 1) process take control of the behavior. The second parameter (a) provides the probability given that an analytic (type 2) process takes control of the behavior. The third parameter, which I called α, describes the probability that a type 2 rather than type 1 process will take control, resulting in the simple additive probability model:

$$P(R) = \alpha \cdot a = (1 - \alpha) \cdot h$$

As Evans (2007b) demonstrated it is possible to devise both parallel and sequential forms of dual-process theory that generate this equation. In the parallel form both type 1 and 2 processes operate independently and problems arise only if their outcomes conflict. In this case, α represents the probability that they are resolved in favor of the type 2 process. In the sequential, or default-interventionist, form of dual-process theory α represents the probability that an analytic process intervenes after the heuristic process has proposed its default. Perhaps implausibly, however, this model only produces equation (1) on the assumption that intervention likelihood is independent of the outcome of heuristic processing.

The point I wish to develop here is that no dual-process theory in the cognitive literature appears to have proposed a third kind of process or system that corresponds to α. What happens instead is that System 2 gets overburdened with the responsibility of allocating control and resolving conflict. I say overburdened because the primary function of type 2 processing is rule-based reasoning, something quite different. In Kahneman and Frederick's (2002) theory, as an earlier quote shows, System 2 has the task of monitoring the output of System 1 and deciding whether to intervene. Of course, it also has the different task of executing the rule based reasoning should intervention occur. Evans, Over, and Stanovich have made similar proposals. The same dual function is required of System 2 in parallel dual-process models, hence Sloman's Criterion S. Here the problem is worse because the parallel model describes a horse race between a very fast horse (type 1) and a much slower horse (type 2). Not only does the fast horse have to wait for the slow horse to arrive, the slow horse also gets to decide who has won! To fill this gap, I propose to add the following definition: Type 3 processes: resource allocation, conflict resolution, and ultimate control of behavior.

It is important that the control function of type 3 processes not be confused with the so-called 'controlled' nature of type 2 processing, which contrasts with the 'automatic' nature of type 1 processing. Indeed this confusion may have some responsibility for the overburdening of System 2 in current accounts. Type 2 processing is controlled in the sense of being volitional: related to a conscious intention that can be stated and reflected upon. Volition is tricky topic in itself, however, with strong arguments for the view that 'conscious will' is illusory (Bargh and Ferguson 2000; Wegner 2002). The experience of having willed something is not, in fact, reliable evidence that it is under type 2 control (see Wegner 2002). The point I am making here, however, is that in a dual-process model a more basic notion of control is that of whether a type 1 or 2 process determines behavior in any particular instance. This form of cognitive control is *not* a type 2 function but a separate type 3 function (see also Conrey et al. 2005 for discussion of related issues in dual-process models of social cognition).

I am defining type 3 processes (and if you like a potential System 3) here by function rather than character. However, one reason for separating them out from System 2 is that they cannot, in general, be conscious. We may feel subjectively that consciousness is 'in control' but it does not take much reflection to realize that working memory resources and controlled attention are largely recruited by preconscious systems. For example, if when driving my car and talking to the passenger a hazardous situation is encountered (e.g. the car in front brakes sharply) then my conscious attention immediately switches to the road situation. The system responsible for monitoring hazards and recruiting working memory cannot be working memory itself. Nor should we confuse the 'executive function' property of working memory with the kind of control I am talking about here (see also Stanovich, this volume).

The hybrid model, incorporating type 3 processing is shown in Figure 2.2. The two branches represent parallel form dual-process theories with implicit knowledge and associative (type 1) processing on the left and with explicit knowledge and rule-based (type 2) processing (though working memory) on the right. The right hand side also incorporates other kind of type 1 processing described by sequential dual-process theories: those attached to the perceptual, language, and memory systems that provide content for working memory form. However, the two branches are now seen as flowing through a type 3 processing system which is responsible for (optionally) recruiting working memory and type 2 processing, and for resolving conflict, if required, between the two systems.

An immediate advantage of adding such preconscious type 3 processes is that it resolves the main paradox of conflict resolution in the parallel model. No longer need

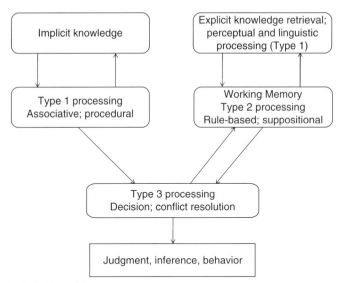

Fig. 2.2 The hybrid model.

the fast horse necessarily wait for the slow horse, as 'System 3' can 'decide' to pass on the fast response immediately without recruiting or waiting for System 2 processing to complete. Only when a problem is detected need the system involve the slow and capacity-limited type 2 processing. Interestingly, recent evidence suggests that the mind does detect conflicts, even when we are not conscious that it is doing so. For example, although participants never describe 'belief bias' as the basis for their decision in syllogistic reasoning, they do spend more time inspecting the premises of belief-logic conflict problems (Ball et al. 2006). In a recent study, De Neys and Glumicic (2007) also found that indirect measures such as memory recall indicated additional processing of base-rate information in statistical reasoning problems which put heuristic and analytic processing into conflict, even though there was no reference to this in the verbal protocols recorded.

A couple of examples of hybrid dual-process accounts already exist in the literature. For example, the dual-process model of causal conditional reasoning presented by Verschueren et al. (2005) includes two distinct influences of belief. One is graded degree of connection between antecedent and consequent and might be regarded as an associative process on the left hand side of the hybrid model. The other is a prompting of counterexample cases that are recruited into working memory for explicit reasoning—which looks like the kind of memory retrieval envisaged on the right hand side of the diagram.

Similar theoretical proposals have been made in recent years to account for belief biases in syllogistic reasoning. Several authors have noted that there appears to be (a) a 'response bias' effect in which people simply accept believable conclusions and reject unbelievable ones without any regard to the logic of the argument, but also (b) a process of biased search for counterexamples (Evans 2007a; Evans et al. 1999;

Klauer et al. 2000; Oakhill et al. 1989) to account for why belief bias is stronger on invalid arguments. Perhaps (a) is an autonomous process reflecting *implicit* beliefs and only (b) involves explicit knowledge in a heuristic-analytic interaction

Although the explicit identification of type 3 processes is new, dual-process research has already revealed quite a lot about them. This is indicated by studies that are focused on shifting the balance between type 1 and 2 processing. We know, for example, that this balance can be shifted towards type 1 by the use of time limits and concurrent working memory loads and towards type 2 by instructional emphasis on logical reasoning. We also know that the balance is influenced by both the cognitive ability and the dispositional thinking style of participants. It may also be related to metacognitive feelings (see Thompson, this volume). In addition, we know that a particular region of the brain, the anterior cingulate cortex, seems to be directly involved in conflict detection and recruitment of controlled attention (see, e.g. Lieberman, this volume). However, the implications for the nature of type 3 processing and the underlying cognitive architecture are yet to be explored explicitly and this seems a fruitful area for new research.

Conclusions

In answer to the question posed by my chapter title, we cannot manage with just one kind of dual-process theory to incorporate the many that have been proposed in different fields of psychology. Dual-system theories try to do too many things at once. There are dual-process distinctions that are to do with automatic and controlled processes and those that are to do with the implicit system support for working memory. There are also theories that really do with thinking styles—two forms of 'controlled' processing—and there are combinations and confusions of all of the above to be found.

I suggest that the talk of Systems 1 and 2 should now be discouraged, as it creates more problems than it solves. At the very least we would need to add a System 3 to deal with conflict and control issues and recognize that System 2 involves type 1 as well as type 2 processing. I do not apologize for my role in creating the dual-system concept, however, because I think it was a necessary developmental stage in our quest to understand the mind. Certainly, it was only by testing the dual-system theory to its limits and exposing its problems (Evans 2006a) that I came to the views expressed in this chapter. I think that the old/new mind distinction has some validity but cannot be mapped onto Systems 1 and 2 that perform exclusively type 1 and type 2 processes. The only part of the mind that operates in the type 2 manner is working memory and this surely cannot be a new mind all on its own, without the range of modular support systems that it requires, and the essential ability to construct and access explicit forms of knowledge, all of which require type 1 processes. On the other hand there is some accuracy in the proposal that autonomous control of behavior, mediated by implicit forms of knowledge is older and more animal-like. It is also the case that we often have alternative and potentially conflicting routes to control of our behavior and so can genuinely be said to be 'in two minds'.

Acknowledgments

I would like to thank Keith Stanovich, Keith Frankish, and Shira Elqayam for their helpful comments on an earlier draft of this chapter. The writing of this chapter was supported by research fellowship awarded to the author by the Economic and Social Research Council of the United Kingdom (RES–000–27–0184).

References

Ball, L.J., Wade, C.N., and Quayle, J.D. (2006) Effects of belief and logic on syllogistic reasoning: Eye-movement evidence for selective processing models. *Experimental Psychology*, **53**, 77–86.

Bargh, J.A. (2006) (ed.) *Social psychology and the unconscious*. Psychology Press, New York.

Bargh, J.A. and Ferguson, M. J. (2000) Beyond behaviorism: On the automaticity of higher mental processes. *Psychological Bulletin*, **126**, 925–45.

Barrett, H.C. and Kurzban, R. (2006) Modularity in cognition: Framing the debate. *Psychological Review*, **113**, 628–47.

Barrett, L.F., Tugade, M.M., and Engle, R.W. (2004) Individual differences in working memory capacity and dual-process theories of the mind. *Psychological Bulletin*, **130**, 553–73.

Carruthers, P. (2006) *The architecture of the mind*. Oxford University Press, Oxford.

Chaiken, S. (1980) Heuristic versus systematic information processing and the use of source versus message cues in in persuasion. *Journal of Personality and Social Psychology*, **39**, 752–66.

Chen, S. and Chaiken, S. (1999) The heuristic-systematic model in its broader context. In S. Chaiken and Y. Trope (eds) *Dual-process theories in social psychology,* 73–96. Guilford Press, New York.

Colom, R., Rebollo, I., Palacios, A., Juan-Espinosa, M., and Kyllonen, P.C. (2004) Working memory is (almost) perfectly predicted by g. *Intelligence*, **32**, 277–96.

Conrey, F.R., Gawronski, B., Sherman, J.W., Hugenberg, K., and Groom, C.J. (2005) Separating multiple processes in implicit social cognition: The quad model of implicit task performance. *Journal of Personality and Social Psychology*, **89**, 469–87.

Cosmides, L. and Tooby, J. (1996) Are humans good intuitive statisticians after all? Rethinking some conclusions from the literature on judgment under uncertainty. *Cognition*, **58**, 1–73.

Cosmides, L. and Tooby, J. (2000) Consider the source: The evolution of adaptations for decoupling and metarepresentation. In D. Sperber (ed.) *Metarepresentations,* 53–115. Oxford University Press, Oxford.

De Neys, W. (2006) Dual processing in reasoning: Two systems but one reasoner. *Psychological Science*, **17**, 428–33.

De Neys, W. and Glumicic, T. (2007) Conflict monitoring in dual process theories of thinking. *Cognition*, **106**, 1248–99.

Epstein, S. (1994) Integration of the cognitive and psychodynamic unconscious. *American Psychologist*, **49**, 709–24.

Epstein, S. and Pacini, R. (1999) Some basic issues regarding dual-process theories from the perspective of cognitive-experiential theory. In S. Chaiken and Y. Trope (eds) *Dual-process theories in social psychology,* 462–82. Guildford Press, New York.

Evans, J.St.B.T. (1977) Toward a statistical theory of reasoning. *Quarterly Journal of Experimental Psychology*, **29**, 297–306.

Evans, J.St.B.T. (1984) Heuristic and analytic processes in reasoning. *British Journal of Psychology*, **75**, 451–68.

Evans, J.St.B.T. (1989) *Bias in human reasoning: causes and consequences*. Erlbaum, Brighton.

Evans, J.St.B.T. (2003) In two minds: Dual-process accounts of reasoning. *Trends in Cognitive Sciences*, **7**, 454–9.

Evans, J.St.B.T. (2005) *How to do reserach: A psychologist's guide*. Psychology Press, Hove.

Evans, J.St.B.T. (2006a) Dual-system theories of cognition: Some issues. Proceedings of the 28th Annual Meeting of the Cognitive Science Society, Vancouver, http://www.cogsci.rpi.edu/CSJarchive/proceedings/2006/docs/p202.pdf, 202–7.

Evans, J.St.B.T. (2006b) The heuristic-analytic theory of reasoning: Extension and evaluation. *Psychonomic Bulletin and Review*, **13**, 378–95.

Evans, J.St.B.T. (2007a) *Hypothetical thinking: Dual processes in reasoning and judgement*. Psychology Press, Hove.

Evans, J.St.B.T. (2007b) On the resolution of conflict in dual-process theories of reasoning. *Thinking & Reasoning*, **13**, 321–9.

Evans, J.St.B.T. (2008) Dual-processing accounts of reasoning, judgment and social cognition. *Annual Review of Psychology*, **59**, 255–78.

Evans, J.St.B.T. and Curtis-Holmes, J. (2005) Rapid responding increases belief bias: Evidence for the dual-process theory of reasoning. *Thinking & Reasoning*, **11**, 382–9.

Evans, J.St.B.T. and Over, D.E. (1996) *Rationality and Reasoning*. Psychology Press, Hove.

Evans, J.St.B.T., Barston, J.L., and Pollard, P. (1983) On the conflict between logic and belief in syllogistic reasoning. *Memory & Cognition*, **11**, 295–306.

Evans, J.St.B.T., Over, D.E., and Handley, S.J. (2003) A theory of hypothetical thinking. In D. Hardman and L. Maachi (eds) *Thinking: Psychological perspectives on reasoning, judgement and decision making*, 3–22. Wiley, Chichester.

Evans, J.St.B.T. Handley, S.J., Harper, C., and Johnson-Laird, P.N. (1999) Reasoning about necessity and possibility: A test of the mental model theory of deduction. *Journal of Experimental Psychology: Learning, Memory and Cognition*, **25**, 1495–513.

Evans, J.St.B.T., Handley, S.J., Perham, N., Over, D.E., and Thompson, V.A. (2000) Frequency versus probability formats in statistical word problems. *Cognition*, **77**, 197–213.

Fodor, J. (1983) *The Modularity of Mind*. Crowell, Scranton, PA.

Fodor, J. (2001) *The mind doesn't work that way*. MIT Press, Cambridge, MA.

Forgas, J.P., Williams, K.R., and von Hippel, W. (2003) (eds) *Social judgments: Implicit and explicit processes*. Cambridge University Press, New York.

Frankish, K. (2004) *Mind and supermind*. Cambridge University Press, Cambridge.

Gilinsky, A.S. and Judd, B.B. (1994) Working memory and bias in reasoning across the life-span. *Psychology and Aging*, **9**, 356–71.

Girotto, V. and Gonzalez, M. (2001) Solving probabilistic and statistical problems: A matter of information structure and question form. *Cognition*, **78**, 247–76.

Goel, V. (2005) Cognitive neuroscience of deductive reasoning. In K. Holyoak and R.G. Morrison (eds) *The Cambridge handbook of thinking and reasoning*, 475–92. Cambridge University Press, Cambridge.

Goel, V. (2007) Anatomy of deductive reasoning. *Trends in Cognitive Sciences*, **11**, 435–41.

Goel, V. and Dolan, R.J. (2003) Explaining modulation of reasoning by belief. *Cognition*, **87**, B11–B22.

Goldstein, D.G. and Gigerenzer, G. (2002) Models of ecological rationality: The recognition heuristic. *Psychological Review*, **109**, 75–90.

Hammond, K. R. (1996) *Human judgment and social policy*. Oxford University Press, New York.

Kahneman, D. and Frederick, S. (2002) Representativeness revisited: Attribute substitution in intuitive judgement. In T. Gilovich, D. Griffin, and D. Kahneman (eds) *Heuristics and biases: The psychology of intuitive judgment,* 49–81. Cambridge University Press, Cambridge.

Kahneman, D. and Frederick, S. (2005) A model of heuristic judgment. In K. Holyoak and R.G. Morrison (eds) *The Cambridge handbook of thinking and reasoning,* 267–94. Cambridge University Press, Cambridge.

Klaczynski, P.A. and Cottrell, J.M. (2004) A dual-process approach to cognitive development: The case of children's understanding of sunk cost decisions. *Thinking and Reasoning*, **10**, 147–74.

Klauer, K.C., Musch, J., and Naumer, B. (2000) On belief bias in syllogistic reasoning. *Psychological Review*, **107**, 852–84.

Klauer, K.C., Stahl, C., and Erdfelder, E. (2007) The abstract selection task: New data and an almost comprehensive model. *Journal of Experimental Psychology: Learning, Memory and Cognition*, **33**, 680–703.

Krauth, J. (1982) Formulation and experimental verification of models in propositional reasoning. *Quarterly Journal of Experimental Psychology*, **34A**, 285–98.

Lieberman, M.D. (2003) Reflective and reflexive judgment processes: A social cognitive neuroscience approach. In J.P. Forgas, K.R. Williams, and W. von Hippel (eds) *Social judgments: Implicit and explicit processes,* 44–67. Cambridge University Press, New York.

Mithen, S. (1996) *The prehistory of the mind*. Thames and Hudson, London.

Newstead, S.E. (2000) Are there two different kinds of thinking? *Behavioral and Brain Sciences*, **23**, 690–1.

Nisbett, R., Peng, K., Choi, I., and Norenzayan, A. (2001) Culture and systems of thought: Holistic vs analytic cognition. *Psychological Review*, **108**, 291–310.

Oakhill, J., Johnson-Laird, P.N., and Garnham, A. (1989) Believability and syllogistic reasoning. *Cognition*, **31**, 117–40.

Oppenheimer, D. M. (2003) Not so fast! (and not so frugal!): Rethinking the recognition heuristic. *Cognition*, **90**, B1–B9.

Osman, M. (2004) An evaluation of dual-process theories of reasoning. *Psychonomic Bulletin and Review*, **11**, 988–1010.

Over, D.E. (2003) From massive modularity to metarepresentation: The evolution of higher cogntion. In D.E.Over (ed.) *Evolution and the psychology of thinking: The debate,* 121–44. Psychology Press, Hove.

Reber, A.S. (1993) *Implicit Learning and Tacit Knowledge*. Oxford University Press, Oxford.

Reyna, V. F. (2004) How people make decisions that involve risk: A dual-processes approach. *Current Directions in Psychological Science*, **13**, 60–6.

Samuels, R. (2000) Massively modular minds: Evolutionary psychology and cognitive architecture. In P. Carruthers and A. Chamberlain (eds) *Evolution and the human mind,* 13–46. Cambridge University Press, Cambridge.

Sloman, S.A. (1996) The empirical case for two systems of reasoning. *Psychological Bulletin*, **119**, 3–22.

Sloman, S.A. (2002) Two systems of reasoning. In T. Gilovich, D. Griffin, and D. Kahneman (eds) *Heuristics and biases: The psychology of intuitive judgment*, 379–98. Cambridge University Press, Cambridge.

Sloman, S.A., Over, D.E., and Slovack, L. (2003) Frequency illusions and other fallacies. *Organizational Behavior and Human Decision Processes*, **91**, 296–309.

Smith, E.R. and DeCoster, J. (2000) Dual-process models in social and cognitive psychology: Conceptual integration and links to underlying memory systems. *Personality and Social Psychology Review*, **4**, 108–31.

Sperber, D. (2000) Metarepresentations in an evolutionary perspective. In D. Sperber (ed.) *Metarepresentations*, 117–38. Oxford University Press, Oxford.

Sperber, D. and Wilson, D. (1995) *Relevance, 2nd ed.* Basil Blackwell, Oxford.

Stanovich, K.E. (1999) *Who is rational? Studies of individual differences in reasoning.* Lawrence Erlbaum Associates, Mahwah, NJ.

Stanovich, K.E. (2004) *The robot's rebellion: Finding meaning the age of Darwin.* Chicago University Press, Chicago, IL.

Stanovich, K.E. and West, R.F. (2003) Evolutionary versus instrumental goals: How evolutionary psychology misconceives human rationality. In D.E. Over (ed.) *Evolution and the psychology of thinking*, 171–230. Psychology Press, Hove.

Stevenson, R.J. (1997) Deductive reasoning and the distinction between implicit and explicit processes. *Current Psychology of Cognition*, **16**, 222–9.

Strack, F. and Deutsch, R. (2004) Reflective and impulsive determinants of social behavior. *Personality and Social Psychology Review*, **8**, 220–47.

Toates, F. (2004) 'In two minds'—Consideration of evolutionary precursors permits a more integrative theory. *Trends in Cognitive Sciences*, **8**, 57.

Toates, F. (2006) A model of the hierarchy of behaviour, cognition and consciousness. *Consciousness and Cognition*, **15**, 75–118.

Tooby, J. and Cosmides, L. (1992) The psychological foundations of culture. In J.H. Barkow, L. Cosmides, and J. Tooby (eds) *The adapted mind: Evolutionary psychology and the generation of culture*, 19–136. Oxford University Press, New York.

Velmans, M. (2000) *Understanding consciousness.* Routledge, London.

Verschueren, N., Schaeken, W., and d'Ydewalle, G. (2005) A dual-process specification of causal conditional reasoning. *Thinking & Reasoning*, **11**, 239–78.

Wason, P.C. and Evans, J.St.B.T. (1975) Dual processes in reasoning? *Cognition*, **3**, 141–54.

Wegner, D. M. (2002) *The illusion of conscious will.* MIT Books, Cambridge, MA.

Weidenfeld, A., Oberauer, K., and Hornig, R. (2005) Causal and noncausal conditionals: An integrated model of interpretation and reasoning. *Quarterly Journal of Experimental Psychology*, **58**, 1479–513.

Wilson, T.D. (2002) *Strangers to ourselves: Discovering the adaptive unconscious.* Belknap Press, Cambridge, MA.

Chapter 3

Distinguishing the reflective, algorithmic, and autonomous minds: Is it time for a tri-process theory?

Keith E. Stanovich

In a recent book (Stanovich 2004), I spent a considerable effort trying to work out the implications of dual-process theory for the great rationality debate in cognitive science (see Cohen 1981; Gigerenzer 1996; Kahneman and Tversky 1996; Stanovich 1999; Stein 1996). In this chapter, I wish to advance that discussion, first by discussing additions and complications to dual-process theory and then by working through the implications of these ideas for our view of human rationality.

Dual-process theory and human goals: Implications for the rationality debate

My previous proposal (Stanovich 1999, 2004; Stanovich and West 2000, 2003) was that partitioning the goal structure of humans in terms of dual-process theory would help to explicate the nature of the disputes in the great rationality debate in cognitive science. The proposal was that the goal structures of System 1 and System 2 were different, and that important consequences for human self-fulfillment follow from this fact. The analytic system is more attuned to the person's needs as a coherent organism than is System 1, which is more directly tuned to the ancient reproductive goals of the subpersonal replicators (likewise, it is also the case that System 1 is more likely to contain memes that are nonreflectively acquired; see Blackmore 1999; Distin 2005; Stanovich 2004). In the minority of cases where the outputs of the two systems conflict, people will often be better off if they can accomplish an analytic system override of the System 1-triggered output. Such a system conflict is likely to be signaling a vehicle/replicator goal mismatch and, statistically, such a mismatch is more likely to be resolved in favor of the vehicle (which all of us should want) if the System 1 output is overridden. This is why in cases of response conflict, override is a statistically good bet.

From within this framework, I have previously criticized some work in evolutionary psychology and adaptive modeling for implicitly undervaluing instrumental rationality by defending non-normative responses made by many subjects in reasoning experiments. Evolutionarily adaptive behavior is not the same as rational behavior.

Evolutionary psychologists obscure this by sometimes implying that if a behavior is adaptive it is rational. Such a conflation represents a fundamental error of much import for human affairs. Definitions of rationality must be kept consistent with the entity whose optimization is at issue. In order to maintain this consistency, the different 'interests' of the replicators and the vehicle must be explicitly recognized. I think a conflation of these interests is at the heart of the disputes between researchers working in the heuristics and biases tradition and their critics in the evolutionary psychology camp.

My research group has shown that while the response that is consistent with many evolutionary analyses (optimal foraging and so forth) is the modal response on many heuristics and biases tasks, the most cognitively able subjects give the response that is instrumentally rational (Kokis et al. 2002; Stanovich and West 1998a, 1998b, 1998c, 1998d, 1999; West and Stanovich 2003; see also De Neys 2006a, 2006b). Our interpretation of this data pattern was that the evolutionary psychologists are probably correct that most System 1 responses are evolutionarily adaptive. Nevertheless, their evolutionary interpretations do not impeach the position of the heuristics and biases researchers that the alternative response given by the minority of subjects is rational at the level of the individual. Subjects of higher analytic intelligence are simply more prone to override System 1 in order to produce responses that are epistemically and instrumentally rational. This rapprochement between the two camps that West and I have championed has also by advocated in several papers by Samuels and Stich (Samuels and Stich 2004; Samuels et al. 2002; Samuels et al. 1999) who have argued for a similar synthesis (see also, Evans, 2007). Indeed, such a synthesis could be said to be implicit within the early writings of the original heuristics and biases researchers themselves (Kahneman and Frederick 2002; Kahneman and Tversky 1982a, 1996; Tversky and Kahneman 1974, 1983). As Kahneman (2000) notes, 'Tversky and I always thought of the heuristics and biases approach as a two-process theory' (p.682).

Complicating the generic dual-process model

The main purpose of this chapter, though, is to add some complications to the dual-process view articulated in Stanovich (2004). First to a complication that I believe should generate little controversy. Evans (2006a, this volume) and Stanovich (2004) have both argued that although many theorists use terms such as System 1 or heuristic system as if they were talking about a singular system, this is really a misnomer (see also Carruthers 2006). In actuality, the term used should be plural because it refers to a *set* of systems in the brain that operate autonomously in response to their own triggering stimuli, and are not under the control of the analytic processing system. I thus have suggested the acronym TASS (standing for The Autonomous Set of Systems) to describe what is in actuality a heterogeneous set.[1]

---

[1] Evans (this volume) revives the type 1/type 2 process terminology of Wason and Evans (1975) and I am largely in sympathy with his suggestion. As with the TASS terminology, Evans' (this volume) usage allows that there may be many different type 1 processes.

For example, many TASS processes would be considered to be modular, as that construct has been discussed by evolutionary psychologists and other cognitive scientists, but TASS is not limited to modular subprocesses that meet all of the classic Fodorian criteria. Along with the Darwinian mind of quasi-modules discussed by the evolutionary psychologists, TASS contains domain *general* processes of unconscious implicit learning and conditioning. Also, TASS contains many rules, stimulus discriminations, and decision-making principles that have been practiced to automaticity (e.g. Shiffrin and Schneider, 1977). And finally, processes of behavioral regulation by the emotions are also in TASS (on the types of processes in TASS, see Brase 2004; Carruthers 2002; Cosmides and Tooby 1992; Evans 2003, this volume; Sperber 1994). Thus, TASS processes are conjoined in this category on the basis of autonomy, not modularity—specifically TASS processes respond automatically to triggering stimuli; their execution is not dependent upon input from, nor is it under the control of, the analytic processing system (System 2); and finally TASS can sometimes execute and provide outputs that are in conflict with the results of a simultaneous computation being carried out by System 2.

Theoretically, this complication to dual-process models serves to remind us that learned information is in TASS as well as modules that are the result of evolutionary adaptation. This learned information can be just as much a threat to rational behavior—that is, just as in need of override by System 2—as are evolutionary modules that fire inappropriately in a modern environment. Rules learned to automaticity can be overgeneralized—they can autonomously trigger behavior when the situation is an exception to the class of events they are meant to cover (Arkes and Ayton 1999; Hsee and Hastie 2006).

The next complication I wish to introduce concerns the conceptualization of System 2 and it is of perhaps more theoretical import. I will argue that System 2 needs to be understood in terms of two levels of processing—the algorithmic level and the reflective level. We can see this if we consider the logic of TASS override. TASS will implement its short-leashed goals unless overridden by the algorithmic mechanisms implementing the long-leash goals of the analytic system. But override itself is initiated by higher level control. That is, the algorithmic level of the analytic system is conceptualized as subordinate to the higher-level goal states and epistemic thinking dispositions, some of which have been studied empirically (e.g. Cacioppo et al. 1996; Stanovich and West 1997, 2007). These goal states and epistemic dispositions exist at what might be termed the reflective level of processing—a level containing control states that regulate behavior at a high level of generality. Such high-level goal states are common in the intelligent agents built by artificial intelligence researchers (Franklin 1995; Pollock 1995; A. Sloman 1993; A. Sloman and Chrisley 2003). My attempt to differentiate System 2 into the two levels of processing was the reason for the provocative title of this chapter which was meant to raise the question of how seriously we should take a tripartite model. In Figure 3.1, I have presented the tripartite proposal in a simple form. In the spirit of Dennett's (1996) book *Kinds of minds*, I have labeled the traditional TASS (or System 1) as the autonomous mind, the algorithmic level of System 2 the algorithmic mind, and the reflective level of System 2 the reflective mind.

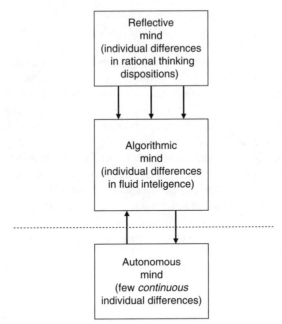

Fig. 3.1 Individual differences in the tripartite structure.

Differentiating the algorithmic and the reflective mind

In fact, artificial intelligence researchers take the possibility of a tripartite structure quite seriously (see A. Sloman and Chrisley 2003; Samuels 2005). Are there any other reasons, aside from the precedent in AI research, for accepting this alternative structure? First, it must be acknowledged that there is no way that the distinctions between the algorithmic and reflective mind will cleave as nicely as those that have traditionally differentiated System 1 and 2 (the dashed line in Figure 3.1 signals this) because the algorithmic and reflective mind will both share properties (capacity-limited serial processing for instance) that differentiate them from the autonomous mind.

Nonetheless, there are some reasons for giving the algorithmic/reflective distinction some consideration. My research group has found that individual differences in some very important critical thinking pitfalls such as the tendency toward myside thinking and the tendency toward one-sided thinking are relatively independent of intelligence (Stanovich and West 2007, 2008). We take this to indicate that the critical thinking skills necessary to avoid myside bias and one-side bias are instantiated at the reflective level of the mind as opposed to the algorithmic level. Second, across a variety of tasks from the heuristics and biases literature, it has consistently been found that rational thinking dispositions will predict variance in these tasks after the effects of general intelligence have been controlled (Bruine de Bruin et al. 2007; Klaczynski and Lavallee 2005; Kokis et al. 2002; Parker and Fischhoff 2005; Stanovich and West 1997, 1998c, 2000; Toplak and Stanovich 2002, 2003). Thinking disposition measures are telling us about the individual's goals and epistemic values—and they are indexing broad tendencies of pragmatic and epistemic self-regulation at the intentional level of analysis. The empirical studies cited indicate that these different types of cognitive predictors are tapping separable variance, and the reason that this is to be expected is because cognitive capacity measures such as intelligence and thinking dispositions map on to different levels of analysis in cognitive theory.

Figure 3.1 reflects the theoretical conjecture (Stanovich 2002, in press). It is proposed that variation in fluid intelligence (see Carroll 1993) largely indexes individual differences in the efficiency of processing of the algorithmic mind. In contrast, thinking dispositions index individual differences at the intentional level—that is, in the reflective mind. In the empirical studies cited above, the rational thinking dispositions examined have encompassed assessments of epistemic regulation such as actively open-minded thinking and dogmatism (Stanovich and West 1997, 2007), assessments of response regulation such as the Matching Familiar Figures Test (Kagan et al. 1964), and assessments of cognitive regulation such as need for cognition (Cacioppo et al. 1996).

The proposal is thus that just as System 1 has been pluralized into TASS, we might now need to recognize two aspects of System 2, the reflective and algorithmic. One reason for endorsing a tripartite structure is that breakdowns in cognitive functioning in the three kinds of minds manifest very differently. For example, disruptions in algorithmic-level functioning are apparent in general impairments in intellectual ability of the type that cause mental retardation (Anderson 1998). And these disruptions vary quite continuously. In contrast, continuous individual differences in the autonomous mind are few. The individual differences that do exist largely reflect damage to cognitive modules that result in very discontinuous cognitive dysfunction such as autism or the agnosias and alexias. Importantly, Bermudez (2001; see also Murphy and Stich 2000) notes that they are traditionally explained by recourse to subpersonal functions (see Davies 2000, for a discussion of personal and subpersonal constructs). In complete contrast are many psychiatric disorders (particularly those such as delusions) which implicate intentional-level functioning (that is, functioning in what I here call the reflective mind). Bermudez (2001) argues that the 'impairments in which they manifest themselves are of the sort that would standardly be explained at the personal level, rather than at the subpersonal level. In the terms of Fodor's dichotomy, psychiatric disorders seem to be disorders of central processing rather than peripheral modules … Many of the symptoms of psychiatric disorders involve impairments of rationality—and consequently that the norms of rationality must be taken to play a vital role in the understanding of psychiatric disorders' (pp.460, 461).

Thus, there is an important sense in which rationality is a more encompassing construct than intelligence—it concerns both aspects of System 2. The reason is that rationality is an organismic-level concept. It concerns the actions of an entity in its environment that serve its goals. To be rational, an organism must have well-calibrated beliefs (reflective level) and must act appropriately on those beliefs to achieve its goals (reflective level). The organism must, of course, have the algorithmic-level machinery that enables it to carry out the actions and to process the environment in a way that enables the correct beliefs to be fixed and the correct actions to be taken.

Thus, individual differences in rational thought and action can arise because of individual differences in intelligence or because of individual differences in thinking dispositions. To put it simply, the concept of rationality encompasses two things (thinking dispositions and algorithmic-level capacity) whereas the concept of intelligence—at least as it is commonly operationalized—is largely confined to algorithmic-level capacity.

Intelligence tests and critical thinking tests: Partitioning the algorithmic from the reflective mind

The difference between the reflective mind and the algorithmic mind is captured operationally in the distinction that psychologists make between tests of intelligence and tests of critical thinking. To a layperson, the tasks on tests of cognitive capacities (intelligence tests or other aptitude measures) might seem superficially similar to those on tests of critical thinking (in the educational literature, the term critical thinking is often used to cover tasks and mental operations that a cognitive scientist would term indicators of rational thought). An outsider to psychometrics or cognitive science might deem the classification of tasks into one category or the other some-what arbitrary. In fact, it is far from arbitrary and actually reflects the distinction between the reflective mind and the algorithmic mind.

Psychometricians have long distinguished typical performance situations from optimal (sometimes termed maximal) performance situations (Ackerman and Heggestad 1997; Ackerman and Kanfer 2004). Typical performance situations are unconstrained in that no overt instructions to maximize performance are given, and the task interpretation is determined to some extent by the participant. In contrast, optimal performance situations are those where the task interpretation is determined externally (not left to the participant), the participant is instructed to maximize per-formance, and is told how to do so. All tests of intelligence or cognitive aptitude are optimal performance assessments, whereas measures of critical or rational thinking are often assessed under typical performance conditions. What this means is that tests of intelligence are constrained at the level of reflective processing (an attempt is made to specify the task demands so explicitly that variation in thinking dispositions is minimally influential). In contrast, tests of critical or rational thinking are not con-strained at the level of reflective processing (or at least are much less constrained). Tasks of the latter but not the former type allow high-level personal goals (and epis-temic goals) to become implicated in performance.

Consider the type of syllogistic reasoning item usually examined by cognitive psychologists studying belief bias effects (see Evans et al. 1983; Evans and Curtis-Holmes 2005):

Premise 1: All living things need water.

Premise 2: Roses need water.

Therefore, Roses are living things.

Approximately 70% of the university students who have been given this problem incorrectly think that the conclusion is valid (Markovits and Nantel 1989; Sá et al. 1999;

Stanovich and West 1998c). Clearly, the believability of the conclusion is interfering with the assessment of logical validity.

The important point for the present discussion is that it would not be surprising to see an item such as the 'rose' syllogism (that is, an item that pitted prior belief against logical validity) on a critical thinking test. Such tests do not constrain reflective-level thinking dispositions, and in fact attempt to probe and assess the nature of such cognitive tendencies to bias judgments in the direction of prior belief or to trump prior belief with new evidence (see, e.g. certain exercises in the *Watson-Glaser critical thinking appraisal*, Watson and Glaser 1980).

In using items with such content, critical thinking tests create (even if the instructions attempt to disambiguate) ambiguity about what feature of the problem to rely upon—ambiguity that is resolved differently by individuals with different epistemic dispositions. The point is that on an intelligence test, there would be no epistemic ambiguity created in the first place. Such tests attempt to constrain reflective-level functioning in order to isolate processing abilities at the algorithmic level of analysis. It is the efficiency of computational abilities under optimal (not typical) conditions that is the focus of IQ tests. Variation in thinking dispositions would contaminate this algorithmic-level assessment.

I do not wish to argue that intelligence tests are entirely successful in this respect—that they entirely eliminate reflective-level factors; only that the constructors of the tests *attempt* to do so. Additionally, it is certainly the case that some higher-level strategic control is exercised on intelligence test items, but this tends to be a type of micro-level control rather than the activation of macro-strategies that are engaged by critical thinking tests. For example, on multiple-choice IQ-test items, the respondent is certainly engaging in a variety of control processes such as suppressing responses to identified distracter items. Nonetheless, if the test is properly designed, they are not engaging in the type of macro-level strategizing that is common on critical thinking tests—for example, deciding how to construe the task or how to allocate effort across differing construals.

Thus, you will not find an item like the 'rose' syllogism on an intelligence test (or any aptitude measure or cognitive capacity measure). For example, on a cognitive ability test, a syllogistic reasoning item will be stripped of content (all As are Bs, etc.) in order to remove any possible belief bias component. In complete contrast, in the reasoning and rational thinking literature, conflict between knowledge and validity is often deliberately *created* in order to study belief bias. Thus, cognitive ability tests eliminate the conflict between epistemic tendencies to preserve logical validity and the tendency to project prior knowledge. In contrast, critical thinking tasks deliberately leave reflective-level strategic decisions unconstrained, because it is precisely such epistemic regulation that they wish to assess. Of course this is why debates about the normative response on rational thinking measures have been prolonged in a way that has not characterized IQ tests (Cohen 1981; Gigerenzer 1996; Kahneman and Tversky 1996; Manktelow 2004; Over 2002, 2004; Shafir and LeBoeuf 2002; Stanovich 1999; Stein 1996). The more a measure taps the reflective-level psychology of rationality, the more it will implicate normative issues that are largely moot when measuring algorithmic-level efficiency.

The key functions of the reflective mind and the algorithmic mind that support human rationality

The reflective mind and the algorithmic mind both have a key function that serves to support human rationality. Both functions relate to an aspect of reasoning that has received considerable attention in parts of the dual-process literature—hypothetical thinking (Evans 2003, 2006b, 2007, this volume; Evans and Over 1996, 2004). One idea is that 'the analytic system is involved whenever hypothetical thought is required' (p.379, Evans 2006b). Stated in the form of a conditional, we might say that: If hypothetical thought is required, then the analytic system is involved. Such a formulation preserves an important point I will make later—that not all analytic system thought involves hypothetical thinking.

Hypothetical thinking is the foundation of rationality because it is tightly connected to the notion of TASS override (see Stanovich 2004). The analytic system must be able to take early response tendencies triggered by TASS offline and be able to substitute better responses. But where do these better responses come from? One answer is that they come from a process of cognitive simulation (e.g. Buckner and Carroll 2007; Byrne 2005; Kahneman and Tversky 1982b; Nichols and Stich 2003; Oatley 1999). Responses that have survived a selective process during simulation are often a better choice than the TASS-triggered response. So the key mechanism of the *reflective* mind that supports human rationality is the mechanism that sends out a call to begin cognitive simulation or hypothetical reasoning more generally. It is conjectured that individual differences in the operation of this mechanism contribute to the differences in rational thinking examined in some of the studies cited above (e.g. Stanovich and West 1998c).

Correspondingly, there is a key operation of the algorithmic mind that supports hypothetical thinking and that is characterized by large individual differences. Simply put, cognitive simulation and hypothetical reasoning is dependent upon the operation of cognitive decoupling carried out by the algorithmic mind. Cognitive decoupling has been discussed in related and somewhat differing ways by a large number of different investigators coming from a variety of different perspectives, not limited to: developmental psychology, evolutionary psychology, artificial intelligence, and philosophy of mind (Cosmides and Tooby 2000; Dienes and Perner 1999; Jackendoff 1996; Nichols and Stich 2003; Perner 1991; Sperber 2000). I shall emphasize the origins of the concept in developmental psychology because of a useful theoretical link to important models of the origins of System 2 (see Mithen 1996).

In a famous article in the early theory of mind literature, Leslie (1987) provided a model of pretence that made use of the concept of cognitive decoupling. Leslie's (1987) model can best be understood by adopting a terminology later used by Perner (1991). In the latter's view, a primary representation is one that is used to directly map the world and/or is also rather directly connected to a response. Leslie (1987) modeled pretense by positing a so-called secondary representation (to use Perner's [1991] terms) that was a copy of the primary representation but that was decoupled from the world so that it could be manipulated—that is, be a mechanism for simulation. Nichols and Stich (2003) model this cognitive decoupling as a separate 'possible world box' (PWB) in which the simulations are carried out without contaminating the relationship between the world and primary representation.

For Leslie (1987), the decoupled secondary representation is necessary in order to avoid so-called representational abuse—the possibility of confusing our simulations with our primary representations of the world as it actually is. The cognitive operation of decoupling, or what Nichols and Stich (2003) term cognitive quarantine, prevents our representations of the real world from becoming confused with representations of imaginary situations. For example, when considering an alternative goal state different from the current goal state, one needs to be able to represent both. To engage in these exercises of hypotheticality and high-level cognitive control, one has to explicitly represent a psychological attitude toward the state of affairs as well as the state of affairs itself. Thus, decoupled representations of actions about to be taken become representations of potential actions, but the latter must not infect the former while the mental simulation is being carried out.

Decoupling operations must be continually in force during any ongoing simulations, and I have conjectured (Stanovich 2001, 2004) that the raw ability to sustain such mental simulations while keeping the relevant representations decoupled is likely the key aspect of the brain's computational power that is being assessed by measures of fluid intelligence (on fluid intelligence, see Carroll 1993; Horn and Noll 1997; Kane and Engle 2002).

Decoupling—outside of certain domains such as behavioral prediction (so-called 'theory of mind' where evolution has built content-specific machinery)—is a cognitively demanding operation. Any mindware that can aid this computationally expensive process is thus immensely useful, and language appears to be one such mental tool. Language provides the discrete representational medium that greatly enables hypotheticality to flourish as a culturally acquired mode of thought. For example, hypothetical thought involves representing assumptions, and linguistic forms such as conditionals provide a medium for such representations (Carruthers 2002; Evans 2007; Evans and Over 2004).

Decoupling skills vary in their recursiveness and complexity. The skills discussed thus far are those that are necessary for creating what Perner (1991) calls secondary representations—the decoupled representations that are the multiple models of the world that enable hypothetical thought. At a certain level of development, decoupling becomes used for so-called meta-representation—thinking about thinking itself (there are many subtleties surrounding the concept of metarepresentation; see Dennett 1984; Perner 1991; Sperber 2000; Whiten 2001). Decoupling processes enable one to distance oneself from representations of the world so that they can be reflected upon and potentially improved. The use of metarepresentational abilities in such a program of cognitive reform would be an example of what has been termed the quest for broad rationality—the cognitive critique of the beliefs and desires that are input into the implicit calculations that result in instrumental (Humean) rationality (see Stanovich 2004).

I propose that cognitive decoupling is the key function of the algorithmic mind that supports human rationality and that it is the operation that accounts for several other features of what we have been calling System 2—in particular its seriality and most importantly its computational expense. In short, we are beginning to understand the key computational function of the algorithmic mind—which is to maintain decoupling among representations while carrying out mental simulation. This is becoming clear from converging work on executive function (Baddeley et al. 2001; Duncan et al. 2000; Hasher et al. 1999; Kane 2003; Kane and Engle 2002; Salthouse et al. 2003) and working memory (Conway et al. 2003; Engle 2002; Geary 2005; Kane et al. 2001; Kane and Engle 2003; Kane et al. 2005).

First, there is a startling degree of overlap in individual differences on working memory tasks and individual differences in measures of fluid intelligence. Secondly, it is becoming clear that working memory tasks are only incidentally about memory. Or, as Engle (2002, p.20) puts it,

> WM capacity is just as important in retention of a single representation, such as the representation of a goal or of the status of a changing variable, as it is in determining how many representations can be maintained. WM capacity is not directly about memory—it is about using attention to maintain or suppress information. WM capacity is about memory only indirectly. Greater WM capacity does mean that more items can be maintained as active, but this is a result of greater ability to control attention, not a larger memory store.

Hasher et al. (2007) concur with this view when they conclude that 'our evidence raises the possibility that what most working memory span tasks measure is inhibitory control, not something like the size of operating capacity' (p.231).

Lepine et al. (2005) report an experiment showing that working memory tasks with simple processing components are actually better predictors of high-level cognitive performance than are working memory tasks with complex processing requirements—as long as the former are rapidly paced to lock up attention. Their results are consistent with Engle's (2002) review of evidence indicating that working memory tasks really tap the preservation of internal representations in the presence of distraction or, as I have termed it—the ability to decouple a secondary representation (or metarepresentation) from a primary representation and manipulate the former. For example, he describes an experiment using the so-called antisaccade task. Subjects must look at the middle of a computer screen and respond to a target stimulus that will appear on the left or right of the screen. Before the target appears, a cue is flashed on the opposite side of the screen. Subjects must resist the attention-capturing cue and respond to the target on the opposite side when it appears. Subjects scoring low on working memory tasks were more likely to make an eye movement (saccade) in the direction of the distracting cue than were subjects who scored high on working memory task.

That the antisaccade task has very little to do with memory is an indication of why investigators have reconceptualized the individual difference variables that working memory tasks are tapping. Individual differences on such tasks are now described with a variety of different terms (attentional control, resistance to distraction, executive control), but the critical operation needed to succeed in them—and the reason they are the prime indicator of fluid intelligence—is that they reflect the ability to sustain decoupled representations. Such decoupling is an important aspect of behavioral control that is related to rationality (see De Neys 2006a, 2006b).

So-called 'executive functioning' measures tap the algorithmic mind and not the reflective mind

One interesting implication that follows from the distinction between the algorithmic mind and reflective mind is that the measures of so-called executive functioning in the neuropsychological literature actually measure nothing of the sort. The term 'executive' implies that these tasks assess the highest level of cognitive functioning— the reflective level. However, a consideration of the tasks most commonly used in the neuropsychological literature to assess executive functioning (see Pennington and Ozonoff 1996; Salthouse et al. 2003) reveals that almost without exception they are optimal performance tasks and not typical performance tasks and that most of them rather severely constrain reflective-level functioning. Thus, because reflective-level functioning is constrained, such tasks are largely assessing individual differences in algorithmic-level functioning. This is the reason why several studies have shown very strong correlations between executive functioning and fluid intelligence (Conway et al. 2003; Kane et al. 2005; Salthouse et al. 2003; Unsworth and Engle 2005).

Consider some of the classic tasks in the neuropsychological literature on executive function (see Pennington and Ozonoff 1996; Salthouse et al. 2003). In the critical part of the Trail Making Test the subject must, in the shortest time possible, connect with a line a series of numbered and lettered circles going from 1 to A to 2 to B to 3 to C, and so on. The rule is specified in advance and there is no ambiguity about what constitutes optimal performance. There is no higher-level task interpretation required of the subject. Cognitive decoupling is required though, in order to keep the right sequence in mind and not revert to number sequencing alone or letter sequencing alone. Thus, the task does require algorithmic-level decoupling in order to suppress TASS from disrupting performance by defaulting to an overlearned rule. But the task does not require reflective control in the sense that I have defined it here (or it does in only the most basic sense by requiring a decision to comply with the tester or experimenter).

The situation is similar regarding another test of executive functioning from the neuropsychological literature, the Stroop Test. The subject is explicitly told to name the color and not read the word, and optimal performance is clearly defined as going as fast as possible. Algorithmic-level decoupling is needed in order to suppress the automatic response from TASS to read the word. But higher-level reflective control never enters the picture. The response requirements of the task are very basic and the task set is dictated externally. It is a test of suppression via algorithmic-level decoupling pure and simple. Fluency tasks are also commonly used to measure executive functioning (Salthouse et al. 2003). Here, the subject simply articulates as many words as they can from a specified category (words beginning with the letter F, names of red things, etc.). Again, in such a task there is no reflective choice about what rule to use. The task requirements are entirely specified in advance and the assessment concerns merely the efficiency of execution.

A widely used measure of executive functioning, the Wisconsin Card Sorting Test (Heaton et al. 1993), does begin to tap more reflective processes, although variance in suppression via decoupling is still probably the dominant individual difference component that it taps. In the WCST the subject sees a set of target cards containing shapes varying in color, form, and number. The instructions are to sort new cards in a deck correctly by grouping them with the correct target card. The subject must discover the dimension (color, form, or number) that should be the basis of the sort, and at predetermined points the correct dimension of sort is changed on the subject without warning. Although the basic task structure is set by the examiner, there may well be some reflective involvement in the rule discovery stages of the task. Nevertheless, once the rule is switched, suppression of the tendency to sort by the previous rule is probably the dominant influence on performance. This suppression is carried out by algorithmic-level decoupling abilities and is probably why the task is correlated with fluid intelligence (Salthouse et al. 2003).

The tasks I have discussed so far come from the neuropsychological literature. However, more precise experimental tasks have been used in the literature of cognitive psychology to measure exactly the same construct as the neuropsychological executive function measures. These more precise tasks—stop signal paradigms, working memory paradigms, time-sharing paradigms, inhibition paradigms of various types (see Salthouse et al. 2003)—are all subject to exactly the same arguments just made regarding the neuropsychological measures. The more precise experimental measures are optimal performance tasks (not typical performance tasks) and they severely constrain reflective-level functioning. All measure algorithmic-level decoupling power, which is why they display a considerable degree of overlap with fluid intelligence (Kane and Engle 2002; Salthouse et al. 2003). Individual differences in the reflective mind are only tangentially implicated. This is because tapping reflective processes requires measures of typical performance so that individual differences in epistemic regulation and cognitive allocation (e.g. need for cognition) become implicated in performance beyond simply the computational power to sustain decoupling operations. This point about the laboratory measures has been made before by Salthouse et al. (2003): 'The role of executive functioning may also be rather limited in many laboratory tasks because much of the organization or structure of the tasks is provided by the experimenter and does not need to be discovered or created by the research participant' (p.569).

In short, my argument is that executive processes are misnamed in the psychological literature. Executive functioning measures are nothing of the kind—at least as most people would understand the word 'executive'. These tasks might instead be better termed measures of *supervisory* processes. They assess the ability to carry out the rules instantiated not by internal regulation (*true* executive control) but by an external authority that explicitly sets the rules and tells the subject what constitutes maximal performance. Subjects do not set the agenda in these tasks (as is the case in many tasks in the rational-thinking and critical-thinking literatures) but instead attempt to optimize criteria explicitly given to them. The processes assessed by such tasks do involve algorithmic-level decoupling (which is why they are so highly related to fluid intelligence), but they are supervisory in nature—decoupling is used to screen out distracting stimuli (i.e. suppress via decoupling irrelevant inputs from the autonomous mind) and make sure the externally-provided rule remains the goal state.

In contrast, processes of the reflective mind operate to set the goal agenda or they operate in the service of epistemic regulation (i.e. to direct the sequence of information pickup). Such processes that set and regulate the goal and epistemic agendas are little engaged by so-called executive function tasks. The term 'executive' thus can lead to theoretical confusion in the literature. More importantly, it contributes to the tendency to overlook the importance of measuring variation in the reflective mind. The term 'executive' mistakenly implies that everything 'higher up' has been taken care of, or that there is no level higher than what these executive functioning tasks measure.

Serial associative cognition with a focal bias

The current tripartite view of the mind has begun to look somewhat like that displayed in Figure 3.2. Previous dual-process theories have emphasized the processing sequence where the reflective mind sends out a call to the algorithmic mind to override the TASS response by taking it offline. An alternative response that is the result of cognitive simulation is substituted for the TASS response that would have been emitted. The override function has loomed large in dual-process theory but less so the simulation process that computes the alternative response that makes the override worthwhile. Figure 3.2 explicitly represents the simulation function as well as the fact that the call to initiate simulation originates in the reflective mind. The decoupling operation itself is carried out by the algorithmic mind. Recall that two different types of individual differences are associated with the initiation call and the decoupling operator—specifically, rational-thinking dispositions with the former and fluid intelligence with the latter.

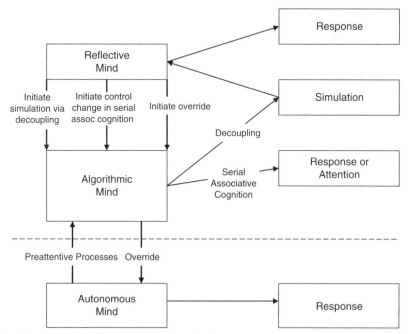

Fig. 3.2 A more complete model of the tripartite structure.

The model in Figure 3.2 defines a third critical function for the algorithmic mind in addition to TASS override and enabling simulation. The third is a function that in the Figure is termed serial associative cognition. This function relates to my point mentioned previously, that: all hypothetical thinking involves the analytic system (Evans and Over 2004), but not all analytic system thought involves hypothetical thinking. Serial associative cognition represents this latter category. It can be understood by considering a discussion of the selection task in a recent theoretical paper on dual processes by Evans (2006b; see also Evans and Over 2004). Here, and in Evans and Over (2004), it is pointed out that the previous emphasis on the matching bias evident in the task (Evans 1972, 1998, 2002; Evans and Lynch 1973) might have led some investigators to infer that the analytic system is not actively engaged in the task. In fact, matching bias might be viewed as just one of several such suggestions in the literature that much thinking during the task is non-analytic (see Margolis 1987; Stanovich and West 1998a; Tweney and Yachanin 1985). In contrast, however, Evans (2006b) presents evidence indicating that there may be analytic system involvement during the task—even on the part of the majority who do not give the normatively correct response but instead give the PQ response.

First, in discussing the card inspection paradigm (Evans 1996) that he pioneered (see also Lucas and Ball 2005; Roberts and Newton 2001), Evans (2006b) notes that although subjects look disproportionately at the cards they will choose (the finding leading to the inference that heuristic processes were determining the responses), the lengthy amount of time they spend on those cards suggests that analytic thought is occurring (if only to generate justification for the heuristically-triggered choices). Secondly, in verbal protocol studies, subjects can justify their responses (indeed, can justify *any* set of responses they are told are correct, see Evans and Wason 1976) with analytic arguments—arguments that sometimes refer to the hidden side of cards chosen.

I think it is correct to argue that analytic cognition is occurring in this task, but I also want to argue that it is not full blown cognitive simulation of alternative world models. It is thinking of a shallower type (see Frankish 2004). In Figure 3.2 I have termed it serial associative cognition—cognition that is not rapid and parallel such as TASS processes, but is nonetheless rather inflexibly locked into an associative mode that takes as its starting point a model of the world that is *given* to the subject. In the inspection paradigm, subjects are justifying heuristically-chosen responses (P and Q for the standard form of the problem), and the heuristically-chosen responses are driven by the model given to the subject by the rule.

Likewise, Evans and Over (2004) note that in the studies of verbal protocols subjects making an incorrect choice referred to the hidden sides of the cards they are going to pick, but referred only to verification when they did so. Thus, the evidence suggests that subjects accept the rule as given, assume it is true, and simply describe how they would go about verifying it. The fact that they refer to hidden sides does not mean that they have constructed any alternative model of the situation beyond what was given to them by the experimenter and their own assumption that the rule is true. They then reason from this single focal model—systematically generating associations from this focal model but never constructing another model of the situation.

This is what I would term serial associative cognition with a focal bias. It is how I would begin to operationalize the satisficing bias in the analytic system posited by Evans (2006b, 2007; Evans et al. 2003).

One way in which to contextualize the idea of focal bias is as the second stage in a framework for thinking about human information processing that is over 30 years old—the idea of humans as cognitive misers (Dawes 1976; Taylor 1981; Tversky and Kahneman 1974). Krueger and Funder (2004) characterize the cognitive miser assumption as one that emphasizes 'limited mental resources, reliance on irrelevant cues, and the difficulties of effortful correction' (pp.316–17). More humorously, Hull (2001) has said that 'the rule that human beings seem to follow is to engage the brain only when all else fails—and usually not even then' (p.37).

There are in fact several aspects of cognitive miserliness. Dual-process theory has heretofore highlighted only Rule 1 of the Cognitive Miser: default to TASS processing whenever possible. But defaulting to TASS processing is not always possible—particularly in novel situations where there are no stimuli available to domain-specific evolutionary modules, nor perhaps any information with which to run overlearned and well-compiled procedures that TASS has acquired through practice. Analytic processing procedures will be necessary, but a cognitive miser default is operating even there. Rule 2 of the Cognitive Miser is that, when analytic processing is necessary: default to serial associative cognition with a focal bias (*not* fully decoupled cognitive simulation). [Rule 3 might be deemed the tendency to start cognitive simulation but not complete it—that is, override failure.]

Evans (2006b) draws attention to Rule 2 in the model of humans as cognitive misers by emphasizing a satisficing principle in his conception of the analytic system. The notion of focal bias is a way of conceiving of just what satisficing by the analytic system is in terms of actual information-processing mechanics. The proposal is, simply, that it amounts to a focal bias with an additional tendency *not* to interrupt serial associative cognition with a decoupling call from the reflective mind.

The notion of a focal bias conjoins several closely related ideas in the literature—Evans et al.'s (2003) singularity principle, Johnson-Laird's (1999, 2005) principle of truth, focusing (Legrenzi et al. 1993), the effect/effort issues discussed by Sperber et al. (1995), and finally, the focalism (Wilson et al. 2000) and belief acceptance (Gilbert 1991) issues that have been prominent in the social psychological literature. My notion of focal bias conjoins many of these ideas under the overarching theme that they all have in common—that humans will find any way they can to ease the cognitive load and process less information. Focal bias combines all of these tendencies into the basic idea that the information processor is strongly disposed to deal only with the most easily constructed cognitive model.

So the focal model that will dominate processing—the only model that serial associative cognition deals with—is the most easily constructed model. The focal model tends to represent: only one state of affairs (the Evans et al. 2003, singularity idea), it accepts what is directly presented and models what is presented as true (e.g. Gilbert 1991; Johnson-Laird 1999), it is a model that minimizes effort (Sperber et al. 1995), it ignores moderating factors (as the social psychological literature has demonstrated, e.g. Wilson et al. 2000)—probably because taking account of those factors would necessitate modeling several alternative worlds and this is just what a focal processing allows us to avoid. And finally, given the voluminous literature in cognitive science on belief bias and the informal reasoning literature on myside bias, the easiest models to represent clearly appear to be those closest to what a person already believes in and has modeled previously (e.g. Evans and Feeney 2004; Stanovich and West 2007).

Thus, serial associative cognition is defined by its reliance on a single focal model that triggers all subsequent thought. So framing effects, for instance, are a clear example of serial associative cognition with a focal bias. As Kahneman (2003) notes, 'the basic principle of framing is the passive acceptance of the formulation given' (p.703). The frame presented to the subject is taken as focal, and all subsequent thought derives from it rather than from alternative framings because the latter would necessitate more computationally expensive simulation operations.

In short, serial associative cognition is serial and analytic (as opposed to holistic) in style, but it relies on a single focal model that triggers all subsequent thought. Such a view is consistent with the aforementioned discussion of thinking during the selection task and the conclusion that analytic cognition does indeed take place even for the incorrect responders (see Evans 2006b; Evans and Over 2004). Incorrect responders are engaging in serial associative cognition with a focal bias, but reflective processes are not prone to send additional decoupling calls in order to explore alternative models to the focal one. A final factor that might differentiate serial associative cognition from fully decoupled simulation is the tendency for the focal model in the former to become 'unclamped'—that is, to be replaced by another model suggested by the serial stream of consciousness.

In the tripartite model proposed here, the decoupling operation is uniquely a function of the algorithmic mind—it is not a function of TASS (outside the theory of mind module). It is also the main source of variance in computational assessments of the algorithmic mind (such as tests of fluid intelligence). But again I would stress that what is assessed on such measures is the ability to *sustain* cognitive decoupling when the necessity for decoupling is clearly communicated to the subject. Such measures do not in fact assess the natural *tendency* to simulate alternative models—they do not assess the tendency of the reflective mind to send out an instruction to decouple from the focal model.

The preceding discussion might be taken to define three different functions of cognitive decoupling. In the override case, decoupling involves taking offline the connection between a primary representation and response programming in TASS. In the second case, the case of comprehensive simulation, it involves segregating from representational abuse multiple models undergoing simultaneous evaluation and transformation. Of course these two are related—TASS responses are often decoupled pending a comprehensive simulation that determines whether there is a better response.

A third type of decoupling involves interrupting serial associative cognition—that is, decoupling from the next step in an associative sequence that would otherwise direct thought. This third type of decoupling might shunt the processor to comprehensive simulation or may not in fact replace the focal model but simply start a new associative chain from a different starting point *within* the focal model.

Paralleling the three types of decoupling are three initiate signals from the reflective mind (see Figure 3.2): initiating override operations; initiating cognitive simulation; and initiating an interrupt of serial associative cognition.[2]

Dual-process theory and knowledge structures

One aspect of dual-process theory that has been relatively neglected is that the simulation process is not simply procedural but instead utilizes content—that is, it uses declarative knowledge and strategic rules (linguistically-coded strategies) to transform a decoupled representation. In the previous dual-process literature, override and simulation have been treated as somewhat disembodied processes. The knowledge bases and strategies that are brought to bear on the secondary representations during the simulation process have been given little attention.

In fact, each of the levels in the tripartite model described in this chapter has to access knowledge to carry out its operations (see Figure 3.3). The reflective mind not only accesses general knowledge structures but, importantly, accesses the person's opinions, beliefs, and reflectively acquired goal structure (considered preferences, see Gauthier 1986). The algorithmic mind accesses micro-strategies for cognitive operations and production system rules for sequencing behaviors and thoughts. Finally, the autonomous mind accesses not only evolutionarily-compiled encapsulated knowledge bases, but also retrieves information that has become tightly compiled due to overlearning and practice.

It is important to note that what is displayed in Figure 3.3 are the knowledge bases that are *unique* to each mind. Algorithmic- and reflective-level processes also receive inputs from the computations of the autonomous mind. As Evans (this volume) notes, TASS processes that supply information to the analytic system are sometimes termed preattentive processes. His chapter contains a particularly good discussion of the importance of these preattentive processes in fixing the content of analytic thought.

The rules, procedures, and strategies that can be retrieved by the analytic system (the algorithmic and reflective minds) and used to transform decoupled representations have been referred to as mindware, a term coined by David Perkins in a 1995 book (Clark 2001, uses it a slightly different way from Perkins' original coinage). The mindware available for the analytic system to substitute during TASS override is in part the product of past learning experiences. Indeed, if one is going to trump a TASS-primed response with conflicting information or a learned rule, one must have previously learned the information or the rule. If, in fact, the relevant mindware is not available because it has not been learned, then we have a case of missing mindware rather than a TASS-override failure. This distinction in fact represents the beginning of a taxonomy of the causes of cognitive failure related to rational behavior that I am currently using to organize the heuristics and biases literature and to classify various practical problems of rational thinking—for example, to understand the thinking problems of pathological gamblers (Toplak et al. 2007).

---

2 These three functions of decoupling are interestingly parallel to three executive process functions (see Miyake et al. 2000) that have been discussed in the literature: inhibition, updating, and set shifting.

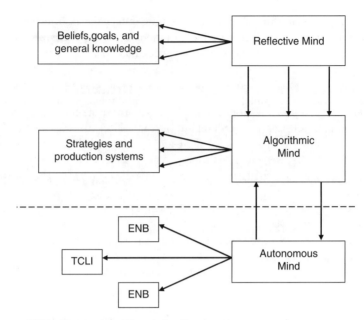

ENB = Encapsulated Knowledge Base
TCLI = Tightly Compiled Learned Information

Fig. 3.3 Knowledge structures in the tripartite model.

A taxonomy applied to the heuristics and biases literature

My taxonomy recognizes several different categories of cognitive failure termed: TASS override failure; mindware gaps; contaminated mindware; defaulting to the autonomous mind; and defaulting to serial associative cognition with a focal bias.[3] The first is the well-known category—the one we are all familiar with from the dual-process literature: situations where the TASS-primed responses must be

---

[3] I have discussed a fifth category elsewhere (Stanovich 2009; Toplak et al. 2007), but because it relates less to classifying the heuristics and biases literature, I omit it here. The fifth category derives from the possibility of not too much TASS output (as in override failure) but too little. Cognitive neuroscientists have uncovered cases of mental pathology that are characterized by inadequate behavioral regulation from the emotion modules in TASS—for example, Damasio's (1994, 1996; Bechara et al. 1994; Eslinger and Damasio 1985) well-known studies of patients with damage in the ventromedial prefrontal cortex. These individuals have severe difficulties in real-life decision making but do not display the impairments in sustained attention and executive control that are characteristic of individuals with damage in dorsolateral frontal regions (e.g. Bechara 2005; Duncan et al. 1996; Kimberg et al. 1998; McCarthy and Warrington 1990; Pennington and Ozonoff 1996). Instead, they are thought to lack the emotions that constrain the combinatorial explosion of possible actions to a manageable number based on somatic markers stored from similar situations in the past.

overridden by the analytic system if the optimal response is to be made and the analytic system fails to override. As just mentioned though, this category is interestingly related to the second. Note that there are two reasons for what previously has been termed a failure of TASS override, but most discussions in the dual-process literature simply tacitly default to one of them. Most previous discussions of TASS override have simply assumed that mindware was available to be employed in an override function by the analytic system. If, in fact, the mindware is not available because it has not been learned or at least not learned to the requisite level to sustain override, then I am suggesting in this taxonomy that we call this not override failure but instead a mindware gap.

Note one interesting implication of the relation between TASS override and mindware gaps—the fewer gaps one has, the more 'at risk' one will be for a case of override failure. Someone with considerable mindware installed will be at greater risk of failing to use it in a propitious way. Of course, the two categories trade off in a continuous manner with a fuzzy boundary between them. A well-learned rule not appropriately applied is a TASS override failure. As the rule is less and less well instantiated, at some point it is so poorly compiled that it is not a candidate to override the TASS response and thus the processing error becomes a mindware gap. The study of pathological gambling behavior, for instance, has focused on a class of missing mindware of particular relevance to that condition: knowledge and procedures for dealing with probability and probabilistic events (Keren 1994; Toplak et al. 2007; Wagenaar 1988). Many studies now administer to such subjects measures of knowledge of regression to the mean, outcome bias, covariation detection, the gambler's fallacy, probability matching, baserate neglect, Bayesian probabilistic updating, and covariation detection.

Although mindware gaps may lead to sub-optimal reasoning, the next category in the taxonomy is designed to draw attention to the fact that not all mindware is helpful—either to goal attainment or to epistemic accuracy. In fact, some acquired mindware can be the direct cause of irrational actions that thwart our goals. Such effects thus define another category in the taxonomy of cognitive failures: contaminated mindware. Although the idea of contaminated mindware is controversial (see Aunger 2000) many theorists speculating on the properties of cultural replication would admit such a possibility (Blackmore 1999, 2005; Dennett 1991, 2006; Distin 2005; Hull 2000; Mesoudi et al. 2006).

Two further categories are defined by two effort-minimizing strategies that reflect cognitive miserliness. One is the tendency to engage in serial associative cognition with a focal bias (see Evans 2006b, on satisficing during analytic processing). This represents a tendency to over-economize during analytic processing—specifically, to fail to engage in the full-blown simulation of alternative worlds or to engage in fully disjunctive reasoning (Shafir 1994; Toplak and Stanovich 2002). Another effort minimizing strategy is the tendency not to engage in System 2 reasoning at all (not even serial associative cognition)—specifically, to default to the processing options offered by the autonomous mind.

Figure 3.4 displays the different classes of cognitive dysfunction. Many useful distinctions are captured in the Figure. For example, it helps to illustrate the importance of distinguishing between TASS override failure and situations where System 2 is not engaged at all. In my use of the term, for something to be considered a TASS override

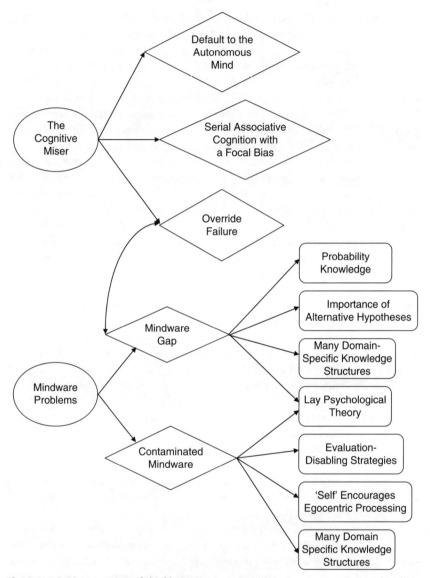

Fig. 3.4 A basic taxonomy of thinking errors.

failure, the analytic system must lose in a conflict of discrepant outputs. If the analytic system is not engaged at all, then we have a case of defaulting to the autonomous mind. In fact, the early heuristics and biases researchers were clearer on this point than many later dual-process theorists. The distinction between impressions and judgments in the early heuristics and biases work (see Kahneman 2003; Kahneman and Frederick 2002, 2005, for a discussion) made it clearer that non-normative responses often resulted not from a TASS/System 2 struggle but from intuitive impressions that are left uncorrected by System 2 rules and strategies. In fact, in many cases that have been called TASS override failure in the literature, the subject probably does not even consider overriding the TASS-based response (even when the mindware to do so is readily available and well learned). The subject does not recognize the need for override, or chooses not to sustain the necessary decoupling and simulation with alternative mindware that would make override possible.

The category of true override failure in my taxonomy would encompass what folk theory would call problems of willpower or the problem of multiple minds (see Ainslie 2001, for a nuanced discussion of this folk concept in light of modern cognitive science). But there is more than just willpower issues in this category. Heuristics and biases tasks can also trigger the problem of multiple minds. Sloman (1996) points out that at least for some subjects, the Linda conjunction problem (see Tversky and Kahneman 1983) is the quintessence of dual-process conflict. He quotes Stephen Gould's introspection that 'I know the [conjunction] is least probable, yet a little homunculus in my head continues to jump up and down, shouting at me—"but she can't be a bank teller; read the description"' (Gould 1991, p.469). For sophisticated subjects such as Gould, resolving the Linda problem clearly involves a TASS/analytic system conflict, and in his case a conjunction error on the task would represent a true TASS override failure. However, for the majority of subjects, there is no conscious introspection going on—System 2 is either not engaged or engaged so little that there is no awareness of a cognitive struggle. Instead, TASS-based heuristics such as representativeness or conversational pragmatics trigger the response (the detailed controversies about the Linda task are beyond the scope of the present chapter; for that large literature, see Adler 1984, 1991; Girotto 2004; Lee 2006; Mellers et al. 2001; Politzer and Macchi 2000). Analytic processing has not lost a struggle when it has not been called into the battle.

Defaulting to the autonomous mind is a more miserly type of thinking error than is override failure. In the former, sustained decoupling is not even attempted, whereas in the latter decoupling is initiated but is not sustained until completion. Intermediate between these two is System 2 processing taking place without sustained decoupling: serial associative cognition with a focal bias. In Figure 3.4 it is displayed between the other two. Figure 3.4 thus displays three types of cognitive miserliness and, below them, two types of mindware problem. The first mindware category in Figure 3.4 is the category of mindware gaps. The double-headed arrow indicates its aforementioned relation to TASS override. Some representative areas where important mindware gaps occur are illustrated. I have not represented an exhaustive set of knowledge partitionings—to the contrary, I have represented a minimal sampling of a potentially large set of coherent knowledge bases in the domains of probabilistic reasoning, causal reasoning, logic, and scientific thinking, the absence of which could result in irrational thought or behavior. I have represented mindware categories that have been implicated in research in the heuristics and biases tradition: missing knowledge about probability and probabilistic reasoning strategies; and ignoring alternative hypotheses when evaluating hypotheses. The latter would encompass the phenomenon of evaluating hypotheses in a way that implies that one is ignoring the denominator of the likelihood ratio in Bayes' rule—the probability of D given ~H [$P(D/\sim H)$]. These are just a few of many mindware gaps that have been suggested in the literature on behavioral decision making. There are many others, and the box labeled 'Many Domain-Specific Knowledge Structures' indicates this.

Finally, at the bottom of the Figure is the category of contaminated mindware. Again, the curved rectangles do not represent an exhaustive partitioning (the mindware-related categories are too diverse for that), but instead represent some of the mechanisms that have received some discussion in the literature. One is a subcategory of contaminated mindware that is much discussed in the memetics literature—memeplexes that contain evaluation-disabling memes (Blackmore 1999; Dennett 1991, 2006; Lynch 1996; Stanovich 2004). Some of the evaluation-disabling memes that help keep some memeplexes lodged in their hosts are: memes that promise punishment if the memeplex is questioned; those that promise rewards for unquestioning faith in the memeplex; or those that thwart evaluation attempts by rendering the memeplex unfalsifiable.

Another subcategory of contaminated mindware has been suggested by memetic theorists such as Dennett (1991, 1995) and Blackmore (1999) who consider the self to be a memetic construct. Among its many properties is the fact that the self serves to encourage egocentric thinking. Thus, the self is a mechanism that fosters one characteristic of focal bias: that we tend to build models of the world from a single myside perspective. Nevertheless, if should not be forgotten that the egocentrism of memeplex self must be a very adaptive cognitive style—both evolutionarily adaptive and adaptive in the sense of our personal (that is, vehicle) goals. However, for many of the same reasons that TASS heuristics often are non-optimal in a technological environment different from the environment of evolutionary adaptation, the decontextualizing demands of modernity increasingly require such characteristics as: fairness, rule-following despite context, even-handedness, nepotism prohibitions, unbiasedness, universalism, inclusiveness, contractually-mandated equal treatment, and discouragement of familial, racial, and religious discrimination. These requirements are difficult ones probably for the reason that they override processing defaults related to the self.

Finally, the last subcategory of contaminated mindware pictured in Figure 3.4 (labeled Many Domain-Specific Knowledge Structures) is meant to represent what is actually a whole set of categories: mindware representing specific categories of information or maladaptive memeplexes. Like the missing mindware category, there may be a large number of misinformation-filled memeplexes that would support irrational thought and behavior. For example, the gambler's fallacy and many of the other misunderstandings of probability that have been studied in the heuristics and biases literature would fit here. Of course, this example highlights the fact that the line between missing mindware and contaminated mindware might get fuzzy in some cases and the domain of probabilistic thinking is probably one such case.

Problems with people's lay psychological theories are represented as both contaminated mindware *and* a mindware gap in Figure 3.4. Mindware gaps are the many things about our own minds that we do not know; for example, how quickly we will adapt to both fortunate and unfortunate events (Gilbert 2006). Other things we think we know about our own minds are wrong. These misconceptions represent contaminated mindware. An example would be the folk belief that we accurately know our own minds. This contaminated mindware accounts for the incorrect belief that we always know the causes of our own actions (Nisbett and Wilson 1977) and the tendency to think that although others display thinking biases, we ourselves have special immunity from the very same biases (Pronin 2006).

Finally, Table 3.1. illustrates how the various cognitive characteristics and processing styles that exemplify the category cash out in terms of well-known effects and tasks in the thinking and reasoning literature. This again is not an exhaustive list, and I have detailed some categories more than others to reflect my interests and the biases of the field. The grain-size of the Table is also arbitrary. For example, both vividness and affect substitution (e.g. Slovic et al. 2002) could be viewed as simply specific aspects of the general phenomenon of attribute substitution discussed by Kahneman and Frederick (2002, 2005).

Some tasks are cognitively complex, and it is no surprise that some of the most complex tasks are those that are among the most contentious in the heuristics and biases literature. Thus, the taxonomy argues indirectly that non-normative responding on some of these tasks is overdetermined. For example, conjunction errors on tasks such as the Linda problem could result from attribute substitution in the manner that Tversky and Kahneman (1983) originally argued, from conversational defaults of the type discussed by a host of theorists (Adler 1984, 1991; Girotto 2004; Mellers, Hertwig, and Kahneman 2001; Politzer and Macchi 2000), and/or such errors could be exacerbated by missing mindware—that is, inadequately instantiated probabilistic mindware that impairs not just probabilistic calculations but also the tendency to see a problem in probabilistic terms.

It is likewise with the selection task. The Table illustrates the conjecture that focal bias of the type exemplified in the emphasis on the matching bias (Evans 1972, 1998; Evans and Lynch 1973) is implicated in selection task performance, as are the interpretational defaults emphasized by many theorists (Margolis 1987; Oaksford and Chater 1994; Osman and Laming 2001). But the Table also captures the way the task was often treated in the earliest years of research on it—as a proxy for Popperian falsifiability tendencies. From this latter standpoint, problems in dealing with the task might be analyzed as a missing mindware problem. Certainly training programs in the critical thinking literature consider the generation of alternative hypotheses and falsification strategies as learnable mindware (Nickerson 2004; Nisbett 1993; Perkins 1995).

Of course, Table 3.1 is not meant to be exhaustive. It is very much a preliminary sketch and it is not meant to be the final word on many definitional/conceptual issues. The taxonomy is meant to serve an organizing function, to provoke research on the conjectures implicit within it, and to demonstrate how a framework deriving from dual-process theory (as I conceive it) might bring some order to the unwieldy heuristics and biases literature.

Conclusion

In summary, what has been termed System 2 in the dual-process literature is composed of (at least) the distinct operations of the reflective and algorithmic level of analysis. Rationality is a function of processes at both the reflective and algorithmic levels—

Table 3.1 A basic taxonomy of rational thinking errors

Tasks, Effects, and Processing Styles	The Cognitive Miser			Mindware Gaps (MG)		MG & CM	Contaminated Mindware (CM)	
	Default to the Autonomous Mind	Focal Bias	Override Failure	Probability Knowledge	Alternative Thinking	Lay Psychological Theory	Evaluation Disabling Strategies	Self and Egocentric Processing
Vividness effects	X							
Affect substitution	X							
Impulsively associative thinking	X							
Framing effects		X						
Anchoring effects		X						
Belief bias			X					
Denominator neglect			X					
Outcome bias			X					
Hindsight bias ('curse of knowledge' effects)			X					
Self-control problems			X					
Noncausal baserates				X				

Tasks, Effects, and Processing Styles	The Cognitive Miser			Mindware Gaps (MG)		MG & CM	Contaminated Mindware (CM)	
	Default to the Autonomous Mind	Focal Bias	Override Failure	Probability Knowledge	Alternative Thinking	Lay Psychological Theory	Evaluation Disabling Strategies	Self and Egocentric Processing
Gambler's fallacy				X				
Bias blind spot						X		
Causal baserates			X	X				
Conjunction errors	X			X				
Ignoring P(D/~H)		X			X			
Four card selection task	X	X			X			
Myside processing		X						X
Affective forecasting errors		X				X		
Confirmation bias		X			X		X	
Overconfidence effects		X						X
Probability matching		X		X				
Pseudoscientific beliefs					X		X	
Evaluability effects		X				X		

specifically, thinking dispositions and fluid intelligence. In terms of human individual differences, rationality is thus a more encompassing construct than intelligence. Theoretical and empirical evidence for a tripartite structure was presented. Empirically, thinking dispositions and fluid intelligence predict unique portions of variance in performance on heuristics and biases tasks. Theoretically, it was argued that it makes sense to distinguish the cognitive control signal to begin decoupling operations from the ability to sustain decoupled representations. A distinct type of System 2 processing—serial associative cognition—was also defined. The importance of the knowledge bases recruited by each system in the tripartite model was stressed. All of these insights were fused into a taxonomy for classifying the thinking problems that people have on heuristics and biases tasks.

References

Ackerman, P.L. and Heggestad, E.D. (1997) Intelligence, personality, and interests: Evidence for overlapping traits. *Psychological Bulletin*, **121**, 219–45.

Ackerman, P.L. and Kanfer, R. (2004) Cognitive, affective, and conative aspects of adult intellect within a typical and maximal performance framework. In D.Y. Dai and R.J. Sternberg (eds) *Motivation, emotion, and cognition: Integrative perspectives on intellectual functioning and development*, 119–41. Lawrence Erlbaum Associates, Mahwah, NJ.

Adler, J.E. (1984) Abstraction is uncooperative. *Journal for the Theory of Social Behaviour*, **14**, 165–81.

Adler, J.E. (1991) An optimist's pessimism: Conversation and conjunctions. In E. Eells and T. Maruszewski (eds) *Probability and rationality: Studies on L. Jonathan Cohen's philosophy of science*, 251–82. Editions Rodopi, Amsterdam.

Ainslie, G. (2001) *Breakdown of will*. Cambridge University Press, Cambridge.

Anderson, M. (1998) Mental retardation, general intelligence, and modularity. *Learning and Individual Differences*, **10**, 159–78.

Arkes, H. R. and Ayton, P. (1999) The sunk cost and Concorde effects: Are humans less rational than lower animals? *Psychological Bulletin*, **125**, 591–600.

Aunger, R. (ed.) (2000) *Darwinizing culture: The status of memetics as a science*. Oxford University Press, Oxford.

Baddeley, A., Chincotta, D., and Adlam, A. (2001) Working memory and the control of action: Evidence from task switching. *Journal of Experimental Psychology: General*, **130**, 641–57.

Bechara, A. (2005) Decision making, impulse control and loss of willpower to resist drugs: A neurocognitive perspective. *Nature Neuroscience*, **8**, 1458–63.

Bechara, A., Damasio, A.R., Damasio, H., and Anderson, S. (1994) Insensitivity to future consequences following damage to human prefrontal cortex. *Cognition*, **50**, 7–15.

Bermudez, J.L. (2001) Normativity and rationality in delusional psychiatric disorders. *Mind & Language*, **16**, 457–93.

Blackmore, S. (1999) *The meme machine*. Oxford University Press, New York.

Blackmore, S. (2005) Can memes meet the challenge? In S. Hurley and N. Chater (eds) *Perspectives on imitation*, Vol. 2, 409–11. MIT Press, Cambridge, MA.

Brase, G.L. (2004) What we reason about and why: How evolution explains reasoning. In K.I. Manktelow and M.C. Chung (eds) *Psychology of reasoning: Theoretical and historical perspectives*, 309–31. Psychology Press, Hove.

Bruine de Bruin, W., Parker, A.M., and Fischhoff, B. (2007) Individual differences in adult decision-making competence. *Journal of Personality and Social Psychology*, **92**, 938–56.

Buckner, R.L. and Carroll, D. C. (2007) Self-projection and the brain. *Trends in Cognitive Sciences*, **11**, 49–57.

Byrne, R.M.J. (2005) *The rational imagination: How people create alternatives to reality*. MIT Press, Cambridge, MA.

Cacioppo, J.T., Petty, R.E., Feinstein, J., and Jarvis, W. (1996) Dispositional differences in cognitive motivation: The life and times of individuals varying in need for cognition. *Psychological Bulletin*, **119**, 197–253.

Carroll, J. B. (1993) *Human cognitive abilities: A survey of factor-analytic studies*. Cambridge University Press, Cambridge.

Carruthers, P. (2002) The cognitive functions of language. *Behavioral and Brain Sciences*, **25**, 657–726.

Carruthers, P. (2006) *The architecture of the mind*. Oxford University Press, New York.

Churchland, P.M. (1988) *Matter and consciousnes* revised ed. MIT Press, Cambridge, MA.

Clark, A. (2001) *Mindware: An introduction to the philosophy of cognitive science*. Oxford University Press, New York.

Cohen, L. J. (1981) Can human irrationality be experimentally demonstrated? *Behavioral and Brain Sciences*, **4**, 317–70.

Conway, A.R.A., Kane, M.J., and Engle, R.W. (2003) Working memory capacity and its relation to general intelligence. *Trends in Cognitive Science*, **7**, 547–52.

Cosmides, L. and Tooby, J. (1992) Cognitive adaptations for social exchange. In J. Barkow, L. Cosmides, and J. Tooby (eds) *The adapted mind,* 163–228. Oxford University Press, New York.

Cosmides, L. and Tooby, J. (2000) Consider the source: The evolution of adaptations for decoupling and metarepresentation. In D. Sperber (ed.) *Metarepresentations: A multidisciplinary perspective*, 53–115. Oxford University Press, Oxford.

Damasio, A.R. (1994) *Descartes' error*. Putnam, New York.

Damasio, A.R. (1996) The somatic marker hypothesis and the possible functions of the prefrontal cortex. *Philosophical Transactions of the Royal Society (London)*, **351**, 1413–20.

Davies, M. (2000) Interaction without reduction: The relationship between personal and sub-personal levels of description. *Mind & Society*, **1**, 87–105.

Dawes, R.M. (1976) Shallow psychology. In J. S. Carroll and J. W. Payne (eds) *Cognition and social behavior,* 3–11. Erlbaum, Hillsdale, NJ.

De Neys, W. (2006a) Automatic-heuristic and executive-analytic processing during reasoning: Chronometric and dual-task considerations. *Quarterly Journal of Experimental Psychology*, **59**, 1070–100.

De Neys, W. (2006b) Dual processing in reasoning—Two systems but one reasoner. *Psychological Science*, **17**, 428–33.

Dennett, D.C. (1984) *Elbow room: The varieties of free will worth wanting*. MIT Press, Cambridge, MA.

Dennett, D.C. (1991) *Consciousness explained*. Little Brown, Boston, MA.

Dennett, D.C. (1995) *Darwin's dangerous idea: Evolution and the meanings of life*. Simon & Schuster, New York.

Dennett, D.C. (1996) *Kinds of minds: Toward an understanding of consciousness*. Basic Books, New York.

Dennett, D.C. (2006) From typo to thinko: When evolution graduated to semantic norms. In S. C. Levinson and P. Jaisson (eds) *Evolution and culture* (133–45). MIT Press, Cambridge, MA.

Dienes, Z. and Perner, J. (1999) A theory of implicit and explicit knowledge. *Behavioral and Brain Sciences*, **22**, 735–808.

Distin, K. (2005) *The selfish meme*. Cambridge University Press, Cambridge.

Duckworth, A.L. and Seligman, M.E.P. (2005) Self-discipline outdoes IQ in predicting academic performance of adolescents. *Psychological Science*, **16**, 939–44.

Duncan, J., Emslie, H., Williams, P., Johnson, R., and Freer, C. (1996) Intelligence and the frontal lobe: The organization of goal-directed behavior. *Cognitive Psychology*, **30**, 257–303.

Duncan, J., Seitz, R.J., Kolodny, J., Bor, D., Herzog, H., Ahmed, A., Newell, F.N., and Emslie, H. (2000) A neural basis for general intelligence. *Science*, **289**, 457–60.

Engle, R.W. (2002) Working memory capacity as executive attention. *Current Directions in Psychological Science*, **11**, 19–23.

Eslinger, P.J. and Damasio, A.R. (1985) Severe disturbance of higher cognition after bilateral frontal lobe ablation: Patient EVR. *Neurology*, **35**, 1731–41.

Evans, J.St.B.T. (1972) Interpretation and matching bias in a reasoning task. *Quarterly Journal of Experimental Psychology*, **24**, 193–9.

Evans, J.St.B.T. (1996) Deciding before you think: Relevance and reasoning in the selection task. *British Journal of Psychology*, **87**, 223–40.

Evans, J.St.B.T. (1998) Matching bias in conditional reasoning: Do we understand it after 25 years? *Thinking & Reasoning*, **4**, 45–82.

Evans, J.St.B.T. (2002) The influence of prior belief on scientific thinking. In P. Carruthers, S. Stich, and M. Siegal (eds) *The cognitive basis of science,* 193–210. Cambridge University Press, Cambridge.

Evans, J.St.B.T. (2003) In two minds: Dual-process accounts of reasoning. *Trends in Cognitive Sciences*, **7**, 454–9.

Evans, J.St.B.T. (2006a) Dual system theories of cognition: Some issues. *Proceedings of the 28th Annual Meeting of the Cognitive Science Society,* Vancouver, 202–7.

Evans, J.St.B.T. (2006b) The heuristic-analytic theory of reasoning: Extension and evaluation. *Psychonomic Bulletin and Review*, **13**, 378–95.

Evans, J.St.B.T. (2007) *Hypothetical thinking: Dual processes in reasoning and judgment.* Psychology Press, New York.

Evans, J.St.B.T. and Curtis-Holmes, J. (2005) Rapid responding increases belief bias: Evidence for the dual-process theory of reasoning. *Thinking & Reasoning*, **11**, 382–9.

Evans, J.St.B.T. and Feeney, A. (2004) The role of prior belief in reasoning. In J. P. Leighton and R. J. Sternberg (eds) *The nature of reasoning,* 78–102. Cambridge University Press, Cambridge.

Evans, J.St.B.T. and Lynch, J.S. (1973) Matching bias in the selection task. *British Journal of Psychology*, **64**, 391–7.

Evans, J.St.B.T. and Over, D.E. (1996) *Rationality and reasoning.* Psychology Press, Hove.

Evans, J.St.B.T. and Over, D.E. (1999) Explicit representations in hypothetical thinking. *Behavioral and Brain Sciences*, **22**, 763–4.

Evans, J.St.B.T. and Over, D. E. (2004) *If.* Oxford University Press, Oxford.

Evans, J.St.B.T. and Wason, P.C. (1976) Rationalization in a reasoning task. *British Journal of Psychology*, **67**, 479–86.

Evans, J.St.B.T., Over, D.E., and Handley, S.J. (2003) A theory of hypothetical thinking. In D. Hardman and L. Macchi (eds) *Thinking: Psychological perspectives on reasoning, judgment and decision making.* John Wiley, New York.

Evans, J.St.B.T., Barston, J., and Pollard, P. (1983) On the conflict between logic and belief in syllogistic reasoning. *Memory & Cognition*, **11**, 295–306.

Frankish, K. (2004) *Mind and supermind*. Cambridge University Press, Cambridge.

Franklin, S. (1995) *Artificial Minds*. MIT Press, Cambridge, MA.

Gauthier, D. (1986) *Morals by agreement*. Oxford University Press, Oxford.

Geary, D.C. (2005) *The origin of the mind: Evolution of brain, cognition, and general intelligence.* American Psychological Association, Washington, DC.

Gigerenzer, G. (1996) On narrow norms and vague heuristics: A reply to Kahneman and Tversky (1996). *Psychological Review*, **103**, 592–6.

Gilbert, D. (1991) How mental systems believe. *American Psychologist*, **46**, 107–19.

Gilbert, D. (2006) *Stumbling on happiness*. Alfred A. Knopf, New York.

Girotto, V. (2004) Task understanding. In J.P. Leighton and R.J. Sternberg (eds) *The nature of reasoning,* 103–25. Cambridge University Press, Cambridge.

Gould, S.J. (1991) *Bully for the Brontosaurus*. Norton, New York.

Hasher, L., Lustig, C., and Zacks, R. (2007) Inhibitory mechanisms and the control of attention. In A. Conway, C. Jarrold, M. Kane, A. Miyake, and J. Towse (eds) *Variation in working memory,* 227–49. Oxford University Press, New York.

Hasher, L., Zacks, R.T., and May, C.P. (1999) Inhibitory control, circadian arousal, and age. In D. Gopher and A. Koriat (eds) *Attention and performance XVII, cognitive regulation of performance: Interaction of theory and application,* 653–75. MIT Press, Cambridge, MA.

Heaton, R., Chelune, G., Talley, J., Kay, G., and Curtiss, G. (1993) *Wisconsin Card Sorting Test,* Revised and expanded. Psychological Assessment Resource, Lutz, FL.

Horn, J.L. and Noll, J. (1997) Human cognitive capabilities: Gf-Gc theory. In D. Flanagan, J. Genshaft, and P. Harrison (eds) *Contemporary intellectual assessment: Theories, tests, and issues,* 53–91. Guilford Press, New York.

Hsee, C.K. and Hastie, R. (2006) Decision and experience: Why don't we choose what makes us happy? *Trends in Cognitive Sciences*, **10**, 31–7.

Hull, D.L. (2000) Taking memetics seriously: Memetics will be what we make it. In R. Aunger (ed.) *Darwinizing culture: The status of memetics as a science,* 43–67. Oxford University Press, Oxford.

Hull, D.L. (2001) *Science and selection: Essays on biological evolution and the philosophy of science*. Cambridge University Press, Cambridge.

Jackendoff, R. (1996) How language helps us think. *Pragmatics and Cognition*, **4**, 1–34.

Johnson-Laird, P.N. (1999) Deductive reasoning. *Annual Review of Psychology*, **50**, 109–35.

Johnson-Laird, P.N. (2005) Mental models and thought. In K.J. Holyoak and R.G. Morrison (eds) *The Cambridge handbook of thinking and reasoning,* 185–208. Cambridge University Press, New York.

Kagan, J., Rosman, B.L., Day, D., Albert, J., and Philips, W. (1964) Information processing in the child: Significance of analytic and reflective attitudes. *Psychological Monographs*, **78**, 578.

Kahneman, D. (2000) A psychological point of view: Violations of rational rules as a diagnostic of mental processes. *Behavioral and Brain Sciences*, **23**, 681–3.

Kahneman, D. (2003) A perspective on judgment and choice: Mapping bounded rationality. *American Psychologist*, **58**, 697–720.

Kahneman, D. and Frederick, S. (2002) Representativeness revisited: Attribute substitution in intuitive judgment. In T. Gilovich, D. Griffin, and D. Kahneman (eds) *Heuristics and biases: The psychology of intuitive judgment*, 49–81. Cambridge University Press, New York.

Kahneman, D. and Frederick, S. (2005) A model of heuristic judgment. In K.J. Holyoak and R.G. Morrison (eds) *The Cambridge handbook of thinking and reasoning*, 267–93. Cambridge University Press, New York.

Kahneman, D. and Tversky, A. (1982a) On the study of statistical intuitions. *Cognition*, **11**, 123–41.

Kahneman, D. and Tversky, A. (1982b) The simulation heuristic. In D. Kahneman, P. Slovic, and A. Tversky (eds) *Judgment under uncertainty: Heuristics and biases*, 201–8. Cambridge University Press, Cambridge.

Kahneman, D. and Tversky, A. (1996) On the reality of cognitive illusions. *Psychological Review*, **103**, 582–91.

Kahneman, D. and Tversky, A. (eds) (2000) *Choices, values, and frames*. Cambridge University Press, Cambridge.

Kane, M.J. (2003) The intelligent brain in conflict. *Trends in Cognitive Sciences*, **7**, 375–7.

Kane, M.J. and Engle, R.W. (2002) The role of prefrontal cortex working-memory capacity, executive attention, and general fluid intelligence: An individual-differences perspective. *Psychonomic Bulletin and Review*, **9**, 637–71.

Kane, M.J. and Engle, R.W. (2003) Working-memory capacity and the control of attention: The contributions of goal neglect, response competition, and task set to Stroop interference. *Journal of Experimental Psychology: General*, **132**, 47–70.

Kane, M.J., Hambrick, D.Z., and Conway, A.R.A. (2005) Working memory capacity and fluid intelligence are strongly related constructs: Comment on Ackerman, Beier and Boyle (2005). *Psychological Bulletin*, **131**, 66–71.

Kane, M.J., Bleckley, M., Conway, A., and Engle, R.W. (2001) A controlled-attention view of WM capacity. *Journal of Experimental Psychology: General*, **130**, 169–83.

Keren, G. (1994) The rationality of gambling: Gamblers' conceptions of probability, chance and luck. In G. Wright and P. Ayton (eds) *Subjective probability*, 485–99. Wiley, Chichester.

Kimberg, D.Y., D'Esposito, M., and Farah, M.J. (1998) Cognitive functions in the prefrontal cortex—working memory and executive control. *Current Directions in Psychological Science*, **6**, 185–92.

Klaczynski, P.A. and Lavallee, K.L. (2005) Domain-specific identity, epistemic regulation, and intellectual ability as predictors of belief-based reasoning: A dual-process perspective. *Journal of Experimental Child Psychology*.

Kokis, J., Macpherson, R., Toplak, M., West, R.F., and Stanovich, K.E., (2002) Heuristic and analytic processing: Age trends and associations with cognitive ability and cognitive styles. *Journal of Experimental Child Psychology*, **83**, 26–52.

Krueger, J. and Funder, D.C. (2004) Towards a balanced social psychology: Causes, consequences and cures for the problem-seeking approach to social cognition and behavior. *Behavioral and Brain Sciences*, **27**, 313–76.

Lee, C.J. (2006) Gricean charity: The Gricean turn in psychology. *Philosophy of the Social Sciences*, **36**, 193–218.

Legrenzi, P., Girotto, V., and Johnson-Laird, P.N. (1993) Focussing in reasoning and decision making. *Cognition*, **49**, 37–66.

Lepine, R., Barrouillet, P., and Camos, V. (2005) What makes working memory spans so predictive of high-level cognition? *Psychonomic Bulletin & Review*, **12**, 165–70.

Leslie, A.M. (1987) Pretense and representation: The origins of 'Theory of Mind'. *Psychological Review*, **94**, 412–26.

Lucas, E.J. and Ball, L.J. (2005) Think-aloud protocols and the selection task: Evidence for relevance effects and rationalisation processes. *Thinking & Reasoning*, **11**, 35–66.

Lynch, A. (1996) *Thought contagion*. Basic Books, New York.

Manktelow, K.I. (2004) Reasoning and rationality: The pure and the practical. In K.I. Manktelow and M.C. Chung (eds) *Psychology of reasoning: Theoretical and historical perspectives,* 157–77. Psychology Press, Hove.

Margolis, H. (1987) *Patterns, thinking, and cognition*. University of Chicago Press, Chicago.

Markovits, H. and Nantel, G. (1989) The belief-bias effect in the production and evaluation of logical conclusions. *Memory & Cognition*, **17**, 11–17.

McCarthy, R.A. and Warrington, E.K. (1990) *Cognitive neuropsychology: A clinical introduction*. Academic Press, San Diego, CA.

Mellers, B., Hertwig, R., and Kahneman, D. (2001) Do frequency representations eliminate conjunction effects? An exercise in adversarial collaboration. *Psychological Science*, **12**, 269–75.

Mesoudi, A.,Whiten, A., and Laland, K.N. (2006) Towards a unified science of cultural evolution. *Behavioral and Brain Sciences*, **29**, 329–83.

Mithen, S. (1996) *The prehistory of mind: The cognitive origins of art and science*. Thames and Hudson, London.

Miyake, A., Friedman, N., Emerson, M.J., and Witzki, A.H. (2000) The utility and diversity of executive functions and their contributions to complex 'frontal lobe' tasks: A latent variable analysis. *Cognitive Psychology,* **41**, 49–100.

Murphy, D. and Stich, S. (2000) Darwin in the madhouse: Evolutionary psychology and the classification of mental disorders. In P. Carruthers and A. Chamberlain (eds) *Evolution and the human mind: Modularity, language and meta-cognition*, 62–92. Cambridge University Press, Cambridge.

Nichols, S. and Stich, S.P. (2003) *Mindreading: An integrated account of pretense, self-awareness, and understanding other minds*. Oxford University Press, Oxford.

Nickerson, R.S. (2004) Teaching reasoning. In J.P. Leighton and R. J. Sternberg (eds) *The nature of reasoning,* 410–42. Cambridge University Press, Cambridge.

Nisbett, R.E. (1993) *Rules for reasoning*. Lawrence Erlbaum Associates, Hillsdale, NJ.

Nisbett, R.E. and Wilson, T.D. (1977) Telling more than we can know: Verbal reports on mental processes. *Psychological Review*, **84**, 231-59.

Oaksford, M. and Chater, N. (1994) A rational analysis of the selection task as optimal data selection. *Psychological Review*, **101**, 608–31.

Oatley, K. (1999) Why fiction may be twice as true as fact: Fiction as cognitive and emotional simulation. *Review of General Psychology*, **3**, 101–17.

Osman, M. and Laming, D. (2001) Misinterpretation of conditional statements in Wason's selection task. *Psychological Research*, **65**, 128–44.

Over, D.E. (2002) The rationality of evolutionary psychology. In J.L. Bermudez and A. Millar (eds) *Reason and nature: Essays in the theory of rationality,* 187–207. Oxford University Press, Oxford.

Over, D.E. (2004) Rationality and the normative/descriptive distinction. In D.J. Koehler and N. Harvey (eds) *Blackwell handbook of judgment and decision making*, 3–18. Blackwell Publishing, Malden, MA.

Parker, A.M. and Fischhoff, B. (2005) Decision-making competence: External validation through an individual differences approach. *Journal of Behavioral Decision Making*, **18**, 1–27.

Pennington, B.F. and Ozonoff, S. (1996) Executive functions and developmental psychopathology. *Journal of Child Psychology and Psychiatry*, **37**, 51–87.

Perkins, D.N. (1995) *Outsmarting IQ: The emerging science of learnable intelligence*. Free Press, New York.

Perner, J. (1991) *Understanding the representational mind*. MIT Press, Cambridge, MA.

Politzer, G. and Macchi, L. (2000) Reasoning and pragmatics. *Mind & Society*, **1**, 73–93.

Pollock, J.L. (1995) *Cognitive carpentry: A blueprint for how to build a person*. MIT Press, Cambridge, MA.

Pronin, E. (2006) Perception and misperception of bias in human judgment. *Trends in Cognitive Sciences*, **11**, 37–43.

Roberts, M.J. and Newton, E.J. (2001) Inspection times, the change task, and the rapid-response selection task. *Quarterly Journal of Experimental Psychology*, **54A**, 1031–48.

Rokeach, M. (1960) *The open and closed mind*. Basic Books, New York.

Sá, W., West, R.F., and Stanovich, K.E. (1999) The domain specificity and generality of belief bias: Searching for a generalizable critical thinking skill. *Journal of Educational Psychology*, **91**, 497–510.

Sá, W., Kelley, C., Ho, C., and Stanovich, K.E. (2005) Thinking about personal theories: Individual differences in the coordination of theory and evidence. *Personality and Individual Differences*, **38**, 1149–61.

Salthouse, T.A., Atkinson, T.M., and Berish, D.E. (2003) Executive functioning as a potential mediator of age-related cognitive decline in normal adults. *Journal of Experimental Psychology: General*, **132**, 566–94.

Samuels, R. (2005) The complexity of cognition: Tractability arguments for massive modularity. In P. Carruthers, S. Laurence, and S. Stich (eds) *The innate mind*, 107–21. Oxford University Press, Oxford.

Samuels, R. and Stich, S.P. (2004) Rationality and psychology. In A.R. Mele and P. Rawling (eds) *The Oxford handbook of rationality*, 279–300. Oxford University Press, Oxford.

Samuels, R., Stich, S.P., and Bishop, M. (2002) Ending the rationality wars: How to make disputes about human rationality disappear. In R. Elio (ed.) *Common sense, reasoning and rationality*, 236–68. Oxford University Press, New York.

Samuels, R., Stich, S.P., and Tremoulet, P.D. (1999) Rethinking rationality: From bleak implications to Darwinian modules. In E. Lepore and Z. Pylyshyn (eds) *What is cognitive science?*, 74–120. Blackwell, Oxford.

Sanfey, A.G., Loewenstein, G., McClure, S.M., and Cohen, J.D. (2006) Neuroeconomics: Cross-currents in research on decision-making. *Trends in Cognitive Sciences*, **10**, 108–16.

Shafir, E. (1994) Uncertainty and the difficulty of thinking through disjunctions. *Cognition*, **50**, 403–30.

Shafir, E. and LeBoeuf, R.A. (2002) Rationality. *Annual Review of Psychology*, **53**, 491–517.

Shiffrin, R.M. and Schneider, W. (1977) Controlled and automatic human information processing: II. Perceptual learning, automatic attending, and a general theory. *Psychological Review*, **84**, 127–90.

Sloman, A. (1993) The mind as a control system. In C. Hookway and D. Peterson (eds) *Philosophy and cognitive science,* 69–110. Cambridge University Press, Cambridge.

Sloman, S.A. (1996) The empirical case for two systems of reasoning. *Psychological Bulletin,* **119**, 3–22.

Sloman, S.A. (2002) Two systems of reasoning. In T. Gilovich, D. Griffin, and D. Kahneman (eds) *Heuristics and biases: The psychology of intuitive judgment,* 379–96. Cambridge University Press, New York.

Sloman, A. and Chrisley, R. (2003). Virtual machines and consciousness. *Journal of Consciousness Studies,* **10**, 133–72.

Slovic, P., Finucane, M.L., Peters, E., and MacGregor, D.G. (2002) The affect heuristic. In T. Gilovich, D. Griffin and D. Kahneman (eds) *Heuristics and biases: The psychology of intuitive judgment,* 397–420. Cambridge University Press, New York.

Sperber, D. (1994) The modularity of thought and the epidemiology of representations. In L.A. Hirschfeld and S.A. Gelman (eds) *Mapping the mind: Domain specificity in cognition and culture,* 39–67. Cambridge University Press, Cambridge.

Sperber, D. (2000) Metarepresentations in evolutionary perspective. In D. Sperber (ed.) *Metarepresentations: A Multidisciplinary Perspective,* 117–37. Oxford University Press, Oxford.

Sperber, D., Cara, F., and Girotto, V. (1995) Relevance theory explains the selection task. *Cognition,* **57**, 31–95.

Stanovich, K.E. (1999) *Who is rational? Studies of individual differences in reasoning.* Erlbaum, Mahwah, NJ.

Stanovich, K.E. (2001) Reductionism in the study of intelligence: Review of 'Looking Down on Human Intelligence' by Ian Deary. *Trends in Cognitive Sciences,* **5**, 91–2.

Stanovich, K.E. (2002) Rationality, intelligence, and levels of analysis in cognitive science: Is dysrationalia possible? In R.J. Sternberg (ed.) *Why smart people can be so stupid,* 124–58. Yale University Press, New Haven, CT.

Stanovich, K.E. (2003) The fundamental computational biases of human cognition: Heuristics that (sometimes) impair decision making and problem solving. In J.E. Davidson and R. J. Sternberg (eds) *The psychology of problem solving,* 291–342. Cambridge University Press, New York.

Stanovich, K.E. (2004) *The robot's rebellion: Finding meaning in the age of Darwin.* University of Chicago Press, Chicago, IL.

Stanovich, K.E. (2009) *What IQ tests miss: The cognitive science of rational and irrational thinking.* Yale University Press, New Haven, CT.

Stanovich, K.E. (in press) *Rationality and the reflective mind: Toward a tri-process model of cognition.* Oxford University Press, New York.

Stanovich, K.E. and West, R.F. (1997) Reasoning independently of prior belief and individual differences in actively open-minded thinking. *Journal of Educational Psychology,* **89**, 342–57.

Stanovich, K.E. and West, R.F. (1998a) Cognitive ability and variation in selection task performance. *Thinking & Reasoning,* **4**, 193–230.

Stanovich, K.E. and West, R.F. (1998b) Individual differences in framing and conjunction effects. *Thinking & Reasoning,* **4**, 289–317.

Stanovich, K.E. and West, R.F. (1998c) Individual differences in rational thought. *Journal of Experimental Psychology: General,* **127**, 161–88.

Stanovich, K.E. and West, R.F. (1998d) Who uses base rates and P(D/~H)? An analysis of individual differences. *Memory & Cognition,* **26**, 161–79.

Stanovich, K.E. and West, R.F. (1999) Discrepancies between normative and descriptive models of decision making and the understanding/acceptance principle. *Cognitive Psychology*, **38**, 349–85.

Stanovich, K.E. and West, R.F. (2000) Individual differences in reasoning: Implications for the rationality debate? *Behavioral and Brain Sciences, 23,* 645–726.

Stanovich, K.E. and West, R.F. (2003) Evolutionary versus instrumental goals: How evolutionary psychology misconceives human rationality. In D. Over (ed.) *Evolution and the psychology of thinking: The debate,* 171–230. Psychology Press, Hove.

Stanovich, K.E. and West, R.F. (2007) Natural myside bias is independent of cognitive ability. *Thinking & Reasoning*, **13**, 225–47.

Stanovich, K.E. and West, R.F. (2008). On the relative independence of thinking biases and cognitive ability. *Journal of Personality and Social Psychology,* **94**, 672–95.

Stein, E. (1996) *Without good reason: The rationality debate in philosophy and cognitive science.* Oxford University Press, Oxford.

Suddendorf, T. and Whiten, A. (2001) Mental evolution and development: Evidence for secondary representation in children, great apes, and other animals. *Psychological Bulletin*, **127**, 629–50.

Taylor, S.E. (1981) The interface of cognitive and social psychology. In J.H. Harvey (ed.) *Cognition, social behavior, and the environment,* 189–211. Erlbaum, Hillsdale, NJ.

Toplak, M. and Stanovich, K.E. (2002) The domain specificity and generality of disjunctive reasoning: Searching for a generalizable critical thinking skill. *Journal of Educational Psychology*, **94**, 197–209.

Toplak, M.E. and Stanovich, K.E. (2003) Associations between myside bias on an informal reasoning task and amount of post-secondary education. *Applied Cognitive Psychology*, **17**, 851–60.

Toplak, M., Liu, E., Macpherson, R., Toneatto, T., and Stanovich, K.E. (2007) The reasoning skills and thinking dispositions of problem gamblers: A dual-process taxonomy. *Journal of Behavioral Decision Making*, **20**, 103–24.

Tversky, A. and Kahneman, D. (1974) Judgment under uncertainty: Heuristics and biases. *Science*, **185**, 1124–31.

Tversky, A. and Kahneman, D. (1983) Extensional versus intuitive reasoning: The conjunction fallacy in probability judgment. *Psychological Review*, **90**, 293–315.

Tweney, R.D. and Yachanin, S. (1985) Can scientists rationally assess conditional inferences? *Social Studies of Science*, **15**, 155–73.

Unsworth, N. and Engle, R.W. (2005) Working memory capacity and fluid abilities: Examining the correlation between Operation Span and Raven. *Intelligence*, **33**, 67–81.

Wagenaar, W.A. (1988) *Paradoxes of gambling behavior.* LEA, Hove.

Wason, P.C. and Evans, J.St.B.T. (1975) Dual-processes in reasoning? *Cognition*, **3**, 141–54.

Watson, G. and Glaser, E.M. (1980) *Watson-Glaser critical thinking appraisal.* Psychological Corporation, New York.

West, R.F. and Stanovich, K.E. (2003) Is probability matching smart? Associations between probabilistic choices and cognitive ability. *Memory & Cognition*, **31**, 243–51.

Whiten, A. (2001) Meta-representation and secondary representation. *Trends in Cognitive Sciences*, **5**, 378.

Wilson, T.D., Wheatley, T., Meyers, J.M.,Gilbert, D.T., and Axsom, D. (2000) Focalism: A source of durability bias in affective forecasting. *Journal of Personality and Social Psychology*, **78**, 821–36.

Chapter 4

Systems and levels: Dual-system theories and the personal–subpersonal distinction

Keith Frankish

Introduction

There is now abundant evidence for the existence of two types of processing in human reasoning, decision making, and social cognition—one type fast, automatic, effortless, and non-conscious, the other slow, controlled, effortful, and conscious—which may deliver different and sometimes conflicting results (for a review, see Evans 2008). More recently, some cognitive psychologists have proposed ambitious theories of cognitive architecture, according to which humans possess two distinct reasoning systems—two minds, in fact—now widely referred to as *System 1* and *System 2* (Evans 2003; Evans and Over 1996; Kahneman and Frederick 2002; Sloman 1996, 2002; Stanovich 1999, 2004, this volume). A composite characterization of the two systems runs as follows. System 1 is a collection of autonomous subsystems, many of which are old in evolutionary terms and whose operations are fast, automatic, effortless, non-conscious, parallel, shaped by biology and personal experience, and independent of working memory and general intelligence. System 2 is more recent, and its processes are slow, controlled, effortful, conscious, serial, shaped by culture and formal tuition, demanding of working memory, and related to general intelligence. In addition, it is often claimed that the two systems employ different procedures and serve different goals, with System 1 being highly contextualized, associative, heuristic, and directed to goals that serve the reproductive interests of our genes, and System 2 being decontextualized, rule-governed, analytic, and serving our goals as individuals.

This is a very strong hypothesis, and theorists are already recognizing that it requires substantial qualification and complication (Evans 2006a, 2008, this volume; Stanovich, this volume; Samuels, this volume). There are numerous issues. Do the various features mentioned really divide up into just two groups in the neat way suggested? Are the features ascribed to each system exclusive to that system, and are they essential to it? Are the systems completely separate or do they share processing resources? Do they operate in parallel and compete for control of behavior, or do they cooperate, with System 1 generating default responses that are then assessed and sometimes overridden by System 2? There are also related questions about the memory systems associated with each system. Does each system have its own knowledge base and goal structure, and if so, do the two sets of states differ in their formal characteristics?

This chapter aims to shed light on these issues from a perhaps surprising source, namely philosophy of mind. Philosophy does not, of course, supply new data, but it can offer new ways of conceptualizing data, and philosophers of mind have been active in interpreting psychological data and theorizing about cognitive architecture. In what follows I shall outline a new way of conceptualizing the distinction between the two systems and consider its implications for the issues mentioned. The key suggestion will be that the distinction between the two putative systems is primarily one of *levels*, rather than systems, and the result will be a sympathetic reinterpretation of the dual-systems hypothesis.

Personal reasoning and subpersonal reasoning

I want to begin with a distinction that will be familiar to philosophers, though perhaps less so to psychologists. It is the distinction between *personal* and *subpersonal* levels, introduced in its contemporary form by Daniel Dennett in his 1969 book *Content and consciousness*. Dennett introduces the distinction to do specific philosophical work, but I shall adapt it for my own purposes.

Personal-level states and events are ones that are properly attributed to a person or creature as a whole, rather than to some organ or subsystem. Examples include being English, seeing a sunset, singing, feeling a pain in one's toe. These are states and activities of people, not their subsystems. If a personal-level event is motivated and caused in the right way by the subject's beliefs and desires, then it counts as an *intentional action*. ('Intentional' here means 'performed for a reason', and the contrast is with involuntary movements, such as reflexes.) So feeling a pain is a personal-level event but not an intentional action, whereas singing is a personal-level event that is also an intentional action. Subpersonal states and events are ones that are properly attributed to some organ or subsystem rather than to the person as a whole. Examples are having a high concentration of sodium ions, secreting adrenalin, regulating blood sugar level. These are not states of us or activities that we perform; rather they are states of parts of us and things that our subsystems do.

Now, we can make a personal–subpersonal distinction in the mental realm. Everyday 'folk-psychological' mental concepts are typically personal-level ones: it is people who have thoughts, feelings, and desires, and who recall events, work things out, and make decisions. People also perform mental actions. Think of trying to remember a phone number, imagining a purple cow, reciting a poem silently to oneself. Like other actions, these are things we do and can be motivated to do. Not all mental states and events are personal ones, however. Modern cognitive psychology posits a vast array of subpersonal mental states and processes, which are invoked to explain personal-level phenomena. Examples include having a Mentalese sentence stored in the belief box, building a mental model of a set of premises, constructing a representation of the logical form of a heard sentence, creating a 2.5D sketch of the visual scene. These are states and activities of neural systems, not of persons. (I shall assume that what distinguishes subpersonal *mental* states and processes from non-mental ones is the possession of informational content; subpersonal mental states are ones that carry information about things, and subpersonal mental processes are ones involving such states (Dennett 1981).) In the case of mental *processes* at least, the distinction between personal and subpersonal corresponds roughly with that between conscious and non-conscious. We are typically conscious of our personal mental processes, but not of our subpersonal ones.

There are some complex philosophical debates surrounding the interpretation and application of the personal–subpersonal distinction (see the papers in Bermúdez and Elton 2000). There is no space to address these here, so I shall confine myself to clarifying how I understand the distinction. First, the notion of a *person* employed here is a minimal one, without any of the connotations of personal identity, selfhood, moral responsibility, and so on, that the concept often carries. A person in the present sense is simply a human being, or other creature, considered as a unified entity, and a personal–subpersonal distinction could be made for animals or even robots. Likewise, I do not mean to suggest that only personal-level states are important to personal identity—that they constitute the real *self*, as it were. As understood here, the subpersonal–personal distinction is not a distinction between what is part of the self and what is not, but simply between levels of organization within a human being.

Second, the personal–subpersonal distinction has sometimes been employed by philosophers with an anti-reductionist agenda. Some theorists argue for the irreducibility of personal-level psychological explanation as a way of insulating common-sense psychology from scientific refutation (e.g. Baker 1987; Hornsby 2000). I do not share this agenda. I shall assume that personal-level states are realized in subpersonal ones and that it will always be possible, in principle, to reductively explain personal-level phenomena by identifying the realizing states.

Third, I want to say something about the concepts of belief and desire, which are central to the definition of intentional action. In everyday usage these concepts are personal-level ones (it is people that have beliefs and desires, not their brains). However, many theorists assimilate them to the theoretical concepts of subpersonal cognitive psychology, holding that they refer to functionally defined states of the cognitive system (e.g. Botterill and Carruthers 1999; Fodor 1987; Lewis 1972). For present purposes I shall follow this view, though my considered position on the relation between folk psychology and cognitive psychology is actually more complex and qualified (see Frankish 2004).[1] I shall also assume that intentional actions can be caused by beliefs and desires that have not been consciously brought to mind. So construed, the concepts of belief and desire correspond to the psychologist's concepts of knowledge (or memory) and goal structure. Later, I shall introduce concepts of distinctively personal-level forms of belief and desire, which contrast with these subpersonal ones.

Finally, since I linked the personal–subpersonal distinction with consciousness, let me clarify what I mean by this term. For present purposes, I shall assume a global workspace theory, according to which information is conscious in virtue of occupying working memory and being the focus of selective attention (Baars 1988, 1997). It is

---

[1] In the terms of my 2004, beliefs and desires in the present sense are states of the *sub-mind*—the level of subpersonal psychology that supports the multi-track behavioral dispositions that constitute the *basic mind*.

arguable that this theory does not adequately address the so-called 'hard problem' of consciousness—the nature of qualia—but this issue will not be the focus here.

With the personal–subpersonal distinction in place, we can now make a distinction between personal and subpersonal *reasoning*. (I use the term 'reasoning' in a generic sense to include both practical reasoning, which terminates in decisions to act, and theoretical reasoning, which terminates in new beliefs.) Personal reasoning is reasoning that is done by people; subpersonal reasoning is reasoning that is done by neural subsystems. As a simple example, take long division. Imagine someone with a natural talent for arithmetic. We ask them, what is 21,582 divided by 11, and they immediately respond with the answer, '1962'. We ask them how they worked it out, and they say they don't know—the answer just came to them. Here the reasoning involved in arriving at the answer was subpersonal. Of course *answering* the question was an intentional action, motivated by the subject's desire to comply with the request; but *working out* the answer was not. The subject did not *do* anything to work it out; the operations involved were entirely subpersonal, though they culminated in a personal-level event. This, is of course, an artificial example; few people can do long division in this way. But it is almost certain that there are subpersonal reasoning systems of very complex kinds. Indeed, cognitive science is largely devoted to offering subpersonal computational accounts of basic human abilities—pattern recognition, concept acquisition, learning, problem solving, goal seeking, and so on.

Now contrast this with another case. Here we ask someone the same question, but instead of simply answering, they start doing other things. They get a pencil and paper, write down the numbers, then perform a sequence of simpler divisions and subtractions—dividing 21 by 11, writing the integer part of the answer above the '21' and the remainder below, and so on, in the usual style. Finally, they read off the number along the top as their answer. This is a personal-level reasoning process. It involves a series of personal actions which collectively implement an algorithm for solving the problem and which are individually motivated by the desire to find the solution and the belief that the strategy being followed will produce it. Of course, each step in this process itself involves reasoning—solving simple problems of division, subtraction, and so on—and these processes may themselves be either personal or subpersonal. Take the step where the subject has to divide 105 by 11. The answer may come to them in a flash or they may write down some intervening steps. Ultimately, however, the process breaks down into actions that are the product of subpersonal rather than personal reasoning. For example, when confronted with the task of multiplying 11 by 9 most of us will write down the answer straight off without engaging in any personal reasoning.

A few points of clarification are in order. First, the actions involved in doing long division are overt and involve the use of external props. This is often necessary in mathematical reasoning, owing to the limitations of working memory, but these features are not essential to personal reasoning *per se*. The defining feature of personal reasoning is that it constitutively involves the performance of one or more intentional actions that are designed to generate a solution to a problem and motivated by a desire to find it. And, as already noted, intentional actions can be covert; we can talk to ourselves silently, for example, or deliberately visualize a diagram. (In calling these actions *covert*, I do not, of course, mean that they belong to a private subjective realm, merely that they have no easily observable manifestations.) And personal reasoning can also be covert, involving the formation and manipulation of mental images rather than external symbols. These actions will be motivated in the same way as their overt counterparts, by a desire to find a solution to some problem and a belief that they may generate one.

Second, I assume that personal reasoning involves attention and the use of working memory, and that it is therefore conscious. (In theory, some repetitive personal reasoning tasks might be performed with little or no attention; think, for example, of doing a series of long divisions using pencil and paper. But such cases will be rare and I shall ignore them.) I shall also assume that personal reasoning will require the exercise of various metacognitive abilities, including the ability to focus one's attention, monitor one's reasoning activities, and evaluate the strategies one is using.

Third, although personal reasoning itself is conscious, the beliefs and desires that motivate it typically will not be. Actions can be consciously performed even if we do not consciously reflect on the reasons for performing them. For example, I am currently conscious of pressing various keys on my computer keyboard. I press these keys because I desire to type certain words and believe that pressing them will achieve that. But I do not consciously entertain those beliefs and desires as I type; I just think about the content of what I am typing. The same goes, I assume, for most personal reasoning activities.

When we think about the mind in a pretheoretical way, we tend to focus on personal reasoning, which is the kind of which we are conscious, rather than the subpersonal variety. But most of our behavior is generated without the involvement of personal reasoning. Think about the actions involved in such everyday activities as driving a car, holding a conversation, or playing sports. These are intelligent actions, which are responsive to our beliefs and desires (think of how beliefs about the rules of the game shape the actions of a football player), and a great deal of complex mental processing must be involved in generating them. Yet, typically, they are performed spontaneously with no prior conscious thought or mental effort. Indeed, giving conscious thought to such activities is a good way to disrupt their fluidity. Even everyday 'folk' psychology recognizes this; we find it perfectly natural to give belief-desire explanations for routine behavior, such as that involved in driving a car, which we know is not the product of conscious thought. (For example, we would say that the driver pressed the indicator stalk because they wanted to signal a turn, and believed that pressing it would do that.) Personal reasoning, by contrast, is an effortful form of cognitive activity, which we engage in only when properly motivated—perhaps because subpersonal reasoning has failed to deliver a satisfactory response, or because we have reason to take special care.

What forms can personal reasoning take? The most obvious, perhaps, is the construction of arguments in inner speech, following learned rules of inference, either deductive or inductive. In doing this, one might draw on explicit knowledge of logical principles, consciously recalling a rule and then constructing an argument in accordance with it. But explicit knowledge is not required; one could also draw on practical skills in the construction of good arguments—procedural, as opposed to declarative, knowledge, embedded in linguistic skills. For example, through practice in public argumentation one might learn to recognize and produce utterance patterns that instantiate *modus ponens* and to regard them as normatively correct argumentative moves, even though one has never been taught the rule explicitly. Such skills could then be deployed in one's private personal reasoning, enabling one to generate sequences of inner utterances that conform to the rule; just saying the premises over to oneself might prompt one to supply the conclusion. Skills of this kind can be used to generate extended sequences of personal reasoning, as when we reason something out in interior monologue. Argument construction can also be supported by skills in the manipulation of sensory imagery. For example, one might visualize a Venn diagram to aid reasoning with quantifiers.

We can also deliberately apply rules of thumb, such as the recognition heuristic ('If you have to say which of two items best satisfies some criterion, then choose the one you recognize'). There is, of course a large psychological literature on the role of innate heuristics in non-conscious subpersonal reasoning, but heuristics can also be learned and applied in conscious personal reasoning (Evans, this volume). Again, the knowledge involved might be either declarative or procedural. (Even when procedural, this knowledge of heuristics is different from that involved in subpersonal reasoning, since it is embedded in skills in the construction of arguments at a personal level, in overt or covert speech.)

Argument construction may be the paradigm form of personal reasoning, but it is not the only one. Personal reasoning includes any intentional actions designed to further problem solving and decision making, and the range of these is wide. (For convenience, I shall focus on actions that can be performed covertly 'in the head'; if we were to include ones involving the use of external props, then the range would be even wider.) For example, one might deliberately direct one's attention to certain aspects of a situation, guided by normative beliefs about the relevant factors (see Buchtel and Norenzayan, this volume). Or one might engage in thought experiments involving the deliberate manipulation of sensory imagery, such as that used by Galileo to refute the Aristotelian view of gravitational attraction (e.g. Gendler 1998). Or one could use sensory imagination as a handy substitute for empirical investigation. For example, if you want to know how many chairs there are in your house, then a quick way to find out is to visualize each room and count them.

Sensory imagery is also central to a broad class of personal reasoning techniques which Daniel Dennett has dubbed *autostimulation* (Dennett 1991, ch.7). By this Dennett means the trick of generating self-directed stimuli—words and images—as a way of eliciting reactions from oneself that may be useful in solving problems. Originally, Dennett suggests, the actions involved would have been overt ones—talking aloud to oneself, drawing diagrams, and so on—but our ancestors learned the trick of covert autostimulation using inner speech and other forms of sensory imagery. In particular, Dennett stresses the benefits of *self-interrogation*. A self-generated question, he argues, will be processed by subpersonal comprehension systems in a similar way to an externally-generated one, and may evoke an instinctive verbal reply containing information that we would otherwise have been unable to access. This reply will then be processed in turn, giving global neural publicity to the information it carries.

Dennett focuses on the role of self-interrogation in broadcasting information stored in isolated neural subsystems, but it is plausible to think that it can also be a creative process, stimulating subpersonal reasoning to generate new inferences and novel responses.

Self-interrogation is, I suspect, a very common feature of human mental life. We often deliberately *try* to work something out, even though we do nothing more explicit than 'thinking'. This seems to be an intentional action (we can do it at will, and it requires motivation and effort), and what we are doing at such moments, I suggest, is engaging in self-interrogation: articulating a problem and challenging ourselves to come up with a solution to it, just as another person might challenge us, and thereby deliberately focusing our subpersonal reasoning abilities on to the task. If successful, this will culminate in a further personal event, such as an episode of inner speech or the occurrence of a visual image, carrying relevant information. Since self-interrogation is an intentional action, this counts as a personal reasoning process, even though all the real work is done subpersonally. From a personal-level perspective, the process is an associative one, and it may be one of the mechanisms underlying what Stanovich (this volume) calls *serial associative cognition*.

Of course, self-interrogation is not a very reliable problem-solving strategy, but it would be a useful way of generating hypotheses for subsequent evaluation, as part of an extended personal reasoning process. In particular, it would facilitate kinds of reasoning for which there are no formal procedures, such as abductive reasoning (inference to the best explanation). We could focus on our data, ask ourselves what could explain it, and then test out any hypotheses that come to mind—comparing them with rival ones, exploring their consequences, and so on. Similarly, we could use self-interrogation to evaluate a model by actively searching for counterexamples.

Another form of autostimulation is the mental rehearsal of action—imagining oneself performing some action. Peter Carruthers has argued that this can play an important role in practical reasoning (Carruthers 2006, this volume). Mentally rehearsing an action, Carruthers argues, generates perceptual and proprioceptive feedback which is then globally broadcast to subpersonal inferential and motivational subsystems, producing cognitive, motivational, and emotional reactions similar to those the action itself would produce. By this means, Carruthers suggests, a creature would be able to calculate some of the consequences of contemplated actions, thereby vastly extending its problem-solving abilities.

This is not intended as an exhaustive list of possible personal reasoning techniques, and of course empirical investigation would be needed to know which ones people actually employ. Some of the skills involved may have an innate basis (Dennett suggests that this is the case with autostimulation), but there are likely to be large differences between individuals in the particular skills used and the ways they are deployed, reflecting differences in people's normative beliefs about the nature of good reasoning—differences which may show considerable cultural variation. (Much of the data on thinking styles from cross-cultural psychology is, I suggest, best construed as relating to personal-level reasoning.) There may also be individual differences in the development of the metacognitive dispositions required to support personal reasoning, and cultural influences may play an important role here, too.

A two-levels view

The proposal I want to make will already be obvious. It is that the distinction between System 1 processes and System 2 processes is to be identified with that between subpersonal and personal reasoning. This view is, arguably, implicit in some existing accounts of the distinction. System 2 processes are typically characterized as *controlled* and sometimes as *volitional* (e.g. Evans 2003, this volume), and the characterization of System 2 processes as intentional actions is one way of spelling out this claim. At any rate, the features of subpersonal reasoning and personal reasoning coincide closely with the core features of the two putative systems. Subpersonal reasoning is typically fast, automatic, effortless, and non-conscious, whereas personal reasoning is typically slow, controlled, effortful, and conscious. Personal reasoning is also serial, shaped by culture and formal tuition, and, since it typically requires attention, demanding of working memory. By contrast, there is no reason to think that subpersonal reasoning will possess these features, and if it is effected by a collection of specialized, task-specific subsystems operating independently of consciousness, then it will not.

There are also theoretical advantages to the proposed identification. In particular, it explains why the features ascribed to System 2 form a natural kind (Samuels, this volume). Personal reasoning is typically slow, effortful, conscious, serial, and demanding of working memory *because* it involves the performance of sequences of intentional actions. And it is shaped by culture and formal tuition because it is guided by beliefs and desires which culture and tuition impart. The proposed view also offers an attractive framework for thinking about the evolution of System 2 reasoning, as I shall explain shortly.

The proposal is not a completely bland one, however, and it dictates some revisions to the standard characterization of the two systems. The most important of these concerns the procedures used by System 2. System 2 is often characterized as decontextualized, rule-based, analytic, and normatively correct. The proposed view partially vindicates this, since personal reasoning can involve the construction of valid arguments in accordance with formal rules of inference. (Indeed, it may be that decontextualized reasoning like this occurs *only* at the personal level.) But, as I explained, a range of other techniques can be employed in personal reasoning, including quick-and-dirty heuristics, selective direction of attention, and forms of autostimulation, some of which involve deliberately contextualizing a problem or exploiting associative subpersonal processes. Moreover, even when it is rule-based, personal reasoning may fail to be normatively correct. People can learn incorrect rules or apply correct ones carelessly. Other qualifications to the characterization of System 2 are dictated, too. By identifying intentional control as the defining feature of System 2 reasoning, the proposal demotes the other features to the status of, at most, typical but non-necessary features. Thus, most personal reasoning activities are slow and effortful, but in the right circumstances some could be quick and effortless. This emphasis on the varied character of System 2 processes harmonizes well with recent work in dual-process tradition (Buchtel and Norenzayan, this volume; Evans 2006b, this volume; Stanovich, this volume).

The proposal also has important implications for our view of the architectural relations between the two systems. System 1 and System 2 are often regarded as separate neural systems, operating either in sequence or in parallel. On the proposed view, however, System 2 is not a neural system at all, but a *virtual* one, constituted by states and activities of the whole agent. (If we ask what it is that implements personal reasoning processes, then the *immediate* answer is that it is the person themselves.) Moreover, on this view System 2 will be heavily dependent on System 1. There are several aspects to this.

First, System 2 will be dependent on System 1 for its *inputs*. Conscious, personal-level reasoning can begin only after a great deal of preconscious processing has been completed—processing that determines which problems become the focus of attention and what information is consciously recalled for use in solving them. (It is true that we sometimes deliberately *try* to recall things, as when we *rack our brains* for a piece of information, but this is, I assume, simply a form of self-interrogation, and its outcome is dependent on subpersonal processes.) This sort of dependency is a key feature of heuristic-analytic versions of dual-process theory, according to which heuristic (System 1) processes select information that is then made available for processing by the analytic system (System 2) (e.g. Evans 2006b, 2007), and in this respect the present proposal can be regarded as a variant of such theories.

Second—and more controversially—System 2 will be *causally* dependent on System 1. The intentional actions involved in personal reasoning will themselves be generated by subpersonal cognitive processes. These will include the processes involved in deciding to initiate personal reasoning, choosing reasoning strategies, directing attention, selecting, generating, and manipulating inner speech and other sensory imagery, together with the mechanisms of language comprehension, self-monitoring, self-regulation, and many other processes, depending on the nature of the task. (For detailed suggestions about the subpersonal underpinnings of personal reasoning, see Carruthers 2006, this volume.)

Third, System 2 can be *instrumentally* dependent on System 1. As already noted, we can deliberately engage in various forms of autostimulation, which allow us to exploit our subpersonal reasoning abilities and employ their deliverances in extended sequences of personal reasoning.

Finally, System 2 will be dependent on System 1 processes to make its *outputs* effective. I assume that conscious reasoning can affect our actions, perhaps overriding default responses generated non-consciously. This is not to deny that some conscious reasoning may be confabulatory, serving merely to rationalize intuitive responses generated by non-conscious processes. There is good evidence that much of it is (e.g. Gazzaniga 1998; Wegner 2002; Wilson 2002). But it is implausible to hold that *all* conscious reasoning is confabulatory. Yet, if such reasoning takes the form I have proposed, it is not easy to see how it could guide action. The termination of an episode of personal reasoning will typically be itself an action—an utterance in inner speech, say—which expresses the conclusion reached. And such actions will have no *direct* effect on further action. Saying that one will do something does not immediately cause one to do it. For example, thinking about the best way to get to a friend's house, I may conclude by saying to myself 'I'd better get a taxi'. This utterance is itself simply a behavioral response; if it is to have any effect on my journey, then mediating processes will be required. Some of these may also be intentional actions. For example, I may remind myself of my decision during subsequent personal reasoning.

But these actions, too, will require mediation if they are to affect my subsequent behavior, and the mediating events must ultimately be subpersonal ones. This is a conceptual point; the mediating process cannot involve an endless sequence of personal actions. (And of course any mediating intentional actions will themselves be generated by subpersonal processes.) For similar reasons, subpersonal mediation will be required if a conclusion arrived at in one episode of personal reasoning is to be recalled and used as a premise in later episodes. Thus on the proposed view System 2 depends for its efficacy on System 1 processes.

Let me say a little more about this. What might the subpersonal mediating mechanisms be? How could saying to myself that I will take a taxi influence my subpersonal systems to initiate that action and implement the decision? One possible mechanism is autostimulation: conclusions articulated in inner speech might be processed by the speech comprehension system and interpreted as instructions or reports, which are then adopted as intentions or beliefs in subpersonal reasoning (Carruthers 2006, ch.6, this volume.) Such processes may play a role, but unless one is preternaturally suggestible, it is unlikely that they will ensure that conscious decisions are reliably implemented. (Of course, such decisions are not *always* implemented; but they often are, and it is doubtful that autostimulation alone would be sufficient to secure this.)

A more plausible suggestion appeals to the role of metacognitive attitudes in subpersonal reasoning (Frankish 2004). Suppose we have a strong desire to act upon the results of our personal reasoning, executing any decisions and relying on any conclusions. (I shall say something shortly about why we might have this desire.) Then this desire could play the mediating role through its influence in subpersonal reasoning. The idea is this. At a subpersonal level, my utterance of 'I'd better get a taxi' is interpreted as a decision to take a taxi, and this, together with a general desire to act upon my personal-level decisions, strongly influences my subsequent subpersonal reasoning, leading me to phone for a taxi. The subpersonal metacognitive attitudes make the personal decision effective. Of course, I would not normally explain my action by citing these metacognitive attitudes; I would simply cite the attitudes involved in my personal reasoning. And this commonsense explanation would be not wrong, since those attitudes did play an important role. But it would not be the whole story.

One attraction of this view is that it offers an account of how conflicts between the two systems are resolved. It is a basic tenet of dual-system theories that the two systems may deliver conflicting results. In the standard scenario, System 1 generates an intuitive response that is adaptive but non-normative, whereas System 2 generates a more considered response that is in line with one's normative theories. On existing theories, the result will be either that the two systems compete for behavioral control, or that System 2 attempts to override System 1. The present proposal offers a different perspective, however, on which the conflict will be resolved at the System 1 level. Schematically, the story goes like this. Suppose that our subpersonal processes generate a desire to perform some action X, but that before performing it, we engage in personal reasoning which terminates in a decision to perform some incompatible action Y. Since we have a general desire to act on our personal decisions, we shall then be motivated to perform Y. So we shall have competing desires at the subpersonal level: a first-order desire to perform X and a second-order desire to act on our personal decision to perform Y. The resolution of the conflict will be determined simply by which desire is stronger. (Cases where the first-order desire outweighs the second-order one are, I suggest, cases of what we call *weakness of will*; see Frankish 2004, ch.8.)

I turn now to some further issues raised by the proposed view. First, given the complex dependency of personal reasoning on subpersonal reasoning, does it make sense to think of personal reasoning as constituting a distinct *system*? Why not speak simply of System 1 characteristics and System 2 characteristics, and say that we have a suite of subpersonal systems with System 1 characteristics, and that some of these systems occasionally cooperate to sustain personal reasoning processes with System 2 characteristics?

Such a description would not be inaccurate, and indeed on the present view the core distinction is one between processes rather than systems. However, I think we can retain talk of a distinct System 2, and that it is useful to do so as a way of highlighting the *functional autonomy* of personal reasoning. We can think of personal reasoning as a functionally defined system that takes representations (typically sentences of inner speech), manipulates them in accordance with procedures designed to implement various forms of inference, and generates further representations, which assume the causal role of conclusions or decisions. It is true that this system is dependent on lower-level reasoning systems, but from a functional perspective this is irrelevant, and the reasoning tasks performed at the two levels during an episode of personal reasoning will typically be quite different. The higher-level system will be devoted to a first-order problem of some kind, the lower-level systems to the task of how to access and implement procedures to solve this problem.

The suggestion, then, is that System 2 is a reasoning system constructed out of other reasoning systems—a sort of super-system. (Elsewhere I have dubbed it a 'supermind'.) Is this view compatible with the claim that System 2 is a recent system? After all, the various subpersonal systems involved in supporting personal reasoning will be of different evolutionary ages—some, such as the visual system, very old; others, such as the language system, much more recent. However, there may still be a sense in which System 2 is recent. Perhaps it is not the *components* of the system that are recent, but their *assembly*. It is possible that most, if not all, of the resources involved in supporting personal reasoning (working memory, language, sensory imagination, metacognitive abilities, etc.) evolved independently, and that personal reasoning emerged only when these disparate resources were co-opted to serve a new task, perhaps with some minor additional adaptations. (We might compare it to the emergence of reading and writing.)[2] And the crucial developments may have been cultural rather than biological, involving the discovery of skills in argumentation and self-stimulation and the formation and transmission of a body of normative beliefs about good reasoning.[3] From an evolutionary perspective this account has an attractive

---

[2] Steven Mithen has also argued that flexible intelligence—which seems linked to System 2 reasoning—developed from the co-ordination of previously isolated specialized intelligences (Mithen 1996).

[3] For another approach which also connects System 2 reasoning with argumentation, see Mercier and Sperber, this volume.

economy, and if it is right, System 2 may be very recent (compare Dennett 1991; Jaynes 1976).

A corollary of this view is that we may well be innately disposed to form the metacognitive desires that drive personal reasoning and make it effective, including desires to set explicit goals for ourselves, to engage in personal reasoning about how to achieve them, and to act upon the conclusions of this reasoning. To borrow a metaphor from Daniel Dennett (1991), these attitudes are part of the software required to program the brain to engage in personal reasoning, and thereby create a flexible, decontextualized, reasoning system. Assuming there was selective pressure to develop such a system, there would also have been pressure to develop a disposition to form the required attitudes.

A further attraction of the proposed view is that it has the resources to accommodate new distinctions that have recently been introduced by theorists in the dual-systems tradition. I shall briefly consider proposals by Jonathan Evans and Keith Stanovich.

Evans (this volume) now recommends reverting to talk of processes rather than systems, and he identifies the use of working memory as the key functional distinction underlying dual-process approaches. He distinguishes *type 1* processes, which do not require working memory, and are, consequently, fast, automatic, and effortless, and *type 2* (or *analytic*) processes, which manipulate explicit representations in working memory. He also makes a distinction among type 1 processes, distinguishing *autonomous* processes, which control behavior directly, without the involvement of working memory, and *preattentive* processes, which supply content to working memory. Thus, on this view, there are two different dual-process distinctions to be made: between autonomous and analytic processes, which work competitively and in parallel, and between preattentive and analytic processes, which work co-operatively and in sequence. Evans notes that existing dual-systems accounts fail to make this distinction, leading to confusion and cross-talk. Evans also introduces a third category of processes, *type 3* processes, which are responsible for initiating type 2 processing and resolving conflicts between autonomous and analytic processes, and which have ultimate control of behavior.

There is of course much more detail to Evans's picture, but his basic distinctions at least can be accommodated within the framework I have proposed. Personal reasoning, unlike the subpersonal type, requires attention and the use of working memory, so the distinction between type 1 and type 2 processes corresponds closely to that between subpersonal and personal reasoning. And the distinction between autonomous and preattentive processes corresponds to that between those subpersonal reasoning processes that guide action directly and those that provide inputs to personal reasoning. (There are, of course, other ways in which subpersonal processes are involved in supporting personal reasoning, corresponding to the other kinds of dependency mentioned earlier, and we could make further distinctions among type 1 processes to reflect this.) Finally, Evans's type 3 processes correspond to the subset of subpersonal processes involved in deciding when to initiate personal reasoning and whether or not to act on the outputs of any given episode of it. On the view proposed earlier, decisions of the latter kind will often involve competition between a general second-order desire to act on the outcomes of our personal reasoning and specific first-order desires to perform other, incompatible actions.

Whereas Evans makes a distinction among type 1 processes, Stanovich has recently argued for a division within System 2, between what he calls the *reflective mind* and the *algorithmic mind* (this volume). These correspond to two different levels of processing. The reflective mind is the top level and consists of goals and beliefs which exert high-level control of behavior. Importantly, these include *epistemic* goals and values, which exert reflective control over our reasoning, together with 'thinking dispositions' such as openmindedness, impulsiveness, and willingness to engage in effortful thought, which are manifested in our decisions about how to interpret tasks, what strategies to adopt, what rules to apply, and so on. (Stanovich adopts the term 'mindware' for the learned rules, procedures, and strategies that guide System 2 processes.) The algorithmic mind is a subordinate level, and consists of the processing machinery that supports these reflective-level states. Support for the reflective–algorithmic distinction comes from tasks studied in the heuristics-and-biases literature. Measures of general intelligence are known to predict variation on these tasks; this is taken to reflect differences in System 2 functioning. But there is further variation in performance once general intelligence has been controlled for, and measures of thinking dispositions predict this. Stanovich argues that tests of general intelligence measure the processing efficiency of the algorithmic mind, whereas measures of thinking dispositions reflect individual differences in the reflective control of reasoning.

Again, in outline at least, this distinction maps easily on to the picture I have sketched. The reflective mind corresponds to personal reasoning. It is plausible to regard thinking dispositions, such as openmindedness, as personal-level states, which manifest themselves in our personal reasoning activities. And it is our personal reasoning over which we can exercise reflective control, since it is precisely intentional actions that are responsive to reason. The algorithmic mind, by contrast, corresponds to the subpersonal processing resources which support personal reasoning and over which we cannot exercise reflective control. This view also accords with the data on individual differences. We should expect there to be variation in personal reasoning abilities independent of variation in cognitive capacity, reflecting individual differences in knowledge of reasoning strategies, normative beliefs about good reasoning, metacognitive dispositions, and so on—differences in mindware rather than hardware.

There are also differences between the pictures, however. Stanovich treats the algorithmic-level processes that support the reflective mind as an aspect of System 2, so, assuming these processes are subpersonal, personal reasoning cannot be identified with System 2 in Stanovich's sense. To some extent, this difference is terminological: Stanovich's System 2 can be identified with the personal reasoning system *together with* the subpersonal processes that support it. There is a case, however, for restricting the term 'System 2' to the personal, reflective-level processes themselves, since it is they, rather than the subpersonal algorithmic-level mechanisms, that exhibit the distinctive properties of System 2 processes (controlled, effortful, conscious, etc.). (This reflects the general point that functional systems can be realized in lower-level processes of a very different character; for example connectionist networks can be modelled on digital computers.) There is a more substantive issue here too. Can we make a sharp distinction between those subpersonal resources that are involved in supporting the reflective mind and those that are not? In retaining a distinction between systems, in addition to the distinction between levels, Stanovich implies that we can. Now there is good reason for this: there are heritable individual differences in the capacity of the cognitive mechanisms supporting System 2 reasoning—tapped by measures of general intelligence—which are not found in the autonomous subsystems grouped under the System 1 banner. However, it does not follow that such variation is found in *all* the mechanisms involved in supporting System 2 reasoning; it might be exhibited by just one or two key components, such as working memory. And some autonomous subsystems might be involved, including language and theory of mind, which do not display such variation. Indeed, different subsets of subpersonal mechanisms might be involved on different occasions, depending on the nature of the task. If this is right, then it will not be possible to draw a hard-and-fast distinction between the subpersonal mechanisms associated with Systems 1 and 2. If we are looking for a simple binary division, then the personal–subpersonal division may be the only one available.

Finally in this section, I shall address a possible objection to the proposal I have made. It goes like this. The aim of cognitive psychology is to provide reductive explanations of personal-level phenomena in terms of the underlying subpersonal states and processes. The two-systems hypothesis is an attempt to do this: dual reasoning systems were posited in order to explain why people respond as they do on various reasoning tasks. So to reclassify one of the systems as a personal one is to take a step backwards in this explanatory project. Now I agree that the aim of cognitive psychology is to provide reductive explanations, but it does not follow that the proposal is a backward step—or at least that it is an unnecessary one. For we need to have the right explanandum for subpersonal theory. Take a sporting ability, such as being able to play a good round of golf. From a psychological point of view this is not a single skill, and we would not seek to explain it directly in subpersonal terms (Clark 1993, p.203). Rather, we would explain it as the product of a cluster of more basic skills—at driving, chipping, putting, gauging distance, and so on. And it is these more basic skills for which we would then seek reductive explanations. And the same may go for some of our reasoning abilities: they may involve the deployment of a cluster of personal skills in constructing explicit arguments, applying heuristics, autostimulation, and so on, which are the proper targets for reductive explanation. Thus the present proposal is not incompatible with the search for subpersonal explanations, and may be a needed corrective to the tendency to seek them prematurely.

Dual mental states

A dual-systems theory of reasoning may need to be supplemented with a dual-systems theory of memory, according to which the two reasoning systems have separate suites of beliefs and desires (knowledge bases and goal structures), differing in content and functional characteristics. Such a view is a corollary of theories which treat the two systems as operating in parallel, and may be implicit in other versions, too. The case for dual memory systems is also supported by social-psychological work on persuasion and attitude change, which has led several theorists to distinguish two independent memory systems: an implicit system, which is non-conscious, automatic, and slow-learning, and an explicit system, which is conscious, effortful, and fast-learning (e.g. Smith and Collins, this volume; Smith and DeCoster 2000; Wilson et al. 2000; see also Sun et al., this volume). The distinction between subpersonal and personal reasoning is also associated with a distinction of mental states, similar to that between implicit and explicit, and in this final section I shall sketch this briefly.[4]

Beliefs are states that serve as premises in reasoning, and we can distinguish two broad types of belief, depending on whether the reasoning in question is subpersonal or personal. The former will be subpersonal states of the cognitive system, whereas the latter will be behavioral dispositions of the whole person. (Personal reasoning is an activity, and to have a personal-level belief is be disposed to conduct this activity in a certain way, taking the content of the belief as a premise.) For convenience, we can refer to these as *subpersonal belief* and *personal belief* respectively. (I should add a caveat here. As noted earlier, there is a sense in which all beliefs are personal; it is people who believe things, not their brains. The proposed terminology is designed to underscore the claim that there are two very different ways in which a person can believe something, defined by the relative roles of subpersonal and personal factors in the processing of the belief in question. It is also worth stressing that the distinction between the two kinds of belief is not drawn in terms of content, and that 'personal' does not mean 'relating to oneself'.)[5] We can make a similar distinction for desire, with personal desire consisting in a disposition to take the desired outcome as a goal in one's personal reasoning. The beliefs and desires that motivate and guide personal reasoning are subpersonal ones, whereas those that form its content are personal ones.[6]

I assume there will be numerous subdivisions to be drawn within each category of belief. In particular, just as there are likely to be many subpersonal reasoning systems, so there are likely to be many subpersonal memory systems (Carruthers 2006, ch.2). However there are also certain fundamental differences between the two. The first relates to consciousness. Subpersonal beliefs are operative at a non-conscious level, whereas personal ones are entertained as premises in episodes of conscious reasoning. (This is not to say that we are not aware of possessing our subpersonal beliefs; we may, for example, infer their existence from our own behavior; but we do not employ them in our conscious reasoning.) The second difference relates to mode of formation. Subpersonal beliefs are formed passively, by subpersonal processes.

---

[4] What follows draws on Frankish 2004, to which the reader is referred for detailed discussion.

[5] My use of the term 'personal belief' should be distinguished from that in the social-psychological literature, where personal beliefs are often contrasted with shared cultural stereotypes (e.g. Devine 1989). Personal beliefs in this sense will, however, often be personal in my sense, too.

[6] There may be another difference with Stanovich here. For Stanovich (this volume), the reflective mind seems to include both the attitudes that figure as premises and goals in System 2 reasoning and the epistemic attitudes that guide this reasoning. By contrast, I am suggesting that the two sets of attitudes are located at different levels.

Often, I assume, this will be a gradual process, involving repeated exposure to relevant environmental regularities. Personal beliefs, on the other hand, can be actively formed, by one-off decisions. Since personal reasoning is under intentional control, we shall be able to make decisions about which propositions to take as premises in it. If we think a proposition is well-warranted—say, because we have been told on good authority that it is true or because we have inferred it from something else we believe—then we can decide to adopt it as a premise for use in subsequent personal reasoning on relevant topics. (As with other personal-level decisions, such decisions will become effective in virtue of subpersonal metacognitive attitudes—specifically, a belief that one has decided to adopt the proposition in question as a premise and a general desire to act on one's personal-level decisions.) A third contrast relates to degree. It is plausible to think of subpersonal beliefs as graded states, corresponding to subjective probability assignments. Much human reasoning can be analyzed as probabilistic in character, even though we rarely make explicit assessments of probability (e.g. Evans and Over 2004; Oaksford and Chater 2007). Personal beliefs, on the other hand, are ungraded, all-or-nothing attitudes. To have the personal belief that p is to be disposed to take p as a premise in one's personal reasoning, and one either has this disposition or not; there is no halfway house. (Of course, the *content* of a personal belief may be a probability claim—for example, that there is a 75% chance of rain today—but the attitude towards this content remains ungraded.)[7]

The distinction between subpersonal and personal belief corresponds closely to one drawn by some philosophers between *belief* and *acceptance*—the former being a passive, graded state, and the latter a voluntary, all-or-nothing one (e.g. Bratman 1992; Cohen 1992; Engel 2000). Accepting a proposition involves deciding to treat it as true for certain reasoning purposes, and writers on the subject stress that the attitude can be adopted for pragmatic reasons as well as epistemic ones, and that it can be restricted as to context. For example, a lawyer might accept that their client is innocent for the purposes of deciding how to conduct their defence, even though they strongly believe that they are guilty. Personal belief is very similar to acceptance, and I assume that it, too, can be pragmatically motivated and restricted in context. (We might hesitate to call pragmatically-motivated attitudes *beliefs tout court,* but we could think of them as *professional,* or *pragmatic* beliefs.) This serves to emphasize the essentially *hypothetical* character of personal belief and personal reasoning. In forming a personal belief and using it in personal reasoning, one is adopting and exploring a working hypothesis, and one can be motivated to do this for a variety of reasons.

I shall conclude this section with some remarks about the relation between the two levels of belief, where it is plausible to see a constitutive dependency relation. A personal belief is a behavioral disposition—a disposition to conduct one's personal reasoning in a

---

7 Note that to say that our personal beliefs are ungraded is not to say that we treat them as *certain*. One can be disposed to take a proposition as a premise in one's personal reasoning without being disposed to rely on it in all contexts, no matter what is at stake (see Frankish 2004, ch.4). Note, too, that we can have varying degrees of *attachment* to our personal beliefs, reflecting how reluctant we would be to revise or abandon them.

certain way, taking the believed proposition as a premise. And this disposition (assuming it is not simply a reflex) will exist in virtue of subpersonal beliefs and desires that make the behavior in question attractive. These might be the belief that one has decided to take p as a premise (formed as result of having made such a decision) and the desire to act on one's personal decisions, or the belief that p is well-warranted and the desire to take well-warranted propositions as premises. Such metacognitive subpersonal attitudes would constitute, or *realize*, the first-order personal belief that p.

It may be objected that if personal beliefs are constituted by subpersonal ones, then they are not a distinct type of belief. The objection is similar to one discussed earlier in relation to the personal reasoning system itself, and a similar response is in order. The claim is not that personal beliefs *are* metacognitive subpersonal beliefs, but that they are functional states that are *realized in* metacognitive subpersonal beliefs; a person exhibits the premising dispositions in which personal beliefs consist in virtue of having the appropriate subpersonal attitudes. And, as just noted, there will be significant functional differences between the realized and realizing states—differences relating to consciousness, mode of formation, and degree. It is true that if personal beliefs constitutively involve subpersonal ones, then it must be the case that some subpersonal beliefs can be formed quickly, as personal ones can. However, the subpersonal beliefs in question will be ones about one-off events, to the effect that we have decided to adopt this or that proposition as a premise, and it is plausible to think that subpersonal beliefs of this kind can be formed quickly (e.g. Smith and DeCoster 2000).

Conclusion

I have argued that the distinction between System 1 and System 2 corresponds to that between subpersonal and personal reasoning. But even if the distinctions do not align in this way, a weaker claim still stands. The distinction between personal and subpersonal reasoning marks *one* broad binary division in human reasoning, and one that needs to be acknowledged in psychological theory. Indeed, it may be the *only* such division. Most dual-systems theorists accept that System 1 is actually a suite of systems, and several contributors to the present volume suggest that System 2 may also fragment in various ways (Evans, this volume; Samuels, this volume; Stanovich, this volume). Indeed, there could be hybrid systems at a subpersonal level, with some System 1 properties and some System 2 properties. Personal reasoning, on the other hand, constitutes a distinct level of mental activity, which can be clearly distinguished from the lower, subpersonal one.

Of course, those interested in the nuts and bolts of cognition may regard personal reasoning as a superficial phenomenon. In a sense it is, but it is a real one, and one that must be recognized in psychological theorizing, if only to avoid the error of premature reduction. And in the end, it may be the main source of the remarkably widespread intuition that there is a fundamental duality in human reasoning.

Acknowledgments

I should like to thank Jonathan Evans for many fruitful discussions of dual-process theory and for his detailed comments on earlier drafts of this chapter. Thanks are also due to Peter Carruthers, Maria Kasmirli, Richard Samuels, and Keith Stanovich for their comments and advice. The writing of this chapter was supported by a research leave award from the UK's Arts and Humanities Research Council.

References

Baars, B.J. (1988) *A cognitive theory of consciousness*. Cambridge University Press, Cambridge.

Baars, B.J. (1997) *In the theater of consciousness: The workspace of the mind*. Oxford University Press, Oxford.

Baker, L.R. (1987) *Saving belief: A critique of physicalism*. Princeton University Press, Princeton, NJ.

Bermúdez, J.L. and Elton, M. (eds) (2000) *Philosophical Explorations,* vol. 3(1): Special issue: *The personal/sub-personal distinction*. Van Gorcum, Assen.

Botterill, G. and Carruthers, P. (1999) *The philosophy of psychology*. Cambridge University Press, Cambridge.

Bratman, M.E. (1992) Practical reasoning and acceptance in a context. *Mind*, **101**, 1–15.

Carruthers, P. (2006) *The architecture of the mind*. Oxford University Press, Oxford.

Clark, A. (1993) *Associative engines: Connectionism, concepts, and representational change*. MIT Press, Cambridge, MA.

Cohen, L.J. (1992) *An essay on belief and acceptance*. Oxford University Press, Oxford.

Dennett, D.C. (1969) *Content and consciousness*. Routledge and Kegan Paul, London.

Dennett, D.C. (1981) Three kinds of intentional psychology. In R Healey (ed.) *Reduction, time and reality*, 37–61. Cambridge University Press, Cambridge.

Dennett, D.C. (1991) *Consciousness explained*. Little Brown and Co., Boston, MA.

Devine, P.G. (1989) Stereotypes and prejudice: Their automatic and controlled components. *Journal of Personality and Social Psychology*, **56**, 5–18.

Engel, P. (ed.) (2000) *Believing and accepting*. Kluwer, Dordrecht.

Evans, J.St.B.T. (2003) In two minds: Dual-process accounts of reasoning. *Trends in Cognitive Sciences*, **7**, 454–9.

Evans, J.St.B.T. (2006a) Dual system theories of cognition: Some issues. *Proceedings of the 28th Annual Meeting of the Cognitive Science Society,* Vancouver, 202--7.

Evans, J.St.B.T. (2006b) The heuristic-analytic theory of reasoning: Extension and evaluation. *Psychonomic Bulletin and Review*, **13**, 378–95.

Evans, J.St.B.T. (2007) *Hypothetical thinking: Dual processes in reasoning and judgement*. Psychology Press, Hove.

Evans, J.St.B.T. (2008) Dual-processing accounts of reasoning, judgment, and social cognition. *Annual Review of Psychology*, **59**, 255–78.

Evans, J.St.B.T. and Over, D.E. (1996) *Rationality and reasoning*. Psychology Press, Hove.

Evans, J.St.B.T. and Over, D.E. (2004) *If*. Oxford University Press, Oxford.

Fodor, J.A. (1987) *Psychosemantics: The problem of meaning in the philosophy of mind*. MIT Press, Cambridge, MA.

Frankish, K. (2004) *Mind and supermind*. Cambridge University Press, Cambridge.

Gazzaniga, M.S. (1998) *The mind's past*. University of California Press, Berkeley, CA.

Gendler, T.S. (1998) Galileo and the indispensability of scientific thought experiment. *The British Journal for the Philosophy of Science*, **49**, 397–424.

Hornsby, J. (2000) Personal and sub-personal: A defence of Dennett's early distinction. *Philosophical Explorations*, **3**, 6–24.

Jaynes, J. (1976) *The origins of consciousness in the breakdown of the bicameral mind*. Houghton Mifflin, Boston, MA.

Kahneman, D. and Frederick, S. (2002) Representativeness revisited: Attribute substitution in intuitive judgement. In T. Gilovich, D. Griffin, and D. Kahneman (eds) *Heuristics and biases: The psychology of intuitive judgement*, 49–81. Cambridge University Press, Cambridge.

Lewis, D. (1972) Psychophysical and theoretical identifications. *Australasian Journal of Philosophy*, **50**, 249–58.

Mithen, S. (1996) *The prehistory of the mind: A search for the origins of art, religion and science*. Thames and Hudson, London.

Oaksford, M. and Chater, N. (2007) *Bayesian rationality*. Oxford University Press, Oxford.

Sloman, S.A. (1996) The empirical case for two systems of reasoning. *Psychological Bulletin*, **119**, 3–22.

Sloman, S.A. (2002) Two systems of reasoning. In T. Gilovich, D. Griffin, and D. Kahneman (eds) *Heuristics and biases: The psychology of intuitive judgment*, 379–96. Cambridge University Press, Cambridge.

Smith, E.R. and DeCoster, J. (2000) Dual-process models in social and cognitive psychology: Conceptual integration and links to underlying memory systems. *Personality and Social Psychology Review*, **4**, 108–31.

Stanovich, K.E. (1999) *Who is rational? Studies of individual differences in reasoning*. Lawrence Erlbaum Associates, Mahwah, NJ.

Stanovich, K.E. (2004) *The robot's rebellion*. University of Chicago Press, Chicago, IL.

Wegner, D.M. (2002) *The illusion of conscious will*. MIT Press, Cambridge, MA.

Wilson, T.D. (2002) *Strangers to ourselves: Discovering the adaptive unconscious*. Belknap Press, Cambridge, MA.

Wilson, T.D., Lindsey, S., and Schooler, T.Y. (2000) A model of dual attitudes. *Psychological Review*, **107**, 101–26.

Chapter 5

An architecture for dual reasoning

Peter Carruthers

This chapter takes for granted the existence of some sort of real distinction between System 1 and System 2 reasoning processes, and asks how they are realized in the human mind–brain. In contrast with the usual view of the two systems as distinct from one another, it is argued that System 2 is partly realized in cycles of operation of System 1. But System 2 is also distinctive in being action-based. It is mental rehearsals of action that generate and sustain the cycles of operation of System 1 that constitute System 2. A number of advantages of the proposed account will be detailed, together with some implications for future research.

Introduction

Dual-system theories of human reasoning are now quite widely accepted, at least in outline (Evans and Over 1996; Frankish 2004; Kahneman 2002; Sloman 1996, 2002; Stanovich 1999). I shall begin by delineating the contrasting sets of properties of the two systems that I propose to take as my explanatory target. (These are summarized in Table 5.1.)

Most researchers agree that System 1 is really a collection of different systems that are fast and unconscious, operating in parallel with one another. The principles according

Table 5.1 The properties of the two systems

System 1	System 2
A set of systems	A single system
Fast	Slow
Parallel	Serial
Unconscious	Conscious
Not easily altered	Malleable
Universal amongst humans	Variable (by culture and by individual)
Mostly shared with other animals	Uniquely human
Impervious to verbal instruction	Responsive to verbal instruction
Independent of normative beliefs	Influenced by normative beliefs
Heuristic based	Can involve the application of valid rules

to which these systems function are, to a significant extent, universal to humans, and they aren't easily altered (e.g. by verbal instruction). (I should emphasize that in my view it is only the general principles of operation of System 1 systems that are hard to alter, rather than their contents. For many of these systems have been designed for *learning*, enabling us to extract new information from our environment in quick and reliable-enough ways. See Carruthers 2006.) Moreover, the principles via which System 1 systems operate are, for the most part, heuristic in nature ('quick and dirty'), rather than deductively or inductively valid. It is also generally thought that most, if not all, of the mechanisms constituting System 1 are evolutionarily ancient and shared with other species of animal.

In addition, however, some researchers maintain that System 1 processes are associative in character (Sloman 1996, 2002). I disagree. I believe that System 1 is a collection of semi-independent modules whose internal processes are, rather, computational in nature (Carruthers 2006). I should stress, however, that those who are associationists about System 1 should face no obstacles in accepting the proposed architecture for the two systems that I shall outline and defend in the present chapter. I merely want to emphasize that by defending the reality of the System 1/System 2 distinction I am *not* intending to defend an account of the distinction that links it to the contrast between associative and rule-governed (nor between irrational and rational) forms of cognition.

System 2, on the other hand, is generally thought to be a single system which is slow, serial, and conscious. The principles according to which it operates are variable (both across cultures and between individuals within a culture), and can involve the application of valid norms of reasoning. (Indeed, some seem to believe that System 2 always and exclusively instantiates logical principles. This is not part of the view that I shall defend. I maintain that System 2, too, can involve the use of heuristics.) These System 2 principles are malleable and can be influenced by verbal instruction, and they often involve normative beliefs (that is, beliefs about how one *should* reason). Moreover, System 2 is generally thought to be uniquely human.

It seems likely that the mechanisms that constitute System 1 belong to at least three distinct kinds. There will be systems that issue in new beliefs, systems that issue in new goals, and systems concerned with swift decision making in the light of one's beliefs and goals. For there is good reason to think that System 1 will exemplify a belief/desire/decision making architecture (Carruthers 2006, ch.2). This System 1 architecture is depicted in Figure 5.1 (which also incorporates the dual visual systems hypothesis of Milner and Goodale (1995), according to which the ventral/temporal-lobe system makes its outputs available for belief-formation and planning, while the dorsal/parietal-lobe system is concerned with the on-line guidance of movement).

One might then expect System 2 to carve up into three distinct sub-components also: one charged with conscious, reflective, belief-fixation; one subserving conscious, reflective, goal-adoption; and one of which takes conscious decisions (thereby forming new intentions) in the light of one's conscious beliefs and goals. For there certainly appear to be tasks of each of these three types (e.g. reasoning tasks versus decision-making tasks) which would be categorized as involving the operations of System 2. I shall argue later, however, that there is actually just a single system constituting System 2, which can nevertheless operate in different 'modes' corresponding to belief, desire, and decision making.

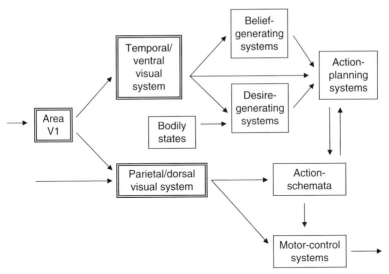

Fig. 5.1 The System 1 architecture.

It is generally assumed that System 1 and System 2 are (largely) distinct from one another. But then one immediate challenge for dual-system theory concerns the relationships between the two (sets of) systems. How, if at all, do they interact with one another? How is it possible for System 2 to override the operations of System 1 in controlling behavior? And how are we to imagine that System 2 could have evolved? If System 2 is charged with generating new beliefs, desires, and decisions, then how could it have evolved alongside a set of mechanisms (System 1) that already possessed precisely those functions? And what evolutionary pressures could have led to such a wholesale change in our cognitive architecture—effectively creating a new, species-specific, belief/desire/decision-making system alongside of a more ancient set of belief/desire/decision-making systems shared with the rest of the animal kingdom? The problem is further exacerbated if one allows—as we surely should—that there are a number of other species-unique cognitive adaptations that humans possess, including a language faculty, a sophisticated mind-reading faculty, a system for normative reasoning and motivation, and perhaps others besides (Carruthers 2006, ch.3).

Another set of challenges for dual-system theory concerns the ways in which System 2 operates. For it appears that the acquisition of new beliefs (especially normative beliefs) must somehow be capable of creating and/or rewriting the algorithms governing our System 2 reasoning. But it is hard to understand how this can happen. How is it possible for processes of belief-formation, for example, to be guided by acquired beliefs? (Put differently: how can you build a learning mechanism *out of beliefs*?) And how, moreover, can reasoning be controlled by beliefs about how one *ought* to reason? Likewise, how can reasoning be guided by verbal instruction? It looks as if System 2 reasoning must somehow be under our intentional control (Frankish 2004, this volume). And that means, in turn, that it should somehow be action-based or action-involving. For it is actions *par excellence* that are under the control of beliefs and desires, and that can be directly guided by verbal instruction. But this is then puzzling in its own right: how can a system of *reasoning* be constituted by *actions*?—for actions are the sorts of things that rather *issue from* prior reasoning (see Figure 5.1).

My goal in this chapter is to answer these challenges. I shall outline an architecture for System 2 that sees it as realized in cycles of operation of System 1 (rather than existing alongside the latter). On the account that I shall provide, mental rehearsals of action lead to globally broadcast images of those actions, which are in turn received as input by all of the System 1 mechanisms for the formation of beliefs, desires, and emotions, leading to a changed cognitive and affective landscape which forms the context and partial cause for the next mental rehearsal. And because action-selection in general is under intentional control, so is System 2. In the second to fifth sections I shall explain the various components of the account, showing that they are independently motivated. I shall then, in the sixth section, describe the ways in which System 2 issues in new beliefs and intentions, before detailing the advantages of the account in the seventh section. In the eighth section I shall draw attention to a number of testable predictions, before outlining some implications for researchers in the field in the ninth.

The mental rehearsal of action

The uses of 'forward models' of action for fine-grained action control are now quite well understood (Wolpert and Flanagan 2001; Wolpert and Ghahramani 2000; Wolpert et al. 2003). At the same time as an activated motor schema issues motor commands to the muscles to initiate a movement, an 'efferent copy' of those commands is created and compared with the initial motor intention, thus allowing for swift self-correction before the movement itself has even begun. But the efferent copy is also transformed via one or more 'emulator systems' that model the kinematics of the body (Grush 2004) so as to match the incoming proprioceptive and other (e.g. visual) perceptual representations of the action as it is executed, again allowing for fast on-line correction. (This is thought to be one of the main functions of the dorsal–parietal visual system, represented in the lower half of Figure 5.1, and its equivalent in other sense modalities.)

Efferent copies are not confined to the dorsal-parietal system, however, yielding bare representations of bodily movement. They are also used to drive visual imagery within the ventral-temporal system (and its equivalent for other forms of perception). These images can then interact with the inferential systems that normally operate on the basis of ventral input, so as to generate predictions of the likely immediate consequences of the movement. This allows for a comparison between predicted effects and perceived effects as the action unfolds, again allowing for correction of the original motor schema. (And note that in general it is the effects of our movements that interest us, rather than those movements themselves.) For example, someone lifting a jug to pour coffee into a cup will need to predict where, precisely, to position the spout of the jug in relation to the cup; but if the coffee is observed to fall too close to the edge of the cup as it begins to pour, the position of the hand and arm can be adjusted accordingly.

There is now robust evidence of the contribution of motor and pre-motor cortex to the generation and transformation of conscious visual images located in temporal cortex (Ganis et al. 2000; Kosslyn et al. 2001; Lamm et al. 2001; Richter et al. 2000; Schubotz 2007; Turnbull et al. 1997). Although images are also frequently

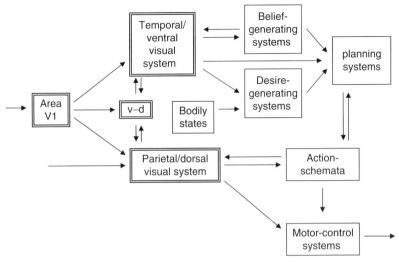

Fig. 5.2 Two visual systems with back-projecting pathways.

created in temporal cortex for purposes of object recognition (Kosslyn 1994), it is motor cortex that initiates the generation of images in the absence of any relevant visual stimulus, and which moves and transforms the images created. This happens via an area of ventro-dorsal cortex that is probably best thought of as a common functional component of the two primary visual systems. The area in question is the superior temporal sulcus and area FP in the rostral part of the inferior parietal lobule. These are strongly interconnected with each other, and also with area F5 in the pre-motor cortex (Rizzolatti 2005).[1] See Figure 5.2 (in which 'vd' stands for 'ventro-dorsal') for a depiction of this more complex version of the System 1 architecture.

The systems described above are probably quite ancient, and evolved initially for purposes both of controlling movement and anticipating its effects so that one can monitor and prepare to respond to those effects in turn. But these systems are also ideally suited to subserve the mental *rehearsal* of action, independently of any overt movement. When operated in this mode one activates an action schema 'off line', with the normal set of instructions to the muscles suppressed. The efferent copy of this activated schema is then used to drive representations of the action and its likely effects for purposes of decision making. By 'trying out' actions in imagination

---

[1] These areas form part of the so-called 'mirror neuron' system in humans and monkeys (Gallese et al. 1996; Rizzolatti et al. 2000). There are neurons within this system that fire *both* when the monkey perceives someone performing a quite specific movement (such as grasping a piece of food with the whole hand), *and* when the monkey executes just such a movement for itself. Much of the discussion of the function of these neurons has concerned their possible role in enabling us to understand the actions and goals of others (Gallese and Goldman 1998; Goldman 2006). But they are just as well positioned to enable us to map our own intended movements onto visual representations of movement.

we can test whether they are likely to achieve our goals, and by creatively activating and rehearsing actions from our repertoire we can sometimes hit upon novel solutions to problems. There is some evidence of the use of mental rehearsal when problem solving by other apes (especially chimpanzees; see Carruthers 2006, ch.2). And there is robust evidence of mental rehearsal of action amongst members of *Homo ergaster* from over a million years ago, which enabled them to create stone tools of fine symmetry. For the only known way of producing such tools, out of materials that always vary in detail from case to case, involves mentally rehearsing the likely effects of a given strike on the core, thus enabling the stone knapper to plan several blows ahead (Mithen 1996; Wynn 2000; Carruthers 2006, ch.2).

The global broadcast of rehearsed actions

What becomes of the representations in ventral-temporal cortex that result from the mental rehearsal of an action? Under certain conditions (e.g. when attended to) those representations are 'globally broadcast' to a wide range of consumer systems for forming new beliefs and memories, for creating new desires and emotions, and for practical reasoning (see Figure 5.2). Initially proposed by Baars (1988), there is now robust and varied evidence of the global broadcasting of the outputs of the ventral-temporal visual system and of the coincidence of such broadcasts with conscious experience (Baars 2002, 2003; Baars et al. 2003; Dehaene and Naccache 2001; Dehaene et al. 2001, 2003, 2006; Kreiman et al. 2003).

It is worth stressing that global broadcasting theory is consistent with a variety of different accounts of the nature of consciousness itself. First-order theorists of consciousness like Dretske (1995) and Tye (1995, 2000), for example, can claim that perceptual and imagistic contents become conscious *in virtue of* being globally broadcast. For such theorists maintain that consciousness consists in the immediate availability of such contents to first-order processes of belief-formation and decision making. (These processes are described as 'first order' because the resulting beliefs and decisions are about the worldly events represented in perception, rather than about those perceptual states themselves.) Higher-order theorists of consciousness like Lycan (1987, 1996), Carruthers (2000, 2005), and Rosenthal (2005), in contrast, will maintain that only a single aspect of global broadcasting is really relevant to the conscious status of the percepts and images in question, which is their availability (via global broadcast) to the mind-reading system. For such theorists maintain that conscious perceptions are those that we are aware of having at the time, in a higher-order way.

It is also worth emphasizing that it is only the perceptual *contents* that get globally broadcast that are conscious. The cognitive processes that underlie and sustain those broadcasts certainly aren't. And many of the processes that issue in a content being globally broadcast aren't conscious either, whether these are 'bottom-up' (such as the mechanism that identifies one's name in an unattended conversation at a cocktail party, causing it to pop into awareness) or rather involve top-down forms of attention. The only exception would be that *sometimes* a decision to direct attention at a stimulus or type of stimulus can be conscious (as when I remind myself when doing a jigsaw puzzle, 'I must pay attention to the shape'). But the intervening processes that begin from a conscious thought of this sort and issue in a globally broadcast perception or image won't themselves be conscious ones.

It is likely that the mechanisms underlying the global broadcast of attended perceptual events are evolutionarily ancient. Indeed, they provide a core aspect of the System 1 cognitive architecture. (see Figure 5.1). Global broadcast enables perceptual contents to be made available as input simultaneously to the full range of System 1 systems. Some of these have been designed to draw inferences from the input, generating new beliefs. Others have been designed to create new desires and emotions. (Think how seeing a piece of chocolate, even when one is replete, can give rise to a desire to eat chocolate; and think how the sight of a snake rippling through the grass can give rise to a shiver of fear.) And yet others are charged with the creation of new plans for achieving one's goals in relation to the perceived environment. ('I'll go around *that* way and pick up *that* one.')

When the globally broadcast representations are, not percepts of external events, but rather images resulting from the mental rehearsal of an action, the System 1 systems process those representations as normal (at least initially). Mentally rehearsed actions, too, generate inferences and emotional reactions. But it is important that those inferences should *not* issue in beliefs as they usually would. When the *sight* of a hand pushing a vase gives rise to the prediction that the vase will fall, it is appropriate for the subject to believe (in advance of it doing so) that the vase will fall. (This belief might then lead the subject to leap to catch the vase to prevent it breaking.) But when the *image* of a hand pushing the vase is generated through mental rehearsal of a pushing action-schema directed at the vase, and the same prediction results, the subject should *not* believe that the vase will, actually, fall. For the vase will only fall if it is actually pushed. What should be believed, rather, is a conditional: it will fall if pushed like that. This might lead subjects to go ahead and execute the pushing schema, or to abandon it and begin a search for some alternative means of moving the vase, depending on their purposes.

Notice that mental rehearsal of an action is the functional equivalent of *supposing* that the act is performed. Inferences drawn from the rehearsal must therefore be tagged, somehow, as dependent upon a self-produced mental rehearsal, in such a way that the conclusions reached aren't believed outright. Although small, this was by no means a trivial alteration in the mode of operation of the set of System 1 systems. For the result was the creation of what Nichols and Stich (2003) call a 'possible worlds box'—a workspace where possibilities can be tested and explored in advance of action.

Soma-sensory monitoring of the effects of mental rehearsal

While the images resulting from mentally rehearsed actions don't give rise to real beliefs when they are received as input by the System 1 belief-generating systems (except perhaps conditional beliefs), they do appear to give rise to real emotions and motivations. As is familiar, imagined sex acts can make you sexually aroused, by imagining yourself eating a piece of chocolate cake you can make yourself hungry, and so forth. So the impact of imagery on System 1 motivational systems appears somewhat different from its impact on belief systems. But even here, something a bit

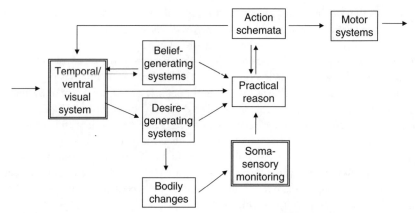

Fig. 5.3 Mental rehearsal and soma-sensory monitoring.

like tagging of conclusions to display their dependence on a supposition would appear to be involved, since the functional roles of the emotions caused via mental rehearsal are distinctively different from normal.

According to Damasio (1994, 2003) our emotional responses to mentally rehearsed actions and their predicted consequences give rise to a variety of physiological changes, such as altered heart rate, respiratory rate, and so on.[2] (See also Rolls 1999. For a related but distinct account, see Schroeder 2004.) These somatic changes are in turn perceived, and are used to ratchet up, or down, the desirability of the rehearsed action. If the overall somatic effects of the rehearsal of the action are positively valenced then a desire to perform that action will generally result (unless the rehearsal in question is a mere fantasy, unrelated to any current project or possibility); whereas if the overall effects are negatively valenced, then we are motivated *not* to perform the action (see Figure 5.3).

Consider a particular example. Looking at my monthly credit card statement, I realize that I need more money. After reviewing some options, I hit upon the idea of going to ask my boss for a raise. I mentally rehearse the action of walking into his office and broaching the question of salary. The resulting images are globally broadcast, and are elaborated by System 1 inferential systems to include my boss' likely response (the glowering face, the harsh words). The result is that I feel fear and disappointment. And that leads me to abandon any thought of asking for a raise, and returns me to considering other options.

We spend much of our waking lives, as adults, in mental rehearsals of this sort, often to good effect. (And yet sometimes *not* to good effect—see Gilbert 2005, for discussion of the ways in which our imaginings can lead us astray in our reasoning about the future.) Initially promising plans can turn out to be disastrous when rehearsed; and plans whose success at first seems implausible can turn out to be much more likely to succeed. Moreover, when the frontal-lobe systems concerned with soma-sensory monitoring are

---

[2] Damasio (1994) also argues that these systems can operate in swifter 'as if' mode, during which physiological changes are predicted and responded to without actually needing to occur.

damaged, our capacities for medium and long-term planning are severely interfered with (Damasio 1994). The patients in question can *reason*, theoretically, about practical matters in perfectly sensible ways, but their decision making in light of that reasoning is very poor. In consequence their practical lives are often in a terrible mess.

Inner speech

As we noted above, a distinction somewhat similar to that between the ventral-temporal and dorsal–parietal visual systems has been confirmed for other sense modalities (Michel and Peronnet 1980; Paillard et al. 1983; Rossetti et al. 1995). And we also know that mental rehearsal of actions can give rise to conscious imagery of other sorts besides vision. More specifically, rehearsal of speech actions gives rise to imagery, resulting in so-called 'inner speech'. (Most often these images are auditory, representing the sounds that would result if those speech actions were executed. But they can also be articulatory or—in the case of deaf signers—visual.) And here, too, one function (and perhaps the original function) of the systems underlying inner speech is fast on-line repair of action itself (Levelt 1989).

It is commonly accepted that the language faculty contains distinct production and comprehension sub-systems, each of which can draw on a common database of linguistic knowledge (Chomsky 1995). In that case the systems underlying the phenomenon of inner speech can be seen depicted in Figure 5.4. (It should be noted that there is evidence that both the language production and the language comprehension areas of the cortex are active during inner speech. See Paulescu et al. 1993; Shergill et al. 2002.) Here is how it works. In light of the subject's beliefs and goals, a speech action-schema is formulated by the language production sub-system. While overt action is suppressed, an efference copy of the motor instructions is transformed via an emulator system into an auditory representation of the sounds that would have resulted had the action been carried out. This representation is globally broadcast in the manner of conscious images generally, and is received, *inter alia,* by the language comprehension sub-system. The latter constructs an interpretation of the utterance in the normal way, and presents that (attached to the sounds) to the various other System 1 inferential systems. Hence, just as is the case with external speech, we seem to hear the meaning of the imagined sounds of inner speech (the message expressed) as well as hearing those imagined sounds themselves.

Hurlburt (1990, 1993) has demonstrated the near ubiquity of inner speech in the waking lives of normal people. Subjects in his studies wore headphones during the course of the day, through which they heard, at various intervals, a randomly generated series of bleeps. When they heard a bleep, they were instructed to immediately 'freeze' what was passing through their consciousness at that exact moment and then make a note of it, before elaborating on it later in a follow-up interview. Although frequency varied widely, all normal (as opposed to schizophrenic) subjects reported experiencing inner speech on some occasions—with the minimum being 7% of occasions sampled, and the maximum being 80%. Most subjects reported inner speech on more than half of the occasions sampled. (The majority of subjects also reported the occurrence of visual images and emotional feelings—on between 0% and 50% of

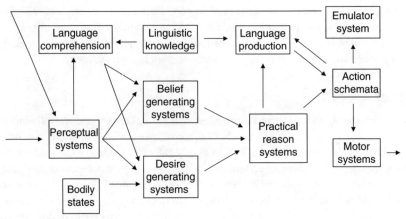

Fig. 5.4 The metnal rehearsal of speech.

occasions sampled in each case.) This is an extremely high proportion of time to devote to mental rehearsal of a single type of activity.

Mental rehearsals of speech, like mental rehearsals of action generally, are often undertaken to test whether or not the utterance should actually be made, overtly. We often 'try out' utterances in imagination in advance of making them, allowing our various System 1 inferential systems to evaluate the likely effects on our audience, while reacting emotionally to those effects. But this is by no means the most common way for inner speech to be utilized. More often we are interested in the content of imagined utterances, rather than in (the effects of) those utterances themselves. And we take those imagined utterances to express, or to be constitutive of, our thought processes. This is a large part of the foundation on which System 2 thinking and reasoning is built.

Putting it all together

One set of advantages of this account of System 2 should be readily apparent. For there is no need to postulate a distinct belief/desire/decision-making system alongside of System 1. Rather, System 2 is *realized in* cycles of operation of System 1. We have independent reasons to believe in the existence of many of the component mechanisms and processes utilized in such cycles, and it is likely that they evolved initially for other purposes. The basic capacity for mental rehearsal of action when problem solving is probably shared with other great apes. And when a language faculty, a more sophisticated mind-reading faculty, and some kind of system for normative reasoning and motivation were added to the System 1 architecture alongside its other components, it would have taken but small changes for the full range of System 2 processes to come into existence.

We do need to explain, however, how System 2 beliefs, goals, and decisions emerge out of the cyclical operations of System 1. The easy case is the mental rehearsal of action (whether bodily action or speech action) which eventuates in an evaluation of the consequences of that action. In such a case a schema for the action in question is activated and rehearsed, giving rise to a globally-broadcast imagistic representation of the act. This is received as input by the System 1 inferential and motivational modules, some of which may elaborate it to include some likely consequences. Our bodily/emotional reactions to the envisaged act and its consequences are monitored, with the desirability of the action being adjusted up or down. Such a newly created desire to perform the action may then be sufficient in the circumstances to issue in an intention to perform it (either immediately or when the envisaged circumstances arise), utilizing our regular System 1 decision-making procedures.

More challenging, however, is to explain how mentally rehearsed speech acts can give rise to new beliefs in the propositions expressed by those acts, or to novel intentions to act as described. For here it isn't the consequences of *performing* the speech acts in question that need to be evaluated, but rather the *contents* of those acts. I shall defend a pluralist position. It seems to me that there are a variety of ways in which inner speech can issue in new beliefs, goals, and intentions. I shall begin, however, with the proposal made by Frankish (2004, this volume).

On Frankish's account the mind reading system has a crucial role to play. If it interprets a given utterance in inner speech, in the circumstances, as a *commitment*, or a 'making up of mind', then the functional equivalent of a new belief, desire, or intention will be the result (depending on the sort of commitment that gets attributed), provided that there exists a standing System 1 desire to execute one's commitments. Suppose, first, that an utterance is interpreted as a commitment to the truth of the proposition that it expresses. The subject therefore forms a System 1 belief that a commitment of that kind has been made. This will then in future interact with the System 1 desire to honor commitments, issuing in further overt or covert verbalizations. If asked whether he believes the proposition in question, for example, the subject will reply that he does. For one of the things one ought to be prepared to do, if one has committed oneself to the truth of a proposition, is assert it. And likewise, during one's System 2 practical or theoretical reasoning one will be prepared to rely upon the sentence in question as a premise. For if one has committed oneself to the truth of a proposition then one ought also to commit oneself to any other proposition that one believes follows from it. And so on.

Frankish provides a similar account of the formation of System 2 goals and intentions. Let me here just work through the case of intention. Suppose that a sequence of System 2 reasoning concludes with an inner verbalization of a sentence of the form, 'So, I shall do *P*.' This is globally broadcast and received as input by the mind-reading system *inter alia*. The latter interprets it as expressing a *commitment* to do *P*, and stores a record of this commitment in memory. Later, when the time to act arrives, this memory is activated, and it combines with the subject's standing (System 1) desire to execute his commitments in such a way as to issue in a (System 1) decision to do *P*. Notice that on this account, although the initial verbalization wasn't, itself, the formation of an intention, by being interpreted as committing the subject to act in a certain way it becomes the System 2 functional equivalent of an intention to act.

I have no doubt that System 2 belief formation and intention formation sometimes work in these ways. Sometimes, for example, I might quite naturally report what took place by saying, 'I realized that I had been thinking long enough, and that I had better commit myself to believing/doing *something*, so I made up my mind to believing/doing *P*.' But there is a problem about claiming that System 2 attitude formation is *always* a matter of commitment. For on other occasions I might report what took place by saying, 'After thinking about the matter for a while, I realized that *P*' or by saying, 'After thinking about it for a while, I realized that I should do *P*.' Here there is no mention of commitment, or anything resembling commitment.

Frankish (2004, this volume) can (and does) respond that the beliefs about commitment that realize System 2 believing and intending are often unconscious ones, and so aren't reportable in speech. But this is problematic. For although System 1 *processes* aren't conscious, the beliefs and intentions in which those processes issue generally are. (While there are multiple memory systems within System 1, in general many of the beliefs that I express in speech are formed via the operations of System 1.) In particular, when my mind-reading system (operating unconsciously for the most part, at the System 1 level) issues in a belief about the beliefs or intentions of other people, I can generally express that belief in speech. So why should it be so different when the belief produced by the mind-reading system is a belief about my own commitments? Why should the latter beliefs so often be 'screened off' from consciousness and verbal report?

In (some of) the cases where Frankish's commitment-based account fails to apply, it might be better to see System 2 as driven by beliefs about one's own beliefs or intentions, together with a desire for *consistency*. When I say to myself at the conclusion of a period of System 2 reasoning, 'So, P is the case', I will interpret myself as having formed the belief that *P*. (And I might quite naturally express that second-order belief in speech by saying that at that moment I realized/formed the belief that *P*.) Hence, I shall thereafter believe that I believe that *P*. In my later reasoning and planning, this higher-order belief may become activated. But I also have the normative belief that, if I believe *P*, I should think and act in ways that are appropriate in the circumstances. Wanting to think and act as I should, or wanting my thinking and acting to be consistent with what I believe myself to believe, I am motivated to think and act just as if I believed that *P*. This account has the advantage of not requiring me to have any beliefs or goals that I couldn't articulate, or that I would be unwilling to attribute to myself.

System 2 thinking might also issue in beliefs and intentions more directly and simply, however. (See Carruthers 2006, ch.6, for elaboration of the idea sketched here.) Entertaining in inner speech the sentence, 'P', the content of that utterance is extracted and evaluated much as if it were the testimony of another person. It is checked for consistency and coherence with existing beliefs, for example. If it meets the appropriate standards, and there are no reasons *not* to believe *P*, the content that *P* is accepted and stored in whatever manner is usual for a belief of that type.

Advantages of the account

In addition to removing any need to regard System 1 and System 2 as distinct, existing alongside one another, a further advantage of the account presented in this chapter is that it explains why System 2 processes should be comparatively slow and serial, and why (some of) its operations should be conscious. Since System 2 is realized in *cycles* of operation of System 1 it will be slow by comparison. And since only one action can be mentally rehearsed and globally broadcast at a time, System 2 will be serial in its operation (but utilizing the parallel-process functioning of System 1). And since the images that result from mental rehearsal of each action in the cycle are globally broadcast, and we know that such broadcasts correlate closely with consciousness, we can explain why each such stage in each cycle should be conscious. (The other stages, by contrast, will be *un*conscious, including the processes that select a given action-schema for rehearsal, and those that draw inferences from, or generate emotional reactions to, the broadcast image.)

In addition, this account can explain some of the individual variation that exists in people's capacity to solve System 2 tasks, specifically the variation that correlates with 'cognitive style' (Stanovich 1999; see also Stanovich, Evans, Buchtel, and Norenzayan, this volume). For this can result from individual differences in the likelihood of utilizing System 2 at all, or of activating it when problem solving. A disposition to be reflective, for example, which correlates with success in System 2 tasks, will consist in a capacity to suppress one's initial response generated by System 1, mentally rehearsing it and other alternatives that come to mind, hence allowing the knowledge that is stored across the various System 1 systems to influence the eventual outcome.

Moreover, since on this account System 2 is action-based, it predicts that System 2 processes should be malleable and subject to learning in any of the ways that action itself is. We acquire behavioral skills and abilities by imitation of others, by receiving verbal instruction, and by forming normative beliefs about the ways in which one should behave. So we can predict that System 2 thinking skills should be acquirable by imitation and by instruction, and that sequences of System 2 reasoning should be shaped by beliefs about the ways in which one *should* reason. Each of these predictions is borne out, I believe.

In support of the first of these predictions (that System 2 skills should be acquirable by imitation) one can cite the common belief—held by many teachers—that one way of teaching intellectual skills is by *exhibiting* them. Many university professors (especially in philosophy) hope that by *thinking through* a problem in the presence of the students, some of the ways in which one should think will thereby be imitated and acquired. Likewise, this is a plausible construal of what happens in scientific lab meetings. It is by talking through problems and potential solutions in the presence of undergraduate and graduate students that the more senior researchers impart many of the intellectual skills necessary for science. And this is consistent with the widely recognized fact that much of what younger scientists have to acquire is *know how* of various sorts, in addition to specific facts and theories.

Another skill acquisition mechanism is explicit instruction. People can *tell* me what actions and sequences of action to perform in the service of a given goal. Thus a logic teacher might tell me what steps to take in order to evaluate the truth of a conditional, just as an experienced kayak maker might tell a novice how to prepare and shape the materials for use in the frame. And in both cases the beliefs thus acquired can be recalled at the point of need, and used to guide novel instances of the activity in question (evaluating a conditional, building a kayak).

People also learn normative facts, and come to believe that there are certain things that they *should* or *should not* do. And in many cultures these normative beliefs concern the processes of (System 2) reasoning itself. Since it is a general fact about normative beliefs that they are apt to give rise to an intrinsic motivation to perform (or refrain from) the action required (or forbidden; Sripada and Stich 2006), this will mean that people will be intrinsically motivated to rehearse sequences of action that will constitute certain abstract patterns of System 2 thinking.

Consistent with this prediction, people do seem to be intrinsically motivated to entertain or to avoid certain types of thought or sequence of thought. Thus if someone finds himself thinking that *P* while thinking that $P \supset Q$, then he will feel *compelled*, in consequence, to think that *Q*. And if someone finds herself thinking that *P* while also thinking that ~*P*, then she will feel herself *obligated* to eliminate one or other of those two thoughts. The explanation is that the system for normative reasoning and belief has acquired a rule requiring sequences of thought/action that take the form of *modus ponens*, as well as a rule requiring the avoidance of contraction, and is generating intrinsic motivations accordingly.

As should be clear from the above, the present account also predicts that there should be wide variations in the patterning of System 2 reasoning across cultures, just as there is variation in both skilled behavior and normative belief and behavior. For of course cultures will vary in their beliefs about which sequences of System 2 reasoning are likely to be successful; and they will differ in their beliefs about what sequences are normatively required or forbidden. A significant part of what has changed in the history of science, for example, consists in culturally shared beliefs about the ways in which one *should* reason scientifically, and the ways in which one *should* evaluate hypotheses. Just think, for instance, of the impact that statistical methods have increasingly had in the social sciences over the last century.

Finally, it should also be stressed that the present account is fully consistent with the fact that 'think aloud' protocols are reliable indicators of the ways in which subjects actually solve System 2 tasks, as demonstrated by task analysis combined with timing and error patterns (Ericsson and Simon 1993). As Ericsson and Simon emphasize, it is crucial that experimenters should *not* ask subjects to report *on* their thoughts while working on the problem. For this meta-reflection will (and demonstrably does) interfere with the conduct of the first-order reasoning in question. Rather, they should be asked to 'think their thoughts aloud', articulating in an unreflective way the reasoning that they go through. This should be predicted not to interfere with the task if, but only if, that task is normally conducted in inner speech. For otherwise the cognitive resources necessary to formulate into speech the underlying reasoning should have an effect on task performance.

Some predictions

What is distinctive of the theory of System 2 reasoning presented here is that it is *action-based*. According to this account, it is mentally rehearsed actions that initiate and sustain System 2 reasoning, thereby recruiting and utilizing the mechanisms that also subserve System 1 reasoning, as well as activating normative beliefs about proper reasoning, together with the stored schemata for skilled action sequences, and so forth. This leads to a number of clear predictions.

The first prediction is that patients with Huntington's disease, which attacks especially motor and pre-motor cortex, should be much weaker at System 2 than System 1 tasks in comparison with other brain-damaged populations. Forms of brain damage that interfere with System 1 mechanisms will tend also to interfere with System 2 processes, on the account provided here. For example, damage to the 'association areas' of temporal cortex that underlie many forms of intuitive inference will also interfere with System 2 tasks that recruit those inferences. Moreover, damage to the areas of the frontal lobes concerned with 'executive function' will also interfere with

System 2 tasks that recruit those same decision making mechanisms. (All System 2 tasks will implicate System 1 decision making, of course, since these are the mechanisms that select amongst available action schemata for activation and rehearsal.)

Damage to motor and pre-motor cortex, in contrast, should leave System 1 reasoning mechanisms intact. Patients should still be capable of forming swift and intuitive inferences in the light of perceptual data, they should still display swift emotional reactions in response to that data, and they should still be capable of making swift and unreflective decisions. But because they will have difficulty activating and rehearsing action schemata, they should have problems with System 2 tasks, which crucially involve such rehearsals, if the account that I have provided is correct.

Essentially the same prediction could also be tested more directly by temporarily 'freezing' motor and pre-motor cortex by trans-cranial magnetic stimulation (provided that subjects can be given some means for indicating their responses, of course). What we should find is that performance on System 2 tasks should suffer dramatic collapse, while System 1 tasks should be left relatively untouched. In contrast, 'freezing' areas of cortex implicated in System 1 should have an effect on both systems equally; and 'freezing' of other areas (e.g. primary visual cortex) should have no effects on either system.

We can also predict that subjects who are required to 'shadow' speech while conducting many forms of System 2 task (even 'nonsense speech' that doesn't require comprehension) should perform much more poorly than subjects who are required to 'shadow' a complex rhythm that places equivalent demands on working memory. (See Hermer-Vazquez et al. 1999, for an example of this paradigm used for another purpose.) For speech shadowing will tie up the resources of the language production sub-system, thus making it difficult for subjects to engage in inner speech, whereas rhythm shadowing, while utilizing the resources of motor cortex broadly construed, should have no effect on speech production.

Implications for System 1/System 2 research

Many researchers in the field think that it is distinctive of System 1 processes that they should be triggered automatically by perceptual cues (in 'bottom-up' fashion), and that they should operate outside of intentional control. DeSteno et al. (2002), for example, argue that jealousy isn't a System 1 system on the grounds that it is sensitive to cognitive load manipulation. Their view is that System 1 systems, because automatic and non-intentional, should continue to operate in ways that are unaffected by whatever may be occurring elsewhere in the cognitive system. (See Barrett et al. (2006) for an extended critique of DeSteno et al.'s methodology from an evolutionary psychology perspective.)

The account defended in this chapter shows quite clearly what is wrong with this way of thinking of the relationship between System 1 and System 2, however. If System 1 systems are organized around the global broadcast of perceptual output (as depicted in Figure 5.1), then whether any given System 1 system gets 'turned on' in a given context will depend crucially on what the agent is attending to. For we know that top–down attention is one of the main determinants of whether or not a given perceptual content becomes globally broadcast (Dehaene et al. 2006). So to the extent that the agent's attentional resources are occupied elsewhere, to that extent we should expect that the processing of stimuli giving rise to jealousy—and hence the emotion of jealousy itself—will be negatively affected.

Moreover, on the account presented here, System 1 systems can get turned on by imagistic representations as well as by external cues. And since the former are characteristically under our intentional control, System 1 processing of this sort will likewise be under intentional control. By actively generating and maintaining images that give rise to the emotion of jealousy, the causing and sustaining of such feelings can be under the agent's intentional control, even if (as I believe) the system that issues in jealousy belongs to System 1. Once again, therefore, we should predict that feelings of jealousy will be highly sensitive to cognitive load manipulations of various sorts. For to the extent that agents are occupied with other cognitive tasks, to that extent they will be unlikely to maintain the imagery necessary (in the absence of attention-grabbing external cues) for a strong emotional response.

One general point that this brings out, I think, is that some care needs to be taken in how we characterize System 2 tasks. In particular, we shouldn't classify as 'System 2' all tasks whose solution requires processing that is under the intentional control of the agent. For although this will, indeed, implicate System 2 (because involving the mental rehearsal of action), it shouldn't be counted as a System 2 *task* if System 1 processing, activated from the task instructions via mental rehearsal and global broadcast, is sufficient for a solution. Rather, System 2 tasks should either require the recall and rehearsal of some appropriate culturally-acquired item of information (e.g. a normative belief), or they should require the controlled activation of sequences of mental rehearsal in accordance with learned rules, or they should implicate practices of self-interrogation (e.g. asking oneself, 'What should I do next?'). Merely being prompted to imagine one's spouse being unfaithful, for example, and creating and sustaining the appropriate images, shouldn't count.

Conclusion

I suspect many people have been puzzled about how there could be two distinct systems in the human mind–brain for reasoning and decision making, each of which must replicate the functionality of the other to a significant degree. In this chapter I have aimed to remove that puzzlement, thereby providing a defense of one sort of dual-system theory. I have shown that there are good reasons for thinking that System 2 is realized in cycles of operation of System 1, utilizing mechanisms and processes that we have independent reason to believe in. The resulting account of System 2 is action-based, since it is activations and mental rehearsals of action schemata that initiate and sustain its operations.[3]

....

[3] Previous versions of this paper were presented at the *In Two Minds* conference held in Cambridge in July 2006, at the *Inter-University Workshop on Philosophy and Cognitive Science* held in Palma de Mallorca in May 2007, and at the Max Planck Center for Adaptive Behavior and Cognition (Berlin) in July 2007. I am grateful to all those who gave me feedback on those occasions (with special thanks to Gerd Gigerenzer), and also to Jonathan Evans and Keith Frankish for their written comments on an earlier draft.

References

Baars, B. (1988) *A cognitive theory of consciousness*. Cambridge University Press, Cambridge.

Baars, B. (2002) The conscious access hypothesis: origins and recent evidence. *Trends in Cognitive Science*, **6**, 47–52.

Baars, B. (2003) How brain reveals mind: neuroimaging supports the central role of conscious experience. *Journal of Consciousness Studies*, **10**, 100–14.

Baars, B., Ramsoy, T., and Laureys, S. (2003) Brain, consciousness, and the observing self. *Trends in Neurosciences*, **26**, 671–5.

Barrett, H., Frederick, D., Haselton, M., and Kurzban, R. (2006) Can manipulations of cognitive load be used to test evolutionary hypotheses? *Journal of Personality and Social Psychology*, **91**, 513–18.

Carruthers, P. (2000) *Phenomenal consciousness: A naturalistic theory*. Cambridge University Press, Cambridge.

Carruthers, P. (2005) *Consciousness: Essays from a higher-order perspective*. Oxford University Press, Oxford.

Carruthers, P. (2006) *The architecture of the mind: Massive modularity and the flexibility of thought*. Oxford University Press, Oxford.

Chomsky, N. (1995) *The minimalist program*. MIT Press, Cambridge, MA.

Damasio, A. (1994) *Descartes' error: Emotion, reason and the human brain*. Papermac, London.

Damasio, A. (2003) *Looking for Spinoza: Joy, sorrow, and the feeling brain*. Harcourt, New York.

Dehaene, S. and Naccache, L. (2001) Towards a cognitive neuroscience of consciousness: Basic evidence and a workspace framework. *Cognition*, **79**, 1–37.

Dehaene, S., Sergent, C., and Changeux, J. (2003) A neuronal network model linking subjective reports and objective physiological data during conscious perception. *Proceedings of the National Academy of Science*, **100**, 8520–5.

Dehaene, S., Changeux, J-P., Naccache, L., Sackur, J., and Sergent, C., (2006) Conscious, preconscious, and subliminal processing: A testable taxonomy. *Trends in Cognitive Sciences*, **10**, 204–11.

Dehaene, S., Naccache, L., Cohen, L., Bihan, D., Mangin, J., Poline, J., and Riviere, D. (2001) Cerebral mechanisms of word priming and unconscious repetition masking. *Nature Neuroscience*, **4**, 752–8.

DeSteno, D., Bartlett, M., Braverman, J., and Salovey, P. (2002) Sex differences in jealousy: Evolutionary mechanisms or artifact of measurement? *Journal of Personality and Social Psychology*, **83**, 1103–16.

Dretske, F. (1995) *Naturalizing the mind*. MIT Press, Cambridge, MA.

Ericsson, A. and Simon, H. (1993) *Protocol analysis: Verbal reports as data*, revised ed. MIT Press, Cambridge, MA.

Evans, J.St.B.T. and Over, D.E. (1996) *Rationality and reasoning*. Psychology Press, Hove.

Frankish, K. (2004) *Mind and supermind*. Cambridge University Press, Cambridge.

Gallese, V. and Goldman, A. (1998) Mirror neurons and the simulation theory of mind-reading. *Trends in Cognitive Sciences*, **12**, 493–501.

Gallese, V., Fadiga, L., Fogassi, L., and Rizzolatti, G. (1996) Action recognition in the pre-motor cortex. *Brain*, **119**, 593–609.

Ganis, G., Keenan, J., Kosslyn, S., and Pascual-Leone, A. (2000) Transcranian magnetic stimulation of primary motor cortex affects mental rotation. *Cerebral Cortex*, **10**, 175–80.

Gilbert, D. (2005) *Stumbling on happiness*. Vintage Books, New York.

Goldman, A. (2006) *Simulating minds: The philosophy, psychology, and neuroscience of mind-reading*. Oxford University Press, Oxford.

Grush, R. (2004) The emulation theory of representation: Motor control, imagery, and perception. *Behavioral and Brain Sciences*, **27**, 377–442.

Hermer-Vazquez, L., Spelke, E., and Katsnelson, A. (1999) Sources of flexibility in human cognition: Dual-task studies of space and language. *Cognitive Psychology*, **39**, 3–36.

Hurlburt, R. (1990) *Sampling normal and schizophrenic inner experience*. Plenum Press, New York.

Hurlburt, R. (1993) *Sampling inner experience with disturbed affect*. Plenum Press, New York.

Kahneman, D. (2002) Maps of bounded rationality: A perspective on intuitive judgment and choice. Nobel laureate acceptance speech. Available at: http://nobelprize.org/economics/laureates/2002/kahneman-lecture.html.

Kosslyn, S. (1994) *Image and brain*. MIT Press, Cambridge, MA.

Kosslyn, S., Thompson, W., Wraga, M., and Alpert, N. (2001) Imagining rotation by endogenous versus exogenous forces: distinct neural mechanisms. *NeuroReport*, **12**, 2519–25.

Kreiman, G., Fried, I., and Koch, C. (2003) Single neuron correlates of subjective vision in the human medial temporal lobe. *Proceedings of the National Academy of Science*, **99**, 8378–83.

Lamm, C., Windtschberger, C., Leodolter, U., Moser, E., and Bauer, H. (2001) Evidence for premotor cortex activity during dynamic visuospatial imagery from single trial functional magnetic resonance imaging and event-related slow cortical potentials. *Neuroimage*, **14**, 268–83.

Levelt, W. (1989) *Speaking: From intention to articulation*. MIT Press, Cambridge, MA.

Lycan, W. (1987) *Consciousness*. MIT Press, Cambridge, MA.

Lycan, W. (1996) *Consciousness and experience*. MIT Press, Cambridge, MA.

Michel, F. and Peronnet, F. (1980) A case of cortical deafness: clinical and electro-physiological data. *Brain and Language*, **10**, 367–77.

Milner, D. and Goodale, M. (1995) *The visual brain in action*. Oxford University Press, Oxford.

Mithen, S. (1996) *The pre-history of the mind*. Thames and Hudson, London.

Nichols, S. and Stich, S. (2003) *Mindreading: An integrated account of pretence, self-awareness, and understanding other minds*. Oxford University Press, Oxford.

Paillard, J., Michel, F., and Stelmach, G. (1983) Localization without content: A tactile analogue of 'blind-sight'. *Archives of Neurology*, **40**, 548–51.

Paulescu, E., Frith, D., and Frackowiak, R. (1993) The neural correlates of the verbal component of working memory. *Nature*, **362**, 342–5.

Richter, W., Somorjat, R., Summers, R., Jarnasz, N., Menon, R., Gati, J., Georgopoulos, A., Tegeler, C., Ugerbil, K., and Kim, S. (2000) Motor area activity during mental rotation studied by time-resolved single-trial fMRI. *Journal of Cognitive Neuroscience*, **12**, 310–20.

Rizzolatti, G. (2005) The mirror neuron system and imitation. In S. Hurley and N. Chater (eds) *Perspectives on imitation: From neuroscience to social science*, Volume 1, MIT Press, Cambridge, MA.

Rizzolatti, G., Fogassi, L., and Gallese, V. (2000) Cortical mechanisms subserving object grasping and action recognition: A new view on the cortical motor functions. In M. Gazzaniga (ed.) *The new cognitive neurosciences*, 2nd ed. MIT Press, Cambridge, MA.

Rolls, E. (1999) *The brain and emotion*. Oxford University Press, Oxford.

Rosenthal, D. (2005) *Consciousness and mind*. Oxford University Press, Oxford.

Rossetti, Y., Rode, G., and Boissson, D. (1995) Implicit processing of somaesthetic information. *Neurological Reports*, **6**, 506–10.

Schroeder, T. (2004) *Three faces of desire*. Oxford University Press, Oxford.

Schubotz, R. (2007) Prediction of external events with our motor system: Towards a new framework. *Trends in Cognitive Sciences*, **11**, 211–18.

Shergill, S., Brammer, M., Fukuda, R., Bullmore, E., Amaro, E., Murray, R., and McGuire, P. (2002) Modulation of activity in temporal cortex during generation of inner speech. *Human Brain Mapping*, **16**, 219–27.

Sloman, S. (1996) The empirical case for two systems of reasoning. *Psychological Bulletin*, **119**, 3–22.

Sloman, S. (2002) Two systems of reasoning. In T. Gilovich, D. Griffin, and D. Kahneman (eds) *Heuristics and biases: The psychology of intuitive judgment*. Cambridge University Press, Cambridge.

Sripada, C. and Stich, S. (2006) A framework for the psychology of norms. In P. Carruthers, S. Laurence and S. Stich (eds) *The innate mind: Culture and cognition*. Oxford University Press, Oxford.

Stanovich, K. (1999) *Who is rational? Studies of individual differences in reasoning*. Lawrence Erlbaum Associates, Mahwah, NJ.

Turnbull, O., Carey, D., and McCarthy, R. (1997) The neuropsychology of object constancy. *Journal of the International Neuropsychology Society*, **3**, 288–98.

Tye, M. (1995) *Ten problems of consciousness*. MIT Press, Cambridge, MA.

Tye, M. (2000) *Consciousness, color, and content*. MIT Press, Cambridge, MA.

Wolpert, D. and Flanagan, R. (2001) Motor prediction. *Current Biology*, **11**, 729–32.

Wolpert, D. and Ghahramani, Z. (2000) Computational principles of movement neuroscience. *Nature Neuroscience*, **3**, 1212–17.

Wolpert, D., Doya, K., and Kawato, M. (2003) A unifying computational framework for motor control and social interaction. *Philosophical Transactions of the Royal Society of London*, **B358**, 593–602.

Wynn, T. (2000) Symmetry and the evolution of the modular linguistic mind. In P. Carruthers and A. Chamberlain (eds) *The Evolution of the human mind*. Cambridge University Press, Cambridge.

Chapter 6

The magical number two, plus or minus: Dual-process theory as a theory of cognitive kinds

Richard Samuels

A central explanatory objective of much cognitive science is to provide an account of our *mental architecture*: to characterize the various systems and structures from which the human mind is composed. In this regard dual-process theories are unremarkable. For they too are in the business of providing (at least partial) answers to questions about what cognitive systems there are, and what properties they possess. Indeed dual-process theorizing has proven extraordinarily fruitful, and resulted in the development of a broad array of hypotheses about the systems responsible for such apparently disparate phenomena as learning (Reber 1993), deductive reasoning (Evans 2002), probabilistic judgment (Barbey and Sloman 2007), decision making (Kahneman and Frederick 2002) and social cognition (Chaiken and Trope 1999; Lieberman 2003).

Whilst these hypotheses are strikingly similar, they also differ in crucial respects. Not only do they concern different domains of cognition, they also attribute different properties to the cognitive processes and systems they seek to explain. This raises some quite fundamental issues about dual-process theories in general. Most obviously, it raises the issue of how best to think about the relationship between the various hypotheses currently on offer. There are two broad options. According to the first, extant hypotheses are merely related by family resemblance—for example, in positing two processes or systems with broadly similar characteristics. According to the second, the various extant hypotheses are instances of some generic dual-process account of cognition. No doubt, there are dual-process theorists who would settle for the first of these options. Yet the second is clearly the more intriguing, and moreover one that's more or less explicit in the research of some prominent dual-process theorists (e.g. Evans 2008; Stanovich 2004). In what follows, it is this second option—the prospect of a generic dual-process account—that I focus on. Specifically, I consider the question of whether there is some general, distinctive and plausible dual-process thesis about cognition. I argue that there is such an account—what I call the *type* (or cognitive kinds) version of dual-process theory.

Here's how I'll proceed. In the first section, I identify a substantive and interesting class of hypotheses worthy of the 'dual-process' label and contrast them with some other rather more banal claims. Then in the second section, I distinguish between two

ent versions of the hypothesis: one on which dual-process theory is con-
hesis about cognitive tokens (or particulars), the other on which it is a
.uesis about cognitive types (or kinds). These two versions of dual-process theory differ considerably in plausibility. Or so I maintain. In the third section, I sketch the reasons for rejecting the cognitive tokens version of dual-process theory; and in the
fourth section, I highlight the virtues of the cognitive types version. Finally, I conclude in the fifth section by arguing that given a clear understanding of the cognitive
types proposal we can deflect the main general objections to dual-process theorizing.

How to understand dual-process theories

The dual-process proposal is, I maintain, a bold and substantive one. But to see this
we need to get clearer on its commitments and distinguish it from some superficially
similar ones. Let me start, then, by saying what the dual-process proposal is not.

Dual-process accounts claim far more than that there is some bipartite division of cognitive processes

Though dual-process theories may sometimes appear to say no more than this, the
appearance is (fortunately) misleading. If this were the view, it would be a banal and
uninteresting one. There are always *lots* of ways of dividing up processes. This is true
not only of cognitive process, but processes quite generally. (Exercise: Think of all the
ways of subdividing a process, such as making chocolate.) How many processes one
acknowledges will depend on the *granularity* of the distinctions one draws; and it is
very easy to find *some* bipartite distinction or other for almost any (kind of) process.

One respect in which dual-process theories go beyond the above banal claim is in
characterizing mental processes in terms of a menu of distinctions that are widely
regarded as important to understanding cognition, such as the distinctions between
associative and rule-based processes, and between conscious and unconscious ones.
As we will see later, dual-process theorists vary in the distinctions they invoke. But
Table 6.1 contains the most common ones: what I'll call the *Standard Menu* of distinctions. (For the moment, ignore the 'S1' and 'S2' labels. I'll come back to these very soon.)

Single and covariant factors

Dual-process theories do not claim merely that cognitive processes can be divided in
terms of single dichotomies on the Standard Menu. No doubt some cognitive
processes are more automatic than others, some faster than others, and so on.
No doubt, some of these distinctions are more interesting than others; and some of
them harder to specify with precision. (Further: some of the pairs of terms on the
Standard Menu almost certainly correspond to more than just one distinction.) But it
should be relatively uncontentious that *some* such distinctions can be drawn. So, a
theory that claimed merely that such distinctions can be drawn—that there are, for
example, relatively fast and relatively slow processes—would be a rather uninteresting
one. But fortunately, the dual-process theorist's position is far bolder than this. What
they claim is that such distinctions *line-up*: that processes which exhibit one property
from a column typically, though not invariably, possess the others. According to this

Table 6.1 The standard menu. Distinctions between cognitive processes

S1	S2
Associative	Rule-based
Heuristic	Analytic
Parallel	Serial
Automatic	Controlled
Unconscious	Conscious
Low demands on cognitive capacity	High demands on cognitive capacity
Relatively fast	Relatively slow
Contextualized	Decontextualized
Evolutionarily old	Evolutionarily new
Conserved across species	Unique to humans

view, then, the properties listed under 'S1' and the properties listed under 'S2' form *clusters* of *co-varying* properties. Thus a central and far from banal commitment of dual-process theories is that cognitive processes—either generally or within some domain, such as reasoning—can be divided in two: those that possess the S1-property cluster and those that possess the S2-property cluster.

So what? From property clusters to cognitive mechanisms

Why should it matter whether S1-properties and S2-properties tend to cluster? One important reason is that it provides the basis for a familiar (and wholly respectable) kind of argument for the existence of a division between cognitive *systems*. Thus the existence of clusters bears on what I earlier identified as perhaps the central project of cognitive science: the task of characterizing the mind's architecture.

Let me spell out the argumentative strategy. By assumption, S1-properties and S2-properties form co-varying clusters. But the members of each cluster are not logically dependent on each other in the way that, for example, being a bachelor is logically dependent on being unmarried. Nor is the clustering plausibly viewed as a product of mere coincidence. So, *why* do the properties form clusters? Some kind of explanation is required; and one very common, general strategy is to posit an underlying suite of mechanisms to explain co-variation. This is a specific instance of what philosophers call an inference to the best explanation. In the present case, dual-process theorists propose a division between cognitive mechanisms that subserve processes exhibiting the S1 cluster and those that subserve S2-exhibiting processes. Moreover, to the extent that the explanation is the best one, we have reason to accept it. Thus according to dual-process theorists, not only do cognitive processes exhibit disjoint clusters of properties, but this putative fact also provides reason to posit a bipartite division between cognitive *mechanisms*.

Here's a philosophically more loaded way to put the point. The existence of cognitive processes that exhibit distinct property clusters enables us to identify a bipartite division in the *natural kinds* that underwrite cognition. The expression 'natural kind' has of course been explicated in many different ways. But the most popular, and to my mind most plausible, view to have emerged from recent philosophy of science is that natural kinds are *homeostatic property clusters* (Boyd 1991). Roughly put, according to this view, a kind is natural if:

- ◆ It is associated with a range of characteristics or symptoms, which tend to be co-instantiated by instances of the kind, but need not be genuine necessary conditions for membership.

- ◆ There is some set of underlying causal mechanisms and constraints—a 'causal essence', if you will—whose operation explains the co-instantiation of these various symptoms.

- ◆ To the extent that there is any real definition of what it is for something to be a member of the kind, it is not symptoms but causal essence that defines membership.

Consider an illness such as influenza. Influenza is, on the homeostatic cluster view, a plausible candidate for natural kind status. First, it is associated with a range of characteristic symptoms—coughing, elevated body temperature, and so on—even though these symptoms do not *define* what it is to have flu. Second, there is a causal mechanism—roughly, the presence of the flu virus—whose operation explains the occurrence of the symptoms. Finally, to the extent that influenza has a definition, it is the presence of the virus—or better, the presence of the virus producing some symptoms—but not the symptoms as such, that make it the case that one has flu.

The proposal is intended to capture paradigmatic examples of natural kinds, such as water and influenza. But it also comports quite well with the project of cognitive science where researchers are often in the business of characterizing the mechanisms that subserve the various cognitive processes on which our behavior depends. More specifically, it comports well with the explanatory objectives of dual-process theorists since precisely what they do is posit underlying causal mechanisms in order to explain the existence of processes that exhibit distinct property clusters.

Two versions of dual-process theory: Cognitive tokens and cognitive types

So far we have seen that dual-process theorists endorse the following pair of claims:

- ◆ Dual-Cluster Thesis: cognitive processes tend to exhibit either the S1 or S2 property clusters.

- ◆ Dual-Systems Thesis: there is a division in our cognitive architecture—a division between cognitive systems—that explains this clustering effect.[1]

From here on, I will assume that any version of dual-process theory worthy of the name is committed to these generic claims. Yet there are two rather different ways of

---

[1] Note: The first claim could be adopted without endorsing the second; but canonically they go together. Further, it is the endorsement of the latter that gives dual-process theory much of its import and substance.

developing this generic formulation of dual-process theory: what I'll call the token and type theses.

To a first approximation, what the *Token Thesis* maintains is that each mind contains two *particular* cognitive mechanisms or systems. The first, sometimes called *System 1*—though also variously and more expressively, the 'heuristic', 'implicit', or 'associative' system—subserves those cognitive processes that tend to exhibit the S1-property cluster. The second mechanism, often called *System 2*—though also variously referred to as the 'analytic', 'explicit', or 'rule-based' system—subserves those cognitive processes that tend to exhibit the S2-property cluster. On this view, then, each human mind exhibits a fundamental, bipartite division into particular systems.

According to the second, *Type Thesis*, each mind is comprised of two types or *kinds* of cognitive system. Systems of the first kind—type-1 systems—subserve processes that tend to exhibit the S1 cluster. Systems of the second kind—type-2 systems—subserve processes that tend to exhibit the S2 cluster. Such a view is logically weaker than the Token Thesis: the Token Thesis implies the Type Thesis but not vice versa. Even so, the Type Thesis still makes a bold and substantive claim about our minds, namely that each exhibits a fundamental, bipartite division into kinds or types of cognitive system. If the view were correct, then it would identify a central division in the systems which comprise our minds. The question I now wish to consider is this: is either version of dual-process theory plausible

The Token Thesis: Dual-process theory as a theory of cognitive tokens

Let's start with the Token Thesis. Though the proposal comes in a variety of forms, I maintain that none are attractive. Indeed, it's unclear how to formulate the thesis so as to avoid rendering it either highly implausible or else trivial.

Refining the Token Thesis

One initial, though obviously unsatisfactory, formulation of the Token Thesis is that our minds contain exactly two cognitive systems: System 1 and System 2. But literally construed this turns dual-process theory into a straw man. One reason is that cognitive scientists quite generally, and dual-process theorists in particular, routinely advocate a strategy of functional decomposition which conceives of relatively complex systems as hierarchically decomposable into relatively simple component subsystems. On any remotely plausible version of this story, there are going to be *far more* than two systems.

The point should be obvious even if we restrict ourselves to, for example, the human vision system. Here, it is overwhelmingly likely that the overall system is organized into subsystems, including, for example, for depth perception, color identification, and categorization (Palmer, 1999). Further, it is likely that these subsystems are themselves composed of further subsystems, which further decompose into smaller units, and so on. If anything like this story is correct—and virtually all vision scientists assume it is—then there are obviously going to be more than two systems. Indeed, if we focus on lower levels in the hierarchy of decomposition, we should expect to find *loads* of them—still more if we are permitted to sum mechanisms across all the different levels in the decomposition hierarchy. So, even if we restrict ourselves to a particular region of cognition, there are likely to be lots of mechanisms; and I presume that no dual-process theorist would seriously claim otherwise.[2]

Of course, none of the above shows that the Token Thesis is false. My aim is merely to eliminate an obvious misreading: one that, if accepted, would turn the thesis into a straw man. But how ought it to be formulated so as to avoid such obvious pitfalls? One possibility is to relativize dual-process theory to a specific level of decomposition. On this suggestion, dual-process theory would not claim there are two systems *tout court* but that there are two systems relative to some—presumably quite abstract—level of decomposition. Yet even at quite abstract levels of decomposition, it's just not plausible that our minds contain only two systems. On any plausible decomposition, there are likely to be a great many systems for a wide range of different mental processes, including perception, memory, reasoning, emotion, language, and no doubt many others. Moreover, it's not plausible to treat all these devices as constituting just two systems. Not, at any rate, unless one is prepared to countenance systems that are wildly heterogeneous in character.

Again, the present observation does not refute the Token Thesis so much as indicate a need for further refinement. And the obvious addition is to restrict the domain to which one's theory is supposed to apply. In doing so, one ceases to treat dual-process theory as a view of cognition in general, and instead reformulates it as a thesis about some specific region of cognition. *Which* region? Clearly, there are many possibilities. Perhaps the most common—and the one most relevant for the purposes of this volume—would be to restrict the claim to the domain of *reasoning*. On such a proposal, what dual-process theories (of reasoning) claim is that relative to some appropriate—presumably quite abstract—level of decomposition, there are exactly two *reasoning* systems.

Two reasoning systems?

So, the present suggestion is that there are two specific reasoning systems, one whose processes exhibit the S1 cluster, the other whose processes exhibit the S2 cluster. On the face of it, this appears to be a plausible Token Thesis; and moreover, one that some prominent dual-process theorists advocate. So, for example, Steven Sloman appears to defend such a view in his widely cited 'The empirical case for two systems of reasoning' (Sloman 1996).

Yet the proposal is hardly free from difficulty. The claim that there are two reasoning systems is not supposed to be mere stipulation, but a substantive and plausible empirical hypothesis. For this to be so, however, there needs to be some way of

---

[2] This is not, of course, to say that visual processing doesn't also divide up in ways that are conducive to some version of the dual-process theory. So, for example, Milner and Goodale (1995) suggest a dichotomous division within vision –roughly put, a distinction between a system for fast action in the world and another for object recognition—that seems broadly consonant with dual-process approaches to cognition.

distinguishing reasoning—or a reasoning system—from the rest of cognition so that there are plausibly just two reasoning systems. The problem is that it is far from clear that this can be done. Consider what appear to be the main options:

Suggestion 1. Any inferential device is a reasoning system. Problem: this will not do for the purposes of the Token Thesis since it includes too much. Inference of some sort appears to be a pervasive feature of much cognition, including perception and action guidance. Thus on this construal of reasoning systems, there are going to be too many—i.e. more than two.

Suggestion 2. Any system that subserves conscious deliberative inference is a reasoning system. Problem: though commonplace amongst philosophers and sometimes adopted by psychologists (e.g. Haidt 2001), this characterization of reasoning will not do because it obviously excludes too much. In particular, on such a view, System 1 itself would not count as a reasoning system since it is supposed to subserve automatic and largely unconscious processes.

Suggestion 3: Any device involved in paradigmatic reasoning tasks is a reasoning system. Problem: again, this will not do because it includes too much. A paradigmatic reasoning task—such as a deductive reasoning problem or probabilistic judgment—draws on many psychological capacities, including perception, motor control, language, and perhaps much more. In which case, on this view of reasoning systems, there will be too many.

Suggestion 4: Reasoning systems are to be identified with so-called 'central' systems. Problem: this is a fudge. Though the distinction between central systems—roughly, those responsible for 'higher' cognition—and non-central systems may be useful for heuristic purposes, it's hard to draw with any precision. Sometimes the distinction is characterized in terms of those systems that subserve reasoning and those that do not (Samuels 1998). But this clearly won't do for present purposes since it is reasoning that we seek to characterize. Another approach is to characterize central systems as those that deploy *conceptual* representations. Yet this tells us little in the absence a clear distinction between conceptual and non-conceptual representation: a distinction that is notoriously hard to draw.

Suggestion 5: 'If you've got to ask, you're never going to know.' A final suggestion is that we waive the demand for any explicit characterization of reasoning. Instead one insists that, as with many areas of enquiry, our intuitive notions are good enough to give us a reasonable purchase on the phenomena we seek to understand. On this view, our intuitive notion of reasoning—though no doubt rough and ready and largely implicit—is good enough for government purposes: sufficiently precise to permit the identification of *bona fide* reasoning systems.

Well maybe so.[3] But if one takes this line, then it's very far from clear there that there are just two reasoning systems. This is because reasoning as we intuitively construe it seems to include a great many kinds of process for which there are good empirical grounds for supposing the existence of distinct cognitive systems.

---

[3] Though it should be noted that I have doubts that our intuitive grasp of reasoning is really all that clear.

Though there is not the space to discuss the evidence in detail here, plausible candidates include: arithmetic inference (Dehaene 1997; Gelman and Butterworth 2005), probabilistic reasoning, decision making, planning, spatial reasoning, reasoning about social phenomena, ethical judgment (Greene and Haidt 2002), reasoning about the minds of others (Leslie et al. 2004), enumerative induction, and abductive inference. Intuitively, all these things appear to involve kinds of reasoning; and there is little or no reason to suppose that they all depend on just two systems. In short: though possible, the present suggestion lacks empirical plausibility.

One-way or two-way collapse?

It's worth stressing that the closing point of the previous section is very widely acknowledged amongst dual-process theorists (Stanovich 2004; Evans 2008). But the most common response is to adopt a view on which the Token Thesis is only *half* wrong. On this view, though the Token Thesis is wrong to claim that there is a single System 1, it is right about System 2: there really is just one per mind. As Keith Stanovich has put it:

> I have used terms such as System 1 or heuristic system as if I were talking about a singular system … However, using a term such as heuristic system—which implies a single cognitive system—is really a misnomer. In actuality, the term used should be plural because it refers to a (probably large) *set* of systems in the brain that operate autonomously in response to their own triggering system, and are not under control of the analytic processing system (Stanovich 2004, p.37).

In short: the collapse of the Token Thesis only goes in one direction.

Why suppose the collapse is unidirectional: that there is still just one System 2 per head? This is unclear; and of late, some dual-process theorists have suggested the need for additional systems. Stanovich has, for example, tentatively proposed a division within System 2 between algorithmic and reflective systems (Stanovich, this volume). But it seems to me that there are at least two considerations that militate in favor of a more extensive plurality.

Consideration 1: the first depends on an observation about the present state of research within the dual-process tradition. As noted earlier, dual-process theorizing has been applied to a wide range of cognitive domains, including learning, deductive reasoning, probabilistic judgment, decision making, and social cognition. In each domain one finds apparently well motivated empirical hypotheses that seek to explain the available range of data for that domain. Moreover, these various hypotheses posit systems and processes that bear striking similarities to each other. Yet the processes and mechanisms posited in each domain are *not* characterized in identical fashion. They also *differ* in crucial respects. For instance, they differ in how they characterize what the systems are supposed to do—execute rules, as opposed to exert executive control, for example. Moreover, their processes are not characterized in terms of the very same properties from the Standard Menu. So, for example, in the domain of social cognition, Lieberman and colleagues have posited a mechanism for controlled social cognition—the C-System—whose processes exhibit much of the S2 cluster but also differ in various respects from the analogous system(s) posited by researchers working on, say, deductive reasoning (Lieberman 2003). Now one possibility is that different researchers are groping towards the identification of a single System 2 for reasoning that is operative across all these various domains. But an alternative is that researchers in different domains may well be identifying different mechanisms that subserve processes of the same general type—i.e. those exhibiting the S2 cluster. Further, this is, I maintain, a *preferable* view. For unlike the single-system view, it does not demand on general grounds that we treat the differences between dual-process hypotheses as steeped in error. Instead it permits us to take seriously not only the similarities but also the differences between these more specific—and empirically more motivated—hypotheses. And this, it seems to me, is a *prima facie* reason for not adopting the single System 2 position.

Consideration 2: a second *prima facie* reason for not adopting the single System 2 position is that the processes allegedly subserved by this system appear to exhibit precisely the sorts of *heterogeneity* that should lead us to suspect that they depend on multiple systems. On many versions of the dual-process theory, there is a wide variety of cognitive processes—including, planning, decision making, deductive inference, the construction of self narrative, causal-mechanical reasoning, and the production of explanation—that are, at least some of the time, subserved by System 2 (Stanovich 2004). Given a commitment to a single System 2, this inclusiveness seems wholly appropriate. For by assumption, System 2 is supposed to subserve all S2-exhibiting processes, which routinely include instances of the above sorts of processes. For example, there are many occasions when our planning and deductive inference is slow, controlled, conscious, serial, and cognitively demanding. *Mutatis mutandis* for explanation, causal reasoning, self-narrative, and the rest. Even so, I maintain that it is not at all plausible to view all S2-exhibiting instances of planning, deductive inference, causal explanation, and the like, as the products of a single cognitive mechanism. On the contrary, these processes differ in precisely those respects that should lead us to conclude that they involve different cognitive systems. Specifically, they differ in ways that are typically taken as relevant to the *individuation* of cognitive mechanisms.

First, they differ considerably in *functional* respects. Consider planning, for example. In contrast to, say, deductive inference or causal explanation, planning is centrally concerned with the guidance of action—with identifying sequences of behaviors that collectively facilitate the attainment of our goals. Moreover (and presumably because of this) planning involves a quite different mapping from inputs to outputs than those found in deductive inference or causal reasoning. Most obviously, a planning process takes both beliefs and goals (or desires) as input and generates plans (or intentions) as output, whereas other sorts of process—deductive inference or causal explanation, for example—do not.

Second, and equally importantly, the *computational* demands of the various processes appear to be quite different. At any rate, the most plausible computational models to have emerged from cognitive science and artificial intelligence—for planning, deductive reasoning, causal explanation, and so on—vary considerably both in the sorts of computations that are taken to be relevant and the representational formats that are used (Russell and Norvig 2003). But if this is so, then to the extent that we take attempts at computational modeling seriously, we should suppose such processes differ in important computational respects.

Now, of course, it is quite possible for a single system to underwrite multiple processes. But the present point is not merely that various S2-exhibiting processes differ, but that they differ in *precisely* those respects that militate in favor of multiple systems. For psychological mechanisms are, by very widespread consensus, individuated by their functional and computational properties. And if this is so, then the assumption that, for example, planning and causal explanation depend on the very same system is implausible. It would thus seem that there is *prima facie* reason for skepticism about the claim that all instances of S2-exhibiting processes are subserved by a single System 2.

The Type Thesis: Dual-process theory as a theory of cognitive types

In the preceding section I argued that the Token Thesis is implausible. There is unlikely to be just one System 1 or just one System 2. What of the Type Thesis? How plausible is the claim that our minds are composed of two different *kinds* of cognitive mechanism—type-1 systems that exhibit the S1-cluster and type-2 systems that exhibit the S2-cluster?

The short answer is that it's simply too early to tell. Our understanding of cognitive architecture is at best radically incomplete; and nowhere more so than when it comes to the study of such 'higher' cognitive capacities as reasoning. Nonetheless, I maintain that the Type Thesis remains a genuine contender—a plausible thesis worthy of serious consideration. My reasons for this claim are straightforward. Dual-process theorizing is worthy of serious consideration because it earns its *explanatory keep*. In particular, it has generated a wide array of fruitful explanations for many phenomena. To select some examples more or less at random:

- *Belief bias:* in the psychology of deductive reasoning, dual-process theorizing constitutes perhaps the standard approach to explaining belief bias. Roughly put, it explains our tendency to assess the validity of arguments quite differently depending on the believability of their conclusions (Evans and Over 1996).

- *Interpersonal variation in reasoning:* dual-process theories have proven fruitful in explaining interpersonal variation on standard reasoning tasks and, moreover, explaining why performance correlates with such factors as psychometric intelligence and cognitive style (Stanovich 1999; Stanovich and West 1998).

- *Probabilistic judgment:* dual-process theories have been invoked to explain the patterns of data surrounding such phenomena as base-rate neglect and the conjunction fallacy (Barbey and Sloman 2007).

- *Cross-cultural variation:* dual-process accounts have held centre stage in recent attempts to explain cross-cultural differences in cognition, such as those characteristic of Western and South-East Asian subjects (Norenzayan et al. 2002).

Though there is not the space to defend the claim here, I maintain that these and other examples of dual-process theorizing have resulted in plausible empirical hypotheses. But as I have already argued, the Token Thesis is implausible because it seems likely that there are both many system 1s and many system 2s. In which case, if dual-process theories are worthy of serious attention, then it would seem that we are committed to the Type Thesis.

Of course, such an argument would the undermined if the Token Thesis were required for the above kinds of explanations to work. But this is not the case. On the contrary, the commitment to just two particular systems is gratuitous. In the case of belief bias, for example, what's required to explain the fact that we're more likely to assess arguments as valid when their conclusions are plausible is not the assumption of *exactly* two (reasoning) systems. What's required is that, when assessing the validity of arguments, two competing systems are involved. But this is wholly consistent with these two systems being two systems amongst many others. Thus not only is the Type Thesis the only plausible available version of dual-process theory, but it would also seem to suffice for the explanatory purposes that make dual-process approaches attractive in the first place.

Some challenges

I have suggested that the Type Thesis is a plausible one worthy of serious consideration. Nonetheless, the claim is not without its problems. As one might expect, much of the action concerns the details of specific empirical hypotheses and the nature of the evidence that has been invoked in their defense. But there are also some quite general concerns that have been expressed by both opponents and friends of dual-process theorizing (Evans 2006). I propose to close by considering three such problems. I maintain that whilst each calls for substantial further research, none pose insurmountable problems for the type version of dual-process theory.

Problem 1: The specification problem

In characterizing dual-process theory, I have so far alluded vaguely to two different property clusters, S1 and S2. But this is an oversimplification. Though there is substantial overlap between different formulations of dual-process theory, the characteristics invoked by different versions are not identical. In view of this, an obvious question arises: What precise characterizations of the S1 and S2 property clusters ought we to adopt?

In fact, there are two closely-related issues here. The first, 'conceptual problem', concerns how to characterize in a precise and appropriate manner the various dichotomies invoked by dual-process theorists. This problem arises, in large measure, because the distinctions have been characterized in a variety of non-equivalent ways. So, for example, there exist a variety of formulations of the distinction between controlled and automatic processes (Moors and De Houwer 2006). A fully developed version of dual-process theory should presumably address this worry.

The second, 'inclusion problem', concerns which distinctions should figure in our characterization of the two property clusters. Should we invoke, for example, a distinction between parallel and serial processes, as Sloman does (1996), or should we resist this suggestion, as Evans does (2008)? *Mutatis mutandis* for conscious versus unconscious, controlled versus automatic, evolutionarily ancient versus novel, and so on. Again, a fully developed version of dual-process theory should presumably address this worry.

To what extent should the above be a cause for concern? The answer is, I think, not much. There are two reasons for this. First, on the assumption that the Type Thesis is correct, the lack of clarity about property clusters is unsurprising. This is because it is quite possible for distinct, individual mechanisms to differ in *some* respects even if they are members of the same broad class of mechanisms.[4] Second, even waiving this consideration, the fact that the property clusters require revision and clarification is hardly reason to reject dual-process approaches. On the contrary, the need to refine general hypotheses in this way is just a commonplace feature of many scientific enterprises. That is, in the course of time, general hypotheses get refined and elaborated. At this time, there is no reason to suppose that dual-process theorizing is any different in this regard. In effect the present problems are just that: problems for future research, and not substantive objections.

Problem 2: The crossover problem

There is, however, a second, closely-related worry about dual-process theories that on the face of it poses a more serious challenge. According to this worry, the problem is not merely that dual-process accounts are underspecified or that some extant formulations are incorrect. Rather the concern is that no interesting type-1/type-2 distinction can be drawn because the characteristics exhibited by cognitive processes are not amenable to a clean bipartite division into two property clusters. On this view, the worry is that there are many 'crossover' processes that exhibit a combination of both S1 *and* S2 properties. Consider the property of evolutionary recency, for example. According to many standard formulations of dual-process theory, processes that exhibit the S1 property cluster are evolutionarily ancient, whilst those that exhibit the S2 cluster are paradigmatically recent and unique to humans. Yet there appear to be evolutionary recent processes that possess many S1 properties. So, for example, judgments of numerical magnitude involving familiar, conventional numeral systems—such as Arabic numerals—possess many S1 properties. For instance, they are relatively fast ($\approx$200ms); and appear to be automatic in that they exhibit Stroop-like effects—so-called 'number Stroop'—where we automatically access our sense of the numbers designated by numerals and order them by number size, even when number size is irrelevant to the task at hand. (Girelli et al. 2001). Nevertheless, the process so characterized is presumably an evolutionarily recent one since it depends on cultural innovations—conventional numeral systems—which are themselves very recent. Thus the process involved in judgments of numerical magnitude would appear to exhibit both S1 and S2 properties.

How serious is this crossover problem? In particular, should the existence of crossovers lead us to reject dual-process theory? The answer is, I maintain, that it poses no serious problem, so long as crossovers are not too numerous or too extreme. One possibility is that they merely indicate the need to drop some notions—for example, evolutionary recency—from our characterization of the property clusters.

---

[4] Thanks to Chris Viger for this point.

And as already noted, such modest revisions are both commonplace in science and provide no serious grounds for rejecting the Type Thesis as such.

A second, and more interesting possibility is that crossovers can be tolerated without any modification whatsoever to the assumed property clusters. As I noted in the first section, dual-process theorists are most plausibly construed as being in the business of identifying some of the cognitive natural kinds that underlie our mental processes. But on such a view, the members of S1 and S2 are not necessary conditions on the activity of their associated systems. That is, the presence and activity of some system 1 (or system 2) does not require that all members of its associated property cluster obtain, any more than, say, the presence of all the typical symptoms of influenza is a necessary condition for having flu. The point is that, for natural kinds quite generally, the relationship between underlying mechanism and associated characteristics is far weaker than this. In which case, saddling dual-process theorists with the requirement that system activity is always accompanied by all members of its associated property cluster is simply too demanding.

The unity problem

The final problem that I discuss here is what I call the *unity problem*. Though positing mechanisms is a standard strategy for explaining the existence of property clusters, it does not, by itself, constitute a satisfactory explanation. Rather one needs to specify those features of the proposed mechanisms that account for such clustering effects. In the present case, we need to specify those characteristics of type-1 systems that yield S1-exhibiting processes, and those properties of type-2 systems that yield S2-exhibiting processes. Again, this does not strike me as a serious objection so much as a challenge for future research—one that requires a more detailed account of the systems responsible for type-1 and type-2 processes. Nevertheless it is a significant explanatory challenge that has not, to date, been fully addressed. In what follows I comment briefly on three of the more plausible recent suggestions.

Proposal 1: associative and rule-based systems. One general approach to explaining the type-1/type-2 distinction would be to assume the cognitive mechanisms that underlie them operate according to different computational principles. Such a view is suggested, for example, by Steven Sloman's version of dual-process theory.[5] According to this view, the existence of distinct S1 and S2 property clusters can be explained on the assumption that the mind has a hybrid classical/connectionist architecture—one in which type-1 systems are connectionist (associative) mechanisms, and type-2 systems are classical computational (rule-based) ones.

This suggestion is not without its virtues. First, the general form of the proposal is of the right sort to address the unity problem. If the style of computation implemented by type-1 systems were appropriately different from that of type-2 systems, then it would also be unsurprising that the character of their respective processes differed significantly. Second, the solution would be a theoretically elegant and simple one since it would reduce the type-1/type-2 distinction to the distinction between classical and connectionist

---

[5] I say 'suggested' because it's not at all clear Sloman endorses the suggestion.

computational devices. Finally, the idea that cognition depends on both classical and connectionist devices is not without plausibility; and many recent theories of the mind incorporate some version of this suggestion (Anderson 2003; Sloman 1996).

For all that, there is little reason to accept the proposed solution to the unity problem. First, aside from theoretical elegance, there is currently no reason to suppose that the type-1/type-2 distinction corresponds to the connectionist/classical divide. So, for example, special purpose learning mechanisms of the sort studied by Gallistel and his collaborators—for dead reckoning, path integration and geometric inference, for example—are often treated by dual-process theorists as paradigmatic examples of type-1 systems (Sloman 1996; Evans 2008). But is it far from clear that such mechanisms have a connectionist architecture. Indeed, Gallistel's own account of these mechanisms is militantly classical in character (Gallistel 1990).

Another problem is that it's very unclear how the classical/connectionist distinction is supposed to explain many of the properties associated with type-1 and type-2 processes. Why, for example, should only classical processes be consciously accessible and controlled? Clearly, neither are essential properties of classical systems. Indeed it is hard to see why classical processes should be any more controlled or accessible to consciousness than connectionist ones. Conversely, why should connectionist processes be more automatic or less cognitively demanding than classical ones? On the face of it, there is no reason to suppose that they should. In short: it is, to put it mildly, obscure why connectionist processes should exhibit the S1 cluster whilst classical ones exhibit the S2 cluster. But absent an explanation of this (putative) fact, presenting the classical/connectionist distinction as a solution to the Unity problem is mere hand waving: a gesture at explanation almost wholly lacking in content.

Proposal 2: cyclic realization of type-2 processes. A second possible approach to the Unity problem, recently suggested by Peter Carruthers and Keith Frankish, is that the difference between the characteristics of type-1 and type-2 processes results from the fact that system-2 is realized by cycles of system-1 operations (Carruthers, this volume; Frankish, this volume). On this approach, the distinctiveness of type-2 processes is explained by providing an empirically rich account of how different type-1 processes combine to realize type-2 systems. For example, Carruthers sketches an elaborate and intriguing account on which System-2 is realized by complexly interacting type-1 systems for language, perception, practical reasoning, and many other things besides.

What are we to make of such proposals? First, it's worth stressing that the general claim that type-2 systems depend on type-1 systems—or at any rate mechanisms very much like them—should be relatively uncontentious amongst cognitive scientists. This is because it is widely assumed that (a) complex cognitive systems decompose into simpler mechanisms—ultimately into primitive processors—and (b) that cognitive explanations proceed by explaining the behavior of complex systems in terms of the operations and interactions of their parts (Bechtel and Richardson 1993). Primitive processors are more or less by definition automatic, unconscious, and cognitively undemanding. This much is required to avoid a range of familiar homunculi regress worries. (For instance, if each system responsible for conscious thought were, in turn, dependent upon the activity of conscious subsystems, then a regress would appear to threaten, where each system is dependent on the activity of some further conscious system.) Further, on the plausible assumption that evolution operates by reusing pre-existing types of structure (Marcus 2004), primitive processors are likely to be evolutionarily more ancient and more widely conserved across species than the more complex systems they realize.

So, the general idea that type-2 systems are realized by mechanisms very much like type-1 seems plausible. But it is one thing to accept this general claim—what amounts to little more than an endorsement of standard methodology in cognitive science—quite another to provide a detailed response to the unity problem. And at this time such suggestions are, at best, highly speculative. Consider Carruthers' view, for example. Though this is not the place for detailed discussion, I do think that it possesses some notable virtues. Most obviously, it makes a good attempt at explaining the clustering of S2 characteristics. (See Carruthers, this volume.) But in order to do so, Carruthers helps himself to a very rich 'boxology' of cognitive mechanisms. And this comes at an obvious cost. Many of the assumptions he makes about our cognitive systems, their properties and relations to each other concern matters about which little is known, and are consequently highly speculative and contentious. Here's a fairly characteristic example. In developing his view, Carruthers provides a central role for inner speech, and then attempts to explain how inner speech operates:

> Here is how it works. In light of the subject's beliefs and goals, a speech action-schema is formulated by the language production sub-system. While overt action is suppressed, an efference copy of the motor instructions is transformed via an emulator system into an auditory representation of the sounds that would have resulted had the action been carried out. This representation is globally broadcast in the manner of conscious images generally, and is received *inter alia* by the language comprehension sub-system. The latter constructs an interpretation of the utterance in the normal way, and presents that (attached to the sounds) to the various other System 1 inferential systems. Hence, just as is the case with external speech, we seem to hear the meaning of the imagined sounds of inner speech (the message expressed) as well as hearing those imagined sounds themselves. (Carruthers, this volume.)

Now I do not wish to claim that this story is incorrect. (I have no idea.) Nor do I wish to claim that a response to the unity problem which incorporates such a story is without merit. On the contrary, as an answer to a 'how possible' question— 'How could a system exhibiting the S2 cluster be built from a suit of subsystems?'—such an account may well be useful. My point is merely that such proposals are highly speculative and lack much in the way of empirical confirmation. In short: the proposal buys the ability to explain the properties of type-2 processes at the cost of lacking empirical support.

Proposal 3: working memory. The final response to the unity problem that I will discuss here is that the existence of the S1 and S2 clusters depends crucially on the nature of human working memory (Evans 2008, this volume). According to this proposal, what generates the division between type-1 and type-2 processes is that the latter, but not the former, 'require access to a single, capacity limited central working memory resource' (Evans 2008). As a consequence, type-2 processes possess certain characteristics lacking in type-1 processes. For example, type-2 processes are slow, sequential, and capacity limited because they inherit these characteristics from central working memory.

I think that the present suggestion is worthy of very serious consideration. Indeed it is the most plausible response to the unity problem that I know of. One virtue is that it readily explains some core aspects of type-2 processes. So, for example, on the present view, the sequential character of type-2 reasoning turns out to be a direct consequence of the fact that working memory imposes a sequential 'bottleneck' on the processing of information. A second virtue is that the proposal helps explain what might otherwise appear to be puzzling facts about cognition. So, for example, it suggests an explanation of the fact that individual differences in working memory capacity, in reasoning and in psychometric g are highly intercorrelated (Stanovich 1999; Evans 2008). Roughly put, on the present proposal, these variables are highly correlated because they all depend to a significant degree on the operation of a central working memory system whose capacity varies from individual to individual. A third virtue of the present view is that it comports well with the position defended in this paper—that there are many type-2 systems—since it is quite possible for many distinct systems to share central working memory resources. Finally, and in contrast to the proposals discussed earlier, the present response to the unity problem requires only relatively austere assumptions about our cognitive architecture—viz. the existence of a sequential, capacity limited working memory—assumptions that are both widespread amongst cognitive psychologists and well supported by empirical research (Baddeley 2007; Barrett et al. 2004). In short: the working memory proposal seems to be an elegant and empirically well-motivated response to the unity problem.

For all that, the present proposal is clearly in need of further development; and in current form, it fails fully to address the unity problem. A first and relatively minor worry is that although the proposal does a good job of explaining some features of type-2 processes—for example, their serial and capacity-limited character—it is far less clear how it is supposed to accommodate others. So, for example, it is less clear why type-2 processes should be more accessible to consciousness or more readily under cognitive control. To explain these putative features of type-2 processes, far more would need to be said about the nature of working memory. My point is not that this cannot be done. Indeed there are clearly possible ways to develop the account. My point is merely that such additions to the proposal are required.

A second and more serious worry about the working memory proposal is that in its present form it really only addresses one half of the unity problem. To address the unity problem it is not enough to specify those characteristics of type-2 systems that yield S2-exhibiting processes. One must also explain why type-1 systems yield S1-exhibiting processes. Moreover, to do this, it is not enough merely to make the more or less definitional point that type-1 systems tend to yield such processes. What is required is some account of the characteristic properties of type-1 systems that tend to yield processes of this sort. But in its current form the working memory proposal is almost entirely silent on this matter. Instead type-1 systems are merely characterized by exclusion—as those systems that do *not* rely on central working memory. My point is that even if the present proposal is broadly right about type-2 systems, we still require a substantial account of why systems that operate independently of working memory yield processes that exhibit the S1 cluster. Why, for example, are they relatively fast? Why are they not decontextualized? Why are they not under conscious control? And so on. In the absence of such an explanation, the present proposal is, at best, incomplete.

Conclusion

This chapter has been concerned with the issue of whether or not there exists some generic version of dual-process theory that is both interesting and plausible. I started by identifying those characteristics that an interesting version of the theory would need to possess. I then argued that the most plausible view of this sort is one that reconstructs the original System 1/System 2 distinction as a distinction between kinds or *types* of psychological system. Moreover, I argued on grounds of explanatory value that dual-process theorizing quite generally is worth taking seriously and, consequently, that—by virtue of being the most plausible version of the theory—the Type Thesis is worthy of very serious consideration. Of course, this hardly establishes the truth of the view. As we have seen, there are a number of conceptual and empirical problems that need to be addressed. Nonetheless, if the arguments of the last section are correct, then these problems are not so much reasons to reject the Type Thesis as issues that call for further research.

References

Anderson, J.R. and Lebiere, C. (2003) The Newell Test for a theory of cognition. *Behavioral and Brain Sciences*, **26**, 587–601.

Baddeley, A.D. (2007) *Working memory, thought and action*. Oxford University Press, Oxford.

Barbey, A.K. and Sloman, S.A. (2007). Base-rate respect: From statistical formats to cognitive structures. *Behavioral and Brain Sciences*, **30**, 287–92.

Barrett, L.F., Tugade, M.M., and Engle, R.W. (2004) Individual differences in working memory capacity and dual-process theories of the mind. *Psychological Bulletin*, **130**, 553–73.

Bechtel, W. and Richardson, R.C. (1993) *Discovering complexity: Decomposition and localization as strategies in scientific research*. Princeton University Press, Princeton, NJ.

Boyd, R. (1991) Realism, anti-foundationalism and the enthusiasm for natural kinds. *Philosophical Studies*, **61**, 127–48.

Chaiken, S. and Trope, Y. (1999) (eds) *Dual-process theories in social psychology*. Guildford Press, New York.

Dehaene, S. (1997) *The number sense*. Oxford University Press, New York.

Evans, J.St.B.T. (2002) Logic and human reasoning: An assessment of the deduction paradigm. *Psychological Bulletin*, **128**, 978–96.

Evans, J.St.B.T. (2003) In two minds: Dual process accounts of reasoning. *Trends in Cognitive Sciences*, **7**, 454–9.

Evans, J.St.B.T. (2008) Dual-processing accounts of reasoning, judgment and social cognition. *Annual Review of Psychology*, **59**, 255–78

Evans, J.St.B.T. and Over, D.E. (1996) *Rationality and reasoning*. Psychology Press, Hove, MA.

Gallistel, C.R. (1990) *The organization of learning*. Bradford Books/MIT Press, Cambridge, MA.

Gelman, R. and Butterworth, B. (2005) Number and language: How are they related? *Trends in Cognitive Sciences*, **9**, 6–10.

Girelli, L., Sandrini, M., Butterworth, B., and Cappa, S. (2001) Number Stroop performance in normal aging and Alzheimer's type dementia. *Brain and Cognition*, **46**, 144–9.

Greene, J. and Haidt, J. (2002) How (and where) does moral judgment work? *Trends in Cognitive Sciences*, **6**, 517–23.

Haidt J. (2001) The emotional dog and its rational tail: A social intuitionist approach to moral judgement. *Psychological Review*, **108**, 814–34.

Kahneman, D. and Frederick, S. (2002) Representativeness revisited: Attribute substitution in intuitive judgement. In T. Gilovich, D. Griffin, and D. Kahneman (eds). *Heuristics and biases: The psychology of intuitive judgment*, 49–81. Cambridge University Press, Cambridge.

Leslie, A.M., Friedman, O., and German, T.P. (2004). Core mechanisms in 'theory of mind'. *Trends in Cognitive Sciences*, **8**, 528–33.

Lieberman, M.D. (2003) Reflective and reflexive judgment processes: A social cognitive neuroscience approach. In J.P Forgas, K.R. Williams, and W. von Hippel (eds). *Social judgments: Implicit and explicit processes*, 44–67. Cambridge University Press, New York.

Marcus, G. (2004) *The birth of the mind: How a tiny number of genes creates the complexities of human thought*. Basic Books, New York.

Moors, A. and De Houwer, J. (2006) Automaticity: A theoretical and conceptual analysis. *Psychological Bulletin*, **132**, 297–326.

Norenzayan, A., Smith, E.E., Kim, B., and Nisbett, R.E. (2002) Cultural preferences for formal versus intuitive reasoning. *Cognitive Science*, **26**, 653–84.

Palmer, S. (1999) *Vision science: Photons to phenomenology*. MIT Press, Cambridge, MA.

Reber, A.S. (1993) *Implicit learning and tacit knowledge*. Oxford University Press, Oxford.

Russell, S. and Norvig, P. (2003) *Artificial intelligence: A modern approach* 2nd ed. Prentice Hall, Upper Saddle River, NJ.

Samuels, R. (1998) Evolutionary psychology and the massive modularity hypothesis. *British Journal for the Philosophy of Science*, **49**, 575–602.

Sloman, S.A. (1996) The empirical case for two systems of reasoning. *Psychological Bulletin*, **119**, 3–22.

Stanovich, K. (1999) *Who is rational? Studies of individual differences in reasoning*. Laurence Erlbaum Associates, Mahwah, NJ.

Stanovich, K. (2004) *The robot's rebellion: Finding meaning in the age of Darwin*. University of Chicago Press, Chicago, IL.

Stanovich, K.E. and West, R.F. (1998) Cognitive ability and variation in selection task performance. *Thinking and Reasoning* **4**, 193–230.

Part 2

Perspectives

Chapter 7

Intuitive and reflective inferences

Hugo Mercier and Dan Sperber

Introduction

Experimental evidence on reasoning and decision making has been used to argue both that human rationality is adequate and that it is defective. The idea that reasoning involves not one but two mental systems (see Evans and Over 1996; Sloman 1996; Stanovich 2004 for reasoning, and Kahneman and Frederick 2005 for decision making) makes better sense of this evidence. 'System 1' reasoning is fast, automatic, and mostly unconscious; it relies on 'fast and frugal' heuristics (to use Gigerenzer's expression (Gigerenzer et al. 1999)) offering seemingly effortless conclusions that are generally appropriate in most settings, but may be faulty, for instance in experimental situations devised to test the limits of human reasoning abilities. 'System 2' reasoning is slow, consciously controlled and effortful, but makes it possible to follow normative rules and to overcome the shortcomings of system 1 (Evans and Over 1996).

The occurrence of both sound and unsound inferences in reasoning experiments and more generally in everyday human thinking can be explained by the roles played by these two kinds of processes. Depending on the problem, the context, and the person (the ability for system 2 reasoning is usually seen as varying widely between individuals, see Stanovich and West (2000)) either system 1 or system 2 reasoning is more likely to be activated, with different consequences for people's ability to reach the normatively correct solution (Evans 2006). The two systems can even compete: system 1 suggests an intuitively appealing response while system 2 tries to inhibit this response and to impose its own norm-guided one.

Much evidence has accumulated in favor of such a dual view of reasoning (Evans 2003, in press; for arguments against, see Osman 2004). There is, however, some vagueness in the way the two systems are characterized. Instead of a principled distinction, we are presented with a bundle of contrasting features—slow/fast, automatic/controlled, explicit/implicit, associationist/rule-based, modular/central— which, depending on the specific dual-process theory, are attributed more or less exclusively to one of the two systems. As Evans states in a recent review, 'it would then be helpful to have some clear basis for this distinction'; he also suggests that 'we might be better off talking about type 1 and type 2 processes' rather than systems (Evans 2008).

We share the intuitions that drove the development of dual-system theories. Our goal here is to propose in the same spirit a principled distinction between two types of inferences: 'intuitive inference' and 'reflective inference' (or reasoning proper). We ground this distinction in a massively modular view of the human mind where metarepresentational modules play an important role in explaining the peculiarities of human psychological evolution. We defend the hypothesis that the main function of reflective inference is to produce and evaluate arguments occurring in interpersonal communication (rather than to help individual ratiocination). This function, we claim, helps explain important aspects of reasoning. We review some of the existing evidence and argue that it gives support to this approach.

Inferential processes and massive modularity

Dual-process theories stand in contrast to more traditional monistic views that assume that reasoning is governed by a single system, be it one of rules (Braine 1990; Rips, 1994), or mental models (Johnson-Laird 1983). At first blush, dual-process theories also stand in contrast to massively modular views of human cognition (Barrett and Kurzban 2006; Carruthers 2006; Sperber 1994; Tooby and Cosmides 1992). Massive modularists are neither monists nor dualists, they are pluralists. They see the human mind as made up of many specialized modules, each autonomous, each with a distinct phylogenetic and/or ontogenetic history, and each with its own input conditions, specific procedures, and characteristic outputs.

In the human case, most innate modules are learning modules (e.g. the language faculty) and perform their function by using environmental inputs to construct acquired modules (e.g. the grammar of a particular language). Given the prevalence of these innate learning modules, massive modularity does not imply massive innateness of mental modules: many or most of them are the output of an acquisition process. This is not the place to argue in detail for the massive modularity thesis (but see Sperber 1994, 2001b, 2005). What we want to do rather is to explore some implications of the thesis for the psychology of reasoning, and in particular for the interpretation of the kind of phenomena that has inspired dual-process theories.

Massive modularists assume that inferences are carried out not by one or two systems but by many domain-specific modules that take advantage of the peculiar regularities of their specific domains to apply inferential procedures that would be inappropriate in other domains.

If, for instance, we had seen two objects being put behind an opaque screen, we are surprised to see only one object when the screen is lifted (and so are 12-month-old infants, Wynn 1992). We expected there would be at least two objects. An expectation is the outcome of an inference. In drawing this inference (in a typically unconscious manner) we do not use as a premise the assumption that solid objects persist through time. We passively ignore rather than actively deny the possibility of their vanishing or blending with one another. This assumption of persistence is built into a domain-specific mechanism we use to draw inferences about solid objects. No such assumption is built into the way we draw inferences about, say, liquids. If we see two liquids being poured in the same opaque vessel, we are not surprised to discover only one liquid when the content of the vessel is made visible.

Similarly we have different built-in assumptions about the fall of objects and their other changes of location (Spelke 1990), about the movement of animate and inanimate objects respectively (Leslie 1995), and about the relevance of information unintentionally made available and that of information intentionally communicated (Sperber and Wilson 2002).

Massive modularity may seem incompatible with the sense we have that our think- Core .
ing is a unitary and integrated process. However, this vague introspective datum is of
no serious evidential value. More relevant is the fact that we can and do reason on premises that pertain to more than one cognitive domain. For instance, when we see a small child (but not a cat) sitting on window sill (but not on a low bench), we infer that there is a serious and pressing danger, unproblematically integrating premises from our knowledge of child psychology and form our commonsense knowledge of physics. A sensible massive modularity theory must however assume that the same premise can be processed successively or in parallel by several modules, just as the same food can be decomposed successively or in parallel by several enzymes (for a development of the analogy between enzymes and modules suggested in Sperber 1994; see Barrett 2005) Multi-domain inferences can be the joint work of several domain-specific modules.

Fodor (2001) has developed a more serious objection to the idea that human inferences could be performed by a massively modular mind. Individual modules, by their very nature, have very little or no context-sensitivity. Human inference on the contrary is characterized by high context-sensitivity: the same input can yield quite different conclusions in different contexts. Another way to put the same point is that human inference tends to process not just any available inputs but only the most relevant ones in the situation, and tends moreover to contextualize each of these inputs in a way that maximizes its relevance. This is arguably a major feature of human cognition (described in Sperber and Wilson 1995 as the 'cognitive principle of relevance'). If one assumes, as does Fodor, that the operations of modules are mandatory, in the sense that they automatically process any input that meets their input condition, then human cognition should be stimulus-driven, with the same stimuli triggering the same inferences in all contexts, and the output of these inferences triggering the same higher level inferences in all contexts, and so forth. The high context-sensitivity actually exhibited by human inferences provides a powerful argument against the view that the human mind is massively modular in the way envisaged and criticized by Fodor.

In fact, however, it is dubious that any cognitive processes can be considered mandatory in the intended sense. As studies on attentional blindness demonstrate, even when the psychophysical conditions for perception are fully met, some outstanding stimuli may remain unperceived (e.g. a person disguised as a gorilla moving in full view in the middle of a few basketball players; see Simons and Chabris 1999). Thus even perceptual mechanisms—which for Fodor are prototypical modules—do not automatically process every input that meets their input conditions. This is easily explained. Human cognition is characterized by the fact that, at any moment, it is monitoring the environment and has available in memory much more information than it could simultaneously process. 'Attention' refers to the dynamic selection of some of the available information from the environment and from memory for deeper processing.

From a modularist point of view, attentional selection might be best seen, not as the output of a distinct attention mechanism allocating resources to specific modules, but as the result of a process of competition for such resources among modules.

Some modules, for instance danger detectors, may be permanently advantaged in this competition because their inputs have a high expected relevance. Other modules may be advantaged at a given time because of a decision to attend to their potential inputs. For instance, face recognition is on the alert when waiting for a friend at the train station. Leaving aside these permanent bottom-up biases and temporary top-down biases, modules with the highest level of immediate activation both from upstream and downstream modules should be winners in the competition (with ongoing changes in these levels of activation resulting in shifts of attention).

A competitive system of this type fine-tuned both in phylogenetic evolution and in individual development would go a long way towards explaining how human cognition can, in practice, tend toward high context-sensitivity or, equivalently, towards the maximisation of the relevance of the inputs it processes.

Still, there seem to be some inferential processes that are truly domain-general. For example, people seem to be able to infer Q from P-or-Q and *not-P* whatever the content of P and Q, be it concrete or abstract, factual or imaginary. Similarly, people are able to infer from X *believed that P* and X *now believes that not-P* that X has changed her mind regarding the subject matter of P, whatever this subject matter. Or again, people are capable of inferring what a speaker means from what she utters, whatever she is talking about. Are these genuine instances of domain-generality (and therefore of non-modularity)? A more careful examination of the inferential mechanisms involved reveals that they are as domain-specific as any other cognitive mechanisms; they just happen to draw inferences warranted by the properties of a very peculiar kind of objects: conceptual representations.

There is a standard distinction between *perceptual* mechanisms that have as input sensory data and as output representations of distal stimuli, and *conceptual* mechanisms that have representations both as input and as output. Still, just as perceptual mechanisms are not drawing inferences about sensory data but about perceived objects, conceptual mechanisms are not drawing inferences about the properties of the representations they process but about the properties of the objects or states of affairs represented in these representations. For instance, inferring from the perceived presence of dark clouds that it will rain is not an inference about that perception but about the clouds themselves and their likely effects.

Representations, be they mental (e.g. beliefs) or public (e.g. utterances), are also objects in the world. They have properties qua representations. The belief that it will rain is a mental representation held by John at a given time and given up by him at another; it may be consistent or inconsistent with some of his other beliefs; it may be true or false; and so on. Consistency and truth are properties not of the state of affairs represented but of the belief itself. Mary's utterance is a public representation that may be grammatical or not, relevant or not, addressed to John or to Jean. These are properties not of the state of affairs talked about but of the utterance itself. The inference of a conclusion of the form Q from a pair of premises of the form P-or-Q and *not-P* is warranted not by the state of affairs described by these premises but by the formal properties of these representations considered in the abstract.

Humans are aware of the existence of representations in the world, and a good part of their behavior is aimed either at influencing the mental representations of others or at improving their own mental representations. From a modularist point of view, it is

sensible to expect that the special properties of representations (c
representations) should be exploited by modules that specialize in ᴠ
about representations. For this, representations have themselves to b
means of second-order representations, or metarepresentations (see Sp

Modules that draw inferences about representations are metarepresentᴠ
ules. The representations about which metarepresentational modules draw
can themselves be about any subject matter within or across any cognitive ᴠ   ᴠns.
Inferences about representations on a given subject matter may often provide reasons
to accept specific conclusions about that subject matter. For instance, knowing that a
competent meteorologist believes that it will rain is a reason to believe that it will rain.
Or knowing that a set of premises entails a conclusion is a reason to believe that conclusion if one believes the premises.

The fact that metarepresentational inferences may indirectly yield conclusions that
belong to the domains of the representations metarepresented results in a semblance of
domain-generality. However, since metarepresentational mechanisms only process
specific properties (e.g. who is entertaining a given representation or what a set of representations entails) of a specific kind of objects (representations), this is only an *indirect and virtual* domain-generality. Metarepresentational modules are as specialized
and modular as any other kind of module. It is just that the domain-specific inferences
they perform may result in the fixation of beliefs in any domain. In this respect,
metarepresentational inferences are comparable to visual or auditory perception.
Visual perception mechanisms are highly specialized and attend to special properties of
highly specific optical inputs and yet they may fixate beliefs in most cognitive domains.

Massive modularity is clearly incompatible with a monistic view of inference: if
inferential procedures are carried out by many different modules using a variety of
procedures, then it is pointless to ask how inference in general is performed or to try
to generalize from the properties of inference in a given domain to all inferential
process. For instance, it could be that spatial reasoning of some kind is performed by
means of mental models but that, nevertheless, mental models play no role in most or
even all other inferential processes. Is massive modularity similarly incompatible with
a dualistic view? We will argue that it is not and that, in fact, a modularist approach
provides a principled way to develop such a view.

Intuitive and reflective inference

Inferential modules alter—and if things go well, improve—the information available
to an individual by adding new beliefs, updating or erasing old ones, or modifying the
strength, or the subjective probability, of existing beliefs. These modifications occur at
what Dennett called the 'subpersonal' level (Dennett 1969; see also Frankish, this volume) They are the output of processes that take place inside individuals without
being controlled by them. The modification of the stock of beliefs (or the 'data base')
that results from spontaneous inference occurs without the individual's attending to
what justifies this modification, just as in the case of perceptual processes.

As we pointed out, there are different kinds of representations. Some properties are
shared by all representations, others are specific to one given kind. From a modularist
point of view, it is sensible to ask whether the different inferential opportunities

offered by various types of representations are taken advantage of by several distinct metarepresentational modules. Yet, in the literature, metarepresentational abilities are generally equated with a single 'Theory of Mind', 'mentalization', or 'mindreading' module. 'Metarepresentational' (i.e. about representations) is treated as more or less synonymous with 'metapsychological' (i.e. about mental representations). This is both too broad and too narrow.

It is too broad because some types of attributions of mental states are best performed by means of specialized inferential routines rather than by a unitary general mindreading ability. For instance the intention of another person to establish joint attention with you can be inferred from a fairly simple, possibly repeated, action sequence in which eye contact with you is followed by staring at the intended target of joint attention. Nine-month-old infants are capable of using this behavioral pattern to attribute an intention of this kind. For this, they do not use a general mindreading ability but a much more specialized module with, presumably, a strong genetic basis (Baron-Cohen 1995; Tomasello 1999).

Treating 'metarepresentational' as synonymous with 'metapsychological' is also too narrow since metarepresentations are used to represent not just mental representations but also public representations, such as utterances (Wilson 2000), and representations considered in the abstract, independently of their mental or public instantiations, as in logical or mathematical reasoning.

There are good evolutionary reasons (discussed in the next section) to make the assumption that, among metarepresentational modules, there is one specialized in argumentative relationships among conceptual representations (Sperber 2000a, 2001a). Often, we are interested not just in some claim (for instance the claim that it will rain this afternoon) but also in reasons to accept it (for instance the fact that there are heavy clouds) or to reject it (for instance the fact that last weather bulletin forecasted clouds but not rain). This occurs in two types of situations: somebody is making a claim that would be relevant to us if it were true but we are not disposed to accept it just on trust, and so we look at reasons to accept or reject it; or we are trying to convince an interlocutor of a claim that she won't accept just on trust, and therefore we have to give her reasons to accept it.

What the argumentation module does then is to take as input a claim and, possibly, information relevant to its evaluation, and to produce as output reasons to accept or reject that claim. The workings of this module are just as opaque as those of any other module, and its immediate outputs are just as intuitively compelling. We accept as self-evident that a given pair of accepted assumptions of the form *P-or-Q* and *not-Q* justifies accepting the conclusion *P*, but this compelling intuition would be hard to justify.[1] We accept as self-evident that, everything else being equal, we are likely to be

----

[1] Arguing that the inference is justified by the logical properties of the connectives 'or' and 'not' is not enough. Arthur Prior has imagined a connective, 'tonk', defined by two rules: (1) $[P \rightarrow (P \text{ tonk } Q)]$; (2) $[(P \text{ tonk } Q) \rightarrow Q]$. With 'tonk', one may then infer any proposition Q from any proposition P. This is of course inacceptable and illustrates the point that only appropriate connectives permit sound inferences. This in turn raises the difficult question of what makes a connective appropriate (see Bonnay and Simmenauer 2005; Engel 2006; Prior 1960).

better off betting on a horse that has won many races than on a horse that has won few races, but as philosophers since Hume have argued at length, we would be hard put to justify this type of compelling intuition (see Vickers 1988). Still, the argumentation module provides us with reasons to accept conclusions, even though we may be unable to articulate why we accept these reasons as reasons.

The direct output of all inferential modules, including the argumentation module, is intuitive in the clear sense that we just trust our own mental mechanisms and that we are disposed to treat as true their output without attending to reasons for this acceptance, or even without having access to such reasons.

In the case of the argumentation module, however, there is a subtle twist that, if not properly understood, may cause confusion. The intuitive output of the argumentation module consists in the representation of a relationship between a conclusion and reasons to accept it. This representation is produced by a communicator aiming at convincing her audience, and evaluated by her audience unwilling to be convinced without good grounds. Here, for reasons of space, we consider only the audience's perspective. For the audience, intuitively accepting the *direct* output of the argumentation module, that is the representation of an argument-conclusion relationship, provides explicit reasons to accept on its own the conclusion embedded in it. The acceptance of this embedded conclusion, when it occurs, is an *indirect* output of the argumentation module.

At the level of personal psychology, there is a major difference between intuitively accepting some representation as a fact, and accepting some claim because of explicit reasons. In the second case only, do we experience engaging in a mental act that results in a conscious decision to accept. At the level of subpersonal cognitive psychology, disembedding a conclusion from the argument that justifies it is not, properly speaking, an inferential operation—it does not result in a new conclusion—but a data management one. It allows a conclusion that has already been derived to be stored and used on its own.[2] What, at a personal level, looks like a decision to accept a conclusion, is, we suggest, realized at the subpersonal level by this data management operation. This indirect output of the argumentation module—the disembedded conclusion—is quite unlike the direct output of this and all of other inferential modules in that we mentally represent a reason to accept it. Conclusions accepted for a reason are not intuitive but are, we will say, 'reflective' (Sperber 1997) and the mental act of accepting a reflective conclusion through an examination of the reasons one has to do so is an act of reflection.[3]

There is thus, within a massive-modularist framework, a subtle but unambiguous way to distinguish two categories of inferences: intuitive inferences the conclusion of which are the direct output of all inferential modules (including the argumentation module), and reflective inferences the conclusions of which are an indirect output

[2] Dan Sperber (1985, ch. 2) has suggested that there are conditions of intelligibility on such disembeddings and that poorly understood conclusions are stored inside their validating context and not on their own.

[3] Several philosophers (Cohen 1992; Engel 2000; Stalnaker 1984; see also de Sousa 1971; Dennett 1981) have proposed a contrast between belief and acceptance that is interestingly similar to ours between intuitive and reflective conclusions.

embedded in the direct output the argumentation module. Since reflective inferences involve the representation of reasons, they well deserve the name of reasoning proper.

In this perspective, the sense we have that reasoning is a slow and effortful mental process does not come from the difficulty of the individual reflective steps involved, but from the fact that typical reasoning involves a series of such reflective steps. The conclusion embedded in an output of the argumentation module is disembedded and used as part of the input for another operation of the same module, and this can be reiterated many times. The difficulty of reasoning comes from the attentional or 'concentration' effort needed to maintain long enough an expectation of relevance strong enough to keep the argumentation module active throughout this series of steps when other modules are competing for energetic resources. A deliberate reiterated use of a perception module, for instance of the face recognition module when looking for a specific face in a crowd, is also slow and effortful without this implying in any way that the basic mechanism involved is non-modular.

It is tempting at this stage to equate system 1 reasoning with intuitive inferences and system 2 reasoning with reflective inferences. Some analogies seem obvious. Both system 2 and reflective inference are characterized by control, effortfulness, explicitness and, (at least virtual) domain-generality. They contrast in all these respects with system 1 and with intuitive inference.

There are also important disanalogies between the two ways of partitioning inferences. To begin with, the intuitive/reflective contrast is not one between two systems operating at the same level. Intuitive inferences are the direct output of many different modules. Reflective inferences are an indirect output of one of these modules. Hence, there are two ways to spell out the contrast. One may contrast the whole cognitive system, which delivers intuitive inferences through its many component subsystems, with one of these subsystems—the argumentation module—which, like all other inferential modules, directly delivers intuitive inferences, but which also indirectly delivers reflective inferences. One may also contrast a variety of processes carried out by different modules in many different ways, with the processes carried out in a more systematic way by a single one of these modules. These two ways of spelling out the contrast are of course compatible. They highlight the clear asymmetry between a first type of inferences—system 1 or intuitive—found in all animals endowed with rich enough cognitive systems, and a second type of inferences—system 2 or reflective—that may well be absent in non-human animals and that, even in humans, are used much more sparingly than the first type.

The argumentation module, being an ordinary module (different from other modules just as every module is different from all the others), shares to a greater or lesser extent many properties with many other modules. In particular, rather than being unique in requiring high attention (at least when its operations are reiterated in an inferential chain), the argumentation module may just stand towards one end of a particular gradient on which all modules are situated, a gradient defined by the respective role of bottom-up and top-down triggering factors in the activation of the module.

Some modules—we have mentioned danger detectors—have an inbuilt expectation of relevance and get activated in a bottom-up way. Our rich cognitive lives are possible, however, only to the extent that stimuli capable of pre-empting attention the way danger detectors do not occur too frequently in our environment. The full activation of most modules depends on a combination of bottom-up and top-down factors of attention. Consider for instance the detection of mood on the basis of facial cues. In ordinary social life, we are often surrounded by many people with different moods, but typically we pay attention only to the moods of some individuals who particularly matter to us, either in a relatively permanent way, or because of our interaction with them at that moment. So, modern humans can live in an urban environment and encounter new faces continually without having their attention preempted by these stimuli, even if they have dedicated modules to interpret them.

The fact that the full activation of modules depends to a greater or lesser extent on top-down control of attention does not mean at all that we choose consciously which modules to activate. After all, we are not even aware of the existence of our mental modules (or else the modularity thesis would not be controversial). What it means is that, by attending in a more or less voluntary way to some possible inputs and not to others, we modify their relative ease of processing (those that are already being attended to requiring less processing effort), thereby increasing their expected relevance (which is an inverse function of expected effort), and thereby the probability of their being fully processed by specific modules. So, the argumentation module is not unique in being much less dependent on bottom-up than on top-down factors of activation, even if it is likely to be towards one end of this particular gradient. One consequence of this relative and indirect controllability, is that the argumentation module should exhibit greater individual and situational variations than modules at the other extreme of the gradient. Another consequence of controllability is that the outputs of the argumentation module are particularly likely to be consciously attended.

As we already suggested, outputs of modules—unlike modular processes—may be conscious. They are particularly likely to be so when the process of which they are an output results from controlled attention, as in the case of reasoning proper. Moreover, since reasoning takes the form of a series of inferential steps the output of each of which consists in a justification for inferring a given conclusion, reasoning may appear to consciousness as a series of epistemically justified operations performed on explicit representations. This conscious representation of reasoning is partly misleading: what appears to consciousness is at best the series of intermediate and final conclusions with their justification, that is, a derivation in the formal, abstract sense of the term of the ultimate conclusion from the initial premises, and not a derivation in the concrete sense of a process with a series of sub-processes, (a distinction underscored by Harman 1986). Moreover, quite often, some of the intermediate steps may not be consciously entertained at all, so that the derivation is in fact enthymematic. Our approach thus clarifies in what interesting but limited sense reflective inference, or 'system 2 reasoning', may seem conscious, in contrast with intuitive inference or 'system 1 reasoning'. This approach does not suggest that 'consciousness' as such enables reflective inference or plays a causal role in it.

The function of reflective inference

General considerations and experimental evidence give us good reasons to distinguish two types of inferential processes, be they described as system 1 and system 2 reasoning or as intuitive and reflective inference. Still, one would want such a distinction to provide more novel theoretical insights, allow more new analyses of available evidence, and suggest more groundbreaking experimental research than it has done so far.

In this search for greater theoretical and empirical import, it should be fruitful to consider the different functions of these two types of inference, and in particular of reflective inference (the general function of intuitive inference is, we take it, better understood; interesting issues at that level have to do rather with the function of individual domain-specific modules). We assume that these forms of inference are evolved capacities, or at least capacities for the development of which there is an evolved disposition. Ernst Mayr's oft-quoted remark is relevant here (extending his point from physiology to psychology): 'The adaptationist question, "What is the function of a given structure or organ?" has been for centuries the basis for every advance in physiology' (Mayr 1983, p.328). So what, if anything, made the structures underlying different forms of inference advantageous over evolutionary time? The founders of dual-system theory have proposed at best cursory answers to this question.

In his 1996 article, Steven Sloman alluded to the question of the two systems' function. He offered two suggestions: the first is that 'the systems serve complementary functions. The associative system is able to draw on statistical structure, whereas a system that specializes in analysis and abstraction is able to focus on relevant features.' The second suggestion draws on Freudian psychology: on the one hand, the pain principle motivates us to seek gratification and avoid pain (system 1); on the other hand, we sometimes have to repress these impulses because gratification would otherwise escape us (system 2).

In their book on dual-system theory, Jonathan Evans and David Over state that 'consciousness [i.e. system 2 reasoning] gives us the possibility to deal with novelty and to anticipate the future' (Evans and Over 1996, p.154). In a more recent article, Evans says that 'interesting though such [evolutionary] speculations are, they may seem to have little immediate relevance to thinking and reasoning researchers attempting to account for the results of their experiments' (Evans 2006).

In *The robot's rebellion*, Keith Stanovich offers a somewhat more elaborate evolutionary account. He states that system 2 is 'where the genes gave up direct control and instead said (metaphorically, by the types of phenotypic effect that they created) "things will be changing too fast out there, brain, for us to tell you exactly what to do—you just go ahead and do what you think is best given the general goals (survival, sexual reproduction) that we have inserted"' (Stanovich 2004). He claims that system 1 reasoning is built by our genes to serve them directly by way of contextualized rules of the form: when in situation X, do Y (because it tends to maximize fitness). By contrast, system 2 reasoning is built to favor the individual. To that end, it should be able to fight some of the urges of system 1, by being decontextualized (so that it can find solutions that are not so context-dependent) and by having a strong inhibitory power.

These three views on the evolution and function of system 2 reasoning concur in seeing it as a way to compensate for some of the shortcomings of system 1 and to enhance individual cognition. This is consistent with the view of classical philosophers, Descartes in particular, according to which reasoning (by which they mean conscious reasoning) is the only reliable way to acquire knowledge.

There are, however, strong reasons to doubt that conscious or system 2 reasoning—here we will call it 'reasoning' *tout court*—evolved to enhance individual cognition.

The view that its function is to permit delaying gratification is puzzling for two reasons. The ability to delay gratification when it is advantageous to do so is a widespread feature of animal cognition—in hoarding food for instance—and not a specifically human trait. In humans, the ability to delay gratification seems to be a personality trait related to emotions and is dissociated from the ability to reason, as illustrated by the famous story of Phineas Gage and other better-documented similar cases discussed by Damasio (Damasio 1994).

The view that the function of reasoning is to enhance the ability to deal with novelty is not compelling either. Humans tend to accumulate in memory information of no immediate practical relevance which they can exploit to imagine possible novel situations. This is a more plausible basis for the ability to deal with novelty. The role of reasoning proper, as opposed to intuitive inference, in memory and imagination can hardly be described as central.[4]

The 'Cartesian' view that reasoning is *the* road to knowledge, or the more cautious view that the function of reasoning is to enhance cognition are also questionable. The issue is one of costs and benefits: those of reasoning have to be compared with those of intuitive inference. All theorists agree that reasoning is a relatively slow and costly process. Moreover, reasoning is difficult and prone to a variety of performance errors. So how might such a fallible and costly system still be advantageous? By providing a check on the inferences of system 1? System 1 inferences are on the whole reliable, and it remains to be demonstrated that checking them by means of reasoning, i.e. correcting some mistakes at a high cost and at the risk of further mistakes, would be advantageous. Is reasoning advantageous by allowing the mind to go where it would not intuitively? Many such extensions of the domain of knowledge that make a crucial use of reasoning come to mind, in the sciences in particular, but they typically involve social procedures and institutions where only few individuals make groundbreaking contributions. It is unclear that, at the individual level, the value of reasoning lies in its opening new intellectual vistas.

As an alternative to the view that the basic function of reasoning is to enhance individual cognition, we want to explore the hypothesis that reasoning has a primarily social function and, more specifically, that it is linked to the massive human reliance on communicated information.

Communication is found in a large number of species. For communication to evolve, the cost for the communicator of emitting a signal, and the cost for the receiver of responding to the signal must, on average, be inferior to the benefits. Often, however, the interests of the communicator and of the receiver do not

---

4 There is one kind of contingency that does call for a special form of reasoning, and that is strategic planning in social interaction. According to the Machiavellian hypothesis (Byrne and Whiten 1988; Whiten and Byrne 1997), this is in fact a driving force in the evolution of mindreading. To what extent it has evolved as a distinct module (or submodule of mindreading) is an open question. While strategic thinking has features in common with standard reasoning, in particular its metarepresentational complexity, we suggest that it is the work of a module other than the argumentation module.

coincide: communicators commonly have an interest in deceiving, whereas receivers' interest is best served by reliable, honest signals. If dishonest signals were frequent to the point of making communication disadvantageous to receivers, receivers would stop responding to them, and emitting these signals would cease to be advantageous to the communicators too (Krebs and Dawkins 1984). In other words, communication would be selected out. There is a variety of mechanisms that ensure honest signalling in animal species. The signal may involve a cost that only an honest signaller is in a position to incur (Zahavi and Zahavi 1997). A peacock, for instance, signals its fitness to peahens by displaying a magnificent tail, the cost of which could not be supported by an unfit peacock. Individuals may store information about past communication events and cease to trust communicators that have proved unreliable. Several species of monkey, for instance, are known to recognize the vocalizations of different members of their group; if an individual 'cries wolf' (by using a vocalization in a context that does not warrant it), the other members will soon stop reacting to this individual's vocalizations, or at least to the specific vocalization that has been improperly used (Cheney and Seyfarth 1990; Gouzoules et al. 1996).

Non-human animals, however, communicate only very simple information about a narrow range of matters, so that simple ad hoc mechanisms may evolve to enforce honesty. Humans, on the other hand, communicate complex information on an unbounded variety of matters and rely much more on communicated information than any other species. This reliance, hugely advantageous as it may be, is also a source of vulnerability to misinformation and deception. In other terms, there has been among humans a strong selective pressure for ways to filter communicated information so as to come as near as possible to accepting all and only reliable information. We assume that this pressure has caused not one but a variety of mechanisms of what may be called 'epistemic vigilance' (Sperber et al. submitted) to evolve. Some of the mechanisms have to do with selectively trusting or distrusting different sources of information on the basis of what is otherwise known of their competence and benevolence towards their audience, their past record in communication, and even behavioral indices of honesty or dishonesty (even if these are only marginally reliable; see (DePaulo et al. 2003; Ekman 2001). Other mechanisms have to do with properties of the information communicated which make it more or less credible.

A possible way to help calibrate one's trust is for the receiver to check the coherence of what is being said against his own knowledge base. The communicator would then have to adjust her signals if she wants them to be accepted. One way is to stay within the boundaries of what the receiver will be willing to accept on trust.[5] In some cases however, the communicator might want to communicate some information that the

---

[5] To put it another way: when a trusted communicator communicates something that is not totally coherent with the receiver's beliefs, the receiver has to choose between revising his beliefs regarding the content of what is being communicated or revising his trust in the speaker. He will tend to choose the solution that brings less incoherence, and this will often be to lower trust in the speaker.

receiver will not accept on trust. Here a strategy for the communicator can be to show the receiver how the information she communicates is in fact coherent with what he already believes—how, in fact, it would be incoherent for him not to accept it. To show this, the communicator must present information that the receiver is already disposed to accept or is willing to accept on trust and that provides premises from which the less easily accepted information follows.

The communicator can moreover highlight the logical or evidential links between the acceptable premises and the intended conclusion. The receiver will then be in a position to evaluate the strength or the validity of these links. Why would he put in such effort? First, it should be noted that most of the effort will be on the communicator's side: it is advantageous for her to make her argument as plain, simple and understandable as possible if she wants to convince the receiver by this means. But the receiver also has something to gain from using a more selective, finer-grained filtering mechanism. Communicators whose benevolence or competence in the matter at hand cannot be taken for granted may nevertheless have valuable information to transmit; it is useful in such cases to be able to bypass or overcome selective distrust. Also, because one's previously held beliefs may be wrong, it can be useful to be able to go beyond a simple check of coherence with these beliefs.

If this scenario is correct, there may have been selection pressures favoring the evolution of capacities that allow communicators and receivers to evaluate evidential, logical and coherence relationships between different pieces of information, i.e. selection pressures for reflective inference. Reflective inference so understood is geared to deal with specific problems concerning the acceptance or rejection of claims in communication. The effectiveness of the argumentation module, like that of any other module, should depend on the expected relevance of its operations in a given situation. In particular, situations characterized by the need to convince others or by that of not being too easily convinced should trigger more efficient reasoning—a prediction quite specific to this approach.

Reasoning and argumentation: Some evidence

Abstract versus argumentative contexts

If our approach is right, reasoning should be more easily triggered in argumentative situations. We should therefore expect better performances on reasoning tasks where the participants are placed in such situations. Standard theories make no such prediction. If anything, argumentative contexts should increase the cognitive load since they involve taking into account different opinions.

It is now well established that performances on computationally trivial logical problems can be dismal. As Evans states in his review of the literature on deductive reasoning: 'it must be said that logical performance in abstract reasoning tasks is generally quite poor'(Evans 2002, p.981). The simplest way to compare the abstract context of a classical reasoning experiment with an argumentative context is to get the participants to discuss the problem in groups.

Among the great many studies on group decision making, the most relevant are those bearing on problems that have a demonstrably correct answer—and are thus analogous to the tasks used in most reasoning experiments. It has now been repeatedly shown that, provided certain minimal conditions are met (the good answer must be accessible to at least one of the participants for instance), what is observed is that in such contexts, if one of the participants has the correct answer, then the other members will get to it too. This has been shown for mathematical tasks (Laughlin and Ellis 1986; Stasson et al. 1991), 'Eureka' problems (in which the correct solution seems obvious in retrospect—Laughlin et al. 1975), and Mastermind problems (from the board game—Bonner et al. 2002). In all these cases the performance of groups tends to be at the level of the best participants taken individually. The experiments carried out by Moshman and Geil (1998) illustrate this point dramatically. The experimenters had participants solve the Wason selection task, either first individually and then in groups, or directly in groups. In both cases, the performance of the groups was impressively higher than that of the participants who were solving the problem individually: 75% of the groups found the right answer, compared with 14% in the solitary condition.[6]

According to the theory advocated here, this dramatic improvement is due to the fact that when they have to solve the problem in groups, participants have to argue and debate, and that this activates their reasoning abilities in such a manner that they are able either to come up with the correct solution, or at least to accept it and reject the incorrect ones.

Of course, this is not the only possible interpretation of these results. An alternative interpretation might be that the smartest participant gets it right and the others recognize her competence and accept her answer without reasoning (explanation hinted at by (Oaksford et al. 1999). Another possible interpretation is that the participants are simply sharing information, and not reasoning. These explanations are hard to reconcile with the following facts. First of all, information sharing is often insufficient to solve the task. For example, in the Wason selection task, it will often be the case that a participant has wrongly selected a card and another has rightly rejected it. In that case, sharing information won't do the trick: participants have conflicting pieces of information, and they have to pick the correct one. This means that conflicts and debate should occur. An analysis of the transcripts of such experiments will show that such is indeed the case (Moshman and Geil 1998; Trognon 1993), and there is a large literature showing that conflict is often the crucial factor that allows groups to outperform individuals (see the references in Schulz-Hardt et al. 2006). In some cases, conflicts will even lead a group in which no individual had the correct answer towards it—provided that not everyone makes the same mistake to start with (this happened in some of the groups studied by Moshman and Geil and is known in developmental psychology as 'two wrongs make a right' (Glachan and Light 1982; Schwarz et al. 2000) and as the 'assembly bonus effect' in social psychology (Kerr et al. 1996). The explanation based on the recognition of an expert is also hard to reconcile with the presence and importance of

---

[6] A similar effect—if a bit less dramatic—was observed by (Maciejovsky and Budescu 2007).

such conflicts. One could even argue that the opposite in fact happens: a person is recognized as an expert because she uses good arguments—so participants must use reasoning to discern good arguments in the first place (see Littlepage and Mueller 1997 for evidence in that direction).

Finally, we can also rule out an explanation based on general motivation: one might think that participants are more motivated—will make greater effort—to solve any task in group. This would be quite surprising, however, given the importance of social loafing in groups (Karau and Williams 1993). Moreover, if motivation was the problem, it should be alleviated by monetary incentives. However, in line with the general observation that money tends to have no effect on performances in decision making tasks (Camerer and Hogarth 1999), it has been shown that monetary incentives do not increase the performance in the Wason selection task (Johnson-Laird and Byrne 2002; Jones and Sugden 2001)—a result in sharp contrast with the dramatic improvement in group settings.

Biases in reasoning

The biases that plague reasoning provide further evidence in favor of our approach. We concentrate here on two twin biases that have been reported time and again: the confirmation bias and the disconfirmation bias. Both biases apply when we have to evaluate a belief or a hypothesis: instead of objectively evaluating it, we seek to confirm it if we agree with it in the first place, and to disconfirm it if we don't. This can hardly be sanctioned by a normative theory and is all the more disquieting in that it seems to be extremely widespread: 'smart' people do it (Stanovich and West 2007); open-minded people do it (Stanovich and West 2007); and physicians, judges and scientists do it (see Fugelsang and Dunbar 2005; Nickerson 1998; and references within). From an argumentative viewpoint, these biases are hardly surprising. In fact, they could be predicted on the grounds that when we try to persuade someone that something is true (or false), a confirmation (or disconfirmation) bias may help us achieve our goal.

The experiment that has done the most to promote the idea of the confirmation bias is Wason's 2, 4, 6 task (Wason 1960). In this task, participants have to find the rule governing the formation of triplets of numbers, knowing that 2, 4, 6 is such a triplet. They can test their hypothesis by proposing their own triplets and being told whether they fit the rule. Participants can propose triplets and suggest tentative rules until they have found the correct rule or have given up. Participants typically show a strong confirmation bias in using triplets that conform to their hypothesis in order to test for it rather than triplets that might falsify it (Tweney et al. 1980; Wason 1960). Whether the strategy of the participant is really non-normative has been debated (Klayman and Ha 1987; Koehler 1993), but two elements point to a real bias and fit with our hypothesis. First, 'psychological experiments that have strongly instructed participants to take a falsification approach to the 2, 4, 6 task have in fact had little effect in improving performance (Poletiek 1996; Tweney et al. 1980)' (Evans 2006). If the tendency to confirm wasn't a deep-rooted bias, these instructions should be much more effective. Even more interestingly, there seems to exist a simple solution to get participants to use a falsifying strategy: when told that they were testing someone else's hypothesis, participants used the falsifying strategy four times more often and abandoned the hypothesis sooner (Cowley and Byrne 2005).[7]

Just as we tend to confirm claims we agree with, we tend to disconfirm claims that don't fit our views. The classical demonstration of this disconfirmation bias comes from a study by Lord et al. (1979) in which people had to evaluate studies either in favor or against the death penalty. Participants who supported the death penalty were much more critical of the study arguing against it, and conversely. It has later been shown that people not only put in more effort in examining studies whose conclusions they don't agree with: they are strongly biased towards critical thoughts (Edwards and Smith 1996). Here, too, urging participants to be objective isn't very efficient (Lord et al. 1984). However, when participants are told to imagine that a given study they agree with has in fact the opposite conclusion, they become quite adept at critically examining it (Lord et al. 1984).

Another well known effect in the psychology of reasoning is the belief bias, thought to be a consequence of the disconfirmation bias. Some experiments have pitted the believability of the conclusion of an argument against its logical validity. The main effect is one of believability: people will tend to use believability instead of validity to judge the argument, a finding easy to interpret in terms of epistemic vigilance: believability provides a reason to believe and unbelievability a reason to disbelieve. This effect is stronger for believable conclusions: with them, validity barely makes a difference. Validity, on the other hand, is taken into greater account in th case of unbelievable conclusions. It seems then that when the conclusion of an argument is believable, participants hardly bother to evaluate its validity, but when it is unbelievable, they try to find the flaw, as they should if what motivates is epistemic vigilance. When they fail to find any flaw because the argument is valid, they accept it, again, as they should. Epistemic vigilance is what explains that people are more sensitive to validity when the conclusion is unbelievable (Evans et al. 1993; Klauer et al. 2000; Newstead et al. 1992).

In a nutshell, the confirmation, disconfirmation, and believability biases behave much as the argumentative theory would predict: one cannot suppress them with instructions to be objective, but if one can get participants to change their mind about the claim to be evaluated, then the biases can disappear or even be reversed.

Are people good at arguing?

If argumentation has been so important in evolutionary history, then humans should be good at it. The first large scale study of the 'skills of argument' by Deanna Kuhn (1991) concluded, however, that people are rather poor at argumentation. We remain unconvinced for the following reasons. To begin with, the context of her experiments was quite artificial: people were asked to argue about topics of which they had very limited knowledge (e.g. the causes of school failure, or of relapse into delinquency after prison), with an experimenter who wasn't really arguing with them. It has later

---

[7] Even though due to the limited number of participants this difference failed to reach significance.

been shown that when participants are more knowledgeable about the topics they stop making some of the mistakes noted by Kuhn (such as using explanation—some kind of naive theory—instead of genuine evidence (Brem and Rips 2000). More importantly, most of the shortcomings Kuhn attributed to participants were in fact instances of the confirmation bias: for example, participants often had trouble finding alternative theories or rebuttals to their own hypothesis. So they were indeed doing what one should expect if reasoning was used not to get at the truth, but to persuade.

Other studies have since tended to show that participants do possess the skills necessary to understand and take part in an argument. They can follow the commitments of the different speakers and determine, at any given point of the argument, who has the burden of proof (Bailenson and Rips 1996; Rips 1998). They understand the macrostructure of arguments (Ricco 2003). They are often able to spot the classical fallacies of argumentation, such as ad hominem, *petitio principii* (begging the question), or circular reasoning (Neuman et al. 2004; Neuman et al. 2006; Rips 2002; Weinstock et al. 2004).

Note that these 'fallacies' can sometimes be quite appropriate – for example, when someone uses her authority to make a point, then a good ad hominem may be effective. Oaksford, Hahn, and their colleagues have used Bayesian statistics to pinpoint which features of a given argument make it more or less fallacious (Hahn and Oaksford 2007). For example, the validity of a slippery slope argument depends—among other things—on the conditional probability of each step of the slope given the preceding step. Instead of the mere ability to spot fallacies, a more accurate measure of people's argumentative skills is a measure of the fit between their evaluations of arguments and their actual validity (as indexed by these statistics). In a set of experiments, these researchers tested these predictions for a set of such 'fallacies': argument from ignorance (Oaksford and Hahn 2004), slippery slope arguments and circular reasoning (Hahn and Oaksford 2006). In all of these experiments, participants' ratings of the strength of different arguments were indeed correlated with factors that reflected the actual statistical validity of the arguments.

Finally, researchers who have looked at real arguments—between participants debating for instance—have been 'impressed by the coherence of the reasoning displayed. Participants … appear to build complex argument and attack structure. People appear to be capable of recognizing these structures and of effectively attacking their individual components as well as the argument as a whole' (Resnick et al. 1993). The contrast between these observations and the dismal results of simple reasoning tasks could not be sharper.

Conclusion

In this chapter we have tried to outline an original view of reasoning, seeing it as an aspect of social, and more specifically communicative competence. This view is embedded in an evolutionary psychology framework and in particular in a massive modularist view of the human mind. At its core is the distinction between two types of inferences: intuitive inferences that are the direct output of inferential modules and take place without attention to reasons for accepting them; and reflective inferences that are an indirect output of a particular metarepresentational module, the argumentation module, the direct output of which is an argument for or against a given conclusion. Being a distinction between two types of inferences, this view has obvious analogies with other dual-process accounts of reasoning, but some serious differences were also noted.

An evolutionary argument was put forward to explain what the function of the argumentation module might be—namely, to regulate the flow of information among interlocutors through persuasiveness on the side of the communicator and epistemic vigilance on the side of the audience. Testable predictions follow from such an account. We have argued that some puzzling findings in the psychology of reasoning and state of the art work in the psychology of argumentation confirm these predictions. Further confirmation will have to come from novel experiments specifically designed to test these theoretical claims.

Acknowledgments

We thank Jonathan Evans, Keith Frankish, Katherine Kinzler, and Deirdre Wilson for their useful comments. This work was made possible in part thanks to the support of the Center for the Study of the Mind in Nature (University of Oslo).

References

Bailenson, J.N. and Rips, L.J. (1996) Informal reasoning and burden of proof. *Applied Cognitive Psychology*, **10**, 3–16.

Baron-Cohen, S. (1995) *Mindblindness*. MIT Press, Cambridge, MA.

Barrett, H.C. (2005) Enzymatic computation and cognitive modularity. *Mind and language*, **20**, 259–87.

Barrett, H.C. and Kurzban, R. (2006) Modularity in cognition: Framing the debate. *Psychological Review*, **113**, 628–47.

Bonnay, D. and Simmenauer, B. (2005) Tonk strikes back. *Australasian Journal of Logic*, **3**, 33–44.

Bonner, B.L., Baumann, M.R., and Dalal, R.S. (2002) The effects of member expertise on group decision making and performance. *Organizational Behavior and Human Decision Processes*, **88**, 719–36.

Braine, M.D.S. (1990) The 'natural logic' approach to reasoning. In W.F. Overton (ed.) *Reasoning, necessity and logic: Developmental perspectives*, Vols. 133–57. Lawrence Erlbaum Associates Inc, Hillsdale, NJ.

Brem, S.K. and Rips, L.J. (2000) Explanation and evidence in informal argument. *Cognitive Science*, **24**, 573–604.

Byrne, R. and Whiten, A. (eds) (1988) *Machiavellian intelligence: Social expertise and the evolution of intellect in monkeys, apes, and humans*. Oxford University Press, Oxford.

Camerer, C. and Hogarth, R.M. (1999) The effect of financial incentives on performance in experiments: A review and capital-labor theory. *Journal of Risk and Uncertainty*, **19**, 7–42.

Carruthers, P. (2006) *The architecture of the mind*. Oxford University Press, Oxford.

Cheney, D.L. and Seyfarth, R.M. (1990) *How monkeys see the world*. Chicago University Press, Chicago, IL.

Cohen, L.J. (1992) *An essay on belief and acceptance*. Clarendon Press, Oxford.

Cowley, M. and Byrne, R.M.J. (2005) *When falsification is the only path to truth*. Paper presented at the Twenty-Seventh Annual Conference of the Cognitive Science Society, Stresa, Italy.

Damasio, A.R. (1994) *Descartes' error: emotion reason, and the human brain*. G.P. Putnam's Sons, New York.

de Sousa, R. (1971) How to give a piece of your mind: Or, the logic of belief and assent. *Review of Metaphysics*, **25**, 52–79.

Dennett, D.C. (1969) *Content and consciousness*. Routledge and Kegan Paul, London.

Dennett, D.C. (1981) *Brainstorms: Philosophical essays on mind and psychology*. MIT Press, Cambridge, MA.

DePaulo, B.M., Lindsay, J.J., Malone, B.E., Muhlenbruck, L., Charlton, K., and Cooper, H. (2003) Cues to deception. *Psychological Bulletin* **129**, 74–118.

Edwards, K. and Smith, E.E. (1996) A disconfirmation bias in the evaluation of arguments. *Journal of Personality and Social Psychology*, **71**, 5–24.

Ekman, P. (2001) *Telling lies*. Norton, New York.

Engel, P. (2000) *Believing and accepting*. Kluwer Academic Publishers, Dordrecht.

Engel, P. (2006) Logic, reasoning and the logical constants. *Croatian Journal of Philosophy* **2**, 219.

Evans, J.St.B.T. (2002) Logic and human reasoning: An assessment of the deduction paradigm. *Psychological Bulletin*, **128**, 978–96.

Evans, J.St.B.T. (2003) In two minds: Dual-process accounts of reasoning. *Trends in Cognitive Sciences*, **7**, 454–9.

Evans, J.St.B.T. (2006) The heuristic-analytic theory of reasoning: Extension and evaluation. *Psychonomic Bulletin and Review*, **13**, 378–95.

Evans, J.St.B.T. (2008) Dual-processing accounts of reasoning, judgment and social cognition. *Annual Review of Psychology*, **59**, 255–78.

Evans, J.St.B.T. and Over, D.E. (1996) *Rationality and reasoning*. Psychology Press, Hove.

Evans, J.St.B.T., Newstead, S.E., and Byrne, R.M. J. (1993) *Human reasoning: The psychology of deduction*. Lawrence Erlbaum Associates Ltd, Hove.

Fodor, J. (2001) *The mind doesn't work that way*. MIT Press, Cambridge, MA.

Fugelsang, J.A. and Dunbar, K.N. (2005) Brain-based mechanisms underlying complex causal thinking. *Neuropsychologia*, **43**, 1204–13.

Gigerenzer, G., Todd, P.M., and ABC Research Group. (1999) *Simple heuristics that make us smart*. Oxford University Press, Oxford.

Glachan, M. and Light, P. (1982) Peer interaction and learning: Can two wrongs make a right? In G. Butterworth and P. Light (eds) *Social cognition: Studies in the development of understanding*, 238–62. University of Chicago Press, Chicago, IL.

Gouzoules, H., Gouzoules, S., and Miller, K. (1996) Skeptical responding in rhesus monkeys (Macaca mulatta). *International Journal of Primatology*, **17**, 549–68.

Hahn, U. and Oaksford, M. (2006) A Bayesian approach to informal argument fallacies. *Synthese*, **152**, 207–36.

Hahn, U. and Oaksford, M. (2007) The rationality of informal argumentation: A Bayesian approach to reasoning fallacies. *Psychological Review*, **114**, 704–32.

Harman, G. (1986) *Change in view: Principles of reasoning*. MIT Press, Cambridge, MA.

Johnson-Laird, P. N. (1983) *Mental models*. Cambridge University Press, Cambridge.

Johnson-Laird, P.N. and Byrne, R.M.J. (2002) Conditionals: A theory of meaning, pragmatics, and inference. *Psychological Review*, **109**, 646–78.

Jones, M. and Sugden, R. (2001) Positive confirmation bias in the acquisition of information. *Theory and Decision*, **50**, 59–99.

Kahneman, D. and Frederick, S. (2005) A model of heuristic judgment. In K. Holyoak and R.G. Morrison (eds) *The Cambridge handbook of thinking and reasoning*, 267–94. Cambridge Univiversity Press, Cambridge.

Karau, S.J. and Williams, K.D. (1993) Social loafing: A meta-analytic review and theoretical integration. *Journal of Personality and Social Psychology*, **65**, 681–706.

Kerr, N.L., Maccoun, R.J., and Kramer, G.P. (1996) Bias in judgement: Comparing individuals and groups. *Psychological Review*, **103**, 687–719.

Klauer, K.C., Musch, J., and Naumer, B. (2000) On belief bias in syllogistic reasoning. *Psychological Review*, **107**, 852–84.

Klayman, J. and Ha, Y. (1987) Confirmation, disconfirmation, and information in hypothesis testing. *Psychological Review*, **94**, 211–28.

Koehler, J.J. (1993) The influence of prior beliefs on scientific judgments of evidence quality. *Organizational Behavior and Human Decision Processes*, **56**, 28–55.

Krebs, J.R. and Dawkins, R. (1984) Animal signals: Mind-reading and manipulation? In J.R. Krebs and N.B. Davies (eds) *Behavioural ecology: An evolutionary approach,* 2nd ed, 390–402. Basil Blackwell Scientific Publications, Oxford.

Kuhn, D. (1991) *The skills of arguments*. Cambridge University Press, Cambridge.

Laughlin, P.R. and Ellis, A.L. (1986) Demonstrability and social combination processes on mathematical intellective tasks. *Journal of Experimental Social Psychology*, **22**, 177–89.

Laughlin, P.R., Kerr, N.L., Davis, J.H., Halff, H.M., and Marciniak, K.A. (1975) Group size, member ability, and social decision schemes on an intellective task. *Journal of Personality and Social Psychology*, **33**, 80–8.

Leslie, A.M. (1995) A theory of agency. In D. Sperber and D. Premack (eds) *Causal cognition: A multidisciplinary debate*. Oxford University Press, New York.

Littlepage, G.E. and Mueller, A.L. (1997) Recognition and utilization of expertise in problem-solving groups: Expert characteristics and behavior. *Group Dynamics*, **1**, 324–8.

Lord, C.G., Lepper, M.R., and Preston, E. (1984) Considering the opposite: A corrective strategy for social judgment. *Journal of Personality and Social Psychology*, **47**, 1231–43.

Lord, C.G., Ross, L., and Lepper, M.R. (1979) Biased assimilation and attitude polarization: The effects of prior theories on subsequently considered evidence. *Journal of Personality and Social Psychology*, **37**, 2098–2109.

Maciejovsky, B. and Budescu, D.V. (2007) Collective induction without cooperation? Learning and knowledge transfer in cooperative groups and competitive auctions. *Journal of Personality and Social Psychology*, **92**, 854–70.

Mayr, E. (1983) How to carry out the adaptationist program. *The American Naturalist*, **121**, 324–34.

Moshman, D. and Geil, M. (1998) Collaborative reasoning: Evidence for collective rationality. *Thinking and Reasoning*, **4**, 231–48.

Neuman, Y., Glassner, A., and Weinstock, M. (2004) The effect of a reason's truth-value on the judgment of a fallacious argument. *Acta Psychologica*, **116**, 173–84.

Neuman, Y., Weinstock, M.P., and Glasner, A. (2006) The effect of contextual factors on the judgement of informal reasoning fallacies. *The Quarterly Journal of Experimental Psychology*, **59**, 411–25.

Newstead, S.E. Pollard, P. Evans, J.St.B.T. and Allen, J.L. (1992) The source of belief bias effects in syllogistic reasoning. *Cognition*, **45**, 257–84.

Nickerson, R.S. (1998) Confirmation bias: A ubiquitous phenomena in many guises. *Review of General Psychology*, **2**, 175–220.

Oaksford, M. and Hahn, U. (2004) A Bayesian approach to the argument from ignorance. *Canadian Journal of Experimental Psychology*, **58**, 75–85.

Oaksford, M., Chater, N., and Grainger, R. (1999) Probabilistic effects in data selection. *Thinking and Reasoning*, **5**, 193–243.

Osman, M. (2004) An evaluation of dual-process theories of reasoning. *Psychonomic Bulletin and Review*, **11**, 988–1010.

Poletiek, F.H. (1996) Paradoxes of falsification. *Quarterly Journal of Experimental Psychology*, **49**, 447–62.

Prior, A.N. (1960) The runabout inference-ticket. *Analysis*, **21**, 38, 39.

Resnick, L.B., Salmon, M., Zeitz, C.M., Wathen, S.H., and Holowchak, M. (1993) Reasoning in conversation. *Cognition and Instruction*, **11**, 347–64.

Ricco, R.B. (2003) The macrostructure of informal arguments: A proposed model and analysis. *Quarterly Journal of Experimental Psychology*, **56**, 1021–51.

Rips, L.J. (1994) *The psychology of proof: Deductive reasoning in human thinking*. MIT Press, Cambridge, MA.

Rips, L.J. (1998) Reasoning and conversation. *Psychological Review*, **105**, 411–41.

Rips, L.J. (2002) Circular reasoning. *Cognitive Science*, **26**, 767–95.

Schulz-Hardt, S., Brodbeck, F.C., Mojzisch, A., Kerschreiter, R., and Frey, D. (2006) Group decision making in hidden profile situations: dissent as a facilitator for decision quality. *Journal of Personality and Social Psychology*, **91**, 1080–93.

Schwarz, B.B., Neuman, Y., and Biezuner, S. (2000) Two wrongs make a right … if they argue together! *Cognition and Instruction*, **18**, 461–94.

Simons, D.J. and Chabris, C.F. (1999) Gorillas in our midst: Sustained inattentional blindness for dynamic events. *Perception*, **28**, 1059–74.

Sloman, S.A. (1996) The empirical case for two systems of reasoning. *Psychological Bulletin*, **119**, 3–22.

Spelke, E.S. (1990) Principles of object perception. *Cognitive Science*, **14**, 29–56.

Sperber, D. (1985) *On anthropological knowledge*: Cambridge University Press, Cambridge.

Sperber, D. (1994) The modularity of thought and the epidemiology of representations. In L.A. Hirschfeld and S.A. Gelman (eds) *Mapping the mind: Domain specificity in cognition and culture*, 39–67. Cambridge University Press, Cambridge.

Sperber, D. (1997) Intuitive and reflective beliefs. *Mind and Language*, **12**, 67–83.

Sperber, D. (2000a) Metarepresentations in an evolutionary perspective. In D. Sperber (ed.) *Metarepresentations: A multidisciplinary perspective*, 117–37. Oxford University Press, Oxford.

Sperber, D. (ed.) (2000b) *Metarepresentations: A multidisciplinary perspective*. Oxford University Press, Oxford.

Sperber, D. (2001a) An evolutionary perspective on testimony and argumentation. *Philosophical Topics*, **29**, 401–13.

Sperber, D. (2001b) In defense of massive modularity. In E. Dupoux (ed.) *Language, brain and cognitive development: Essays in honor of Jacques Mehler*, 47–57. MIT Press, Cambridge, MA.

Sperber, D. (2005) Modularity and relevance: How can a massively modular mind be flexible and context-sensitive? In P. Carruthers, S. Laurence, and S. Stich (eds) *The innate mind: Structure and contents*.

Sperber, D., Clément, F., Mascaro, O., Mercier, H., Origgi, G., and Wilson, D. (submitted). Epistemic vigilance.

Sperber, D. and Wilson, D. (1995) *Relevance: Communication and cognition*. Blackwell, Oxford.

Sperber, D. and Wilson, D. (2002) Pragmatics, modularity and mind-reading. *Mind and Language*, **17**, 3–23.

Stalnaker, R.C. (1984) *Inquiry*. MIT Press, Cambridge, MA.

Stanovich, K.E. (2004) *The robot's rebellion*. Chicago University Press, Chicago, IL.

Stanovich, K.E. and West, R.F. (2000) Individual differences in reasoning: Implications for the rationality debate. *Behavioral and Brain Sciences*, **23**, 645–726.

Stanovich, K.E. and West, R.F. (2007) Natural myside bias is independent of cognitive ability. *Thinking and Reasoning*, **13**, 225–47.

Stasson, M.F., Kameda, T., Parks, C.D., Zimmerman, S.K., and Davis, J.H. (1991) Effects of assigned group consensus requirement on group problem solving and group members' learning. *Social Psychology Quarterly*, **54**, 25–35.

Tomasello, M. (1999) *The cultural origins of human cognition*. Harvard University Press, Cambridge, MA.

Tooby, J. and Cosmides, L. (1992) The psychological foundations of culture. In J.H. Barkow, L. Cosmides, and J. Tooby (eds) *The adapted mind*, 19–136. Oxford University Press, Oxford.

Trognon, A. (1993) How does the process of interaction work when two interlocutors try to resolve a logical problem? *Cognition and Instruction*, **11**, 325–45.

Tweney, R.D., Doherty, M.E., Warner, W.J., and Pliske, D.B. (1980) Strategies of rule discovery in an inference task. *Quarterly Journal of Experimenal Psychology*, **32**, 109–24.

Vickers, J.M. (1988) *Chance and structure: An essay on the logical foundations of probability*. Clarendon Press, Oxford.

Wason, P.C. (1960) On the failure to eliminate hypotheses in a conceptual task. *Quarterly Journal of Experimental Psychology*, **12**, 129–37.

Weinstock, M., Neuman, Y., and Tabak, I. (2004) Missing the point or missing the norms? Epistemological norms as predictors of students' ability to identify fallacious arguments. *Contemporary Educational Psychology*, **29**, 77–94.

Whiten, A. and Byrne, R.W. (eds) (1997) *Machiavellian intelligence II: Extensions and evaluations*. Cambridge University Press, Cambridge.

Wilson, D. (2000) Metarepresentation in linguistic communication. In D. Sperber (ed.) *Metarepresentations: A multidisciplinary perspective*. Oxford University Press, Oxford.

Wynn, K. (1992) Addition and subtraction in human infants. *Nature*, **358**, 749–50.

Zahavi, A. and Zahavi, A. (1997) *The handicap principle: A missing piece of Darwin's puzzle*. Oxford University Press, Oxford.

Chapter 8

Dual-process theories: A metacognitive perspective

Valerie A. Thompson

The core assumption of Dual-Process Theories (DPT) is that reasoning and decision making are accomplished by the joint action of two types of processes, differing in terms of the degree to which they are characterized as fast and automatic or slow and conscious (e.g. Evans 2006; Kahneman 2003; Sloman 2002; Stanovich 2004). Automatic System 1 (S1) processes give rise to a highly contextualized representation of the problem and attendant judgments that are seldom analyzed extensively by the more deliberate, decontextualized System 2 (S2) processes. Even in cases where analytic processes are engaged, the representations formed by System 1 may omit relevant information that is not salient in the environment, so that the processes engaged by System 2 may focus on a selected subset of relevant information. Together with the assumption that System 2 processes have limited abilities, variously attributed to poor monitoring, limited working memory resources, absence of good normative models, and a tendency to 'satisfice', DPT potentially explain so-called biases and errors in a broad range of reasoning tasks.

In terms of predicting the outcome of any given reasoning attempt, the crucial questions for DPT are when and to what extent does S2 intervene? To date, a number of variables have been suggested (see Evans 2006 for a summary). With few exceptions, these variables deal with global characteristics of the reasoner, such as cognitive capacity (Stanovich 1999; De Neys 2006b) or aspects of the environment including the amount of time allotted to complete the task (Evans and Curtis-Holmes 2005; Finucane et al. 2000) and the instructions provided to the reasoner (Newstead et al. 1992; Evans et al. 1994; Daniel and Klaczynski 2006; Vadenoncoeur and Markovits 1999). Missing from this analysis is a description of the properties of the stimulus that are more or less likely to trigger S2 intervention. That is the goal of the current paper.

The theoretical framework

In this chapter, I develop a framework for predicting S2 intervention that is based on metacognitive experiences associated with S1 processes. In particular, I develop the argument that the outcome of a given reasoning attempt is determined not only by the content of the information that is retrieved by S1 and analyzed by S2, but also by a second-order judgment. This metacognitive judgment is largely based on the experience associated with the execution of S1 and S2 processes and it is this judgment that determines whether, and how S2 processes are engaged. A diagram of the complete model is presented in Figure 8.1.

The major difference between the model presented in Figure 8.1 and extant models is the inclusion of metacognitive processes. Other aspects of the model, namely the generation of heuristic responses and that execution of analytic processing have been extensively discussed by others. In the current chapter, I argue that metacognitive processes provide an important link between the heuristic processes represented on the left and the analytic processes described on the right.

To illustrate this approach, consider the following two formulations of a problem. The first is one of the items from Frederick's (2005) Cognitive Reflection Test (CRT). The second is an isomorphic version of the same problem:

If it takes 5 machines 5 minutes to make 5 widgets, how long would it take 100 machines to make 100 widgets?

_____ minutes

If it takes 5 machines 2 minutes to make 10 widgets, how long would it take 100 machines to make 100 widgets?

_____ minutes

The first problem strongly cues the response '100', which is, in fact, erroneous but often given as an answer (Fredrick 2005). In the language of DPT, System 1 has produced a heuristic response that is accepted with little, if any, analysis by System 2. In contrast, the second problem does not directly cue a response from S1, and instead invites one to take out a pencil and paper and attempt a solution via algebra.

Put in these terms, the widget example draws attention to several issues. The first concerns the circumstances under which S1 is cued to produce a heuristic response.

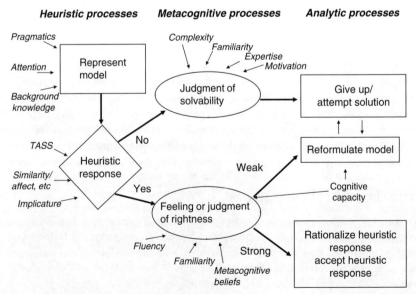

Fig. 8.1 A metacognitive framework of reasoning.

Second, once such a response is cued, under what circumstances is that response modified? Again, there are at least two facets to this question. The first concerns the properties of the retrieval process that trigger awareness of the need to reanalyze the problem. The second concerns the nature of the analysis that is triggered. Finally, in the absence of a strong heuristic response, what determines S2 intervention? That is, under what circumstances will the reasoner take out the pencil and paper and attempt the algebra needed to solve the widget problem?

What triggers a strong heuristic response?

Although this is a important question, I will address it only briefly, given that it has been extensively analyzed by others. Indeed, three recent approaches to explaining heuristic responding have been proposed; although they differ in terms of specifics, they share the basic assumption that heuristic responses are cued automatically by perceptual or cognitive input and that these responses form the basis of subsequent judgments and decisions.

Kahneman (2003) proposed that heuristic responses consist of impressions formed about the objects of perception and thought. These impressions, which he called *natural assessments*, are formed automatically, in that they are not subject to voluntary control; further, the origins of these impressions are not available to introspection. The accessibility of these natural assessments is thought to be determined by the skill of the reasoner, properties of the stimulus, physical salience, framing, and priming. For example, framing an outcome in terms of survival rates promotes a more positive evaluation than does a framing in terms of mortality rates, presumably because the former primes positive thoughts whereas the latter primes negative ones. Reasoners then form an impression or a natural assessment based on the emotional valence of the primed thoughts and this natural assessment subsequently forms the basis of a judgment.

According to Kahneman, the domain of natural assessments includes physical properties such as size, distance, and loudness, as well as more abstract properties such as similarity, surprisingness, affective valence, etc. These assessments become judgments by a process of attribute substitution in which an individual makes a judgment about one attribute (i.e. probability) by substituting a judgment about a different attribute (such as affective valence) that is more accessible. In this view, the role of S2 is to monitor this process; analytic processes are engaged when the substitution is detected.

Stanovich (2004) offers a somewhat different view of heuristic processes. He argues that what is referred to as 'System 1' is really a multiplicity of systems that function automatically in response to triggering stimuli; these he collectively refers to as The Autonomous Set of Systems (TASS). These systems include domain-specific processes, such as those involved in language and perception, domain-general processes, such as those involved in associative and implicit learning, and skills that have been learned to the point of automaticity. These processes, while constrained to operate within the strict limits of their triggering stimuli, are fast, efficient and can operate in parallel. S2, in this view, is responsible for monitoring the outputs of the TASS subsystems and to intervene when TASS produces responses that conflict with the reasoner's goals.

Alternatively, S1 processes can be viewed as the processes that construct a model of the problem (Evans 2006); this model may contain only a subset of relevant information, include irrelevant information, and may be contaminated by prior beliefs and expectations. In this view, S1 processes are those used to contextualize input, that is, they are the processes by which relevant background knowledge and beliefs are recruited (Evans 2006; Evans et al. 2003; Stanovich 1999). These processes give rise to belief-bias and other related effects. For example, listeners often rely on conversational implicatures to embellish and interpret a reasoner's speech. In the context of deductive reasoning, for example, a reasoner's interpretation of logical quantifiers may be guided by conversational principles that gives them a different meaning than intended by logicians (Begg and Harris 1982; Feeney et al. 2004; Newstead 1989) and this interpretation plays a functional role in the inferences that they draw (Roberts et al. 2001; Schmidt and Thompson 2008). For instance, the meaning of 'some' is logically consistent with 'all' even though most listeners would find such usage infelicitous. In other cases, pragmatic and linguistic processes highlight the relevance of some information, and omit others from the representation (Evans 1998; 2006). In this view, S2 operates on potentially biassed or incomplete representation, and decisions are usually based on the information that is heuristically cued (Evans 2006). Although the analytic system may scrutinize those choices, it will not do so unless there is a compelling reason.

In summary, all three views suggest that heuristic judgments are strongly cued, automatic and largely implicit (i.e. their origins are not available to introspection). For a variety of reasons, these judgments are often accepted with little further analysis by the analytic system. In the following sections, I turn to the question of why these heuristic judgments are readily accepted, and propose criteria by which S2 is triggered to intervene with those heuristic judgments.

Properties of the retrieval process that trigger awareness of the need to reanalyze the problem

Do you feel the need to reread the forgoing paragraphs? The answer to this question is guided by a metacognitive judgment of the degree to which you have adequately understood the text. Metacognitive judgments are routinely used to assess the workings of our cognitive processes, and in particular, the degree to which such processes have functioned or will function correctly. Just as importantly, these judgments are causally relevant in the decision to stay with the current output or seek another (e.g. Mazzoni and Cornoldi 1993; Son and Metcalfe 2000; Nelson 1993; Son 2004). If you are confident that you have understood the text, you will not reread it. If you are confident that you have correctly remembered the name of a person you have just run into, you will address that person by name; if not, you may choose a more generic greeting. If you are not confident that you will remember the milk on the way home, you might arrange a cue or trigger to jog your memory. In all cases, the accuracy of performance depends not only on the accuracy of one's memory but also on metamemory, that is, one's ability to monitor one's mental processes and take appropriate actions on that basis (Koriat and Levy-Sadot 1999).

The Feeling of Rightness

Although studied extensively in other domains, the role of metacognitive processes in reasoning have been relatively neglected. However, it is almost certain that they play the same kind of role as they do in other judgments; namely, to provide a means to assess the output of one's cognitive processes and determine whether further action should be taken. Under this view, the explanation for the compellingness of many cognitive illusions is that the heuristic response is generated with a strong intuition that the answer is correct. It is this intuition, or Feeling of Rightness (FOR), that is the reasoner's cue to look no further afield for the answer.

During the preparation of this paper, I asked several of my colleagues to solve the misleading version of the widget problem above. A typical response was something like 'Well the answer has to be 100, doesn't it? What else can it be?' The answer '100' is cued with a very strong FOR, so that even when told the answer was incorrect, people suspected me of pulling their leg. Sloman (2002) has made a similar point about the famous 'Linda' problem. Even knowing that it is impossible for the probability of being a feminist bank teller to be less than the probability of being a bank teller, one is left with the feeling that Linda *has* to be a feminist. That is, one has a strong FOR that Linda is a feminist and this feeling persists, even after the logical contradiction is understood.

Determinants of the Feeling of Rightness

What creates a strong FOR? As above, such metacognitive experiences have not been extensively studied in the context of reasoning, but there is a large literature on analogous processes in the domain of memory. That is, retrieving an answer from memory is accompanied by a Feeling of Familiarity (FOF), which is the cue that the retrieved item is the one that was sought. For example, what is the capital city of England? Of Peru? Do these memories arrive with the same feeling of certainty? As illustrated by the case of the person whose name you are uncertain of, the strength of this FOF provides a basis for subsequent action. A number of related concepts have been extensively studied, including the Feeling of Knowing (FOK), that is the judged probability that an unrecalled item will be correctly recognized, and Judgment of Learning (JOL), that is, the judged probability that a recently studied item will be correctly recalled at a later time.

This family of metacognitive experiences provides a good analogy to the FOR because, as above, it is assumed that heuristic attributes and accompanying natural assessments are retrieved from memory. Moreover, the FOF, like the FOR, can produce erroneous judgments. We know, for example, that people can express high degrees of confidence in completely false or inaccurate memories (Roediger and McDermott 1995; Sporer et al. 1995). The reason for this is that metacognitive experiences are based on properties of the retrieval processes that produce memories, rather than on the contents of memory *per se* (e.g. Benjamin et al. 1998; Busey et al. 2000; Jacoby, Kelley, and Dywan 1989; Koriat 1995, 1997, Koriat and Levy- Sadot 1999; Schwartz et al. 1997). For example, familiarity of the retrieval cues, as opposed to familiarity of the answer (Reder and Ritter 1992; Schunn et al. 1997; Vernon and Usher 2003) determines FOK, as does the amount of ancillary information that is brought to mind during the retrieval attempt (Koriat 1993, 1995; Koriat et al. 2003).

Of particular relevance to the current discussion is the determining role played by fluent retrieval in metacognitive experiences (e.g. Benjamin et al., 1998; Jacoby et al. 1989; Kelley and Jacoby 1993, 1996; Matvey et al. 2001; Whittlesea and Leboe 2003). That is, easy or efficient processing of an item gives rise to the attribution that the item has been previously experienced, *even when it has not* (e.g. Jacoby et al. 1989; Whittlesea et al. 1990). Fluency of processing has also been demonstrated to underlie numerous other attributions (see Schwarz 2004; Whittlesea 1993 for summaries) including aesthetic pleasure (Reber et al. 2004) and judgments of truth (Reber and Schwarz 1999).

Evidence that metacognitive experiences are based on the fluency of processing is twofold: First are cases in which the experimenter manipulates fluency, either by degrading the stimulus (Whittlesea and Jacoby 1990; Reber and Schwarz 1999), by secretly enhancing fluency, as by masked priming (Jacoby and Whitehouse 1989; Rajaram 1993) or by implicit activation of a target stimulus (Dewhurst and Hitch 1997; Roediger and McDermott 1995). The second concerns item- or task-specific properties of the stimulus. For example, the longer a participant takes to generate the answer to a question, the more difficult they predict it will be to recall later (Benjamin et al. 1998; Kelley and Jacoby 1996; Matvey et al. 2001). Indeed, the fluency of processing gives rise to a perception of difficulty, regardless of the actual relationship between the speed of initial retrieval and subsequent recall (Benjamin et al. 1998). In sum, there is a great deal of evidence to support the conclusion that metacognitive feelings are mediated by the fluency with which the information is brought to mind (see Whittlesea and Leboe 2003 for a summary of the evidence).

On this view, the key to understanding the basis of the FOR is to understand that it is produced by a retrieval experience. That is, heuristic outputs are retrieved from memory, and this retrieval is accompanied by metacogntive experience based on properties of that retrieval experience, such as the fluency of processing. Moreover, given that heuristic attributes are highly accessible (Kahneman 2003), even processed ballistically (Stanovich 2004), the experience should be very fluent and result in a strong FOR. It is important to note, however, that such experiences exist along a continuum, such that some are perceived to be more fluent than others. Thus, more effortful, less efficient processes should produce a weaker FOR.

Affect and the Feeling of Rightness

How is it that fluent processing should produce a sense of rightness? Although the reasons are not well understood, there is ample evidence that fluent processing is associated with positive affect, as the extensive literature on the 'mere exposure' effect illustrates (see Zizak and Reber 2004 for a recent review): Stimuli that have been previously encountered are liked better than unfamiliar stimuli. Moreover, this increase in liking is associated with physiological indicators of positive affect, such as increased activity in the zygomatic cheek muscles associated with smiling (Harmon-Jones and Allen 2001; Winkielman et al. 2006). Several explanations for this relationship have been offered (see Winkielman et al. 2003 for a review). For example, as described above, fluency is a cue that a stimulus has previously been encountered; the positive valence may result from a predisposition towards caution when encountering unfamiliar and potentially hazardous objects. Alternatively, fluent processing may be a sign that a target has been successfully recognized and interpreted.

How does the FOR trigger S2 intervention?

Thus far, I have made the case that heuristic outputs are delivered into conscious awareness accompanied by a metacognitive experience that is largely, although not exclusively, determined by the fluency with which the output was retrieved. In the next section, I will argue that the strength of the FOR determines the probability that S2 is engaged to analyze or rethink the decision based on the heuristic output. On this account, the explanation for the compellingness of many so-called reasoning biases and illusions is the strength of the FOR that accompanies the heuristic response. In cases where the FOR is weaker, the probability of S2 intervention should be higher.

This section has three parts. The first consists of a discussion of the types of intervention that can be engaged in by S2. The second concerns the relation between strength of a FOR and the probability and type of S2 intervention. The third concerns factors that may moderate the link between FOR and the probability of S2 intervention.

Types of S2 intervention

There are many different responses that could be classified as S2 intervention. I will consider four here, acknowledging that further options are possible. The first is that the heuristic judgment might be considered with little or no further analysis (Kahneman 2003). This entails the most minimal commitment of analytic resources, and amounts to little more than an explicit acceptance of the answer generated by implicit processes. A related option, requiring a minimally larger degree of S2 engagement, involves an explicit attempt to consider whether the heuristic judgment seems reasonable. Assuming that it satisfies the current goal state and is otherwise plausible, again, it is likely to be accepted without further analysis (Evans 2006; Roberts 2004). If it is not, it may be rejected with little further analysis, or may be subject to re-evaluation (see option three below).

A second alternative is that analytic processes may be engaged to rationalize or justify the heuristic judgment. That is, S2 process might be engaged to explain why the heuristic judgment is correct. There is ample evidence that such processes occur. For example, not all reasoners give more normatively correct responses when allowed ample time to respond than when forced to answer quickly; many participants in the free-time condition produce the same answer as those in the forced-time condition (Evans and Curtis-Holmes 2005; Roberts and Newton 2001; Shynkaruk and Thompson 2006). In other words, for many reasoners, the answer that would be given when allowed extra time to think is the same answer that would be given under time pressure, even if the original answer was incorrect.

What, then, do people do with the extra time if they are not rethinking their answer? Evans (1996) suggests that they are engaged in justifying their initial responses. In support of this hypothesis, he found that on Wason's four-card selection task, people spent the majority of their time attending to the cards they were going to select, rather than to the cards they were going to reject (see also Ball et al. 2003; Lucas and Ball 2005). In other words, people appeared to spend time deliberating about options already identified by heuristic processes, presumably to rationalize them, rather than considering the potential relevance of the items not identified. Similarly, when presented with hypothetical solutions to Wason's four-card problem, participants are just as confident in their explanations for why the not-q card is a correct choice as for why it is an incorrect one (Evans and Wason 1976). Wason and Evans (1975; Evans and Wason 1976) speculated that the decision about which card to choose in the selection task was generated by a non-conscious matching bias, so that when asked to justify an answer, they were forced to rely on rationalizations. Indeed, there is evidence to suggest that the processes underlying many choices, judgments, and attitudes are implicit and not easily available to conscious introspection, such that the role of consciousness might be limited to trying to create explanations for why such choices, judgments, and attitudes have been made (see Stanovich 2004, ch. 2; Wilson and Dunn 2004 for review).

A third way in which S2 might intervene is to attempt to reformulate the initial model or representation of the premises, with the goal of deriving a different solution (Evans 2006; Johnson-Laird and Byrne 1991; Torrens et al. 1999). For example, a reasoner given the first version of the widget problem above may distrust the initial response, and so instead try to reason out how long it takes each machine to produce a widget. This is clearly the most effortful option, and success at this stage is tied to traditional measures of cognitive capacity such as IQ (see Stanovich 1999 for review) and WM (e.g. De Neys 2006a, b; Gilhooly et al. 2002). For this reason, it is possible for a reasoner to acknowledge the need to rethink the problem, but judge that he/she lacks the wherewithal or motivation to do so (see the section on judgments of solvability, below).

A fourth possibility is that there is an attempt at S2 intervention that fails, such that the heuristic response generated by S1 determines much of the response (see Bargh 2007 for an extensive discussion of this phenomena in social psychology). For example, S2 processes might be engaged and produce an alternative answer that is less compelling than the S1 output, so that the heuristic response is generated. Similarly, the S1 output may be generated with a sufficiently strong FOR that it casts doubt on the answer generated by S2, undermining the confidence with which it is held. Another mechanism by which the S1 output might contaminate S2 judgments is by anchoring. That is, the S1 output might provide a reference point or a starting point for any simulation attempted by S2; thus, the final value of the answer generated by S2 may be shaded towards the initial value generated by S1 (see Chapman and Johnson 2002; Epley 2004 for recent reviews of anchoring and adjustment phenomena).

Link between S2 and FOR

Under this proposal, one should be able to predict the type and degree of S2 intervention based on the strength of the FOR. At the extremes, very strong FORs should be correlated with the inclination to accept the heuristic judgment, and weak FORs with the inclination to reject the heuristic judgment or to reformulate the problem.

It is less clear what the relationship between the FOR and the probability of S2 rationalisation should be, although in the absence of evidence to the contrary, it seems reasonable to hypothesize that such rationalization is engaged for a purpose. That is, the attempt at explanation should be made when there is a perceived need for one, either because the experimenter has requested one, because the instructions suggest a need for certainty, or because the FOR is not high enough to accept the heuristic judgment without additional warrant.

Factors that may moderate the link between S2 and FOR

Although a weak FOR should be a sufficient basis to engage S2, and a strong FOR a sufficient basis to retain S1, there are several factors that may mediate this relationship. Specifically, reasoners' theories about the origins of the FOR should moderate the relationship between that intuition and the probability of S2 intervention. For example, if one believes that the experimenter is trying to be deceptive or tricky, one might engage analytic thinking even if the heuristic judgment cues a strong FOR. Thinking dispositions, such as those measured by the Actively Openminded Thinking questionnaire (AOT; Stanovich 1999, this volume) might also moderate this relationship: reasoners who enjoy analytic thinking or believe that good thinking requires analysis of more than one option might be more inclined to engage S2 even with strong FOR. Additionally, an internal metric such as the difference between the state of confidence produced by the FOR and a reasoner's desired level of confidence, may also determine how and when reasoners act on a weak FOR (Chen and Chaiken 1999).

Finally, reliance on the FOR as a cue may vary as a function of individual differences in monitoring and control (Hertzog and Robinson 2005 for review, Stanovich this volume for a related view). That is, individuals differ with respect to how good they are at monitoring their cognitive processes for errors. Did you catch the typo in last sentence? If so, that is an example of successful monitoring. Generally speaking, individual differences in monitoring skills are linked to successful task performance in a variety of domains, such as reading (e.g. Lin et al. 2001; Pressley 2003), learning optical principles (Prins et al. 2006), and mathematical problem solving (Desoete and Roeyers 2006; Lucangeli et al. 1998).

Metacognition and the quality versus quantity of S2 intervention

The link between monitoring skills and task performance may provide an answer to another contentious question, namely, whether cognitive capacity predicts the probability that S2 is engaged to overturn a heuristic output or whether cognitive capacity predicts the success of S2 intervention once it has occurred (e.g. De Neys 2006a; Klaczyski and Robinson 2000; Stanovich 2008, this volume; Torrens et al. 1999). Evans (2007) refers to these possibilities as the quantity and the quality hypotheses respectively. In the metacognitive framework outlined here, evidence that demonstrated a link between cognitive capacity and monitoring skill would favor the quantity hypothesis. That is, the quantity hypothesis suggests that high capacity reasoners should have better monitoring skill; this, in turn, means that they are more likely to initiate S2 analysis of a heuristic response.

There is good reason to suppose that such monitoring and inhibitory abilities are linked to IQ (e.g. Prins et al. 2006; Veenman et al. 2005). For example, Nęcka and Orzechowski (2005) documented evidence that IQ is linked to the ability to suppress automatic responses on tasks such as the Stroop. On this task, participants need to inhibit a highly automatic response in favor of a less available one, such as naming the ink color of a printed word (e.g. the word blue printed in red ink). Similarly, the probability of suppressing the modal response on the widget and other problems is likewise linked to measures of cognitive capacity (Frederick 2005) as is the ability to suppress irrelevant counter examples in conditional reasoning (De Neys et al. 2005; Markovits and Doyon 2004).

Based on these findings, one might proffer the hypothesis that cognitive capacity and IQ have both direct and indirect links to S2. The direct link reflects the fact that high capacity reasoners are more likely to correctly solve a problem once a heuristic response has been suppressed. The second link may be mediated by monitoring skill, in that high ability reasoners have better metacognitive skill (and are thus more likely to inhibit a heuristic response) than low ability reasoners.

Nonetheless, it is important to note that cognitive capacity may explain only a small part of the relationship between monitoring skill and propensity to engage S2 processes. Indeed, the available evidence suggests that the ability to inhibit heuristic responses (Markovits and Doyon 2004; Handley et al. 2004) and skill at monitoring cognitive processes (Prins et al. 2006; Veenman et al. 2005) predict an independent portion of the variance in problem solving skills after accounting for the effects of IQ. Moreover, the data suggest that many biases, such as belief-bias and myside bias may be independent of IQ (Klaczynski and Robinson, 2000; Torrens et al., 1999; Stanovich and West 2007). Thus, while IQ might explain part of the relationship between monitoring and S2 processes, much of the variance is yet to be explained.

Stanovich (this volume) proposes that the remaining variance can be accounted for by what he calls the 'reflective' mind. The reflective mind encapsulates an intentional level of behavior, such as goal- and belief-states. The reflective mind shares many properties with System 2, such as limited-capacity serial processing. Nonetheless, he proposes that intentional states occupy a different level of analysis in cognitive theory than do algorithmic processes (i.e. those processes associated with the execution of S2 analyses). This proposal shares many assumptions with the metacogntive framework advance here, namely, that the regulation of S2 intervention requires a third type of process that is not captured by the S1/ S2 distinction. The key difference lies in the notion of intentionality. Stanovich's description of the reflective mind emphasizes conscious processes that are available to introspection; these processes can therefore be adequately indexed using self-report measures of thinking dispositions that tap reasoners' epistemic values and goals. In contrast, the proposal outlined above emphasizes the role of implicit processes in monitoring, allowing a relatively smaller role for intentional processes.

Finally, it is assumed that the answer endorsed by S2 is endorsed with a final estimate of confidence. This final judgment should reflect both the initial FOR as well as the influence of the moderating factors described above. For example, in cases where the answer is based on the heuristic output, confidence should vary positively with the strength of the initial FOR. One might speculate that when S2 is engaged to rationalize the heuristic judgment, that the final confidence judgment is stronger than the initial FOR. In cases where the reasoner has an alternative theory for the source of the FOR, there might be no relationship between the strength of that initial response and the final judgment of confidence. Similarly, in cases where S2 is engaged to reformulate the problem, one would expect relatively little relationship between the initial FOR and the final confidence judgment; confidence in this latter case should be determined by the factors discussed in the section dealing with judgments of solvability.

Metacognitive judgments and the feeling of rightness

In the forgoing discussion, I have been careful to refer to metacognitive experiences when discussing the FOR, as opposed to metacognitive judgments. As described above, the FOR is assumed to be an affective response that carries little cognitive content and that is generated by implicit processes whose origins are not likely available to conscious processes (Koriat and Levy-Sadot 1999). It is the interpretation of that feeling or affective response that produces a judgment.

I will use the term *Judgment of Rightness* (JOR) to differentiate the interpretation of the FOR from the affective response itself. Note that use of the term judgment does not imply extensive analysis. Indeed, in most cases, it is assumed that the FOR will be a sufficient basis for judgment, such that one's JOR is completely determined by the strength of the FOR with little, if any, conscious effort. Thus, like many other metacognitive judgments, the JOR may be little more than the awareness of a feeling of confidence that carries little or no information about the basis of that confidence.

The interpretive basis of the JOR

Although in most cases, the strength of the FOR should be a sufficient basis for judgment, there will be circumstances in which the FOR may be explicitly discounted. For example, if participants are given an alternative explanation for the basis of their metacognitive experience, they are less likely to rely on fluency of retrieval as a cue (e.g. Jacoby and Whitehouse 1989; Kelley and Jacoby 1996; Schwarz and Vaughn 2002; Whittlesea and Jacoby 1990). Schwarz and his colleagues have provided many demonstrations of this phenomena (Rothman and Schwarz 1998; Sanna and Schwarz 2003; Schwarz et al. 1991). In these studies, participants are asked to generate either short or long lists of exemplars, for example, of instances in which they have recently been assertive. They are then asked to make a judgment about a quality relevant to those instances (i.e. their assertiveness). A typical finding is that those who generate short lists provide more extreme ratings than those who generate long lists. For example, participants who are asked to generate six instances of assertive behavior rate themselves as more assertive than participants who are asked to generate 12 instances, even though they have less objective evidence to support their judgment (Schwarz et al. 1991). This relationship presumably represents a metacognitive judgment regarding the ease with which instances are generated: six instances are more fluently generated than 12. Participants who generated many instances presumably found it difficult, and inferred the cause of that difficulty to be the absence of the quality under judgment rather than the properties of the task. However, this trend reverses if they are given a different explanation about why it is relatively difficult to generate instances, such as the background music or unfamiliarity with the task (Schwartz and Vaughn 2002).

Explicit cues to the JOR

Thus far, I have discussed only implicit aspects of the JOR. By analogy to other memory-based judgments, such as the Feeling of Knowing and the Judgment of Learning, it is assumed that the JOR reflects two sources of information (e.g. Kelley and Jacoby 1996; Koriat and Levy-Sadot 1999; Koriat et al. 2004; Schwarz 2004; Brewer and Sampaio 2006; Matvey et al. 2001). The first source is the FOR; it is assumed to be cued automatically and the origins of the response (e.g. as a feeling of fluency) are assumed to be unavailable to introspection (e.g. Brewer and Sampaio 2006; Koriat et al. 2004; Matvey et al. 2001; Schwartz 2004). The second source consists of a reasoner's metacognitive beliefs. These can be accessed explicitly, although it is not assumed that the reasoner is necessarily aware of their contribution to a judgment. For example, beliefs about how memory deteriorates over time can moderate confidence in memory retrievals (Koriat et al. 2004), although such beliefs may be difficult to access in a particular context and so have limited effect.

Shynkaruk and Thompson (2006) found evidence that confidence in syllogistic reasoning performance may be moderated by these types of metacognitive beliefs. Reasoners were asked to evaluate the conclusions to syllogistic arguments and to provide confidence ratings on two occasions: the first in response to an initial, fast assessment of the conclusion and the second after more deliberation. They observed that confidence increased from first to second response, regardless of whether accuracy increased, decreased, or the answer did not change. The authors argued that the increase in confidence was a function of reasoner's metacognitive beliefs that decisions considered over time are superior to those made under pressure.

Other source of metacognitive beliefs may be a reasoner's global assessment of their reasoning ability or thinking style as indexed by measures such as the Rational Experiential Inventory (REI), a 40-item self-report inventory (Pacini and Epstein 1999). The REI measures self-reported tendency to engage in rational (i.e. reliance on analytic approaches to solving problems) and/or experiential thinking (i.e. reliance on past experiences or intuition). Consistent with this hypothesis, Prowse-Turner and Thompson (2007) observed that those who scored high on the rationality portion of the REI expressed a high degree of confidence in their evaluation of syllogistic arguments, even though they were no more accurate than those who scored low in rationality (see also Dunning et al. 2003; Jonsson and Allwood 2003).

Another basis of metacognitive beliefs concerns the extent of one's domain- specific knowledge about a topic. That is, if one believes that one knows a lot about a particular domain, one may be prone to confidence in judgments associated with that domain (Cowley 2004; Costermans et al. 1992; Gill et al. 1998; Morgan and Cleave-Hogg 2002). Shynkaruk and Thompson (2006) posited that these types of beliefs may also play a role in reasoning judgments: in a syllogistic reasoning task, reasoners expressed more confidence in conclusions to which they could apply pre-existing knowledge (i.e. that were believable or unbelievable) than ones that were neutral, even though they were no more accurate with the believable than the neutral conclusions.

In sum, it is proposed that the JOR, like other memory-based metacognitive judgments, is multiply determined by both implicit and explicit cues. Implicit cues are based on properties of the retrieval experience, such as its fluency; explicit cues are derived from beliefs that are accessible to conscious introspection. Note that, as is the case with decisions based on heuristic outputs, metacognitive decisions may be based on implicit cues, even when a more accurate judgment could be derived from explicit sources (Koriat et al. 2004).

JORs, FORs, and the control of cognition

Figure 8.1 allows for the possibility that S2 intervention may take place either on the basis of a JOR or a FOR. As above, a JOR is more complex than a FOR, at minimum, reflecting an interpretation of the cues giving rise to the FOR; it may include variety of beliefs about the tasks, one's own reasoning ability, etc. That cognitive functions can be controlled by these types of judgments is well documented (see Koriat 2007 for an excellent summary).

Less clear is whether a judgment per se is required to initiate S2 intervention. That is, can S2 be initiated without conscious intent to do so? Or, put another way, is awareness of the FOR necessary to initiate S2 intervention? Although the term 'metacognition' is generally understood to imply conscious awareness, there are those who argue that monitoring and control processes can be initiated without such awareness (again, see Koriat 2007). This possibility is allowed for in Figure 8.1.

Under this view, S2 analysis could be initiated by a weak FOR without the need for an explicit evaluation of that feeling. This type of direct association was implied by the discussion on rationalization. This could still be true in those circumstances where the reasoner undertakes a reanalysis of the problem; whilst it is possible for the reasoner to be aware of the particular circumstances that motivated their reanalysis, it might also be prompted by a vague unease about the heuristic output. That is, it is not necessary to assume that the reasoner has any more conscious awareness about why they are analysing the heuristic output than they do about the sources of that output.

In the absence of a strong heuristic response, what determines degree of S2 involvement?

In the preceding sections, I addressed the situation in which the content or context of the problem provokes a heuristic judgment and attendant FOR. In this section, I examine the situation in which the combined activities of S1 do not suggest a compelling solution or decision. That is, in many cases there will be little contextualization provided by the heuristic systems; in other cases, there might be some but not enough on which to base an answer.

In those cases where the heuristic systems do not deliver a compelling response, I propose that the probability with which reasoners will engage analytic processes varies according to the strength of a prospective metacognitive judgment that I will term the Judgment of Solvability (JOS). Less is understood about these kinds of judgments than about the processes that give rise to the experiential judgments discussed above, although there is evidence that such prospective judgments predict accuracy for some types of problem-solving situations (Metcalfe and Wiebe 1987) but not others (Metcalfe 1986a). As with the JOR, it is proposed that initial JOSs determine the type and extent of analytic engagement. Initially, the choice is to attempt a solution or not; during the course of problem solving, the choice is to continue with the current strategy, start anew, or abandon the attempt.

A few obvious candidates suggest themselves as the basis for this JOS. For example, reasoners may undertake an initial estimate of problem difficulty (Efklides et al. 1999; Kruger 1999). Although there is little evidence to indicate how such estimates are derived, variables such as self-assessed ability in a particular domain certainly mediate such estimates (see Hertzog and Robinson 2005 for a review). One might also speculate that the reasoner's goals and motivation might determine the strength of the JOS, such that problems that might be deemed solvable in some circumstances might not be attempted in others (Efklides et al. 1999).

Other bases for JOSs can be derived by analogy to prospective memory estimates, such as Judgments of Learning. Such judgments are moderated a quick assessment of solvability (Son and Metcalfe 2005), fluency of reading (as above), and familiarity with problem components (Reder and Ritter 1992; Rehder 1999; Vernon and Usher 2003). There is also evidence that JOSs are made at several points during a problem solving episode, such that initial estimates of difficulty are continuously revised and updated (Efklides et al. 1999; Vernon and Usher 2003).

Outstanding issues

In this final section, I attempt to address several questions raised by the preceding analysis: First, given that heuristic processes are associated with processes that comprehend and represent information, the next logical question concerns how that information is represented. In the paragraphs below, I suggest some lines of enquiry that might be fruitful in elucidating this issue. Second, at a fundamental level, one might query the adaptive value of relying on metacognitive processes that so often produce reasoning biases. Third, I discuss the 'levels of representation' issue with respect to the JOR and FOR. Finally, I offer some suggestions about how these constructs could be operationalized and tested experimentally.

Comprehension, attention, and representation

Earlier, it was proposed that heuristic responses are derived from impressions of attributes of the objects of perception and thought such as similarity, suprisingness, affective valence, and so on (Kahneman 2003) or from the operation of quasi-modular systems that subserve language comprehension, perception, and learning (Stanovich 2004). Both views make an explicit link between the information that is extracted and represented from a stimulus and a heuristic output. Moreover, even given that the analytic system has been engaged, its operation is largely restricted to the contents of the representation formulated by S1 unless a deliberate effort is made (Evans 2006; Markovits and Quinn 2002; Verschueren et al. 2005).

Consequently, the next level of theorizing needs to be explicit about the information that is extracted from a stimulus and the processes by which representations are formed (Newstead 2000; Thompson 2000). A possibly fruitful line of enquiry would be to frame the issue in terms of basic comprehension processes. That is, one way to look at the problem is to view heuristic processes as the output of processes used to contextualize representations, that is, to make meaning out of input (Evans 2006; Stanovich 1999). For example, processes of semantic priming have been used to elucidate the mental representations underlying such diverse phenomena as conditional reasoning (Markovits and Quinn 2002; Thompson 1995, 2000), anchoring and adjustment (Chapman and Johnson 2002) and analogical reasoning (Krendl et al. 2006).

In addition to deriving meaning from input, S1 processes also act as a filter for incoming information, so that S2 processes often operate on incomplete information (Arbuthnott et al. 2005; Evans and Over 1996; Stanovich, this volume). Thus, another potentially fruitful line of enquiry would be to examine the role played by basic attentional processes in constraining and determining the information that is represented. For example, our attentional processes are largely driven by information that is present in the environment; missing or absent information, no matter how relevant to the current goal, is detected only with difficulty (see Hearst 1991 for a review and Brockmole and Henderson 2005 for a recent demonstration). Attention can also be driven by pragmatic and linguistic factors, as numerous experiments with Wason's four-card selection task demonstrate (e.g. Evans 1998; Sperber et al. 1995; Thompson 2000).

The utility of metacognitive judgments

What is the adaptive value of metacognitive processes, if they so often lead us astray? The fact that metamemory experiences, such as the FOF, give rise to judgments that are based on aspects of the retrieval experience rather than the contents of memory per se, means that people can have high confidence in completely false memories. As above, I have argued that similar properties of the FOR explain why S2 fails to intervene, even when it is appropriate to do so.

A straightforward answer to the adaptiveness question is that these feelings are, in fact, normally accurate. In the case of feelings of familiarity, for example, it is true that recently encountered events will be recalled more fluently than distant ones, that highly frequent events are recalled more fluently than less frequent ones, and so on. Thus, basing judgments of familiarity on processing fluency is usually a reliable cue to the contents of memory.

Moreover, as Gigerenzer and colleagues have argued (e.g. Gigerenzer et al. 1991; Todd and Gigerenzer 2000, 2003) experimenters are very good at designing studies that show people's intuitions in a poor light. They argue that processes that produce dismal performance under laboratory conditions are optimized to take advantage of the structure of the everyday world, and perform well under normal circumstances. Indeed, even in difficult laboratory environments, there is a positive correlation between metacognitive judgments and performance (Burson et al. 2006; Metcalfe 1986b; Schraw et al. 1995; Nelson and Dunlosky 1991) especially when participants are asked to estimate their overall performance rather than make item by item judgments (Dunning et al. 2003; Stankov 2000; Shynkaruk and Thompson 2006; Prowse-Turner and Thompson 2007).

A less optimistic explanation for the unreliability of metacognitive judgments is the one argued in the current paper, namely that metacognitive judgments, like most other cognitive processes are based on implicit inputs. Consequently, one may have access to the outputs of those processes, but seldom to their inputs (Hertzog and Robinson 2005; Stanovich 2004). The resulting metacognitive judgments are based on a number of cues that vary in terms of their diagnositicity, but because they are implicit, the diagnosticity of these cues is unknowable (Koriat 1995, 1997). Indeed, several researchers have suggested that training in a domain needs to address not only the skills necessary to solve problems, but also needs to provide information about how to monitor those processes (Hertzog and Robinson 2005; Dunning et al. 2003; Prowse-Turner and Thompson 2007; Pressley 2003; Desoete et al. 2003).

Theory of mind

In the opening section to this chapter, I referred to metacognitive judgments as second-order judgments, that is, as judgments about judgments. Specifically, a JOR is a judgment about the heuristic judgment delivered by S1. In that way, it is similar to other metacognitive constructs, which are often viewed as 'representations of representations'. The judgments themselves have propositional content, and express beliefs about the workings of one's cognitive processes, such as 'that answer feels right' or 'I should be more confident of this judgment than the first one because I have had more time to think about it.'

The same cannot be said about many of the processes that give rise to the JOR. As discussed at length, the FOR likely resembles other metacognitive experiences whose origins are not available to introspection. Koriat (2007, p.315) refers to them as 'sheer subjective feelings, which (although they) lie at the heart of consciousness, may themselves by the product of unconscious processes.'

One might be tempted to thereby classify the FOR as a heuristic output that bears more similarity to the automatic, implicit responses generated by S1 than to a true metacognitive judgment. Indeed, Kahneman (2003) argued that the accessibility of a heuristic attribute is, in and of itself, a natural assessment. A metacognitive account shares with Kahneman's the assumption that experience of accessibility, or fluency, gives rise to an attribution that is causally relevant to the outcome of any judgment or decision. However, the metacogntive account assumes that the assessment of fluency (and other cues that give rise to a FOR) is qualitatively different than other types of natural assessments, because the FOR is really an assessment about an assessment. That is, the process of retrieving a heuristic attribute, such as a stereotype, produces two outcomes: The first is the natural assessment of the perceived similarity of the target to that stereotype, and the second is an assessment of the fluency with which this information is retrieved. The former produces a heuristic judgment, the latter, the feeling that this judgment is right (i.e. FOR).

Methodological considerations

To wrap up, I will offer suggestions for how the constructs and hypotheses developed in this chapter might be operationalized and tested. The first goal, of course, will be to develop a measure of the FOR. The second will be to establish the link between the FOR and the probability and type of S2 engagement. From there, one has the tools to evaluate the many specific predictions that fall out of the framework I have sketched.

Given its similarity to other metacognitive experiences, it would be reasonable to adapt methods from the metacognitive literature for measuring the FOR. The normal approach for measuring Feelings of Knowing or Judgments of Learning is to ask the reasoner to self-report. The difference between the FOR and these other jugdments is that it pertains to an event that has already occurred, whereas the others pertain to events that will happen in the future (i.e. the probability that an unrecalled item will be recognized or the probability that a just learned item will be subsequently recalled). Thus, the measurement will have to be modified.

Specifically, the FOR is defined as the feeling of certainty associated with the answer produced by S1. Under the assumption that S1 are automatic processes, the first answer (A1) should be produced rapidly, whereas answers generated by S2 require deliberation and should be slower. Thus, measuring the FOR will require reasoners to respond quickly, giving the first answer that comes to mind and then to rate their certainty that this answer is the right one.

Two related predictions can then be tested. The first is that the FOR accompanying A1 responses predicts the probability with which it is given as a final answer. Consequently, participants will need to be asked to produce a second answer (A2) without time constraint. FORs should be correlated with the probability that A1 occurs as A2. This method allows for within-individual estimates, but runs the risk that asking reasoners to articulate A1 changes the response that would normally be given at Time 2. Thus, a between-subjects design will also be needed in which one group generates generate fast answers and another works without time pressure. Items that produce high FOR in the fast condition should be answered with A1 in the free time condition.

The second prediction is that low FORs promote S2 processes. For this, one needs a measure of S2 intervention. Several possibilities offer themselves. For example, low FORs should be associated with a high probability that A2 is normatively correct. However, given that S2 may not always produce normatively correct answers, converging evidence will be required. For example, under the assumption that S2 processes take time to implement, low FORs should be associated with longer RTs to produce a final answer. Moreover, given that S2 processes, by definition, involve conscious deliberation, they should therefore be available to introspection. Thus, think aloud protocols and strategy choice paradigms (which of the following strategies did you use to solve the problem?) should be diagnostic of S2 processing.

Summary

A crucial issue for DPT concerns the circumstances under which analytic processes intervene to alter a heuristic output. I have proposed that the process by which reasoners become aware of the need for such intervention is a metacognitive one. Stimuli that produce a strong Feeling of Rightness are not likely to be further scrutinized, whereas those that produce a weaker feeling are more likely to trigger S2 analysis.

Framed in that way, the next question to be addressed concerns the variables that moderate the strength of a FOR. By analogy to the memory literature, several hypotheses were offered. Specifically, it was proposed that the FOR is mediated by implicit cues that are largely based on experience of retrieving heuristic output; these include variables such as fluency of retrieval and familiarity with the retrieval cues. Judgments based on the FOR may also incorporate cues that are available to introspection, although it is not assumed that the reasoner necessarily applies them in a deliberate manner to a given problem-solving episode. These include metacognitive theories, beliefs about one's own competence, attributions about the problem-solving environment, and so on.

This analysis supplements current theories in several ways. First, it allows for another set of tools for predicting the probability of analytic system engagement by focusing on a different level of analysis than is currently common. That is, rather than global characteristics of the reasoner and the problem-solving environment, analysis of both the FOR and JOS invite us to consider the experience of processing a stimulus and interpretations of that experience as causally relevant dimensions.

Finally, a metacognitive framework may also offer a means to explain the relationship between cognitive capacity and reasoning performance. For example, cognitive capacity might determine the efficacy of S2 once it has been triggered. However, the key question concerns whether or not cognitive capacity also determines the likelihood that S2 is engaged in a particular situation. It was argued that S2 intervention is linked to metacognitive processes of monitoring and control, and that these metacognitive processes are in turn linked to cognitive capacity. That is, it is possible that the link between capacity and intervention can be explained by a shared link to metacognitive efficiency.

Acknowledgments

I would like to acknowledge the contributions of several people who provided valuable advice and input to the current manuscript. First and foremost, I would like to thank Jamie Campbell for his support and advice during all phases of the project. I would also like to thank Jonathan Evans for several stimulating discussions, and in particular, for his observations about the nature of S2 intervention, confabulation, the adaptive value of metacognitive judgments, and the role of consciousness in the FOR. Thanks to Simon Handley for his ideas about the role of inhibition and IQ in S2 intervention and to Shira Elqayam for suggesting the importance of the gap between a reasoner's desired and actual confidence. Finally, thanks to Jamie Campbell, Erin Beatty, and Jamie Prowse Turner for comments on an earlier draft of this manuscript, to Nicole Robert for her patient help in assembling the reference section, and to Jonathan Evans, Keith Frankish, and Keith Stanovich for their many useful suggestions.

References

Arbuthnott, K.D. Arbuthnott, D.W., and Thompson, V.A. (2005) *The mind in therapy: Cognitive science for practice.* Lawrence Erlbaum Associates: Mahwah, NJ.

Ball, L.J., Lucas, E.J., Miles, J.N.V., and Gale, A.G. (2003) Inspection times and the selection task: What do eye-movements reveal about relevance effects? *Quarterly Journal of Experimental Psychology A: Human Experimental Psychology,* **56**, 1053–77.

Bargh, J.A. (2007) Social psychological approaches to consciousness. In P.D. Zelazo, M. Moscovitch, and E. Thompson (eds). *The Cambridge handbook of consciousness*, 555–69. Cambridge University Press, Cambridge.

Begg, I. and Harris, G. (1982) On the interpretation of syllogisms. *Journal of Verbal Learning and Verbal Behavior*, **21**, 595–620.

Benjamin, A.S., Bjork, R.A., and Schwartz, B.L. (1998) The mismeasure of memory: When retrieval fluency is misleading as a metamnemonic index. *Journal of Experimental Psychology: General*, **127**, 55–68.

Brewer, W.F. and Sampaio, C. (2006) Processes leading to confidence and accuracy in sentence recognition: A metamemory approach. *Memory*, **14**, 540–52.

Brokmole, J.R. and Hendersen, J.M. (2005). Object appearance, disappearance, and attention prioritization in real-world scenes. *Psychonomic Bulletin & Review*, **12**, 1061–7.

Burson, K.A., Larrick, R.P., and Klayman, J. (2006) Skilled or unskilled, but still unaware of it: How perceptions of difficulty drive miscalibration in relative comparisons. *Journal of Personality and Social Psychology*, **90**, 60–77.

Busey, T.A., Tunnicliff, J., Loftus, GR., and Loftus, E.F. (2000) Accounts of the confidence-accuracy relation in recognition memory. *Psychonomic Bulletin & Review*, **7**, 26–48.

Chapman, G.B. and Johnson, E.J. (2002) Incorporating the irrelevant: Anchors in judgments of belief and value. In T. Gilovich, D. Griffin, and D. Kahneman (eds) *Heuristics and biases: The psychology of intuitive judgment*, 120–38. Cambridge University Press, New York.

Chen, S. and Chaiken, S. (1999) The heuristic-systematic model in its broader context. In S. Chaiken and Y. Trope (eds) *Dual-process theories in social psychology*, 73–96. The Guilford Press, New York.

Costermans, J., Lories, G., and Ansay, C. (1992) Confidence level and feeling of knowing in question answering: The weight of inferential processes. *Journal of Experimental Psychology: Learning, Memory, and Cognition*, **18**, 142–50.

Cowley, E. (2004) Recognition confidence, recognition accuracy and choice. *Journal of Business Research*, **57**, 641–6.

Daniel, D.B. and Klaczynski, P.A. (2006) Developmental and individual differences in conditional reasoning: Effects of logic instructions and alternative antecedents. *Child Development*, **77**, 339–54.

De Neys, W. (2006a) Automatic-heuristic and executive-analytic processing during reasoning: Chronometric and dual-task considerations. *Quarterly Journal of Experimental Psychology*, **59**, 1070–100.

De Neys, W. (2006b) Dual processing in reasoning: Two systems but one reasoner. *Psychological Science*, **17**, 428–33.

De Neys, W., Schaeken, W., and d'Ydewalle, G. (2005) Working memory and counterexample retrieval for causal conditionals. *Thinking & Reasoning*, **11**, 123–50.

Desoete, A. and Roeyers, H. (2006) Metacognitive macroevaluations in mathematical problem solving. *Learning and Instruction*, **16**, 12–25.

Desoete, A., Roeyers, H, and De Clercq, A. (2003) Can offline metacognition enhance mathematical problem solving? *Journal of Educational Psychology*, **95**, 188–200.

Dewhurst, S.A. and Hitch, G.J. (1997) Illusions of familiarity caused by cohort activation. *Psychonomic Bulletin & Review*, **4**, 566–71.

Dunning, D., Johnson, K., Ehrlinger, J., and Kruger, J. (2003) Why people fail to recognize their own incompetence. *Current Directions in Psychological Science*, **12**, 83–7.

Efklides, A., Samara, A., and Petropoulou, M. (1999) Feeling of difficulty: An aspect of monitoring that influences control. *European Journal of Psychology of Education*, **14**, 461–76.

Epley, N. (2004) A tale of tuned decks? Anchoring as accessibility and anchoring as adjustment. In Koehler, D.E. and Harvey, N. (eds). *Blackwell Handbook of judgment and decision-making*, 240–57. Blackwell Publishing, Malden, MA.

Evans, J.St.B.T. (1996) Deciding before you think: Relevance and reasoning in the selection task. *British Journal of Psychology*, **87**, 223–40.

Evans, J.St.B.T. (1998) Matching bias in conditional reasoning: Do we understand it after 25 years? *Thinking & Reasoning*, **4**, 45–82.

Evans, J.St.B.T. (2006) The heuristic-analytic theory of reasoning: Extension and evaluation. *Psychonomic Bulletin and Review*, **13**, 378–95.

Evans, J.St.B.T. (2007) On the resolution of conflict in dual process theories of reasoning. *Thinking & Reasoning*, **13**, 321–9.

Evans, J.St.B.T. and Curtis-Holmes, J. (2005) Rapid responding increases belief bias: Evidence for the dual-process theory of reasoning. *Thinking & Reasoning*, **11**, 382–9.

Evans, J.St.B.T. and Over, D.E. (1996) *Rationality and reasoning*. Psychology Press, Hove.

Evans, J.St.B.T. and Wason, P.C. (1976) Rationalization in a reasoning task. *British Journal of Psychology*, **67**, 479–86.

Evans, J.St.B.T., Handley, S., and Over, D.E. (2003) Conditionals and conditional probability. *Journal of Experimental Psychology: Learning, Memory and Cognition*, **29**, 321–55.

Evans, J.St.B.T., Newstead, S.E., Allen, J.L., and Pollard, P. (1994) Debiasing by instruction: The case of belief bias. *European Journal of Cognitive Psychology*, **6**, 263–85.

Feeney, A., Scrafton, S., Duckworth, A., and Handley, S.J. (2004) The story of *some*: Everyday pragmatic inference by children and adults. *Canadian Journal of Experimental Psychology*, **58**, 121–32.

Finucane, M.L., Alhakami, A., Slovic, P., and Johnson, S.M. (2000) The affect heuristic in judgments of risks and benefits. *Journal of Behavioral Decision Making*, **13**, 1–17.

Frederick, S. (2005) Cognitive reflection and decision making. *Journal of Economic Perspectives*, **19**, 25–42.

Gigerenzer, G., Hoffrage, U., and Kleinbolting, H. (1991) Probabilistic mental models: A Brunswikian theory of confidence. *Psychological Review*, **98**, 506–28.

Gilhooly, K.J., Wynn, V., Philips, L.H., Llogie, R.H., and Della Sala, S. (2002) Visuo-spatial and verbal working memory in the five-disc Tower of London task: An individual differences approach. *Thinking & Reasoning*, **8**, 165–78.

Gill, M.J., Swann, W.B. Jr., and Sivera, D.H. (1998) On the genesis of confidence. *Journal of Personality and Social Psychology*, **75**, 1101–14.

Handley, S.J., Capon, A., Beveridge, M., Dennis, I., and Evans, J.St.B.T. (2004) Working memory, inhibitory control and the development of children's reasoning. *Thinking & Reasoning*, **10**, 175–95.

Harmon-Jones, E. and Allen, J.J.B. (2001) The role of affect in the mere exposure effect: Evidence from psychophysiological and individual differences approaches. *Personality and Social Psychology Bulletin*, **27**, 889–98.

Hearst, E. (1991) Psychology and nothing. *American Scientist*, **79**, 432–43.

Hertzog, C. and Robinson, A. E. (2005) Metacognition and intelligence. In O. Wilhelm and R.W. Engle (eds) *Handbook of understanding and measuring intelligence*, 101–23. Sage Publications, Inc, Sage.

Jacoby, L.L. and Whitehouse, K. (1989) An illusion of memory: False recognition influenced by unconscious perception. *Journal of Experimental Psychology: General*, **118**, 126–35.

Jacoby, L.L., Kelley, C.M., and Dywan, J. (1989) Memory attributions. In H.L. Roediger III, and F.I.M. Craik (eds) *Varieties of memory and consciousness: Essays in honour of Endel Tulving*, 391–422. Lawrence Erlbaum Associates, Inc, Hillsdale, NJ.

Johnson-Laird, P.N. and Byrne, R.M.J. (1991) *Deduction*. Lawrence Erlbaum Associates, Inc, Hillsdale, NJ.

Jonsson, A.C. and Allwood, C.M. (2003) Stability and variability in the realism of confidence judgements over time, content domain, and gender. *Personality and Individual Differences*, **34**, 559–74.

Kahneman, D. (2003) A perspective on judgment and choice: Mapping bounded rationality. *American Psychologist*, **58**, 697–720.

Kelley, C.M. and Jacoby, L.L. (1993) The construction of subjective experience: Memory attributions. In M. Davies and G. W. Humphreys (eds) *Consciousness: Psychological and philosophical essays*, 74–89. Blackwell Publishing, Malden, MA.

Kelley, C.M. and Jacoby, L.L. (1996) Adult egocentrism: Subjective experience versus analytic bases for judgment. *Journal of Memory and Language*, **35**, 157–75.

Klaczynski, P.A. and Robinson, B. (2000) Personal theories, intellectual ability, and epistemological beliefs: Adult age differences in everyday reasoning biases. *Psychology and Aging*, **15**, 400–16.

Koriat, A. (1993) How do we know that we know? The accessibility model of the feeling of knowing. *Psychological Review*, **100**, 609–39.

Koriat, A. (1995) Dissociating knowing and the feeling of knowing: Further evidence for the accessibility model. *Journal of Experimental Psychology: General*, **124**, 311–33.

Koriat, A. (1997) Monitoring one's own knowledge during study: A cue-utilization approach to judgments of learning. *Journal of Experimental Psychology: General*, **126**, 349–70.

Koriat, A. (2007) Metacognition and consciousness. In P.D. Zelazo, M. Moscovitch, and E. Thompson (eds) *The Cambridge handbook of consciousness*, 289–326. Cambridge University Press, Cambridge.

Koriat, A. and Levy-Sadot, R. (1999) Processes underlying metacognitive judgments: Information-based and experience-based monitoring of one's own knowledge. In S. Chaiken, and Y. Trope (eds) *Dual-process theories in social psychology*, 483–502. Guilford Press, New York.

Koriat, A., Bjork, R.A., Sheffer, L., and Bar, S.K. (2004) Predicting one's own forgetting: The role of experience-based and theory-based processes. *Journal of Experimental Psychology: General*, **133**, 643–56.

Koriat, A., Levy-Sadot, R., Edry, E., and de Marcas, S. (2003) What do we know about what we cannot remember? Accessing the semantic attributes of words that cannot be recalled. *Journal of Experimental Psychology: Learning, Memory, and Cognition*, **29**, 1095–105.

Krendl, A.C., Macrae, C.N., Kelley, W.M., Fugelsang, J.A., and Heatherton, T.F. (2006) The good, the bad, and the ugly: An fMRI investigation of the functional anatomic correlates of stigma. *Social Neuroscience*, **1**, 5–15.

Kruger, J. (1999) Lake Wobegon be gone! The 'below-average effect' and the egocentric nature of comparative ability judgments. *Journal of Personality and Social Psychology*, **77**, 221–32.

Lin, L.M., Moore, D., and Zabrucky, K.M. (2001) An assessment of students' calibration of comprehension and calibration of performance using multiple measures. *Reading Psychology*, **22**, 111–28.

Lucangeli, D., Tressoldi, P.E., and Cendron, M. (1998) Cognitive and metacognitive abilities involved in the solution of mathematical word problems: Validation of a comprehensive model. *Contemporary Educational Psychology*, **23**, 257–75.

Lucas, E.J. and Ball, L.J. (2005) Think-aloud protocols and the selection task: Evidence for relevance effects and rationalisation processes. *Thinking & Reasoning*, **11**, 35–66.

Markovits, H. and Doyon, C. (2004) Information processing and reasoning with premises that are empirically false: Interference, working memory, and processing speed. *Memory & Cognition*, **32**, 592–601.

Markovits, H. and Quinn, S. (2002) Efficiency of retrieval correlates with 'logical' reasoning from causal conditional premises. *Memory & Cognition*, **30**, 696–706.

Matvey, G., Dunlosky, J., and Guttentag, R. (2001) Fluency of retrieval at study affects judgements of learning (JOLs): An analytic or nonanalytic basis for JOLs? *Memory and Cognition*, **29**, 222–33.

Mazzoni, G. and Cornoldi, C. (1993) Strategies in study time allocation: Why is study time sometimes not effective? *Journal of Experimental Psychology: General*, **122**, 47–60.

Metcalfe, J. (1986a) Feeling of knowing in memory and problem solving. *Journal of Experimental Psychology: Learning, Memory, and Cognition*, **12**, 288–94.

Metcalfe, J. (1986b) Premonitions of insight predict impending error. *Journal of Experimental Psychology: Learning, Memory, and Cognition*, **12**, 623–34.

Metcalfe, J. and Wiebe, D. (1987) Intuition in insight and noninsight problem solving. *Memory & Cognition*, **15**, 238–46.

Morgan, P.J. and Cleave-Hogg, D. (2002) Comparison between medical students' experience, confidence and competence. *Medical Education*, **36**, 534–9.

Nęcka, E. and Orzechowski, J. (2005) Higher-order cognition and intelligence. In R.J. Sternberg and J.E. Pretz (eds) *Cognition and intelligence: Identifying mechanisms of the mind*, 122–41. Cambridge University Press, Cambridge.

Nelson, T.O. (1993) Judgments of learning and the allocation of study time. *Journal of Experimental Psychology: General*, **122**, 269–73.

Nelson, T.O. and Dunlosky, J. (1991) When people's judgments of learning (JOLs) are extremely accurate at predicting subsequent recall: The 'delayed-JOL effect'. *Psychological Science*, **2**, 267–70.

Newstead, S.E. (1989) Interpretational errors in syllogistic reasoning. *Journal of Memory and Language*, **28**, 78–91.

Newstead, S.E. (2000) What is an ecologically rational heuristic? *Behavioral and Brain Sciences*, **23**, 759–60.

Newstead, S.E., Pollard, P., and Evans, J.S. (1992) The source of belief bias effects in syllogistic reasoning. *Cognition*, **45**, 257–84.

Pacini, R. and Epstein, S. (1999) The relation of rational and experiential information processing style to personality, basic beliefs and the ratio-bias phenomenon. *Journal of Personality and Social Psychology*, **76**, 972–87.

Pressley, M. (2003) Metacognition and self-regulated comprehension. In A. Farstrup and J. Samuels (eds) *What Research has to say about Reading Instructions*, 291–309. International Reading Association, Newark.

Prins, F.J., Veenman, M.J., and Elshout, J.J. (2006) The impact of intellectual ability and metacognition on learning: New support for the threshold of problematicity theory. *Learning and Instruction*, **16**, 374–87.

Prowse-Turner, J. and Thompson, V.A. (2007) Factors affecting the confidence-accuracy relationship in deductive reasoning. Manuscript under review.

Rajaram, S. (1993) Remembering and knowing: Two means of access to the personal past. *Memory & Cognition*, **21**, 89–102.

Reber, R. and Schwarz, N. (1999) Effects of perceptual fluency on judgments of truth. *Consciousness and Cognition*, **8**, 338–42.

Reber, R., Schwarz, N., Winkielman, P. (2004) Processing fluency and aesthetic pleasure: Is beauty in the perceiver's processing experience? *Personality and Social Psychology Review*, **8**, 364–82.

Reder, L.M., and Ritter, F. E. (1992) What determines initial feeling of knowing? Familiarity with question terms, not with the answer. *Journal of Experimental Psychology: Learning, Memory and Cognition*, **18**, 435–51.

Rehder, B. (1999) Detecting unsolvable algebra word problems. *Journal of Educational Psychology*, **91**, 669–83.

Roberts, M.J. (2004) Heuristics and reasoning I: Making deduction simple. In J. P. Leighton and R. J. Sternberg (eds) *The Nature of Reasoning*, 234–72. Cambridge University Press, Cambridge.

Roberts, M.J. and Newton, E.J. (2001) Inspection times, the change task, and the rapid-response selection task. *Quarterly Journal of Experimental Psychology A: Human Experimental Psychology*, **54**, 1031–48.

Roberts, M.J., Newstead, S.E., and Griggs, R.A. (2001) Quantifier interpretation and syllogistic reasoning. *Thinking & Reasoning*, **7**, 173–204.

Roediger, H.L. and McDermott, K.B. (1995) Creating false memories: Remembering words not presented in lists. *Journal of Experimental Psychology: Learning, Memory, and Cognition*, **21**, 803–14.

Rothman, A.J. and Schwarz, N. (1998) Constructing perceptions of vulnerability: Personal relevance and the use of experiential information in health judgments. *Personality and Social Psychology Bulletin*, **24**, 1053–64.

Sanna, L.J. and Schwarz, N. (2003) Debiasing the hindsight bias: The role of accessibility experiences and (mis)attributions. *Journal of Experimental Social Psychology*, **39**, 287–95.

Schmidt, J. and Thompson, V.A. (2008) 'At least one' problem with 'some' formal reasoning paradigms. *Memory & Cognition*, **36**, 217–29.

Schraw, G., Dunkle, M.E., Bendixen, L.D., and Roedel, T.D. (1995) Does a general monitoring skill exist? *Journal of Educational Psychology*, **87**, 433–44.

Schunn, C.D., Reder, L.M., Nhouyvanisvong, A., Richards, D.R., and Stroffolino, P. J. (1997) To calculate or not to calculate: A source activation confusion model of problem familiarity's role in strategy selection. *Journal of Experimental Psychology: Learning, Memory, and Cognition*, **23**, 3–29.

Schwarz, N. (2004) Metacognitive experiences in consumer judgment and decision making. *Journal of Consumer Psychology*, **14**, 332–48.

Schwarz, N. and Vaughn, L.A. (2002) The availability heuristic revisited: Ease of recall and content of recall as distinct sources of information. In T. Gilovich, D. Griffin, and D. Kahneman (eds) *Heuristics and biases: The psychology of intuitive judgment*, 103–119. Cambridge University Press, New York.

Schwartz, B.L., Benjamin, A.S., and Bkork, R.A. (1997) The inferential and experiential bases of metamemory. *Current Directions in Psychological Science*, **6**, 132–7.

Schwarz, N., Bless, H., Strack, F., Klumpp, G., Rittenauer-Schatka, H., and Simons, A. (1991) Ease of retrieval as information: Another look at the availability heuristic. *Journal of Personality and Social Psychology*, **61**, 195–202.

Shynkaruk, J.M. and Thompson, V.A. (2006) Confidence and accuracy in deductive reasoning. *Memory & Cognition*, **34**, 619–32.

Sloman, S.A. (2002) Two systems of reasoning. In G. D. Griffin and D. Kahneman (eds) *Heuristics and biases: The psychology of intuitive judgment*, 379–96. Cambridge University Press, New York.

Son, L.K. (2004) Spacing one's study: Evidence for a metacognitive control strategy. *Journal of Experimental Psychology: Learning, Memory, and Cognition*, **3**, 601–4.

Son, L.K. and Metcalfe, J. (2000) Metacognitive and control strategies in study-time allocation. *Journal of Experimental Psychology: Learning, Memory, and Cognition*, **26**, 204–21.

Son, L.K. and Metcalfe, J. (2005) Judgments of learning: Evidence for a two-stage process. *Memory & Cognition*, **33**, 1116–29.

Sperber, D., Cara, F., and Girotto, V. (1995) Relevance theory explains the selection task. *Cognition*, **57**, 31–95.

Sporer, S.L., Penrod, S., Read, D., and Cutler, B. (1995) Choosing, confidence, and accuracy: A meta-analysis of the confidence-accuracy relation in eyewitness identification studies. *Psychological Bulletin*, **118**, 315–27.

Stankov, L. (2000). Complexity, metacognition, and fluid intelligence. *Intelligence*, **28**, 121–43.

Stanovich, K.E. (1999) *Who is rational?: Studies of individual differences in reasoning.* Lawrence Erlbaum Associates Publishers, Mahwah, NJ.

Stanovich, K.E. (2004) *The robot's rebellion: Finding meaning in the age of Darwin.* University of Chicago Press, Chicago, IL.

Stanovich, K.E. and West, R.F. (2007) Natural myside bias is independent of cognitive ability. *Thinking & Reasoning*, **13**, 225–47.

Thompson, V.A. (1995) Conditional reasoning: The necessary and sufficient conditions. *Canadian Journal of Experimental Psychology*, **49**, 1–60.

Thompson, V.A. (2000) The task-specific nature of domain-general reasoning. *Cognition*, **76**, 209–68.

Todd, P.M. and Gigerenzer, G. (2000) Precis of simple heuristics that make us smart. *Behavioral and Brain Sciences*, **23**, 727–80.

Todd, P.M. and Gigerenzer, G. (2003) Bounding rationality to the world. *Journal of Economic Psychology*, **24**, 143–65.

Torrens, D., Thompson, V.A., and Cramer, K.M. (1999) Individual differences and the belief bias effect: Mental models, logical necessity, and abstract reasoning. *Thinking & Reasoning*, **5**, 1–28.

Vadeboncoeur, I. and Markovits, H. (1999) The effect of instructions and information retrieval on accepting the premises in a conditional reasoning task. *Thinking & Reasoning*, **5**, 97–113. Taylor & Francis, Oxford.

Veenman, M.V.J., Kok, R., and Blöte, A.W. (2005) The relation between intellectual and metacognitive skills in early adolescence. *Instructional Science*, **33**, 193–211.

Vernon, D. and Usher, M. (2003) Dynamics of metacognitive judgments: Pre- and post-retrieval mechanisms. *Journal of Experimental Psychology: Learning, Memory, and Cognition*, **29**, 339–46.

Verschueren, N., Schaeken, W., and D'Ydewalle, G. (2005) Everyday conditional reasoning: A working memory-dependent tradeoff between counterexample and likelihood use. *Memory & Cognition*, **33**, 107–19.

Wason, P.C. and Evans, J.St.B.T. (1975) Dual processing in reasoning? *Cognition*, **3**, 141–54.

Whittlesea, B.W.A. (1993) Illusions of familiarity. *Journal of Experimental Psychology: Learning, Memory, and Cognition*, **19**, 1235–53.

Whittlesea, B.W. and Jacoby, L.L. (1990) Interaction of prime repetition with visual degradation: Is priming a retrieval phenomenon? *Journal of Memory and Language*, **29**, 546–65.

Whittlesea, B.W. Jacoby, L.L., and Girard, K. (1990) Illusions of immediate memory: Evidence of an attributional basis for feelings of familiarity and perceptual quality. *Journal of Memory and Language*, **29**, 716–32.

Whittlesea, B.W.A. and Leboe, J.P. (2003) Two fluency heuristics (and how to tell them apart). *Journal of Memory and Language*, **49**, 62–79.

Wilson, T.D. and Dunn, E.W. (2004) Self-knowledge: Its limits, value, and potential for improvement. *Annual Review of Psychology*, **55**, 493–518.

Winkielman, P., Halberstadt, J., Fazendeiro, T., and Catty, S. (2006) Prototypes are attractive because they are easy on the mind. *Psychological Science*, **17**, 799–806.

Winkielman, P., Schwarz, N., Fazendeiro, T.A., and Reber, R. (2003) The hedonic marking of processing fluency: Implications for evaluative judgment. In J. Musch and K.C. Klauer (eds) *The psychology of evaluation: Affective processes in cognition and emotion*, 189–217. Lawrence Erlbaum Associates, Mahwah, NJ.

Zizak, D.M. and Reber, A.S. (2004) Implicit preferences: The role(s) of familiarity in the structure mere exposure effect. *Consciousness and Cognition*, **13**, 336–62.

Chapter 9

Dual-process models: A social psychological perspective

Eliot R. Smith and Elizabeth C. Collins

People are constantly processing information about the world and adjusting their behavior accordingly. Everyday observation as well as careful research suggests that people often use a sort of quick and dirty approach to information processing, arriving at (usually) reasonable answers efficiently and effortlessly. For example, arguments presented by an expert source with statistical evidence are often correct, and are often accepted without much deliberation. However, people can also think deeply about things, such as an argument presented by an expert, and such scrutiny may reveal that the argument is specious or flawed.

Many dual-process models have been developed in specific topic areas within social psychology over the years (Brewer 1988; Chaiken 1980; Devine 1989; Epstein 1991; Fazio 1986; Fiske and Neuberg 1988; Gilbert 1989; Martin et al. 1990; Petty and Cacioppo 1986; Wegener and Petty 1995). Smith and DeCoster (2000) proposed a generalized dual-process model that integrates most of the earlier models. Since Smith and DeCoster's integration, Strack and Deutsch (2004) proposed an extended model explaining how behavior can be controlled by different processes under different situations. In this paper we will describe a few of the more influential social psychological dual-process models and give an in-depth review of the integrative models. We will then compare the general characteristics of dual-process models in social psychology with similar models in other areas of psychology, and discuss implications of this comparison for several conceptual issues.

Examples of prominent social psychological dual-process models

Dual-process models in social psychology were initially suggested to explain specific phenomena in individual domains. More recently, theorists have begun to look at how those explanations for distinct phenomena might fit together into more broadly integrated models of dual processing in general. In this section we review some of the more important models of specific phenomena. In the next section we examine some of the integrated models.

Dual-process models have been very influential in the field of persuasion and attitude change, which focuses on the processes involved when an individual receives a persuasive message such as an ad for a consumer product or an advocacy for a social policy. Petty and Cacioppo (1981) and Chaiken (1980) proposed broadly similar models regarding two types of processing of persuasive messages. In the Chaiken model (Chen and Chaiken 1999) *heuristic* processing involves the use of simple, well learned and readily accessible associations. (Chaiken termed these associations 'heuristic rules', a term that has unfortunately suggested to some that she was postulating deliberative or rule-based processing. We regard her heuristic processing as associative in nature, and use that term here for clarity.) For example, someone might agree with a persuasive message delivered by an attractive, likable source simply because positive feelings are aroused by the source, or agree with a majority's position because in the individual's past experience, majorities have usually turned out to be correct. Heuristic processing is the default processing mode, but people perform *systematic* processing when they have the motivation, time, and cognitive capacity allowing for more effortful processing. This involves the active, effortful scrutiny of all relevant information, requiring considerable cognitive capacity and potentially leading to more enduring attitude change. Systematic processing (to the extent that it occurs) is assumed to take place in addition to and simultaneously with heuristic processing, rather than replacing it. Systematic processing is initiated or terminated on the basis of an intuitive 'sufficiency criterion'—people are assumed to process systematically until their subjective confidence in their judgment reaches a threshold.

Petty and Cacioppo's (1986) Elaboration Likelihood Model (ELM) focuses on the relative balance of what are termed 'central' and 'peripheral' processing. Elaboration likelihood is the extent to which the impact of a persuasive message is caused by the individual's thoughtful cognitive responses to the arguments contained in the message (high elaboration), versus peripheral aspects of the message, its source, or the situation (low elaboration). When people are low in capacity or motivation they will not engage in much elaboration, so judgments will be based mostly on salient peripheral cues. When people possess both capacity and motivation they assess the arguments in detail, and may attempt to correct for potentially biasing effects of peripheral cues. During elaborative processing people can still be affected by peripheral cues, although their influence is mediated by conscious consideration of their relevance (Petty and Wegener 1999).

Literally hundreds of studies have used one general research design to test these dual-process models of persuasion (Petty et al. 2003). (A) Argument strength is manipulated, so that some research participants read a message containing strong, compelling arguments and others see only weak, specious arguments. The assumption is that only systematic or elaborative processing enables people to detect and be influenced by these differences in argument strength. (B) A more peripheral or heuristic cue, such as the attractiveness of the message source, is also manipulated. (C) Some aspect of the participant's motivation or ability to process the message in depth is either manipulated or measured. Manipulations include personal relevance of the issue targeted by the message, distraction, or cognitive load imposed by a secondary task. Measurement often involves the 'need for cognition' construct (Cacioppo and Petty 1982), a stable individual difference in the extent to which people enjoy complex thinking.

Typical results from such a study indicate that when processing motivation or ability is low, the peripheral cue has a strong effect on the participant's final agreement with the message, while argument strength has little or no effect (because participants in this condition do not process the arguments in any depth). In contrast, when ability and motivation are high, participants agree much more with strong than with weak arguments, while attractiveness or other peripheral cues have little effect. Many studies also obtain subsidiary evidence regarding the type of processing by using a 'thought-listing' measure, which asks participants to write down the thoughts they have while processing the argument. Evidence for systematic or elaborative processing includes (a) a high proportion of message-relevant thoughts (e.g. 'That argument makes sense to me') and (b) a statistical relationship between the favorability or unfavorability of the listed thoughts and the participant's final agreement with the message.

Dual-process models are also found outside the area of persuasion in social psychology. Devine (1989) proposed a model in the area of stereotyping which follows the general dual-process framework. She holds that virtually everyone within a culture learns common stereotypes (beliefs about the typical characteristics of social groups) from other people or the media. These well-learned associations are automatically activated merely by encountering or thinking about a group or group member. However, an additional process may occur as a second sequential stage in individuals who are low in prejudice. These people may effortfully override the automatic activation of stereotypes by accessing and considering their relatively more favorable 'personal beliefs' about the group's characteristics (a process essentially similar to systematic or elaborative processing).

Devine's model illustrates social psychologists' long-standing interest in prejudice and stereotyping, a domain where there is well-founded suspicion that people often distort explicit self-reports of their attitudes. In order to measure prejudiced responses, as well as other responses potentially subject to self-presentational concerns, researchers have developed measures that do not rely on self-report. Often termed 'implicit' measures (Fazio and Olson 2003), these use various means (e.g. speeded responses, subliminal presentation of stimuli) that make it very difficult or impossible for people to intentionally control their responses. Several different types of implicit measures are in wide use. One example is evaluative priming: an attitude object is presented as a prime, followed by positive or negative words as targets. The speed with which the participant can classify the target words by valence depends on his or her evaluation of the prime, and hence a response-time index can be used as a measure of this implicit evaluation (Fazio et al. 1995). Research has often assumed that such implicit measures tap the results of automatic, associative, or System 1 processes with little contamination by intentional efforts to control responses. Recent studies by Ranganath et al. (2008) suggest that specific types of self-report measures, including instructions to report one's 'gut feelings' or self-reports obtained under time pressure, can also tap more automatic, associative responses to stimuli.

Wilson et al. (2000) proposed a dual-process model explaining how implicit and explicit attitudes or evaluations of the same object can sometimes be dissociated. For example, someone might reveal negative attitudes about a racial group on an implicit test, yet self-report positive attitudes with all evident sincerity. Their model posits that well learned associations do not simply disappear when an attitude is changed. For example, someone may be persuaded by compelling arguments, and develop a new attitude about the object (similar to Devine's (1989) unprejudiced 'personal beliefs'). However, the former attitude does not vanish but continues to exist as a nonconscious association that can reveal itself on subtle, indirect measures.

Gawronski and Bodenhausen (2006) expanded on Wilson et al.'s (2000) model, giving a detailed explanation of several ways implicit and explicit attitudes can influence each other according to their Associative-Propositional Evaluation (APE) model. They hold that implicit evaluations are built up by repeated association of a concept with positive or negative concepts, whereas propositional evaluations are influenced by a logical analysis of the truth of a thought or situation. Associative (implicit) and propositional (explicit) attitudes may influence each other and each may shape the individual's behavior, depending on the situation. The effects depend on how automatic associations and logical/propositional reasoning are triggered and influenced by the situation. For example, repeated exposure to positive words paired with exemplars of a negatively stereotyped group will influence a participant's implicit attitudes (associations) toward the group (Karpinski and Hilton 2001). However this manipulation does not influence propositional or explicit attitudes, since no meaningful arguments were presented.

Conceptually integrative models

Smith and DeCoster's Model

Smith and DeCoster (2000) advanced a conceptual integration, placing a number of dual-process models from social and cognitive psychology into a common framework. They proposed that the two processes posited in many dual-process theories have a structural basis in two separate memory systems with distinct properties (Sherry and Schacter 1987). They base this argument on evidence that humans have two memory systems that use fundamentally different principles of operation: one is a slow-learning memory system, the other a rapid-learning memory system (for a review, see McClelland et al. 1995).

The two processing modes draw in different ways on those two memory systems. The *associative processing mode* is based directly on the properties of the slow learning system, which operates essentially as a pattern-completion mechanism. After knowledge has been accumulated from a large number of experiences into the slow learning memory system, the associative process uses that knowledge to automatically add to the information available in the situation. It does so by reactivating information that has previously been observed, or affective reactions that have previously been experienced, in situations that resemble the current one. In contrast, the *rule-based processing mode* uses symbolically represented and culturally transmitted knowledge which it processes analytically. It rests on human linguistic and logical abilities, which in turn draw on *both* underlying memory systems. Rules may be stored in either processing system, depending on such factors as how frequently they have been encountered (i.e. rarely or frequently), and over what length of time.

Associative processing

In general, social psychological dual-process theories agree that processing in the associative mode amounts to the automatic access of knowledge or affective reactions that have become associated with a cue (such as stereotypes that have been repeatedly paired with a social group, or positive reactions to an attractive message source), when the cue is salient in the current stimulus or context. The buildup or learning of such an association is assumed to require repeated pairings over time. Activation of the knowledge is automatic and preconscious, so that it becomes subjectively part of the stimulus information (rather than being seen as part of the perceiver's own interpretation of it). The associated knowledge therefore has the potential to affect judgments and behavior without the individual's awareness.

Smith and DeCoster's (2000) integrative model captures these features. Associative processing is quick, automatic, and preconscious (Bargh 1994), leading to the experience of intuitive and affective responses to objects or events. It uses knowledge that is retrieved from memory in response to currently available cues, filling in unobserved details or even changing the way people interpret existing features of an object. Finally, associative processing uses general, overall similarity between the cues and stored information to guide retrieval, allowing superficial or irrelevant similarities to the current cues to guide retrieval (see Gilovich 1981; Lewicki 1985 for social psychological demonstrations of this property). For example, one may have a 'gut reaction' of liking or disliking a stranger on first encounter, based on that person's physical resemblance to a liked or disliked known individual (Andersen and Berk 1998).

Rule-based processing

Most social psychological dual-process models share the view that rule-based processing, such as the systematic evaluation of persuasive arguments, is consciously controlled and effortful, and involves search, retrieval, and use of task-relevant information (see Petty and Cacioppo 1981; Fiske and Neuberg 1988). Rule-based processing is assumed to be strategic, and its exact nature will vary depending on the specifics of the task, the individual's goals, or situational constraints. When it occurs, this type of processing generally gives rise to a higher level of perceived validity of the conclusion or judgment and to more long-lasting effects (Chaiken et al. 1989). For Smith and DeCoster (2000) the other defining feature of rule-based processing is that it uses symbolically represented and intentionally accessed knowledge as rules to guide processing. This processing may use information stored in *either* the fast-learning *or* the slow-learning memory system. Symbolic knowledge that has been encountered just once can be stored in the fast learning memory system, and then explicitly retrieved and used to guide processing: the processing *uses* or *follows* rules, rather than merely *conforming to* them. This interpretive rule-use process is necessarily sequential and relatively slow and effortful (in contrast to the fast, parallel constraint-satisfaction process that can be used with associative knowledge representations). Rule-based processing also tends to be analytic, rather than based on overall or global similarity. For example, judgments may be made about a person based on specifically relevant and applicable information (such as their behaviors), rather than on their overall resemblance to a known person.

The symbolic rules used by Smith and DeCoster's (2000) rule-based processing system may constitute a formal system, such as the laws of arithmetic or of logical inference, that is supported and accorded validity by social consensus in a way that goes beyond its inherent persuasiveness for any given individual (Smolensky 1988; Sloman 1996; Wood 2000). In other cases, rules may be idiosyncratically learned, applied by a particular individual who finds them useful even in the absence of social/normative support (e.g. 'Never eat at a place called "Mom's"'). The fast-learning memory system's ability to rapidly bind together multiple cognitive elements into new combinatorial structures (e.g. to put together concepts into new combinations) underlies the ability to dynamically construct and change knowledge representations. Symbolic language permits great flexibility, allowing for comprehension and expression of impossible events, alternative realities, future possibilities, and so on. The rule-based system maintains and uses explicit representations of rules to derive its conclusions. The individual may be aware of discrete, sequential steps in this process and may be able to verbally report on the rules that were used (Sloman 1996). This ability to 'backtrack' provides a basis for explaining or justifying a conclusion, which makes it more socially recognized as valid.

Interactions between processing modes

Repeated use of symbolic rules creates the conditions for associative learning, so eventually the same answer that is generated by the rule-based system can be retrieved by pattern-completion in the associative system, rendering the step-by-step procedure superfluous (Logan 1988; Sloman 1996). Thus, after months or years of practice with effortful counting, simple facts about addition (such as $3 + 4 = 7$) become directly and immediately retrievable from memory. However, a newly learned rule should be unable to affect associative processing until it has been extensively practiced. Information from the associative system can direct the construction of new information in the rule-based system, as when people intentionally reflect on their past experiences and summarize them as a symbolically represented rule. This process allows for knowledge to be used flexibly, applied to other contexts, or communicated to other people.

Whether a person will rely on the associative or rule-based processing system for responses depends on motivation and capacity, because using the rule-based system requires attentional resources. However, rule-based processing may not always be evenhanded and unbiased, and when it is biased, it may produce less accurate conclusions compared to the results of associative processing. Rule-based processing also generally takes longer than associative processing (Logan 1988), and because it requires attention, is more subject to disruption by distraction, interference, etc. Thus, responses that are made quickly or when the perceiver is busy or distracted will likely be controlled by the associative system (this is the principle underlying interpretations of implicit measures).

In addition to motivation and capacity three other things may also affect which processing mode is relied on: (1) type of judgment; (2) generality or specificity of stimuli or judgment targets; and (3) mood. Judgments involving how one subjectively feels about an object or event appear to be more associatively driven, compared to more analytic, rational judgments such as those about causation. Specific, concrete stimuli seem to be better cues for responses from the associative system, while more abstract stimuli often elicit use of symbolic rules (Kahneman and Miller 1986; Epstein 1991). Finally, findings suggest that positive mood elicits more reliance on the associative system, whereas negative mood appears to promote reliance on rule-based processing (Bless 2001).

Under many circumstances Smith and DeCoster assume that both systems function in parallel, since the associative system works automatically, and without effort. When the working of the associative system is unnoticed by the individual, the information arising from that system may exert an unwanted biasing influence on the rule-based processing. If the individual becomes aware of such an effect (e.g. from a well-learned but explicitly rejected stereotype), rule-based processing may attempt to correct or overcome the bias.

Beyond integrating earlier models, Smith and DeCoster's (2000) model explains many dissociations that have been noted in social psychology. Hastie and Park (1986) noted that the judgments people make about an object based on a body of information may have little relationship to the specific items of information that the person can recall. This is because judgments about an object may be formulated in the slow-learning associative system, while explicit memory of the information upon which the judgment was based would depend on the fast-learning system. Our frequent inability to verbalize some types of knowledge, especially procedural knowledge, can also be explained by the distinction between the two processing systems: the associative processor is responsible for skilled performance, while verbal reports are generated by the rule-based system. Sloman (1996) showed evidence that people are sometimes aware of holding simultaneous contradictory beliefs, which can be explained by different responses arising from different processing modes, each having its own subjective 'pull' on the individual.

Strack and Deutsch's Model

An integrative model proposed by Strack and Deutsch (2004) also focuses on the functioning of two systems: an impulsive system that is similar to the associative system of Smith and DeCoster (2000) and a reflective system, similar to the rule-based system. The major addition made by Strack and Deutsch's (2004) model is to explain how behavior can be affected directly by either system.

Strack and Deutsch (2004) propose that each system can exert control over action. The reflective system can process information and come to a decision on a behavioral action, which will then be acted upon. However, behavioral schemata can also be encoded into the impulsive system over time. These can then be activated by associated stimuli (physical states or familiar situations or objects) causing action without reflection. Strack and Deutsch (2004) posit that the two systems compete for control of behavior. Thus, when the impulsive system's behavioral motivation is strong, individuals may act in ways that contradict their stated values or long term goals (for example, cheating on a diet).

The other major contribution made by Strack and Deutsch (2004) is in the exploration of how specific behaviors can elicit specific cognitions, because of associations that have built up over time in the impulsive system. The 'embodied cognition' perspective (Semin and Smith 2008) holds that behavior often shapes cognition: over time physical actions can become associated with specific states or stimuli, eventually causing the cognitions to be automatically triggered by the physical action, even when inappropriate. An example (Cacioppo et al. 1993) is that participants who were asked to flex their arm (pull toward themselves) while examining Chinese ideographs later rated the ideographs more positively than those who examined the ideographs while extending their arm (pushing away from themselves). This effect is interpreted as resulting from an association between arm flexion movements and bringing positive things closer to the self, and arm extension movements and pushing negative things away. Thus, the arm movements activate the corresponding evaluations.

Potential contributions of social psychological dual-process models

As chapters in this volume make clear, a number of dual-process models sharing similar general outlines have been developed in several areas of cognitive and social psychology, but with little cross-referencing or mutual influence. The social psychological models reviewed above typically make little reference to models from cognitive psychology, other than Smith and DeCoster's (2000) discussion of Sloman's (1996) model and the McClelland et al. (1995) dual memory systems proposal. Equally few citations of the social psychological models are found in the cognitive dual-process literature. Here we discuss some of the insights from the social psychological models that might be of value to dual-process thinking more generally.

Relations of the assumed two processing modes

Social psychological models make diverse assumptions regarding the relations between the two processing modes. Some (e.g. Smith and DeCoster 2000; Chaiken 1980) assume that the two types of processing occur in parallel and can affect each other. Others (e.g. Gilbert 1989) assume that processing is sequential, with quick associative processing followed (and potentially corrected) by rule-based processing. Still other models (e.g. Petty and Cacioppo 1986) assume that either one or the other type of processing is used in a given situation.

An important recent development is presented in a paper by Conrey et al. (2005). They argue that more than one specific process of either type can contribute to performance for a particular task. To illustrate their argument, consider a priming paradigm where a photo of a black or white male is presented, followed by a photo of a tool or handgun (Payne 2001). The participant has to decide as rapidly and accurately as possible whether the second photo is a tool or gun. In this paradigm, people make more misidentifications of tools as weapons when they are preceded by a black prime. Conrey and colleagues assume that four processes contribute to task performance. Each is characterized by a parameter describing the probability of the process occurring; the parameter values can be estimated from task performance data. The processes are:

Activating an association: the prime photo may automatically activate a well-learned stereotype of blacks as violent/criminal.

Overcoming bias: the participant may be able to intentionally inhibit this information (if it is activated) so that it does not control the response.

Discrimination: the participant may be able to intentionally discriminate whether the object is a tool or weapon.

Guessing: if there is no association activated AND no ability to discriminate, the participant may guess either the 'tool' or 'weapon' response.

Postulating 4 processes permits finer-grained analyses of exactly how correct or erroneous responses are generated. Further, investigators can analyze how various manipulations produce shifts in responding. For example, Lambert and colleagues (Lambert et al. 2003) have conducted studies showing that putting people in a public situation as they do this task (so they are concerned about whether stereotype-driven misjudgments might reveal their own prejudice) actually makes performance more likely to be driven by stereotypes. Model-based analyses make it possible to see whether this is because the public situation increases the probability of activating the association, decreases the ability to discriminate, etc.

This framework could also be informative if applied to other tasks, for example the belief/syllogistic reasoning task that has been prominent in the cognitive literature (Evans 2008). In this task, people are presented with logically valid or invalid syllogisms, whose conclusions are (independently) either believable or not believable based on general knowledge. Although the task is to evaluate the logical validity of the conclusion, believability tends to bias these judgments. The processes would be:

◆ Activating an association: the person may notice that the conclusion is believable or not.

◆ Overcoming bias: the person may intentionally inhibit this information (if it is activated) so that it does not control the response.

◆ Discrimination: the person may intentionally use the rules of logic to determine whether the syllogism is valid.

◆ Guessing: if neither belief nor validity information is available, the person may guess 'valid' or 'invalid'.

The Conrey et al. (2005) model may also shed light on the distinction made by Evans (2008, this volume) between 'parallel/competitive' and 'default/interventionist' models. Parallel/competitive models are those in which automatic and controlled processes run in parallel and (if they arrive at different responses) compete for control of the final overt behavior. Default/interventionist models are those in which automatic processes supply a default behavioral response, which can be replaced by a different response if controlled processing intervenes. We do not see that distinction as very clear-cut. If (as we believe) two processes operate in parallel (e.g. activation of an association and efforts to intentionally discriminate the right answer), the overt response will depend on competition between those processes (e.g. in their respective speed), as well as on whether the person can intentionally intervene to inhibit or overcome the unwanted bias ('overcoming bias' process in the Conrey et al. 2005 model). This whole chain of events could equally well be described either as parallel/competitive or default/interventionist in nature.

Another way of thinking about this issue is to observe that the extent of systematic processing varies tremendously across people and situations, being near zero when motivation or opportunity is very low. In this case, people may simply use an available associative cue as a default judgment (e.g. use their positive or negative mood to make a positive or negative judgment about an object). They presumably make only the most minimal kind of plausibility check before doing so (e.g. people refrain from making mood-based judgments if their attention is called to some obvious extraneous cause of their mood; Martin 2001). Although, in general, systematic and associative processing run in parallel, because systematic processing is minimal in this case it seems apt to say that associative processing furnishes a default that is used as the person's judgment unless some (rare) intervention is made. Kahneman and Frederick's (2005) model in which heuristic judgments are made available by System 1, but may be altered by optional System 2 processing, appears to be similar to this description.

Multiple potential roles for a single type of information

Theorists in the ELM tradition have been especially interested in pointing out that a given type or item of information may play multiple roles in the process of evaluating and responding to a persuasive message (Wegener and Petty 1996). That is, a specific factor is not inherently tied to one or the other processing mode, but may affect judgments through different pathways. Like the insights of the Quad Model, this principle may also have broader implications beyond social psychological dual-process models. We illustrate this principle by considering a frequently studied factor, the person's positive or negative mood. First, when elaborative processing is low, mood may act as a simple heuristic cue, leading to favorable judgments when mood is positive or unfavorable judgments when mood is negative (Petty et al. 1993). Second, when elaborative processing is high, mood can bias that processing. For example, positive mood has been shown to increase people's judgments of the likelihood of favorable consequences of some action or policy (DeSteno et al. 2000), which may well bias their attitude toward the action. Finally, when the extent of elaborative processing is not constrained, mood can influence the extent of processing: people think more about messages when they are sad than when they are happy (Bless et al. 1990). Therefore, a message with strong arguments should be more persuasive to sad than to happy people, while a message with weak arguments will be more persuasive for those who are happy than those who are sad. As this example illustrates, it would be a mistake to identify a particular cue or factor (such as mood) with a specific type or mode of processing, because, at least in principle, any type of information can play multiple roles in the processing sequence.

Origin of biases in processing

As we hope the preceding discussion makes clear, most social psychological models do not assume that biases arise *solely* from the use of associative processing. Rather, systematic or rule-based processing can also be biased by the perceiver's motives, by priming, or by other factors (e.g. current mood) that make certain cognitive structures more or less accessible. Thus, biases can influence processing in either mode.

In this regard, we agree with Evans (2008), whose review questions the idea that biased responses (e.g. responses to valid or invalid syllogisms that are biased by the believability of the conclusion) are a 'signature' of System 1 processing.

In fact, research in social psychology demonstrates that intentional efforts to correct bias may even lead to further bias. Wegener and Petty (1997) described how people use intuitive theories of bias in an effort to correct judgments that they believe might be biased. For example, someone might be asked to evaluate the prospect of a week's vacation in Paris, followed by a week in Columbus, Ohio. Many people hold the intuitive idea that the latter judgment might be biased in a contrastive fashion (made more negative by the implicit comparison with the more desirable Paris vacation) and therefore they might attempt to correct their judgment by making it more positive. Of course, to the extent that such intuitive theories of bias are inaccurate, such efforts at correction might fail to remove biases in judgment, or even exacerbate them.

Potential different information-processing properties in two modes

Many dual-process models assume that the two systems involve qualitatively different information-processing rules or properties. For example, a frequent assumption is that System 1 makes use of associations that are built up through repeated experiences, while System 2 can use information that is learned on only a single occasion. Smith and DeCoster (2000), as discussed earlier, relate this difference to the properties of slow-learning and fast-learning memory systems (following McClelland et al. 1995). Research bears out these general assumptions. For example, Petty and colleagues (Petty et al. 2006) exposed people on repeated trials to positive information about one target person and negative information about another. They then told the participants that a mistake had been made, and the two target persons had erroneously been switched. Participants were able to use the information about the mistake to correct explicit responses (driven by System 2): they reported that they liked the person who had been presented unfavorably more than the one who had been presented favorably. However, the repeatedly presented positive or negative information continued to control responses to the targets that were driven by the associative System 1—in this study, responses on an implicit attitude measure, an adaptation of the Implicit Association Test (IAT, Greenwald et al. 1998).

Another difference between the two systems in information-processing properties has been recently discovered by Betsch et al. (2006). In their studies, participants watched 'stock symbols' move across the bottom of a TV screen, accompanied by numbers representing price gains. If participants focused on the stocks as their explicit task, their later reports of how favorably they evaluated each 'stock' corresponded well to the *average* of the price gains they had seen for that stock. In contrast, in another condition participants watched and tried to memorize 20 videotaped ads, which distracted their attention from the stock price information on the bottom of the screen. When their attitudes toward the stocks were later assessed, results showed that the participants had absorbed some information even though the stocks were not their focus of attention. However, the attitudes correlated with the *sum* rather than the average of the price gains that had been displayed. In other words, explicit and implicit evaluations may involve different information-integration rules of averaging versus summation (respectively). The authors hold that when there is an intention to form an attitude or other judgment, conscious consideration of each item of information results in a judgment that is an overall average of the items. In contrast, when evaluatively relevant information is processed without an explicit intention to form a judgment, the information is simply accumulated without being normalized by the sample size, resulting in a judgment that reflects the sum (not the average) of the items.

Systematic processing not inherently superior to associative processing

Dual-process models vary in the extent to which they imply an evaluative distinction between the two processing modes. Some social psychological models identify associative processing with bias and general badness, and rule-based processing with accuracy and general goodness. Abelson (1994) suggested that the evaluative difference between the two processes implied by some models arises from both the general Western bias toward rational instrumentalism, and also the focus within social psychology on the study of racial prejudice, which is often associatively learned but overridden by rule-based processing. Evans (2008) notes that in cognitive models as well, System 2 processing is often seen as an ideal and System 1 processing is attributed only the pragmatic virtues of speed and efficiency.

In contrast, other models have little or no connotation of an evaluative distinction between the two processing modes. Smith and DeCoster (2000) propose that each type of processing has appropriate and adaptive effects, just as each can produce bias. In general, recent years have seen an increased emphasis on the idea that more affective, intuitive judgments are often useful and accurate, rather than being condemned simply because they are not narrowly 'rational'. Examples of thinkers who hold positions of this sort are Damasio (especially in *Descartes' error* 1994), Haidt (with his work on the emotional basis of moral judgments, e.g. 2001), work on fast, effective judgments by domain experts (Klein 1999), and in social psychology, Wilson and Schooler's (1991) work showing that intuitive attitude judgments can be more adaptive for the perceiver than more deliberative attitude judgments.

Nature and capabilities of nonconscious (implicit) processing

Motivated by general acceptance of the dual-process framework, social psychological researchers and theorists have focused much attention on nonconscious or implicit processes and representations in recent years. Here we briefly discuss developments in the measurement of implicit attitudes, and investigations of other properties of nonconscious processing and regulatory systems.

From the perspective of dual-process models, many social psychologists believe that implicit attitude measures tap, in relatively pure form, the evaluative associations that people have for a particular object. By the same token, implicit measures are thought to be relatively impervious to strategic control, hence relatively unaffected by conscious motives such as the motive to present oneself in a favorable light by appearing nonprejudiced. Hundreds of studies using these measures establish several important generalizations that provide evidence for their validity (see Fazio and Olson 2003). First, implicit measures successfully predict a range of social behaviors (e.g. non-verbal behavior), over and above the predictive power offered by explicit self-report measures. Second, implicit and explicit attitudes toward the same object are sometimes highly correlated, but in other situations show low or negligible correlations (Nosek 2007). The latter case suggests that at least sometimes, associations in memory differ substantially from the explicit responses that people would make given adequate time and cognitive control (e.g. on a questionnaire). Important questions remain largely unanswered, such as whether implicit responses represent the way people *know* they feel but choose not to report, or represent tendencies of which people are *honestly unaware* and thus unable to report. In general, continued development and refinement of implicit measures promises to provide new approaches to investigating properties of dual-process models.

As just noted, people sometimes have congruent or similar implicit and explicit attitudes, while in other circumstances they may be incongruent or dissimilar. Some research has focused on examining the consequences for the individual of implicit-explicit attitude congruence on an important topic. One intriguing study hints that inconsistent implicit and explicit evaluations of the self (i.e. self-esteem) are associated with more negative mood states (Robinson et al. 2003). Thus, not only may people at times feel subjective conflict between products of distinct processing systems (e.g. in the case of visual illusions; Sloman 1996), the conflict may actually have meaningful negative consequences for affect and subjective well-being.

A third area of active investigation is the properties of nonconscious (or implicit) processing systems. Much research has focused on the effects of implicit goal activation (Dijksterhuis and Bargh 2001). Studies have used manipulations of which participants are unaware (often subliminal priming manipulations) to activate concepts that represent goals. Such manipulations are found to influence people's behavior in ways that suggest the operation of nonconscious self-regulatory systems. Effects of goal activation are sharply distinct from the effects of simply activating a semantic concept (Förster et al. 2007). For example, goal activation has effects that persist or even increase over time as long as the goal remains unfulfilled, then drop rapidly upon goal fulfillment. In contrast, semantic activation diminishes monotonically over time. Also, goal activation produces activation and shifts in the evaluation of other concepts that are instrumentally related to the goal, even if they are not generally semantically related to the goal concept. For example, if a child's birthday party is approaching and it is important to pick up the cake at the bakery, activation of 'party' or 'cake' as a goal may cause activation of 'car', because driving is instrumental in accomplishing that goal, even if 'cake' and 'car' are not generally semantically related. Again, research on nonconscious goal attainment and nonconscious self-regulatory processes can potentially extend our knowledge about the properties of dual-processing systems, in ways that have been relatively little studied in the context of dual-process models in cognitive psychology.

Some of these recent findings suggest that nonconscious processing can be quite powerful. In a similar vein, Dijksterhuis and his colleagues (2006) recently advanced the startling claim that implicit or nonconscious processing is of a deliberative nature (similar to conscious, reflective, or System 2 processing), and even that it can lead to superior decisions. In their studies, people obtain information relevant to a decision, and then either deliberate on the information or are prevented from deliberating by a distracting task before making their decision. Participants who were distracted are found to make normatively better decisions. However, we question the conclusion drawn by Dijksterhuis et al. (2006). This paradigm cannot show that nonconscious deliberative processing occurred in the distraction condition. Rather, simpler associative processes could give rise to overall impressions of the evaluative quality of the decision alternatives. These and other similar studies (e.g. Wilson and Schooler 1991) do, however, support the provocative idea that conscious reflection can sometimes impair the quality of judgments.

Broader view of the motives behind systematic processing

System 2 processing is optional and effortful; thus, its extent may vary every time an individual makes a judgment or decision, and sometimes it may not take place at all. At the broadest level, the extent of such processing is controlled by two factors: ability to process (e.g. whether the person has necessary background information to scrutinize a message in depth; freedom from distraction; adequate time to process), and motivation to process. While dual-process models in cognitive psychology have often assumed that the sole significant motivation is accuracy (i.e. to form judgments that are valid and normatively correct), social psychological models have taken a broader view of possibly relevant motives. Wood (2000) argues that three fundamental social motives can each lead to increased processing. For example, consider someone who is processing a persuasive message on some topic. *Accuracy* motivation, the desire to form attitudes that will be valid and functional guides to reality (e.g. leading to approach of beneficial objects and avoidance of dangerous ones), could certainly motivate in-depth scrutiny of the message. The motive to *belong* or to be *connected* to others could also motivate processing, in cases where holding the same attitude as other individuals or groups is important—for example, one might carefully process a message from one's favored political party to determine what attitudes it is appropriate to hold as a party member. Finally, the motive to *maintain a valued identity* can also motivate processing, in situations where attitudes are important and self-relevant. For example, a message that challenged an important self-view would no doubt be subject to intensive (probably biased) scrutiny. The bottom line is that multiple social motives can lead people to engage in effortful processing; accuracy is not the only goal that people care about, nor necessarily the ultimate result of extensive processing.

Summary and conclusions

There is substantial convergence between the basic assumptions of dual-process models from cognitive and social psychology. Evans' (2008) review makes this point, which is underlined by Smith and DeCoster's (2000) integration of the memory systems framework of McClelland et al. (1995) and the reasoning model of Sloman (1996), as well as several social-psychological models. The conceptual convergence means that several aspects of dual-process research and theory from social psychology might be valuable to researchers in other traditions as well.

Most important in our view is social psychologists' large and productive research investment in implicit measures, which aim to tap the output of associative (System 1) processing in relatively direct ways, at least more direct than conventional self-report measures. Although important questions yet remain unanswered (see Fazio and Olson 2003), at a minimum it seems clear that implicit measures can provide additional windows into human processing systems, offering valuable complements to what can be learned with self-report questionnaires and other explicit, controllable responses. In particular, research identifying specific topics and conditions under which implicit and explicit responses are correlated versus dissociated (Nosek 2007) seems likely to shed much light on the interrelations of System 1 and System 2 processing.

Because of the important place held by prejudice, stereotypes, and other negatively regarded phenomena in the social-psychological dual-process literature, research attention has been devoted to the conditions under which implicit attitudes or associations can change. For example, Blair (2002) demonstrated that a few minutes intentionally forming mental images of a 'strong woman' can weaken or reverse the stereotypical implicit association between women and weakness (compared to men and strength).

The Quad model of Conrey et al. (2005) also represents a significant direction for further exploration. It advances beyond a typical dual-process framework by postulating four distinct processes, most importantly by distinguishing the intentional effort to inhibit or overcome automatic associations that may bias responses from the intentional effort to arrive at the correct response *per se*. These two forms of controlled processing, presumably both part of System 2, may be found to have distinct antecedents and consequences.

The multiple roles idea, that a single factor such as the individual's current mood may influence processing in more than one way, also seems important for the dual-process literature more broadly (Wegener and Petty 1996). Often researchers identify an effect of a particular factor (such as the believability of a syllogism's conclusion in the belief-bias paradigm) with the functioning of a particular system. Instead, it may be more productive to consider the different pathways through which such a factor might affect judgments. The believability of a conclusion might operate as a simple cue, directing judgments with little thought. Or believability might be explicitly and intentionally used to answer the problem (e.g. if the participant finds the logical rules too complex to understand). Finally, believability might even motivate participants to engage in extensive thought (if people feel that conclusions that are unbelievable are not worth much processing effort). These three distinct information-processing roles might all be found in different circumstances, and would mean that an empirically observed effect of believability could not be directly identified with the operation of a specific processing system.

Finally, a significant message from the social psychological literature is that people care about other goals besides understanding the world accurately. Multiple motives may lead people to engage in effortful System 2 processing, including not only a desire for accuracy, but also a desire to relate and connect to other people, and a desire to attain valued identities (Wood 2000). Not only can motives other than accuracy lead to extensive processing, it is also the case that extensive processing does not always result in increased accuracy. This is because the processing may be biased in various ways (e.g. Wegener and Petty 1996).

At the broadest level, dual-process models fit comfortably with the current emphasis on situated cognition (Smith and Semin 2004). That is, instead of holding that people have stable, autonomous information-processing propensities that they apply to whatever situations or stimuli come their way, the key insight of dual-process models is that people are flexible and responsive to situational demands. Some situations call for rapid, 'good-enough', low-effort responses, others for full and effortful scrutiny of all available information. Work in the dual-process framework is giving researchers important clues as to the ways intuitive, implicit processes compete with, complement, or interact with explicit, thoughtful deliberation as people make judgments and decisions in the course of navigating their lives. They also represent a key area for advancing understanding of the interactions of cognitive processing systems and motivational goals, which can sometimes induce people to engage in effortful processing.

References

Abelson, R.P. (1994) A personal perspective on social cognition. In P.G. Devine, D.L. Hamilton, and T.M. Ostrom (eds) *Social cognition: Impact on social psychology*, 15–37. Academic Press, San Diego, CA.

Andersen, S.M. and Berk, M.S. (1998) The social-cognitive model of transference: Experiencing past relationships in the present. *Current Directions in Psychological Science,* **7**, 109–15.

Bargh, J.A. (1994) The four horsemen of automaticity: Awareness, intention, efficiency, and control in social cognition. In R.S. Wyer and T.K. Srull (eds) *Handbook of social cognition*, 2nd ed., vol. 1, 1–40. Lawrence Erlbaum Associates, Mahwah, NJ.

Betch, T., Kaufmann, M., Lindow, F., Plessner, H., and Hoffmann, K. (2006) Different principles of information integration in implicit and explicit attitude formation. *European Journal of Social Psychology,* **36**, 887–905.

Blair, I.V. (2002) The malleability of automatic stereotypes and prejudice. *Personality and Social Psychology Review,* **6**, 242–61.

Bless, H. (2001) Mood and the use of general knowledge structures. In L.L. Martin and G.L. Clore (eds) *Theories of mood and cognition: A user's guidebook*. 9–26. Lawrence Erlbaum Associates, Mahwah, NJ.

Bless, H., Bohner, G., Schwarz, N., and Strack, F. (1990) Mood and persuasion: A cognitive response analysis. *Personality and Social Psychology Bulletin,* **16**, 331–45.

Brewer, M.B. (1988) A dual process model of impression formation. In R.S. Wyer and T.K. Srull (eds) *Advances in social cognition*, vol. 1, 1–36. Lawrence Erlbaum Associates, Mahwah, NJ.

Cacioppo, J.T. and Petty, R.E. (1982) The need for cognition. *Journal of Personality and Social Psychology*, **42**, 116–31.

Cacioppo, J.T., Priester, J.R., and Berntson, G.G. (1993) Rudimentary determinants of attitudes:
II. Arm flexion and extension have differential effects on attitudes. *Journal of Personality and Social Psychology*, **65**, 5–17.

Chaiken, S. (1980) Heuristic versus systematic information processing and the use of source versus message cues in persuasion. *Journal of Personality and Social Psychology*, **39**, 752–66.

Chaiken, S., Liberman, A., and Eagly, A.H. (1989) Heuristic and systematic information processing within and beyond the persuasion context. In J.S. Uleman and J.A. Bargh (eds) *Unintended thought*, 212–52. Guilford, New York.

Chen, S. and Chaiken, S. (1999) The heuristic-systematic model in its broader context. In S. Chaiken and Y. Trope (eds) *Dual-process theories in social psychology,* 73–96. Guilford, New York.

Conrey, F.R., Sherman, J.W., Gawronski, B., Hugenberg, K., and Groom, C.J. (2005) Separating multiple processes in implicit social cognition: The quad model of implicit task performance. *Journal of Personality and Social Psychology*, **89**, 469–87.

Damasio, A.R. (1994) *Descartes' error: Emotion, reason, and the human brain.* Avon Books, New York.

DeSteno, D., Petty, R.E., Wegener, D.T., and Rucker, D.D. (2000) Beyond valence in the perception of likelihood: The role of emotion specificity. *Journal of Personality and Social Psychology*, **78**, 397–416.

Devine, P.G. (1989) Stereotypes and prejudice: Their automatic and controlled components. *Journal of Personality and Social Psychology*, **56**, 5–18.

Dijksterhuis, A. and Bargh, J.A. (2001) The perception-behavior expressway: Automatic effects of social perception on social behavior. In M.P. Zanna (ed.) *Advances in experimental social psychology,* vol. 33, 1–40. Academic Press, San Diego, CA.

Dijksterhuis, A., Bos, M.W., Nordgren, L.F., and van Baaren, R.B. (2006) On making the right choice: The deliberation-without-attention effect. *Science*, **311**, 1005–7.

Epstein, S. (1991) Cognitive-experiential self-theory: An integrative theory of personality. In R. Curtis (ed.) *The self with others: Convergences in psychoanalytical, social, and personality psychology*, 111–37. Guilford Press, New York.

Evans, J.St.B.T. (2008) Dual-processing accounts of reasoning, judgment and social cognition. *Annual Review of Psychology*, **59**, 255–78.

Fazio, R.H. (1986) How do attitudes guide behavior? In R.M. Sorrentino and E.T. Higgins (eds) *Handbook of motivation and cognition*, 204–43. Guilford Press, New York.

Fazio, R.H. and Olson, M.A. (2003) Implicit measures in social cognition research: Their meaning and uses. *Annual Review of Psychology*, **54**, 297–327.

Fazio, R.H., Jackson, J.R., Dunton, B.C., and Williams, C.J. (1995) Variability in automatic activation as an unobtrusive measure of racial attitudes: A bona fide pipeline? *Journal of Personality and Social Psychology*, **69**, 1013–27.

Fiske, S.T. and Neuberg, S.L. (1988) A continuum model of impression formation: From category-based to individuating processes as a function of information, motivation, and attention. In M.P. Zanna (ed.) *Advances in experimental social psychology,* **23**, 1–108. Elsevier Academic Press, San Diego, CA.

Förster, J., Liberman, N., and Friedman, R.S. (2007) Seven principles of goal activation: A systematic approach to distinguishing goal priming from priming of non-goal constructs. *Personality and Social Psychology Review*, **11**, 211–33.

Gawronski, B. and Bodenhausen, G.V. (2006) Associative and propositional processes in evaluation: An integrative review of implicit and explicit attitude change. *Psychological Bulletin*, **132**, 692–731.

Gilbert, D.T. (1989) Thinking lightly about others: Automatic components of the social inference process. In J.S. Uleman and J.A. Bargh (eds) *Unintended thought*, 189–211. Guilford, New York.

Gilovich, T. (1981) Seeing the past in the present: The effect of associations to familiar events on judgments and decisions. *Journal of Personality and Social Psychology*, **40**, 797–807.

Greenwald, A.G., McGhee, D.E., and Schwartz, J.L.K. (1998) Measuring individual differences in implicit cognition: The implicit association test. *Journal of Personality and Social Psychology*, **74**, 1464–80.

Haidt, J. (2001) The emotional dog and its rational tail: A social intuitionist approach to moral judgment. *Psychological Review*, **108**, 814–34.

Hastie, R. and Park, B. (1986) The relationship between memory and judgment depends on whether the judgment task is memory-based or on-line. *Psychological Review*, **93**, 258–68.

Kahneman, D. and Frederick, S. (2005) A model of heuristic judgment. In K.J. Holyoak and R.G. Morrison (eds) *The Cambridge handbook of thinking and reasoning*, 267–93. Cambridge University Press, New York.

Kahneman, D. and Miller, D.T. (1986) Norm theory: Comparing reality to its alternatives. *Psychological Review*, **93**, 136–53.

Karpinski, A. and Hilton, J.L. (2001) Attitudes and the implicit association test. *Journal of Personality and Social Psychology*, **81**, 774–88.

Klein, G. (1999) *Sources of power*. MIT Press, Cambridge, MA.

Lambert, A.J., Payne, B.K., Jacoby, L.L., Shaffer, L.M., Chasteen, A.L., and Khan, S.K. (2003) Stereotypes as dominant responses: On the 'social facilitation' of prejudice in anticipated public contexts. *Journal of Personality and Social Psychology*, **84**, 277–95.

Lewicki, P. (1985) Nonconscious biasing effects of single instances of subsequent judgments. *Journal of Personality and Social Psychology*, **48**, 563–74.

Logan, G.D. (1988) Toward an instance theory of automatization. *Psychological Review*, **95**, 492–527.

Martin, L.L. (2001) Mood as input: A configural view of mood effects. In L.L. Martin and G.L. Clore (eds) *Theories of mood and cognition: A user's guidebook*, 135–57. Lawrence Erlbaum Associates, Mahwah, NJ.

Martin, L.L., Seta, J.J., and Crelia, R.A. (1990) Assimilation and contrast as a function of people's willingness and ability to expend effort in forming an impression. *Journal of Personality and Social Psychology*, **59**, 27–37.

McClelland, J.L., McNaughton, B.L., and O'Reilly, R.C. (1995) Why there are complementary learning systems in the hippocampus and neocortex: Insights from the successes and failures of connectionist models of learning and memory. *Psychological Review*, **102**, 419–57.

Nosek, B. (2007) Implicit-explicit relations. *Current Directions in Psychological Science*, **16**, 65–9.

Payne, B.K. (2001) Prejudice and perception: The role of automatic and controlled processes in misperceiving a weapon. *Journal of Personality and Social Psychology*, **81**, 181–92.

Petty, R.E. and Cacioppo, J.T. (1981) *Attitudes and persuasion: Classic and contemporary approaches*. Wm. C. Brown, Dubuque, IA.

Petty, R.E. and Cacioppo, J.T. (1986) The Elaboration Likelihood Model of persuasion. In L. Berkowitz (ed.) *Advances in experimental social psychology*, vol. **19**, 123–205. Academic Press, New York.

Petty, R.E. and Wegener, D.T. (1999) The Elaboration Likelihood Model: Current status and controversies. In S. Chaiken and Y. Trope (eds) *Dual-process models in social psychology*, 41–72. Guilford Press, New York.

Petty, R.E., Wheeler, S.C., and Tormala, Z.L. (2003) Persuasion and attitude change. In T. Millon and M.J. Lerner (eds) *Handbook of psychology: Personality and social psychology*, vol. 5, 353–82. John Wiley and Sons, Hoboken, NJ.

Petty, R.E., Schumann, D.W., Richman, S.A., and Strathman, A.J. (1993) Positive mood and persuasion: Different roles for affect under high- and low-elaboration conditions. *Journal of Personality and Social Psychology*, **64**, 5–20.

Petty, R.E., Tormala, Z.L., Binol, P., and Jarvis, W.B.G. (2006) Implicit ambivalence from attitude change: An exploration of the PAST model. *Journal of Personality and Social Psychology*, **90**, 21–41.

Ranganath, K.A., Smith, C.T., and Nosek, B.A. (2008) Distinguishing automatic and controlled components of attitudes from direct and indirect measurement methods. *Journal of Experimental Social Psychology*, **44**, 386–96.

Robinson, M.D., Vargas, P,. and Crawford, E.G. (2003) Putting process into personality, appraisal, and emotion: Evaluative processing as a missing link. In J. Musch and C. Klauer (eds) *The psychology of evaluation: Affective processes in cognition and emotion*, 275–306. Lawrence Erlbaum Associates, Mahwah, NJ.

Semin, G.R. and Smith, E.R. (eds) (2008) *Embodied grounding: Social, cognitive, affective, and neuroscientific approaches*. Cambridge University Press, New York.

Sherry, D.F. and Schacter, D.L. (1987) The evolution of multiple memory systems. *Psychological Review*, **94**, 439–54.

Sloman, S.A. (1996) The empirical case for two systems of reasoning. *Psychological Bulletin*, **119**, 3–22.

Smith, E.R. and DeCoster, J. (2000) Dual-process models in social and cognitive psychology: Conceptual integration and links to underlying memory systems. *Personality and Social Psychology Review*, **4**, 108–31.

Smith, E.R. and Semin, G.R. (2004) Socially situated cognition: Cognition in its social context. In M.P. Zanna (ed.) *Advances in experimental social psychology*, vol. 36, 53–117. Elsevier Academic Press, San Diego, CA.

Smolensky, P. (1988) On the proper treatment of connectionism. *Behavioral and Brain Sciences*, **11**, 1–74.

Strack, F. and Deutsch, R. (2004) Reflective and impulsive determinants of social behavior. *Personality and Social Psychology Review*, **8**, 220–47.

Wegener, D.T. and Petty, R.E. (1995) Flexible correction processes in social judgment: The role of naive theories of correction for perceived bias. *Journal of Personality and Social Psychology*, **68**, 36–51.

Wegener, D.T. and Petty, R.E. (1996) Effects of mood on persuasion processes: Enhancing, reducing, and biasing scrutiny of attitude-relevant information. In L.L. Martin and A. Tesser (eds) *Striving and feeling: Interactions among goals, affect, and self-regulation*, 329–62. Lawrence Erlbaum Associates, Mahwah, NJ.

Wegener, D.T. and Petty, R.E. (1997) The flexible correction model: The role of naïve theories of bias in bias correction. In M.P. Zanna (ed.) *Advances in experimental social psychology,* vol. 29, 141–208. Academic Press, San Diego, CA.

Wilson, T.D. and Schooler, J.W. (1991) Thinking too much: Introspection can reduce the quality of preferences and decisions. *Journal of Personality and Social Psychology,* **60,** 181–92.

Wilson, T.D., Lindsey, S., and Schooler, T.Y. (2000) A model of dual attitudes. *Psychological Review,* **107,** 101–26.

Wood, W. (2000) Attitude change: Persuasion and social influence. *Annual Review of Psychology,* **51,** 539–70.

Chapter 10

Thinking across cultures: Implications for dual processes

Emma E. Buchtel and Ara Norenzayan

In *A history of God*, Karen Armstrong describes a division, made by fourth-century Christians, between *kerygma* and *dogma*: 'religious truth … capable of being expressed and defined clearly and logically', versus 'religious insights [that] had an inner resonance that could only be apprehended by each individual in his own time during … contemplation' (Armstrong 1993, p.114). This early dual-process theory had its roots in Plato and Aristotle, who suggested a division between 'philosophy', which could be 'expressed in terms of reason and thus capable of proof', and knowledge contained in myths, 'which eluded scientific demonstration' (Armstrong 1993, pp.113–14). This division—between what can be known and reasoned logically versus what can only be experienced and apprehended—continued to influence Western culture through the centuries, and arguably underlies our current dual-process theories of reasoning.

In psychology, the division between these two forms of understanding has been described in many different ways. The underlying theme of 'overtly reasoned' versus 'perceived, intuited' often ties these dual-process theories together. In Western culture, the latter form of thinking has often been maligned (Dijksterhuis and Nordgren 2006; Gladwell 2005; Lieberman 2000). Recently, cultural psychologists have suggested that although the distinction itself—between reasoned and intuited knowledge—may have precedents in the intellectual traditions of other cultures, the privileging of the former rather than the latter may be peculiar to Western cultures (e.g. Lloyd 1996; Nakamura 1960/1988; Nisbett 2003). The Chinese philosophical tradition illustrates this difference of emphasis. Instead of an epistemology that was guided by abstract rules, 'the Chinese in esteeming what was immediately perceptible—especially visually perceptible—sought intuitive instantaneous understanding through direct perception' (Nakamura 1960/1988, p.171). Taoism—the great Chinese philosophical school besides Confucianism—developed an epistemology that was particularly oriented towards concrete perception and direct experience (Fung 1922; Nakamura 1960/1988). Moreover, whereas the Greeks were concerned with definitions and devising rules for the purposes of classification, for many influential Taoist philosophers, such as Chuang Tzu, '… the problem of … how terms and attributes are to be delimited, leads one in precisely the wrong direction. Classifying or limiting knowledge fractures the greater knowledge' (Mote 1971, p.102).

Drawing on a distinction between 'analytic' and 'holistic' thinking, cultural psychologists have argued that these two systems of thinking are unevenly distributed across cultures—the former is more prevalent in Western cultures, whereas the latter is more prevalent in East Asian cultures. While other conceptualizations of human thinking across cultures have also been made (e.g. Cole and Scribner 1974; Medin and Atran 2004; Witkin and Berry 1975), the analytic-holistic distinction appears to be directly relevant to dual-process theories. But are the cultural psychologist's Holistic and Analytic the same thing as Systems I and II (Kahneman 2003; Stanovich 1999), or Associative and Analytic (Sloman 1996), or Intuitive-Experiential and Analytical-Rational (Epstein et al. 1996), or any of the many similar divisions that have been made in the Western cognitive psychology literature? While acknowledging the similarities between their distinction and the dual-process models (e.g. Nisbett et al. 2001; Norenzayan et al. 2007), most cross-cultural researchers have not explicitly dealt with the issue of how the analytic-holistic distinction maps on dual-process models of reasoning, an issue which is the main topic of the present chapter.

In this paper, we will examine how analytic and holistic thinking have been defined by cultural psychologists, and briefly review the studies in this new tradition. We will suggest that holistic and analytic thinking are in many ways very similar to the dual-process theories that have been described by Western cognitive psychologists, and in fact the cross cultural evidence supports the plausibility of this distinction. However, the emphasis on holistic thinking that has occurred in East Asian societies may also have led to the development of a more sophisticated kind of non-analytic thinking than in the West. In particular, different cultural norms for thinking may have encouraged explicit, contextualized thinking in a way that is less common in the West, and in a way that is not fully captured by some aspects of popular dual-process theories. By attending to the forms of thinking that have been shown to be particularly East Asian, we may be led to a greater understanding of how humans can develop our fundamental cognitive abilities to better adapt to the particular demands of cultures.

Holistic versus analytic modes of thought: A brief overview

In the 1990s, Richard Nisbett and colleagues began to examine the idea that one's cultural background could influence not only the content of one's thoughts (beliefs), but also the very information processing strategies used to know the world (for extensive reviews, see Nisbett 2003; Nisbett et al. 2001; Norenzayan et al. 2007). These studies showed that East Asians had a greater tendency to rely on context to make decisions, while, under identical task conditions, Westerners tended to de-contextualize, using feature-based and rule-based strategies (Nisbett et al. 2001). Further studies have extended this work in the directions of covariation detection (Ji et al. 2000), tendency to use abstract rules versus experience in categorization and deductive reasoning (Norenzayan et al. 2002), and tendency to use dispositional (i.e. information attached to a decontextualized individual) versus situational (i.e. contextual) information to explain behavior (Choi et al. 1999; Masuda and Kitayama 2004; Miyamoto and Kitayama 2002; Morris and Peng 1994; Norenzayan et al. 2002). These cultural differences do not emerge only in the conceptual domain, but also have been found in attention and perception. Eye-tracking experiments indicate that Americans fixate more on focal objects than do Chinese and Japanese (Chua et al. 2005; Masuda et al. 2007; Masuda et al. 2008). These and similar findings (Kitayama et al. 2003; Masuda and Nisbett 2006) support the idea that cultural experiences affect what people actually perceive in a scene.

The evidence for cultural variation in cognition and perception is robust and reliable—these differences emerge from a variety of unrelated paradigms and methodologies, with a variety of samples, and many artefactual explanations have been ruled out (see Nisbett and Masuda 2003; Nisbett et al. 2001; Norenzayan et al. 2007). A meta-analytic review of studies comparing East Asians (Chinese, Koreans, Japanese) and North Americans (excluding Asian North Americans) indicated that the overall effect size of the cultural difference is moderate to large, and this effect size is as strong for attentional and perceptual tasks as it is for tasks that involve language-based conceptual processes (Miyamoto et al. 2006, January). Not surprisingly, East Asians tested in East Asian countries diverged more strongly than East Asians tested in North America.

While initial studies did not specify the particular moderators of these cultural differences, cultural differences in individualism versus collectivism were theorized to be a partial cause. Subsequent work has supported these theories, showing that priming independent versus interdependent self-concepts (e.g. thinking of 'I' versus 'We' pronouns) causes participants to temporarily adopt analytic versus holistic thinking styles and skills (e.g. Cha 2007; K. Kim and Markman 2006; Kühnen and Oyserman 2002). In addition to these general cultural effects, holistic and analytic thinking can also be transmitted through formal education in a specific society or philosophy, such as Oriental Medicine (Koo and Choi 2005). Similar studies have shown that exposure to Western-style formal education in non-Western cultures increases the tendency to decontextualize deductive arguments (Cole and Scribner 1974). These studies suggest that (1) the cultural differences are best conceptualized as differences in *habits of thought*, rather than differences in the actual availability of information processing strategies in the cognitive repertoire, and that (2) holistic and analytic ways of thinking can be differentially encouraged in their development and use by different cultural and situational constraints, and that these cultural differences can be seen both in habits of basic processing as well as culturally-elaborated epistemic beliefs and lay theories.

Definitions: Is holistic-analytic the same as System 1 and 2?

It is important to note that the primary focus of the holistic-analytic difference has been on differences in attending to *contextual*, relational/associative information, versus attending to *focal* objects, divided from the context. As we will see below, literature on dual-process thinking often focuses on these differences. However, the dual-process literature also concentrates on other elements of the definitions that are not usually attended to by cultural psychologists, such as contrasting effortful versus effortless thinking, with the associative processes depending more on effortless heuristics (Evans 2003, 2006; Verschueren et al. 2005). In a recent review, Evans (2008) defines four 'clusters' of characteristics that are commonly used to define System 1 and System 2 processes. The cultural definitions of analytic and holistic modes appear to closely parallel the 'functional characteristics' cluster, defined by contrasts such as associative versus rule-based, or contextualized versus abstract. But do the other clusters of common characteristics—such as unconscious versus conscious, or shared with animals versus uniquely human, or independent of versus linked to general intelligence—also reflect the holistic-analytic division? We would suggest not. In fact, cultural psychology studies may show that contextualized versus decontextualized thinking is functionally separable from the other clusters of System 1 and System 2 attributes.[1]

Similarities: Contextualizing versus decontextualizing, relational versus not

Describing System 1 as 'contextualized' and System 2 as 'decontextualized' is a common theme in definitions given by dual-systems theorists, as can be seen in summaries of the literature (e.g. Epstein 1991; Evans 2008; Kahneman 2003; Sloman 1996; Stanovich and West 2000). Classic tests of System 1 versus System 2 often test whether or not participants will ignore 'irrelevant' contextual cues. In belief bias tests, System 1 is said to be evident in 'the tendency to contextualize all problems with reference to prior knowledge elicited by contextual cues' (Evans 2006, p.380). Stanovich and West have described System 1 as a 'radical contextualizer', while System 2 works to 'decontextualize and depersonalize' (Stanovich and West 2000, p.659).

Similarly, and as will be reviewed in detail below, a major emphasis in the cultural analytic–holistic literature has been on cultural differences in attention to context, such as visually attending more to the context of objects (e.g. Masuda et al. 2007; Masuda et al. 2008; Masuda and Nisbett 2001, 2006; Miyamoto, Nisbett, and Masuda 2006), attributing more causal power to context (e.g. Lam et al. 2005; Masuda and Kitayama 2004; Masuda et al. 2008; Miller 1984; Miyamoto and Kitayama 2002; Morris and Peng 1994), automatically binding objects to the context (Masuda and Nisbett 2001), and being more subject to belief-bias effects (Norenzayan et al. 2002). In regards to this element of System 1–2 differences, then, the similarities with cultural psychology's definitions of holistic-analytic differences are striking.

Another (weaker) link between dual-processing and cultural psychology definitions of the two systems is how they are connected to social relations. System 1 has sometimes been described as 'interactional intelligence', and as resulting in task construals that assume conversational norms (Stanovich and West 2000). In the cultural psychology literature, a strong connection between holistic processing and attention to social relationships has been noted. The relative emphasis on holism in the East

---

[1] In the following pages, 'analytic' and 'holistic' will be used to describe the modes of thought elaborated on by cultural psychologists; and as with many other authors in this book, we will use 'System 1 and 2' to refer to dual-process theories, as variously defined as they are.

and analytical thinking in the West is proposed to have roots in these cultures' differing emphasis on interpersonal relationships (Nisbett et al. 2001). In the relatively collectivistic cultures of East Asia, attention paid to social relationships—both relationships between 'objects' (people) and one's role within the social field—may train similar habits of processing when attending to non-social objects. In the relatively individualistic cultures of the West, on the other hand, the cultural training to regard oneself as independent of others is reflected in the cognitive tendency to attend to decontextualized objects. Priming studies have supported this cultural explanation. Temporary increases in holistic processing can be brought about simply by asking participants to think of themselves as parts of social relationships, while similar increases in analytic processing are brought about by thinking about oneself as independent of others (e.g. Cha 2007; K. Kim and Markman 2006; Kühnen and Oyserman 2002). It is social situations, where one is considering one's relationships with others, that seem to bring holistic processing to the fore.

Differences: Automatic versus controlled, natural versus normative

Despite these similarities, there are other aspects of the dual-process literature that do not match neatly with the holistic-analytic theories of the cultural psychologists. System 2 is generally defined as more than simply a decontextualizing way of thinking. It is also described as more deliberative (i.e. explicit and time-consuming), and its use is associated with greater intelligence, ability to control one's thoughts and follow directions, and 'cognitive flexibility' (e.g. Evans, 2003, this volume; Sloman 1996, 2002; Smith et al. 1992; Stanovich and West 2002, p.438; Stanovich, this volume). For example, Evans states that 'it is [both] abstract reasoning and the ability to comply with instructions' that characterizes those high in System 2 use (Evans 2003, p.457). Especially in this volume (e.g. Evans, Stanovich), System 2 is overwhelmingly described as a method of overriding the 'default responses' given by System 1. Stanovich and West have called our automatic tendency to contextualize problems a 'fundamental computational bias' that System 2 allows us to control (Stanovich 1999; Stanovich and West 2000, 2002). System 2 is seen as the controlled, effortful, generally explicit thinking that can, but does not always, override the results of System 1 thinking, checking if the latter produces 'sensible' output.

Stanovich and West have shown (among Western populations) that although greater intelligence leads to a greater ability to use System 2 thinking, the actual use of System 2 thinking is also greatly dependent on personal preference or 'thinking style' (e.g. Stanovich and West 2000, p.707). Evans (2006; this volume) has suggested that analytic and holistic might be best understood as thinking styles. By this conceptualization, Holistic is not System 1, and Analytic System 2; instead, they are individual variation in using System 2: 'Styles are … a (variable) property of the system (System 2) that employs epistemic and response regulation because its goals are flexible' (Stanovich and West 2000, p.708). By this definition, while everyone can and does engage in System 1 thinking, the use of System 2 thinking is dependent on, first, ability, and secondly, choice: '… some people do have the cognitive flexibility to decouple unneeded systems of knowledge and some do not … those who do have the requisite flexibility are somewhat higher in cognitive ability and in actively open-minded thinking' (Stanovich and West 2000, p.662). Similarly, Evans has described thinking style as being largely a matter of choosing, or not choosing, to engage in effortful re-checking of intuitive assumptions: 'Intuitive thinkers, for example, may be predisposed by personality or by cultural context to accept uncritically default judgments that are generated heuristically, whereas analytic thinkers may be more inclined to check them out with explicit reasoning' (Evans 2006, p.383).

The idea that cultural differences in analytic-holistic thinking reflect different preferences for object versus context-oriented thinking—i.e. differences in normative style rather than innate ability—is not problematic for cultural psychologists. However, the characterization of holistic thinking as no more than a choice to not engage in System 2 thinking is theoretically problematic. Rather than conceiving of holistic thinking as being the absence of System 2 thinking, cultural psychologists have traditionally conceived of holistic thinking, as it is observed in East Asian contexts, as a trained, culturally-elaborated form of thinking in its own right.

This culturally-learned aspect of the analytic-holistic definitions suggests another disconnect between the dual-process and cultural psychology conceptualizations. Both Sloman (1996) and Stanovich and West (2000), for example, propose that System 2 thinking is taught formally and has its source in culture, while System 1 thinking is learned simply through exposure or personal experience. Similarly, Sloman cites Evans and Over (1996) as describing System 2 as 'adept at ensuring that one's conclusions are sanctioned by a normative theory' (Sloman 2002, p.382). These characterizations of System 2 imply that if a way of thinking has its source in one's culture, and one checks one's System 1 thinking for whether or not it fits the culture's norms, then that is a kind of System 2 thinking, whether or not the actual norm is 'decontextualization'. In the cultural psychology literature, both analytic and holistic thinking are seen as elaborated in different philosophical and scientific cultural products, and taught both implicitly and explicitly through the culture (Koo and Choi 2005; Nisbett et al. 2001). Presumably, East Asians may check their initial conclusions to see if they fit norms; but these norms may be holistic and dialectical, rather than analytical. If we take the 'culturally taught' aspect of System 2 definitions seriously, then holistic thinking may be a different cultural form of deliberate, System 2 thinking; contextualizing, but taught.

Cultural psychologists do agree that Western culture has encouraged the use and elaboration of a decontextualizing thinking process in a way that other cultures have not. It seems unlikely, however, that only Western culture encourages effortful, deliberative thinking to 're-check' one's initial thinking. It seems more likely that the decontextualizing System 2 described by dual-process theorists is one version of a normative form of effortful thinking, and that in other cultures with other norms, other forms of effortful second-guessing of System 1 thinking may occur. In this case, we suggest that while East Asian culture may not encourage decontextualized thinking as much as Western culture encourages it, conversely, Western culture does not encourage holistic, dialectical thinking. These culturally different norms for 'good thinking' may both sometimes lead to effortful corrections of initial models, though in opposite directions on the contextualizing/decontextualizing continuum. Moreover (and perhaps less controversially), as culturally-trained modes of thinking, both holistic and analytic modes of thinking can become automatic and effortless: over-learned cultural rules that have become habits.

However, these are differences in theories. Is there evidence that East Asian think-ing, while holistic, is not merely an effortless 'default' to intuitive thinking; and that Western analytical thinking is not necessarily effortful, explicit thinking? In the fol-lowing pages, we will see that the terms 'holistic' and 'analytic' are umbrella terms for cultural differences found in a large number of different cognitive tasks. These tasks vary in their applicability to traditional dual-process models. While some of these cognitive tasks offer evidence that holistic thinking may sometimes be less effortful than analytical thinking, not all of these tasks fall easily into analytic-effortful, holistic-effortless categories.

Review of relevant research

Rule-based versus associative thinking

Our own past research has, in fact, assumed a strong correspondence between dual-process reasoning theories and the analytic-holistic differences found in cultural research. Based mainly on Sloman's (1996) descriptions of 'associative' versus 'rule-based' reasoning, and the contextualizing/decontextualizing aspects of these definitions, Norenzayan, Smith et al. (2002) hypothesized that East Asian participants would be more likely to show biases towards giving contextualized, associative System 1 answers to classic tests. A series of studies (Norenzayan, Smith et al. 2002) showed that when contextual information led to conflict with abstract rules, East Asians did show larger effects of exemplars, concept prototype, category family resemblance, and belief plausibility compared to North Americans, even when (1) no differences were found in abstract deductive reasoning abilities with no content; and (2) told explicitly to follow an abstract rule.

For example, in one study (Norenzayan, Smith et al. 2002, Study 1), participants were given the task of categorizing objects, such as novel 'alien' animals, according to a rule that determined category membership (whether the animal lived in Saturn or Venus). Koreans and European Americans showed equal performance; until, as par-ticipants became more familiar with the task, information from exemplars occasion-ally conflicted with the rule (e.g. an alien that looked very similar to previous Saturnian was in fact a Venutian by the rule). In these cases, Americans erroneously followed the exemplar rather than the rule about 11% of the time; Koreans showed an exaggerated effect of the influence of the exemplar, ignoring the rule about 25% of the time. In this task, both Koreans and Americans knew that the explicit directions were to follow a complex rule in order to classify the objects. From these results, it appears that Koreans found the exemplar information more 'tempting' to use than did Americans. It appeared that Koreans were less used to subduing associative informa-tion such as exemplars in favor of abstract rules, and so this may be seen as a test of the ability to disregard contextual information.

In a second study of 'spontaneous' categorization strategies, participants were asked to categorize objects as being similar to one or another group of objects (Norenzayan,

Smith et al. 2002, Study 2). Participants could either note that one attribute (e.g. stem length) was the same across all members of the group, and use that one feature as the basis of classification, or they could use family resemblance (similarity based on several features that were more common in one group than the other, without any one feature being necessary for group membership). Results showed that participants who had more exposure to East Asian culture were more likely to use family resemblance than the single attribute as a method of classification, suggesting that East Asian culture encouraged attention to family resemblance structure rather than attending to one deterministic feature only.

In two more studies, Norenzayan, Smith et al. (2002) also showed that participants with more exposure to East Asian culture were relatively more sensitive to the content of the conclusion of an argument, rather than its underlying abstractly logical nature, in evaluating convincingness and logical correctness. For example, it is commonly found that an argument extending arbitrary features (e.g. having an 'ulnar artery') from a superordinate category (e.g. birds) to subordinate categories is seen as more convincing when the members are typical (e.g. eagles), rather than atypical (e.g. penguins) (Sloman 1996). This tendency to attend to content to evaluate convincingness (instead of evaluating the argument on purely abstract, logical grounds) was exaggerated among Koreans and, to a lesser extent, Asian Americans, as compared to European Americans. Similar results were obtained with the classic 'belief bias' test. When evaluating arguments for logical consistency, Koreans were more likely than Americans to mark unbelievable but logically correct arguments as logically invalid, showing greater 'belief bias' in their evaluations. However, it is important to note that when evaluating abstract forms of these arguments (with letters and nonsense words, rather than content), there were no cultural differences in accuracy in logical reasoning. It is only when the believability of the content of the argument conflicted with the logical correctness of the argument that Koreans were, on average, more influenced by the believability of the conclusions. Once again, these studies suggested that exposure to Western culture influences participants to more easily, and more commonly, separate content and past experience from abstract rules.

In sum, these studies showed that when put in the position of choosing between sensitivity to contextual cues and associations of features *or* abstract rules and a single deterministic feature, participants who were closer to East Asian cultures were more sensitive to the former than were participants who were less influenced by East Asian culture. Though no mediators of this difference were measured other than cultural background, similar performance in control tasks suggests that it is unlikely that this is a difference of intelligence or general self-control. Instead, it is most likely that it was a result of differential levels of practice in ignoring contextual, holistic, and experience-based information in favor of abstract rules.

Perception: Evidence for automatic analysis and expert holism

The above studies used classic decontextualization tests to examine hypotheses based firmly on dual-process theories, specifically looking at what happens when context and decontextualized rules are in conflict, and the normative response is to follow the rule.

The majority of research in the analytic-holistic tradition, however, has looked not at conflicts between context and abstract rules, but at differential attention to objects versus to the context.

Some of the most productive and interesting work to come out of the holistic-analytic paradigm has been in the area of perception. Multiple studies have shown that even at the basic level of attention and vision, exposure to Western culture appears to facilitate attention *primarily* to focal objects, automatically separated from their context, while exposure to East Asian culture facilitates attention to context as well as focal objects, automatically associating objects with their context. As opposed to many dual-process tasks where the normative response is decontextualizing, tasks have been developed in which the normative response requires attention to context. As one might expect if East Asians have been trained to take better account of context and relationships, East Asians tend to do better on these tasks; when given tasks that require attending to focal objects and ignoring their relationship to context, Westerners tend to do better.

Some of the first hints of these attentional differences came from work by Masuda and Nisbett (2001). In one study, Japanese and American college students were simply asked to describe a scene similar to the now common 'aquarium' screen savers. Japanese participants tended to describe background objects such as the aquarium floor or small, unmoving snails much more than did Americans, while Americans and Japanese were equally likely to mention the animals placed at the foreground of the aquarium scene, such as large fish and energetic newts. These open-ended descriptions of the scene suggested that Americans were relatively 'context-blind' compared to Japanese, who were attentive to both focal and background objects. Masuda et al. (2001) come to the surprising conclusion that 'Japanese may simply see far more of the world than do Americans'. Further work by Masuda and colleagues (2008) has extended this work, showing that the differential attention is motivated by what is regarded as relevant information. Eye-tracking studies showed that when Americans and Japanese judged the emotion of a central figure in a group of people, Japanese participants looked at the emotions on the faces of other figures more than did Americans, and took this information into account when judging the emotion of the central figure (Masuda et al. 2008). This kind of higher-level task suggests that Japanese were following a 'holistic rule'; they believed that in order to accurately judge a focal object, its relation to objects in the context must be taken into account. Americans, on the other hand, did not find the contextual information to be as important, as indicated both by their pattern of eye movements and also by the fact that they did not take others figures' emotions into account when judging the emotion of the central figure.

Though in the above studies the choice to attend to contextual information (or not) appears to be volitional, other studies have indicated that both of these culturally-influenced tendencies can be difficult to control. Masuda and Nisbett (2006) carried out a series of 'change blindness' tests, where participants looked at pairs of scenes that were slightly different from each other, and tried to identify all differences between them. The average time taken to notice changes in the focal objects was the same among Japanese and Americans, but Japanese took significantly less time to note the contextual changes than did Americans, leading to them noticing more changes overall. Although both groups knew that changes could be occurring in the context, Americans took longer to drag their attention away from the focal objects, suggesting that ignoring context was habitual and automatic. On the other hand, eye-tracking studies testing the ability *not* to attend to the context replicated the results of Norenzayan, Smith et al. (2002): just as East Asians had trouble ignoring contextual information in conceptual problems, they also had trouble ignoring context in perceptual problems. When participants were requested to keep their eye on a central dot and ignore dots that occasionally flashed in the surrounding area, eye-tracking revealed that Japanese were less able than Americans to prevent their attention from wandering to the surrounding flashing dots (Masuda et al. 2007). In other words, while contextualization in the area of perception may be automatic for many East Asians, decontextualization (ignoring of the context) appears to be automatic for many Westerners.

Another lesson of the above studies is that different training in contextualization can result in individual differences in the *ability* to pay attention to context. While many dual-processing paradigms test for individual differences in the ability to decontextualize, testing the ability to take context into account also reveals individual differences. For example, the 'Framed Line Task' measures both contextualizing and decontextualizing abilities separately (Kitayama et al. 2003). Looking first at a square with a line drawn down its center, participants are given the task of drawing a similar line inside a blank, differently sized square. Participants are instructed to either draw a line that is the same size as the first, *relative* to the square; or they are instructed to draw a line that is *absolutely* the same length as the first, regardless of the size of the squares. The accuracy with which they perform these two tasks, one of which requires taking relative object-context comparisons into account and one of which requires ignoring context, is compared. In these tests, Japanese participants perform better than Americans on the relative task, while Americans perform better than Japanese on the absolute task.

In sum, the above studies provide evidence for the rather amazing idea that cultural experiences can influence our visual perception of the world around us—what we see. They also show that decontextualization, which is the principal feature of analytic thinking by the cultural definition, is sometimes a habit that takes effort to overcome; and that contextualization can be measured as a skill, with individual differences in ability.

Person perception: Direct evidence for effortful holism

But what about more conceptual kinds of information? Do East Asians consider more information in general than do Westerners? And how well do these higher-level processes map on to dual-process definitions?

Analytic and holistic ways of thinking have also been shown in person perception, where Americans tend to ignore situational information more than East Asians. As seen above, analytic thinking causes an automatic concentration on objects as separated from their context; in person perception, this translates to a concentration on personality and disposition (internal, situationally invariable attributes of each person), and a disregard for the effects of the situation. As a result, Western participants are more likely to be subject to the Correspondence Bias (or the Fundamental Attribution Error): the tendency to attribute a person's actions to their disposition, while discounting the effect of the situation (Choi et al. 1999; Masuda and Kitayama 2004).

In a series of studies examining prediction of behavior, Norenzayan, Choi, and Nisbett (2002) found that Koreans predicted stronger situational effects on behavior than did Americans. For example, if a person was considering giving a dollar to someone needing to buy a bus ticket, Koreans predicted that practical constraints—such as whether or not he had more money for his own bus ticket—would have a stronger effect on his behavior than did Americans. Koreans and Americans also had different 'lay theories' about behavior, with Koreans more likely to state that behavior was strongly controlled by the situation than Americans. This cultural difference was also found in studies on *explanation* of behavior (Choi et al. 2003). For example, when Koreans and Americans read about a graduate student who had killed his advisor, and then were given a list of about 100 pieces of information that might be relevant for explaining the muderer, Koreans considered a larger number of the clues to be relevant than did Americans: when asked to exclude clues that were definitely not relevant, Americans expurgated about 60% of the items, while Koreans excluded only about 30%.

In these studies, it is important to note that the choice to attend to situational information appears to be conscious and deliberate. East Asian and Western cultures teach different lay theories about the importance of the situation, which participants then use to decide what information is relevant for predicting and explaining others' behavior. This is commonly part of the definition of System 2 thinking (Sloman 1996; Stanovich and West 2000). Contrary to most definitions of System 2 processes, however, in East Asian culture the rule is to *attend* to situational information, not to 'decontextualize' the person from the situation.

More direct evidence that holistic use of conceptual information can be motivated and effortful comes from research on cultural differences in the Fundamental Attribution Error (FAE) and Correspondence Bias (CB). In the Western literature on the FAE or CB, the choice to contextualize the person—to pay attention to situational constraints on a person's behavior—has been shown to be an effortful, cognitively demanding process, as participants correct for their automatic dispositional attributions (Gilbert et al. 1988). East Asians have been shown to be less likely to exhibit FAE and CB (Choi et al. 1999; Masuda and Kitayama 2004; Morris and Peng 1994). Does this mean that East Asians are engaging in an effortful correction for a dispositional attribution, or does it mean that East Asians are less likely to make the analytical dispositional attribution in the first place? The evidence, as we will see below, suggests that East Asians also make an automatic dispositional attribution, and then explicitly correct for it; the correction itself, however, is partially automatic as well, likely a trained response.

In Masuda and Kitayama (2004) and Miyamoto and Kitayama (2002), the correspondence bias—assuming that one's actions reflect one's disposition, rather than the situation—is shown to be a more persistent bias among Americans than Japanese. In the classic CB tests, participants read an essay that, they are told, was written by another student who was asked to make a certain argument in their essay. After reading the essay, participants are asked how much the student actually believes what he/she said in the essay. American participants tended to display more CB than Japanese participants, attributing the student's behavior to his/her own opinion, and being unaffected by knowledge of situational constraints.

Seeking direct evidence that the cultural difference in CB was due to explicit consideration of situational constraints by Japanese participants, Miyamoto and Kitayama (2002) asked participants to list the thoughts that led to their rating of the student's true belief. Japanese listed more cognitions about the situational constraints than Americans did. Moreover, at the individual level, the number of situation-referencing cognitions mediated the cultural difference, suggesting that the decision to use contextual information explains the cultural difference. This indication of explicit, effortful holism is also supported by the fact that under cognitive load, Japanese began to show evidence of adopting a situation-blind view (showing CB). However, even under cognitive load, Japanese still showed CB to a significantly smaller degree than did Americans, suggesting that the cultural difference may also be partially due to an *automatic* tendency to attend to situational information among Japanese. In these studies, then, a situational attribution is more effortful for both cultures, and is more often made by Japanese; but among Japanese, the situational attribution appears to be somewhat resistant to cognitive load, suggesting that it may also be partially an automatic process.

More evidence that situational corrections for dispositional attributions can be automatic came from research by Knowles and colleagues (Knowles et al. 2001), where Hong Kong students put under cognitive load did *not* make more dispositional attributions than Hong Kong students not under cognitive load. American students under cognitive load, on the other hand, made a much larger dispositional attribution than American students not under cognitive load. This showed that for the American students, that situational correction was an effortful process, while for Hong Kong students, the situational correction was automatic, occurring even when they were cognitively busy. However, because Hong Kong students did not become *more* situational under cognitive load, the authors concluded that for both Hong Kong and American students, the initial automatic attribution was in fact to the disposition, and then both cultures later made a situational correction for that attribution; the difference between the cognitive load conditions was caused by the Hong Kong students' practiced situational attribution, which, presumably due to cultural influence, had become automatic.

The fully-automatic situational correction among Hong Kong students and partially-automatic situational correction among Japanese students appears to be evidence for an 'overlearned' rule, one that has become part of the automatic habits of thought but had to be learned through cultural influence. Americans, on the other hand, must always engage in effortful thought to make a situational attribution, presumably because of the cultural emphasis on ignoring context. These cultural differences in CB are especially important for showing how tasks attributed to analytic-holistic thinking styles can be quite different from the definitions usually given to System 1 (holistic *and* automatic) and System 2 (analytic *and* effortful). In the case of CB and FAE, Westerners must engage effortful thinking in order to overcome an automatic, analytical attribution; East Asians show evidence of consciously thinking about the situation in order to overcome what would otherwise also be an automatic dispositional attribution, and show evidence of having learned an attention-to-situation rule in order to correct initial dispositional attributions.

Norms: Culturally-elaborated and learned holism

A further reason to believe that the cultural definition of holistic thinking may not be the same thing as System 1 thinking lies in the way a culturally-elaborated holistic way of thinking can be learned. As previously discussed, in some dual-process accounts of reasoning, System 1 is not defined as a kind of thinking that needs to be taught, but only avoided or not depending on use of System 2 (Evans 2003, 2006; Stanovich and West 2000). In the cultural psychology literature, however, holistic thinking is conceptualized as something that can be developed, learned and trained. This kind of culturally-elaborated holistic thinking involves greater attention to context, and also includes dialectical thinking: expectations of flux and contradiction, rather than linear change. In Koo and Choi (2005), for example, in which Korean students in Oriental Medicine were compared to Korean students in psychology, longer training in Oriental Medicine (but not in psychology) was associated with more dialecticism (i.e. predictions of dialectical, rather than linear, change, as in Ji et al. 2001), and also with endorsement of more clues as possibly relevant to solving a crime (as in Choi et al. 2003). Students of Oriental Medicine had been taught to adopt a consciously holistic and dialectical stance: they were trained to attend to 'maintain[ing] the dynamic balance of organs', and to interpret symptoms as results of holistic interrelations among organs (Koo and Choi 2005, p.1265).

A new Analysis-Holism Scale (AHS, Choi et al., 2007) has also shown that holistic thinking can be an explicitly adopted set of beliefs. The AHS measures individual differences in endorsement of four subscales: holistic Causality (e.g. 'Everything in the world is intertwined in a causal relationship'), dialectical Attitudes towards Contradictions (e.g. 'It is more desirable to take the middle ground than go to extremes'), dialectical Perception of Change (e.g. 'Current situations can change at any time'), and holistic Locus of Attention (e.g. 'It is more important to pay attention to the whole than its parts') (Choi et al. 2007, p.694). As expected, endorsement of AHS items was higher among Korean than American students, and also higher among Korean students studying Oriental Medicine than other Korean students. Among Koreans, individuals with higher AHS scores tended to score higher on other measures of relevant thinking styles (such as 'attributional complexity', a 'global' thinking style, and a 'compromising' approach to conflict), were more likely to categorize objects based on family resemblance (as in Norenzayan, Smith et al. 2002), and were less willing to exclude 'irrelevant' clues in a murder case (as in Choi et al. 2003). These findings suggest that holistic thinking can consist of an explicitly adopted, culturally taught set of beliefs about the proper way to react to conflict, predict change, attend to context, and perceive causal relationships in the world.

But one more potential similarity: Nonverbal thinking?

Another commonly mentioned (though also controversial; e.g. Evans, this volume) difference between System 1 and 2 thinking is how *explicit* it is. System 1 processes are generally seen as ones that cannot be 'actively perceived' by the conscious mind; only the results of these processes can be brought consciously to mind (Evans 2003; Sloman 2002). In contrast, System 2 thinking is supposed to progress through a consciously controlled route, each step occurring in the conscious mind and therefore explicit and verbalizable.

H. S. Kim and colleagues (2002) have shown that in comparison with East-Asian Americans, Caucasian Americans are more likely to identify talking with intelligence and 'good thinking'. This suggests that part of the reason that System 2 is often identified as being a 'verbal', 'conscious' system may be because of a Western, pro-verbal bias to associate intelligent thought with verbalization (though see Evans, this volume, for caveats on the System 2–explicit thinking connection).

Perhaps coincidentally, then, H.S. Kim (2002) has indeed found evidence that Westerners are more likely to verbalize thought than East Asians. In these studies, participants were asked to complete Raven's Matrices tests, either silently or by speaking their thoughts aloud. East Asian Americans' thinking was disrupted by speaking their thoughts aloud, as reflected in poorer performance on Raven's Matrices, while European Americans' performance was not. Moreover, when required to recite the alphabet while solving Raven's Matrices (thus suppressing other forms of verbal thought), European Americans' performance was disrupted, but East Asian Americans' performance was left intact (both groups were students at Stanford University, and all indicated that their native/dominant language was English). These studies suggested that at least when carrying out the thinking required to solve Raven's Matrices, East Asian Americans' internal thought processes were less likely to be verbal. East Asian Americans were also more likely to describe their own natural thinking as less 'verbal' than were Americans. In fact, individual differences in self-reported internal verbalization of thought, as well as self-reported views on the connection between speaking and intelligence, were found to mediate the effect of culture on the disruptive effect of speaking one's thoughts aloud.

The exact connection between thinking 'holistically' and thinking non-verbally was not made in these studies. However, the studies do show that one's culture can influence whether talking is seen as an indication of good thinking, and, consequently, how much internal (and external) verbalization takes place when one thinks. Whether or not this is causally connected to using associative, contextualizing, holistic thought processes that require non-verbalization—versus a different set of cultural effects, related directly to verbalization—is still an open question.

Similarities and differences: Summary

Although not fully exhaustive of all research that has been done in the analytic-holistic cultural psychology tradition, the above summary of studies shows some important similarities and differences to common conceptualizations of dual-process models. Similar to theories that concentrate on the 'decontextualizing' aspect of System 2 and the 'associative, holistic, contextualizing' aspect of System 1, holistic East Asians have been shown to have more difficulty ignoring past experience in favor of abstract rules or logic, and to more easily shift to categorizing based on family resemblance rather than single features (Norenzayan, Smith et al. 2002); East Asians also are more likely to automatically bind an object with its context, while Westerners are more likely to decontextualize the object (Masuda and Nisbett 2001). In agreement with theories that describe System 1 as only posting the end result of a thinking process to the conscious mind while System 2 processes are fully conscious, there is evidence that East Asians may think less verbally than Westerners (H. S. Kim 2002). And in agreement with descriptions of System 2 as being an ability to control attention to context, East Asians find it more difficult to avoid looking at contextual flashing dots than do Westerners (Masuda et al. 2007).

However, there are many aspects of the above studies that do not fit neatly into the dual-process categories. Though dual-process theories identify the tendency to contextualize as an automatic process, we have seen evidence that paying attention to context can be done deliberately, consciously and in line with lay theories of what one ought to attend to (Choi et al. 2003; Masuda and Kitayama 2004; Masuda et al. 2008; Miyamoto and Kitayama 2002; Norenzayan Choi et al. 2002), and as a correction to an automatic decontextualization (Gilbert et al. 1988; Knowles et al. 2001; Miyamoto and Kitayama 2002). Though dual-process theories identify the decontextualizing System 2 as the only thinking process that is taught through formal education, we have seen that dialectical, holistic attitudes are learned by students of Oriental Medicine (Koo and Choi 2005), and that holistic beliefs are culturally elaborated (Choi et al. 2007). Though dual-process tests generally test one's ability to decontextualize, we have seen that the *skill* of paying attention to context and relational information is better developed among East Asians (Kitayama et al. 2003; Masuda and Nisbett 2006). Overall, holistic thinking does not appear to be best described as a tendency 'to accept uncritically default judgments that are generated heuristically' (Evans 2006, p.383); instead, it can be conscious and norm-following, but with an eye to paying *more* attention to context rather than *less*.

Implications

These connections and disconnects have implications both for analytic-holistic and dual-process theories. First, cultural psychologists may benefit from clearer distinctions between four categories: automatic holistic and analytic habits of thought, versus more conceptual, conscious, rule-following holistic and analytic thinking (see Table 10.1). It is possible that examining these four categories in turn would lead to better explanations for the sources of cultural differences, as different elements of cultures may influence the development of less and more cognitively demanding kinds of analytic and holistic thinking. Though East Asian holistic thinking does encourage cultural participants to attend to context and relationships, this way of thinking is not necessarily intuitive or unconscious, and not all descriptions of System 1 thinking apply to all kinds of East Asian holistic thinking. Secondly, dual-process theorists could begin to explore the question of under what circumstances System 2-like

Table 10.1 Selected cultural psychology references illustrating four categories of analytic and holistic thinking

	Decontextualized	Contextualized
Effortful/volitional/skilled/culturally taught/verbal	Choi et al. 2003 H.S. Kim 2002 Kitayama et al. 2003 Norenzayan, Smith et al. 2002 Norenzayan, Choi et al. 2002	Choi et al. 2003 Choi et al. 2007 Kitayama et al. 2003 Koo and Choi 2005 Miyamoto and Kitayama 2002 Norenzayan, Choi et al. 2002
Effortless/automatic/nonverbal	Masuda and Nisbett 2006 Miyamoto and Kitayama 2002 Knowles et al. 2001	Norenzayan, Smith et al. 2002 Masuda et al. 2007 Knowles et al. 2001 H.S. Kim 2002

thought processes (namely, effortful and deliberative) might actually involve contextualization rather than decontextualization. This suggestion to cross 'effortful/deliberative' and 'contextualizing' echoes Moshman (2000), who suggested that crossing heuristic/rule-following and automatic/explicit dimensions could better explain certain evidence about reasoning in the developmental literature.

Further directions: Effortless, but aware, thinking?

In our effort to elaborate on how holistic thinking can be rule-following and deliberative, however, we do not want to fall into a possible trap of applying Western values about effortful thinking to East Asian thinking. It is possible that the East Asian concentration on absorbing more, rather than less, information necessarily leads to the use of a more unconscious, general-use associative system that has greater processing capacity than deliberate thought. Though we have a large amount of evidence that suggests that East Asians are better able, and more likely, to pay attention to more (contextual) information, we do not have very good insight into what process of thinking this conscious choice leads to. In studies on the advantages of unconscious thinking, Dijksterhuis and colleagues have suggested that decisions requiring consideration of more information are best processed unconsciously (Dijksterhuis et al. 2006). Even if not all forms of what cultural psychologists call 'holistic thinking' are the associative, effortless processes described in many System 1 theories, it is very possible that even the conscious holistic thinking that has been detailed above leads to more use of unconscious, less effortful thinking. Moreover, it is possible that this kind of thinking is seen as advantageous in East Asian cultures. Recent evidence that East Asians are more admiring of decision making based on intuitions than are Westerners is supportive of this proposal (Buchtel and Norenzayan in press).

Generally speaking, a differential emphasis on the usefulness of intuition versus logic has been noted in East Asian versus Western philosophy (Becker 1986; Lloyd 1990, 1996). The development of formal logic, as well as other rule-based systems such as Euclidian geometry and theoretical models to explain physical and biological phenomena, was a feature of Greek philosophy that heavily influenced the development of Western thought (Lloyd 1990). Expert analytic thinking may be advantageous in situations where argumentation and the cutting away of irrelevancies are emphasized, and thus lionized in societies where debate is important, such as the Ancient Greek-influenced West, or where objective and analytical thought is expected, such as in many work situations in the West (Sanchez-Burks 2002).

As the idea of expert analytic thinking was elaborated on in the West, the idea of expert intuitive (and effortless) thinking may have been developed in the East. For example, the Taoist and Confucian spiritual ideal of 'wu-wei' or 'effortless action' is a kind of intuition, and yet is more complex and sophisticated than the Western idea of intuition as a 'snap judgment' (Dijksterhuis and Nordgren 2006, p.106; Slingerland 2000, p.300). Epitomized by Confucius' reputed ability, perfected at the age of 70, to perform rituals and to interact with others in an effortlessly harmonious and flexible way, 'effortless action' is a kind of expert intuition that allows one to engage in perfect, effortless deliberation and immediate response. Similarly, meditation practices in the Buddhist tradition emphasize a kind of non-directed awareness of thoughts, a kind of thinking that is not effortful, and yet is conscious (Marlatt 2006). Effortless thinking, then, may be held in higher regard in East Asian society because of philosophical traditions in which intuition is understood as complex and based on expert knowledge.

Another reason that intuition and holistic thinking might be more valued in East Asian than Western culture is that expert (i.e. informed by experience, automatic) forms of this kind of thinking may be objectively more successful at solving the social-environmental problems that are more prevalent in East Asian societies than Western societies. Among those factors believed to create and sustain the cultural differences in cognition is the degree to which different cultures encourage interpersonal modes of being (Fiske et al. 1998; Nisbett et al. 2001). Cultures such as those of East Asia may require greater attention to 'relationships and subtle changes in social situations' (Masuda and Nisbett 2001, p.923), thus favoring holistic habits of thinking.

Consistent with this reasoning, as briefly described above, Western subjects exhibit increases in holistic cognitive processing after being primed with an interdependent self-construal, while East Asian subjects move towards analytic thinking when primed with independent self-construal (Cha et al. 2005; Kühnen et al. 2001; Kühnen and Oyserman 2002). The link between intuitive processing and successful social inference, such as detection of nonverbal cues, has also been supported by their mutual dependence on brain structures required for implicit learning (Lieberman 2000). Importantly, recent studies have suggested that in complex situations, intuitive, holistic thinking has a distinct advantage over conscious, analytic reasoning (Dijksterhuis, 2004; Dijksterhuis et al. 2006; Dijksterhuis and Nordgren 2006; Dijksterhuis and van Olden 2006). Societies in which social success depends on attentiveness to subtle social cues in complex interpersonal environments may explicitly encourage the mode of thinking that leads to better detection of such cues, namely unconscious, automatic, holistic thinking.

Conclusion

The strongest lesson that cultural psychologists wish to communicate is that in order to make conclusions about the 'human mind', researchers must expand the net of their research to include humans from cultures other than their own. Given the Western cultural emphasis on analytical thinking, it behooves us to consider to what extent our own culture has biased the development of dual-process reasoning theories. Are analytical, effortful, deliberative, and explicit thinking processes always tied up with each other, or is that more likely to occur in Western minds than others? Conversely, there is room for dual-process theories of thinking to inform cross cultural research in a more systematic manner (reflecting System 2 reasoning, one might say!). Such cross-fertilization between cultural research and cognitive models of the mind can expand the reach of dual-process theories, and refine the cultural psychologist's operationalization of human thinking across cultures.

Dual-process theories are certainly still in a period of development (as evidenced by new advances described in this volume). We hope that this summary of studies, showing cultural variation in reasoning, encourage dual-process theorists to test out their theories in non-Western cultures. The particular combinations of historical and social environments that characterize different cultures may have given rise to particular ways of thinking that are worthy of exploration. Common Western definitions of System 1 and System 2 thinking may be only one of them.

References

Armstrong, K. (1993) *A history of God: The 4,000-year quest of Judaism, Christianity and Islam.* Ballantine Books, New York.

Becker, C.B. (1986) Reasons for the lack of argumentation and debate in the Far East. *International Journal of Intercultural Relations,* **10**, 75–92.

Buchtel, E.E. and Norenzayan, A. (in press) Which should you use, intuition or logic? Cultural differences in injunctive norms about reasoning. *Asian Journal of Social Psychology.*

Cha, O. (2007) 'I' see trees, 'we' see forest: Cognitive consequences of independence vs. interdependence. *Dissertation Abstracts International: Section B: The Sciences and Engineering,* **67**, 4155.

Cha, O., Oyserman, D., and Schwarz, N. (2005) *Turning Asians into Westerners: Priming an independent self-construal in Korea II.* Paper presented at the annual meeting of the Society for Personality and Social Psychology, New Orleans, LA.

Choi, I., Koo, M., and Choi, J.A. (2007) Individual differences in analytic versus holistic thinking. *Personality and Social Psychology Bulletin,* **33**, 691–705.

Choi, I., Nisbett, R.E., and Norenzayan, A. (1999) Causal attribution across cultures: Variation and universality. *Psychological Bulletin,* **125**, 47–63.

Choi, I., Dalal, R., Kim-Prieto, C., and Park, H. (2003) Culture and judgement of causal relevance. *Journal of Personality and Social Psychology,* **84**, 46–59.

Chua, H.F., Boland, J., and Nisbett, R.E. (2005) Cultural variation in eye movements during scene perception. *Proceedings of the National Academy of Sciences, USA,* **102**, 12629–33.

Cole, M. and Scribner, S. (1974) *Culture and thought: A psychological introduction.* Wiley, New York.

Dijksterhuis, A. (2004) Think different: The merits of unconscious thought in preference development and decision making. *Journal of Personality and Social Psychology,* **87**, 586–98.

Dijksterhuis, A. and Nordgren, L. F. (2006) A theory of unconscious thought. *Perspectives on Psychological Science,* **1**, 95–109.

Dijksterhuis, A. and van Olden, Z. (2006) On the benefits of thinking unconsciously: Unconscious thought can increase post-choice satisfaction. *Journal of Experimental Social Psychology,* **42**, 627–31.

Dijksterhuis, A., Bos, M.W., Nordgren, L.F., and van Baaren, R.B. (2006) On making the right choice: The deliberation-without-attention effect. *Science,* **311**, 1005–7.

Epstein, S. (1991) Cognitive-experiential self-theory: An integrative theory of personality. In R. C. Curtis (ed.) *The relational self: Theoretical convergences in psychoanalysis and social psychology,* 111–37. Guilford Press, New York.

Epstein, S., Pacini, R., Denes-Raj, V., and Heier, H. (1996) Individual differences in intuitive-experiential and analytical-rational thinking styles. *Journal of Personality and Social Psychology,* **71**, 390–405.

Evans, J.St.B.T. (2003) In two minds: Dual-process accounts of reasoning. *Trends in Cognitive Sciences,* **7**, 454–9.

Evans, J.St.B.T. (2006) The heuristic-analytic theory of reasoning: Extension and evaluation. *Psychonomic Bulletin and Review,* **13**, 378–95.

Evans, J.St.B.T. (2008) Dual-processing accounts of reasoning, judgment, and social cognition. *Annual Review of Psychology,* **59**, 255–78.

Evans, J.St.B.T. and Over, D.E. (1996) *Rationality and reasoning.* Psychology/Erlbaum (UK) Taylor and Francis, Oxford.

Fiske, A.P., Kitayama, S., Markus, H.R., and Nisbett, R.E. (1998) The cultural matrix of social psychology. In D.T. Gilbert, S.T. Fiske, and G. Lindzey (eds) *The handbook of social psychology,* Vols. 1 and 2, 4th ed., 915–81. McGraw-Hill, New York.

Fung, Y.-I. (1922) Why China has no science. *International Journal of Ethics,* **32**, 237–63.

Gilbert, D.T., Pelham, B.W., and Krull, D.S. (1988) On cognitive busyness: When person perceivers meet persons perceived. *Journal of Personality and Social Psychology,* **54**, 733–40.

Gladwell, M. (2005) *Blink: The power of thinking without thinking.* Little, Brown and Co, New York.

Ji, L.-J., Nisbett, R.E. and Su, Y. (2001) Culture, change, and prediction. *Psychological Science,* **12**, 450–6.

Ji, L.-J., Peng, K., and Nisbett, R.E. (2000) Culture, control, and perception of relationships in the environment. *Journal of Personality and Social Psychology,* **78**, 943–55.

Kahneman, D. (2003) A perspective on judgment and choice: Mapping bounded rationality. *American Psychologist,* **58**, 697–720.

Kim, H. S. (2002) We talk, therefore we think? A cultural analysis of the effect of talking on thinking. *Journal of Personality and Social Psychology,* **83**, 828–42.

Kim, K. and Markman, A.B. (2006) Differences in fear of isolation as an explanation of cultural differences: Evidence from memory and reasoning. *Journal of Experimental Social Psychology*, **42**, 350–64.

Kitayama, S., Duffy, S., Kawamura, T., and Larsen, J.T. (2003) Perceiving an object and its context in different cultures: A cultural look at new look. *Psychological Science*, **14**, 201–6.

Knowles, E.D., Morris, M.W., Chiu, C., and Hong, Y. (2001) Culture and the process of person perception: Evidence for automaticity among East Asians in correcting for situational influences on behavior. *Personality and Social Psychology Bulletin*, **27**, 1344–56.

Koo, M. and Choi, I. (2005) Becoming a holistic thinker: Training effect of Oriental medicine on reasoning. *Personality and Social Psychology Bulletin*, **31**, 1264–72.

Kühnen, U. and Oyserman, D. (2002) Thinking about the self influences thinking in general: Cognitive consequences of salient self-concept. *Journal of Experimental Social Psychology*, **38**, 492–9.

Kühnen, U., Hannover, B., and Schubert, B. (2001) The semantic-procedural interface model of the self: The role of self-knowledge for context-dependent versus context-independent modes of thinking. *Journal of Personality and Social Psychology*, **80**, 397–409.

Lam, K.C.H., Buehler, R., McFarland, C., Ross, M., and Cheung, I. (2005) Cultural differences in affective forecasting: The role of focalism. *Personality and Social Psychology Bulletin*, **31**, 1296–309.

Lieberman, M.D. (2000) Intuition: A social cognitive neuroscience approach. *Psychological Bulletin*, **126**, 109–37.

Lloyd, G.E.R. (1990) *Demystifying mentalities*. Cambridge University Press, New York.

Lloyd, G.E.R. (1996) Science in antiquity: The Greek and Chinese cases and their relevance to the problems of culture and cognition. In D.R. Olson and N. Torrance (eds) *Modes of thought: Explorations in culture and cognition*, 15–33. Cambridge University Press, New York.

Marlatt, G.A. (2006) Mindfulness meditation: Reflections from a personal journey. *Current Psychology: Developmental, Learning, Personality, Social*, **25**, 155–72.

Masuda, T. and Kitayama, S. (2004) Perceiver-induced constraint and attitude attribution in Japan and the US: A case for the cultural dependence of the correspondence bias. *Journal of Experimental Social Psychology*, **40**, 409–16.

Masuda, T. and Nisbett, R. E. (2001) Attending holistically versus analytically: Comparing the context sensitivity of Japanese and Americans. *Journal of Personality and Social Psychology*, **81**, 922–34.

Masuda, T. and Nisbett, R. E. (2006) Culture and change blindness. *Cognitive Science*, **30**, 381–99.

Masuda, T., Akase, M., Radford, H.B., and Wang, H. (2007) *The effect of contextual factors on the patterns of eye-movement: Comparing context sensitivity between the Japanese and Westerners*. Manuscript submitted for publication.

Masuda, T., Ellsworth, P.C., Mesquita, B., Leu, J., Tanida, S., and Van de Veerdonk, E. (2008) Placing the face in context: Cultural differences in the perception of facial emotion. *Journal of Personality and Social Psychology*, **94**, 365–81.

Medin, D.L. and Atran, S. (2004) The native mind: Biological categorization and reasoning in development and across cultures. *Psychological Review*, **111**, 960–83.

Miller, J.G. (1984) Culture and the development of everyday social explanation. *Journal of Personality and Social Psychology*, **46**, 961–78.

Miyamoto, Y. and Kitayama, S. (2002) Cultural variation in correspondence bias: The critical role of attitude diagnosticity of socially constrained behavior. *Journal of Personality and Social Psychology*, **83**, 1239–48.

Miyamoto, Y., Kitayama, S., and Talhelm, T. (2006) *A meta-analytic review of cultural differences in cognitive processes*. Poster presented at the 6th Conference of the Society for Personality and Social Psychology, January. Palm Springs, CA.

Miyamoto, Y., Nisbett, R.E., and Masuda, T. (2006) Culture and the physical environment: Holistic versus analytic perceptual affordances. *Psychological Science*, **17**, 113–19.

Morris, M.W. and Peng, K. (1994) Culture and cause: American and Chinese attributions for social and physical events. *Journal of Personality and Social Psychology*, **67**, 949–71.

Moshman, D. (2000) Diversity in reasoning and rationality: Metacognitive and developmental considerations. *Behavioral and Brain Sciences*, **23**, 689–90.

Mote, F. W. (1971) *Intellectual foundations of China*. Alfred A. Knopf, New York.

Nakamura, H. (1960/1988). *The ways of thinking of Eastern peoples*. Greenwood Press, New York.

Nisbett, R.E. (2003) *The geography of thought*. The Free Press, New York.

Nisbett, R.E. and Masuda, T. (2003). *Culture and point of view*. Proceedings of the National Academy of Sciences, USA, 100, 11163–70.

Nisbett, R.E., Peng, K., Choi, I., and Norenzayan, A. (2001) Culture and systems of thought: Holistic versus analytic cognition. *Psychological Review*, **108**, 291–310.

Norenzayan, A,. Choi, I. and Nisbett, R.E. (2002) Cultural similarities and differences in social inference: Evidence from behavioral predictions and lay theories of behavior. *Personality and Social Psychology Bulletin*, **28**, 109–20.

Norenzayan, A., Choi, I., and Peng, K. (2007) Cognition and perception. In S. Kitayama and D. Cohen (eds) *Handbook of cultural psychology,* 569–94. Guilford Publications, New York.

Norenzayan, A., Smith, E.E., Kim, B.J., and Nisbett, R.E. (2002) Cultural preferences for formal versus intuitive reasoning. *Cognitive Science*, **26**, 653–84.

Sanchez-Burks, J. (2002) Protestant relational ideology and (in)attention to relational cues in work settings. *Journal of Personality and Social Psychology*, **83**, 919–29.

Slingerland, E. (2000) Effortless action: The Chinese spiritual ideal of Wu-wei. *Journal of the American Academy of Religion*, **68**, 293–328.

Sloman, S. A. (1996) The empirical case for two systems of reasoning. *Psychological Bulletin*, **119**, 3–22.

Sloman, S.A. (2002) Two systems of reasoning. In T. Gilovich, D. Griffin, and D. Kahneman (eds) *Heuristics and biases: The psychology of intuitive judgment,* 379–96. Cambridge University Press, New York.

Smith, E.E., Langston, C., and Nisbett, R.E. (1992) The case for rules in reasoning. *Cognitive Science: A Multidisciplinary Journal*, **16**, 1–40.

Stanovich, K.E. (1999) *Who is rational?: Studies of individual differences in reasoning*. Lawrence Erlbaum Associates Publishers, Mahwah, NJ.

Stanovich, K.E. and West, R.F. (2000) Individual differences in reasoning: Implications for the rationality debate? *Behavioral and Brain Sciences*, **23**, 645–726.

Stanovich, K.E. and West, R.F. (2002) Individual differences in reasoning: Implications for the rationality debate? In T. Gilovich, D. Griffin, and D. Kahneman (eds) *Heuristics and biases: The psychology of intuitive judgment*, 421–40. Cambridge University Press, New York.

Verschueren, N., Schaeken, W., and d'Ydewalle, G. (2005) A dual-process specification of causal conditional reasoning. *Thinking & Reasoning*, 11, 239–78.

Witkin, H.A. and Berry, J.W. (1975) Psychological differentiation in cross-cultural perspective. *Journal of Cross-Cultural Psychology*, 6, 4–87.

Chapter 11

The two systems of learning: An architectural perspective

Ron Sun, Sean M. Lane, and Robert C. Mathews

This chapter is concerned with theoretical views and models that posit the existence of two systems of learning, and focuses on one particular theoretical model that emphasizes the representational difference between the two systems of learning (Sun et al. 2005). This chapter discusses how such theoretical views/models may be developed into a coherent and generic computational cognitive model—that is, a 'cognitive architecture' (Newell 1990; Sun 2002). The resulting computational model (CLARION) can account for a wide range of psychological data.

To present these ideas, first, in the opening section, historical thinking about the existence of two systems of learning is briefly reviewed. Then, in the second section, some details of two-systems learning models are explicated. In the third section, a cognitive architecture is developed based on a two-system model. In the fourth section, implications and comparisons are discussed. Finally, the fifth section provides concluding remarks.

Some historical perspectives on two systems of learning

The notion of dual processes has been well accepted in several domains including reasoning (e.g. Evans 2003; Sun 1994), social judgment (e.g. Lieberman 2000), and decision making (e.g. Stanovich 1999). However, the notion that there are dual systems in learning has received great resistance. Why is this the case? One possibility has to do with the revered concept of working memory. Cognitive psychologists have often been resistant to the idea that any form of knowledge can exist in the mind without first being consciously noted and processed through working memory (Baddeley 1986). Therefore, the two claims often associated with implicit learning have been frequently criticized: the notion that something can be learned nonconsciously and the notion that implicit learning requires no (conscious) working memory (Sun 2002).

The idea of two separate systems has roots earlier than the current distinction between implicit and explicit learning. Early studies of learning focused on operant and classical conditioning, and the issue of possible conditioning without awareness was raised (e.g. Greenspoon 1955). Arthur Reber deserves credit as the 'father' of research on implicit learning (as well as a leading influence on dual-system theory generally—see Frankish and Evans, this volume). Reber's early work (1976) demonstrated that subjects could memorize letter strings that followed certain patterns (i.e. they followed the rules of a finite state grammar, in an *artificial grammar learning* task) and later discriminated new valid from invalid strings without awareness of how they were doing it. He eventually made three central claims about implicit learning (Reber 1993). The claims were that implicit learning: (a) can occur without awareness that anything was learned, (b) occurs automatically, without requiring central resources, and (c) involves abstracting the inherent structure of the stimuli at the time of encoding. Reber also made an evolutionary argument for the existence of dual learning systems. Essentially, he argued that human (like other animals) evolved the ability to learn from interactions with the environment long before symbolic thought evolved. Thus, conscious thinking is an 'add-on' that came much later than the more basic implicit learning mechanisms. He supported this claim with several lines of evidence, including research suggesting greater robustness of implicit learning to various types of brain damage that sharply reduced the ability to explicitly learn new tasks (e.g. Squire and Frambach 1990).

Reber's theoretical claims spurred three decades of research attempting to support or argue against these claims. For instance, implicit learning has been studied in the context of the serial reaction time paradigm. This task evolved from early work by Donald Hebb (1961), who found that people's memory for sequences of numbers improved if certain sequences were repeated, even when they were unaware of the repetition. A typical study of this type involves seeing letters that appear in various locations on a screen. Subjects press a key corresponding to the quadrant of the screen where a target letter will appear. If there is a pattern to the sequence of locations, subjects speed up their responses, yet are unable to describe the pattern (see Goschke 1997 for a review). To study the issue of central resources, secondary tasks are added to test whether this disrupts implicit learning of the sequences. The results of these studies are mixed, although in some situations, disruption does occur. Researchers largely agree that the evidence for the claim that implicit learning requires no central resources is currently inconclusive (Shanks 2005; but see Sun et al. 2005).

The claim that implicit knowledge is abstract has been studied primarily in the artificial grammar learning paradigm. As noted above, the primary finding in this literature is that subjects can distinguish between exemplars and non-exemplars of a grammar without being able to articulate how they are making such decisions. Although Reber (1993) argued that this finding indicated that subjects must be abstracting their knowledge of the grammar during learning, others disagreed. However, some argued that implicit learning does not involve abstracting any knowledge at encoding (e.g. Brooks and Vokey 1991). Rather, task knowledge merely consists of remembered exemplars (strings) of the grammar. The abstraction required to identify a new valid string occurs at the retrieval time, by comparing new items to all the remembered strings in memory. Thus, although a number of researchers have evidence that abstraction does occur because subjects show transfer to new letter sets or modalities, some argue that abstraction occurs at retrieval rather than encoding (e.g. Brooks and Vokey 1991).

The issue of abstraction has also been studied in the context of research using a dynamic control task. The original version of this task (Berry and Broadbent 1984) asked subjects to attempt to control the production of sugar in a simulated factory. On each trial, subjects change the number of workers deployed in order to maintain sugar output at a target level. The output on the next trial depends on the number of workers assigned plus the current level of output, and it includes a small noise factor (random variation). This task is difficult to learn, but eventually subjects improve their ability to control the system, although they often demonstrate poor explicit knowledge of how to control it. One prominent view of performance on this task involves remembered past instances (e.g. Dienes and Fahey 1995). In research motivating this view, subjects who had practiced the task showed above-chance performance at test only on system states where they had previously made a correct input. Thus, it was argued that specific correct instances were stored in memory and used when those same situations occurred again (although such representations were thought to be implicit; Dienes and Fahey 1995). Furthermore, this knowledge was argued to be highly specific based on the fact that it did not transfer to other possible situations (e.g. nearby system states). However, recent work suggests that this conclusion may be limited to experiments where subjects have little experience with the task, becuase subjects do show transfer to some new situations after extensive training (Lane et al. 2008). In summary, the claim that implicit learning involves abstraction has received support (Sun et al. 2005). However, there is still much disagreement about whether such abstraction occurs at encoding or retrieval.

Perhaps the longest and most protracted debate has been concerned with whether people are consciously aware of implicit knowledge (Sun 1997, Sun 2002, ch. 7). The strongest support for the complete lack of conscious awareness of acquired implicit knowledge probably comes from the work of Lewicki (e.g. Lewicki 1986). Lewicki's studies involve a training phase where subjects are exposed to a secret covariation (e.g. between hair length and personality dimensions) under the cover story of learning about other relationships. After training, subjects are tested on new stimuli to see if they use the covariation provided during training. The consistent finding of this research is that subjects pick up and respond to these covariations without being able to report them. Furthermore, in all the implicit learning paradigms discussed above, subjects have difficulty explaining what they have learned. However, they sometimes, in some tasks, demonstrate some degree of awareness when forced to explain what they know (e.g. Perruchet and Pacteau 1990; Sun et al. 2001). Other support for the lack of conscious awareness comes from the process dissociation procedures (see Destrebecqz and Cleeremans 2001 for details).

In summary, all three of Reber's (1993) claims about implicit learning have received some support, but there is no incontrovertible demonstration of complete lack of awareness of what is supposedly learned implicitly, no demonstration that implicit learning always occurs without central resources, and no evidence of abstract encoding of implicit knowledge that could not possibly occur at retrieval. Although these findings have been used to argue against a dual-systems view of learning, the pattern of results evidently does not rule out a dual-systems approach (see, e.g. Mathews 1997; Sun 2002). Furthermore, the focus on finding tasks that can be performed in the complete absence of conscious knowledge or without any access to central resources ('process-pure' tasks) has led many researchers to errorneously assume independence between explicit and implicit processes. The focus on the specific claims has led researchers to neglect possible interactions between the two systems (Mathews 1997; Sun 2002; Sun et al. 2005). We believe that the interactions are crucial for the development of skills and expertise (e.g. Sun 2002; Sun et al. 2001, 2005). Overall, we believe that the findings discussed above can be seen as consistent with a dual-systems perspective. For example, people may become aware of the knowledge acquired implicitly through the implicit/explicit interactions (Sun et al. 2001). Furthermore, the notion of abstraction in implicit knowledge may be substantiated through a dual-systems (dual-representational) perspective (Sun 2002).

Theoretical models of two systems of learning

As reviewed above, some researchers have proposed the view that there are two complementary systems of learning—one implicit and one explicit. Here, we will focus on one particular such view that is better developed than others (e.g. in terms of representation-based explanation, computational modeling, and empirical test).

A plausible theoretical model of two systems of learning

In Sun et al. (2001), Sun et al. (2005), and Sun (2002), a theoretical model concerning two separate learning systems, implicit and explicit, was proposed. Below, we discuss this model that incorporates both types of learning processes in one unified framework based on representations.

Representation

Let us consider the representations of a model incorporating the distinction between implicit and explicit learning processes. First, we note that the inaccessible nature of implicit knowledge can be suitably captured by (subsymbolic) distributed representations provided by, for example, a backpropagation neural network model (Rumelhart et al. 1986). This is because representational units in a distributed representation (e.g. in the hidden layer of a backpropagation network) are capable of accomplishing tasks but are subsymbolic and generally not individually meaningful (see Rumelhart et al. 1986; Sun 1994, 2002). This characteristic of distributed representation accords well with the relative inaccessibility (relative lack of conscious awareness) of implicit knowledge. (Although it is generally not the case that distributed representations are completely inaccessible, they are definitely less accessible, not as direct and immediate as symbolic or localist representations. Distributed representations, however, may be accessed through indirect, transformational processes.) Furthermore, this type of representations may encompass both prototype-based and exemplar-based encoding (as demonstrated before in the neural networks literature; Rumelhart et al. 1986). In contrast, explicit knowledge may be best captured in computational modeling by a symbolic or localist representation (Clark and Karmiloff-Smith 1993), in which each unit is more easily interpretable and has a clearer conceptual meaning. This characteristic captures the property of explicit knowledge being more consciously accessible and manipulable (Sun 1994, 2002). This difference in the representations of the two types of knowledge leads to a two-level theoretical model (initially proposed in Sun 1997), whereby each 'level' using one kind of representation captures one corresponding type of process (either implicit or explicit). Sun (1994, 1997, 2002), Dreyfus and Dreyfus (1987), and Smolensky (1988) presented relevant theoretical arguments for such two-level models.

At each level of the model, there are multiple modules—both *action-centered* modules and *non-action-centered* modules (Moscovitch and Umilta 1991; Schacter 1990). The reason for having both action-centered and non-action-centered modules at both levels is because, as it should be obvious, action-centered knowledge (roughly, procedural knowledge) is not necessarily inaccessible (directly), and non-action-centered knowledge (roughly, declarative knowledge) is not necessarily accessible (directly). (Although it has been argued by some that all procedural knowledge is inaccessible and all declarative knowledge is accessible, such a clean mapping of the two dichotomies is untenable in our view. See Sun 2002.)

At the bottom level, action-centered knowledge is highly modular, with each module adapted to a specific modality, task, or input stimulus type. This is consistent with the well-known modularity claim (Fodor 1983; Karmiloff-Smith 1986), and is also similar to Shallice's (1972) idea of a multitude of action systems competing with each other. The existence of multiple modules at the bottom level has significant implications for the resources issues.

The non-action-centered modules (at both levels) represent more static, declarative, and generic types of knowledge. This knowledge includes what is commonly referred to as semantic memory (i.e. general knowledge about the world).

Learning

The learning of implicit action-centered knowledge at the bottom level of the model can be accomplished through trial-and-error interactions with the world (Heidegger 1927; Sun et al. 2001; Sun 2002). This can be accomplished mechanistically in a variety of ways consistent with the nature of distributed representations. In particular, reinforcement learning can be used (e.g. Q-learning implemented with backpropagation neural networks; Watkins 1989). Such learning methods, with repeated, incremental numerical tuning (Rumelhart et al. 1986), are theoretically justified. For example, Cleeremans (1997) argued that implicit learning could not be captured by symbolic models but could be captured by neural networks (see also Sun 2002). Furthermore, this type of learning may lead to both prototype-based and exemplar-based encoding of information (as demonstrated in the neural networks literature; Rumelhart et al. 1986). The learning of implicit non-action-centered knowledge is similarly based on repeated, incremental numerical tuning (see, e.g. Sun and Zhang 2006).

The explicit action-centered knowledge at the top level of the model can also be learned in a variety of ways in accordance with the localist/symbolic representation used. Because of its representational characteristics, one-shot learning based on hypothesis testing (Bruner et al. 1956; Sun 2002; Sun et al. 2001) is needed. With such learning, individuals explore the world and dynamically acquire representations and modify them as needed, reflecting the dynamic, ongoing nature of skill learning (Heidegger 1927; Sun 2002). In so doing, the implicit knowledge already acquired in the bottom level can be used in learning explicit knowledge (through 'bottom-up learning'; Sun et al. 2001). The basic idea of such bottom-up learning is that explicit knowledge (e.g. explicit action rules) may be acquired on the basis of implicit knowledge already acquired in the bottom level when such implicit knowledge has been used to direct actions. When an action decided by the bottom level is successful (according to some criteria), then explicit knowledge may be established that corresponds to that action decision. Newly acquired explicit knowledge may be tested and refined through its application in action decision making. In addition, explicit knowledge may also be acquired through independent hypothesis testing learning (independent from the bottom level; Bruner et al. 1956). The explicit non-action-centered knowledge can also be learned in these different ways (although not based on the actions taken, but based on the invocation of relevant implicit knowledge; see Sun 2003; Sun and Zhang 2006).[1]

Moreover, learning can also occur the other way around—from the top-down (learning first explicit knowledge and then implicit knowledge on that basis), when explicit knowledge is readily available or easily learnable (more on top-down learning later).

Interaction

The two levels may interact in many different ways. The bottom level is often faster than the top level, in addition to their representational and learning differences, all of which lead to interesting possibilities for interaction (Sun 2003). One particularly important way of interaction is the final selection of an action based on 'combining' the action recommendations generated by the two levels respectively. This can be accomplished in a variety of different ways in different circumstances. One of the simplest ways involves stochastically selecting the action from either the top level or the bottom level based on a probability distribution. As will be discussed later, such interactions may lead to synergy, that is, improved overall performance due to the interaction/combination of levels, compared with using either level alone.

Summary

Here is a list of the basic hypotheses of the theoretical model (see Figure 11.1):

◆ Representational difference: the two levels use two different types of representations and thus have different degrees of accessibility (i.e. different potentials for conscious awareness).

◆ Learning difference: different learning methods are used for the two levels (in part due to the representational difference of the two levels), leading to different encoding.

◆ Bottom-up and top-down learning: when there is no sufficient prior explicit knowledge available, learning may be bottom-up. When explicit knowledge is provided from external sources or is easily learnable, learning may be top-down.

◆ Combined action decision making: action decision making is in general the result of 'combining' the recommendations from the two levels.

----

[1] The learning difference of the two levels is somewhat analogous to that hypothesized between the corticostriatal habit system and the corticolimbic memory system as proposed by Mishkin et al. (1984).

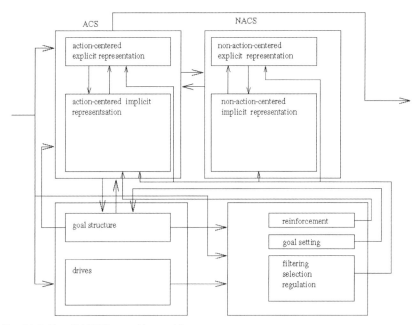

Fig. 11.1 The CLARION cognitive architecture.

A detailed computational model implementing this theory will be described in the next section. But before that, let us look into some data and arguments in favor of the assumptions and the implications of this theory.

Some relevant data and arguments

Separation of implicit and explicit learning

Can implicit and explicit learning really be separated as two different processes empirically? Human skill learning data suggest that the answer to this question is yes. Berry and Broadbent (1988) demonstrated this point using two dynamic control tasks that differed in the degree to which the pattern of correct responding was salient to subjects. Subjects in the two different conditions learned the tasks in different ways; subjects in the non-salient condition learned the task implicitly while subjects in the salient condition learned the task more explicitly. Lee (1995) found a similar difference using manipulations of task complexity instead of saliency. Cohen et al. (1990) described a similar situation in serial reaction time tasks: When complex hierarchical relations were needed to make predictions, subjects tended to use implicit learning, but explicit learning was more evident when simpler relations were involved. Research using artificial grammar learning tasks has similarly found dissociations between learning simple relations and learning complex hierarchical relations (Mathews et al. 1989).

Another line of evidence resulted from contrastive manipulations of implicit and explicit processes. First of all, through instructions that encourage explicit search, a more explicit mode of learning may be employed by subjects. The effect of such a mode change varies, depending on task difficulty (e.g. the salience of stimulus materials). In the case of salient relations/regularities in stimuli, explicit search may be more successful and thus may improve performance (e.g. Cohen et al. 1990). In the case of nonsalient relations, explicit search may fail and thus lead to performance decrement (e.g. Berry and Broadbent 1988). This contrast accentuates the differences between the two types of processes, and some tasks appear more amenable to explicit processes than others. Second, a more explicit learning mode may be introduced by requiring verbalization, because verbalization focuses subjects' attention explicitly on the relations/regularities in stimulus materials. Verbalization usually leads to comparable or improved performance (Sun et al. 2001), but may sometimes lead to worsened performance when the task involves difficult-to-verbalize information (Lane and Schooler 2004; Sun et al. 2001). Third, through using dual-tasks conditions (having subjects perform two tasks at the same time), a more implicit mode of learning may be attained (because, as has been argued in the literature, such manipulation affects explicit processes more than implicit processes). Dual-tasks conditions often lead to worsened performance, which may mainly reflect the reduction of contributions from explicit processes in task performance. Moreover, under dual-tasks conditions, performance differences between subjects with explicit knowledge and those without may disappear (Curran and Keele 1993). Contrasting these manipulations, we see the role played by explicit processes: enhancing explicit processes often helps performance and weakening explicit processes hinders performance.

This interpretation of human data accords well with the theoretical model sketched earlier. Within the theoretical model, one can select one type of learning or the other, by engaging or disengaging the top level (and its learning mechanisms), or the bottom level (and its learning mechanisms). The question now is how a subject 'decides' this on the fly and how the theoretical model accomplishes this 'decision'.

Division of labor

A general pattern discernible from the human data (especially those from the implicit learning literature) is that, if to-be-learned relations are simple and the number of input dimensions is small (in other words, if the relations are salient to subjects), explicit learning usually prevails; if more complex relations and a larger number of input dimensions are involved, implicit learning becomes more prominent (Mathews et al. 1989; Seger 1994; Sun et al. 2005). This pattern has been demonstrated in artificial grammar-learning tasks, serial reaction-time tasks, and dynamic control tasks. Seger (1994) further pointed out that implicit learning was biased toward structures with a system of statistical relations. Thus, the implicit learning mechanism appears more structurally sophisticated and able to handle more complex situations.

This observation can be predicted by the theoretical model sketched earlier. While explicitness of knowledge at the top level allows for a variety of explicit processing, it does not lend itself easily to the learning of complex structures (because of crisp representation and selective hypothesis-testing learning process). On the other hand, in the bottom level, the distributed representation (e.g. in a backpropagation network) that incorporates gradedness and temporal information handles complex relations (including complex sequential relations) and high dimensionality better (Sun 2002).

Therefore, although both levels are present, the bottom level prevails in such circumstances. This correspondence supports the two-level framework.

This explanation implies that it is not necessary to deliberately and a priori decide when to use implicit or explicit learning. When complex relations and high dimensionalities are involved and the top level fails to learn (or is slow to learn), then we can expect a reliance on implicit learning at the bottom level. When the stimulus materials involved are simple, the top level may handle them better and therefore be more readily utilized. This accords well with the fact that, in most circumstances, both types of learning are involved with varying amounts of contributions from each (Seger 1994; Sun et al. 2005).[2]

Bottom-up learning

Let us turn to the possibility of bottom-up learning. As we know, subjects' ability to verbalize is often independent of their performance on implicit learning (Berry and Broadbent 1988). Furthermore, performance typically improves before explicit knowledge can be verbalized by subjects (Stanley et al. 1989). For instance, in dynamic control tasks, although the performance of subjects quickly rose to a high level, their verbal knowledge improved far slower; subjects could not provide usable verbal knowledge until near the end of their training (see, e.g. Stanley et al. 1989). A more recent study of bottom-up learning was conducted by Sun et al. (2001) using a more complex minefield navigation task. In all of these tasks, it appears easier to acquire implicit skills than explicit knowledge (hence the delay in the development of explicit knowledge). In addition, the delay indicates that explicit learning may be triggered by implicit learning, and the process may be described as delayed explication of implicit knowledge. Explicit knowledge is, in a way, extracted from implicit skills. Explicit learning can thus piggyback on implicit learning.

In the context of discovery tasks, Bowers et al. (1990) also showed evidence of explication of implicit knowledge. When subjects were given patterns to complete, they showed implicit recognition of correct pattern completions, even though they could not explicitly recognize a correct completion. Implicit recognition performance improved over time and eventually explicit recognition was achieved. Stanley et al. (1989) and Seger (1994) suggested that, since explicit knowledge lagged behind but improved along with implicit knowledge, explicit knowledge could be viewed as obtained from implicit knowledge. Cleeremans and McClelland (1991) also pointed out this possibility in analyzing their data.

Several developmental theorists have considered a similar delayed explication process in child development. For example, Karmiloff-Smith (1986) suggested that

---

[2] There have also been other views concerning division of labor, for example, in terms of procedural versus declarative processes (Anderson 1983; Anderson and Lebiere 1998), non-selective versus selective processing (Hayes and Broadbent 1988), algorithms versus instances (Stanley et al. 1989), or uni-dimensional versus multi-dimensional systems (Keele et al. 2003). However, these alternative views are not as generically applicable as the implicit/explicit distinction, although each of them may be supported in specific contexts (see Sun 2002; Sun et al. 2005 for further discussions).

developmental changes involved 'representational redescription'. On this view, children first form low-level implicit representations of stimuli; then, when more knowledge is accumulated and stable behavior patterns develop, more abstract representations are formed through a redescription process, which transforms low-level representations and makes them more explicit. Such theories and data testify to the ubiquity of the implicit-to-explicit transition.

The theoretical model sketched earlier captures this kind of bottom-up process. In the model, the bottom level develops implicit skills, on its own, through trial and error, while the top level may extract explicit rules through bottom-up learning (see Sun 2002; Sun et al. 2001). Thus, delayed bottom-up learning naturally falls out of the model.

There is also evidence that explicit knowledge may develop independently (with little or no correlation with implicit skills), under some circumstances. Willingham et al. (1989) reported data that were consistent with the parallel development of implicit skills and explicit knowledge. Correspondingly, in the theoretical model described earlier, explicit hypothesis testing can be employed for learning rules in the top level, independent of the bottom level (as explained earlier), when to-be-learned materials are not overly complex.

Knowledge interaction

With regard to the use of explicit knowledge to affect implicit processes (top-down information), the existing literature suggests that explicit knowledge may help subjects to learn when it directs subjects to focus on relevant features, or when it heightens subjects' sensitivity to relevant information (see Reber 1989; see also later discussions of recent experiments). However, as Reber (1989) pointed out, explicit knowledge may also hamper implicit learning, especially when (1) explicit prior instructions induce an explicit learning mode in a task that is not suitable for explicit learning (e.g. Schooler et al. 1993), or (2) explicit knowledge conflicts with the implicit representations acquired by subjects (Roussel 1999).

On the other hand, we know less about how implicit knowledge is used to affect explicit processes (bottom-up information). We posit that implicit knowledge is used in explicit learning and explicit performance, and this reverse influence, given proper circumstances, can be strong. As discussed above, implicit processes often handle more complex relations and can thus support explicit processes by providing relevant information. Implicit processes are also better at keeping track of statistical information and thus may aid explicit processes in useful ways (Lewicki 1986). However, during explicit tasks (e.g. verbal reasoning), subjects might ignore information from implicit processes when it contradicts their explicit knowledge (Seger 1994).

As explained before, such interactions of explicit and implicit processes are allowed for in the theoretical model described earlier (and, furthermore, embodied in the cognitive architecture CLARION, with its two-level dual-representational framework and the inter-level interaction mechanism), which allows a proper mixture of the top and the bottom level that captures the 'superimposition' of the effects of the two levels (see discussions of CLARION later). Conflicts between the two types of knowledge occur either when the development of explicit knowledge lags behind that of implicit one (e.g. when bottom-up learning is used), or when the top level acquires explicit knowledge independent of the bottom level (when independent hypothesis testing learning methods are used). When conflicts occur, the inter-level interaction mechanism of the model may ignore the bottom level (e.g. in explicit reasoning), or ignore the top level (e.g. in implicit skilled performance), in ways consistent with the above interpretation of human data.

Synergy

Why are there two separate (although interacting) levels? There need to be reasons other than mere redundancy (e.g. for the sake of fault-tolerance). The discussion earlier concludes that there is a division of labor between explicit and implicit processes. We further hypothesize that there may be a synergy between the two types of processes (partially on the basis of dissociations between the two types of processes as discussed earlier). Such a synergy may show up, under right circumstances, by speeding up learning, improving performance, and facilitating transfer of learned skills.

There is indeed some evidence in support of this hypothesis. In terms of speeding up learning, Willingham et al. (1989) found that those subjects who acquired more explicit knowledge in serial reaction time tasks appeared to learn faster. Stanley et al. (1989) reported that in a dynamic control task, subjects' learning improved if they were asked to generate verbal instructions for other subjects during learning. That is, a subject is able to speed up his/her own learning through an explication process that generates explicit knowledge. Sun et al. (2001) showed a similar effect of verbalization in a minefield navigation task. Mathews et al. (1989) showed that better performance could be attained if a proper mix of implicit and explicit learning was used.

In addition, in terms of task performance, Stanley et al. (1989) found that subjects who verbalized while performing a dynamic control task were able to attain a higher level of performance than those who did not verbalize, because the requirement that they verbalized their knowledge prompted the formation and utilization of explicit knowledge. Squire and Frambach (1990) reported that initially, amnesic and normal subjects performed comparably in a dynamic control task and equally lacked explicit knowledge. However, with more training, normals achieved better performance than amnesics and also better scores on explicit knowledge measures, which led to the conjecture that it was because normal subjects were better able to acquire explicit knowledge that they achieved better performance. Even in high-level skill acquisition, similar effects have been observed (see Sun et al. 2005 for reviews). Taken together, research suggests the importance of explicit processes for performance.[3]

We note that it has been demonstrated (Sun et al. 2001, 2005) that the theoretical model described earlier (as implemented in the cognitive architecture CLARION, which will be discussed later) can produce similar synergy effects (as well as other effects) that are discernable through verbalization or dual-tasks manipulations. See Sun et al. (2001, 2005) and Sun (2002) for further details.

---

[3] Note that synergy effects are not universal (i.e. they are task-dependent). Even so, it should be recognized that explicit processes play important cognitive functions as reviewed above. Explicit processes also serve additional functions, such as facilitating verbal communication and acting as gatekeepers (e.g. enabling conscious veto).

Some contrasting views and arguments

Implicit learning is a controversial topic. But the existence of implicit learning processes is not in question—what is in question is their extent and importance (Seger 1994; Cleeremans et al. 1998). We allow for the possibility that both types of processes and both types of knowledge coexist and interact with each other to shape learning and performance, so we go beyond the controversies that focused mostly on the minute details of implicit learning.

As discussed in the first section, some criticisms of implicit learning focused on the alleged inability to isolate processes of implicit learning (e.g. Perruchet and Pacteau 1990; Shanks and St.John 1994). Such methodological problems are not relevant to the theoretical model outlined earlier, because in that model, we recognize that both implicit and explicit learning are present and that they are likely to influence each other in a variety of ways. Criticisms of implicit learning also focused on the degree of cognitive involvement in implicit learning tasks (e.g. Shanks and St. John 1994). These criticisms are not relevant to the theoretical model either, because it makes no claim in this regard. Yet another strand of criticisms concerned the fact that implicit learning was not completely autonomous and was susceptible to the influence of explicit cues, attention, and intention to learn (e.g. Curran and Keele 1993). These findings are actually consistent with the theoretical model of two interacting systems as presented earlier (because explicit processes do affect implicit performance according to the model).

Recent psychological explorations

The two-system (two-level) theoretical model as described above has been explored in a number of empirical studies. Recent research focused on the issue of how the two systems interact—a theoretically very important question. Most prior research on implicit/explicit learning has tried to isolate a given process within a particular experimental task, under the assumption that individuals rely exclusively on one process during learning. Because of this assumption, the question of whether and how these processes interact has largely been neglected (as pointed out in Sun 2002).

Recent work explored this issue. For example, a set of studies used an artificial grammar learning task in which subjects learn multi-consonant strings (artificial 'words') that follow a set of rules (a grammar). One unique aspect of these studies is that they assessed subjects' ability to produce strings that are consistent with the grammar (rather than simply recognize them). At test, subjects attempt to generate valid strings by performing a 'fill-in-the-blank' task in which they are presented with a set of blanks with two letters present as cues. Importantly, this cued-generate test allows for assessments of accuracy and speed of production. Domangue et al. (2004) used this paradigm to attempt to create highly accurate and quickly retrieved artificial grammar knowledge by training subjects with mixtures of experience-based and model-based learning. Briefly, experience-based learning involves the acquisition of knowledge directly from exposure to exemplars while model-based learning involves acquiring grammar knowledge from explicit representations of the rules by which the exemplars are generated

The results of Domangue et al. (2004) can be summarized simply as follows: experience-based training led to fast but relatively inaccurate production, and model-based training led to slow but more accurate production. Integrated training (with both types together) led to intermediate levels of accuracy and speed. Groups who had a mixture of model- and experience-based training (interleaved) ended up showing the relatively fast but inaccurate performance associated with experience-based learning. Thus, Domangue et al.'s results demonstrated that it was difficult to obtain both fast and accurate performance in artificial grammar learning even with extensive training. In addition, model- and experience-based processing demonstrated a tradeoff between accuracy and speed, in line with the predictions of the theoretical model discussed earlier.

Sallas et al. (2007) tried to distinguish between two possible interpretations of Domangue et al.'s results. On the one hand, some theories of artificial grammar learning view it as primarily a bottom-up process in which associations between pairs of letters are acquired first (lower-level units), followed by identification of mid-level units or chunks (e.g. Perruchet and Pacteau 1990; Servan-Schreiber and Anderson 1990); and as learning continues, subjects may learn about higher-level units (such as which chunks occur together and the specific locations chunks can occupy in valid strings). This interpretation suggests that it might be possible to acquire higher-level knowledge of the grammar by extensive practice and by facilitating the acquisition of lower-level knowledge (because higher-level knowledge is 'built-up' from lower-level knowledge through experience). Thus, according to this interpretation, Domangue et al. failed to find both fast and accurate performance because training conditions failed to facilitate bottom-up processing to a sufficient degree. However, on the other hand, our theoretical model discussed earlier posits that top-down processes may also play a role: high-level grammar knowledge might be best acquired by providing an explicit representation of the grammar along with extensive exposure to exemplars (a combination of model- and experience-based learning). That is, a mixture of top-down and bottom-up processing may lead to both fast and accurate performance (depending on how it is implemented). Specifically, according to this alternative interpretation, Domangue et al. failed to find both fast and accurate performance in their integrated conditions because their training condition (i.e. copying letters from the strings into a grammar diagram) led subjects to focus on how to use the grammar diagram rather than on the implications of the knowledge contained in the grammar diagram for the construction of good exemplars. Based on this second interpretation, Sallas et al. (2007) used animation to emphasize letter-level, chunk-level, or structural-level information during training. The results revealed both fast and accurate performance, and suggest that two critical components for producing enhanced performance are: (1) using the provided explicit model to acquire experience-based knowledge rather than using it directly to generate responses and (2) receiving the explicit model-based knowledge precisely when it is needed during training. Thus, the findings were consistent with our theoretical model outlined earlier, which allows for the complex interactions between explicit and implicit processes.

A cognitive architecture with two systems of learning

Below, we will describe a detailed (but generic) computational model, that is, a 'cognitive architecture', which embodies the theoretical model of the two systems of learning (implicit and explicit) as described earlier. In the cognitive science parlance, a cognitive architecture is a generic computational model of cognition that is aimed to capture the essential processes and structures of the mind (Newell 1990, Sun 2002). This computational model has been named CLARION (Sun et al. 2001; Sun 2002; Sun et al. 2005).

An overview of CLARION

CLARION has been described and justified psychologically in Sun (2002, 2003) (see also Sun et al. 2001, 2005). Overall, CLARION is an integrative architecture, consisting of a number of distinct subsystems (with a dual-representational structure in each subsystem: implicit versus explicit representations). Its subsystems include the action-centered subsystem (the ACS), the non-action-centered subsystem (the NACS), the motivational subsystem (the MS), and the meta-cognitive subsystem (the MCS). The role of the action-centered subsystem is to control actions, regardless of whether the actions are for external physical movements or for internal mental operations. The role of the non-action-centered subsystem is to maintain general knowledge, either implicit or explicit. The role of the motivational subsystem is to provide underlying motivations for perception, action, and cognition, in terms of providing impetus and feedback. The role of the meta-cognitive subsystem is to monitor, direct, and modify the operations of the action-centered subsystem dynamically (as well as the operations of all the other subsystems).

Each of these interacting subsystems consists of two levels of representation (i.e. a dual-representational structure) as posited earlier in the theoretical model: Generally, in each subsystem, the top level encodes explicit knowledge (using symbolic/localist representations, as discussed before) and the bottom level encodes implicit knowledge (using distributed representations, as discussed before). The two levels interact, for example, by cooperating in action decision making, through a combination of the action recommendations from the two levels respectively, as well as by cooperating in learning through a bottom-up and a top-down learning process (as discussed before). See Figure 11.1.

Some details of CLARION

The Action-Centered Subsystem

First, let us look into the action-centered subsystem (the ACS) of CLARION. This is the most important part of CLARION. In the action-centered subsystem, the process for action decision making is essentially the following (Sun et al. 2001): observing the current state of the world, the two levels of processes within the ACS (implicit or explicit) make their separate decisions in accordance with their own knowledge, and their outcomes are somehow 'combined'. Thus, a final selection of an action is made and the action is then performed. The action changes the world in some way. Comparing the changed state of the world with the previous state, the agent learns (e.g. in accordance with Q-learning of Watkins 1989 in the bottom level, as mentioned earlier). The cycle then repeats itself. In this subsystem, the bottom level is implemented with neural networks involving distributed representations, and the top level is implemented using symbolic/localist representations (involving rules).

In the bottom level of the action-centered subsystem (with distributed representations), implicit reactive routines are learned: a state-action value provides an evaluation of the 'quality' of an action in a given state. The agent may choose an action in any state based on these state-action values. To acquire these values, the Q-learning algorithm (Watkins 1989) may be used, which is a reinforcement learning algorithm. It basically compares the values of successive actions and adjusts an evaluation function on that basis. It thereby develops (implicit) sequential behaviors within neural networks (Sun et al. 2001).

The bottom level of the action-centered subsystem is modular; that is, a number of small neural networks co-exist, each of which is adapted to specific modalities, tasks, or groups of input stimuli. As discussed before, this coincides with the modularity claim that much processing is done by limited, encapsulated (to some extent), specialized processors that are highly efficient (Sun, 2002).

In the top level of the action-centered subsystem, explicit conceptual knowledge is captured in the form of rules. See Sun (2003) for representational details. There are many ways in which explicit knowledge may be learned, including independent hypothesis-testing learning and 'bottom-up learning' as discussed below.

Autonomous Generation of Explicit Conceptual Structures. As discussed previously, people are generally able to learn implicit knowledge through trial and error. Further, explicit knowledge can be acquired from ongoing experience in the world, through the mediation of implicit knowledge (i.e. the idea of bottom-up learning as discussed earlier; Sun et al. 2001). The basic algorithm of bottom-up learning is as follows: if an action implicitly decided by the bottom level is successful (according to some statistical criterion), then the agent extracts an explicit rule that corresponds to the action selected by the bottom level and adds the rule to the top level. Then, in subsequent interaction with the world, the agent verifies the extracted rule by considering the outcome of applying the rule: if the outcome is not successful (according to some statistical criterion), then the rule should be made more specific and exclusive of the current case; if the outcome is successful (according to some statistical criterion), the agent may try to generalize the rule to make it more universal (see Sun et al. 2001, 2005 for technical details).

After explicit rules have been learned, a variety of explicit reasoning methods may be used. In addition, learning explicit representations at the top level can also be useful in enhancing learning of implicit reactive routines at the bottom level (see, e.g. Sun et al. 2001, 2005).

Assimilation of Externally Given Conceptual Structures. Although CLARION can learn even when no a priori or externally provided knowledge is available (through trial-and-error and bottom-up learning, or through some other means), it can make use of it when such knowledge is available. To deal with such instructed learning, externally provided knowledge can (1) be combined with existing conceptual structures at the top level (i.e. internalization), and (2) be assimilated into implicit reactive routines at the bottom level (i.e. assimilation). This process is known as top-down learning. See Sun (2003) for more details.

The Non-Action-Centered Subsystem

The non-action-centered subsystem (NACS) is for representing general knowledge about the world (i.e. the 'semantic' memory) and for performing various kinds of memory retrievals and inferences on that basis. Note that the non-action-centered subsystem is under the control of the action-centered subsystem (through its actions).

At the bottom level, 'associative memory' networks encode implicit non-action-centered knowledge. Associations are formed by mapping an input to an output. The regular backpropagation learning algorithm, for example, may be used to establish such associations between pairs of inputs and outputs (Sun 2003).

On the other hand, at the top level of the non-action-centered subsystem, a general knowledge store encodes explicit non-action-centered knowledge. In this network, chunks (i.e. concepts) are specified through dimensional values. A node is set up in the top level to represent a chunk (a concept). The chunk node connects to its corresponding features (dimensional values) represented as individual nodes in the bottom level of the non-action-centered subsystem. Additionally, links between chunks encode explicit associations between concepts, known as associative rules. Explicit associative rules may be learned in a variety of ways (Sun 2003). In addition to applying associative rules, similarity-based reasoning may be automatically carried out through the interaction of the two levels of representation (see Sun 2003).

As in the action-centered subsystem, top-down or bottom-up learning may take place in the non-action-centered subsystem, either to extract explicit knowledge in the top level from the implicit knowledge in the bottom level or to assimilate explicit knowledge of the top level into implicit knowledge in the bottom level.

The Motivational and the Meta-Cognitive Subsystem

The motivational subsystem (the MS) is concerned with drives and their interactions (Toates 1986), which lead to actions. It is concerned with *why* an agent does what it does. Simply saying that an agent chooses actions to maximize gains, rewards, or reinforcements leaves open the question of what determines these things. Dual motivational representations are in place in the motivational subsystem (based on relevant psychological evidence): the explicit goals (such as 'finding food') may be generated based on internal drive states (e.g. 'being hungry'). See Sun (2003) for details of the motivational subsystem.

Beyond low-level drives (concerning physiological needs such as hunger), there are also higher-level drives in the motivational subsystem. Some of them are primary, in the sense of being 'hard-wired' (Reiss 2004). While primary drives are built-in and relatively unalterable, there are also 'derived' drives, which are secondary, changeable, and acquired mostly in the process of satisfying primary drives.

The meta-cognitive subsystem (the MCS) is closely tied to the motivational subsystem. The meta-cognitive subsystem monitors, controls, and regulates cognitive processes for the sake of improving cognitive performance (e.g. Reder 1996; see also ch.8 by Valerie Thompson in this volume). Control and regulation can take the form of setting goals for the action-centered subsystem, setting essential parameters of the action-centered subsystem and the non-action-centered subsystem, interrupting and changing ongoing processes in the action-centered subsystem and the non-action-centered subsystem, and so on. Control and regulation can also be carried out through the setting of reinforcement functions for the action-centered subsystem. All of the above can be done on the basis of drive states and goals in the motivational subsystem (Sun 2003). The meta-cognitive subsystem is also made up of two levels: the top level (explicit) and the bottom level (implicit).

Accounting for psychological data

CLARION has been successful in simulating, accounting for, and explaining a wide variety of psychological data. For example, a number of well known skill learning tasks have been simulated using CLARION that span the spectrum ranging from simple reactive skills to complex cognitive skills. The simulated tasks include serial reaction time tasks, artificial grammar learning tasks, dynamic control tasks, categorical inference tasks, alphabetical arithmetic tasks, and the Tower of Hanoi task (Sun 2002). Among them, serial reaction time and dynamic control tasks are typical implicit learning tasks (mainly involving implicit reactive routines), while Tower of Hanoi and alphabetic arithmetic are high-level cognitive skill acquisition tasks (with significant presence of explicit processes). In addition, we have done extensive work modeling a complex and more realistic minefield navigation task, which involves complex sequential decision making (Sun et al. 2001). We have also worked on reasoning tasks, social simulation tasks, as well as meta-cognitive and motivational tasks. While accounting for various psychological data, CLARION provides explanations that shed new light on cognitive phenomena (see, e.g. Sun et al. 2005; Sun 2002; Sun and Zhang 2006).

Discussion

Implications

Let us explore the implications of the theory described thus far (both the theoretical model and the cognitive architecture). First, we explicate the relationship between the implicit/explicit distinction outlined here and the procedural/declarative distinction proposed in some other theories. In Anderson and Lebiere (1998), procedural knowledge is represented in an action-oriented way (using production rules that can only be used in one direction—from conditions to actions), and declarative knowledge in a non-action-oriented way (i.e. with knowledge chunks that can be used in any possible direction). The difference in action-orientedness seems to be the main factor in distinguishing the two types, while explicit accessibility a secondary factor. A common interpretation is that while procedural knowledge is inaccessible, declarative knowledge consists of both accessible symbolic representations and inaccessible subsymbolic representations. We believe that this view of declarative/procedural knowledge unnecessarily confounds two issues: action-orientedness and accessibility, and can be made clearer by separating the two issues. As in the theoretical model described earlier (and as in CLARION), action-orientedness does not necessarily go with inaccessibility (see, e.g. Sun et al. 2001), and non-action-orientedness does not necessarily go with accessibility either (e.g. priming and implicit memory; see, e.g. Schacter 1987). Thus, we need to posit two *separate* dimensions (procedural versus declarative and implicit versus explicit) in theorizing about cognition as in our theoretical model and CLARION. (See Carruthers, this volume, for a different view, which, nevertheless, might not be able to account for all the data and cognitive phenomena reviewed here.)

The issue of automaticity (automatic vs. controlled processes) is also relevant. The notion of automaticity has been variously associated with (1) the absence of competition for limited resources (attention) and thus the lack of performance degradation in multitask settings, (2) the absence of conscious control/intervention in processes, (3) the general inaccessibility of processes, (4) the general improvement of skilled performance (Hunt and Lansman 1986). The theoretical model (and CLARION) is certainly compatible with these characteristics. The top level can account for controlled processes (the opposite of these above properties), and the bottom level has the potential of accounting for all the aforementioned properties of automatic processes. In prior work, we have in fact separately covered these issues: the improvement of skilled performance (Sun et al. 2001, 2005), the direct inaccessibility of processes at the bottom level, including their ability of running without conscious intervention (Sun 2002), and the lack of resource competition (due to the existence of multiple bottom-level modules that can run in parallel; see Sun 2002, 2003). Thus, in the theoretical model (and in CLARION), automaticity serves as an umbrella term that describes a set of phenomena occurring in implicit processes at the bottom level.

The issue of accessibility should be of major importance to theories of cognition, considering its close relationships to various fundamental dichotomies in cognition (such as implicit vs. explicit, subconceptual vs. conceptual, procedural vs. declarative, automatic vs. controlled, and unconscious vs. conscious). In most existing theories, the difference between accessible and inaccessible representations is simply assumed, without grounding in representational *forms*. In other words, the difference is not intrinsic to representational media. For example, in ACT models (Anderson and Lebiere 1998), both declarative and procedural knowledge are represented in an explicit, symbolic form (one with semantic networks and the other with productions, along with some numerical measures). Thus the ACT models do not explain, from a representational viewpoint, the difference in accessibility between the two types of knowledge. For another instance, SOAR (Rosenbloom et al. 1993) does not separate the two types of knowledge: To account for the difference in conscious accessibility, it assumes the inaccessibility of the inner working of individual productions; thus, implicit and explicit processes are distinguished using the difference of a single production vs. multiple productions. The theoretical model we outlined (and CLARION), on the other hand, accounts for this difference based on the use of two different forms of representations: The inaccessibility of implicit knowledge is captured by (subsymbolic) distributed representations (e.g. provided by a backpropagation network; Rumelhart et al. 1986), while the accessibility of explicit knowledge is captured by symbolic/localist representations, as argued earlier (see also Sun 2002 for further justifications of this reduction). Thus, this distinction in our theory is *intrinsic* instead of *assumed*. This is a more principled way of accounting for the accessibility difference.

The implicit/explicit distinction bears a clear relationship to the study of consciousness, because this distinction involves the issue of awareness, which is the key to consciousness. The study of the implicit/explicit distinction may help us to better understand issues concerning consciousness, by identifying mechanisms and processes correlated with consciousness (Schacter 1987; Reber 1989; Sun 1997, 2002). A central thesis of the theoretical model outlined earlier is that directly accessible representation, along with explicit manipulability (on directly accessible representation), constitutes the essence of consciousness (see Sun 1997, 2002). Thus, it naturally embodies the difference between the conscious and the unconscious through the use of localist/symbolic and distributed representations in different levels of the model, and provides a plausible grounding for the notion of consciousness.

Evans (2008, this volume) distinguishes between parallel and interventionist forms of dual-processes and dual-systems theories. While our theoretical model is compatible with the parallel theories that propose a competitive interaction between implicit and explicit learning, our theoretical model (and CLARION) goes beyond competitive interactions. We propose (and have demonstrated experimentally) that direct positive and negative interactions occur between the two systems (e.g. Sallas et al. 2007; Roussel 1999). For example, explicit knowledge such as explicit rules or instructions can guide implicit learning (e.g. in top-down learning); similarly, acquired implicit knowledge may guide the generation of correct explicit rules (e.g. in bottom-up learning). We believe that understanding these positive and negative interactions is paramount.

Let us now turn to the cognitive architecture CLARION specifically. First, the CLARION cognitive architecture has implications for reasoning, because it contains a subsystem for non-action-centered knowledge (the NACS) and generates inferences with such knowledge based on both implicit and explicit processes. Dual-systems accounts of human reasoning, as embodied in CLARION, are now widely accepted (e.g. Sun 1994; Stanovich 1999; Evans 2003). CLARION has been shown to be able to simulate a great deal of human reasoning data based on the two-systems view (e.g. Sun and Zhang 2006).

In particular, Sloman (1993) presented a model of implicit feature similarity-based reasoning that was almost the same as the bottom half of the model presented in Sun (1994). The latter model was modified to become the NACS of CLARION. Therefore, CLARION has a similar capability of accounting for implicit similarity-based reasoning as Sloman (1993), in addition to accounting for explicit reasoning (Sun and Zhang 2006). Sloman's (1996) theoretical account of two reasoning systems is also quite compatible with the similar account in Sun (1994), and therefore quite compatible with CLARION (Sun 2002, 2003).

Relatedly, CLARION's account of learning is very similar to some dual-processes theories proposed in social psychology (see Smith and Collins, this volume), in that they all posit the existence of both 'associative' and rule-based learning, with similar characterizations of these two types of learning (e.g. compare Smith's chapter in this volume with Sun 1994, 2002).

The theoretical model discussed earlier and the CLARION cognitive architecture derived from it also makes connections to the dual systems of implicit versus explicit memory (e.g. Schacter 1987). In both the action-centered subsystem and the non-action-centered subsystem, two memory systems exist, one implicit and the other explicit. The CLARION cognitive architecture can thus account for many memory phenomena based on the two-systems view of memory (Sun 2003).

The CLARION cognitive architecture makes connections with research on human motivation, because of its inclusion of the motivational subsystem (the MS) in the architecture. In this regard, it supports a dual-representational framework for motivations: on the one hand, there are explicit representations of goals (as in ACT-R; Anderson and Lebiere 1998), and on the other hand, there are also less accessible forms of motivational representations (needs, desires, drives, etc.; Toates 1986). See Sun (2003) for theoretical arguments in support of such a dual-representations (dual-systems) approach towards motivations.

The CLARION cognitive architecture also makes connections with dual-processes accounts of metacognition (e.g. Reder 1996), through its inclusion of a metacognitive subsystem (the MCS) in the architecture. Although more empirical and theoretical research on this topic is needed, CLARION clearly supports a dual-processes and dual-systems account in this regard (Sun 2003).

Most importantly, CLARION shows how different subsystems (action-centered, non-action-centered, motivational, metacognitive, and so on) interact with each other, on top of the interaction of implicit and explicit processes (which is compatible with the view that there are multiple implicit and explicit systems; see Evans 2008). In this regard, it is important to provide an overarching computational framework in order to sort out detailed issues. Of course, this computational framework (cognitive architecture) itself should be subject to empirical verification, along the line of the many simulations mentioned earlier.

Comparisons

We may compare CLARION (which embodies the theoretical model of two systems of learning) with other existing computational models of learning, especially those attempting to capture implicit learning.

First, Cleeremans and McClelland (1991) simulated a serial reaction time task using a recurrent backpropagation network. The model succeeded in matching some human data. However, their success was obtained through introducing additional mechanisms for several types of priming. Their model does not deal with explicit knowledge and its role in learning in serial reaction-time tasks. One general shortcoming of this and similar connectionist models is that, mostly, these models focus only on implicit learning, and they ignore (1) the role of explicit learning in these tasks, (2) the interaction between explicit and implicit processes in learning and performing the tasks, and (3) the possibility of bottom-up learning.

Dienes and Fahey (1995) developed an instance-based model for a dynamic control task. Their model was based on acquiring successful instances from trials supplemented by a set of rules to start with. However, it is not clear how the model can account for gradual explication of implicit knowledge, for example, as reported in Stanley et al. (1989). Dienes and Fahey (1995) also examined an alternative model, which focused instead on hypothesizing and testing rules (without using instances), accomplished via competition among rules. They found that neither model fitted the data completely; while the instance model fitted better the nonsalient version of the task, the rule model fitted better the salient version of the task. This fact suggests that it may be advantageous to include both types of learning in one unified model (as in CLARION). In such a model, the effect of salience results from the interaction of the two learning processes: that is, the top level handles salient tasks well and therefore mostly rules account for the learning (as in the top level of CLARION), but the top level cannot handle nonsalient ones well and therefore instance-based processes (as in the bottom level of CLARION) account for the learning in these cases. Thus, CLARION appears to be a more complete model, and it explains the natural choice between the two types of processes.

Hunt and Lansman (1986) hypothesized a top-down learning process for explaining automatization data (which top-down learning models fitted most naturally). They incorporated two separate components in their model: a production system for capturing controlled processes, and a semantic network for capturing automatic processes. They hypothesized that, through practice, production rules were assimilated into the semantic network, thus resulting in automatic processes (through spreading activation in the semantic network). The implementation of the two types of knowledge is somewhat similar between CLARION and Hunt and Lansman's model. The production system in Hunt and Lansman's model clearly resembles the top level in CLARION, in that explicit rules are used in much the same way. Likewise, the spreading activation in the semantic network in Hunt and Lansman's model resembles the spreading activation in the bottom level of CLARION. However, the direction of learning is different across these two models. While learning in CLARION can be either bottom-up or top-down, learning in their model is only top-down. That is, the working of the production system is assimilated into the semantic network, but the opposite process is not available. This makes their model more limited than CLARION. Similar criticisms can be made of the models by Schneider and Oliver (1991) and, to some extent, Anderson and Lebiere (1998). Evidently, human learning is not exclusively top-down. Exclusively top-down approaches were contradicted by much evidence (e.g. as reviewed in Sun 2002).

Concluding remarks

In this chapter, we highlight the work that stresses the importance of both implicit and explicit learning processes and their interactions (instead of, e.g. focusing on minute details of implicit learning). Such work points to the usefulness of incorporating both explicit and implicit learning processes in a unified model (a theoretical model or a computational cognitive architecture) in theorizing about cognition in general.

In particular, CLARION is such a unified model (a unified computational cognitive architecture). It has been used to examine a variety of relevant data (including those from the implicit learning literature). The examination has generated new theoretical insights (e.g. Sun et al. 2001, 2005; Sun 2002). The main contribution of CLARION lies in capturing and explaining a range of human data in skill learning through the interaction of the two types of learning processes, in addition to capturing other human data (Sun 2002; Sun and Zhang 2006). CLARION also demonstrates the computational feasibility and psychological plausibility of bottom-up learning (in addition to top-down learning), which filled a significant theoretical gap in the literature (see Sun et al. 2001). Importantly, CLARION also shows the possibility of synergy (as well as other effects) that may result from the interaction of implicit and explicit processes (Mathews et al. 1989; Sallas et al. 2007; Sun et al. 2005).

Together with other two-systems models in existence, this work points to the importance of dual systems in various areas of cognition (including perception, skill learning, memory, reasoning, motivation, metacognition, and so on). We hope that the theories and the data reviewed herein help to shed more light on this issue.

References

Anderson, J. and Lebiere, C. (1998). *The atomic components of thought*. Lawrence Erlbaum Associates, Mahwah, NJ.

Baddeley, A. (1986) *Working memory*. Clarendon Press, Oxford.

Berry, D.C. and Broadbent, D.E. (1984) On the relationship between task performance and associated verbalizable knowledge. *Quarterly Journal of Experimental Psychology*, **36**, 209–31.

Berry, D.C. and Broadbent, D.E. (1988) Interactive tasks and the implicit-explicit distinction. *British Journal of Psychology*, **79**, 251–72.

Bowers, K., Regehr, G., Balthazard, C., and Parker, C. (1990) Intuition in the context of discovery. *Cognitive Psychology*, **22**, 72–110.

Brooks, L.R. and Vokey J.R. (1991) Abstract analogies and abstracted grammars: Comments on Reber (1989) and Mathews et al. (1989). *Journal of Experimental Psychology: General*, **120**, 316–23.

Bruner, J., Goodnow, J., and Austin, J. (1956) *A study of thinking*. Wiley, New York.

Clark, A. and Karmiloff-Smith, A. (1993) The cognizer's innards: A psychological and philosophical perspective on the development of thought. *Mind and Language*, **8**, 487–519.

Cleeremans, A. (1997) Principles for implicit learning. In D. Berry (ed.) *How implicit is implicit learning?*, 195–234. Oxford University Press, Oxford.

Cleeremans, A. and McClelland, J. (1991) Learning the structure of event sequences. *Journal of Experimental Psychology: General*, **120**, 235–53.

Cohen, A., Ivry, R., and Keele, S. (1990) Attention and structure in sequence learning. *Journal of Experimental Psychology: Learning, Memory, and Cognition*, **16**, 17–30.

Curran, T. and Keele, S. (1993) Attention and structure in dequence learning. *Journal of Experimental Psychology: Learning, Memory, and Cognition*, **19**, 189–202.

Destrebecqz, A. and Cleeremans, A. (2001) Can sequence learning be implicit? New evidence with the process dissociation procedure. *Psychonomic Bulletin and Review*, **8**, 343–50.

Dienes, Z. and Fahey, R. (1995) The role of specific instances in controlling a dynamic system. *Journal of Experimental Psychology: Learning, Memory and Cognition*, **21**, 848–62.

Domangue, T.J., Mathews, R.C., Sun, R., Roussel, L.G., and Guidry, C.E. (2004) Effects of model-based and memory-based processing on speed and accuracy of grammar string generation. *Journal of Experimental Psychology: Learning Memory, & Cognition*, **30**, 1002–11.

Dreyfus, H. and Dreyfus, S. (1987) *Mind over machine: The power of human intuition*. Free Press, New York.

Evans, J.St.B.T. (2003) In two minds: Dual-process accounts of reasoning. *Trends in Cognitive Science*, **7**, 454–8.

Evans, J.St.B.T. (2008) Dual-processing accounts of reasoning, judgment, and social cognition. *Annual Review of Psychology*, **59**, 255–78.

Fodor, J. (1983) *The modularity of mind*. MIT Press, Cambridge, MA.

Goschke, T. (1997) Implicit learning and unconscious knowledge: Mental representation, computational mechanisms, and brain structures. In K. Lamberts and D. Shanks (eds) *Knowledge, concepts and categories*, 247–333. Psychology Press, Hove.

Greenspoon, J. (1955) The reinforcing effect of two spoken sounds on the frequency of two responses. *American Journal of Psychology*, **68**, 409–16.

Hebb, D.O. (1961) Distinctive features of learning in the higher animal. In J. F. Delafresnaye (ed.) *Brain mechanisms and learning*, 37–46. Blackwell, Oxford.

Heidegger, M. (1927) *Being and time.* English transl. Harper and Row, New York.

Hunt, E. and Lansman, M. (1986) Unified model of attention and problem solving. *Psychological Review*, **93**, 446–61.

Karmiloff-Smith, A. (1986) From meta-processes to conscious access: evidence from children's metalinguistic and repair data. *Cognition*, **23**, 95–147.

Lane, S.M. and Schooler, J.S. (2004) Skimming the surface: The verbal overshadowing of analogical retrieval. *Psychological Science*, **15**, 715–19.

Lane, S.M., Mathews, R.C., Sallas, B., Prattini, R., and Sun, R.(2008). Facilitating interactions of model and experience-based processes: Implications for type and flexibility of representation. *Memory & Cognition*, **36**, 157–69.

Lee, Y.S. (1995) Effects of learning contexts on implicit and explicit learning. *Memory & Cognition*, **23**, 723–44.

Lewicki, P. (1986) Processing information about covariations that cannot be articulated. *Journal of Experimental Psychology: Learning, Memory, and Cognition*, **12**, 135–46.

Lieberman, M.D. (2000) Intuition: A social cognitive neuroscience approach. *Psychological Bulletin*, **126**, 109–37.

Mathews, R.C. (1997) Is research painting a biased picture of implicit learning? The dangers of methodological purity in scientific debate. *Psychonomic Bulletin & Review*, **4**, 38–42.

Mathews, R.C., Buss, R., Stanley, W., Blanchard-Fields, F., Cho, J., and Druhan, B. (1989) Role of implicit and explicit processes in learning from examples: a synergistic effect. *Journal of Experimental Psychology: Learning,Memory and Cognition*, **15**, 1083–100.

Mishkin, M., Malamut, B., and Bachevalier, J. (1984) Memories and habits: Two neural systems. In G. Lynch, J.L. McGaugh, and N.M. Weinberger (eds), *Neurobiology of learning and memory*, 65–77. Guilford Press, New York.

Moscovitch, M. and Umilta, C. (1991) Conscious and nonconscious aspects of memory. In R.G. Lister and H.J. Weingartner (eds), *Perspectives on cognitive neuroscience*, 229–66. Oxford University Press, New York.

Newell, A. (1990) *Unified theories of cognition.* Harvard University Press, Cambridge, MA.

Perruchet, P. and Pacteau, C. (1990) Synthetic grammar learning: implicit rule abstraction or explicit fragmentary knowledge? *Journal of Experimental Psychology: General*, **119**, 264–75.

Reber, A.S. (1976) Implicit learning of synthetic languages: The role of instructional set. *Journal of Experimental Psychology: Human Learning and Memory*, **2**, 88–94.

Reber, A. (1989) Implicit learning and tacit knowledge. *Journal of Experimental Psychology: General*, **118**, 219–35.

Reber, A. (1993) *Implicit learning and tacit knowledge: An essay on the cognitive unconscious.* Clarendon Press, Oxford.

Reder, L. (ed.) (1996) *Implicit memory and metacognition.* Erlbaum, Mahwah, NJ.

Reiss, S. (2004) Multifaceted nature of intrinsic motivation: The theory of 16 basic desires. *Review of General Psychology*, **8**, 179–93.

Rosenbloom, P., Laird, J. and Newell, A., (1993) *The SOAR papers: Research on integrated intelligence.* MIT Press, Cambridge, MA.

Roussel, L. (1999) *Facilitating knowledge integration and flexibility: The effects of reflection and exposure to alternative models.* Unpublished doctoral dissertation. Louisiana State University.

Rumelhart, D., McClelland, J., and the PDP Research Group. (1986) *Parallel distributed processing: Explorations in the microstructures of cognition.* MIT Press: Cambridge, MA.

Sallas, B., Mathews, R.C., Lane, S.M., and Sun, R. (2007) Developing rich and quickly accessed knowledge of an artificial grammar. *Memory & Cognition*, **35**, 2118–33.

Schacter, D. (1987) Implicit memory: History and current status. *Journal of Experimental Psychology: Learning, Memory, and Cognition*, **13**, 501–18.

Schacter, D. (1990) Toward a cognitive neuropsychology of awareness: Implicit knowledge and anosognosia. *Journal of Clinical and Experimental Neuropsychology*, **12**, 155–78.

Schneider, W. and Oliver, W. (1991) An instructable connectionist/control architecture. In K. VanLehn (ed.) *Architectures for intelligence*, 113–45. Erlbaum, Hillsdale, NJ.

Schooler, J., Ohlsson, S., and Brooks, K. (1993) Thoughts beyond words: When language over-shadows insight. *Journal of Experimental Psychology: General*, **122**, 166–83.

Seger, C. (1994) Implicit learning. *Psychological Bulletin*, **115**, 163–96.

Servan-Schreiber, E. and Anderson, J.R. (1990) Learning artificial grammars with competitive chunking. *Journal of Experimental Psychology: Learning, Memory, & Cognition*, **16**, 592–608.

Shallice, T. (1972) Dual functions of consciousness. *Psychological Review*, **79**, 383–93.

Shanks, D.R. (2005) Implicit learning. In K. Lamberts and R.L. Goldstone (eds) *Handbook of cognition*, 202–20. Sage Publications, London.

Shanks, D. and St. John, M. (1994) Characteristics of dissociable learning systems. *Behavioral and Brain Sciences*, **17**, 367–94.

Sloman, S. (1993) Feature based induction. *Cognitive Psychology*, **25**, 231–80.

Sloman, S. (1996) The empirical case for two systems of reasoning. *Psychological Bulletin*, **119**, 3–22.

Smolensky, P. (1988) On the proper treatment of connectionism. *Behavioral and Brain Sciences*, **11**, 1–74.

Squire, L. and Frambach, M. (1990) Cognitive skill learning in amnesia. *Psychobiology*, **18**, 109–17.

Stanley, W., Mathews, R., Buss, R., and Kotler-Cope, S. (1989) Insight without awareness: On the interaction of verbalization, instruction and practice in a simulated process control task. *Quarterly Journal of Experimental Psychology*, **41**, 553–77.

Stanovich, K. (1999) *Who is rational?: Studies of individual differences in reasoning*. Lawrence Erlbaum Associates Publishers, Mahwah, NJ.

Sun, R. (1994) *Integrating rules and connectionism for robust common-sense reasoning*. John Wiley and Sons, New York.

Sun, R. (1997) Learning, action, and consciousness: A hybrid approach towards modeling consciousness. *Neural Networks* (special issue on consciousness), **10**, 1317–31.

Sun, R. (2002) *Duality of the mind*. Lawrence Erlbaum Associates, Mahwah, NJ.

Sun, R. (2003) *A tutorial on CLARION*. Technical report, Cognitive Science Department, Rensselaer Polytechnic Institute, http://www.cogsci.rpi.edu/~rsun/sun.tutorial.pdf.

Sun, R. and Zhang, X. (2006) Accounting for a variety of reasoning data within a cognitive architecture. *Journal of Experimental and Theoretical Artificial Intelligence*, **18**, 69–191.

Sun, R., Merrill, E., and Peterson, T. (2001) From implicit skills to explicit knowledge: A bottom-up model of skill learning. *Cognitive Science*, **25**, 203–44.

Sun, R., Slusarz, P., and Terry, C. (2005) The interaction of the explicit and the implicit in skill learning: A dual-process approach. *Psychological Review*, **112**, 59–192.

Toates, F. (1986) *Motivational systems*. Cambridge University Press, Cambridge.

Watkins, C. (1989) *Learning with delayed rewards*. Ph.D Thesis, Cambridge University, Cambridge.

Willingham, D., Nissen, M., and Bullemer, P. (1989) On the development of procedural knowledge. *Journal of Experimental Psychology: Learning, Memory, and Cognition*, **15**, 1047–60.

Part 3

Applications

Chapter 12

Cognitive and social cognitive development: Dual-process research and theory

Paul A. Klaczynski

The scant attention cognitive and social psychologists pay to developmental research is both confusing and disconcerting. For far too long, it has long appeared as though theorists believe that research involving 18-year-old college students is sufficient to understand the myriad intricacies and variations of thought. I note here but four of the many reasons for considering more seriously developmental findings and using these to construct more encompassing theories of cognition and social cognition than currently exist.

First, the past decade has witnessed an increase in attempts to integrate dual-process theories with evolutionary approaches to cognition (Evans 2008; Toates 2004). Because the age at which different evolved psychological processes express themselves varies, development may be a particularly fertile testing ground for dual-process theories and, in particular, the widespread assumption that various domain-specific implicit processing systems emerge (phylogenetically) prior to an explicit, higher-order processing system. Second, dual-process theorists assume that implicit and explicit processing systems are generally independent. Research has yet to address such issues as, if both types of processing are present at birth, do they become increasing independent with age? If we are born with only implicit processing systems, how does an explicit system emerge and does it originate in one or more implicit processing systems (see Karmiloff-smith 1992)? Third, cognitive neuroscientists have identified distinct areas of the brain associated with implicit and explicit processing. Claims that these areas do, in fact, underlie different processing systems would be strengthened if, for example, the maturation of these areas (e.g. prefrontal cortex) paralleled age changes in different processing systems.

Finally, insights into the reasoning of purportedly mature thinkers can be gained by examining the antecedents of adults' response failures on 'heuristics and biases' tasks. Although many of the biases observed in adults have been explored in children, this research has been referenced infrequently in the adult literature. Perhaps one reason for neglecting developmental research is the implicit assumption that, if adults perform poorly on reasoning and decision making tasks, children's performance must be even worse. It may therefore come as a surprise that children sometimes make *better* decisions and *less* biased judgments, and thus may (sometimes) be more rational, than adults.

In this chapter, I describe some of these counterintuitive age trends, present a developmental dual-process theory that affords a more parsimonious interpretation of these trends than offered by traditional theories of development, and survey a research program intended to test developmental predictions derived from dual-process theories. I begin by outlining evidence that contravenes traditional, unidirectional theories of development and then present an amended version of the developmental dual-process theory I have advocated in recent years. Next, I present research that has upheld several dual-process predictions, challenges black-and-white conceptions of rationality, and supports the 'levels of rationality' approach advocated by Reyna and her colleagues (Reyna and Farley 2006; Reyna et al. 2003). I conclude by discussing briefly some theoretical and methodological shortcomings of developmental dual-process theories.

Through most of this chapter, I refer to two forms of processing, 'experiential' (Epstein 1994) and 'analytic' (Evans 1989) processing. In part, I use the experiential/analytic distinction because it better reflects what the two systems do and how they operate than implicit/explicit distinctions, the System 1/System 2 distinction (Stanovich 1999), or other distinctions made in cognitive and social psychology (see Evans 2008). In addition, neither 'implicit processing' nor 'System 1 processing' refers to a single processing system. Rather, it is now clear that there exist multiple types (implicit memory, associative learning, etc.) of managing input and output preconsciously (Evans 2008, this volume; Stanovich, this volume). In the term 'experiential processing', my intent (usually) is to implicate *acquired* automatically-activated heuristics, biases, and beliefs. Thus, my focus is on the automatic operation and development of a particular system, with the caveats that (a) humans are likely biologically predisposed to acquire some systems more rapidly than others (Hejmadi et al. 2004), (a) there are multiple implicit systems (Stanovich 2004, this volume), (c) information is likely fed into the experiential system through an explicit, analytic processing system *and* from other implicit processing systems (e.g. associative learning, perceptual processing), and (d) to varying degrees, experiential output affects other processing systems.

In part because explicit cognition has been the almost exclusive focus of post-infancy research, development is often construed as a unidirectional process, proceeding from relatively immature cognition to relatively mature cognition. However, satisfactory accounts of intellectual growth must explain observations that within-child variability is the norm in cognitive and social cognitive development and inverse relationships between age and performance on various logic and judgment problems. Traditional, unidirectional theories cannot explain counterintuitive age trends on various cognitive and social cognitive tasks or, more specifically, indications of two developmental trends on superficially different, but logically-isomorphic, tasks. Whereas most evidence indicates age increases in normative responses, age is also associated with increases in non-normative responses and violations of formal rules of inference. Neither the coexistence of these age trends nor the fact that these trends are generally statistically independent has found an adequate explanation in conceptualizations of development that focus on explicit cognition.

A developmental dual-process theory

Dual-process theorists have argued that information processing involves simultaneous operations in both experiential and analytic processing. Motivations, beliefs, intellectual dispositions, task features, and situational characteristics (e.g. time constraints) collude to determine which system is *predominant* at a particular moment. When analytic processing predominates, adult thinking often (but not necessarily; see Evans 2008) involves attempts to decontextualize structure from potentially misleading contents and base subsequent inferences, judgments, and decisions on the resultant representation. This computationally burdensome processing more often results in normative responses than when the faster and more cognitively-economical experiential system predominates. However, considerable care should be exercised to avoid equating normative responses with analytic predominance and non-normative responses with experiential predominance (see Evans, this volume; Evans and Over 1996; Klaczynski 2001a; Stanovich, this volume). This precautionary note is particularly important in reviewing developmental research. For instance, developmental differences in non-normative responses may arise from age differences in reliance on experiential processing and/or because younger children have not acquired the same analytic competencies as older children.

Because it likely evolved before the analytic system and expends few cognitive resources, experiential processing predominates most everyday cognitive activity (Evans 2006; Stanovich 1999; see also Reyna and Brainerd 1995). Experiential processing facilitates information mapping onto and assimilation into existing knowledge categories and the conversion of conscious strategies into automatic procedures. Experience predominance automatically cues contextualized task representations which, in turn, activate heuristics and other memories (e.g. procedural, vivid episodic memories) that can serve as the basis for inferences and judgments. The heuristics and other memories activated in the course of experiential processing are acquired through both implicit and explicit processing of experiences; the gist abstracted from experiences often forms serves as the basis for the development of explicit, relatively algorithmic strategies and heuristics. With age, as memories accrue and as conscious strategies are transformed into automatic procedures, repertoires of heuristics become more diverse and more easily activated.

This simple formulation may appear to imply adults rely on heuristics more than children; this is *not*, however, the case. Instead, when experiential processing is predominant, adults' judgments and decisions should reflect more variability in the types of heuristics they use. Although the availability of an increasingly diverse repertoire of heuristics is almost certainly one of the reasons that adults *sometimes* rely more heavily on heuristics than children, access to and activation of this repertoire must be distinguished from its utilization. Thus, an important characteristic of development is an increase in the numbers and types of environments that automatically *activate* heuristics and other procedural memories. However, as discussed subsequently, activation is a necessary but not sufficient condition for utilization.

Developments in experiential processing are accompanied by developments in the analytic processing system. The analytic processing system comprises the consciously-controlled, effortful thinking that enable activation of competencies traditionally considered essential to cognitive development and normative decision making. Unlike experiential processing, analytic processing involves deliberative analysis of task requirements and, under some conditions, the context in which the task is embedded. The representations arising from this reflective processing are then used to draw conclusions, judgments, decisions, and arguments. Unlike experiential processing, analytic processing *may* involve decoupling structure from content, although contexualized representations involving, for instance, coordinating of task requirements with pragmatic considerations, may also be subjected to conscious deliberations. Indeed, as Buchtel and Norenzayan (this volume; also Luria 1976) discuss, the decontextualization of logical structure from context may be a peculiarly Western emphasis, given that adults in Eastern societies rely more on holistic, contextualized representations. Such broad culture differences lead to interesting questions about the development, culture, and representation nexus; for example, early in the development of analytic thought, are children across cultures more similar in their dispositions toward contextualization/decontextualization than later in development, after exposure to different beliefs systems and forms of socialization?

Analytic competencies, such as inductive and deductive reasoning abilities and the metacognitive and executive abilities required for decontextualization and for determining whether decontextualized or contextualized representations are more appropriate in a given situation, do not develop in an all-or-none fashion. Rather, different abilities are acquired at different points in development and at different rates for different children, varying as a function of experiences, culture, biological maturation, and genetic endowments. Regardless, after these abilities have been acquired, their use of often highly effortful, particularly in the early phases of acquisition. Given that, in many everyday circumstances, humans gravitate toward cognitively— and physically—economical strategies, developments in analytic competencies must be accompanied by developments in tendencies to consciously utilize these competences. In other words, the 'mere' acquisition of the *abilities* to inhibit memory-based interference, reflect on one's reasoning, evaluate the quality of decision options, etc., guarantees neither that adolescents and adults *perform* at higher levels than children nor that relatively mature reasoners will opt for the utilization of those competencies they possess. For the latter of occur, developments at the intentional level of analysis are critical (see Stanovich and West 1998, 2000; Stanovich 1999, this volume); specifically, competence development must also include the acquisition of *dispositions* to be cognitive engaged, control impulsive actions, and determine whether to rely on contextualized or decontextualized representations.

Thus, development is marked by, but is not limited to, the acquisition of stereotypes, biases, and heuristics, increases in processing speed and working memory capacity, progressions in computational and reflective thinking abilities, metacognitive skills, and thinking dispositions. Heuristics are used not only because they are 'fast and frugal' (Gigerenzer 1996), intuitive appealing, and activated automatically, but also because they are often harmless and sometimes beneficial. Heuristics can be extremely useful, as is often the case with experts (Reyna and Farley 2006) or disadvantageous, to the self and/or the larger community. Reasoners often have a fleeting awareness that heuristics and other biasing tendencies have been activated, often in the form of the intuitions or 'gut' feelings that they are 'right' (for discussion of 'feelings of rightness' and how these feelings relate metacognition, see Thompson, this volume). In other words, although activation is automatic, at least some heuristics are momentarily available in working memory. This availability affords reasoners the opportunity to reflect on the value of a heuristic, decide upon its use, and, if it is judged inadequate, instead utilize an analytically-derived strategy—a process referred to as 'metacognitive intercession' (Klaczynski 2005; Klaczynski and Cottrell 2004). Even during adulthood, most people do not engage in this type of conscious reflection. However, the occurrence of such reflective analyses illustrates a basic tenet of dual-process theories: When the experiential system is predominant, the analytic system is active, but subordinate.

Interceding in experiential processing likely requires advanced metacognitive abilities and dispositions (Stanovich 1999) and is therefore achieved more effectively by adolescents and adults than children. Most adolescents and adults are not disposed to metacognitively intercede, although individual differences in intercession tendencies do exist (Klaczynski and Fauth 1997). Unfortunately, the distinction between metacognitive competencies and metacognitive dispositions is often blurred. The former involve the abilities to: Reflect on how one knows, evaluate the accuracy of one's knowledge, monitor reasoning for consistency and quality, and plan/select situationally-appropriate strategies. Dispositions are motivational in nature, and reflect beliefs in the value of engaging in effortful analysis. Thus, for instance, among adolescents with nearly identical metacognitive abilities, and who are therefore equally able to inhibit experientially-activated representations and the responses these representations cues, there generally exist large individual differences in the dispositions that motivate metacognitive intercession (Klaczynski 2005).

Empirical support for developmental dual-process theories

With the exception of fuzzy-trace theorists (see Reyna and Brainerd 1995), developmental psychology has lagged behind other areas of psychology (e.g. social, cognitive, clinical) not only in examining predictions based on dual/multiple-process theories but also in refining theoretical descriptions of different processing systems and how these systems change over time. However, a variety of research has been conducted on age trends in memory, judgments and decisions, reasoning, motivated reasoning, stereotypes, and magical thinking. On the one hand, none of this research, examined individually, establishes definitively either the existence or development of two (or more) operating systems. On the other hand, as a whole, an impressive evidential corpus provides compelling reasons for adopting, and further developing, a comprehensive dual-process theory of development.

Memory

Like adults, children sometimes remember information without conscious awareness that they are remembering: Presented incomplete items early in an experiment, children later identify the complete items more quickly and accurately than non-primed items—despite being unaware that they had previously examined the primed items (Hayes and Hennessy 1996; see also Bargh and Chartland 1999). Other evidence similarly suggests that implicit and explicit memory cannot be explained by the same operating system. Newcombe (Lie and Newcombe 1999; Newcombe and Fox 1994), for example, found that few 9–10 year olds accurately recognized preschool classmates. Skin conductance reactivity, used to index implicit memory, was greater for actual classmates than false classmates. In parallel with research on normative and non-normative responses to judgment and reasoning tasks, explicit recognition was unrelated to implicit memory. This independence, findings of few or no age increases in the implicit memory, data linking implicit and explicit memory to different brain systems (Ullman 2004), and clear age increases in the explicit memory (Schneider and Bjorklund 1998) are best explained by dual-process theories. Fuzzy-trace theorists in particular have compiled an impressive set of data, utilizing a variety of methodological paradigms and examining numerous aspects of memory (e.g. the memory-reasoning dissociation, eyewitness memory), that can apparently only be explained by assuming that development occurs in two independent systems.

According to fuzzy-trace theory (Brainerd and Reyna 2001; Reyna and Brainerd 1995), parallel processing allows experiences to be encoded at multiple levels and memories are encoded as both verbatim and gist traces. Verbatim traces of details represent experiences which, in turn, are more likely than gist traces to be governed by conscious attempts to encode and remember. Gist traces are holistic abstractions, imprecise representations of the meaning of experiences, which can serve as prototypes for general categories of events, people, or objects (Reyna and Farley 2006). Development is characterized by increased reliance on gist representations. This verbatim-gist shift has a clear adaptive value: compared with verbatim traces, gist traces are less susceptible to interference and forgetting, are more cognitively economical and, in part because they are less cognitively burdensome, lend themselves more easily to higher-order cognitive operations (Reyna and Brainerd 1995).

A critical finding from fuzzy-trace research is that verbatim memory and reasoning are sometimes independent. This finding contravenes the common assumptions that (a) memory is primarily reconstructive and, therefore, that reasoning is the primary source of memory and (b) memory is necessary for reasoning. For instance, Brainerd and Kingma (1985) showed that memory for premise information on numerous tasks (e.g. transitive inference, class inclusion) and reasoning on those tasks were independent. Thus, verbatim memory for quantitative information does not predict transitive inferences (A > B; B > C; therefore, A > C) or inclusion errors; thus, from four dogs, five horses, and 11 cows, verbatim memory for each category is unrelated to the faulty inference that cows outnumber animals. Such inclusion errors ($p[A_1] > p[A_{1-n}]$) are structurally similar to the conjunction fallacy ($p[AB] > p[A]$) in adult decision making (Reyna 1991). In each case, the probability of a subcategory is inferred to be greater than the probability of the more inclusive category.

Consistent with other dual-process theories, in fuzzy-trace theory, such evidence has been taken to indicate that operations on task structures depend on representations dissociated from the processes responsible for encoding surface-level information. As a result of this dissociation, reasoning becomes increasingly dependent on gist abstraction (similar to, but not identical with, decontextualization) and operates independently from verbatim memory. Together with research described earlier, the independent operations of reasoning and verbatim memory necessitate conceptualizations of development that emphasize parallel processing at the conscious and preconscious levels and different developmental trajectories for inferences that arise from conscious, deep processing and those that arise from preconscious processing.

Decision making

Two general trends have been evident in developmental research on decision making. A first focus has been on the construction of measures of competent decision making and the relationship of scores on these assessments to adolescent judgments of risk (e.g. Parker and Fischhoff 2005). A second trend has focused on the roles of experience and social factors (e.g. peers) on adolescents' decisions and risk assessments and the correlations of these judgments to measures of psychosocial maturity (e.g. self-reported impulse control) and intellectual ability (see Steinberg 2004). These trends have in common the assumptions that adaptive decisions are made explicitly and maladaptive decisions are made with little conscious reflection. In assuming that explicit processes (e.g. deliberate calibration of risks against base rates) are the principle means of making adaptive decisions, the possibility that experiential processing sometimes results in better decisions and risk assessments than analytic processing has not been addressed.

As an example, adolescents often believe that they are less vulnerable to risks than their peers; these invulnerability perceptions increase from adolescence into early adulthood. Even so, adolescents typically overestimate the base rates of deleterious consequences of such behaviors as smoking, drunk driving, and unprotected sex (Millstein and Halpern-Felsher 2002). One explanation for risk overestimation assumes age increases in exposure to messages regarding consequences and 'knowledge' (real and assumed) of peers who experienced these consequences (see Jacobs et al. 1995). This knowledge, preserved as gist, may lead to age increases in reliance on availability. Availability, as opposed to risk calculation based on actual base rates, may trigger 'feelings of wrongness' and thus may serve the adaptive function of inhibiting impulses to engage in risky behaviors.

Similar counterintuitive age trends in judgments and decisions have been reported on various heuristics and biases tasks. For instance, Jacobs and Potenza (1991) found that reliance on statistical evidence on asocial decision tasks (e.g. about bicycles) increased from first grade through adulthood. On logically-isomorphic social problems (e.g. about cheerleaders), the opposite trend was observed: With increasing age, children relied more on the 'representativeness heuristic' and less on statistical evidence. Davidson (1995) similarly reported that, when task contents activated stereotypes of the elderly, older children committed the conjunction fallacy more than younger children—a finding also attributed to increased reliance on representativeness. Developmental increases have also been reported for framing effects (Reyna and Ellis 1994), ignoring denominators on ratio problems (Brainerd 1981), and nonlogical 'transitive' inferences (e.g. 'A is a friend of B. B is a friend of C. Therefore, A and C are friends'; Markovits and Dumas 1999).

The developmental picture is not as simple as these findings suggest, however, primarily because not all decision making research has revealed age increases in biases and heuristic use. Klaczynski (2001a) presented adolescents problems derived from the heuristics and biases literature, including deontic and abstract versions of Wason's (1966) selection task, and problems involving conjunctive reasoning, covariation detection, statistical reasoning, the gambler's fallacy, outcome bias, and hindsight bias. On most problems, middle adolescents gave more normative responses than early adolescents (note, however, that children were not included in Klaczynski's research). Nonetheless, the majority of responses at both ages deviated from traditional prescriptions for normative judgments and decisions. For example, older adolescents were guilty of hindsight bias, committed the conjunction and gambler's fallacies, ignored denominators on covariation problems, and based judgments on personal testimonies instead of more reliable statistical evidence. Many adolescents also gave responses were contradictory on the same problems. For instance, judgments that arguments based on small evidential samples were superior to arguments based on larger samples were accompanied by judgments that for claims based on the former type of arguments were *less intelligent* than the claims based on the latter type of argument.

In contrast to the findings of Stanovich and West (1998), normative responses were not always related to general intellectual ability. For example, statistical judgments and covariation judgments were associated with ability, but outcome biases and hindsight biases were not. Nonetheless, a principle components analyses revealed two interpretable factors, easily interpretable within a dual-process framework. The analytic factor comprised deductive reasoning, covariation judgments, statistical reasoning, and the metacognitive abilities to assess the accuracy of judgments. The experiential factor comprised various non-normative biases (e.g. outcome bias, hindsight bias, the conjunction fallacy). Whereas the analytic factor related positively to age and ability, the experiential factor related negatively to age and was unrelated to ability ($r = 03$).

Stanovich and West (2000) argued that ability is related to performance on heuristics and biases tasks primarily when the experiential and analytic systems are in conflict or 'pull' for different solutions. However, solutions to problems that loaded on the experiential factor in Klaczynski (2001a) were not related to ability, even though the two systems should have pulled for different solutions. Thus, applying the Stanovich and West argument to these problems is difficult. Instead, it could be argued that the variables that loaded on the experiential factor did so because the 'pull' or intuitive appeal of biased and heuristically-based responses was so strong on these problems that cues to engage in analytic processing were overwhelmed, even among high ability adolescents. For example, 'statistical reasoning conflict' occurred when participants relied on vivid personal testimony to make judgments, but then rated simultaneously presented statistical evidence as more intelligent.

Although not related to ability, conflicting judgments and other variables that loaded on the experiential factor decreased with age. Age is not therefore a mere proxy for the abilities measured on intelligence tests. Rather, 'something more' is indexed by age; more precisely, I have argued that age declines in experientially-based responses are not entirely dependent on improvements in basic intellectual abilities, but instead result from developmental progressions in the metacognitive abilities and dispositions associated with inhibiting such responses and deliberating alternatives (Klaczynski 2005). These reflective abilities and dispositions are not utilized often, however, possibly because heuristics and other biased responses are sometimes so appealing that no subjective need for intercession arises (see also Thompson, this volume).

Other investigations illustrate more directly the role of developments in intercession skills. Klaczynski (2001b) presented early adolescents, middle adolescents, and adults a set of tasks involving sunk costs, ratio bias, and counterfactual thinking. As in research by Epstein and his colleagues (e.g. Epstein et al. 1992), half the participants in Klaczynski (2001b) were instructed to respond to the problems as they would normally. In a 'logical instructions' condition, participants were told to adopt the perspective of a 'perfectly logical person'.

Sunk cost decisions involve choices between continued pursuit of actions in which investments have been made, but that were not leading to the intended outcomes (e.g. watching a bad movie for which a non-fundable ticket has been purchased), or taking actions more likely to achieve a desired goal (e.g. leaving the movie and having coffee with a friend). Such problems create a dilemma because, to choose the more rewarding action, prior investments must be forsaken (i.e. 'throwing money down the toilet' versus 'water under the bridge'). The sunk cost fallacy is the decision to 'honor' sunk costs to avoid loss of the investments—a tendency attributed to a 'waste not' heuristic (see Arkes and Ayton 1999).

The ratio bias problems required a choice between two logically identical lotteries (e.g. one winner in 10 tickets versus 10 winners in 100 tickets) or the normative judgment that the options were equally desirable. Finally, the counterfactual thinking problems used were selected because, in adults, they often elicit the 'if only' fallacy. The IO fallacy occurs when behaviors are judged more negatively when it *appears* that a negative consequence could have been easily anticipated, and therefore avoided, in one of two logically identical, equally unpredictable situations. For example:

> When parking his new car in a half-empty parking lot, Tom's wife asked him to park in a spot close to where she wanted to shop. Instead, he parked in a spot closer to where he wanted to shop. When he backed out after shopping, the car behind him backed out at the same time, and both cars sustained about $1000 worth of damage. Robert parked his car in the same parking lot when there was only one parking place available. When he backed out after shopping, the car behind him backed out at the same time, and both cars sustained about $1000 worth of damage (adapted from Epstein et al. 1992).

In neither case did the involved party have control over the accident. Yet spontaneously-activated contextualized representations (e.g. Tom had control, Robert had no control) may activate heuristics that link control to fault (i.e. similar to the 'fundamental attribution error'— overestimating the role of dispositional factors when assessing another's actions). Tom's accident appeared avoidable ('if only he had heeded his wife'); Robert's decision, and the resultant accident, arose from uncontrollable circumstances. Despite the fact that both Tom and Robert were equally responsible/accountable for the accidents, adults typically attribute more foolish behavior to Tom (Denes-Raj and Epstein 1994; Epstein et al. 1992).

In both experiential conditions and across tasks, normative judgments were infrequent. More importantly, on each of the three tasks, normative responses increased with age and were more frequent in the 'logical thinking' than in the 'usual thinking' condition. The frequency of non-normative responses in both frames suggests that experiential processing was predominant, although this predominance was clearly stronger in the 'usual' condition. The effects of the logic instructions suggest, however, that participant attempted to increase the extent to which they engaged in analytic processing. Successful shifts toward increased analytic processing required adolescents to inhibit the 'prepotent' response to a problem, evaluate the quality/appropriateness of the prepotent (heuristic) response against this representation, and consider alternative solutions. Despite these shift (or attempted shifts), performance remained poor. At least in the cases of the ratio and sunk cost problems, this poor performance cannot be attributed to lack of analytic competencies because children are capable of comparing ratios (Krietler and Krietler 1986) and, after training, both children and adolescents understand why sunk costs should be avoided and apply this understanding to novel problems (Klaczynski and Cottrell 2004). Poor performance more likely resulted because participants had trouble decontextualizing the task, perhaps because the logic instructions were weak (e.g. relative to the training given in Klaczynski and Cottrell 2004), participants believed that they were, in fact, responding logically in the 'usual' condition (for evidence supporting this explanation, see Amsel et al. in press) and/or because the heuristics activated by the tasks were too appealing for participants to dismiss easily.

The latter explanation has received preliminary support. In the study similar to Klaczynski and Cottrell (2004), Klaczynski (2007a, Study 1) found age increases in a 'make an exception' heuristic. Specifically, 8, 11, and 14-year-olds (and a comparison sample of adults) were presented two types of problems, each of which involved decisions that could have established negative precedents. In these problems, scenarios contained information about publicly-established rules, a specific rule infraction, and the circumstances surrounding the rule infraction. The circumstances of the infractions either appeared extenuating or fell clearly under the rule. To illustrate a 'no-mitigating circumstance' problem (adapted from Baron et al. 1993):

> Mr. Miller, the coach of the basketball team, says that every person on the team has to go to all of the team's practices if they want to play in the games. If a person misses a practice, then he will not be allowed to play in the next game. Bill is the best player on the team. He missed three practices in a row, just because he wanted to watch TV instead. Bill is *so* good that the team will probably win if he gets to play, but the team will probably lose if Bill doesn't get to play. Now, it's the day before the game. What should Mr. Miller do?

In the absence of mitigating conditions, failure to enforce the rule establishes a negative precedent for future violations. In the example, if the rule is not enforced, the rule may lose its moral force and open the door for Bill and his teammates to legitimately question rule enforcement in the future (see Moshman 1998). When positive precedents are established by enforcing rules, future violations should be deterred; hence, the normative decision in the example is to enforce the rule.

Under some conditions, however, rules can be violated without establishing negative precedents. If, for instance, the conditions surrounding a violation were not anticipated when the rule was created, then the question of whether the violation establishes a negative precedent is more ambiguous (e.g. Bill missed practice because he was doing charity work).

The results shed light on an aspect of decision making (i.e. age trends in precedent decisions) previously investigated only by Baron et al. (1993). Specifically, when problems involved mitigating circumstances, adolescents and adults were more likely than children to advocate rule enforcement. However, in the absence of mitigating conditions, age and the non-normative, 'make an exception' decision was inversely related—suggesting the possibility that, in the absence of strong cues to think analytically, development is marked by an increase in the 'feelings of correctness' (Thompson, this volume) that accompany automatically-activated heuristics. These findings provide yet another demonstration of that, under certain conditions, reliance on heuristics and other cognitively-economical judgment and decision strategies increases with age. At the same time, the findings indicate age increases in cognitive flexibility. That is, whereas adolescents and adults integrated rule understanding with contextual considerations, children's decisions involved more rigid rule adherence. Developments in adolescents' abilities to coordinate social contextual considerations with apparently context-independent rules argues for a developmental progression that parallels, both conceptually and in terms of at ages at which advances are seen, progressions in the metacognitive skills involved in coordinating beliefs and evidence (see Kuhn 2001).

This progression in the ability to integrate considerations of contextual conditions with abstract rules, further supports an earlier point: under some conditions, reliance on contextualized representations, or partially contextualized representations, leads to more adaptive decisions than reliance on decontextualized representations (Buchtel and Norenzayan, this volume). The conflicting age trends found in this research also imply, however, that the challenges involved in overcoming reliance on automatically-cued contextualized representations and avoiding the overgeneralization of the heuristics such representations activate to situations of dubitable relevance become *under certain conditions* more difficult to meet with increasing age. Unfortunately, this issue is one with which theorists and practitioners interested in testing and improving critical thinking and decision making has not yet grappled (see Stanovich, this volume).

Several conclusions can be drawn from developmental research on judgments, risk, and decisions. First, and perhaps foremost, future research needs to utilize more precise methodologies that allow for the disambiguation of biased, fallacious, heuristic, and other non-normative responses from experiential processing predominance. There is a similar clear need to use methods that allow researchers to determine when normative responses are based on experiential processing predominance and when the same responses result from analytic predominance. Second, if, for the present, we assume that the non-normative responses children, adolescents, and adults typically give when first presented decision and judgment tasks cue contextualized representations and experientially-based responses, then extant evidence indicates that instructions can induce experiential→analytic processing shifts. Although Klaczynski (2001b) showed that very simple instructions can lead to such processing shifts, even among early adolescents, these results should not be taken to imply that experiential→analytic shifts can always be so easily accomplished. This point is supported by the fact that, even after instructions, most participants continued responding in non-normative ways, evidence that shifts from experiential to analytic predominance are often short-lived, and findings that, under some instructional conditions, adults and adolescents can be induced not only to make more non-normative decisions than children, but also to believe that these are superior to simultaneously available normative responses. For instance, after exposure to arguments for non-normative precedent setting decisions, adolescents and adults are more likely than children to change from initially normative responses to non-normative, 'make an exception' decisions, even when circumstances surrounding rule violations clearly do not justify allowing rule infractions (Klaczynski 2007a, Study 2). Third, across the studies reviewed here, it is clear that development is not characterized by a shift from experiential to analytic processing predominance—a conclusion supported by repeated findings that adults do not typically rely on analytic processing. Indeed, the case can be made that increased variability is a fundamental characteristic of development (Jacobs and Klaczynski 2002; Klaczynski 2004). Finally, I have made repeated reference to age-related increases in non-normative responding. Because evidence for such increases can be found in numerous domains and across quite disparate methodological paradigms, they cannot be regarded as atypical or as methodological artifacts. Rather, to the extent that non-normative responses are reflective of experiential processing predominance and are indeed less than optimal responses, the data indicate that development is far more complex than is typically assumed. Development occurs in two or, more likely, multiple processing systems; this observations does not, however, mean that age-related changes in any given phenomena— whether decision making, reasoning, memory, or other forms of cognition and social cognition—can be mapped directly onto changes in the underlying systems or the relative predominance of those systems.

Reasoning

Recent developmental research on conditional reasoning (i.e. reasoning about if p, then q premises) has focused on four logical forms—*modus ponens* (MP), *modus tollens* (MT), the *affirmation of the consequent* (AC), and the *denial of the antecedent* (DA). In standard logic, the correct conclusion to MP is that q is true; for MT, the correct conclusion is that p is not true. Because their conclusions are logically necessary and can be drawn with certainty, MP and MT are determinate logical forms. AC and DA are indeterminate forms because no conclusions can be drawn with certainty.

On problems involving MP and MT, 4–5-year-old children often make logically correct inferences (Harris and Nunez 1996; Chao and Cheng 2000). Under certain conditions,

6 and 7-year-olds draw indeterminate conclusions on AC and DA problems (Markovits and Barrouillet 2002). Interpretations of young children's apparent precocity are quite varied, ranging from conclusions that young children possess reasoning capabilities that are fundamentally similar to those of adults to the more cautious interpretation that children's inferences are not based on decontextualized analyses, but instead are reliant on manipulations that facilitate automatic inferences based on pragmatic rule interpretations (Moshman 1998). Nonetheless, such findings appear in different methodological paradigms, including not only children's valid indeterminate inferences on simple reasoning problems, but also judgments of indeterminacy on more complex scientific reasoning problems (Ruffman et al. 1993; Sodian et al. 1991). Extant data thus appear to provide an accurate picture of children's capacities for valid inferences, although these capacities are likely evinced only under rather narrow conditions.

Other research indicates that neither young children's inferences, nor developmental improvements in conditional inferences, are dependent on problem familiarity: Performance is sometimes better on familiarity problems and sometimes worse when problems are more familiar (Janveau-Brennan and Markovits 1999; Klaczynski and Narasimham 1998a). Instead, my colleagues and I have argued that these, and other findings that appear to indicate that children are as (or more) competent reasoners as adults, are best explained from a dual-process perspective (e.g. Daniel and Klaczynski 2006). In most of our research, and that of Markovits and his colleagues (for review, see Markovits and Barrouillet 2002), participants are instructed only to respond based on the information provided in the problem. Because such task instructions are vague, problems can be represented either as intended by the experimenter or as everyday problems on which they are free to use their intuitions (Evans 2002). When not presented explicit instructions to think logically, at least in part because it is cognitively-economical, adults frequently rely on experiential processing and natural language interpretations.

When theorists are more concerned with the mechanisms responsible for performance variability than with determining logical competence, and the ages at which different logical competencies are acquired, examining responses to 'weak' instructions can provide provocative answers concerning development and individual differences in development. Specifically, the inferences 'invited' by natural language or 'pragmatic' interpretations of conditionals sometimes differ from logical inferences. Under a natural language interpretation, the AC premise (q is true) leads to the invited inference (p is therefore true). The invited inference for DA problems (p is not true) is also determinate (q is not true). By contrast, the logical inferences and the invited inferences for MP and MT problems are the same. Consider the conditional, 'If a person eats too much, then she will gain weight' and the MP premise, 'Alice ate too much' and the question, 'Did Alice gain weight?' Both the logical response and the invited response are 'yes'. For AC, 'Alice gained weight', the natural language interpretation leads to the logically fallacious inference, 'Alice ate too much'. Thus, natural language interpretations invite determinate inferences for all four logical forms; logical interpretations should lead to indeterminate responses for AC and DA and determinate responses for MP and MT. Because the invited and logical inferences are the same for

MP and MT and because experiential processing is more cognitively economical than analytic processing, then—regardless of age—the experiential processing should predominate on these forms.

In addition to instructions, an important determinant of whether a conditional is represented logically or pragmatically is the availability of alternative antecedents to a conditional's consequent (Janveau-Brennan and Markovits 1999; Markovits and Barrouillet 2002). Adolescents and adults typically make the natural language interpretations if few alternative antecedents are associated with a consequent. If conditionals have at least one strongly associated alternative antecedent, logical interpretations are more probable. Although adolescents have superior reasoning abilities and more ready access to alternative antecedents, they are also more familiar with natural language interpretations than children. Thus, when conditionals do not readily activate alternative antecedents, pragmatic interpretations are more probable, experiential processing likely predominates, and the chances of age increases in fallacies, such as AC and DA, increases.

Several predictions follow from these conjectures. First, on MP and MT problems, children and adults should make determinate (and logically correct) inferences; age increases should be minimal. On AC and DA problems with strongly associated alternative antecedents, adolescents should make more indeterminate inferences than children. Second, when consequents are weakly associated with alternative antecedents, adolescents should make *fewer* indeterminate inferences on AC and DA problems. Third, correlations between the two determinate forms and the two indeterminate forms should differ for children and adolescents. Specifically, if experiential processing is predominant in children, then determinate inferences should correlate positively across the four forms. For adolescents, if experiential processing is predominant for MP and MT and analytic processing predominates on AC and DA problems (especially problems with few alternative antecedents), AC and DA inferences should be statistically independent from MP and MT inferences.

To test of hypotheses, Klaczynski and Narasimham (1998a) presented 10, 14, and 17-year-olds Wason's (1966) selection task, open-ended syllogisms, and forced-choice conditionals. Across tasks, modest age increases were found for MP and MT. Logically correct inferences increased with age on problems with strongly associated alternative antecedents—problems that were also relatively *less* familiar. By contrast, the AC and DA *fallacies* increased with age on problems with few alternative antecedents and *more* familiar to participants. For instance, on such problems as, 'If a person exercises a lot, then she will be in good shape. Joan is in good shape. Does Joan exercise a lot?' adolescents affirmed the antecedent more often than children and did so more often than on less familiar conditionals (e.g. 'If a person has a healthy diet, the she will be in good shape'). In a similar study involving somewhat younger participants (8, 10, 12, and 14-year-olds), we examined patterns of correlations among inferences on conditionals with strongly and weakly associated alternative antecedents (Klaczynski et al. 2004). Across ages, MP and MT were positively related, as were AC and DA. Critically, whereas determinate responses across all four forms were related positively prior to adolescence, responses on the determinate and indeterminate forms were independent in adolescents and adults.

Although the combined data from these investigations imply that, on MP and MT problems, experiential processing predominated the thinking of both children and adolescents, the findings also point to different conditions under which age-related experiential⟷analytic shifts occur. Age-related shifts from predominantly experiential to predominantly analytic processing are evident and age declines in fallacious inferences are found, for instance, when instructions clearly emphasize the need for logical analyses (Daniel and Klaczynski 2006). Under different conditions (e.g. relatively vague instructions for conditionals with few alternative antecedents), age-related shifts from analytic to experiential processing occur (see Janveau-Brennan and Markovits 1999; Klaczynski and Narasimham 1998a). As for judgments, risk assessments, and decision making, available evidence argues against characterizations of the development of reasoning as involving a general shift from experiential→analytic processing shift.

Belief-motivated reasoning and stereotyping

A similar conclusion can be drawn from developmental research on belief-motivated reasoning and stereotyping. In belief-motivated reasoning, individuals reason about evidence relevant to their beliefs in ways that preserve and perpetuate those beliefs, typically by accepting evidence that supports their beliefs and rejecting evidence that contravenes their beliefs. Belief-biased reasoning is particularly interesting because these reasoning biases (a) illustrate shifts between analytic and experiential processing, (b) suggest the mechanisms that underlie the resilience of beliefs to change, and (c) demonstrate individual differences in analytic/experiential processing predominance and in the abilities/dispositions to override experiential predominance.

My students and I (e.g. Klaczynski and Gordon 1996a, 1996b; Klaczynski and Lavallee 2005; Klaczynski and Narasimham 1998b) have studied how children process logically flawed arguments and scientific evidence (e.g. based on unrepresentative samples, hasty causal inferences, methodologically flawed 'scientific' investigations etc.). The arguments/evidence children are presented leads to conclusions to support, contravene, or has no bearing on strongly-held beliefs (e.g. religion, career goals, social classes, gender). Like adults, children and adolescents scrutinize belief-threatening evidence more carefully than belief-neutral or belief-supportive evidence. Specifically, the evidence is processed analytically, higher-order scientific and statistical reasoning skills are activated, and logical structure is decontextualized from superficial contents. Such processing allows for detection of flaws in the evidence and, as a consequent, the evidence is rejected. When evidence supports beliefs, experiential processing is typically predominant. Evidence is processed at a relatively cursory level and representations are contextualized, triggered by content and based on automatically-activated memories. Justifications for evidence acceptance derive from personal experiences, category exemplars, stereotypes, and simple assertions. Results from several studies (Klaczynski 2000; Klaczynski and Gordon 1996a; Klaczynski and Narasimham 1998a) indicate that reasoning on belief-neutral problems is no more sophisticated than reasoning on supportive problems; reasoning with both belief-supportive and belief-neutral evidence is less complex than reasoning with belief-threatening evidence problems. Such findings support the dual-process hypotheses that people (both children and adults) typically reason experientially and shift to analytic processing only when motivated by evidence that threatens their beliefs.

A somewhat surprising finding from this research is that the extent to which children, adolescents, and adults vacillate between experiential processing on supportive and neutral problems and analytic processing on belief-threatening problems is very similar. In other words, although the amount of experiential processing interference in reasoning varies little with age, the heuristics and higher-order reasoning abilities used to justify evidence ratings are age-related (see Klaczynski 2000; Klaczynski and Fauth 1997). Nonetheless, the extent to which the responding is biased by beliefs is *not* related to age. Across the childhood and into the adult lifespan (Klaczynski and Robinson 2000) and seemingly without conscious awareness, reasoning fluctuates between higher-order reasoning (e.g. when evidence threatens beliefs) and cursory 'reasoning' apparently based on automatically-activated heuristics (e.g. when evidence supports beliefs). That fact that mature adults are no less biased, and are sometimes more biased, than children and adolescents, suggests either that the metamonitoring abilities required to track the course of reasoning for consistency do not develop as fully as unbiased reasoning requires or these metacognitive skills do indeed develop, but consistency may not have been an important intellectual value. Extant evidence supports both possibilities.

Examinations of the effects of extrinsic accuracy motivation on belief-biased reasoning support the first explanation (Klaczynski and Gordon 1996b; Klaczynski and Narasimham 1998b). Adolescents were told that if they gave thoughtless or inaccurate responses, they would have to justify their responses in front of an audience of authorities. Relative to control conditions, the accuracy instructions had a considerable effect: Because reasoning across all problems (i.e. belief-threatening, neutral, and supportive) was more complex (i.e. justification scores increased, rating scores decreased), we argued that the instructions led to increased analytic processing. However, the extent to which reasoning was biased was *not* affected by the instructions. Even though reasoning improved, differences in the quality of reasoning on threatening and supportive problems were as large in the accuracy conditions as in the control conditions. Thus, we further argued that participants could not consciously control *this type* of bias in their reasoning. That is, the improvements in reasoning complexity observed in the accuracy conditions indicates conscious efforts to reason more 'objectively' than in the control conditions. Not only did these efforts fail to reduce biases, but that failure extended across levels of intellectual ability. Note that these studies contrast with Klaczynski's (2001b, 2007a; Klaczynski and Cottrell 2004) studies of decision making, which showed that arguments, and subtle cues to think logically, significantly diminish the interfering effects of experiential processing on analytic processing.

Nonetheless, in each of the aforementioned studies, some participants were *not* biased (for discussion, see Stanovich and West 2000; Stanovich 1999). In most research, intellectual capacity has explained virtually no variance in biases (Kardash and Scholes 1996; Klaczynski 1997, 2000; Klaczynski and Gordon 1996a, 1996b; Klaczynski and Lavallee 2005). Thus, traditional measures of intelligence either do not index the skills required to monitor reasoning for consistency or the thinking dispositions that activate these skills. However, Stanovich and West (1997, 2006) have shown that intellectual capacity *does* predict reasoning biases when participants are instructed to think logically. Such findings are in distinct contrast to our findings with accuracy motivation. A plausible explanation for this difference is that the lack of significant correlations in the research of my colleagues and I may have arisen because the within-subjects design cues responses in line with experimenter expectations (Stanovich and West 2007; Toplak and Stanovich 2003). If this were the case, then *higher* ability individuals, adults and older adolescents—those best able to guess the experiment's intent—should be *more* biased than those with less intellectual capacity and children.

An alternative possibility is that individual differences in belief-motivated reasoning have their origins in the thinking dispositions that index inclinations to metacognitive intercede (Klaczynski 2000; Klaczynski and Lavallee 2005; see also Kardash and Scholes 1996). Consistent with the findings of Stanovich and West (1997, 1998), these dispositions accounted for significant variance in reasoning biases. The dispositional level, rather than level of cognitive capacity, appears to be the locus of individual differences in reasoning biases (for an alternative view, and for discussions of levels of analyses in cognitive psychology and, specifically, the algorithmic and epistemic levels, see Stanovich 1999, 2004, this volume). At least in certain methodological paradigms, dispositions to 'be metacognitive' better predict reasoning biases general intelligence. Whereas research on accuracy motivation is highly suggestive of the difficulties children and adults have in consciously controlling belief-related, automatically-cued interference, findings of individual differences in biases at the epistemic level of analysis suggest that the capacity to control such interference can be learned. Despite calls from interventionists and critical thinking theorists, research dedicated to the development of metacognitive dispositions, and the relationship of developments in these dispositions to various metacognitive and executive function abilities, has been minimal (for discussions, see Hofer and Pintrich 2002; Kuhn et al. 2000).

Belief-motivated reasoning is a basic, and sometimes adaptive, feature of mature cognition. However, its close ties to unrealistic optimism, stereotype maintenance, belief polarization hint at the limits of this adaptive value in technologically-advanced societies (Klaczynski 2000; Klaczynski and Fauth 1996). Developmental research on stereotyping has most often involved examinations of age trends in gender, racial, and more recently, obesity stereotypes, and predictors of these stereotypes (e.g. masculinity, femininity; causal beliefs). Given the centrality of stereotyping to social and developmental psychology, and its relevance to both dual-process theoretic issues and applied issues in education (e.g. critical thinking interventions), it is unfortunate that researchers have been far less concerned with the links between stereotypes and reasoning or methodological innovations that could afford testing dual-process hypotheses. More relevant to issues surrounding dual-process theories, and issues raised in this chapter, is research linking belief-biased reasoning, stereotypes, development, and rationality.

An illustration of the concept of 'degrees of rationality', as discussed by Reyna and her colleagues (2003; Reyna and Farley 2006), is provided by Klaczynski and Aneja (2002). In each of a series of vignettes, 7, 9, and 11-year-old children were presented large samples of boys (or girls) *and* small samples of boys (or girls) engaged in a prosocial, gender-neutral activity, and were asked to indicate the generalizability the behaviors of the children in two samples. Consistent with previous research on gender stereotypes, children generalized more from same-gender scenarios than from other-gender scenarios. Of greatest interest was the finding that, at all three ages, the magnitude of my-gender biases was constrained by sample size. Specifically, on large sample problems, children generalized more from the same-gender than to the other-gender samples; the same was found on small sample problems. However, children generalized more from large samples of the *other*-gender than from *small* my-gender samples. Thus, 7–11-year-old children were rational *to an extent*: generalizations were more extensive from large than from small samples, even when the large evidential samples described the other-gender positively. *Within* sample sizes, however, even the oldest children generalized more from same-gender than from other-gender problems. This demonstration of degrees of rationality is illustrated in Figure 12.1.

The age decline in reasoning biases and gender stereotyping reported by Klaczynski and Aneja (2002) cannot be assumed to reflect either a domain-general or domain-specific developmental trajectory. Although considerable research indicates that gender biases decline during certain age periods (Ruble and Martin 2002), such declines are less apparent in areas less subject to socialization pressures for unbiased self-presentation. As an example, consider obesity.

Obesity stereotypes are present as early as 3 years of age and become stronger during early childhood (Cramer and Steinwert 1998; Musher-Eizenman et al. 2004).

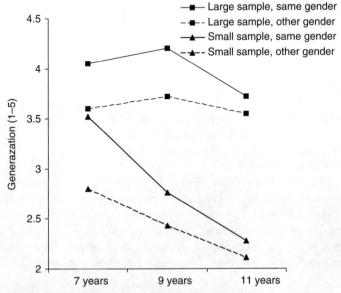

Fig. 12.1 Levels of rationality? Age and sample size effects of same- and other-gender generalizations (adapted from Klaczynski and Aneja 2002).

During later childhood and into adolescence, age increases in 'thin idealization' (Smolak et al. 2001), pressures to be physically attractive, attention to members of the other-sex, and exposure to jokes about the obese, led us to predict that the magnitude of obesity stereotypes would increase further during adolescence.

Recently, Klaczynski and Daniel (in press) presented children and adolescents brief descriptions of obese and average-weight targets. Subsequently to reading each vignette, participants made generalizations to other individuals who 'looked like' the target and completed a personality checklist. Consistent with expectations, anti-obesity biases—differences between average weight generalizations and stereotypes and obese generalizations and stereotypes—increased with age. Importantly, the observed increases in biases could not be explained by variables that, according to most prominent theories of obesity stereotypes, should have mediated the age-obesity bias association (e.g. thin idealization beliefs, beliefs that obesity is caused by characterological flaws, body esteem).

These findings, in combination with research illustrating the early emergence of obesity stereotypes and findings that behavioral avoidance of the obese does not diminish even when explicit stereotypes and attributions change (e.g. from beliefs that obese is caused by within-individual variables, such as laziness, to beliefs that obesity results primarily from uncontrollable physical variables, such as genetic dispositions to metabolize food slowly), indicate that neither obesity stereotypes nor the stigma associated with obesity can be adequately explained by current theories (e.g. attribution theory, social identity theory). Instead, age increases in obesity stereotyping, like age increases in other types and forms of heuristics (e.g. representativeness, 'make an exception') and biases, can be explained by age increases in the strength of an experientially-activated 'thin is in' heuristic. However, increased reliance on such heuristics cannot entirely explain behavioral reactions to obesity—unless activation of these biasing heuristics is also associated with the preconscious belief that 'obesity is contagious'. This explanation, elaborated further in the next section, again argues against black-and-white conceptions of rationality and for the notion that rationality is best conceptualized in terms of levels.

Magical thinking

Traditional theories of magical thinking (e.g. Piagetian, neo-Piagetian) assume that magical thinking declines with age. Support for this claim is available in studies of animism, wherein older children are less likely to attribute human-like qualities to animals and representations (e.g. stuffed toys) of animals. However, despite decreases in beliefs in such characters as Santa Claus, the Easter Bunny, and the Tooth Fairy, most cultures sanction certain magical beliefs (e.g. religious practices). For example, Catholics receive communion, the 'body of Christ' embodied in a wafer. There is little doubt that superstitious beliefs, beliefs that cannot reliably be supported be evidence or logic, are commonplace. Critical questions, are: Do children have magical beliefs beyond those sanctioned by their cultures and do these coexist with (relatively) rational beliefs? How do such beliefs change with age? To the extent that these beliefs persist, what mechanisms underlie their maintenance?

Subbotsky (2000a, p.39) answered the first question in the affirmative, 'phenomenalistic thinking and scientific understanding … coexist throughout the life span'. In a provocative demonstration, children were presented the Muller-Lyer illusion. Not surprisingly, most children claimed that a >—< ruler was longer than a ↔ ruler. Children compared the rulers and determined that they were actually equally long. Next, children were told they could have an interesting stamp, placed just beyond their reach, if they could retrieve it without leaving their seats. Although most children selected the dovetailed ruler, none could provide a rational reason for selecting it.

Both children and adults reject magic at the verbal, conscious level, and yet 'accept' magic in their actions (Subbotsky 2000a, 2000b). For instance, after casting a spell and placing an object in a cleverly designed box, participants open the box and found that the object was badly damaged. When no spell was cast, nothing happened to the object. After then placing a valuable object of their own in the box, neither children nor adults were willing to let the experimenter cast the spell—all the while denying that the spell made a difference.

That adults are susceptible to and affected by implicit magical beliefs has also received support in the work of Rozin and colleagues. For instance, adults will wear washed clothes previously worn by others, but not washed clothes previously worn by AIDS victims. In the latter case, this refusal is accompanied by explicit acknowledgment that AIDS can be contracted only through intimate contact (Rozin et al. 1992). Even preschoolers have a limited understanding of contamination and contagion (Hejmadi et al. 2004; Inagaki and Hatano 2006; Siegal 1988), although young children are prone to overgeneralizing.

Evidence that 5–6 year-old children have a limited understanding of how illnesses are contracted and transmitted, led Klaczynski (2008) to a novel hypothesis regarding the avoidance children exhibit toward the obese. Recall that attribution theory explains neither children's avoidance of obese peers nor developmental increases in stereotypes obesity and generalization biases. Medical evidence indicates that obese individuals display many symptoms similar to those of contagious illnesses. For instance, compared to those of average weight, the obese have more difficulty exerting themselves, more labored breathing, sweat more profusely, fatigue more easily, are more likely to have facial and abdominal discolorations, suffer from more joint pain, and generally are more susceptible to illnesses. Given these similarities to true illnesses, for otherwise naïve children, there may be some adaptive value to avoiding obese children, particularly when the obese children are unfamiliar. Thus, a degree of caution toward and the stigmatization of the obese have a degree of rationality.

By the 'laws of sympathetic contagion' (Nemeroff and Rozin 2000; Rozin and Nemeroff 2002), people avoid contact with people or objects associated with the stigmatized, implicitly believing that contact may lead to the contraction of one of more of the properties associated with the stigma. Untouchables in Indian culture provide one example; the unwillingness of adults to wear clothing previously worn by AIDS victims is another example. Together with the speculations that (a) children recognize some of the basic symptoms of contagious illnesses and (b) obese persons exhibit many of these same symptoms and, therefore, are stigmatized (in this view, stigmas develop *prior* to stereotypes), this information led to the following hypothesis.

Both American children and Chinese children, who are less familiar with obesity, would react more negatively to an object (in this case, a beverage) associated with an obese child than the same object associated with an average weight children. Further, this negativity would (a) increase with age, as children become more exposed to negative depictions of obesity, and (b) be more prominent when children were primed to the ingestion→illness→contagion association than when primed only to ingestion→illness.

Seven and 10-year-old Chinese and American children tasted small samples of identically-flavored drinks, presented by an experimenter purported to represent a company that was testing a new drink. This hypothetical company used children to help make the drink; children's pictures, as a reward for their help, were placed on the labels of the bottles for the drinks they 'created'. Pictures varied by 'creator' gender, ethnicity, and weight (obese, average). After hearing one of two priming stories, children sampled each drink and rated it along several dimensions.

Across cultures and priming conditions, 'obese-created' drinks tasted worse and were more likely to result in illness than 'average-created' drinks. In the illness→contagion condition, the difference between taste ratings for obese-created drinks and average-created drink increased with age (see Figure 12.2). This bias increased with age among Caucasian, but not Chinese, children. Three days later, children were asked to remember the worst tasting drink. Verbatim memory for this drink's creator was poor. However, consistent with fuzzy-trace theory, gist memory—memory for the general category to which the drink creators belonged—was far superior when creators were obese children. Finally, participants more often created the false memory that a child in the priming stories was an obese creator than an average creator.

The effects of obese labels on children's drink preferences, in combination with priming effects and the gist and false memory data, expand research on magical thinking to social contagion and establish a link to memory. That the findings were generally consistent across cultures—one of which, China, has relatively few obese

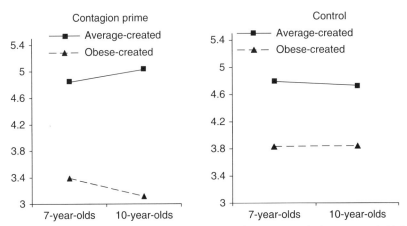

Fig. 12.2 Age and priming effects on taste ratings of average- and obese-created drinks (adapted from Klaczynski 2008).

children, does not publicly endorse negative characterizations of the obese, and does not constantly shower children with depictions of the 'thin ideal' (at least in the rural areas and small cities)—makes difficult an explanation that does not involve experiential processing. Specifically, unless the 'obese creators' left some negative essence on the drinks and unless an implicit belief in this essence existed, then children's reactions should not have differed for these drinks and average-created drinks. That these processes occurred at an implicit level is reinforced by the finding that this effect was stronger when children were primed to the notion that ingestion-related illnesses can be contagious. Of equal importance: to the extent that children's reactions to the obese were founded on perceived similarities with contagious illnesses, their responses were rational … to a degree.

Conclusions and recommendations

Several conclusions follow from the evidence presented in this chapter. First, development cannot be explained without recourse to dual-process theories. These theories have led to and been supported by research in several developmental domains: Memory, decision making, reasoning, motivated reasoning, stereotyping, and magical thinking. Second, development cannot be characterized by an 'all or nothing' shift from predominantly experiential to predominantly analytic processing (or vice versa). Third, dual-process theories currently in vogue can be integrated into a more encompassing developmental theory. However, fuzzy-trace theory distinguishes itself other dual-process models in its focuses on levels of rationality and intuition as advanced reasoning (Reyna and Farley 2006). Fuzzy-trace theory also emphasizes two types of 'quick and easy' thinking: One is similar to experiential processing as discussed here; the second is a form of higher-order reasoning based on gist. These differences do not make fuzzy-trace theory incompatible with the analytic-experiential theory outlined here. Research on gender stereotyping and children's reactions to drinks created by obese children illustrates the utility of viewing responses in terms of degrees of rationality. Similarly, the two forms of rapid reasoning and decision making identified by fuzzy-trace theories are both experiential in nature, but differ in their probabilities of leading to adaptive responses.

To conclude, recent research supports dual-process theories as replacements for unidirectional theories. Despite recent theoretical and empirical advances, dual-process researchers need to establish the conditions under which counterintuitive age trends are to be expected (Klaczynski and Daniel in press) and establish *developmental* criteria for distinguishing between experientially- and analytically-produced responses. The latter issue is particularly important because non-normative responses given by children may well reflect analytic processing errors. Achieving these ends requires careful inspection of the methodologies used to assess age-related change and, subsequently, employing methodologies that afford greater precision. As Thompson (this volume) and Klaczynski (2001a) argue, non-normative responses may be produced experientially or analytically; the same is true of normative responses. For instance, when young children produce correct conditional inferences, current methodologies do not allow conclusions regarding experiential or analytic processing competence. Among other possibilities, new methodologies should attempt to determine the neural and physiological bases of analytic and experiential processes and how these change with age, assess speed of processing to better establish which systems are predominant during different tasks and under different conditions, and increase the use of priming and training techniques.

The range of issues with which developmental dual-process theorists must grapple is extensive, particularly because researchers must consider age changes in the nature and manifestation of different processes. Consider Thompson's (this volume) argument that 'feelings of rightness' often accompany experientially-based output. Determining the ontogeny of such feelings is critical for better understanding developments in decision making and reasoning. However, methodological problems loom large. Familiarity with retrieval cues and fluency of processing, hypothesized determinants of feelings of rightness, increase with age. Increases in the perception that material is easier to process are associated with increases in familiarity and decreases in task difficulty. Because neither perception is necessarily accurate, older children may sometimes spend less time processing material than younger children, not simply because they have superior analytic abilities, but also because they perceive tasks as relatively easy. Age increases in non-normative responding may therefore sometimes arise because of misleading perceptions of task difficulty, misleading 'correctness' feelings, misattributions concerning ability to perform a task (e.g. triggered by ease of processing), and overconfidence (e.g. triggered by feelings of familiarity and rightness). Feelings of rightness may also cue a type of analytic responding not discussed in this chapter: the construction of justifications/rationalizations for an erroneous responses which, in turn, serve to increase response confidence.

Thus, even when the requisite analytic competencies have been acquired, metacognitive intercession by no means guarantees normative responding and, in some cases, may 'backfire'. Further, the application of analyses, such as Thompson's, to developmental phenomena presents numerous methodological challenges. For example, the validity of age comparisons depends on designing instructions and tasks that have equivalent meaning across ages. As task complexity increases, the difficulty of establishing age equivalence increases. The existence of such challenges in no way diminishes the importance of studying age changes in intuitions, the responses that intuitions may trigger, and children's confidence in these responses. Instead, great care must be taken to study development, particularly if our goal is to understand development in multiple processing systems and the mechanisms that afford interactions among these systems.

Acknowledgments

For their comments on earlier versions of this chapter, I am indebted to Eric Peterson, Eric Amsel, Henry Markovits, Keith Frankish, and Jonathan Evans.

References

Arkes, H.R. and Ayton, P. (1999) The sunk cost and Concorde effects: Are humans less rational than lower animals? *Psychological Bulletin*, **125**, 591–600.

Bargh, J.A. and Chartland, T.L. (1999) The unbearable automaticity of being. *American Psychologist*, **54**, 462–79.

Baron, J., Granato, L., Spranca, M., and Teubal, E. (1993) Decision-making biases in children and early adolescence: Exploratory studies. *Merrill-Palmer Quarterly*, **39**, 22–46.

Brainerd, C.J. (1981). Working memory and the developmental analysis of probability judgment. *Psychological Review*, **88**, 463–502.

Brainerd, C.J., and Kingma, J. (1985). On the independence of short-term memory and working memory in cognitive development. *Cognitive Psychology*, **17**, 210–47.

Brainerd, C.J. and Reyna, V.A. (2001) Fuzzy-trace theory: Dual processes in memory, reasoning, and cognitive neuroscience. In H.W. Reese and R. Kail (eds.) *Advances in children development and behavior,* Vol. 28, 41–100. Academic Press, San Diego, CA.

Chao, S-J. and Cheng, P.W. (2000) The emergence of inferential rules: The use of pragmatic reasoning schemas by preschoolers. *Cognitive Development*, **15**, 39–62.

Cramer, P. and Steinwert, T. (1998) Thin is good, fat is bad: How early does it begin. *Journal of Applied Developmental Psychology*, **19**, 429–51.

Daniel, D.B. and Klaczynski, P.A. (2006) Developmental and individual differences in conditional reasoning: Effects of logic instructions and alternative antecedents. *Child Development*, **77**, 339–54.

Davidson, D. (1995). The representativeness heuristic and the conjunction fallacy in children's decision making. *Merrill-Palmer Quarterly*, **41**, 328–46.

Denes-Raj, V. and Epstein, S. (1994) Conflict between intuitive and rational processing: When people behave against their better judgment. *Journal of Personality and Social Psychology*, **66**, 819–29.

Epstein, S. (1994) Integration of the cognitive and psychodynamic unconscious. *American Psychologist*, **49**, 709–24.

Epstein, S., Lipson, A., Holstein, C., and Huh, E. (1992) Irrational reactions to negative outcomes: Evidence for two conceptual systems. *Journal of Personality and Social Psychology*, **62**, 328–39.

Evans, J.B.St.T. (1989) *Bias in human reasoning: Causes and consequences.* Erlbaum, Brighton.

Evans, J.B.St.T. (2002) Logic and human reasoning: An assessment of the deduction paradigm. *Psychological Bulletin*, **128**, 978–96.

Evans, J.B.St.T. (2006) The heuristic-analytic theory of reasoning: Extension and evaluation. *Psychonomic Bulletin & Review*, **13**, 378–95.

Evans, J.B.St.T. (2008) Dual-process accounts of reasoning, judgment, and social cognition. *Annual Review of Psychology*, **59**, 255–78.

Evans, J.B.St.T. and Over, D.E. (1996) *Reasoning and Rationality*. Psychology Press, Hove.

Gigerenzer, G. (1996) On narrow norms and vague heuristics: A reply to Kahneman and Tversky. *Psychological Review*, **103**, 592–6.

Harris, P.L. and Nunez, M. (1996) Understanding of permission rules by preschool children. *Child Development*, **67**, 1572–91.

Hayes, B.K. and Hennessy, R. (1996) The nature and development of nonverbal implicit memory. *Journal of Experimental Child Psychology*, **63**, 22–43.

Hejmadi, A., Rozin. P., and Siegal, M. (2004) Once in contact, always in contact: Contagious essence and conceptions of purification in American and Hindu Indian Children. *Developmental Psychology*, **40**, 467–76.

Hofer, B.K. and Pintrich, P.R. (eds) (2002) *Personal epistemology: The psychology of beliefs about knowledge and knowing.* Erlbaum, Mahwah, NJ.

Inagaki, K. and Hatano, G. (2006) Young children's conception of the biological world. *Current Directions in Psychological Science*, **15**, 177–81.

Jacobs, J.E. and Klaczynski, P.A. (2002) The development of decision making during childhood and adolescence. *Current Directions in Psychological Science*, **4**, 145–9.

Jacobs, J.E. and Potenza, M. (1991) The use of judgment heuristics to make social and object decisions: A developmental perspective. *Child Development*, **62**, 166–78.

Jacobs, J.E., Greenwald, J.P., and Osgood, D.W. (1995) Developmental differences in baserate estimates of social behaviors and attitudes. *Social Development*, **4**, 165–81.

Janveau-Brennen, G. and Markovits, H. (1999) The development of reasoning with causal conditionals. *Developmental Psychology*, **35**, 904–11.

Kalish, C.W. (2002) Essentialist to some degree: Beliefs about the structure of natural kind categories. *Memory & Cognition*, **30**, 340–52.

Kardash, C.M. and Scholes, R.J. (1996) Effects of pre-existing beliefs, epistemological beliefs, and need for cognition on interpretation of controversial issues. *Journal of Educational Psychology*, **88**, 260–71.

Karmiloff-Smith, A. (1992) Beyond modularity: A developmental perspective on cognitive science. MIT Press, Cambridge, MA.

Klaczynski, P.A. (1997) Bias in adolescents' everyday reasoning and its relationship with intellectual ability, personal theories, and self-serving motivation. *Developmental Psychology*, **33**, 273–83.

Klaczynski, P.A. (2000) Motivated scientific reasoning biases, epistemological beliefs, and theory polarization: A two-process approach to adolescent cognition. *Child Development*, **71**, 1347–66.

Klaczynski, P.A. (2001a) Analytic and heuristic processing influences on adolescent reasoning and decision making. *Child Development*, **72**, 844–61.

Klaczynski, P.A. (2001b) Framing effects on adolescent task representations, analytic and heuristic processing, and decision making: Implications for the normative-descriptive gap. *Journal of Applied Developmental Psychology*, **22**, 289–309.

Klaczynski, P.A. (2004) A dual-process model of adolescent development: Implications for decision making, reasoning, and identity. In R.V. Kail (ed.) *Advances in child development and behavior,* vol. 31, 73–123. Academic Press, San Diego, CA.

Klaczynski, P.A. (2005) Metacognition and cognitive variability: A two-process model of decision making and its development. In J.E. Jacobs and P.A. Klaczynski (eds) *The development of decision making in children and adolescents,* 39–76. Erlbaum, Mahwah, NJ.

Klaczynski, P.A. (2007) When (and when not) to make exceptions: When (and when not) to make exceptions: Age, argument evaluation, and understanding negative precedents. Unpublished manuscript. University of Northern Colorado.

Klaczynski, P.A. (2008) There's something about obesity: culture, contagion, rationality, and children's responses to drinks 'created' by obese children. *Journal of Experimental Child Psychology*, **99**, 58–74.

Klaczynski, P.A. and Aneja, A. (2002) The development of quantitative reasoning and gender biases. *Developmental Psychology*, **38**, 208–21.

Klaczynski, P.A. and Cottrell, J.E. (2004). A dual-process approach to cognitive development: The case of children's understanding of sunk cost decisions. *Thinking and Reasoning,* **10**, 147–74.

Klaczynski, P.A. and Daniel, D.B. (in press) Thin idealization, body esteem, causal attributions, and ethnic variations in the development of obesity stereotypes. *Journal of Applied Developmental Psychology*.

Klaczynski, P.A. and Fauth, J.M. (1996) Intellectual ability, rationality, and intuitiveness as predictors of warranted and unwarranted optimism for future life events. *Journal of Youth and Adolescence*, **25**, 755–74.

Klaczynski, P.A. and Fauth, J.M. (1997) Developmental differences in memory-based intrusions and self-serving statistical reasoning biases. *Merrill-Palmer Quarterly*, **43**, 539–66.

Klaczynski, P.A. and Gordon, D.H. (1996a) Goal-directed everyday problem solving: Motivational and general ability influences on adolescent statistical reasoning. *Child Development*, **67**, 2873–91.

Klaczynski, P.A. and Gordon, D.H. (1996b) Self-serving influences on adolescents' evaluations of belief-relevant evidence. *Journal of Experimental Child Psychology*, **62**, 317–39.

Klaczynski, P.A. and Lavallee, K.L. (2005) Reasoning biases as mediators of the relationship between cognition and identity: A dual-process perspective. *Journal of Experimental Child Psychology*, **92**, 1–24.

Klaczynski, P.A. and Narasimham, G. (1998a) The development of self-serving reasoning biases: Ego-protective versus cognitive explanations. *Developmental Psychology*, **34**, 175–87.

Klaczynski, P.A. and Narasimham, G. (1998b) Problem representations as mediators of adolescent deductive reasoning. *Developmental Psychology*, **34**, 865–81.

Klaczynski, P.A and Robinson, B. (2000). Personal theories, intellectual ability, and epistemological beliefs: Adult age differences in everyday reasoning biases. *Psychology and Aging*, **15**, 400–16.

Klaczynski, P.A., Schuneman, M.J., and Daniel, D.B. (2004) Development of conditional reasoning: A test of competing theories. *Developmental Psychology*, **40**, 559–71.

Kreitler, S. and Kreitler, H. (1986). Development of probability thinking in children 5 to 12 years old. *Cognitive Development*, **1**, 365–90.

Kuhn, D. (2001) How do people know? *Psychological Science*, **12**, 1–8.

Kuhn, D., Cheney, R., and Weinstock, M. (2000) The development of epistemological understanding. *Cognitive Development*, **15**, 309–28.

Lie, E. and Newcombe, N.S. (1999) Elementary school children's explicit and implicit memory for faces of preschool classmates. *Developmental Psychology*, **35**, 102–12.

Luria, A. (1976) *Cognitive development: Its cultural and social foundations*. Harvard University Press,Cambridge, MA.

Markovits, H. and Barrouillet, P. (2002) The development of conditional reasoning: A mental model account. *Developmental Review*, **22**, 5–36.

Markovits, H. and Dumas, C. (1999). Developmental patterns of understanding social and physical transitivity. *Journal of Experimental Child Psychology*, **73**, 95–114.

Millstein, S.G. and Halpern-Felsher, B.L. (2002) Judgments about risk and perceived invulnerability in adolescents and young adults. *Journal of Research on Adolescence*, **12**, 399–422.

Moshman, D. (1998). Cognitive development beyond childhood. In D. Kuhn and R. Siegler (eds) *Cognition, perception, and language*, Vol. 2, 947–78. In W. Damon (General Editor), *Handbook of child psychology*, 5th ed.Wiley, New York.

Musher-Eizenman, D.R. Holub, S.C. Miller, A.B., Goldstein, S.E., and Edwards-Leeper, L. (2004) Body size stigmatization in preschool children: The role of control attributions. *Journal of Pediatric Psychology*, **29**, 613–20.

Nemeroff, C. and Rozin, P. (2000) The makings of the magical mind: The nature of function of sympathetic magic. In K.S. Rosengren, C.N. Johnson, and P.L. Harris (eds) *Imagining the impossible: Magical, scientific, and religious thinking in children,* 1–34. Cambridge University Press,New York.

Newcombe, N. and Fox, N. A. (1994) Infantile amnesia: Through a glass darkly. *Child Development*, **65**, 31–40.

Parker, A.M. and Fischhoff, B. (2005) Decision-making competence: External validation through an individual-differences approach. *Journal of Behavioral Decision Making*, **18**, 1–27.

Reyna, V.F. and Brainerd, C.J. (1995) Fuzzy-trace theory: An interim synthesis. *Learning and Individual Differences*, **7**, 1–75.

Reyna, V.F. and Ellis, S.C. (1994) Fuzzy-trace theory and framing effects in children's risky decision making. *Psychological Science*, **5**, 275–9.

Reyna, V.F. and Farley, F. (2006) Risk and rationality in adolescent decision making: Implications for theory, practice, and public policy. *Psychological Science in the Public Interest*, **7**, 1–44.

Reyna, V.F., Lloyd, F.J., and Brainerd, C.J. (2003) Memory, development, and rationality: An integrative theory of judgment and decision-making. In S. Schneider and J. Shanteau (eds.) *Emerging perspectives on decision research*. Cambridge University Press, Cambridge, MA.

Rozin, P. and Nemeroff, C. (2002) Sympathetic magical thinking: The contagion and similarity 'heuristics'. In T. Gilovich, D.Griffin, and D.Kahneman, (eds) *Heuristics and biases: The psychology of intuitive judgment,* 201–16. Cambridge University Press, Cambridge, MA.

Rozin, P., Markwith, M., and Nemeroff, C. (1992) Magical contagion beliefs and fear of AIDS. *Journal of Applied Social Psychology,* **22**, 1081–92.

Ruble, D.N. and Martin, C.L. (2002) Conceptualizing, measuring, and evaluating the developmental course of gender differentiation: Compliments, queries, and quandaries. *Monographs of the Society for Research in Child Development, 67* (Serial No. 269), 148–66.

Ruffman, T., Perner, J., Olson, D.R., and Doherty, M. (1993) Reflecting on scientific thinking: Children's understanding of the hypothesis-evidence relation. *Child Development*, **64**, 1617–36.

Schneider, W. and Bjorklund, D.F. (1998). Memory. In D. Kuhn and R. Siegler (eds) *Cognition, perception, and language*, Vol. 2, 467–521. In W. Damon (General Editor), *Handbook of child psychology,* 5th ed. Wiley, New York.

Siegal, M. (1988) Children's knowledge of contagion and contamination as causes of illness. *Child Development*, **59**, 1153–9.

Smolak, L., Levine, M.P., and Thompson, J.K. (2001) The use of the sociocultural attitudes towards appearance questionnaire with middle school boys and girls. *International Journal of Eating Disorders*, **29**, 216–23.

Sodian, B., Zaitchik, D., and Carey, S. (1991) Young children's differentiation of hypothetical beliefs from evidence. *Child Development*, **62**, 753–66.

Stanovich, K.E. (1999) *Who is rational? Studies of individual differences in reasoning*. Erlbaum: Mahwah, NJ.

Stanovich, K.E. (2004) *The robot's rebellion: Finding meaning in the age of Darwin.* Chicago University Press, Chicago, IL.

Stanovich, K.E. and West, R.F. (1997) Reasoning independently of prior belief and individual differences in actively open-minded thinking. *Journal of Educational Psychology,* **89**, 342–57.

Stanovich, K.E. and West, R.F. (1998) Individual differences in rational thought. *Journal of Experimental Psychology: General,* **127**, 161–88.

Stanovich, K.E. and West, R.F. (1999) Discrepancies between normative and descriptive models of decision making and the understanding/acceptance principle. *Cognitive Psychology,* **38**, 349–85.

Stanovich, K.E. and West, R.F. (2000) Individual differences in reasoning: Implications for the rationality debate? *Behavioral and Brain Sciences,* **23**, 645–65.

Stanovich, K.E. and West, R.F. (2007) Natural myside bias is independent of cognitive ability. *Thinking & Reasoning,* **13**, 225–47.

Steinberg, L. (2004) Risk taking in adolescence: What changes, and why? *Annals of the New York Academy of Sciences,* **1021**, 51–8.

Subbotsky, E. (2000a) Phenomenalistic perception and rational understanding in the mind of an individual: A fight for dominance. In K. S. Rosengren, C. N. Johnson, and P.L. Harris (eds) *Imagining the impossible: Magical, scientific, and religious thinking in children,* 35–74. Cambridge University Press, New York.

Subbotsky, E. (2000b) Phenomenalistic reality: The developmental perspective. *Developmental Review,* **20**, 438–74.

Toates, F. (2004) 'In two minds'—Consideration of evolutionary precursors permits a more integrative theory. *Trends in Cognitive Sciences,* **8**, 57.

Toplak, M.E. and Stanovich, K.E. (2003) Associations between myside bias on an informal reasoning task and amount of post-secondary education. *Applied Cognitive Psychology,* **17**, 851–60.

Ullman, M.T. (2004) Contributions of memory circuits to language: The declarative/procedural model. *Cognition,* **92**, 231–70.

Wason, P.C. (1966) Reasoning. In B. Foss (ed.) *New horizons in psychology.* Penguin Books, Harmondsworth.

Chapter 13

What zombies can't do: A social cognitive neuroscience approach to the irreducibility of reflective consciousness

Matthew D. Lieberman

For the past 30 years, philosophers have debated whether zombies could exist (Kirk 1974). Far from being a detour into the world of horror films, this debate asks a serious question: Could an individual act and speak just like other individuals without having any internal conscious experience? Belief in the possibility of these so-called philosophical zombies serves as a litmus test for whether someone believes in some form of mind-body dualism or materialism. Here, I would like to focus on a related hypothesis that is emerging within psychology which I will refer to as the *psychological zombie hypothesis* (zombie will be used to refer to the psychological variant for the remainder of the chapter). This hypothesis suggests that our behaviors and judgments are produced by an 'inner-zombie' whose mental work does not depend on conscious awareness and that those mental operations that are typically accompanied by conscious awareness do not rely on awareness to generate the operations and their outputs. This hypothesis suggests that mental operations that are typically accompanied by conscious awareness can be produced in the absence of conscious awareness, thus demonstrating the superfluousness of awareness.

At the outset, it is useful to distinguish between two additional terms, reflective and non-reflective, that can be applied to describe consciousness, awareness, and mental processes more generally (Lieberman et al. 2002). These terms will be addressed at length below (see Table 13.1). Generally, reflective awareness involves focusing attention on, considering, or manipulating what previously was part of the moment-to-moment stream of consciousness. If one is looking at a picture of a slightly sad face, one could explicitly think about whether the individual is actually sad and, if so, why. This explicit thought would be considered a reflective process. If on the other hand, one thought about which supermarket to stop at on the drive home from work, then the emotional aspects of the picture that are encoded would be the result of non-reflective processes. It is important to note that non-reflective processes include both those that involve phenomenal awareness such as this example (i.e. the individual saw the face, it just wasn't thought about) and others that do not involve phenomenal awareness (i.e. if the face was presented subliminally, outside of consciousness awareness).

Table 13.1 Characteristics of the X-system and C-system

	X-system	C-system
Phenomenological characteristics	Non-reflective consciousness	Reflective consciousness
	Feels spontaneous or intuitive	Feels intentional and deliberative
	Outputs experienced as reality	Outputs experienced as self-generated
Processing characteristics	Parallel processing	Serial processing
	Fast operating	Slow operating
	Slow learning	Fast learning
	Implicit learning of associations	Explicit learning of rules
	Pattern matching and pattern completion	Symbolic logic and propositional
Representational characteristics	Typically sensory	Typically linguistic
	Representation of symmetric relations	Representation of asymmetric and conditional relations
	Representation of common cases	Representation of special cases (e.g. exceptions)
	Representations are not tagged for time, place, ownership, identity	Representation of abstract features that distinguish (e.g. negation, time, ownership, identity)
Evolutionary characteristics	Phylogenetically older	Phylogenetically newer
	Similar across species	Different in primates or humans
Moderator effects	Sensitive to subliminal presentations	Insensitive to subliminal presentations
	Relation to behavior unaffected by cognitive load	Relation to behavior altered by cognitive load
	Facilitated by high arousal	Impaired by high arousal
Brain regions	Amygdala, ventral striatum, ventromedial PFC, dorsal ACC, lateral temporal cortex	Lateral PFC, medial PFC, lateral PPC, medial PPC, rostral ACC, medial temporal lobe

Support for the psychological zombie hypothesis

To read the New York Times, one might be forgiven for believing the psychological zombie hypothesis should be re-termed the 'law of psychological zombies'. A recent story titled 'Who's minding the mind' (Carey 2007) drew the conclusion that 'the subconscious brain is far more active, purposeful, and independent than previously known.... The brain appears to use the very same neural circuits to execute an unconscious act as it does a conscious one'. This conclusion was probably read by more than a million people and has significant implications for how we understand human behavior.

Only occasionally has the psychological zombie hypothesis been so explicitly posited and defended within the scientific community (Velmans 1991). Nevertheless, in the past few decades, this hypothesis has been gaining steam as neuroscience and social cognition have both interjected themselves into this debate by shedding empirical light on the hypothesis. While neither field has claimed to have created full-blown stand alone zombies, both fields have produced what might be termed partial zombies, individuals with impairments in the ability or tendency to consciously reflect on some aspect of one's own experience. Neuroscience has examined individuals with particular forms of brain damage that render an individual unable to report in a particular domain what would ordinarily be experienced by others, whereas social cognition has used priming paradigms (e.g. subliminal exposure of words related to a concept) to activate mental representations without the individual's awareness, preventing the individual from engaging in any conscious reflective work on those specific representations. In either case, the individuals appear to be zombies with respect to some particular domain of cognition or some particular set of mental representations, at least temporarily. In both cases, the general conclusion has been that partial zombies can be made to perform just as if they were not zombies, affirming the zombie hypothesis and casting doubt on the relevance of reflective consciousness.

Blindsight is one of the neurological conditions described most often to support the zombie hypothesis (Velmans 1991). Blindsight individuals have damage to visual cortical areas associated with conscious perception of the world, but the damage is limited to a region that corresponds to a particular spatial extent in their perception (Weiskrantz et al. 1974). In other words, there is a particular part of the visual field that does not give rise to conscious experience and if an object is placed in that part of the visual field, the patient will not report seeing the object. What many studies have shown, initially to establish the phenomenon and later to rule out artifactual explanations, is that blindsight patients can guess quite accurately which of two objects is in their blind spot despite a lack of conscious experience of the object or the ability to reflect on the identity of the object. Thus, in this small part of visual space, blindsight patients appear to be partial zombies in that they have no reflective awareness of what is in this part of space and yet they show a preserved ability to function like those who have the awareness by accurately identifying what is in the blindsight area of space.

Within social cognition, a different approach to the zombie hypothesis has been taken. As mentioned, social cognition has used priming techniques to activate mental representations of different types (goals, stereotypes, affect) to determine whether non-reflective activation of these representations produces similar consequences as when these same representations are activated explicitly in a way that allows for reflective conscious processing.

A study of memory encoding provides one of the cleanest instantiations of this approach. Chartrand and Bargh (1996) examined the effects of memory versus social encoding mindsets on memory for a written passage. This study was a replication of an earlier study by Hamilton et al. (1980) which found that subjects instructed to form an impression of the individual in the passage ('social encoding mindset') without any memory instructions subsequently demonstrated better memory for the passage than subjects who were instructed to memorize the passage and were informed that there would be a memory test ('memory mindset'). Chartrand and Bargh's zombie-relevant twist was that half of their subjects were given the encoding mindset outside of conscious awareness through priming procedures. Despite the fact that these 'zombie' subjects had no idea that they were induced into either memory encoding or social encoding mindsets, they produced the same memory performance as subjects who were explicitly induced into one of these mindsets. Thus, even though these individuals were zombies with respect to the encoding goal and thus were prevented from reflecting on this goal and intentionally reading the passage in a way that facilitated the goal, they behaved just like non-zombies.

The blindsight and social cognition examples given here are just two of many studies that have produced similar results. These studies commonly prevent subjects from engaging in reflective processing of certain inputs to the system and demonstrate that the lack of reflective awareness does not lead to a change in behavioral performance. In essence, zombie (don't) see, zombie do.

Implications of zombie studies

Findings from the zombie studies are extremely exciting because they counter our naïve expectations about what the brain can do when the conscious mind is not overtly running the show. Indeed, much of the work in social and cognitive psychology over the past two decades clearly establishes an impressive array of computations that can be performed without conscious direction in the forms of implicit memory, implicit learning, and automatic behavior. This work changes our fundamental understanding of the unmonitored mind. Yet the implied subtext of zombie studies goes much further than this. Although many of the researchers conducting 'zombie success' studies are careful to provide circumscribed discussions of the implications of these findings, these studies together, without any study necessarily explicitly stating it, imply that the zombie hypothesis is correct and that perhaps reflective conscious processes have little or no pragmatic value.

These studies give the impression that anything that can be done reflectively can be done non-reflectively and promote the conclusion that reflective conscious processes are identical to non-reflective and non-conscious processes except for the addition of awareness. This statement warrants unpacking before proceeding further because two separate and important implications follow from this single statement. First, this statement implies a neutered reflective consciousness that is valuable only in that it provides our ticket into the theater where we watch the movie of our life. If the added awareness associated with reflective processes has no causal teeth, and it must not if the same input-output relations can be preserved in the absence of awareness, then reflective consciousness is merely epiphenomenal. It may appear to us that our conscious thoughts about our plans, goals, and behaviors have consequences, but a zombie could do the same without having the experience of these thoughts.

Indeed, there is extensive evidence to suggest that the relation of our reflective conscious thoughts about our behavior is often poorly correlated with our behavior and the causes of our behavior (Nisbett and Wilson 1977; Wegner 2003).

The second implication focuses on non-reflective processes. The evidence supporting equivalent input-output relations in reflective and non-reflective processes has been used to suggest that non-reflective processes are actually reflective after all, capable of propositional and intentional processes operating on a host of symbolic representations of the self, others, ones attitudes, beliefs, goals, and motivations—only without the awareness component (Dijksterhuis and Nordgren 2006; Velmans 1991). Note that this is a different claim about non-reflective processes than the one made above about the impressive array of computations that non-reflective processes can support. Here, the claim is much more Freudian in the sense that there seems to be 'an intelligence' or a central voice in the non-conscious capable of explicit thought, only it is a voice that the reflective mind cannot hear.

Together these claims suggest that the reflective mind is less human than we naively believe and that the non-reflective mind is more human. It is interesting to note that the skills now imputed to the non-reflective mind in terms of symbolic processing and propositional logic are simultaneously derived from the putative skills of the reflective mind and yet also used to deny that the reflective mind is really doing those things.

Limitations of zombie studies

While the excitement grows about the power of the non-reflective mind to do anything and everything that the reflective mind does, because it is indeed the same mind minus some mechanism that supports epiphenomenal awareness, there has been very little questioning of whether the zombie studies really provide evidence in support of the zombie hypothesis. Although these studies are fascinating and important, they ultimately fall short of supporting the assumptions that are seeping into our collective understanding of the mind.

Consider the example of blindsight. When asked to discriminate between two potential stimuli in the blindsighted area, these individuals can perform the task successfully. However, there is no report of a blindsighted individual spontaneously identifying or using the information present in that field. These individuals haven't commented to a researcher, 'I know we're not in the middle of a testing session, but did you by chance just hide a $100 bill in my blind spot? I'm not having an experience of it, but I'm feeling compelled to grab for my blind spot as if there was a large denomination bill there.'

In fact, when food is placed in the blind spot of a food-deprived monkey, they make no attempt to reach for it or approach it in any way (Cowey and Weiskrantz 1963). This finding is rarely noted and yet gives a more balanced picture of blindsight as it relates to the zombie hypothesis. These individuals can clearly do some forms of information processing based on information coming through the retina that does not reach visual cortex, but they just as clearly cannot process or use the information in other ways. The information cannot be spontaneously considered and used in light of the individual's current goals and concerns. Thus, blindsight is as much of an indicator of what zombies can't do as what they can do.

More generally, these findings raise the question of whether zombie studies in general are selectively choosing independent and dependent variables such that zombies perform like non-zombies. To demonstrate that a third grader and an adult can both add 3 + 3 does not demonstrate that they have the same math abilities, or even that they use the same mechanisms when performing this particular calculation. To examine whether these individuals have different mathematical abilities, one would want to devise tests where they are likely to differ (e.g. geometry, algebra). Similarly, strong tests of the zombie hypothesis need to consider input-output relations that opponents of the hypothesis would predict zombies to be unable to perform.

I have previously written about two neurocognitive systems, the X-system and the C-system, that are hypothesized to be largely responsible for non-reflective and reflective social cognition, respectively (Lieberman 2007a; Lieberman et al. 2002; Satpute and Lieberman 2006). These systems will be described in detail (see Table 13.1), however, just noting a few of the distinguishing features of the two systems is instructive as far as devising clearer tests of the zombie hypothesis. For instance, one claim about the X-system is that it slowly extracts associative relationships present during perception and logical thought, whereas the C-system is capable of extracting these relationships in a single experience. Thus, the fact that elderly primes lead to slower walking behavior, as if the subject is enacting elderly behavior (Bargh et al. 1996), may be making use of associations that have been repeatedly presented over a lifetime. What if, instead, subjects were exposed to a novel group and information about the group's characteristics? For instance, if subjects learned that a newly discovered tribe, the Nochmani, in Indonesia tend to have a bouncier gate than Americans. Would priming 'Nochmani' lead to a bouncier step in Americans? It's hard to imagine that it would but the zombie hypothesis would need to predict this. To be clear, Bargh et al. have not suggested this would be the case and are not defending the zombie hypothesis. Nevertheless, the concern is how these results are interpreted more broadly within and beyond the scientific community.

Another claim is that the X-system handles affirmative associations (X and Y are associated) but does not explicitly represent non-associations (X and Y are unrelated). Thus, in the C-system 'not tense' and 'relaxed' might be interchangeable descriptors of an individual but in the X-system, 'not tense' cannot be parsed because 'not' is purely symbolic and has no 'associative/sensory referents'.

Deutsch et al. (2006) have provided strong support for the inability of 'not' and negations more generally to be processed non-reflectively. In one study, subjects had to either indicate the valence of a term (e.g. 'a party'; positive valence) or the valence of the negated term (e.g. 'no party'; negative valence). With extensive practice, both tasks became faster suggesting that non-reflective processes which are slow learning but fast acting were at work. Nevertheless, the negation task maintained a constant reaction time disadvantage relative to the basic task. In other words, there appears to have been automatization of several features common to both tasks, but the negation component showed no evidence of becoming automatized. Similarly, in a speeded evaluative priming task, primes had the same valenced priming effects whether shown in normal ('a party') or negated ('no party') form suggesting that non-reflective cognition was unable to integrate negations into its computations.

Another claim is that the C-system, but not the X-system, is capable of propositional reasoning and the representation of asymmetrical relations (i.e. 'If A then B' does not imply 'If B than A'). Although priming of a goal or trait has been shown to affect performance in prime consistent ways (Dijksterhuis and Bargh 2001), DeWall and colleagues (2008) have also shown that prime words related to logic and reasoning do not improve logic and reasoning at all, despite leading to semantic activation of these categories. For a broader discussion, see Evans (2008).

Looking to the brain

Another approach to the zombie hypothesis is to examine the neural mechanisms that are at work when zombies and non-zombies perform a task. There are at least three hypotheses of what this data should look like if the zombie hypothesis is correct. The first is a bit of a straw man and suggests that the same brain mechanisms are activated in identical ways whether a task is performed reflectively or non-reflectively. Although a believer in Cartesian dualism might expect this, I doubt many others would expect this to be how the zombie hypothesis would correspond to brain function. Thus, the first formal hypothesis (*zombie neural hypothesis #1*) is that the same brain mechanisms are activated for both reflective and non-reflective task performance, however, reflective processing is associated with greater activity in these regions (see Figure 13.1a). The implicit assumption behind this claim is that awareness is a function of activation levels. If a neural process or mental representation is more activated then we are more likely to be aware of it because this is the source of awareness. Note that this hypothesis also implies that while greater activity might lead to performance changes because more neural work is being done, none of this additional work is due to the awareness associated with heightened neural activity. The second formal hypothesis (*zombie neural hypothesis* #2) states that additional brain regions may be recruited during reflective processing, compared with non-reflective processing, however, (a) only the brain activity associated with non-reflective processing will relate to performance outcomes regardless of whether the task is performed reflectively or non-reflectively and (b) brain regions associated with non-reflective processing will be at least as active during reflective processing as during non-reflective processing (see Figure 13.1b). This account suggests that awareness may be associated with different brain regions than those involved in non-reflective processing, but that only those involved in non-reflective processing are doing mental work with causal consequences and thus these processes and the activity in the brain regions supporting them should be present regardless of whether reflective awareness is also present.

Data that is inconsistent with these formal hypotheses would provide challenges for them. In addition, we can consider a formal hypothesis that opposes the zombie claim (*anti-zombie neural hypothesis*; see Figure 13.1c). This hypothesis differs from zombie neural hypothesis #2 in two ways. First, this hypothesis claims that activity in brain regions supporting reflective and non-reflective processes are each independently

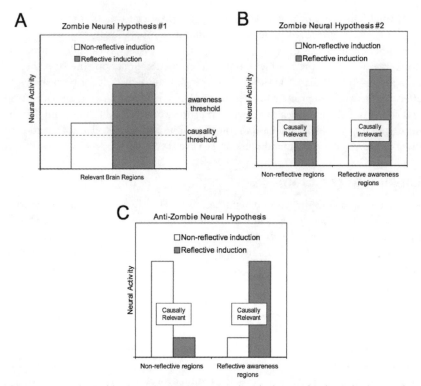

Fig. 13.1 Hypothetical brain activations associated with the zombie hypothesis. Panels A and B depict two possible zombie neural hypotheses. Panel C depicts a neural pattern that would conflict with the zombie hypothesis.

related to performance outcomes under appropriate conditions. Second, this hypothesis claims that under conditions that promote reflective processing, activity in brain regions that support non-reflective processing may be diminished relative to conditions that promote non-reflective processing.

The remainder of this chapter is focused on data, largely from my lab, that bears on the (anti-) zombie neural hypotheses. This work examines how reflective and non-reflective social cognition is instantiated in the brain. In order to transition to this work a bit of exposition is necessary. First, I will describe in more detail the putative differences between reflective and non-reflective social cognition. Second, I will describe the neural model my colleagues and I have developed to examine reflective and non-reflective social cognition in the brain. I will then discuss findings on implicit learning, self-knowledge, emotional processing, social well-being, and attitude change.

Reflective versus non-reflective social cognition

The first step in determining how reflective and non-reflective social cognition are implemented in the brain requires us to declare the characteristics of each system in terms of operating characteristics, mental representation, phenomenology, and the moderators that facilitate or interfere with each system. Our account (Lieberman et al. 2002; Lieberman 2007a, b; Satpute and Lieberman 2006) is greatly influenced by dual-process models (for review see, Chaiken and Trope 1999) and dual-system models (McClelland et al. 1995; Metcalfe and Mischel 1999; Sloman 1996; Smith and DeCoster 1999). In each of these accounts, one system or process is thought to act quickly, potentially without intention, effort, or awareness, based on associations formed incrementally over numerous experiences. Thus, this system can be thought of as a slow learning, fast acting system. In contrast, the second system is thought to act more slowly, typically with intention, effort, and awareness, based on the application of symbolically represented rules that can be learned in a single moment of experience. This system would then be thought of as a fast learning, slow acting system.

Our characterization of the two systems (see Table 13.1) takes these distinguishing characteristics as a starting point and considers a number of additional distinctions between the systems. First, there is a greater focus on the phenomenological aspects of processes emanating from the two systems. Non-reflective processes feel like reality. When we observe one person shoving another, this is experienced as an aggressive act, with the aggressiveness experienced as objectively out there in the world, even though the aggressiveness is constructed psychologically based on a number of characteristics separate from the act itself (Kunda and Sherman-Williams 1993). That is, the aggressiveness is 'seen' as out there in the world, and is not felt as constructed in any part by our minds. In contrast, we typically feel a sense of ownership, construction, and responsibility for our reflective processes. If we see an aggressive behavior and then enumerate the reasons why this behavior may have been morally justified, we believe that this enumeration is our own specific contribution to our understanding of the behavior and the person. We know that this contribution has come from inside ourselves and we are open to the idea that this may not represent reality but our own internal processing.

Although our characterization of the processing characteristics (i.e. how representations are processed) largely conforms to other dual-processing accounts, there are also a number of representational features (i.e. what is represented) that are hypothesized to differ in the systems. The non-reflective system tends to trade in more sensory cues (e.g. images, sounds) and associations that are closely wed to these concrete sensations. In contrast the reflective system is most efficient in dealing with linguistic representations. Sensory and linguistic representations are not exclusively tied to one system or the other, but rather each system appears to be optimized to deal better with one than the other and in any combination. That is, the reflective system is optimized to deal with the overall meaning of multi-word phrases and statements but is less capable of dealing with multiple sensory cues that vary along subtle or complex gradations. In contrast, the non-reflective system is optimized in the opposite way (Deutsch et al. 2006; Greenwald and Liu 1985).

The reflective system is also able to tag various symbolic aspects of a represented entity that distinguish it from other entities in the same class or category, whereas the non-reflective system largely represents commonalities across members of a class or category. The reflective system can represent conditional aspects of an entity (e.g. A has feature B in situation 1 but not situation 2), distinguishing non-present features of an entity (e.g. 'Although he is a professor, unlike most professors he did not graduate from high school'); temporary information (e.g. 'Today my car is parked in a different spot than it usually is'); asymmetrical relationships (i.e. A causes B, but B does not cause A); ownership relations (e.g. 'Jim owns that car'); and explicit representation of identity relations ('That car is a Volvo').

Finally, there are a number of moderators that are thought to affect which system is likely to handle the lion's share of processing at a particular moment. On the one hand, physiological arousal, cognitive load, and subliminal cue presentations will enhance the dominance of non-reflective processing (if non-reflective processes can represent the relevant information), whereas the use of purely symbolic cues and propositional information will enhance the dominance of reflective processing.

X-system and C-system

The aforementioned descriptions of reflective and non-reflective processing are hypothetical models of two systems. These descriptions are not, in themselves, evidence for the existence of the two systems. Instead, these criteria were used to initially identify candidate brain regions for the two systems. The majority of studies that were used to select the candidate brain regions were minimally social or non-social in nature. Although the brain regions are mostly assigned in the same fashion that they were originally (Lieberman et al. 2002), there have been changes along the way in light of numerous studies that have been reported in the field since the initial assignments (see Lieberman 2007a, b; Satpute and Lieberman 2006).

The X-system is hypothesized to handle non-reflective social cognition. The brain regions that are associated with the X-system are the amygdala, basal ganglia (including ventral striatum), ventromedial prefrontal cortex (ventromedial PFC), dorsal anterior cingulate cortex (dorsal ACC), and lateral temporal cortex (including superior temporal sulcus, inferotemporal cortex, and the temporal pole) (see Figure 13.2). The C-system is hypothesized to process reflective social cognition and the brain regions associated with the C-system are lateral PFC (both dorsolateral and ventrolateral PFC), medial PFC (including dorsomedial PFC), lateral posterior parietal cortex (lateral PPC), medial PPC, rostral ACC, and medial temporal lobe (including the hippocampus and surrounding structures). The particular contributions of these brain regions have been discussed extensively elsewhere (Lieberman 2007a; Satpute and Lieberman 2006). Here, it is only critical that these regions are separated into two sets.

Given this hypothetical division, we can then examine whether studies that manipulate variables that alter the tendency for one system or the other to dominate processing also produce neural responses that conform to one of the zombie neural hypotheses or instead fit the anti-zombie pattern. Zombie neural hypothesis #1 (Figure 13.1a) predicts that the X- and C-systems will not be differentially involved in task performance, but rather a single set of relevant brain regions will be activated under both reflective and non-reflective task induction. In both cases, the activity in these brain regions would surpass 'causal threshold' allowing the neural activity to appropriately transform inputs into outputs, whereas activity in the same brain regions would typically surpass a higher 'awareness threshold' only during reflective task inductions.

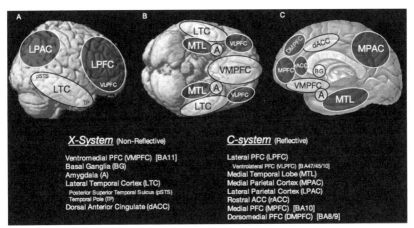

Fig. 13.2 The X-system and C-system responsible for non-reflective and reflective social cognition, respectively. X-system regions are shown in white ovals with black borders. C-system regions are shown in grey ovals with white borders. Panels A–C present lateral, ventral, and mid-sagittal views, respectively.

Zombie neural hypothesis #2 (Figure 13.1b) allows for separate neural networks linked to the X- and C-system. Here regions in the X-system would be expected to be similarly active under reflective and non-reflective task inductions and to be the driving causal force in both cases. C-system activity would be expected to be much greater under reflective than non-reflective task inductions and associated with reflective awareness but not causally relevant to transforming inputs into outputs. The *anti-zombie neural hypothesis* (see Figure 13.1c) differs from hypothesis #2 in two critical ways. First, both X-system and C-system activity can be related to task performance. Second, in at least some cases, X-system activity is reduced during reflective task inductions relative to non-reflective task inductions. This latter point would imply that the brain regions supporting performances under non-reflective task inductions are not still supporting performances under reflective task inductions, even if the same input-output relations are found. Stated differently, this hypothesis, if supported, would indicate that reflective processing would generate performances through different neural mechanisms than those that support non-reflective processes.

Evidence against the zombie hypothesis

Implicit versus explicit learning

The first domain under consideration is implicit and explicit learning. This comparison involves non-reflective and reflective cognition, respectively, but not social cognition per se. However, the results are relevant enough to the zombie hypothesis to deserve inclusion and the distinction has clear implications for social cognition (Lieberman 2000). Numerous behavioral studies have shown that individuals can learn cue sequences that contain task relevant information without having awareness that they are doing so (Reber 1967). Indeed, amnesic patients who are generally unable to remember previous episodes of experience show normal learning on these tasks (Knowlton et al. 1996). In a commonly used implicit learning task, the artificial grammar task, individuals are presented with 'words' from an invented language. The construction of the words follow a set of rules defined in a Markovian grammar chain, but the rules are usually impossible to learn explicitly. After exposure to several examples from the language, individuals are able to successfully guess whether new letter strings constitute legal words in this new language or not. Knowlton and Squire (1996) designed a variant of this task that assesses implicit learning of the grammar as well as explicit learning of simple letter dyads and triads within the words which could be used to make judgments, albeit incorrectly. For instance, a subject might explicitly realize they saw the letter pair 'TV' in some of the training trials and then assume any new string with TV in it is a legal string. This cue may not actually predict legal strings, but it is explicit learning that the subject can reflectively perform and use.

We conducted an fMRI study (Lieberman et al. 2004) in which we examined the neural responses that were more activated on test trials (e.g. 'JTVP') for which explicitly learned cues could be applied (e.g. the test string contains 'TV') but no implicit sequence cues were present relative to other trials in which the implicit sequence cues were present but no explicitly learned cues were present (e.g. 'JVPT'). In other words, the first kind of trial could only be responded to on the basis of reflective knowledge acquired during training and the second kind of trial could only be responded to on the basis of non-reflective knowledge.

In the implicit learning condition, we observed greater basal ganglia activity to valid 'words' than to invalid 'words', when the explicit cues were absent. This X-system activation is consistent with previous motor implicit learning studies (Grafton et al. 1995) which have also implicated the basal ganglia in implicit learning. No C-system activity was observed in this analysis. In contrast, when explicit cues were present, but implicit cues were absent, hippocampal and medial temporal lobe activity was present, both C-system regions, however, no X-system activity was present. Additionally, like a pattern observed in a number of other studies (Packard et al. 1989; Poldrack et al. 2001), we found that activity in the basal ganglia and medial temporal lobes were inversely correlated with one another such that greater activity in one was associated with diminished activity in the other. Thus, while the zombie hypothesis argues that basal ganglia activity, associated here with non-reflective processing, should be equally or more active during reflective processing conditions, this was not observed during reflective processing and was less active to the extent C-system activity was present.

Foerde et al. (2006) provide even more compelling evidence. Subjects trained on an explicit learning task either freely, allowing for reflective processing, or under cognitive load, which impairs reflective cognition but allows non-reflective cognition to proceed. Task performance at test was correlated with brain activity during the training phase. Task performance at test was not significantly different in the two conditions, however, the brain activity during training that predicted test performance differed by training condition. When training occurred without cognitive load, test performance correlated with medial temporal lobe activity during training. When training occurred with cognitive load, test performance instead correlated with basal ganglia activity during training. Importantly, basal ganglia activity in the no load training did not correlate with test performance. This finding directly conflicts with the zombie hypothesis in any of its forms as the region associated with non-reflective performances was not predictive of performances under reflective task conditions.

Reflective versus non-reflective self-knowledge

A number of fMRI studies have examined the neural correlates of self-knowledge (for review, see Lieberman 2007a). Typically medial PFC, in the C-system, is more active when individuals are reflecting on their own personal characteristics than when they are judging the characteristics of another person (Kelley et al. 2002). On its face, this appears to be a reflective process and thus it is not surprising that a C-system structure would be involved. Nevertheless, not all self-knowledge judgments require reflective processing. When Tiger Woods is asked if he is athletic, his response is likely to be automatic and non-reflective. The key question with respect to the zombie hypothesis is whether the same brain regions are active when making self-judgments that do or do not require reflection.

Social psychologists have examined this distinction in the context of self-schemas. In self-schematic domains, like golf or athletics would be for Tiger Woods, a person has a great deal of prior experience and can make judgments about themselves in that domain very quickly (Markus 1977). This characterization is consistent with the non-reflective system as being slow learning, but fast acting. We conducted an fMRI study (Lieberman et al. 2004) to examine the neural correlates of self-knowledge in schematic domains and non-schematic domains to probe non-reflective and reflective self-knowledge, respectively. Individuals were selected to participate in the study either because they were lifelong competitive athletes (i.e. played on the UCLA soccer team) or were long-time actors (i.e. working in Los Angeles), but not both. Additionally, individuals were only classified as schematic if they demonstrated a substantial reaction time advantage for self-judgments in the high experience domain rather than the low experience domain. We then examined which brain regions were differentially activated in the self-schematic and non-schematic domains.

Recall, that in both zombie neural hypotheses, the brain regions invoked during non-reflective processes should be active as much or more during reflective processes, whereas the anti-zombie neural hypothesis predicts that in at least some cases, brain regions that are activated during non-reflective processing will become less activated during reflective processing (because other mechanisms are really at work during reflective processing).

Consistent with all hypotheses, a wide-array of X-system regions were active during self-judgments in the schematic domain, including ventromedial PFC, ventral striatum in the basal ganglia, amygdala and lateral temporal cortex. However, all of these regions were less active during self-judgments in the non-schematic domain and instead, activations in the hippocampus and dorsomedial PFC were present, both C-system regions. This result is inconsistent with either of the zombie neural hypotheses and this study has been largely replicated (Rameson and Lieberman 2007).

We attacked the same question from a different angle by comparing general self-knowledge judgments in children and adults (Pfeifer et al. 2007). Our assumption is that in general, adult self-judgments are less likely to require reflection than the self-judgments of children. In this fMRI study, children (average age = 10.2) and adults (average age = 26.1) reported whether short phrases (e.g. 'I like reading') described themselves or Harry Potter. Harry Potter was chosen as the target of social cognition because both children and adults are familiar with the character and his personality. Both children and adults produced greater activity in medial PFC when making self-judgments than social judgments, however, children produced significantly greater activity in this region than adults consistent with our hypothesis that this task requires more reflective processing for children than adults. Additionally, lateral temporal cortex was significantly active in adults, but not in children. Thus, this X-system region which was more activated for adults in schematic than non-schematic domains (Lieberman et al. 2004) was less active in children for whom self-knowledge judgments are thought to be more reflective. In other words, a region that supports self-knowledge processes in adults to the extent that the process is non-reflective, is not present in children. This, combined with the greater medial PFC activity in children than adults suggests that there may be different mechanisms responsible for self-knowledge judgments to the extent that the judgments invoke reflective or non-reflective processes. As with the self-schema study, these results are inconsistent with either zombie neural hypothesis.

Reflective and non-reflective emotional processing

One of the clearest pieces of evidence we have regarding the zombie hypothesis comes from research on affect labeling (Hariri et al. 2000; Lieberman et al. 2007; Lieberman et al. 2005). In these studies, the emotional aspects of emotionally evocative pictures are either processes reflectively or non-reflectively. The zombie hypothesis would argue that as long as the emotional information gets into the brain, the same brain regions active during non-reflective emotional processing should be at least as active during reflective emotional processing. However, these studies show that merely switching from non-reflective to reflective modes of emotional processing leads to reductions in the neural, physiological, and subjective responses associated with non-reflective emotional processing (for review, see Lieberman 2007b).

In one of these studies (Lieberman et al. 2007), participants were shown negative emotional faces. In the reflective emotional processing condition, participants had to choose from two emotion words presented on the screen with the face, which word described the emotion in the face. In the non-reflective emotional processing condition, participants had to choose which of two names was gender-appropriate for the face. In the non-reflective condition, the emotional stimulus is still present but the emotional aspect is incidental to the task and thus not likely to be reflected upon.

During non-reflective emotional processing, there was a significant response in the amygdala, an X-system region, similar to that seen in previous studies when emotional images are presented subliminally (Whalen et al. 1998) and thus could not have been processed reflectively. However, during reflective emotional processing, the amygdala response was significantly diminished relative to the non-reflective condition. Indeed, all X-system regions (amygdala, VMPFC, ventral striatum in the basal ganglia, dACC, and LTC) were less active during reflective emotional processing than non-reflective emotional processing. In contrast, only a single region of the brain was more active during reflective emotional processing, right ventrolateral PFC, a C-system region. Moreover there was an inverse relationship between the activity in right ventrolateral PFC and the amygdala such that subjects who activated this prefrontal region more during reflective emotional processing also tended to show less activity in the amygdala during reflective processing.

These results are thus inconsistent with the zombie neural hypotheses on two separate accounts. First, all of the X-system regions activated during non-reflective emotional processing showed reduced activation during reflective processing. Second, as in the implicit learning studies above, regions associated with reflective processing appear to be competing with and dampening down activity in regions associated with non-reflective processing. In other words, reflective processing activations appear to occur at the expense of non-reflective processes.

Reflective and non-reflective aspects of social well-being

Kahneman and colleagues (Fredrickson and Kahneman 1993; Kahneman et al. 1993; Redelmeier and Kahneman 1996) have demonstrated in a number of contexts that well-being or distress that an individual reports during the individual moments of an experience ('momentary well-being') often do not correspond in expected ways with an individual's memory of aggregate well-being throughout the entire episode ('retrospective well-being'). One possible reason for this is that the two kinds of self-reports may rely on different processes. Momentary well-being may be the result of a fast, inuitive, non-reflective judgment whereas retrospective well-being may depend on more reflective processes both at retrieval and encoding. That is, retrospection on one's prior well-being integrated over several moments may be a reflective process, but the ability to retrieve those 'to-be-aggregated' moments may depend on those moments having been the subject of reflective processing when they occurred, as this would promote deeper encoding and thus better retrieval (Craik and Tulving, 1975).

We examined this dual-process account of momentary and retrospective well-being in a study (Eisenberger et al. 2007) that combined an fMRI assessment of neural responses to social rejection and an experience sampling study. In the fMRI session, subjects played a virtual game of catch with what they believed were two other players also in MRI scanners. In reality, the two other players were computer players controlled experimentally and programmed to stop throwing the ball to the subject at a set time in order to make the subject feel socially rejected. We had previously observed (Eisenberger et al. 2003) that to the extent that subjects felt 'social pain' during the moment of rejection, they had greater activity in the dorsal ACC which has been associated with physical pain distress in numerous studies (Peyron et al. 1999; Rainville et al. 1997).

At a separate point in time, the same subjects participated in a 10-day experience sampling study. During this time, subjects carried Palm Pilots. Subjects were beeped several times a day and asked to rate their social well-being during their most recent social interaction. At the end of the day, subjects also made retrospective reports of social well-being aggregated over the entire day. Our logic for the study was that individual differences in the neural responses during social rejection in the fMRI session would serve as a proxy for individual differences in neural responses during the individual episodes of experience that subjects were asked to comment on during the experience sampling study. For instance, we expected that an individual who produced high levels of dorsal ACC activity to rejection in the scanner would also tend to report less social well-being during social interactions in their everyday life.

X-system regions dorsal ACC, amygdala, and basal ganglia had activity during rejection in the fMRI session that each predicted the degree of social distress reported when rating their momentary experiences during the day in the experience sampling study. Thus, in a relatively non-reflective task, a host of X-system regions seen in other studies of non-reflective social cognition were again involved. These regions were not correlated with the degree of social distress reported when subjected rated their aggregate experience over the course of the day. Instead, social distress in the aggregate self-reports was associated with activity in the hippocampus and medial PFC, both C-system regions involved in autobiographical memory. It is important to keep in mind that our fMRI data in this study came during an episode of rejection, not during attempts to recall episodes of rejection, so the aggregate analyses are probably more indicative of reflective processes present during the rejection episode itself that produce deeper encoding and thus render the episodic events more retrievable at the time of aggregate judgments.

Once again, we see the brain activations present during non-reflective social cognition, absent during similar judgments involving reflective processing. This is not a process pure manipulation and thus other accounts could be given of the data, but these data are not consistent with the zombie neural hypotheses. It is also notable that these activations were not associated with trying to make judgments of one kind or another, but were associated with the observable outcomes of those judgments. An individual might report, without much reflection, at four separate times during the day that his last social interaction caused him social distress and then at the end of the day, reflect on those different episodes and report that he experienced a great deal of social distress during the day. From the observed self-report alone, one could not be blamed for thinking the same representations were invoved in both cases; however, the fMRI data suggest that the reflective and non-reflective assessments of social well-being were reached through quite different mechanisms.

Reflective and non-reflective attitude change

For half a century, social psychologists have studied post-decisional attitude change in terms of cognitive dissonance reduction (Festinger 1957). The basic finding is that when people make decisions that conflict with existing attitudes, the attitudes tend to change to fit with the decision giving the appearance of rationalization to outside observers. In one common paradigm (Brehm 1956), participants rank their preferences for each member in a set of items (e.g. a set of appliances or a set of art prints). The experimenter then selects two closely ranked items and asks the subject to chose which of these to take home as part of their payment for the experiment. People often, but not always, choose the item that was originally ranked slightly higher. Rationally, people should be thinking to themselves, 'I liked X slightly more than Y, so that's why I chose X over Y. It was a tough choice because the items were similarly matched, but I like X slightly more.' However, when people are asked to re-rank all of the items after the decision has been made, the chosen item goes up in the rankings, and the rejected item goes down. This sudden change in preferences makes what might have been a tough choice in the moment seem like an obvious choice in hindsight.

While this attitude change clearly looks like rationalization from the outside ('Just yesterday, John couldn't decide which job to take because they were so evenly matched, but today he's acting as if he always thought the job he took was the better job'), its unclear how it is experienced from the inside. When this attitude change is occurring, are people reflectively aware that they are shifting their attitudes or is some non-reflective process at work? Of course, the zombie hypothesis suggests that it does not matter and we will return to that shortly.

Most of the classic theories of cognitive dissonance suggest that this form of attitude change is the result of reflective attitude change processes (see Gawronski and Strack 2004). These theories suggest that attitude change results from becoming reflectively aware of the conflict between one's prior attitudes and the decision that is at odds with them and then doing reflective cognitive work to change the attitudes to fit with the decision (for review of these theories with respect to reflective processing, see Lieberman et al. 2001). However, some studies suggest that reflective processing may not be necessary for post-decisional attitude change. Bem and McConnell (1970) found that after subjects' attitudes changed, they had no memory for ever having held different attitudes at the beginning of the study. This suggests that the attitude change took place without reflective processing of the change process. Similarly, Lieberman et al. (2001) found that both amnesic patients who cannot form new memories and individuals under cognitive load showed as much attitude change in a dissonance paradigm as normal control subjects. Thus, amnesic patients who do not remember ranking the items before making a decision and do not remember making a decision that conflicts with their prior attitudes still produced normal levels of post-decisional attitude change suggesting that at least in some cases, reflective processing is not involved in the attitude change process.

We recently examined reflective and non-reflective aspects of post-decisional attitude change in an fMRI study (Jarcho et al. 2007). In the study, we scanned participants while they made several decisions about different pairs of art prints. Each pair of prints had been previously rated by the subject to be roughly evenly matched, thus rendering the choices somewhat in conflict with existing attitudes. After getting out of the scanner, subjects rated all of the prints again so that we could assess attitude change that occurred as a function of their choices. Subjects then saw each art print a final time and were asked to remember what their initial attitude towards the art print had been at the beginning of the study.

We looked at the neural response to just those trials for which attitude change occurred and further subdivided these trials into those for which the subjects remembered that they had previously held a different attitude and those for which the subjects reported that they had always had the same attitude towards the art print that they now hold. Our thinking was that trials for which subjects were aware of the attitude change that took place would be associated with more reflective processing than trials for which they were unaware. The unaware attitude change trials were associated with increased activity in the dorsal ACC and the amygdala, two X-system regions. Repeating the pattern seen through the studies in this chapter, these regions were not active on attitude change trials for which subjects were aware that attitude change had taken place. On the aware trials, which presumably were associated with more reflective cognition during the attitude change process, there was increased activity in several C-system regions including rostral ACC, lateral PFC, and the medial temporal lobe.

One particularly nice feature of this study with respect to the zombie hypothesis is that both the aware and unaware trials produce similar levels of attitude change on average. Thus, whether subjects were reflectively aware that they were changing their attitudes or were zombies with respect to the attitude change, the behavioral effects were similar, but the neural systems supporting the two forms of attitude change are largely distinct from one another.

Other evidence

The preceding sections have provided neurocognitive evidence that I have amassed that relates to the zombie hypothesis and to dual systems of social cognition more generally. Of course, the lion's share of data that bears on this hypothesis comes from other labs. Many of the other studies were not designed with these objectives in mind but because of the methods applied, they either promoted reflective or non-reflective social cognition of some type. This data has been recently reviewed (Lieberman 2007a) and across 21 domains of social cognition, the activations largely conform to the hypothesized distinction between the X-system and the C-system. Figure 13.3 displays a summary of this review. The large gray ovals with white borders represent C-system regions and the large white ovals with black borders represent X-system regions. The small circles represent domains of social cognition with the circles placed in regions only if these activations appeared in multiple studies from that domain. The small black circles represent tasks that induce reflective processing and the small white circles represent tasks that induce non-reflective processing. Of 53 regions of activity associated with reflective and non-reflective processes in 21 domains of social cognition, 49 of the 53 separated into the X- and C-systems as hypothesized.

Evaluating the zombie hypothesis

Conceptually, the zombie hypothesis suggests that reflective cognition is only different from non-reflective cognition in epiphenomenal ways: it might feel different, but the engine under the hood is doing the same things in either case, at least insofar as observable outcomes are concerned. In the terms of this chapter, it suggests that

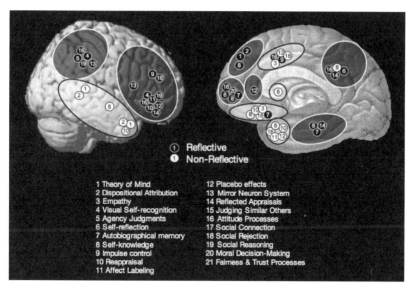

Fig. 13.3 Neural correlates of reflective and non-reflective processes from 21 domains of social cognition overlaid onto the X-system and C-system regions displayed in Figure 13.2.

reflective cognition does not make any contributions that cannot be duplicated by non-reflective cognition. To be honest, I'm not sure who if anyone is truly promoting the zombie hypothesis among empirical psychologists. However, the work that is done precisely in the lab and characterized carefully in research articles can quickly lose its nuance as memes related to the findings spread. Thus, even if those doing zombie studies are conservative in the conclusions they draw, the lesson learned by the research community and the world at large is more expansive.

By reviewing a number of fMRI studies, I hoped to have at least cast doubt on the zombie hypothesis. We have repeatedly observed that the neural mechanisms invoked to support a non-reflective variant of a task are not present when the reflective variant of the same task is performed, even when the observable outputs of the two variants are similar. Instead, we find that the group of brain regions called the X-system tend to be active during non-reflective social cognition and a group of brain regions called the C-system tend to be active during reflective social cognition. Moreover in a number of studies, the degree to which C-system activity is invoked during reflective processes is inversely correlated with X-system activity during reflective processing. The zombie neural hypotheses suggest that the same processes doing the legwork during non-reflective social cognition should also be doing the legwork during reflective social cognition. Our data shows not only are different regions brought on line to do the legwork during reflective social cognition, but that the activation of these reflective processes, far from relying on the neural mechanisms of non-reflective social cognition, seem to prevent the regions involved in non-reflective social cognition from doing any of the legwork.

For full disclosure, I must admit that there is indeed a fourth potential zombie neural hypothesis that was not rejected by the current review: however, on its face it requires tortured logic and suspension of disbelief. The fourth hypothesis is that separate neurocognitive systems (e.g. X- and C-systems) handle what are typically non-reflective and reflective processes, respectively. There are things that each of these systems can do computationally that the other cannot, consistent with the description of processing and representational characteristics listed in Table 13.1. Although the neurocognitive systems that are invoked in reflective processing typically, if not always, occur along with some form of reflective awareness, it is possible that these same processes in the C-system could be invoked without reflective awareness under the right circumstances. This claim starts by admitting that the typical zombie studies do not really support the zombie hypothesis because there really are two systems. It then goes onto suggest that maybe, just maybe, the neurocognitive processes that are always associated with awareness—not those mimicked in typical zombie studies but those neurocognitive processes doing the work that is systematically correlated with reflective awareness—perhaps these processes could be produced without awareness. I must admit that there is no data that rules out this account, but it would be an enormous leap of faith because there is also no data to support this account either. Nevertheless, if someone wanted to provide evidence to support the zombie hypothesis, this is the sort of evidence that would be needed. Non-reflective cognition can mimic a number of the input-output relations produced by reflective cognition. Showing non-reflective production of a reflective process with C-system activation, rather than producing the same outputs, would be strong evidence.

This final zombie hypothesis notwithstanding, one remaining question is why would non-reflective processes so often mimic the outputs of reflective processes, thus giving rise to the empirical support for the zombie hypotheses? One way to think of non-reflective processes is as our own built in 'personal digital assistant' or PDA, like a Palm Pilot. There are various tasks that are relatively simple and straightforward that could each be done by a person but are a relief to hand off to the PDA. People remembered names, dates, addresses, and phone numbers before PDAs and thus can do this, but people also forgot names, dates, addresses, and phone numbers. A PDA can only do certain things but what it can do it can do very reliably and it is designed to work to support our conscious goals and intentions. The X-system may be very much the same way, to serve the goals and intentions of the C-system by taking over repetitive tasks that would be effortful for the C-system to handle sequentially, freeing the C-system up to focus on things the X-system is not suited for. Thus, the X-system may be designed to mimic the C-system to the extent that it can give its own computational constraints and consequently in well-learned domains where associative processes can generate the outputs of interest, both the C-system and X-system are likely to produce results. However, when tasks tap into functions that fit the repertoire of one of the systems, but not the other, outputs should diverge.

Postscript: Interactions of the X- and C-systems

This chapter was intended to show that the neurocognitive systems supporting reflective and non-reflective social cognition could be distinguished from each other in ways that undermine the zombie hypothesis. The picture I've presented is one of independence or even of competition between the systems. Although the systems are separable and can be shown to compete, in many of life's daily experiences, these two systems work together quite closely to achieve the best outcomes. I've presented studies that were intended to differentiate the systems based on their distinguishing features. However, in everyday life, most tasks probably rely on both systems simultaneously.

For instance, there is evidence to suggest that medial PFC and lateral temporal cortex work together in theory of mind (ToM) tasks where the internal mental state of another must be taken into account (Frith and Frith 2003). Lateral temporal cortex appears to support more automatic and non-reflective aspects of ToM (Lieberman 2007a) by responding to facial cues such as facial expressions and eye gaze that relate to mental states in relatively straightforward ways, whereas medial PFC is invoked when an individual is explicitly thinking about the mental state of another. In this case, medial PFC is likely using inputs from lateral temporal cortex as part of the algebraic mental equation used in mental state inference. For instance, smiling is typically associated with positive emotional states without any reflective effort on the part of an observer. However, if the target being observed is a competitor in a poker tournament, then propositional logic may be used by medial PFC to combine these facial cues encoded in lateral temporal cortex with knowledge about situational context to reach the conclusion that this person might be smiling in order to bluff his competition. These high level inferences from medial PFC then may be fed back to lateral temporal cortex to filter incoming facial expressions for relevant information for additional hypothesis testing about the other person's intentions. So while it is possible to separate the contributions of medial PFC and lateral temporal cortex into reflective and non-reflective elements of ToM, respectively, they are also working together in harmony.

In conclusion, the zombie hypothesis may be tantalizing, but evidence from social cognitive neuroscience studies suggests this is not an accurate characterization of the mind. There are two systems, the X-system and the C-system, that are differentially responsible for non-reflective and reflective social cognition respectively. The systems appear to operate upon different principles and are invoked under different conditions. Although the two systems are capable of producing similar outputs in various situations, giving apparent support to the zombie hypothesis, neuroimaging shows that different mechanisms are indeed at work in these cases.

References

Bargh, J.A., Chen, M., and Burrows, L. (1996) Automaticity of social behavior: Direct effects of trait construct and stereotype activation on action. *Journal of Personality and Social Psychology*, **71**, 230–44.

Bem, D.J. and McConnell, H.K. (1970) Testing the self-perception explanation of dissonance phenomena: On the salience of premanipulated attitudes. *Journal of Personality and Social Psychology*, **14**, 23–31.

Brehm, J.W. (1956) Postdecision changes in the desirability of alternatives. *Journal of Abnormal and Social Psychology*, **52**, 384–9.

Carey, B. (2007) Who's minding the mind? *New York Times*, 31 July.

Chaiken, S. and Trope, Y. (1999) *Dual-process theories in social psychology*, Guilford Press, New York.

Chartrand, T.L. and Bargh, J.A. (1996) Automatic activation of impression formation and memorization goals: Nonconscious goal priming reproduces effects of explicit task instructions. *Journal of Personality & Social Psychology*, **71**, 464–78.

Cowey, A. and Weiskrantz, L. (1963) A perimetric study of visual field defects in monkeys. *Quarterly Journal of Experimental Psychology*, **15**, 91–115.

Craik, F.I.M. and Tulving, E. (1975) Depth of processing and retention of words in episodic memory. *Journal of Experimental Psychology: General*, **104**, 268–94.

Deutsch, R., Gawronski, B., and Strack, F. (2006) At the boundaries of automaticity: Negation as reflective operation. *Journal of Personality and Social Psychology*, **91**, 385–405.

DeWall, C.N., Baumeister, R.F., and Masicampo, E.J. (2008) Evidence that logical reasoning depends on conscious processing. *Consciousness and Cognition*, **17**, 628–45.

Dijksterhuis, A. and Bargh, J.A. (2001) The perception-behavior expressway. *Advances in Experimental Social Psychology*, **33**, 1–40.

Dijksterhuis, A. and Nordgren, L.F. (2006) A theory of unconscious thought. *Perspectives on Psychological Science*, **1**, 95–109.

Eisenberger, N.I., Gable, S.L., and Lieberman, M.D., (2007) fMRI responses relate to differences in real-world social experience. *Emotion*, **7**, 745–54.

Eisenberger, N.I., Lieberman, M.D., and Williams, K.D. (2003) Does rejection hurt? An fMRI study of social exclusion. *Science*, **302**, 290–2.

Evans, J.St.B.T. (2008) Dual-processing accounts of reasoning, judgment and social cognition. *Annual Review of Psychology*, **59**, 255–78.

Festinger, L. (1957) *A theory of cognitive dissonance*. Row, Peterson, Evanston IL.

Foerde, K.E., Knowlton, B.J., and Poldrack, R.A. (in preparation) Secondary task effects on classification learning examined using fMRI.

Fredrickson, B.L. and Kahneman, D. (1993) Duration neglect in retrospective evaluations of affective episodes. *Journal of Personality and Social Psychology*, **65**, 45–55.

Frith, U. and Frith, C.D. (2003) Development and neurophysiology of mentalizing. *Philosophical Transactions of the Royal Society of London*, **358**, 459–73.

Gawronski, B. and Strack, F. (2004) On the propositional nature of cognitive consistency: Dissonance changes explicit, but not implicit attitudes. *Journal of Experimental Social Psychology*, **40**, 535–42.

Grafton, S.T., Hazeltine, E., and Ivry, R. (1995) Functional mapping of sequence learning in normal humans. *Journal of Cognitive Neuroscience*, **7**, 497–510.

Greenwald, A.G. and Liu, T.J. (1985) *Limited unconscious processing of meaning*. Presented at annual meeting of the Psychonomic Society, Boston, MA.

Hamilton, D.L., Katz, L.B., and Leirer, V.O. (1980) Cognitive representation of personality impressions: Organizational processes in first impression formation. *Journal of Personality and Social Psychology*, **39**, 1050–63.

Hariri, A.R., Bookheimer, S.Y., and Mazziotta, J.C. (2000) Modulating emotional response: Effects of a neocortical network on the limbic system. *NeuroReport*, **11**, 43–8.

Jarcho, J., Berkman, E., and Lieberman, M.D. (2007) *Neural correlates of post-decisional attitude change*. Poster presented at the Neural Systems of Social Behavior conference, May, Austin, TX.

Kahneman, D., Fredrickson, B.L., Schreiber, C.A., and Redelmeier, D.A. (1993) When more pain is preferred to less: Adding a better ending. *Psychological Science*, **4**, 401–5.

Kelley, W.M., Macrae, C.N., Wyland, C.L., Caglar, S., Inati, S., and Heatherton, T.F. (2002) Finding the self?: An event-related fMRI study. *Journal of Cognitive Neuroscience*, **14**, 785–94.

Kirk, R. (1974) Sentience and behaviour. *Mind*, **83**, 43–60.

Knowlton, B.J., Mangels, J.A., and Squire, L.R. (1996) A neostriatal habit learning system in humans. *Science*, **273**, 1399–402.

Kunda, Z. and Sherman-Williams, B. (1993) Stereotypes and the construal of individuating information. *Personality and Social Psychology Bulletin*, **19**, 90–9.

Lieberman, M.D. (2000) Intuition: A social cognitive neuroscience approach. *Psychological Bulletin*, **126**, 109–37.

Lieberman, M. D. (2007a) Social cognitive neuroscience: A review of core processes. *Annual Review of Psychology*, **58**, 259–89.

Lieberman, M.D. (2007b) The X- and C-systems: The neural basis of automatic and controlled social cognition. To appear in E. Harmon-Jones and P. Winkelman (eds) *Fundamentals of social neuroscience,* 290–315. Guilford, New York.

Lieberman, M.D., Jarcho, J.M., and Satpute, A.B. (2004) Evidence-based and intuition-based self-knowledge: An fMRI study. *Journal of Personality and Social Psychology*, **87**, 421–35.

Lieberman, M.D., Gaunt, R., Gilbert, D.T., and Trope, Y. (2002) Reflection and reflexion: A social cognitive neuroscience approach to attributional inference. *Advances in Experimental Social Psychology*, **34**, 199–249.

Lieberman, M.D., Ochsner, K.N., Gilbert, D.T., and Schacter, D.L. (2001) Do amnesics exhibit cognitive dissonance reduction? The role of explicit memory and attention in attitude change. *Psychological Science*, **12**, 135–40.

Lieberman, M.D., Chang, G.Y., Chiao, J., Bookheimer, S.Y., and Knowlton, B.J. (2004) An event-related fMRI study of artificial grammar learning in a balanced chunk strength design. *Journal of Cognitive Neuroscience*, **126**, 427–38.

Lieberman, M.D., Hariri, A., Jarcho, J.M., Eisenberger, N.I., and Bookheimer, S.Y. (2005) An fMRI investigation of race-related amygdala activity in African-American and Caucasian-American individuals. *Nature Neuroscience*, **8**, 720–2.

Markus, H.R. (1977) Self-schemata and processing information about the self. *Journal of Personalty and Social Psychology*, **35**, 63–78.

McClelland, J.L., McNaughton, B.L., and O'Reilly, R.C. (1995) Why there ae complementary learning systems in the hippocampus and neocortex: Insights from the successes and failures of connectionist models of learning and memory. *Psychological Review*, **102**, 419–57.

Metcalfe, J. and Mischel, W. (1999) A hot/cool system analysis of delay of gratification: Dynamics of willpower. *Psychological Review*, **106**, 3–19.

Nisbett, R.E. and Wilson, T.D. (1977) Telling more than we can know: Verbal reports on mental processes. *Psychological Review,* **84**, 231–59.

Packard, M.G., Hirsh, R., and White, N.M. (1989) Differential effects of fornix and caudate nucleus lesions on two radial maze tasks: Evidence for multiple memory systems. *Journal of Neuroscience*, **9**, 1465–72.

Peyron, R., Garcia-Larrea, L., Gregoire, M., Costes, N., Convers, P., Lavenne, F., Mauguiere, F. Michel, D., and Laurent, B. (1999) Haemodynamic brain responses to acute pain in humans: Sensory and attentional networks. *Brain*, **122**, 1765–79.

Pfeifer, J.H. Lieberman, M.D., and Dapretto, M. (2007) 'I know you are but what am I?!': An fMRI study of self-knowledge retrieval during childhood. *Journal of Cognitive Neuroscience*, **19**, 1323–37.

Poldrack, R.A., Clark, J., Paré-Blagoev, E.J., Shohamy, D., Creso Moyano, J., Myers, C., and Gluck, M.A. (2001) Interactive memory systems in the human brain. *Nature*, **414**, 546–50.

Rainville, P., Duncan, G.H., Price, D.D., Carrier, B., and Bushnell, M.C. (1997) Pain affect encoded in human anterior cingulate but not somatosensory cortex. *Science*, **277**, 968–71.

Rameson, L. and Lieberman, M.D. (2007.) Thinking about the self from a social cognitive neuroscience perspective. *Psychological Inquiry*, **18**, 117–22.

Reber, A.S. (1967) Implicit learning of artificial grammars. *Journal of Verbal Learning and Verbal Behavior*, **6**, 855–63.

Redelmeier, D.A. and Kahneman, D. (1996) Patients' memories of painful medical treatments: Real-time and retrospective evaluations of two minimally invasive procedures. *Pain*, **66**, 3–8.

Satpute, A.B. and Lieberman, M. D. (2006) Integrating automatic and controlled processing into neurocognitive models of social cognition. *Brain Research*, **1079**, 86–97.

Sloman, S.A. (1996) The empirical case for two systems of reasoning. *Psychological Bulletin*, **119**, 3–22.

Smith, E.R. and DeCoster, J. (1999) Associative and rule-based processing: A connectionist interpretation of dual-process models. In S. Chaiken and Y. Trope (eds) *Dual-process theories in social psychology*, 323–36. Guilford, New York.

Velmans, M. (1991) Is human information processing conscious? *Behavioral and Brain Sciences*, **14**, 651–726.

Wegner, D.W. (2003) *The illusion of conscious will*. MIT Press, Cambridge, MA.

Weiskrantz, L., Warrington, E.K., Sanders, M.D., and Marshall, J. (1974) Visual capacity in the hemianopic field, following a restricted occipital ablation. *Brain*, **97**, 709–28.

Whalen, P.J., Rauch, S.L., Etcoff, N.L., McInerney, S.C., Lee, M.B., and Jenike, M.A. (1998) Masked presentations of emotional facial expressions modulate amygdala activity without explicit knowledge. *Journal of Neuroscience*, **18**, 411–18.

Chapter 14

In two minds about rationality?

Clare Saunders and David E. Over

The rationality debate and dual-process theory

Dual-process theories of the mind have become increasingly important in the psychological study of reasoning and decision making. At first the focus was on the relation between dual processes and human rationality (Evans and Over 1996; Sloman 1996; Stanovich 1999). More recently, the topic of rationality has slipped a little from the centre of debate, which is now on dual-process theory as a general account of the mind. However, in this chapter, we will renew our focus on questions about rationality. It is still unclear what dual-process theory should say about rationality. All dual-process theories agree that the mind can come into conflict with itself in some sense, or even that the brain can be 'at war' with itself (Stanovich 2004). Even more strongly, some would claim that individual people have two separate minds that can come into conflict (Evans, this volume). On the other hand, we cannot simply define rationality in terms of subpersonal units, modules, or systems. We also need a notion of the whole self for defining rationality (Stanovich 2004), but dual-process theory has so far said much more about disunited processes or systems than about a unified self. In this chapter, we shall discuss the problems of defining the self and its rationality, in face of the conflict described by dual-process theory. We shall also ask how much unity is necessary for rationality of the self.

Dual-process theory states that the mind contains two different types of mental processes or systems, but there is much disagreement about precisely what the two processes or systems are, and how they should be characterized and distinguished. We will follow those who refer to type 1 and type 2 mental processes (Evans, this volume; Samuels, this volume). These are sometimes said to be in System 1 and System 2, respectively. We will use Evans's (this volume) taxonomy of type 1 processes as fast, automatic, high capacity, and low effort; and of type 2 processes as slow, controlled, limited capacity, and high effort, and as sequential and making use of working memory.

Dual processes, rules, and rationality

An additional distinction, of particular importance to our topic of rationality in dual-process theory, is that between *implicitly conforming to* rules and *explicitly following* rules. Yet dual-process theorists have done little, if anything, to make this distinction clear. Smith et al. (1992) tried to make the distinction outside the context of a dual-process theory; and although their work has been referred to by some dual-process theorists (Evans and Over 1996; Over and Evans 1997), it has not been developed further by them, so for now we will have to continue to rely on Smith et al. (1992) for a psychological account of this central distinction. But we will introduce, as further clarification, examples of type 1 and type 2 processing in particularly strong senses. In these cases, there is the clearest distinction we can think of between implicitly conforming to rules and explicitly following rules.

Suppose that we entered into an agreement with Jack to exchange benefits, but that he turned out to be a cheater. He took a benefit from us without paying the agreed cost later of giving us a benefit back. We will probably find it particularly easy to identify Jack again and, when we do, to feel angry and to be disinclined to have further agreements with him. This example illustrates type 1 processing as understood in a strong way—that is, not only fast and automatic, but possibly the result of an innate domain-specific module that is old in evolutionary terms: a cheater detection module (Cosmides 1989). The module somehow includes, or depends on, other type 1 processes, such as a face-recognition module. It implicitly represents or embodies conditionals, such as 'If the man you are looking at has physical properties XYZ, then he is Jack and cheated in the past'. Thus the module is able to infer implicitly that the man we are looking at is Jack and cheated us in the past, from the processing that identifies Jack and the implicit conditional. It implicitly conforms in its type 1 processing with the logical inference rule of *Modus Ponens* (MP), which is to infer q from p and 'if p then q'.

People cannot, without specialist knowledge, explicitly state the conditional referred to in this example, and they do not use it as part of an explicit inference in MP form. The module does this implicitly for them, and it is no less rational for that. We take an instrumental view of rationality, according to which people are rational to the extent that they reliably achieve their goals. This view is presupposed by most cognitive scientists and has a long history in naturalistic accounts of the mind (Over 2004). People can be rational in this sense whether they are implicitly conforming to rules or explicitly following them. Identifying Jack as a cheater, and reacting to him with anger, could help us to achieve the goal of not being cheated by him again.

We can thus see how a cheater detection module could help us to have instrumental rationality; but such modules do not explain (contra Cosmides 1989) how we can solve certain other types of reasoning task, such as some versions of the Wason selection task, which is a reasoning problem about an explicit conditional (Over 2003). To understand explicit conditionals, and explicitly perform inferences from them, people have to have more general abilities than are implicitly found in domain-specific modules.

Let us now turn to an especially strong example of type 2 processing, using a reasoning problem that we have modified (from Levesque 1986 and Toplak and Stanovich 2002) to be about cheating:

Jack is looking at Ann, but Ann is looking at George.

Jack is a cheater, but George is not.

Is a cheater looking at a non-cheater?

a) Yes; b) No; c) Cannot tell.

Let us call this the Ann problem. Most people answer it incorrectly with 'Cannot tell'—the correct answer is 'Yes'. We can make the Ann problem intuitively easier for everyone by stating explicitly the logical rule that is most helpful for seeing how to solve it. This is the logical rule of the excluded middle, 'p or not-p', and the relevant instance in this case is that Ann is either a cheater or not a cheater.

Logicians would characterize the Ann problem as requiring *non-constructive* reasoning. In this reasoning, we infer a disjunction 'from above' but cannot say which disjunct is true. We solve the Ann problem without knowing whether she is a cheater or, alternatively, not a cheater—only, a priori 'from above', that she is one or the other. We have to reason from both disjuncts. First, *if* Ann is a cheater, then a cheater (Ann) is looking a non-cheater (George). Second, and alternatively, *if* Ann is not a cheater, then again a cheater (Jack) is looking at a non-cheater (Ann). We can therefore infer, 'from above', that the answer to the question is 'Yes'.

Notice that, in this non-constructive reasoning, we must explicitly follow rules in a step by step way in working memory. We infer the conclusion by an explicit representation of the first conditional, and then we infer the conclusion again by an explicit representation of the second conditional. In the whole process, we explicitly follow the rules of the excluded middle and MP. This non-constructive solution to the Ann problem is a particularly strong instance of type 2 processing, having a very high degree of content-independence and domain generality (Over 2007a, b). Even if a dedicated part of the brain—a 'logic module' (Carruthers 2006)—extracts the logical forms, 'p or not-p' and 'if p then q', the valid inferences from these will be content general and not restricted to the specific contents of p and q.

Consider how the two processes can work together. We could infer non-constructively 'from above' that resources are missing and that only one of two people could have taken them by cheating, Jack or George. This reasoning could depend on common sense beliefs or sophisticated technical inferences, as in advanced accounting procedures. In either case, our conclusion is that Jack is the cheater or George is the cheater. We do not know which one is responsible, since the reasoning is so far only non-constructive, but we could now try to identify the cheater using type 1 constructive processing. We could try to watch them both closely, hoping to catch one in the act.

We have presented both processes as working together rationally. There could, however, be tension between them. We could feel tension in the literal sense when we infer using type 2 non-constructive processing that Jack or George is the cheater. Owing to a history of cooperation with both George and Jack, type 1 processing might give us friendly feelings towards them and the firm belief that neither is the cheater. A similar conflict is found in some epistemic paradoxes, such as the preface paradox, in which an author apologizes for mistakes in his book (Sorensen 2006). By writing each sentence 'p1' to 'pn' of the book, he asserts p1 to pn; and yet in the preface he infers non-constructively, in effect, the disjunction 'not-p1 or … or not-pn'. This overall set of sentences is of course inconsistent. The problem is that the author, with a non-constructive justification of the long disjunction, cannot identify which disjunct (or disjuncts) holds, and so where he has made a mistake (or mistakes) in his book. More generally, we may firmly believe non-constructively that some of our beliefs on a matter are mistaken, but also firmly hold to each of these beliefs when considering them constructively one by one. This general kind of problem is only possible for minds that are capable of both type 1 and type 2 processing.

A person can be irrational because of a conflict between type 1 and type 2 processing, but also because the processing of either type is internally biased or fallacious. We might have inferred that cheating is going on in type 2 processing as a result of biased statistical or accountancy practices. We might also 'identify' one of the two men as the cheater in type 1 processing because of implicit prejudices about his social or ethnic group. Type 1 prejudices could cause type 2 reasoning to concentrate too much on only Jack or George as the possible cheater, but type 2 could also draw conclusions from explicit prejudices. A type 1 process can be implicitly biased and a type 2 process can explicitly follow fallacious rules. People sometimes implicitly conform to bad rules and sometimes explicitly follow them.

Why dual-process theories need a unified account of rationality

The two processes have to work well together to achieve full human rationality (see Evans and Over 1996, and Over and Evans 1997, on rationality 1 and rationality 2). Evans and Over (1996, p.1) expressed the view, in the course of stating a dual-process theory, in this way:

> The starting point for any understanding of human rationality must be behavioural: we must ask how decisions taken and actions performed serve the goals of the individual. Formulating and making use of logical and other rules has always had to rest on a more fundamental human ability to achieve behavioural goals.

People's mental processes are rational to the extent that they reliably contribute to goal achievement. Type 1 processing and its implicit rules have often been shaped by natural selection to fulfil goals to do with our well-being (when that was related to reproductive success). It is rational now just as long as we still want those goals, and as long as these processes are well suited to achieving these goals in our twenty-first-century environment.[1] Reliable type 1 processing is necessary for achieving all goals, and type 2 processing always depends on type 1.[2] However, type 2 processes also have their

---

[1] However, natural selection does not always guarantee the reliability of our type 1 reasoning processes —see, for example, Stich (1990, ch.3); Stein (1996, ch.6). Furthermore, even if these processes were adaptive in the 'environment of evolutionary adaptation', they may not always remain so in our rapidly changing world—see especially Stanovich (1999, 2004).

[2] The precise nature of this dependence of type 2 on type 1 processing remains a matter of debate (Evans 2007, this volume). However, there is widespread agreement that, at the

place in human rationality. Type 2 processes explicitly follow rules, and when the rules are good ones, we have good reasons for what we do. Rules, implicit or explicit, are only good as long as they help us to attain our goals, but explicit rule following has something to contribute above and beyond automatically and implicitly conforming to rules. As Nozick (1993, p.64) rather grandly put it (with an echo of Kant 1950/1781), 'Reasons without reliability seem empty, reliability without reasons seems blind' (see also Over and Evans 1997). Type 1 processes can be blind to special circumstances or to longer range goals. But we can at times override these processes or change them with practice or habit, when type 2 processing gives us a good reason to do so.

For example, people may have a module that helps them to identify foods high in fat and sugar, giving them a tendency to select these foods when they are hungry. This module may have been adaptive under primitive conditions (Strassman and Dunbar 1999), but it is blind to the abundance of rich food in advanced technological society and the unhealthy consequences of eating too much of it. Type 2 processing can give us better explicit rules for healthy eating in contemporary society than the implicit one of eating foods high in fat and sugar. Nevertheless, type 2 processing and its reasons are empty if they are not put into effect by reliable type 1 processes.

Evolutionary 'rationality' is inadequate as a unified account of rationality

Type 1 processing that has been shaped by natural selection often implicitly conforms to rules for promoting reproductive success. Conforming to these rules is still a reliable way of achieving many of our goals, but instrumental rationality cannot be reduced to evolutionary 'rationality'. Rode et al. (1999, p.302) argued that:

> One should not expect the cognitive architecture of evolved processes to be 'rational' when rationality is defined as adherence to a normative theory drawn from mathematics or logic. One should expect this cognitive architecture to be ecologically rational: well designed for solving the adaptive problems their ancestors faced during their evolutionary history.

Cosmides and Tooby (1994) criticized Fodor's (1983) dual-process theory and compared the mind with a Swiss army knife. The mind supposedly contains only innate domain-specific modules, in a strong sense, for solving adaptive problems. Gigerenzer and Todd (1999, p.30) also argued for the Swiss army knife model of the mind, holding that the mind is an 'adaptive toolbox' with a 'collection of specialized cognitive mechanisms that evolution has built into the human mind for specific domains of inference and reasoning'. In effect, these theorists have no notion of the rationality of the self, but only of the evolutionary or ecological 'rationality' of the domain-specific modules that supposedly make up the mind and leave no room for anything else.

....

least, some form of pre-attentive thought processes provide the 'input' for type 2 reasoning—in order to solve the 'frame problem' of human cognition (McCarthy and Hayes 1969; Pylyshyn 1987).

One of the deepest problems for evolutionary 'rationality' is its presupposition that the only relevant goal for instrumental rationality is reproductive success (Over 2000, 2004). (It also assumes that the pursuit of reproductive success is monolithic—its massive modularity has no way of adjudicating what evolutionary 'rationality' prescribes in the event that different modules conflict, as we discuss below.) Furthermore, it presupposes, even more strongly, that the only relevant goal is reproductive success in prehistoric environments that are assumed to have been unchanging. Swiss army knife model adaptive modules are blind to novel events or to advances in human society. Explicitly using mathematics and logic can be better now for goal success (whether to do with reproduction or not) than some type 1 processes that gave our primitive ancestors the reproductive edge over other primitive creatures long ago and far away.

More than that, it is wrong to assume that our primitive ancestors could not explicitly follow rules. The study of natural sampling (Kleiter, 1994) shows that people can explicitly follow mathematical and logic rules for operations on sets of objects or propositions, when the relevance of the rules is transparent (Barbey and Sloman 2007; Over 2007a, b). The Ann problem, above, becomes trivial, and it and other problems like it are easy to solve, once the relevance of the logical rule of the excluded middle is made transparent. We have also seen how type 2 non-constructive reasoning could combine with type 1 processing to infer the existence of a cheater and finally to identify him. Swiss army knife domain-specific modules could not provide non-constructive inference (although a system of 'modules' in a much weaker sense, as in Carruthers 2006, might be able to).

Type 2 processing for following and explicitly formulating rules must also have had adaptive value. In the terminology of Stanovich and West (2003), natural selection has put System 1 and its type 1 processing on a 'short leash' and System 2 and its processing on a 'long leash'. People's short-leash domain-specific modules will often automatically aim at the goals of their genes. Their long-leash abilities can achieve their individual goals as well as, and perhaps instead of, those of their genes. Stanovich (2004) shows in Figure 14.1 how this distinction between goals fits into his dual-process framework.

A difference in goals implies a difference in instrumental rationality. Stanovich and West define 'normative rationality' as serving the goals of the individual, and 'evolutionary rationality' as serving the goals of the individual's genes. However, they agree with Evans and Over (1996) that the *primary* notion of rationality is that which is indexed to the goals of the individual. Indeed, Stanovich (2004, p.86) underlines this point by abandoning the label 'evolutionary rationality' in favor of 'evolutionary adaptation', and emphasizing that 'rationality is keyed to the notion of the self. It is defined over a person, not a subpersonal entity (the genes)'.

A challenge for dual-process theories of rationality: conflicting goals

Problems can arise, however, because individuals still often want the goals of short-leash modules, while also desiring the ends pursued by long-leash type 2 processing —and these do not always admit of mutual satisfaction. For example, it is

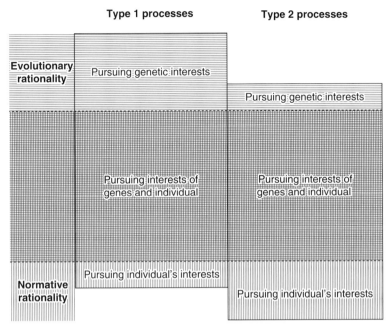

Fig. 14.1 Stanovich's account of the relation between rationality types and reasoning processes; adapted from Stanovich (2004, p.65, figure 2.2).

not only our genes that want chocolate rather than celery for a pleasant snack. We want it as well, and the celery for its health benefits. We cannot always separate, in theoretical or practical reasoning, genetic goals and individual goals. Also, we must be careful not to presuppose that *all* type 1 processing is aimed at genetic and not individual goals, or that *all* type 2 processing is truly in the interests of the self or individual as a whole.

Consider a young woman, already too thin to be healthy, who believes that she needs to lose weight. She consults diet books and works out rules, in type 2 processing, for eating a low calorie diet. She is tempted by the chocolate, thanks to the short-leash module, but also wants to follow her rules and choose the celery instead. She could break her diet for one snack, but decides that, all things considered, she should stick to it. Even so, when the moment of choice comes, she picks the chocolate. The problem for the instrumental view of rationality is that she had two conflicting goals. She achieves one of them, but not the other. She enjoys the chocolate while eating it, but feels guilt and regret afterwards. She would not have got pleasure from the celery, but would not have felt guilt or regret after eating it. Is she rational or not?

Our example is not exactly like a standard illustration of weakness of the will. For that, we would have to say that the young woman needed to lose weight. It would then seem as if her 'better' self, in System 2, and its concern for health, had been over-ridden by a 'base' desire for immediate gratification, in System 1. In this kind of example, we could try to identify the self with the 'better' System 2 processing. That might allow us to argue that people are rational to the extent that they attain the goals of their System 2. However, it is not always possible to identify a better or preferred 'self' with System 2, as our nonstandard example illustrates. The young woman has a natural and, in her case, healthy desire for the chocolate. Perhaps that desire, caused by System 1, represents her 'better' self. But deciding cases like this one by one is no substitute for an account of the self in dual-process theory that will yield an adequate analysis of instrumental rationality. As cognitive scientists, we cannot go back to a Cartesian position and imagine that there is a metaphysical self with unified goals. We must think of the self as in some sense constructed and not as a metaphysical given. But it does not solve the problem to hold that System 1 and System 2 are separate 'systems' in a strong sense—two separate minds in effect—that could have different rationalities to go with different goals.

Perhaps our young woman has had an eating disorder for a long time, and her tendency to choose foods low in calories has become a System 1 habit. Her conflict will then be one in which System 1 appears to be fighting itself. This kind of case is one reason why we must agree with Stanovich (2004) that System 1 is better thought of as 'the autonomous set of systems'. It is equally true that System 2 cannot always be thought of as a unified 'system' in a strong sense, with no conflict in goals. Some of the young woman's type 2 processing about losing weight, to look 'good' in fashionable clothes, could be in conflict with other type 2 processing, about being healthy. She might be in two type 2 minds about which diet is best for her, or have no stable preference for one diet over another.

Furthermore, all of these variants on a 'multiple minds' analysis of our young woman's situation present us with the threat of what Frankfurt (1971) has termed 'wantonness'—they characterize an individual who has various goals and no principled means of choosing amongst them. In Frankfurt's view, such 'wantons' are not persons, because they lack a framework for ordering their goals to express a more or less unified will; there is no such thing as a 'better' or preferred self to which one can appeal in order to resolve the case.

Of course, it is also possible that our young woman is not a 'wanton'—that she does have a preferred self, which is represented by her (type 1 or type 2) pursuit of her goal of dieting, and which seeks to override her type 1 'base' desire for high-calorie foods. She may seek to achieve a unified will by rejecting concerns for health in favor of her pursuit of further weight loss. In such a case her choice of the chocolate does indeed represent an (albeit nonstandard) illustration of weakness of the will.

In the standard account of instrumental rationality, people are rational insofar as they reliably achieve their goals. So a problem arises in applying this account when a person does not have unified and stable goals, insofar as it provides us with no framework to adjudicate between the various goals. Of course, we could just declare that people are 'irrational' if they do not have stable and unified goals; but that is to claim, in effect, that people *should* have stability and unity of goals as a higher level goal, and that they are rational to the extent that they achieve that higher goal. However, there is no basis in instrumental rationality for prescribing ultimate goals, at low or high level, as 'rational'. In the instrumental analysis, goals are simply given and are not prescribed by rationality. Not even the goal of having consistent and true beliefs can be prescribed in general. We should, of course, define science in terms of this goal, but we cannot make adopting it a necessary condition for rationality in ordinary affairs.

Not even scientists have to have the goal of knowing the truth in all aspects of their lives. After all, 'not every fact is worth knowing or even worth having a true belief about' (Nozick 1993, pp.67–8); and indeed one may furthermore have good reason not to seek truth in certain circumstances—for example, one may not want to know the true prognosis for a serious medical condition that one has (Evans and Over 1996).

The instrumental analysis of rationality allows only restricted scope for criticizing goals. The use of reasons or rules to infer goals depends on other goals. Our reason for desiring good health might be to prolong our life, and we achieve that underlying goal by following rules for healthy eating—so, in this case, we could judge our (subordinate) goal of healthy eating to be rational insofar as it helps us to achieve our (ultimate) goal of healthy longevity. However, reasons and rule following cannot give us ultimate or underlying goals in the first place. As Simon (1983, pp.7–8) said:

> Reason is wholly instrumental. It cannot tell us where to go; at best it can tell us how to get there. It is a gun for hire that can be employed in the service of any goals we have, good or bad.

Hume (1978/1739–40, Section III) is the source for contemporary instrumental rationality, and he allowed criticism of goals based on false beliefs. Following him in this, we could criticize the young woman if her goal of losing weight was the result of a false belief that she was overweight. If the belief was definitely false, and impervious to evidence, we could decide that she had a mental illness; her refusal to give informed consent to medical treatment could be set aside, and she be forced into hospital. We might also feel justified in making decisions for her if we considered her too young to act in her best interests. In these cases, we would claim to be striving for the goal she would have if she were well or an adult.

There are, of course, existing criteria for deciding whether people are able to make decisions about their own best interests and give informed consent to medical treatment, but different countries and medical organizations have different criteria (as can be seen by reading the sections on informed consent at the web sites of the UK Department of Health, the General Medical Council, and similar organizations in other countries). This illustrates why the need for an account of the self and its rationality is not a purely academic debate—judgments about rationality are applied not only in abstruse literature on reasoning experiments (for example), but also in real-world decisions, of both everyday and potentially life-changing import. Hence it is crucial that dual-process theory is able to provide a psychologically and theoretically robust account of rationality and the self that will help us to decide cases in general and have practical applications, such as stating criteria for informed consent. We certainly cannot reach this goal of dual-process theory in what remains of this chapter. We will discuss, however, some points that are relevant to it.

Stanovich on rational integration and the dilemma of Huckleberry Finn

The dual-process theorist should provide some account of the self and its rationality, given all the cases of possible mental conflict that such an approach entails. Too much conflict in goals makes assessments of rationality impossible and can destroy, at the extreme, the very notion of the self. However, dual-process theorists should not always assume that completely resolving goal conflict is itself a goal that everyone should have. Adopting the instrumental account of rationality, we cannot simply prescribe as rational the higher level goal of resolving all conflicts in goals. It would be an impossible goal to achieve, for human beings with bounded rationality (Simon 1957, 1990; Baron 1985; Cherniak 1986; Oaksford and Chater 1993, 1995; Stanovich 1999). There will always be some conflict between a type 2 preference for a healthy diet and the type 1 desire for fat and sugar. More generally, there will always be conflicts between longer term goals and the desire for immediate gratification. (See McClure et al. 2004, and McClure et al. 2007, and the evidence they supply for dual processes.)

Nevertheless, dual-process theorists—insofar as they have addressed this problem at all—have tended to argue (or simply assume) that we should at least seek to minimize such conflicts. Indeed, it is often taken to be obvious that 'psychological consistency is itself valuable' (Frankish 2004, p.156); and Stanovich (2004, 2008; drawing upon Nozick 1993) advocates the pursuit of what he calls 'rational integration' of our beliefs and goals. However, as we have already emphasized, instrumental rationality does not allow us simply to prescribe rational goals. We need to establish whether (and if so why) it is instrumentally rational to prefer consistency in our beliefs and goals. Inconsistent beliefs cannot all be true, and inconsistent goals cannot all be successfully achieved. But then people do not have to have the goal of complete truth in their beliefs or complete success in their actions.

It is not difficult to establish the desirability of some stability in goals—radically unstable preferences can render us a 'wanton' or incapable of any action (Frankish 2004). Importantly, however, this does not imply that *complete* consistency or stability is necessary for rationality. We have already established that psychological consistency is unattainable for finite thinkers in a complex environment.

It is impossible to achieve fully Stanovich's rational integration, as he points out himself—furthermore, he suggests (2004, pp.241–3) that there are worse faults than to fall prey to inconsistency such as the hypocrisy of having high ideals that one cannot perfectly fulfil. He holds (p.243) that one achieves 'an additional level of personhood' when 'one notices and is bothered by lack of rational integration'—a level of integration, we note, that only type 2 thought can attain. However, we argue, more strongly, that in order to be rational, one does not always have to be 'bothered' by a lack of integration that one is aware of. One should not unthinkingly disregard such cognitive conflicts, as a wanton does, but sometimes it may be rationally acceptable— and perhaps even desirable—to tolerate this conflict rather than seek a more complete integration.

Consider the moral dilemma of Huckleberry Finn that has been discussed by philosophers and psychologists (Twain 2003/1885; Bennett 1974; McIntyre 1990; Stanovich 2004, 2008). Huck has run away from a brutal father and met a slave, Jim, who has run away from his owner. Jim has become Huck's friend, and Huck's dilemma is whether or not to inform on Jim so he can be returned to his owner, a woman who has tried to help Huck in the past. This is usually presented as a conflict between Huck's conscience, as someone brought up in a slave owning society, and his feelings of friendship for Jim. But Huck's reported thoughts show that he lacks integration in both his type 2 reflections and in his type 1 feelings (in Twain 2003/1885, chs 16 and 31). He thinks that he has obligations to both Jim and Jim's owner, and he has feelings of sympathy for both. After struggling with the dilemma for some time, he decides not to 'bother' about what is the right thing to do any more (ch.16).

Stanovich (2004, 2008) uses Huck's case to illustrate that rational integration need not entail that explicit reasoning should always override type 1 processes. In his view, Huck makes the right decision by relying on his type 1 emotions of friendship. Now we agree that it is sometimes rational, and morally correct, to act on one's type 1 emotion and not type 2 thoughts.[3] However, Huck's case illustrates more than this—it also shows that the pursuit of 'rational' integration is not always appropriate. As we have just pointed out, Huck has conflicts at both the type 1 and type 2 levels, and he gives up trying to resolve these. We believe that Huck was right to give up even trying to achieve integration in his thoughts and feelings, especially as he always does *act*, with impressive resourcefulness and intelligence, to protect Jim. It is far from obvious that Huck would do better to abandon entirely one or the other of his conflicting sympathies for, and obligations to, Jim and his owner; and it would have been extremely difficult for an almost uneducated young boy to reconcile such conflicts inherent in a slave owning society that was supposed to be committed to principles of human equality. It would take a civil war, costing hundreds of thousands of lives, and three constitutional amendments to achieve this resolution in American principles and American minds (McPherson 1988).

There are often conflicts between judgments based on duty or justice and moral emotions like sympathy. We cannot do justice here to the questions raised by these (although see de Sousa 1987; Frank 1988; Damasio 1996; also Smith and Collins, this volume). Our primary concern, for present purposes, is the implication that the pursuit of 'rational' integration is sometimes not just unfeasible, but also undesirable— that it is not always rational for us to try to get into a high level frame of mind where we no longer experience the conflict between (for example) justice and sympathy. Of course, in any particular circumstance we must obey the rules of non-contradiction and excluded middle by deciding one way or the other—either Huck turns Jim in or he does not—and in some circumstances we may indeed wish to reject decisively one or the other of our conflicting desires—no doubt most alcoholics do not wish to identify with their addiction. But we argue that the pursuit of integration is not always more rational than tolerating, and even embracing, our conflicting goals.

One might object that this is an oversimplified characterization of rational integration —that it need not entail abandoning one goal in favor of the other, but rather revising and refining both goals so that they complement rather than conflict with one another. However, we argue that this is an oversimplified picture. Often, one does not (and perhaps cannot) seamlessly meld the two original conflicting goals into a

---

[3] This need not imply that the rational action is always the morally correct one—but that is a topic for another paper.

unified higher-level goal, but rather holds them in creative tension with each other—both goals remain, and continue to pull in opposite directions in many instances, and one is simply required to decide one way or the other in any particular circumstance. Our view of cognitive coherence as a *defeasible* rational requirement (McIntyre 1990) enables us to permit this approach, and we argue further that in some cases this creative tension presents a preferable solution to integration.

Another example helps us to see that a solution which tolerates some degree of cognitive conflict may not only be more 'rational', in the sense of best reflecting the complexity of our situation within our cognitive limits, but may additionally be a more human response. Consider the dilemma, no doubt familiar to many of us, of how to pursue goals both of progressing in our academic field, and of fulfilling our family commitments—the fabled 'work-life balance'. Each of these goals is desirable, and we probably do not regard it as an optimal solution to resolve this conflict by granting one goal priority over the other *tout court*, as rational integration would seem to require. Nor does it seem plausible to suggest, in such cases, that one can straightforwardly refine the goals in order to resolve the conflict—the tension between them is inherent. Rather, rationality of the self requires that we seek a way of somehow managing this conflict whilst avoiding a level of radical cognitive instability or incoherence such that would undermine our status as a unified agent.

It seems plausible to suggest that this is one example where integration would result in loss—that we might prefer to identify with, in part, a tendency to experience the conflict between commitments to work and family; and even to see the capacity to experience such conflicts as part of what it is to be human—in the extreme, to remove the conflict entirely would be to 'cut [ourselves] off from the human condition' (Bennett 1974, p.134). It is far from obvious that such a response is irrational; rather, it could be argued that we display our rationality in recognizing the existence of such conflicts and not in resolving or even wanting to resolve them. This kind of rationality is only possible for creatures with type 2 processing.

So, where does this leave our quest for a unified account of the self and of rationality—is the entire project misguided or doomed to failure? We think not; but that, in order to understand and underpin the unity of the human mind and its rationality, we need to adopt a different perspective.

Minimal rationality

Dual-process theories have tended to focus on particular aspects of human cognition—for example, perception and attention; skilled performance; learning and memory; social cognition; reasoning and decision making. As we have already observed, efforts are now being made to synthesize these approaches and develop a general account of the mind (see especially Evans 2007, this volume). However, all of these theories presuppose a more basic assumption—namely, that humans are to be regarded as agents. We will draw upon arguments from philosophy of mind to demonstrate that this presupposition already builds in a core notion of the self and of rationality.

Philosophers have long regarded our ability to 'read minds' as something of a puzzle. We do not have privileged access to the mental states of others; indeed, we do not necessarily even have privileged access to our own mental states. Yet in everyday life we can attribute mental states to our fellow humans and successfully interpret their behavior, including their verbal behavior and reasoning when using words like 'and' and 'if'. How do we achieve this feat?

There is now widespread agreement that our ability to understand other people as agents (and even perhaps ourselves), and their verbal behavior, is built upon an assumption known as the 'principle of charity' (Quine 1960; Davidson 1984).[4] The argument runs like this:

- We do not have privileged access to the mental states of others.

- Therefore, in order to be able to understand them, we need to rely upon certain background assumptions which enable us to make sense of them.

- This background assumption is the *principle of charity*—we work on the assumption that most of an individual's beliefs are true, and most of his or her inferences are rational.

This principle, it is argued, is a prerequisite for attributing agency—without it, we cannot make sense of people or the words they use. It does not, however, commit us to anything as strong as a rational integration requirement. Agents do not have to be fully consistent, or have a desire to be, in beliefs let alone in goals.

At first blush, this might seem to be a perverse foundation for our account of rationality. One might be tempted to argue that it establishes the unity of the individual agent and his or her rationality at the expense of any claim to normative authority—it seems that 'rationality' is here invoked as an interpretative principle which grants no meaningful scope for an agent to *fail* to meet such standards. If rationality is *assumed* as a prerequisite for agency, how can we make sense of the notion of an irrational agent?

This objection, we argue, holds only against a simplistic version of the principle of charity, and can be avoided if we draw a distinction between minimal rationality (Cherniak 1986) and full normative rationality. The principle of charity does not require us to interpret *all* human cognition as rational in order to understand an agent—intuitively, we *can* make sense of an agent as making cognitive errors; this is, after all, precisely what provoked the 'rationality debate' in the first place. The argument is rather that people must display (only) a *minimal* level of rationality in order for us to understand them as agents at all—we would *not* be able to make sense of an individual who failed to have elementary deductive competence. (See Evans and Over 1996, 1997 and Over and Evans 1997, on people's basic deductive competence.)

....

4 Of course, the principle of charity is not universally accepted—for an influential rival account, see Stich (1990); and for a detailed argument against Stich's position, see for example Stein (1996, ch.4). It lies beyond the scope of the present argument to present a detailed defence here—however, we refer the reader to accounts of its key role in the dominant 'theory–theory' philosophy of mind; and also in an influential strand of the rival (and arguably less rationalist) 'simulation theory' approach (Moran 1994; Heal 2000), for further discussion of the merits of this approach.

It is important to be clear about the strength, and also the limits, of the claim we are advancing here. On this account, minimal rationality is indeed an interpretative principle, insofar as it is a prerequisite for attributing agency; but it is not a *mere* interpretative principle. Rather, it is constitutive of what it is to be an agent who can reason—it simply is part of what it means to be 'in the logical space of reasons' (Sellars 1956; McDowell 1994). According to this view, there are conceptual constraints on the extent to which an agent can fail to be rational—or, as de Sousa (1971, p.77) puts it, 'no one can be *completely* mad' (and still count as an agent).[5]

A comparison with the notion of moral competence may help to clarify this distinction. Unless creatures are first *capable* of morality, they lie beyond the scope of moral assessment—they are *a*moral (non-human animals and infants are often categorized as such, for instance). In order to condemn an agent as *im*moral, by contrast, it must be the case that he or she is capable of morality—and thus falls within the scope of evaluation according to moral criteria—but fails to meet those standards. On this analogy, minimal rationality is comparable to moral competence. Without it, one is not irrational, but simply non-rational, using 'rational' in a sense that can be applied to human agents, but not to non-human animals that stand outside 'the logical space of reasons'. Only once one crosses the threshold of this competence does one become capable of meeting, or failing to meet, human rational standards, and thus count as an (rational or irrational) human agent.

As this analogy also makes clear, however, minimal rationality does not require impeccable cognitive performance—it is, rather, a claim about basic rational competence. For example, in making most decisions, agents must be able to obey the logical rule of the excluded middle and grasp that they must either perform an action or not perform it, and the logical law of non-contradiction and grasp that they cannot both perform the action and not perform it. That does not mean that their beliefs generally must be free of all inconsistency, or that they must always be able to apply the rule of excluded middle to all circumstances (and indeed it may not apply to vague properties or other cases in which there are truth value gaps; see Evans and Over 2004).

We can see a person who fulfils the minimal level of rationality as being an agent and having a mind. After that, there is still scope for saying that the person fails to meet all the non-minimal standards of normative rationality—which are not exhausted by the rules governing minimal competence (although it lies beyond the scope of the current paper to explore this issue in detail). For example, consider the conjunction fallacy (Tversky and Kahneman 1983). People have a tendency in certain contexts to think of a conjunction, 'p and q', as more probable than one of its conjuncts, p. This is normatively incorrect. It violates the elementary logical rule of conjunction elimination: that 'p and q' logically implies p. However, we do not conclude

---

5 Compare Frankish (2004), who argues that the rationality of our 'basic mind' is constitutive of agency, whereas our 'supermind' (the locus of conscious thought and reasoning) is capable of rationality or irrationality. It should be noted, however, that Frankish's account of rationality and reasoning is in other ways quite different to that presented here—although a detailed exploration of these considerations lies beyond the scope of our current argument.

from these results that people do not understand the word 'and'. The reason is that there are many contexts in which people do explicitly follow conjunction elimination; and there are so-called 'transparent contexts' in which people not only explicit follow this logical rule, but also make normatively correct probability judgments (Barbey and Sloman 2007; Over 2007a, b).

Compare human beings with other animals. We can see a kind of instrumental rationality, as successful goal-directed behavior, in many other creatures (Over 2004). Other animals have type 1 mental processes that are often reliable and implicitly conform to logical rules. Animals can implicitly conform to the conjunction rule that 'p and q' logically implies p, and every animal with a conditioned response can be said to comply with MP implicitly. But only human beings have the *ability* to follow conjunction elimination and MP in explicit type 2 thought. This ability is not displayed in all contexts, and people can commit fallacies in their conjunctive and conditional reasoning. They can commit some of these fallacies in their explicit type 2 reasoning: they can explicitly follow fallacious rules in some contexts. But there have to be circumstances in which people explicitly follow the elementary logical rules for 'and' and 'if' in type 2 mental processes, for otherwise they could not be said to understand these constructs any better than a dog or a wasp (see also Dennett 1984; Stanovich 2004, pp.73–8).

Return to the Ann problem for another example. To solve this correctly, as we have pointed out, people must see the relevance of the logical law of the excluded middle and engage in explicit conditional reasoning from alternatives. Many people do not see the relevance of this law and do not do the explicit reasoning, but it does not take exceptional IQ to solve the Ann problem (Toplak and Stanovich 2002). Anyone could solve the Ann problem in transparent contexts and go on to find similar problems trivial (Over 2007b). It is people's ability to follow logical rules when these are transparently relevant to a problem that gives them the minimal rationality that is characteristic of human beings (compare Evans and Over 1996, 1997 and Over and Evans 1997, on rationality).

People can have minimal rationality although they do not always have stable goals or decide a question in consistent ways. They may at times prefer pleasure in their diet and sometimes good health where these conflict. They may at times make a decision using abstract principles of justice and at other times by expressing a moral emotion like sympathy. To have minimal rationality, they do not have to have, or even strive for, fully consistent integration in their beliefs, values, and goals. Once granted this minimal level of rationality, however, there remains scope for agents to fail to meet further rational standards, so the normative value of rationality is preserved.

The dual-process theory of the mind has had conflict built into it from the start. This is one of its (many) positive aspects. Only type 2 rational creatures can have, and be aware of, the conflicts we have been describing. Dual-process theory gives us a framework that recognizes the extent to which people are inconsistent and can have incompatible goals, but it does not yet provide us with a complete account of the whole self and its rationality. If, as we argue, it is neither possible nor necessarily desirable entirely to eliminate conflicting beliefs and desires, then much more has to be discovered about how people do respond to the inconsistencies and conflicts described by dual-process theory. As we learn more about that empirical matter, we can also try to answer the normative question of when one should try to eliminate inconsistencies and conflicts and when one should try to live with them. However, what we should not do is take the simple normative position that inconsistency and conflict in our thoughts and goals should not exist at all.

Acknowledgments

Our thanks are due to Jonathan Evans, Keith Frankish, Leland Saunders, and Keith Stanovich for helpful comments on an earlier version of this paper.

References

Barbey, A.K. and Sloman, S.A. (2007) Base-rate respect: from ecological rationality to dual processes. *Behavioral and Brain Sciences*, **30**, 241–97.

Baron, J. (1985) *Rationality and intelligence*. Cambridge University Press, Cambridge.

Bennett, J. (1974) The conscience of Huckleberry Finn. *Philosophy*, **49**, 123–34.

Carruthers, P. (2006) *The architecture of the mind*. Oxford University Press, Oxford.

Cherniak, C. (1986) *Minimal rationality*. MIT Press, Cambridge, MA.

Cosmides, L. (1989) The logic of social exchange: has natural selection shaped how humans reason? Studies with the Wason selection task. *Cognition*, **31**, 187–276.

Cosmides, L. and Tooby, J. (1994) Better than rational: Evolutionary psychology and the invisible hand. *American Economic Review*, **84**, 327–32.

Damasio, A.R. (1996) *Descartes' error: Reason, emotion and the human brain*. Papermac, London.

Davidson, D. (1984) *Inquiries into truth and interpretation*. Clarendon Press, Oxford.

Dennett, D.C. (1984) *Elbow room: The varieties of free will worth wanting*. MIT Press, Cambridge, MA.

de Sousa, R.B. (1971) How to give a piece of your mind: Or, the logic of belief and assent. *Review of Metaphysics*, **25**, 52–79.

de Sousa, R. (1987) *The rationality of emotion*. MIT Press, Cambridge, MA.

Evans, J.St.B.T. (2007) *Hypothetical thinking: Dual processes in reasoning and judgement*. Psychology Press, Hove.

Evans, J.St.B.T. and Over, D.E. (1996) *Rationality and reasoning*. Psychology Press, Hove.

Evans, J.St.B.T. and Over, D.E. (1997) Rationality in reasoning: The problem of deductive competence. *Current Psychology of Cognition*, **16**, 3–38.

Evans, J.St.B.T. and Over, D.E. (2004) *If*. Oxford University Press, Oxford.

Fodor, J.A. (1983) *The modularity of mind: An essay in faculty psychology*. MIT Press, Cambridge, MA.

Frank, R.H. (1988) *Passions within reason: The strategic role of the emotions*. Norton, New York.

Frankfurt, H.G. (1971) Freedom of the will and the concept of a person. *Journal of Philosophy*, **48**, 5–20.

Frankish, K. (2004) *Mind and supermind*. Cambridge University Press, Cambridge.

Gigerenzer, G., Todd, P.M., and the ABC Research Group (1999) *Simple heuristics that make us smart*. Oxford University Press, Oxford.

Heal, J. (2000) Other minds, rationality and analogy. *Proceedings of the Aristotelian Society,* Supplementary Volume, **74**, 1–19.

Hume, D. (1978/1739–40) *A treatise of human nature*, L. A. Selby-Bigge and P. H. Nidditch (eds), 2nd ed. Clarendon Press, Oxford.

Kant, I. (1950/1781) *The critique of pure reason*, trans. N. Kemp Smith. Macmillan, London.

Kleiter, G. (1994) Natural sampling: Rationality without base rates. In G.H. Fisher and D. Laming (ed.) *Contributions to mathematical psychology, psychometrics and methodology*. Springer-Verlag, New York.

Levesque, H.J. (1986) Making believers of computers. *Artificial Intelligence*, **30**, 81–108.

McCarthy, J. and Hayes, P.J. (1969) Some philosophical problems from the standpoint of artificial intelligence. In B, Meltzer and D, Michie (eds) *Machine intelligence,* vol. 4. Edinburgh University Press, Edinburgh.

McClure, S.M., Laibson, D.I., Loewenstein, G., and Cohen, J.D. (2004) Separate neural systems value immediate and delayed monetary rewards. *Science*, **306**, 503–7.

McClure, S.M., Ericson, K.M., Laibson, D.I., Loewenstein, G., and Cohen, J.D. (2007) Time discounting for primary rewards. *Journal of Neuroscience*, **27**, 5796–804.

McDowell, J. (1994) *Mind and world*. Harvard University Press, Cambridge, MA.

McIntyre, A. (1990) Is akratic action always irrational? In O. Flanagan and A.O. Rorty (eds) *Identity, character and morality: Essays in moral psychology*. MIT Press, Cambridge, MA.

McPherson, J.M. (1988) *Battle cry of freedom: The Civil War era*. Oxford University Press, New York.

Moran, R. (1994) Interpretation theory and the first person. *Philosophical Quarterly*, **44**, 154–73.

Nozick, R. (1993) *The nature of rationality*. Princeton University Press, Princeton, NJ.

Oaksford, M. and Chater, N. (1993) Reasoning theories and bounded rationality. In K.I. Manktelow and D.E. Over (eds) *Rationality: Psychological and philosophical perspectives*. Routledge, London.

Oaksford, M. and Chater, N. (1995) Theories of reasoning and the computational explanation of everyday inference. *Thinking and Reasoning*, **1**, 121–52.

Over, D.E. (2000) Ecological rationality and its heuristics. *Thinking and Reasoning*, **6**,182–92.

Over, D.E. (2003) From massive modularity to meta-representation: the evolution of higher cognition. In D.E. Over (ed.) *Evolution and the psychology of thinking: The debate*. Psychology Press, Hove.

Over, D.E. (2004) Rationality and the normative/descriptive distinction. In D. Koehler and N. Harvey (eds) *Blackwell handbook of judgment and decision making*. Blackwell, Oxford.

Over, D.E. (2007a) Content-independent conditional inference. In J. Maxwell (ed.) *Integrating the mind: Domain general versus domain specific processes in higher cognition*. Psychology Press, Hove.

Over, D.E. (2007b) The logic of natural sampling. *Behavioral and Brain Sciences*, **30**, 277.

Over, D.E. and Evans, J.St.B.T. (1997) Two cheers for deductive competence. *Current Psychology of Cognition*, **16**, 255–78.

Pylyshyn, Z.W. (ed.) (1987) *The robot's dilemma: The frame problem of artificial intelligence*. Ablex, Norwood, NJ.

Quine, W.V.O. (1960) *Word and object*. MIT Press, Cambridge, MA.

Rode, C., Cosmides, L., Hell, W., and Tooby, J. (1999) When and why do people avoid unknown probabilities in decisions under uncertainty? Testing some predictions from optimal foraging theory. *Cognition*, **72**, 269–304.

Sellars, W. (1956) Empiricism and the philosophy of mind. In H. Feigl and M. Scriven (eds) *The foundations of science and the concepts of psychology and psychoanalysis: Minnesota studies in the philosophy of science, I.* University of Minnesota Press, Minneapolis.

Simon, H. (1957) *Models of man.* Wiley, New York.

Simon, H. (1983) *Reason in human affairs.* Stanford University Press, Stanford.

Simon, H. (1990) Invariants of human behavior. *Annual Review of Psychology*, **41**, 1–19.

Sloman, S.A. (1996) The empirical case for two systems of reasoning. *Psychological Bulletin*, **119**, 3–22.

Smith, E.E., Langston, C., and Nisbett, R.E. (1992) The case for rules in reasoning. *Cognitive Science*, **16**, 1–40.

Sorensen, R. (2006) Epistemic paradoxes. *The Stanford encyclopedia of philosophy.* Available at: http://plato.stanford.edu/entries/epistemic-paradoxes//

Stanovich, K. E. (1999) *Who is rational? Studies of individual differences in reasoning.* Lawrence Erlbaum Associates, Mahwah, NJ.

Stanovich, K.E. (2004) *The robot's rebellion: Finding meaning in the age of Darwin.* Chicago University Press, Chicago, IL.

Stanovich, K.E. (2008) Higher-order preferences and the master rationality motive. *Thinking and Reasoning*, **14**, 111–27.

Stanovich, K.E. and West, R.F. (2003) Evolutionary versus instrumental goals: How evolutionary psychology misconceives human rationality. In D. E. Over (ed.) *Evolution and the psychology of thinking: The debate.* Psychology Press, Hove.

Stein, E. (1996) *Without good reason: The rationality debate in philosophy and cognitive science.* Clarendon Press, Oxford.

Stich, S.P. (1990) *The fragmentation of reason: Preface to a pragmatic theory of cognitive evaluation.* MIT Press, Cambridge, MA.

Strassman, B.I. and Dunbar, R.I.M. (1999) Human evolution and disease: Putting the stone age in perspective. In S.C. Stearns (ed.) *Evolution in health and disease.* Oxford University Press, Oxford.

Toplak, M.E. and Stanovich, K.E. (2002) The domain specificity and generality of disjunctive reasoning: Searching for a generalizable critical reasoning skill. *Journal of Educational Psychology*, **94**, 197–209.

Tversky, A. and Kahneman, D. (1983) Extensional versus intuitive reasoning: the conjunction fallacy in probability judgment. *Psychological Review*, **90**, 293–315.

Twain, M. (2003/1885) *Adventures of Huckleberry Finn (Tom Sawyer's Comrade)*, ed. V. Fischer and L. Salamo. University of California Press, Berkeley, CA.

Chapter 15

Reason and intuition in the moral life: A dual-process account of moral justification

Leland F. Saunders

Are moral judgments rational? Many of us think so, and according to one influential research tradition in moral reasoning and moral judgment, they are (Piaget 1932; Kohlberg et al. 1983; Kohlberg 1984). On this view, moral judgments are the conclusions of deductions from consciously held moral principles, such as: Harm is morally bad; *x* is harmful; therefore, *x* is morally bad. Call this the *deductive model* of moral judgment. The deductive model of moral judgment is intended as both a normative theory and a theory of the psychological processes that underlie moral judgment. And notice that both components are necessary to show that moral judgments are rational. We need a normative theory of moral justification that shows that morality is a rational enterprise, and a psychological theory that shows that the normative model is actually implemented in human psychology. A normative theory whose requirements are not psychologically possible for humans cannot establish the rationality of our moral judgments. Likewise, a psychological theory of moral judgment alone cannot provide rational justification of our moral judgments apart from some normative theory.

According to the deductive model, the criteria for the rationality of moral judgments are their logical validity and their relationship to general moral principles. The deductive model has been a dominant psychological paradigm for research on human reasoning in a number of domains (for a review see Evans 2002), including moral reasoning and judgment in the tradition of Piaget and Kohlberg. Moral intuitions, however, raise serious difficulties for the deductive model, because they show that moral judgments can arise in ways ruled out by the psychological theory it posits. Moral intuitions are the sorts of easy and immediate moral judgments that we constantly make without any conscious effort and that strike us with a perception-like quality—characteristics that distinguish them from ordinary deductions that are comparatively slow and effortful. Moreover, unlike moral judgments in the deductive model, the sources of our moral intuitions are opaque, and we do not know what, if any, principles might underlie them. The very term 'moral intuition' is, in fact, meant to distinguish them from the kind of reasoned moral judgment described by the deductive model. These phenomenological differences alone, however, do not show that the deductive model cannot explain moral intuitions, since they may be the result of very quick and perhaps enthymematic deductions.

The real challenge comes from recent findings that show that moral intuitions can leave us 'dumbfounded' (Haidt 2001; Haidt and Hersch 2001; Hauser 2006; Hauser et al. 2007). I will explain the details of this research shortly, but in summary it indicates that moral intuitions are not always immediately responsive to reasons, since they can persist even after subjects recognize compelling reasons to modify or drop them. This is a puzzling result if moral intuitions are thought of as the conclusions of deductions from consciously held moral principles, because deductive conclusions are easily modifiable, especially if one of the premises is shown to be false or in need of modification, as is the case in moral dumbfounding experiments. Moral dumbfounding strongly suggests, then, that the deductive model cannot explain the rational basis of moral intuitions, and by extension it casts doubt on the rationality of morality as a whole.

The challenge, then, is to show how morality can be rational if moral intuitions are resistant to rational reflection. Again, there are two parts to this question, one normative and the other psychological. The normative problem is whether there is a model of moral justification that can show that morality is a rational enterprise given the facts of moral dumbfounding. Appealing to the model of reflective equilibrium for the rational justification of moral intuitions, I argue, fairly easily solves this problem. Reflective equilibrium views the rational justification of morality as a back and forth balancing between moral theory and moral intuition, and therefore does not require that individual moral intuitions be directly responsive to rational reflection. The psychological problem is whether human psychology actually implements the processes required for reflective equilibrium. The psychological problem is far more difficult, and will require appealing to a dual-process view of moral judgment that regards moral intuitions and moral theories as belonging to different mental systems. This allows us to explain the potential gap between moral intuition and moral theory demonstrated by moral dumbfounding, and more importantly, allows us to show how moral intuitions and moral theory can satisfy the requirements of reflective equilibrium.

Moral dumbfounding and rational justification

A striking example of how people can be dumbfounded with respect to their moral intuitions can be found in Haidt's research, using the following vignette:

> Julie and Mark are brother and sister. They are traveling together in France on summer vacation from college. One night, they are staying alone in a cabin near the beach. They decide that it would be interesting and fun if they tried making love. At the very least it would be a new experience for each of them. Julie was already taking birth control pills, but Mark uses a condom just to be safe. They both enjoy making love, but they decide not to do it again. They keep that night as a special secret, which makes them feel even closer to each other. What do you think about that, was it OK for them to make love? (Haidt, 2001)

Most participants in Haidt's research think not, and judge Mark and Julie's actions to be seriously morally wrong. However, when pressed to explain why they are wrong, they are unable to give coherent reasons in support of their judgment. Many start by making appeals to principles of harm—for example, that Julie and Mark will be emotionally traumatized by the experience, or that they will have defective children. Yet, this case excludes the possibility of harm on these fronts, and even when subjects are reminded of this, they nevertheless judge the actions of Mark and Julie to be seriously morally wrong. The judgment of moral wrongness persists even after the participants find that there are no reasons supporting the judgment; this is the phenomenon Haidt labels 'moral dumbfounding'. Though subjects are able to offer some reasons for their judgments, the reasons offered are often confabulated and lack coherence or relevance to the actual vignette—a finding supported by Hauser and colleagues (Hauser 2006; Hauser et al. 2007).

These findings raise serious difficulties for the psychological theory of moral judgment posited by the deductive model. On the deductive model, even if the initial judgment was arrived at through some unconscious or enthymematic reasoning process, the judgment would be responsive to conscious and explicit reasons, since we could consciously entertain the premises, recognize the error in our reasoning, and then modify our judgment accordingly. Yet, in the case of moral dumbfounding, people consciously recognize reasons against their initial judgment, but fail to modify it—something that should be psychologically impossible on the deductive model. Furthermore, if rational justification depends on there being a proper relationship between principles and judgment, then moral intuitions show it is not always psychologically possible to demonstrate the logical validity of that relationship, since we do not know what, if any, moral principles might underlie the moral intuition. The deductive model fails the psychological test, because it cannot provide a plausible psychological theory that implements its normative requirements. If moral judgments are rational, some other model of justification is needed.

One model of moral justification that can quite naturally account for moral dumbfounding is reflective equilibrium (Rawls 1999). According to reflective equilibrium, we use our moral intuitions as a starting point for moral theorizing. From particular moral judgments we begin to theorize about what they have in common—for example, whether they point to any common wrong-making feature or principle. Moral theories are then constructed, guided by constraints of consistency, coherence, and completeness. Of course, not all moral intuitions will accord with the resultant theory, and when intuitions conflict a person will have to decide whether to stick with their theory and revise their intuitions, or to stick with their intuitions and revise their theory. There is no hard and fast rule about when to choose theory over intuition or vice versa, but if the intuition is strongly held, and the change to the theory required to accommodate it is minimal, then it seems reasonable to modify the theory. Conversely, if the theory is general and wide-ranging, and the intuition only mildly held, it seems reasonable to revise the intuition to accord with the theory. The goal of all this back and forth is to achieve maximum consonance between theory and intuition—that is, a reflective equilibrium. Rawls argues that reflective equilibrium counts as rational justification because, '[Rational] justification is a matter of the mutual support of many considerations, of everything fitting together into one coherent view' (Rawls 1999, p.19).

At first glance it may seem that reflective equilibrium faces the same problem with moral dumbfounding as the deductive model, since it too requires that moral intuitions be responsive to reasons to achieve equilibrium with theory. This is true, but a little too simple. Reflective equilibrium does not require that moral intuitions be immediately corrigible by reasoned reflection; rather it requires only that, over time, a person's moral intuitions can be made to conform to their moral theory. This process of reflective modification and endorsement also provides rational justification for occurrent moral intuitions, because the moral intuitions that are modified or endorsed upon reflection inherit the rationality of the process. Thus, if someone has reflectively modified or endorsed a moral intuition prohibiting incest, in accordance with their moral theory, then that intuition is rational, even if, on a given occasion, reasons for it cannot be produced. Moral dumbfounding, therefore, does not raise any difficulties for reflective equilibrium, because it does not require that we be able to articulate reasons for our moral intuitions or that we be able to overrule them; only that they are justified through a rational process of modification and endorsement.

Reflective equilibrium is a plausible normative account of the rationality of moral judgments that is widely accepted (see, for example: Rawls 1999; Smith 1994; Daniels 1996; Kamm 2007), and I propose that we accept it as well. With our normative account of moral judgments in place, we now need to show how the process can be implemented in human psychology.

Two systems and the possibility of reflective equilibrium

Part of what makes reflective equilibrium attractive as a normative theory of moral judgment is that it recognizes a potential gap between moral intuitions and a consciously held moral theory—a gap strikingly demonstrated by moral dumbfounding. Any plausible psychological account of reflective equilibrium needs to explain how that gap is possible. It is important to note that disparities between intuitions and consciously held theories occur with respect to many cognitive domains, not just morality. For example, people often make judgments about probabilities that are in direct conflict with consciously held norms of conjunction (Tversky and Kahneman 1983). It is now a robust finding that humans regularly and persistently make judgments that violate their consciously held norms, even when they have all the resources to reason through a problem carefully and correctly (for a review see Brenner et al. 2002).

The potential disparity between intuitions and consciously held norms cannot be explained by a unified theory of judgment (Gilbert 1999), and the theory of reflective equilibrium also assumes that there are two distinct methods for arriving at a moral judgment—one that is quick, automatic, and nonconscious, and another that is slow, deliberate, and conscious. This fits nicely with dual-process theories of reasoning, according to which humans have two reasoning systems, distinguished by their functional characteristics. System 1 processes are fast, automatic, and nonconscious, whereas System 2 processes are slow, deliberate, and conscious (Evans and Over 1996; Sloman 1996, 2002; Stanovich 1999; Kahneman and Frederick 2002; Wilson 2002).

Beyond this general description, there is little consensus on how best to draw the line between the two different kinds of systems. For example, some theorists have suggested that the two systems differ with respect to evolutionary age, arguing that System 1 is evolutionarily old and shared with other animals, whereas System 2 is evolutionarily recent and distinctively human (Evans and Over 1996; Stanovich 1999). There are good reasons to be skeptical of a cut and dried division of the two systems in terms of evolutionary age (Evans 2008), and it is quite possible that some, if not all, of the processes underlying moral intuitions are evolutionarily recent and distinctively human (Hauser 2006). However, nothing of what follows depends on adopting any particular view about the evolutionary age of the two systems.

Another common claim is that System 1 processes are associative, and System 2 processes are rule-based (Sloman 1996, 2002; Kahneman and Frederick 2002; Strack and Deutsch 2004). But here too there is good reason for thinking that the characterization of the two systems on this basis is too simplistic, and that at least some System 1 operations are indeed rule-governed (Carruthers 2006, this volume; Evans 2008). For example, many researchers claim that System 1 processing involves heuristics, which are not merely associative operations, but rather 'rules of thumb' (Evans 2008). Some System 1 operations may indeed be associative, but not all, and, as we shall see, it is plausible to think that much moral reasoning involves processes of a broadly System 1 kind (fast, automatic, nonconscious) that are nonetheless rule-based.

However, even if the two systems can both employ rules, it is likely that the rules in question will differ in content, and that they are stored in separate memory systems—System 1 rules in a nonconscious implicit system, and System 2 rules in an explicit system, whose contents are available to consciousness (Smith and DeCoster 2000; Evans and Over 1996). The difference in memory systems also has consequences for learning. It takes very little time for System 2 to learn and apply a new rule—for example a rule of logic about how to manipulate symbols to produce valid conclusions—but it takes a great deal of time and repetition for System 1 processes to learn and apply a new rule, if ever. Another consequence of this division is that the two systems can come to different conclusions about the same situation because they draw upon different rules.

When the two systems reach conflicting conclusions, it is possible, in the right circumstances, for a System 1 intuition to be overridden by System 2 reasoning. Indeed, many dual-process theorists characterize System 2 in terms of its role in scrutinizing System 1 intuitions, and either approving or overriding them (Kahneman and Frederick 2002; Gilbert 2002; Stanovich and West 2000; Evans, this volume; Stanovich, this volume). System 2 is not always activated, however, especially if a highly plausible intuition is readily available (Kahneman and Frederick 2002). Moreover, System 2 is easily disrupted by time pressures, multitasking, mood, and time of day (Bodenhausen 1990; Finucane et al. 2000; Kahneman and Frederick 2002). And, even when activated and not disrupted, System 2 cannot always override a strong System 1 intuition (Bargh 1999; Wilson et al. 2000). A System 1 intuition can persist, even when people recognize good reasons to drop or modify it.

A dual-process theory, then, can explain the gaps between moral intuitions and consciously held moral theories. We can think of moral intuitions, like any other kind of intuition, as System 1 judgments, and consciously and explicitly developed moral theories can be thought of as the outcomes of System 2 processes. This suggestion gains further support when we consider possible conflicts between moral intuitions and consciously derived moral judgments. If a moral intuition conflicts with a System 2 moral judgment, or if two moral intuitions conflict, this gives us reason to pause and think through the situation more carefully. These sorts of conflicts are characteristic triggers for reasoning through tricky moral situations, or for that matter even knowing that one is in a tricky moral situation (Cohen 2004).

Furthermore, since dual-process theories recognize that it is possible for System 2 to override a System 1 intuition, but that override is difficult and often fails, dual-process theories provide an explanation for moral dumbfounding, where moral intuitions do not change in response to explicit reasoning about a situation (at least in the short-term). So, moral dumbfounding does not present a problem for a dual-process theory of moral judgment; on the contrary, a dual-process theory of moral judgment explains the facts of moral dumbfounding quite naturally.

Now we need to show how a dual-process theory of moral judgment can satisfy the requirement of reflective equilibrium that our moral intuitions can change to align with our consciously held moral theories. This requirement is much less demanding, in terms of a normative theory, than the deductive model, but it complicates the psychological picture, since we now need to show that System 2 reasoning can, over time, direct changes in System 1 processes to produce moral intuitions that conform to it. This type of change in moral intuitions is different from simply overriding them—it involves changing the kinds of moral intuitions we are disposed to have by changing the rules employed by System 1. We have already seen that many dual-process theories allow for the possibility of learning new rules, over time, by System 1 processes, but we now need to provide a model for how that is possible in the moral case. If we can do that, we will have shown how reflective equilibrium is psychologically possible for minds like ours. To do that, we first need some account of the psychological mechanisms that underlie moral intuitions—that is, a specification of the System 1 processes that give rise to moral intuitions.

A psychology for moral intuitions

If the System 1 operations that give rise to moral intuitions are rule based, then moral intuitions must arise from the application of a set of internalized moral norms. Moral norms have been studied extensively, so there are some fairly robust findings that any psychological model of the System 1 processes underlying moral intuitions must be able to explain. For example, every human society has moral norms, but there is variation in the content of those norms (Brown 1991). Children reliably acquire the prevailing norms of their community from a very early age, and can recognize specifically moral norms between the ages of three and five (Nucci 2001; Turiel 1983). Moral norms have a practical force, which is, perhaps, mediated by emotions, since emotions are somehow involved in, or implicated by, moral intuitions (Greene et al. 2001; Wheatley and Haidt 2005). And lastly, as we have seen, people can be dumbfounded with respect to their moral intuitions (Haidt 2001; Hauser 2006;

Hauser et al. 2007), indicating that at least some of our operative moral norms are not consciously accessible.

Sripada and Stich (2006) offer a plausible psychological model of moral intuitions that synthesizes these findings. Figure 15.1 shows the outlines of the system. In the figure solid lines indicate links for which there is very strong evidence, and the dotted lines indicate links that are more speculative though supported by some evidence.

According to this model, the norms system is divided into two parts: the acquisition system and the execution system. The norms acquisition mechanism allows children to acquire the rules of their community by being sensitive to the appropriate environmental cues, and inferring the norms of their community from them. Sripada and Stich offer no exhaustive list of what the appropriate environmental cues are, but there is evidence that at least some of them are direct verbal admonitions such as, 'Don't hit your sister', and the observation of negative emotional responses in peers and caregivers (Edwards 1987; Turiel 1998). They also give no indication of how much evidence a child needs concerning the content of a rule before he or she acquires it, but it seems highly implausible that only one instance would be sufficient.

After a rule has been inferred, it is stored in the norms database and mapped to a set of perceptual inputs that should invoke it and issue in a judgment. For example, if the rule 'Do not steal' is stored in the norms database, it is mapped to inputs representing the sorts of observable phenomena that count as instances of stealing. Although this example is given in terms of an imperative, Sripada and Stich make no claims about how the rule is represented in the norms database. They offer as possibilities that norms could be represented as prototypes, stereotypes, or narratives. It is also possible that they could be represented as heuristics (Sunstein 2005).

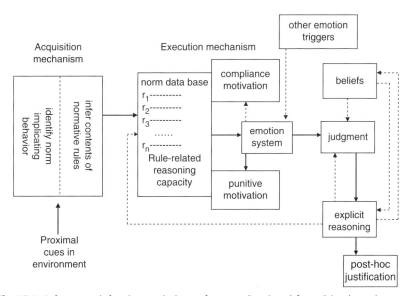

Fig. 15.1 A framework for the psychology of norms. Reprinted from Sripada and Stich (2006).

The database is also connected to the emotion system, which attaches an affective valence to moral judgments—judgments of norm violation have a negative valence, while judgments of norm satisfaction have a positive valence.

There are some limitations to the model that must be mentioned. First, it is incomplete. For example, there is evidence that judgments of intentionality influence our moral intuitions (Núñez and Harris 1998), and that is not included in the Sripada and Stich model. Second, the model is general in scope. That is, the precise details of how the links between various components are accomplished, and what, if any intervening factors may exist are not given. These points are not meant as criticisms, because Sripada and Stich note that their model is a framework, not an exhaustive account, but it is important to recognize that these limitations exist. For our purposes, a plausible framework for the System 1 operations underlying moral intuitions is sufficient, and that is what the Sripada and Stich diagram provides.

Moreover, this framework suggests that the psychology of morality is consistent with a dual-process architecture—a possibility that Sripada and Stich recognize, but do not develop.

> We suspect that some version of the two sets of books hypothesis [that is, dual process theory] is correct ... If the hypothesis is true, it would go a long way towards explaining the commonplace observation that while people do recognize inconsistencies in their moral beliefs and rationally revise certain of them, those changes are often superficial; automatic, intuitive reactions to real-world cases are still governed by the old, inconsistent norms (2006, p.297).

That is all Sripada and Stich say about this possibility, but I think we can do considerably more to explore this suggestion as a working hypothesis, and develop their model in terms of a dual-process theory that could explain the possibility of reflective equilibrium. Our first step is to determine which parts of the diagram belong to System 1, and which parts belong to System 2. Figure 15.2 shows the likely division between the two systems on the Sripada and Stich framework.

The acquisition mechanism most likely belongs to System 1, since young children acquire norms automatically as early as three to five years of age (Nucci 2001; Turiel 1983). Once a norm is acquired, the judgments that result have all the hallmarks of System 1; they are quick, involuntary, and automatic, and strike us with an almost perception-like quality. We simply 'see' the situation as one where a norm is being violated, or where one is being exemplified. We can't help but engage the world in these terms, and this again is a characteristic of System 1 type operations. Also characteristic of System 1 is that people often cannot say *why* they think something wrong, only *that* it is. Often it takes real philosophical work to figure out what rules might underlie such judgments, and often such theories are highly controversial. So, it is plausible that the left part of the diagram up to and including the initial judgment belongs to System 1.

The System 2 portion of the diagram is explicit reasoning and post hoc justification. These operations are conscious and comparatively slow and effortful. Sripada and Stich leave some open questions about what role System 2 plays in moral judgments and in the moral life more generally. For example, they do not discuss whether

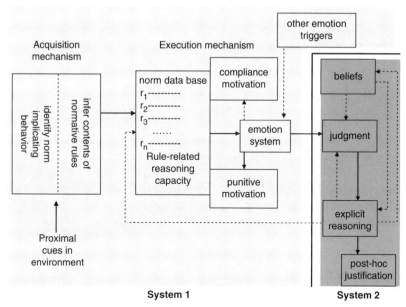

Fig. 15.2 A dual-process framework for the psychology of norms.

System 2 reasoning can result in the modification or rejection of a System 1 intuition. It seems from our discussion of dual-process models that it should be possible at least some of the time, but that it is difficult and often fails, resulting in moral dumbfounding. The only role Sripada and Stich see as being well established by the evidence for System 2 reasoning is post hoc justification, that is, the practice of attempting to justify our moral intuitions by confabulating reasons for them, rather than attempting to derive a justification from an explicit moral theory. Post hoc justification and confabulation are not unique to the moral domain, and some dual-process theorists take the view that System 2 generally operates to provide reasons after the fact for System 1 intuitions (Evans and Over 1996; Wegner 2002; Wilson 2002; Stanovich 2004).

Another possible function of System 2 reasoning that Sripada and Stich see as speculative is that it could have some effect on the contents of the System 1 norms database. This is the critical connection for our purposes, because it could provide the necessary psychological basis for reflective equilibrium. For suppose that we find that some set of our moral intuitions is seriously out of line with the requirements of our moral theory. What we want is to make some System 1 change such that in the future, when confronted with situations that evoke these problematic moral intuitions, we instead come to have moral intuitions that conform to the requirements of our theory. That is, we want to be able to make the 'right' judgments as quickly, unconsciously, and effortlessly as we currently make the wrong ones. If such a change could not be effected, we would be required to overturn those wrong judgments by System 2 processes—a practice which, as we have seen, is effortful and prone to failure. Furthermore, constantly overturning System 1 judgments in this way would require significant cognitive resources—resources that may not always be available. Thus, if we want our moral judgments to be reliable, automatic, and effortless, then they must issue from a System 1 process, rather than a System 2 one. If the norms in the database can be changed by explicit reasoning to produce intuitions that conform to an explicitly held moral theory, then we will have shown how reflective equilibrium is psychologically possible.

One final point before doing that: Sripada and Stich intend the beliefs box in their diagram to represent explicit beliefs that we can consciously entertain and manipulate by System 2 processes. It is important to note, however, that explicit reasoning is likely affected by implicit beliefs, which are stored in different memory systems from those beliefs accessible to explicit reasoning (Smith and DeCoster 2000). Such implicit beliefs are not consciously accessible, and so do not directly enter into explicit reasoning, but they can influence how we frame and undertake deliberation, since they play a role in producing consciously accessible judgments through some System 1 processes (Evans, this volume). To preserve Sripada and Stich's intent, the beliefs box should be thought of as belonging to System 2, since the content will draw on explicit memory, but it is important to keep in mind that implicit beliefs, though they do not figure in explicit reasoning directly, can influence the directions explicit reasoning takes.

Dual-process theory and moral justification

In the preceding section, the term 'norm' was used rather loosely, but to be clear about what kind of effect System 2 reasoning can have on the norms database we need to distinguish between two senses of the term: one psychological and the other evaluative. In the psychological sense, the term 'norm' refers to an action-guiding rule that explains a person's behavior and judgment. Norms, in this sense, are purely descriptive, making no claim as to whether the action-guiding rule is the right one, only that it is the one accepted by the agent. I shall refer to norms of this kind as 'psychological norms'. In the evaluative sense, norms are the standards by which we *should* act and judge. I shall refer to norms of this kind as 'evaluative norms'. Although psychological norms and evaluative norms can prescribe the same behavior, they can also diverge. It is quite possible to act according to a psychological norm that is contrary to an evaluative norm (See Bargh 1999).

The goal of reflective equilibrium is the maximum consonance between psychological and evaluative norms, which requires, *inter alia,* the reflective endorsement or modification of psychological norms. It also requires that we engage in some process for elucidating the correct evaluative norms for morality, which is the goal of moral theory. From a dual-process perspective, developing a moral theory is a System 2 operation, requiring slow, deliberate reasoning, and sometimes university level courses in ethics. It is not an easy thing to do, which is probably why many people never construct anything close to a full-blown moral theory. Quick, intuitive moral judgments, on the other hand, reflect the agent's psychological norms, and issue from System 1 operations. However, our psychological norms are not consciously accessible to us through introspection; we cannot simply look inside the norms database to find the data needed for our System 2 theorizing or to see whether there is a mismatch between our psychological and evaluative norms. So, it may seem that a dual-process model of moral reasoning cannot satisfy the psychological requirements of reflective equilibrium.

That conclusion is too quick, because even though the contents of the norms database are not consciously available, the norms system does produce a plethora of consciously available data in the form of moral intuitions. Such intuitions will not take the form of universal rules, such as 'Harm is bad', but will rather be particular, and often take the form 'This is bad'. But, from many instances of such particular judgments in similar situations, we can infer the underlying rules in our norms database—for example, that things involving harm are bad. Inferring these rules is a System 2 process, as is reasoning about the rules to build moral theories in accordance with our reflective judgments. But what effect, if any, can our System 2 moral theory have on our System 1 moral intuitions? Do we have any reason to think that our psychological norms are alterable?

Indeed we do, if we consider that the norms system is a learning system—that is, although the architecture of the norms system may be hardwired and universal, its *content* is not, but must be acquired. And it is the content that matters when it comes to the sorts of moral intuitions that are made. Thus, if the norms acquisition mechanism were to remain intact and active throughout a person's life, then it would be possible to alter the content of the norms database by acquiring new rules, including ones required by our normative theory. Once such rules were acquired, the norms system would make judgments consistent with the requirements of our theory.

There are some similarities here with language, which is the paradigm of a learning system, that could illuminate how it is possible for System 2 reasoning to alter System 1 rules. For it is possible to acquire a second language that becomes just as natural and easy to use as the first. Moreover, just like the norms system, the architecture of the language system is universal and hardwired, but the lexical content must be acquired from the environment (Chomsky 1988; Crain and Pietroski 2001; Laurence and Margolis 2001), which occurs early in development, usually by around the age of three (Kuhl 2004). Proper language acquisition also needs to take place within a critical period early in life, and failure to be exposed to the proper stimuli within that period means that competency can only be acquired with difficulty (Kuhl 2000; Kuhl et al. 2005)

However, even if a child is exposed to the correct stimuli at the right time, the learning mechanism becomes greatly attenuated, perhaps because of the neural pruning that occurs around three to four years old and then again in early adolescence (Webb et al. 2001). Thus, learning a second language later in life is a much more arduous and explicitly reasoned task than acquiring a first language early in life, requiring drilling, memorization, and lots of practice. Even so, students of second languages can attest to the fact that, once they become familiar enough with it, they are able to 'think' in that language. They are able to 'switch' between languages and converse as easily in the second as they can in the first, in a way that does not require them to explicitly reason through the rules of grammar that they assiduously studied. So, there is some learning mechanism that allows the explicitly studied rules of grammar to modify a System 1 language process, though it takes a significant amount of work to accomplish.

Can an analogous process be at work in the norms acquisition system? If so, it would predict that an evaluative norm endorsed by System 2 reasoning could come to be instantiated in the rules database, but that it would require lots of practice, and would take significantly more time to become 'second nature' than the rules acquired during childhood. Furthermore, just as in the language case, we would expect that during the process of acquisition, the rule would be wrongly or inconsistently applied. There may be one important disanalogy, though, between adult language acquisition and adult norm acquisition. In the case of acquiring a second language, it is possible that there is a different acquisition mechanism in adults than in children (see, for example, Dornyei 2005). And while this might be true for norm acquisition too, it is more likely that the same acquisition mechanism remains in place from childhood to adulthood, though possibly in attenuated form.

Among the reasons for thinking that the norms acquisition mechanism remains intact throughout a person's life, and that it is, perhaps, even more flexible than the language system, is the fact that norms can change within a society during one's lifetime, and that different norms can prevail in different social environments. For example, some behaviors acceptable when one is an undergraduate are not acceptable as a professional. Also, when one becomes a member of a subgroup, it is expected that one will change one's norms to those of the group—an expectation people would not have if it were not possible to change one's norms. Lastly, being able to change one's norms would be very adaptive. In early hunter-gatherer societies, women from conquered communities could be forcibly taken as wives, and being able to adjust to the new norms would be necessary for survival. It would be a short life for a captured woman who habitually and consistently breached the norms of her new community. It might be objected that simply being able to learn instrumental, force-backed rules such as 'If I disobey my new master, I shall be punished', would be enough to ensure survival, but there would be significant benefits to adopting the new norms. One possible benefit is social integration. These women, and their children, would be more likely to become fully integrated members of their new society if they adopted the norms of the community, rather than retaining their previous norms and doing just enough to stay alive. These advantages would increase if the rule could be adopted by a System 1 process, since that would produce quicker, more natural reactions with the appropriate emotional valence and without the heavy cognitive load that would be required if the rule were adopted only by System 2.

Assuming the norms acquisition mechanism remains intact, it becomes, in principle, possible to change our System 1 norms, and this provides the necessary feedback from System 2 that makes reflective equilibrium possible. It should be noted, though, that it would also be possible to acquire a new System 1 norm without System 2 involvement. For example, if a person joins a new community, she may acquire the norms of her community unconsciously. However, these cases are not interesting for the possibility of reflective equilibrium, which requires a conscious, rational process for justifying moral theories and beliefs. What we are looking for is some way for our System 2 reasoning to exploit, perhaps indirectly, the norms acquisition mechanism.

At this point, work on belief by Frankish (2004) may help. Frankish argues that the best way to understand various tensions in our concept of belief, such as that between dispositional beliefs (beliefs you are disposed to act on in the right circumstances) and occurrent beliefs (beliefs you are currently entertaining), is to adopt a two-strand theory, which recognizes the existence of two distinct kinds of belief—'basic beliefs' and 'superbeliefs'. According to Frankish, basic beliefs are those that influence our behavior automatically and unconsciously, while superbeliefs are *commitments* to reason and act in the future as if the proposition believed were true, even if our basic beliefs remain unchanged. Frankish does not make an explicit link between his two-strand theory and dual-process theories (though see Frankish, this volume), but the characteristics he describes map onto it quite easily, with basic beliefs being implicit System 1 beliefs and superbeliefs being explicit System 2 beliefs. On this view, our System 2 beliefs cannot have a direct effect on our System 1 beliefs. Suppose we have a System 1 belief that God exists, but form a System 2 belief that God does not exist. Then what we have really done, on this view, is commit ourselves to reasoning and acting in the future as if God does not exist, even though we continue to have a System 1 belief that God does exist.

Applying this to the moral case, when we develop our moral theory we settle on a number of evaluative norms, and even if they have not been acquired by System 1 operations, we can commit ourselves to reasoning and acting in the future as if our evaluative norms are correct. And there may be a good psychological motivation for forming such moral commitments, perhaps due to a System 1 belief-desire pair—a desire to commit to sound moral principles and a belief that the moral principle in question is a sound one. Or, perhaps simply a System 1 desire to be rational as defined across the whole person (Stanovich 2004; Saunders and Over, this volume).

So, the first part of acquiring a new moral belief via this reflective route is forming a commitment to act in the future as if we had that moral belief, so that even if our initial judgment is not-p, we nevertheless act as though p were true, since we want to follow through on our commitment. Obviously, this is a case of serious cognitive dissonance, and a situation that seems unlikely to persist. Overriding our initial judgments requires serious attention and cognitive resources, and it would not take long for us to return to our initial status quo, just for the sake of ease and cognitive peace. And sometimes this is exactly what we see. People make a serious commitment to act one way, even though they judge another, but it becomes too difficult, and they return to their original state. Perhaps this is just one way of being *akratic*. This seems to me fairly common, and we have a number of ways to excuse ourselves from the requirements of our theory, such as, 'It's just the way I am;' or 'It's just an ideal, I never really expected to live up to it'. Recall from the Sripada and Stich quote above that it is just these sorts of excuses that a dual-process theory of moral judgment should explain.

Yet, at other times, we really do succeed in living up to the requirements of our theory, even when it conflicts with our original intuitions, and over time our intuitions themselves begin to change. Here is how it might happen: when we make a judgment that conflicts with our second-order commitment, we attempt to override our initial judgment, and as we do so, we verbalize our commitment to ourselves, either vocally or silently. This self-verbalization is important, as it provides System 1 with new perceptual inputs in the form of natural language sentences that it can then manipulate in accordance with its own subconscious processing and inferential rules (Carruthers 2006, this volume; Frankish 2004, this volume) So, our self-verbalization of a consciously held moral rule would provide evidence to the System 1 norms acquisition mechanism that there is a new rule in the environment that needs to be inferred and added to the norms database. That is, this practised commitment itself becomes part of the moral environment whereby rules are inferred and added to the rules database. And this might be for no other reason than the fact that when we are thinking about our commitment, we are expressing it to ourselves in a natural language—in effect, lecturing ourselves, as our peers or parents might lecture us about certain norms. As already noted, admonitions expressed in natural language are among the evidences available to the norms acquisition mechanism when inferring a rule from the environment. So, as we repeat this commitment to ourselves in cycles of moral judgment, the self-verbalization of our commitment serves as evidence to the norms acquisition mechanism that there is a new norm that must be added to those already in the database. This process is outlined in Figure 15.3.

Thus, the new rule is acquired through the same mechanism that underlies the acquisition of all other rules, the only difference being that the initial evidence that a rule is in play comes from the self-verbalization of the rule, rather than its verbalization by others. Regardless of its origin, however, the rules acquisition mechanism takes that rule, and through its own operations, places it in the rules database. Once the new rule is acquired, System 1 judgments will be made in accordance with it, just as with any other rule. And this explains how rules in the norms database can be changed, over time, to conform to the requirements of an explicitly held theory.

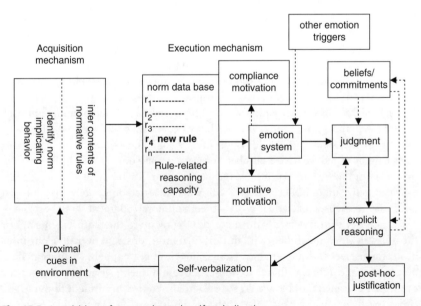

Fig. 15.3 Acquisition of norms through self-verbalization.

There is a limitation to this method of acquiring new rules. According to work by Nucci (2001), rules are not always explicitly stated to children, and so linguistic utterances may not be the most effective type of evidence for norm acquisition. Instead, children usually acquire rules by observing behaviors, especially emotional responses of approval, disapproval, and disgust. So, children between three and five-years-old are probably incapable of acquiring new rules in this reflective fashion, since they are insensitive to explicitly stated rules. However, this fact also points to another possible route for reflective rule acquisition that relies on admonishment and emotional cues.

On this route, we develop a set of System 2 rules and commit ourselves to reasoning and acting as though they were true. Perhaps through weakness of will, we perform an act that we have now committed ourselves to not performing, or vice versa, even though as we do so we quite possibly verbalize to ourselves, 'Don't do it!' When this happens, it is a violation of a very basic rule: 'Do what you have committed yourself to doing'. This seems like one possible formulation of the promise-keeping rule, which is most likely a System 1 rule, given its ubiquity among cultures and early appearance in childhood morality (Brown 1991). The suggestion here is that commitments to act according to some System 2 moral rule are like promises, albeit promises we make to ourselves, but promises nonetheless. In fact, we often talk of having promised ourselves to do, or refrain from doing, something. For example, we promise ourselves to exercise more, or never to take seconds on dessert, and it seems that we can make promises or commitments to ourselves in inner-speech, just as we can make them to other people in overt speech. For psychological purposes, both have the same status, and so, too, do our commitments to explicit System 2 moral beliefs: they are promises made to ourselves in episodes of inner-speech.

This has important an consequence, namely, that when we fail to live up to our own moral commitments, our System 1 norms system interprets our behavior as an occasion where a promise has been broken, and this produces the judgment: 'You broke your promise! That is wrong.' This creates a conflict of judgment, because the System 1 rule that produced the initial judgment determined that the action was permissible, but now, through breaking a commitment, there is a second System 1 judgment that something wrong has been done. However, the judgment that we have done something morally impermissible, that is, broken a promise, feels a certain way to us—it has a very negative emotional valence. In effect, we are disapproving of our behavior. At the same time, we are quite aware of why we disapprove of our behavior, because we feel bad about not doing what we committed to, and say things to ourselves such as, 'I can't believe I did that, when I told myself I shouldn't do it'. Indeed, eighteenth-century British moralists thought that this feeling of self-disapproval was the very heart of moral judgment (see Hutcheson 1728; Shaftsbury 1711). The importance of self-disapproval for our purposes is that it provides evidence to the rules acquisition system in the form of an emotional response, not just self-verbalization.

However, this process does not rely entirely on negative feedback in the form of emotional disapproval. If we act in accordance with our System 2 commitment, this provides us with the positive emotional approval that goes along with keeping our promises, along with self-verbalization of the rule. In time, these negative and positive emotional responses to breaking or adhering to the rule, along with self-verbalization, provide the norms acquisition mechanism with enough evidence to infer the correct norm, and insert it in the rules database. Once that happens, System 1 judgments proceed in the normal way by reference to that rule. Furthermore, it seems that promise making and promise keeping are cultural universals (Brown 1991), so this mechanism of rule acquisition is likely to be universally available. The upshot is that reflective equilibrium can be a universal feature of the moral life, across cultures.

The process of reflective rule acquisition sketched above fulfills both predictions made earlier in this section about modifying psychological norms. The first was that changing intuitions to accord with an explicit theory takes time and practice, and now we can see why. A single cycle of self-verbalization or self-judgment is not sufficient to acquire the new rule, so reflective equilibrium is not something that can be achieved immediately. The second prediction was that during the acquisition period, the new norm would be applied inconsistently, and again this model explains why. The process requires that people consciously entertain their System 2 moral beliefs on those occasions when System 1 produces a judgment that conflicts with them. If the System 2 moral belief is temporally forgotten, it will not trigger episodes of self-verbalization and self-judgment. Since people often fail to recall their commitments, whether to themselves or to others, when a rule is being acquired it will be applied only imperfectly, in starts and stutters, until it is acquired by the System 1 norms system.

Moreover, the process of reflective rule acquisition can account for moral dumbfounding. There is nothing in the process that requires any occurrent moral judgment to be overturned by System 2 processes. There may be some moral intuitions that are so strong—perhaps because of some connection to powerful emotions like disgust—that they persist even when they are no longer warranted. That is perfectly consistent with the process outlined here. The System 1 intuition is corrigible by explicit reasoning, but it will take time and practice, and in the meantime the powerful moral intuition will persist.

A final corollary to this theory of how System 1 rules can be acquired is that it should be much easier to acquire new norms when one is part of a community that endorses them, because the community, through verbal and emotional cues, will increase the volume of evidence available to the norms acquisition system. For instance, if one becomes a member of a religious community later in life it will be much easier to acquire those norms than attempting to do so alone. Not only are the external cues increased, but being part of a community will most likely increase how much attention one pays to the explicitly endorsed theory, so there will be fewer occasions when the commitment is overlooked. There would thus be an increase in both external and internal cues, allowing the norms acquisition mechanism to infer the correct norm much more quickly, with less practice. This is shown in Figure 15.4.

One complication, however, needs to be addressed before concluding: if the newly acquired System 1 rule conflicts with an already existing rule in the norms database, it would seem to follow that, in the presence of the correct stimuli, both rules would be invoked and issue in conflicting judgments of the situation. This would not satisfy the requirements of reflective equilibrium, which requires a consonance between theory and intuition, not merely consonance with theory and one of many intuitions. So, to realize reflective equilibrium fully there must be some way for previously held

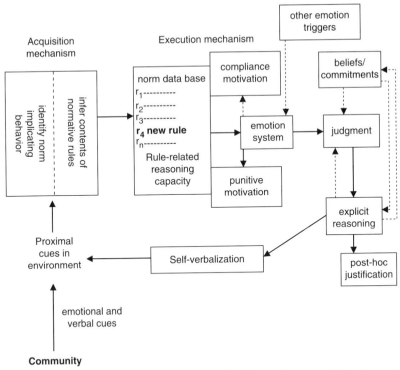

Fig. 15.4 Acquisition of norms through self-verbalization and community involvement.

System 1 norms to cease to issue in intuitions. There are two possibilities here. One is that norms are deleted from the database. That is, once a new rule has been added that conflicts with an existing rule, the old rule is simply erased, and so there is no possibility of conflict. There are reasons to be skeptical of this account. It is unclear that the inferential capacities of the norms database are sensitive to conflicts of this sort, because potential conflicts between norms are fairly common—for example, breaking a promise to meet a colleague for lunch in order to save a drowning child. It is unlikely, therefore, that the inferential mechanism of the norms database will simply delete norms that could potentially conflict.

Another option is that the old norm is *functionally* erased; that is, it remains in the norms database but it is no longer used to produce moral intuitions. Recall that one role of the norms database in the Sripada and Stich framework is to connect norms to sets of perceptual inputs that would invoke them. So, a norm against lying would be connected to many different sets of perceptual inputs indicative of lying, and when any one set is present, the norm is invoked. This would obviously be a very large and diverse collection of sets, and Sripada and Stich do not provide details of how the norms database is connected to perceptual inputs, nor of how the inputs would trigger the activation of a norm to produce a moral intuition. However, it is reasonable to think that for every set of perceptual inputs, there is only one norm with which it is uniquely linked, since if identical inputs triggered more than one norm it would be hard to see how the norms system could fulfill its action-guiding role, as it would issue conflicting advice. It is likely, then, that the inferential mechanisms of the norms database would be sensitive to this kind of conflict, and, when it occurred, would map the inputs to the norm for which there is continuing evidence in the environment, and remove the mappings from the one for which there is not such evidence. So, when a norm is being acquired the environmental evidence available to the norms acquisition mechanism shows that the new rule governs the current social landscape, and so gives it priority when mapping perceptual inputs. The old norm remains, but it is superseded, and thereby functionally erased, because it is no longer mapped to perceptual inputs that would activate it.

If it is, therefore, possible to acquire a System 1 norm based on System 2 reasoning through these processes, then we have what we set out to give, namely, a psychological account of reflective equilibrium; for we have shown how it is possible to reach consonance between theory and judgment. And, if reflective equilibrium is psychologically possible for minds like ours, then we have shown how moral judgments can be rational, since reflective equilibrium provides a normative theory of moral justification. Thus, moral intuitions and the facts of moral dumbfounding do not force us to the conclusion that morality cannot be rationally justified.

Acknowledgments

I would like to thank Peter Carruthers and Keith Frankish for their detailed comments on several drafts of this chapter, which were extraordinarily helpful, and no doubt made it much better. I would also like to thank Jonathan Evans, David Over, and Clare Saunders for their comments.

References

Bargh, J.A. (1999) The cognitive monster: The case against controllability of automatic stereotype effects. In S. Chaiken and Y. Trope (eds) *Dual process theories in social psychology*, 361–82. Guilford Press, New York.

Bodenhausen, G.V. (1990) Stereotypes as judgment heuristics: Evidence of circadian variations in discrimination. *Psychological Science*, **1**, 319–22.

Brenner, L.A. Koehler, D.J., and Rottenstreich, Y. (2002) Remarks on support theory: Recent advances and future directions. In T. Gilovich, D. Griffin, C and D. Kahneman (eds) *Heuristics and biases: The psychology of intuitive judgment*, 489–509. Cambridge University Press, New York.

Brown, D.E. (1991) *Human universals*. Temple University Press, Philadelphia, PA.

Carruthers, P. (2006) *The architecture of mind*. Oxford University Press, New York.

Chomsky, N. (1988) *Language and the problems of knowledge: The managua lectures*. MIT Press, Cambridge, MA.

Cohen, S. (2004) *The nature of moral reasoning: The framework and activities of ethical deliberation, argument and decision making*. Oxford University Press, New York.

Crain, S. and Pietroski, P. (2001) Nature, nurture and universal grammar. *Linguistics and Philosophy*, **24**, 139–86.

Daniels, N. (1996) *Justice and justification: Reflective equilibrium in theory and practice*. Cambridge University Press, New York.

Dornyei, Z. (2005) *The psychology of the language learner: Individual differences in second language acquisition*. Lawrence Erlbaum, Mahwah, NJ.

Edwards, C.P. (1987) Culture and the construction of moral values: A comparative ethnography of moral encounters in two cultural settings. In J. Kagan and S. Lamb (eds) *The emergence of morality in young children*, 123–51. University of Chicago Press, Chicago, IL.

Evans, J.St.B.T. (2002) Logic and human reasoning: An assessment of the deduction paradigm. *Psychological Bulletin,* **128**, 978–96.

Evans, J.St.B.T. (2008) Dual-processing accounts of reasoning, judgment and social cognition. *Annual Review of Psychology,* **59**, 255–78.

Evans, J.St.B.T. and Over, D.E. (1996) *Rationality and reasoning*. Psychology Press, New York.

Finucane, M.L., Alhakami, A., Slovic, P., and Johnson, S.M. (2000) The affect heuristic in judgments of risks and benefits. *Journal of Behavioral Decision Making,* **13**, 1–17.

Frankish, K. (2004) *Mind and supermind*. Cambridge University Press, Cambridge.

Gilbert, D.T. (1999) What the mind's not. In S. Chaiken and Y. Trope (eds) *Dual process theories in social psychology*, 3–11. Guilford, New York.

Gilbert, D.T. (2002) Inferential correction. In T. Gilovich, D. Griffin, and D. Kahneman (eds) *Heuristics and biases: The psychology of intuitive judgment*, 167–84. Cambridge University Press, New York.

Greene, J.D., Sommerville, R.B., Nystrom, L.E., Darley, J.M., and Cohen, J.D. (2001) An fMRI investigation of emotional engagement in moral judgment. *Science,* **293**, 2105–8.

Haidt, J. (2001) The emotional dog and its rational tail: A social intuitionist approach to moral judgment. *Psychology Review,* **108**, 814–34.

Haidt, J. and Hersch, MA. (2001) Sexual morality: The cultures and reasons of liberals and conservatives. *Journal of Applied Social Psychology,* **31**, 191–221.

Hauser, M.D., (2006) *Moral minds: How nature designed our universal sense of right and wrong*. Ecco, New York.

Hauser, M.D., Cushman, F., Young, L., Kang-Xing Jin, R., and Mikhail, J. (2007) A dissociation between moral judgment and justification. *Mind & Language,* **22**, 1–21.

Hutcheson, F. (1728/[2003]) *Essay on the nature and conduct of the passions with illustrations on the moral sense*. Kessinger Publishing, Whitefish, MT.

Kahneman, D. and Frederick, S. (2002) Representativeness revisited: Attribution substitution in intuitive judgment. In T. Gilovich, D. Griffin, and D. Kahneman (eds) *Heuristics and biases: The psychology of intuitive judgment*, 49–81.Cambridge University Press, New York.

Kamm, F.M. (2007) *Intricate ethics: Rights, responsibilities, and permissible harm*. Oxford University Press, New York.

Kohlberg, L. (1984) *The psychology of moral development: The nature and validity of moral stages*. Harper Collins, New York.

Kohlberg, L., Levine, C., Hewer, A. (1983) *Moral stages: A current formulation and response to critics*. Basel, New York.

Kuhl, P.K. (2000) A new view of language acquisition. *Proceedings of the National Academy of Sciences,* **97**, 11850–7.

Kuhl, P.K. (2004) Early language acquisition: Cracking the speech code. *Nature Reviews Neuroscience,* **5**, 831–43.

Kuhl, P.K., Conboy, B.T., Padden, D., Nelson, T., and Pruitt, J. (2005) Early speech perception and later language development: Implications for the 'critical period'. *Language and Learning Development,* **1**, 237–64.

Laurence, S. and Margolis, E. (2001) The poverty of the stimulus argument. *British Journal for the Philosophy of Science*, **52**, 217–76.

Nucci, L. P. (2001) *Education in the moral domain*. Cambridge University Press, New York.

Núñez, M. and Harris, P.L. (1998) Psychological and deontic concepts: Separate domains or intimate connection? *Mind & Language*, **13**, 153–70.

Piaget, J. (1932/[1965]) *The moral judgment of the child*, trans. Marjorie Gabain. Free Press, New York.

Rawls, J. (1999) *A theory of justice*, revised ed. Harvard University Press, Cambridge, MA.

Shaftesbury, A.A.Cooper, Earl of (1711/[2004]), *Characteristics of men, manners, opinions, and times*. Kessinger Press, Whitefish, MT.

Sloman, S.A. (1996) The empirical case for two systems of reasoning. *Psychological Bulletin*, **119**, 3–22.

Sloman, S.A. (2002) Two systems of reasoning. In T. Gilovich, D. Griffin, and D. Kahneman (eds) *Heuristics and biases: The psychology of intuitive judgment*, 379–96. Cambridge University Press, New York.

Smith, E.R. and DeCoster, J. (2000) Dual-process models in social and cognitive psychology: Conceptual integration and links to underlying memory systems. *Personality and Social Psychology Review*, **4**, 108–31.

Smith, M. (1994) *The moral problem*. Blackwell Publishing, Malden, MA.

Sripada, C.S. and Stich, S. (2006) A framework for the psychology of norms. In P. Carruthers, S. Laurence, and S. Stich (eds) *The innate mind: Culture and cognition*, 280–301. Oxford University Press, New York.

Stanovich, K.E. (1999) *Who is rational? Studies in individual differences in reasoning*. Laurence Erlbaum, Mahwah, NJ.

Stanovich, K.E. (2004) *The robot's rebellion*. University of Chicago Press, Chicago, IL.

Stanovich, K.E. and West, R.F. (2000) Individual differences in reasoning: Implications for the rationality debate? *Behavioral and Brain Sciences*, **23**, 645–726.

Strack, F. and Deutsch, R. (2004) Reflective and impulsive determinants of social behavior. *Personality and Social Psychology Review*, **8**, 220–47.

Sunstein, C. (2005) Moral heuristics. *Behavioral and Brain Sciences*, **28**, 531–73.

Turiel, E. (1983) *The development of social knowledge: Morality and convention*. Cambridge University Press, New York.

Turiel, E. (1998) The development of morality. In W. Damon and N. Eisenberg (eds) *Handbook of child psychology. Volume Three: Social, Emotional, and Personality Development*, 5th ed, 863–932. Wiley and Sons, Hoboken, NJ.

Tversky, A. and Kahneman, D. (1983) Extensional vs. intuitional reasoning: The conjunction fallacy in probability judgment. *Psychology Review*, **90**, 293–315.

Webb, S., Monk, C., and Nelson, C. (2001) Mechanisms of postnatal neurobiological development: Implications for human development. *Developmental Neuropsychology*, **19**, 147–71.

Wegner, D.M. (2002) *The illusion of conscious will*. MIT Press, Cambridge, MA.

Wheatley, T. and Haidt, J. (2005) Hypnotic disgust makes moral judgments more severe. *Psychological Science*, **16**, 780–4.

Wilson, T.D. (2002) *Strangers to ourselves: Discovering the adaptive unconscious*. Harvard University Press, Cambridge, MA.

Wilson, T.D., Lindsey, S., and Shooler, T.Y. (2000) A model of dual attitudes. *Psychological Review*, **107**, 101–26.

Name Index

Abelson, R.P. 208
Ackerman, P.L. 60
Adler, J.E. 75, 77
Ainslie, G. 75
Allen, J.J.B. 176
Allwood, C.M. 182
Andersen, S.M. 201
Anderson, J.R. 142, 247, 251, 255–257, 259
Anderson, M. 59
Aneja, A. 282
Annas, J. 2
Arbuthnott, D.W. 185
Arbuthnott, K.D. 185
Arkes, H.R. 57, 273
Armstrong, K. 217
Atkinson, T.M. 12
Atran, S. 218
Aunger, R. 73
Ayton, P. 57, 273

Baars, B.J. 5, 91, 114
Baddeley, A. 10, 64, 144, 239
Bailenson, J.N. 165
Baker, L.R. 91
Ball, L.J. 13, 49, 68, 178
Barbey, A.K. 129, 138, 322, 331
Bargh, J.A. 14, 44, 48, 178, 201, 209, 270, 295–296, 298, 299, 339, 344
Baron, J. 154, 274–275, 326
Baron-Cohen, S. 154
Barrett, H.C. 40, 123, 151–152
Barrett, L.F. 37, 39, 144
Barrouillet, P. 277–278
Barston, J.L. 13
Bechara, A. 72
Bechtel, W. 142
Becker, C.B. 233
Begg, I. 174
Bem, D.J. 309
Benjamin, A.S. 175–176
Berk, M.S. 201
Bermudez, J.L. 59
Berry, J.W. 13, 16, 218, 240, 245–247
Blackmore, S. 55, 73, 76
Blair, I.V. 211
Bless, H. 203, 206
Bodenhausen, G.V. 200, 339
Bonnay, D. 154
Bonner, B.L. 162
Botterill, G. 18, 91
Braine, M.D.S. 151

Brainerd, C.J. 267, 269–270, 272
Brase, G.L. 57
Bratman, M.E. 104
Brehm, J.W. 308
Brem, S.K. 165
Brenner, L.A. 338
Breuer, J. 6
Brewer, W.F. 182
Brewer, M.B. 197
Brown, D.E. 24, 340, 349–350
Buchtel, E.E. 14, 23, 94, 96, 121, 217, 232, 268, 275
Buckner, R.L. 62
Budescu, D.V. 162
Burson, K.A. 185
Busey, T.A. 175
Butterworth, B. 136
Byrne, R.M.J. 62, 163–164, 178
Byrne, R.W. 159

Cacioppo, J.T. 14, 57, 59, 197–198, 201, 204
Carey, B. 294, 311
Carpenter, W.B. 5
Carroll, D.C. 59, 63
Carroll, J.B. 62
Carruthers, P. 12, 18, 22–23, 40, 56–57, 63, 91, 95, 97–98, 103, 107, 109–111, 114, 120, 142–143, 151, 255, 319, 322, 339, 348
Cha, O. 219, 221, 233
Chabris, C.F. 152
Chaiken, S. 36–37, 129, 179, 197–198, 201, 204, 301
Chao, S.-J. 276
Chapman, G.B. 178, 185
Chartland, T.L. 270
Chater, N. 12, 77, 104, 326
Chen, S. 36, 179, 198
Cheney, R. 160
Cheng, P.W. 276
Choi, I. 218–219, 222, 227, 229, 231
Chomsky, N. 10, 117, 345
Chua, H.F. 219
Clark, A. 19, 71, 102, 242
Cleave-Hogg, D. 182
Cloeren, H.J. 3
Cohen, A. 245–246
Cohen, L.J. 20, 55, 61, 104, 155
Cohen, N.J. 12
Cohen, S. 340
Cole, M. 218–219
Colom, R. 33

Index

The index entries appear in word-by-word alphabetical order. Page references in italics indicate figures and tables.